ROBERT E. KRIEGER PUBLISHING COMPANY INC.

MALABAR
FLORIDA 32950

A SOCIAL INTERACTIONAL THEORY
OF EMOTIONS

A SOCIAL INTERACTIONAL THEORY OF EMOTIONS

THEODORE D. KEMPER
St. John's University, New York

A WILEY–INTERSCIENCE PUBLICATION

JOHN WILEY & SONS
New York · Chichester · Brisbane · Toronto

Library of Congress Cataloging in Publication Data

Kemper, Theodore D., 1926-
   A social interactional theory of emotions.

   "A Wiley-Interscience publication."
   Includes index.
   1.   Emotions.   2.   Interpersonal relations.
I.   Title.
BF531.K39   152.4   78-8020
ISBN 0-471-01405-2

Printed in the United States of America

10 9 8 7 6 5 4 3 2

For Nadja

Preface

This book presents a theory of emotions from the viewpoint of a sociologist. It is based on the proposition that most human emotions result from outcomes of interaction in social relationships; hence a complete theory must include the social bases of emotion both descriptively and causally.

In order to investigate the social sources of emotion, we require a comprehensive model of social interaction. Opportunely, empirical work over the past two decades has converged strongly on two analytic dimensions of interaction in social relationships. These dimensions are *power* and *status*, and they locate with unusual precision what we mean sociologically by the term *relationship*. Understood in their relational significance, rather than as attributes of persons, they are extraordinarily functional not only for investigating the social environmental instigators of emotion but also, astonishingly, for better interpreting the data on organismic and psychophysiological concomitants of emotional experience.

Notwithstanding the sociological provenience of the theory of this book, students of emotion in social psychology, experimental psychology, psychophysiology, psychiatry, child development, and similar disciplines will find extensive coverage as well as theoretical integration of the topic. I examine emotions at the social, cognitive, and physiological levels, both as situational responses to social stimuli and as situationally acquired characteristic modes of response. The unifying motif is the power–status model of social relations that I offer as the interactional basis of emotions.

In an important sense I have accepted the invitation implicit in Mandler's (1975) introduction to a recent compendium of knowledge in the field of emotions: "It seems useful not to fall into the trap of trying to explain what 'emotion' *is*. That would be to follow the error of trying to explicate the common language. Nor can one aim yet for a deterministic, mathematical theory. . . . We might start not with the aim of explaining emotion but rather with describing a system that has as its product some of the observations that have been called 'emotions' in the common language." This book presents such a "system" from a sociological position.

I have a second purpose. It overlaps but is not identical to presenting a theory of emotions. I also aim to address sociologists and social psychologists who have a broad interest in social relations, regardless of whether that interest has previously touched on emotions. I believe that the power–status model has general theoretical significance for sociological and social psychological analysis. The model, although focused here specifically on emotions, enables me nonetheless to treat many topics, including the structure of social relations; goals, methods, and outcomes of socialization; social and relational bases of mental and emotional disorder; parent–child relations; a theory and typology of aggression; types and developmental paths of love relationships; theoretical prospects for a discipline of sociophysiology; and relations of social exchange and their limits.

I believe, too, that the power–status model can integrate by means of a common conceptual framework such diverse and often antagonistic perspectives in sociological and social psychological analysis as exchange and reinforcement theory, on the one hand, and the so-called "cognitive" approaches, such as symbolic interaction, *Verstehen*, the ethnographic method, and ethnomethodology, on the other. To exchange theorists this book offers a model of social relations that encompasses domains of interaction excluded by the exchange approach. To cognitive sociologists and social psychologists this book offers the same model as a genotypical category scheme for the classification of a large number of the meanings and motives of action.

The approach taken here also has a home. Perhaps it is most nearly that of reinforcement theory, broadly conceived. But the reader must not conclude that this is a behaviorist tract. If naively understood, behaviorism is at least as much to be eschewed as any other approach. Indeed, one of the merits of the power–status model is that it poses the question of what happens *between* actors in social relationships. For classical behaviorists and for many exchange theorists whose ideas derive from behaviorism (e.g., Homans, 1961), what happens is rewards and punishments. In this book I examine very carefully these concepts, which were developed not in a *relational* analysis, but in the analysis of *individuals*. The individual rat, or the individual man, does indeed act in terms of reinforcements—generally, what will gain rewards and avoid punishments—and ordinary psychological analysis correctly focuses on how the individual acts in terms of reward–punishment contingencies. But this is an inadequate model for what happens in relationships between humans. I differentiate behavior in relationships so that rewards can be understood as being given either *voluntarily* or *involuntarily*—this makes them no less rewards to the recipient, but the type of relationship is greatly changed. The division between voluntary and involuntary action, which articulates with status and power relations, respectively, is ignored in conventional reinforcement analyses. Yet this distinction, I believe, is fundamental to the description of all human social relationships and of their consequences, including emotions. This is a large claim, and I hope the materials presented below provide substance for it.

The first definite formulation of the theory of social relationships of this book emerged for me in conversations with my friend and colleague Louis Wilker. Without the many occasions when he and I sought to obtain a clearer sociological understanding of social psychology, this book could not have been written. I owe him a debt of deep gratitude. I also am grateful to Anthony Costonis and David Schmitt for their willingness to argue at great length with me over sociological issues that are of fundamental importance to this book, though I did not realize this at the time. During the nearly 10 years since the theory was first germinated, many persons have offered comments and encouragement on the work in progress. Among sociologists I want especially to thank David Goslin, Jerald Hage, Robin Badgley, Merijoy Kelner, Reiner Baum, Richard Longabaugh, David Heise, Philip Wexler, Devra Davis, Lauren Seiler, Sheldon Sellers, Howard Aldrich, Bruce Dohrenwend, Marvin Scott, Edgar F. Borgatta, Paul Roman, Edgar Mills, Jr., Rocco Caporale, William Osborne, Rosalyn Bologh, Robert Myers, Mae Meidav, and Tad Krause. Among psychologists, Magda Arnold, Richard Lazarus, and Barbara Dohrenwend encouraged my pursuit of a theory of emotions on the basis of an early paper that contained the first statement of its principles. I thank them for being generous to an outsider seeking to work in the area of their central concern. Arnold Birenbaum, Howard B. Kaplan, David R. Heise, and Louis Wilker provided important insights and critical comments on the entire manuscript. Persons unconnected with the social sciences also have contributed to the understanding I have tried to embody here; I especially acknowledge Rosalyn Kramer and Sonja Ellingson for their different contributions. Naturally, none of the persons mentioned bears responsibility for any of the faults or lacks of this book. To Marie Rogers, Phyllis Zumatto, Susan Cerutti, and Colleen Rochford, who typed the manuscript, I offer a humble thank you.

THEODORE D. KEMPER

Jamaica, New York
February 1978

Acknowledgments

Permission is acknowledged for right to reprint excerpted materials as follows:

In Chapter 2 and Appendices I and II: From Theodore D. Kemper, "The fundamental dimensions of social relationships: A theoretical statement," *Acta Sociologica*, 1973, 41–53; reprinted by permission of Universitetsforlaget.

In Chapter 7: From Daniel Funkenstein, "The physiology of fear and anger," *Scientific American*, 1955 (May), 74–80; reprinted by permission of W. H. Freeman and Co.

In Chapters 7 and 8: From Stanley Schachter and Jerome Singer, "Cognitive, social, and physiological determinants of emotional state," *Psychological Review*, 1962, 62, 379–399; copyright 1962 by the American Psychological Association; reprinted by permission.

In Chapters 12 and 13: From Theodore D. Kemper, "Power, status, and love," pages 180–203 in David R. Heise, ed., *Personality and Socialization*, Chicago: Rand-McNally, 1972; reprinted by permission.

In Chapters 12 and 13: From Max Scheler, *The Nature of Sympathy*; translated by Peter Heath; New Haven, Conn.: Yale University Press, 1954; reprinted by permission of Routledge and Kegan Paul Ltd., Archon Books.

In Chapter 13: From Peter Blau, *Exchange and Power in Social Life*; New York: John Wiley and Sons, 1964; reprinted by permission.

T.D.K.

Contents

Contents

A SOCIAL INTERACTIONAL THEORY
OF EMOTIONS

chapter 1

The Study of Emotions

There are many theories of emotion, but none is sociological. This is astonishing, because in most cases the actions of others toward us, or our actions toward them, have instigated our joy, sadness, anger, or despair. Thus an effort to explain emotions as a product of social interaction is long overdue. This is not to say that sociologists have entirely neglected emotions. Throughout the history of sociological theory, emotions have been a subject of some concern. For example, Marx (1964b) discussed the "mortification" (p. 125) of alienated labor, Durkheim (1915) the religious sentiment, suicide and despair, Weber (1947) the passion of charismatic attachments and the "disenchantment of the world" by the ethos of rationalization (Weber, 1946, p. 155), Simmel (1950) the subtle currents of affect that pass between the sexes, and Homans (1961) the feelings of guilt or anger that ensue from overly favorable or unfavorable outcomes of the rule of "distributive justice" (pp. 75–76). Obviously sociologists have dealt with emotions. Nevertheless a comprehensive theory of emotions from a sociological perspective has yet to be offered.

One reason sociologists pay little systematic attention to emotions is that psychologists have legitimately preempted the field. Emotions are highly appropriate for psychological analysis because the individual is both the unit of emotional expression and undeniably the locus of emotions at the physiological level. Yet there is also a basis for sociological interest in emotions. Social situations influence the expression of emotions, not only in terms of intensity (e.g. the norms that distinguish permissiveness for emotional expression between men and women), but also directly by instigating the qualitatively different emotions themselves. Here a sociological analysis can supplement the basic work on emotions that is done by psychologists whose concern is the psychophysiological or the way emotions are linked to cognitive, motivational, or other aspects of the organism.

A second reason sociologists have not worked extensively in the field of emotions is that a sociological theory of emotions requires a comprehensive model of social interaction. If emotions are produced in the course of social interaction, we must know what is happening there in the first place to predict the emotions produced by interaction. Many current models of social interaction

1

are vacuous in the sense that they tell us very little about what actually goes on *between* the actors. Recently, efforts to develop a comprehensive model of interaction have converged on a few dimensions that can be applied to the problem of emotions. This model is the basis for the theory presented here.

In this chapter I shall consider a number of issues relating to the customary differences between psychological and sociological views of the stimulus and the problem of individual differences in theories of human behavior. In addition there are brief reviews of the major approaches to the study of emotions in psychology and sociology. Chapter 2 presents logical and empirical grounds for a comprehensive model of social interaction that is based on the distinction between *technical activity*, in which actors do their tasks in the division of labor, and *relational activity*, in which the actors direct their behavior toward each other instead of toward the task. Two relational dimensions—*power* and *status*—are explicated and discussed.

The basic statement of the theory of emotions is presented in Chapter 3. The relational dimensions are shown to give rise to three types of emotions: structural, anticipatory, and consequent. The structural emotions are examined in Chapter 3. Chapter 4 takes up the anticipatory emotions. Chapter 5 considers the technical problems that pertain to the identification and naming of the consequent emotions, as well as setting out the method of induction by which the theory is developed. Chapter 6 presents an illustrative set of analyses of certain consequent emotions, particularly fear and anger. In Chapters 7 and 8 I cross several disciplinary boundaries to propose some elements of a *sociophysiology of emotions*. This is a necessary articulation between the sociological level, which provides the stimulus for many emotions, and the physiological, where emotions are most deeply rooted in the organism. A classic problem in the psychophysiology of emotions is examined—organ specificity—and a solution is offered that can perhaps be seen only when the investigator steps as far back from the problem as the sociological level.

In Chapter 9, some speculations on the social relational substrates of the major emotional disorders, namely, schizophrenia and depression, are offered. Chapter 10 examines how particular relational patterns in the socialization process dispose individuals toward guilt, shame, anxiety, and depression. Chapter 11 presents a view of positive outcomes in the socialization process. These are regarded as preventives for guilt, shame, anxiety, and depression. My interest is to establish the positive outcomes as a theoretically based and necessarily interlinked set of goals of socialization and growth. Chapters 12 and 13 deal exclusively with love relationships: types of love relationships—there are seven—and the emotional dynamics of moving into and out of such relationships. The final chapter contains suggestions for the direction of future efforts in the study of emotions and social relations in general.

There are also three technical appendices. The first presents factor-analytic evidence (and criticisms of it) that support the empirical generalization that the two dimensions of power and status are sufficient to account descriptively for social relations. The second explicates the power and status dimensions, compares them with similar concepts used by Homans (1961), Blau (1964), and Thibaut and Kelley (1959), and suggests how they can serve as a general framework for the analysis of social relations. Appendix 3 reviews some methodological problems that must be taken into account when the results of epidemiological studies of emotional and mental disorder are used as a basis for constructing theory. I turn now to the first general question that bears on a social interactional theory of emotions.

APPROACHES TO THE STUDY OF EMOTIONS

Psychological Approaches.   The search for an adequate theory of emotions is one of the oldest quests in psychology. Although the history of this search begins with the pre-Socratics (Cleve, 1969) and includes such luminaries as Aristotle, Descartes, Spinoza, Hobbes, Darwin, Wundt, Nietzsche, Freud, and William James, a team of recent investigators was able to say: "The question of whether emotion is a useful concept for psychology has been much debated in the last several decades, but without satisfactory resolution" (Lazarus, Averill, and Opton, 1970, p. 207). Although an adequate theory of emotion is not the only desideratum in psychology today, it is immediately striking that there are so many perspectives on the question that there is not even agreement on the definition of the principal term.

At least seven distinct approaches to the study of emotion have current proponents and practitioners. These are (1) phylogenetic and innate theories, (2) recognition studies, (3) basic dimension studies, (4) information theory approaches, (5) psychophysiological studies, (6) cognitive theories, and (7) situational approaches. Some of these overlap, but the traditions of work are sufficiently distinct to warrant mention. I do not intend to provide a thorough review and evaluation of the various approaches, but merely to indicate some of the principal persons and issues identified with each of these rubrics so that the place of a sociological approach to emotions can be better understood in the context of current practice in the study of emotions. Comprehensive presentations of the different approaches can be found in Reymert (1950), Plutchik (1962), Arnold (1960, 1970), and Levi (1975).

Phylogenetic and Innate Theories.   Darwin (1873) inaugurated one of the definite traditions in the study of emotions by his observation of certain similarities between animal and human responses, for example, the bared fangs of the angry dog or wolf and the exposed incisors of the sneering man. To explain this evolutionary continuity, Darwin proposed the principle of "serviceable associated habits," namely, that what was useful for adaptation survived. If emotions in animals and men have survival value, they must also in some sense be considered innate qualities, attributes, or capacities of the organism that are transmitted biologically from one generation to the next. All investigations in the Darwinian tradition emphasize this innate character of emotions, in opposition to theories that view emotions as learned.

A strong Darwinian influence pervades the work of Plutchik (1962), Stanley-Jones (1970), and Izard (1972), and all ethological theorists, such as Lorenz (1966) and Eibl-Eibesfeldt (1972, 1974). Plutchik specifically insists that an adequate theory of emotions must "have relevance to basic biological adaptive processes" and deal with emotions that are *"found in some form* at all evolutionary levels" (p. 55, emphasis in original). There is no question that certain responses that can be subsumed under the label of an emotion—fear, for example—are found up and down the phylogenetic scale. Whether this is true for all emotions, for example, altruism, is a question of great interest in this tradition of research (cf. Wilson, 1975).

For humans, the environment for which emotions are presumably adaptive was once more directly that of raw Nature—a habitat of storm, animal attack, and drought—than it is today, but it was always *social* as well. The theories of emotion that have an evolutionary cast must appreciate that social stimulus conditions constitute the largest part of the human environment. Human beings were never isolated and alone phylogentically, and rarely are they so ontogenetically. The nurturing or wrath of a parent, the jealousy or support of siblings, the sexual enticements of men and women for each other, the malice of an enemy, the trust of a child: these conditions of social relationships doubtless existed in earlier stages of human development as they exist today. It is mistaken to look for emotions significant for evolutionary survival that ignore the social environment. Indeed, emotion has no evolutionary significance without a consideration of the social environment.

Theories of emotion based on instinct are another version of emotions as innate. According to Freud (1966) the two basic instincts, *eros* and *thanatos*, produce the two major emotions, love and hostility; anxiety results from a blocking or repression of these. Ambivalent feelings of love and hostility toward another lead, via the process of identification with the other, to hostility turned inward, which is expressed as depression. Guilt is produced by the triumph of instinctual drives over the internalized controls represented by the superego. By and large classical psychoanalytic theory has not moved very far from Freud's view of the biological rootedness of emotions (Freud, 1933, 1936).

McDougall (1933) and Shand (1920), both of whom postulated a variety of emotions, also based emotions on instincts. According to Shand, the instinct of flight and concealment produced fear, the instinct of combat or pugnacity produced anger, the instinct of repulsion produced disgust, and so on. As with all instinct theories, it is easier to name an instinct than to prove it.

Another tradition that sees emotions as innate stems from work with congenitally blind and deaf children, who presumably have very limited opportunities to learn from the sociocultural environment. Goodenough (1932) and Eibl-Eibesfeldt (1974) have argued that many emotions in these children are innate. The reports of their research, however, suggest that there is a good deal more learning through the tactile and olfactory senses than has been considered thus far.

In general the phylogentic and innate approaches to emotions asks whether emotions are acquired through learning or are part of the response structure of the species and are merely released by certain cues and contingencies. Many biologically based theories of emotion—but not all—are quite compatible with a sociological theory of emotion, which assigns to social relational stimuli a major part in the cueing process.

Recognition Studies. The manifest character of emotions in facial and bodily gestures, first propounded by Darwin (1873), has led to a large number of efforts to identify the full roster of human emotions through the analysis of (mainly) facial expressions. Tompkins (1970) proposed that affects are "mainly facial responses" (p. 107) and presents a list of nine primary emotions based on different physiognomical configurations. For example, interest or excitement is distinguished by "eyebrows down, stare fixed or tracking an object," anger by a "frown, clenched jaw and red face" (p. 108). Osgood (1966) also found nine emotions that individuals were able to recognize from photographs. However, other investigators found different numbers (e.g., Frijda, 1970, found five). A remarkable number of such studies have been done to discover both the range of emotions and their characteristics (e.g., intensity, duration, exact body locus, etc.) as well as the reliable signs of each emotion. The usual method is to show judges a set of photographs to be assessed for type, intensity, and other aspects of emotion portrayed by the face in the picture (Ekman, Friesen, and Ellsworth, 1972). The results are often factor analyzed, with varying numbers of factors emerging (Frijda, 1970). Since emotions expressed physiognomically can be treated as communications, they can also be examined for their cognitive "meaning." Osgood (1966) suggested that the meaning components of emotions identified from facial expressions are compatible with the three dimensions of meaning—activity, potency, and affect—derived from applications of the semantic differential.

Basic Dimension Studies. Certainly the longest-term interest in the study of emotions is the search for a fundamental set of emotions. Two modes of inquiry are visible here. First are the nonempirical assertions. This tradition has ancient roots: Aristotle discussed 15 emotions, Descartes offered six primary emotions, and Hobbes proposed seven. Spinoza offered only three primary emotions, but with these he derived 48 additional emotions. Gardiner, Metcalf, and Beebe-Center (1937) present a useful discussion of these philosopher-psychologists' efforts to catalog the emotions. More recently, McDougall (1933) proposed seven emotions derived from seven fundamental instincts. The psychoanalytic tradition has focused on two primary emotions: pleasure and unpleasure. However, other emotions are subsumed under these by Engel (1963). Stanley-Jones (1970) asserted that love and hate, derived from lust and rage, are the primary emotions. Strasser (1970) proposed three emotional tendencies to which he gave the Latin names of *libido* (desire), *securitas* (safety), and *potestas* (power). Arieti (1970) divided emotions into protoemotions, generated by immediate apperception of the environment (there are six protoemotions); these in turn gave rise through the mediation of cognitive processes to second- and third-order emotions. Plutchik (1962) proposed eight primary emotions based on biologically adaptive functions such as protection, destruction, reproduction, and so on.

Obviously there is no dearth of speculative or theoretically derived lists of primary, secondary, and even tertiary emotions. There is, of course, a good deal of overlap, and if consensus were sufficient for the discovery of the basic emotions, there are certainly some emotions that are agreed on by virtually all theorists, for example, fear, anger, and joy.

The second tradition in the basic dimension studies is empirical, either with or without the benefit of factor analysis. Burt (1950) reported three factors, namely, a "general emotionality" factor and two bipolar factors, "demonstrativeness–inhibition" and "euphoria–dyseuphoria." Schlossberg (1954) also proposed a three-dimensional model of emotions: pleasant–unpleasant, degree of attention or rejection, and intensity. These are essentially second-order factors in that they tell less about the basic set of emotions than about the underlying properties of emotions. Plutchik (1970) reported a successful circumplex arrangement of his eight "primary emotions." Nowlis (1970), who discussed emotions under the rubric of mood, proposed 12 basic moods derived from factor analysis. From recognition studies Osgood (1966) reported nine factors, although Frijda (1970) found only five. Nine primary emotions were also found by Tompkins (1970) in facial expressions.

In general the search for dimensions reveals at least two kinds. One involves concrete emotions such as fear, anger, joy, and the like, or, at a minimum, emotional polarities, with pleasurable–unpleasurable the most common. Second, the dimensions point to characteristics of concrete emotions, such as intensity, duration, and purity. Aside from certain obvious convergences, such as that

anger, fear, joy, for example, are distinguishable emotions, there is little fundamental agreement about the basic emotions or their attributes. There is perhaps
no other area in psychology in which there is so much disagreement not only
about how to explain the phenomena in question, but even about how to describe them. This may be due in part to the fact that the search for emotions may
be subject to a crucial, although understandable fallacy, namely, that because
emotions are manifested by individuals, we must examine individuals to discover
the full range of emotions. This view of emotions ignores the fact that the full
realm and range of emotions must be precisely as variegated and subtle as the
range of environmental variability. Some cultures may value particular aspects of
this variability while ignoring others. Untranslatable terms for affect in other
languages show this: for example, *Gemütlichkeit, Schadenfreude, brio*, and so
on. Ultimately these emotions can be explained only by looking outside the
organism to the environment. Indeed, if it is once granted that emotions are
responses to social stimuli, another approach to emotions is through an examination of the full set of possible stimuli. Since these vary, so do emotions. An
experimental approach to the discovery of the full range of human emotions is to
vary stimulus conditions and then observe which emotions occur. Where there
are ethical injunctions against the experimental induction of certain stimuli
(e.g., threatening someone's life), naturalistic accounts can amply fill in the
lacunae.

Information Theories. Since there is good evidence that emotions are
mediated by the brain, and since the brain is also understood to be the locus for
processing information, a number of theories of emotion are based on how the
organism responds to interruptions in information processing. Simonov (1970)
suggested that "negative emotions constitute a special nervous mechanism
thrown into action when a living being lacks the information necessary and
sufficient for organizing the actions that will satisfy a need" (p. 145). Surplus
information, on the other hand, produces enjoyment and pleasure. Pribram
(1970) viewed emotions as "plans, neural programs which are engaged when the
organism is disequilibrated" (p. 43). A similar view is held by Mandler (1962), for
whom one of the central emotions, anxiety, results from the interruption of
on-going plans.

Moss (1973), although not specifically dealing with emotions, which are
absorbed in his view of the overall process of what he calls "biosocial resonation,"
developed a theory of organismic responsiveness to the interaction between two
components of subjective involvement with information. The first is "the degree
to which information available in a given communication network has been
appropriated by a person" (p. 140). The second is the "degree to which one
subjectively evaluates the information learned . . . as accurate and effective in

his milieu" (p. 140). When these two information dimensions are dichotomized and interrelated, they produce four degrees of congruence between the individual and his social systems, ranging from the highly congruent state of identification through lesser states such as autonomy, alienation, and anomie. In these varying states of information congruence the individual experiences greater or lesser susceptibility to harmonious or stressful emotions, ranging from "spiritual ecstacy" (p. 149) to mental illness and suicide.

In yet another approach, Engel (1963) divided emotions into "signal scanning affects" and "drive-discharge affects." The former are "concerned with the regulation of the psychic economy as signal systems for the initiation of defensive and integrative processes within ego" (p. 279). Both positive and negative emotions are included: anxiety, shame, guilt, disgust, sadness and confidence, joy, pride, and hope. Drive discharge affects, on the other hand, include anger, love, affection, and sexual excitement. In general, information-processing models of emotions focus their interest on personality or neurological structures that depend on or process information so that the organism may adapt to the environment.

Psychophysiological Studies. The effort here is to investigate brain and autonomic nervous system causes, concomitants, and sequels of emotions. Much of the work is conducted with animals, since these lend themselves more easily to laboratory manipulation. In the psychophysiological research tradition, one of the most important questions is whether particular emotions are induced or accompanied by the activation of specific organs or by secretion of particular hormones or other chemicals in the body. The classic positions on this question are those of William James (1893), who favored the "specificity" solution, and Walter B. Cannon (1929), who opposed it. Recent investigators (Funkenstein, 1955; Schachter and Singer, 1962; Frankenhaeuser, 1971b) have also taken sides in this debate, and the current evidence appears to lean toward the nonspecificity approach. In chapters 7 and 8, however, I propose a sociological basis for specificity that I believe is supported by the psychophysiological evidence. Further discussion of this approach to the study of emotions is deferred until then.

Cognitive Studies. In the very provocative work by Schachter and Singer (1962) we find some attention given to situational features that might cue emotional response. Schachter and Singer injected their experimental subjects with epinephrine, a drug that induces physiological responses similar to those produced by an activated sympathetic nervous system. They did not, however, tell some of the subjects that they were going to experience such physiological reactions. When exposed to certain of the experimenters' confederates who were somewhat giddy and euphoric, the experimental subjects reported that they too were presumably euphoric; in the presence of angry confederates, the subjects presumably sensed that they themselves were angry. According to Schachter and Singer, the emotional response was a function not only of the physiological substrate, but also of the cognitions of the social situation. (This work is considered extensively in Chapters 7 and 8).

Arnold (1960, 1970) also proposed a cognitive theory based on the notion that there are two components of emotions: "one, static, the appraisal which is a mere acceptance or refusal of the expected effect of the situation on us; another dynamic, the impulse toward what is appraised as good, and away from anything appraised as bad. Accordingly emotion becomes a felt tendency toward anything appraised as good, and away from anything appraised as bad" (Arnold, 1970, p. 176). The appraisal notion is carried further in the work of R.S. Lazarus et al. (1970), where cognitive rehearsal, interpretation, or orientation lead to reduction of stress reactions to stimuli that ordinarily produce stress. Early work of this kind was done by Janis (1966) whose data consisted of postoperative reactions of surgical patients who were variably primed by different cognitive orientations to the prognoses of their cases. At a minimum, the cognitive approach in the study of emotion elevates the empirical and theoretical sights of the investigator to how individuals interpret the situational milieu that cues emotional response. The emphasis, however, is still on the intervening processes of cognition, interpretation, and appraisal—important, of course, in any complete theory of emotion—rather than the conditions of the milieu that are there to be cognized.

Situational Theories. Although the situational approach has not been the most popular mode of inquiry in the psychological study of emotions, there is nonetheless an active tradition. One of the main supports for such a position comes from learning theories. These have perhaps the greatest interest of all psychological approaches in the organism's environment, since that environment is the source of the reinforcement contingencies that instigate the organism's responses. In the words of Gray, "the common element binding the emotions into a class is that they all represent some kind of reaction to a 'reinforcing event' or to signals of impending reinforcing events" (p. 9). Although reinforcing events can be internal and symbolic as well as external, as Wolpe (1973) and others have pointed out, a very large class of reinforcing events are external. Learning theory generally views the events as consisting of "rewards and punishments, including among the punishments the removal of a reward or the failure of an expected reward to occur and [among the rewards] the removal of a punishment or the failure of an expected punishment to occur" (Gray, 1971, p. 9). This approach permits considerable specificity in the prediction of emotions, a feature generally lacking in a number of other approaches. A.A. Lazarus

(1968), for example, proposed that anxiety is the consequence of noxious or threatening stimuli, whereas depression is a reaction to a real or potential deprivation of positive reinforcements. Similarly, Gewirtz (1969) discussed depressed mood as a behavioral response to the absence of environmental reinforcers that ordinarily elicit pleasurable behavior.

Some proponents of the cognitive position in the study of emotions also strongly support a situational approach. Lazarus, Averill, and Opton (1970) provided a useful statement of this view:

> [I]t is necessary to ask two questions: First, what is *the nature of the cognitions* (or appraisals) which underlie separate emotional reactions (e.g. fear, guilt, grief, joy, etc.). Second, what are the determining *antecedent conditions of these cognitions.* Since the analysis is relational or transactional the determining conditions must be of two types: *situational* (referring to environmental factors) and *dispositional* (referring to the psychological structure of the individual, e.g., his beliefs, attitudes, personality traits, etc.) (pp. 218–219, emphasis in original).

This statement can be taken as the general paradigm for all theorists who view the organism's response as an interaction between stimulus properties of the environment and dispositional properties of the individual. Variants on this view are provided by Young (1961), Cattell (1972), and Wolpe (1973).

Unfortunately, even psychologists who are sympathetic to a situational approach can usually do little more than urge us to consider the situation within which emotions are generated, as do Lazarus, Averill, and Opton (1970), without telling much about how to specify the situation. Cattell (1972) discussed two aspects of what he called the "global situation" that determines emotional response: one is the "focal stimulus" to which the person responds in the immediate sense. Another is the "ambient situation" within which the focal stimulus occurs. "For example, the focal stimulus . . . 'Hurry' in an ambient situation . . . 'House on fire' brings a quite different response from the same remark uttered in the same house when it is not on fire" (p. 127). Cattell suggested that we sample from a population of ambient occasions and examine the effects of various focal stimuli within those occasions. Cattell offered "house," "play," and "work" as possible ambient situations that need to be investigated. Indeed, these are situations that undoubtedly produce some variation in response to focal stimuli, but they are merely examples without theoretical foundation, and Cattell provided no typology of occasions or situations that permit more than ad hoc explorations of how occasions affect responses. Wolpe (1973) too, although highly sympathetic to the stimulus view, left the ground somewhat shaky under such an approach by his definition of a stimulus: "a response is a behavioral event. A stimulus is the antecedent of a response" (p. 14). This gives no independent analytical status to the stimulus, since it is knowable only insofar as it produces a response. Since the response may be "imaginal" (p. 15), we may not be able to observe a response to a given stimulus and thus fail to recognize that there is a stimulus. The stimulus in a theory of emotions must have a more independent basis analytically than merely what produces a response.

Young (1961) also advanced a stimulus approach to the study of emotions. "Emotions originate in a psychological situation that always includes an environmental factor . . . " (p. 346). Although this implies the kind of sociological theory of emotions that is proposed here, Young does not tell us how to characterize situations in any systematic way, although he counts on what appears to be implicit knowledge: "How do we recognize and distinguish emotions? First, we rely on our knowledge of the inducing situation . . . " (p. 349). This answer does little to help us understand the situation that produces emotions. With the exception of those approaches that are specifically grounded in a reinforcement-reward-punishment theory, the situational approach is more promise than reality. A comprehensive situational model is lacking that will make it possible to investigate how emotions are induced. Although it seems almost self-evident that such a model must be developed, it will not be greeted with universal acclaim. There are important arguments in psychology that raise serious doubts about the validity of a stimulus approach. These must now be stated and assessed.

THE STIMULUS PROBLEM

A major distinction in the approaches to emotion just reviewed is between those which more or less ignore the stimulus conditions that induce emotional responses and those which do not. In general, moving from least to greatest concern, are physiological studies of emotion, phylogenetic and innate theories, studies of basic dimensions, information theories, recognition studies, cognitive studies, and situational approaches. It is easy to see that the latter types rather than the former are most compatible with a sociological theory of emotions, since it is precisely the sociologist's purported skill and interest to discover how social factors external to individuals evoke emotions. Indeed, the classical definition of a "social fact" is that it is "external" to the individual and it "constrains" him, that is, produces a response (Durkheim, 1938, p. 10). However, some psychologists and sociologists at times do not merely ignore the stimulus, but are actively antagonistic to a stimulus approach. This bears heavily on the reasonableness of pursuing a sociological approach to emotions, and the position must be evaluated.

The Antistimulus Position

Fundamentally two arguments are offered in opposition to a psychological analysis from the point of view of the stimulus. The first is summarized by Bowers (1973) and holds that the so-called "situationists have gone too far in . . .

rejecting . . . organismic or intrapsychic determinants of behavior" (Bowers, 1973, p, 307). The second, which is also taken by some sociologists, is that "a stimulus is a construction established by the individual rather than some external event in any absolute sense" (Koch, cited in Berkowitz, 1973, p. 167). This argument rests on a "phenomenological" basis and in certain sociological versions resists the imputation that the situation of social interaction is a given; rather it is constructed in the course of interaction (e.g. Berger and Luckmann, 1966). These positions are discussed in turn.

Bowers' critique conveniently summarized several points in the argument against stimulus-based theories. First, Bowers claimed that situationism "misidentifies an S-R [stimulus-response] viewpoint with the experimental method [which uses] independent and dependent variable analysis" (Bowers, 1973, p. 310). The objection is that the independent variable is assumed to be *external* to the individual. Bowers said that the S-R approach does not provide an adequate model of causality and is therefore deficient. When S is automatically assumed to be outside the individual, the error is doubly compounded. I call this the *antiexternality* position for purposes of further discussion.

Second, according to Bowers even if S does imply R, this does not necessarily mean that *if* R, *then necessarily* S. Bowers relied here on arguments similar to those put forth by Chomsky (1965) for language acquisition, wherein language is assumed to be acquired because of the operation of certain innate brain mechanisms, not as a result of reinforcement contingencies. At issue is the conflict between the view that the environment has causal and reinforcement properties and a "biocognitive" view in which the environment is only a setting in which internally programmed behavior emerges (cf. Sales, Guydosh, and Iacono, 1974). I call this the *innate* position.

Bowers' third point is that the stimulus itself is as much a part of the person as the environment. Here Bowers discussed the work on "implicit theories of personality" (Cronbach, 1958) that suggests that both preexisting views of personality and a language structure to describe personality are brought to the situation by each actor and thereby help define it. I will call this the *linguistic* position. (This question is also discussed in Appendix 1 in connection with the validity of factor-analytic studies of interaction.)

Variations on the antistimulus theme have been sounded in various ways. Korchin (1967) flatly declared, "For years psychology has known, although periodically it needs to be reminded, that a stimulus as such has no psychological value" (Korchin, 1967, p. 140) or, "A report of exteroceptive stimulation, the awareness of sensation, represents the part of experience which is stimulus bound. This is perhaps the least interesting of the categories of mental phenomena which we must ultimately explain" (John, 1973, p. 320).

Specifically addressing the problem of emotion, Izard (1972) criticized the so-called "cognitive theorists" because they assume that emotion is a response (following a process of cognitive appraisal) to a situation: "search for *the* stimulus [implies] an inexorably oversimplified S-R psychology [and is] a denial of the crucial importance of emotion, an experience defined not by the stimulus but by evolutionary-hereditary processes" (Izard, 1972, p. 73, emphasis in original).

In discussing stress, Arnold (1967) said, "For the scientific investigation of stress, there is a genuine advantage in starting our analysis from the contending or stress emotions rather than from stress itself . . . In starting from emotion, we save ourselves the difficulty of finding a criterion of stress and have the advantage of knowing that a man exposed to stress is really experiencing it" (p. 126).

There is also an antistimulus position in sociology. It concentrates largely on Bowers' third point, namely, the variability of meanings that actors attribute to their situations. In sociology this view stems from the *verstehende* methodology proposed by Weber (1947), for whom meanings are not automatically given by behavioristic accounts, but must be investigated in each case by an effort at empathic understanding of how the actor sees the situation. The Weberian methodological stance is raised to the level of a substantive principle in the symbolic interactionist tradition stemming from the work of Blumer (1962). There, meanings emerge in the course of interaction and are not precisely known beforehand even by the actors. This implies that the actors "construct" the situation as it unfolds from the results of their joint efforts. The ultimate sociological position on the indeterminateness of situations and meanings is found in the work of ethnomethodologists and phenomenologists, for whom meanings are so fluid and situations so susceptible to reinterpretation, that even past situations are "reconstructed" in the light of subsequent developments (Garfinkel, 1967; Berger and Luckmann, 1966; Heap and Roth, 1973; Psathas, 1973).

These methodological and quasiphilosophical views in sociology have their practical side in the critiques by Mechanic (1974) and Brown (1974), who claim that there is insufficent attention to the question of what certain situations "mean" to the actors actually experiencing them. It is a plea for modifying the assumption that particular experiences, for example, the birth of a child, the death of a relative, the loss of a job, or the migration to a new environment, have a constant stimulus value for all persons. I call this the *individual differences* position.

A Response to the Antistimulus View

Four principal objections to a stimulus approach to a theory of emotions are identified in the preceding section. Responses to these are now considered.

The Antiexternality Position.   It is noteworthy that Bowers (1973) said that "situationists" have merely "gone too far . . . in . . . rejecting organismic or intrapsychic determinants of behavior" (p. 307). This signifies that analysis of the situation is not rejected entirely. In Bowers' review of 19 studies in which it was possible to partition explained variance into that accounted for by persons and that accounted for by situations, 11 had higher person variance, and eight had higher situation variance. Also very important was the large amount of person-situation-interaction variance. These results dictate a research strategy in which neither person nor situation can be ignored. Although this seems to be merely a "liberal" response to a situation in which considerable passion has been expended on both sides, it is difficult to see any other sensible course. What eludes us is an adequate theory of person *and* situation. In part this must rest on adequate theories of both person and situation separately, if this is not a logical contradiction. In any event, the theory of the person in the field of emotions is far more extensively developed than the theory of the situation. The theory of this book is an effort to remedy that imbalance.

The Innate Position.   The argument on externality was methodological in the limited sense, in that it can be settled by the straightforward empirical demonstration of the amount of variance that is explained by person, situation, and the interaction effects (see Moos, 1969). However, the innate position is a much more serious and difficult one. What if the external world does not provide the basic functional organization of the person through learning or socialization, but merely provides occasions for the release of innate attributes? It is the old nature versus nurture argument, given new cachet by ethologists, anthropological structuralists, and antibehaviorists. This is not the place to review the full range of these positions. Even if the most extreme of the innate viewpoints were found to be true, there is no denying that the organism releases behavior in an environment. Perhaps he has all his equipment native, so to speak, and does not need to learn very much from the environment, nor even what the environment is and how it is organized—let us say that all of this is innate. Nonetheless, an observer who is constructing a scientific theory must be able to characterize the environment so that when the organism does act, the observer can describe with fidelity and predict with reliability what action the organism takes in that particular environment. From the perspective of a sociological theory of emotions, it does not matter whether the emotions are innate or learned. Either way they will be *emitted* in specific social situations. The sociologist's task is to clarify the nature of those situations and offer predictions about the emotions they elicit.

The Linguistic Position.   Essentially the argument here is like that of the innate position, namely, that persons may create the settings they enter by virtue of the cognitive or linguistic structure they already have. This position has been developed at some length in critiques of the validity of the factor analysis of personality scales and interaction ratings. A good understanding of this question can be obtained in Appendix 1.

The Individual Differences Position.   This is perhaps the most important of the critiques of the antistimulus position, and it can neither be ignored nor permitted to invalidate efforts toward a situational approach.

Any theory of human behavior must confront the fact of individual differences in response to apparently standard stimuli. The best a general theory can do is account for idiosyncratic variation within and between individuals by assigning it to theoretically relevant explanatory categories. With regard to emotions, there are several categories of differentiation that can explain individual variation. Not among these, but important in reducing potential variation in emotions, is the universality of certain human experiences. The ineluctable facts of birth, death, pain, pleasure, although not giving rise to uniform responses across the human species, nonetheless create a universal human foundation for emotion. Some cultures may counsel greater or lesser stoicism when one is in pain (Zborowski, 1952; Zola, 1966), but the facts of pain are common to all humans, and the *emotional* as opposed to the coping or behavorial response may be the same, for example, sadness or grief in the face of death, or joy and happiness in expectation of strong gratification.

Among the categories that account for and reduce idiosyncratic response variation are (1) common cultural and subcultural contexts, (2) common structural conditions for large populations, such as social class, (3) shaping of responses by peer groups, (4) common experiences and demands in social roles, and (5) common levels of physiological responsivity. These are now discussed.

1. Within cultures and large groups, the definitions of what is to be experienced and how it is to be experienced are more or less standardized. Values, norms, sanctions, and symbols guide action toward a common response. Lott and Lott (1974) put the matter well in their discussion of cultural homogeneity in response to reinforcements:

> The fact that reinforcement is relative does not preclude the possibility that we can make reasonable and valid assumptions about the rewarding nature of certain classes of events based on our knowledge of the culture in which particular individuals have been socialized. A head nod or a verbal um-hum may be aversive and annoying to some individuals, but it is likely to be a desirable outcome for most. More often than not we will be correct in assuming that approval, success, and attention, for example, will function as rewards for most Americans (p. 174).

When there are major deviations from the value or normative system, this usually means that a subculture is emerging with a value-norm-sanction and symbol system of its own. Although there are doubtless individual differences even within the smallest subcultures, these must be relatively small, since the smaller the group the more nearly homogeneous the members are likely to be in the pertinent response repertory of that subculture (Durkheim, 1933; Simmel, 1950; Schachter, 1951).

Ethnic subcultures comprise one of the standard categories of societal differentiation and individual homogenization. These are customarily considered to be based on ascriptive criteria such as territory, race, place of origin, and the like, but recent work by Barth (1969) suggests that any group that maintains a distinct "boundary," including occupational and professional groups, can be considered an "ethnic" group and therefore possessed of a subculture of its own that acts to limit response variation.

2. Large populations and subgroups within society can be found that confront social conditions that dispose them toward certain types of responses. These responses are not necessarily normative in the sense that they are prescribed; rather they are the responses virtually anyone in similar circumstances would give. Possibly the largest structural division of this kind in society is that of social class. The conditions of membership are such that individuals in different classes confront different life conditions, which affects their behavior and their responses. Kohn (1969) has shown that the usual conditions of working-class employment settings dispose persons toward a certain pattern of conformity. Miller (1958) has argued that working-class neighborhoods dispose persons toward a pattern of emotional expressivity, especially in terms of anger and violence. In many studies (reviewed in Dohrenwend and Dohrenwend, 1969) it has been shown that the rates of diagnosed emotional disorder differ by socioeconomic status. Although some of these differences may be accounted for by biased judgments imposed by psychiatrists and diagnosticians (Hollingshead and Redlich, 1958), this does not explain the overall higher rates of incidence of symptoms (Langner and Michael, 1963) among those at the lowest socioeconomic level (Mishler and Scotch, 1963; Turner and Wagenfeld, 1967). Although the exact reasons for the different rates of disorder among social classes have not been firmly established, many researchers espouse a social causation explanation (see Dohrenwend and Dohrenwend, 1969). The conditions of working-class life are believed to dispose individual members to emotional turmoil and breakdown more than in other classes. I argue in Chapter 9 that working- and middle-class environments subject individuals to different kinds of stress and that different emotional outcomes and illnessses result from this.

3. Situational conditions common to peer groups, particularly when conditions are extreme, tend to wash out individual differences. This is brought out very well in Bourne's (1971) study of the endocrine secretions of members of an American special forces combat team in Viet Nam: "In small groups with free communication among members of equal standing, there is a tendency for a consensus to develop as to how a stress should be perceived which in turn minimizes individual differences in adrenocortical response . . . As a result, members of a group, when presented with a threatening event, will tend to have

more similar responses in the excretion level of steroids than if they were presented with the same event as isolated subjects" (p. 267). Bourne emphasized
that the norms for responsiveness develop among members of *equal* rank.

4. This produces another condition for the uniformity of response, namely
the common hierarchical position of the actors in the division of labor. In
Bourne's study two officers with the combat team had similar hormonal secretion
patterns, and these differed from the patterns of the enlisted men under their
command. Differences of this nature have also been found in animal studies
between those higher and lower in the dominance hierarchy (Bronson and Desjardins, 1971; Welch and Welch, 1971). Marchbanks (1958) also found endocrine secretion differences between pilots and other air crew members.

5. Finally, common genetic characteristics dispose individuals toward response uniformity. Kugelmass (1973) showed that certain types of autonomic
response vary by territorial ethnic groups. Broverman et al. (1968) and Lacey and
Lacey (1962) have presented important evidence bearing on possible nonacultur-
ally determined differences in autonomic responsivity between males and
females. These differences would significantly influence sex variability in emotional display. Sales et al. (1974) have been able to differentiate between persons
who have relatively high and relatively low threshholds of responsivity to a
standard stimulus. The low-threshhold responders must damp down the intensity
of the stimuli they receive, whereas the high-threshhold types must amplify
them. Sales et al. reasoned that actual response is made to a common level of
stimulus intensity by both high and low types. The common level is attained by
internal adjustments.

Although other categories can be applied to individual emotional response
variation, the ones cited here should account for a substantial portion. This
analysis of variance model is the best we can do at present to reduce idiosyncracy
and explain deviations from the mean emotional response. (I am not, however,
suggesting that individual differences in emotional responses are simply linear-
additive effects that cause deviation from a given numerical value of the grand
mean. Although this may be true in certain instances, differences are also qualitative. Thus one person may feel anger in a certain situation, whereas another
will feel fear.)

Based on the reasoning advanced here, individual differences in emotional
response can be explained by applying to each person various genetic, cultural,
subcultural, peer group, and role templates to obtain a prediction of the response
value of the inducing stimulus. Recently developed multiple-regression
techniques such as Automatic Interaction Detection (Sonquist, 1970) seem particularly well adapted for such analyses. Although I do not know of any studies that
have used this method in the area of emotions, I believe we are ready to

undertake such work and discover how much variation is accounted for by the standard social and genetic categories and how much must be accounted for by other categories and truly idiosyncratic factors.

For heuristic purposes, I assume that once a stimulus has been defined in a social group, the emotion that follows is very nearly identical for all persons who share the same meaning of the stimulus. However, even if emotions are the same, this does not mean that the *action* that follows the emotion is common to all. Again, the social and cultural templates must be applied to learn what standard coping behaviors are prescribed or possible for what emotions.*

The sociological theory of emotions I propose assumes also that the shaping influence of culture, peer groups, social roles, and the like is so powerful that this leads to a *modal* emotional response to given social stimuli. When individuals display unusual, unexpected, or contranormative emotions in response to certain stimuli—for example, laughing at a funeral, crying over ice cream, depression at the receipt of favors from a loved one, or anger when we are given social approval—these are clues to the possibility of emotional disorder. New strategies are called for at such points in dealing with individuals who are emotionally out of tune with the rest of us.

A final point on the question of individual differences may resolve some last doubts. The basic problem of a stimulus approach to the study of emotions is that *standard* stimuli do not universally evoke the same response from all persons. Thus it is argued that we must look not at the stimulus, but at its *meaning* to the person. The logical consequence of this is supposed to be that a stimulus approach must inevitably fail.

This overlooks the fact that most human responses in social relationships are made not to standard stimuli—such as those presented in the experimental laboratory—but to relational stimuli that are often carefully constructed to achieve a certain response. Indeed, the definition of social behavior entails taking the probable response of the other into account, and thereby "the behavior is oriented in its course" (Weber, 1947, p. 88; see also Mead, 1934; Jones and Gerard, 1967, pp. 505–513).

The stimuli most persons receive in interaction have been selected by the other on the basis of the structure and history of the relationship between the actors. These stimuli have meaning in the relationship, and logic suggests that the meaning is *usually* unambiguous in that relationship. Otherwise most interaction would consist merely of discovering the meaning of the previous stimulus. In such a case, no cooperative endeavor between humans would be possible.

---

* Lazarus (1975) gives particular attention to the important distinction between coping and emotion.

This suggests that there are few "standard" *stimuli* in social relationships, but this leaves open the question of whether there are standard *meanings* that convey the important elements of any relationship. In the next chapter I present findings from a body of empirical research that suggest that a standard set of relational meanings does exist and that the overt stimuli each actor directs to the other are indicative of the standard meanings. Since actors rarely mistake those meanings, this also suggests a degree of stimulus commonality within appropriately de-limited social and cultural groups and subgroups that leaves only a relatively small corner for idiosyncracy.

Finally, to avoid present and subsequent misunderstandings, I point out here that I have proposed no restrictions on the term stimulus. It may be a discrete physical act, such as touching, or it may be the omission of a customary act, such as *not* saying, "Good morning" (cf. Weber, 1947, p. 88). The omission becomes prominent because it is a change in pattern, and the change signifies a certain stimulus because the usual pattern signified another. The sociological theory of emotions proposed here does not depend on either a more or less broadly con-ceived view of the stimulus except that some environmental event signifies to the actor the state of social relations between himself and others. This suffices under the conditions to be specified further to instigate an emotion.

A Note on Autonomic Response Stereotypy

Lacey and his colleagues (Lacey and Lacey, 1962; Lacey et al. 1963; Lacey, 1967), have shown that autonomic nervous system activity—involving such fac-tors in emotional response as heart rate, pulse rate, sweating, and the like—varies considerably between individuals. This is observed in two ways: first, there ap-pears to be greater patterning *within* individuals than between them. Thus in response to a particular stimulus, in some individuals heart rate might rise while skin conductance falls; for other individuals, the pattern might be reversed. In addition to this idiosyncratic patterning, individuals also vary in the degree to which their response patterns remain stable or change over time. Given this large amount of inter- as well as intraindividual difference in autonomic response, it may seem almost hopeless to try to formulate a standard set of external stimuli.

The problem here must be understood properly. Let us assume first that autonomic activities are not random and further that they occur only when they have reason to occur—that is, when there are stimuli acting to induce them. With this proviso in mind, if individuals have stereotypically unique response patterns, this suggests that they are responding to stimuli that have a particular configuration of emotional significance for them. Some individuals are phobic to certain stimuli that others may either ignore or regard with mild interest or as a challenge to be overcome. This simply means that the stimulus fits into each individual's configuration of meaning in a different way. However, if the stimulus were seen in the same way by each person, I suggest that the autonomic response pattern would also be the same. Thus what is *fearful* to all would produce in all an autonomic response pattern that could be labeled the fear response.

If individuals are somewhat unreliable in their response patterns, does this suggest that their physiologies are therefore unreliable? Although there are indubitably physiological changes, a more likely explanation is that a particular stimulus now means something different from what it meant on an earlier occasion. One might have been very frightened of the stimulus in the past; now it is less frightening and is seen more as an opportunity for developing the competence to overcome a difficulty; on yet a third occasion one may be relatively indifferent to the stimulus because other interests have succeeded it in priority or attention (cf. Goffman, 1961a).

Lacey (1967) is fully aware of these possibilities. He pointed out, in discussing a pertinent set of data collected by Elliott (1964), that "the correlations [between autonomic indicators] change as a function of many variables. Age is one such variable, possibly, as Elliott points out, because increasing age is correlated with different *perceptions* of and *adjustments* to the experimental situation" (p. 23, emphasis added). Lacey further states, "the source of the response pattern lies with . . . the nature of the subject's set and expectation, of his intended response to the stimulus" (p. 25). This conclusion seems to point us not in the direction of physiology for the answer to the problem of inter- and intraindividual differences in autonomic response, but toward the meaning of the stimulus. This is usually established in the course of social interaction.

Another complicating factor is that there are mixed emotions (Arnold, 1960, Vol. 1; Plutchik, 1962), and an unclear autonomic response pattern may be simply a reflection of a situation that induces multiple and possibly conflicting emotions.

As we consider the kinds of response variability that Lacey and others have found, we must not confuse "an issue of method with an issue of substance" (see Dohrenwend, 1966). Indeed, it may be difficult at present to establish with certainty exactly what aspects of the stimulus field the individual is responding to at a give time, but the methodological difficulties of the quest ought to be seen as such, rather than, perhaps, misunderstood as an inherent variability in the response mechanism, as in the response stereotypy found by Lacey. For the present I propose that response stereotypy can be explained in part by means of a sociological approach to emotions. Thus far very little work has been done to examine response stereotypy in the light of the differentiating and homogenizing conditions of cultural, structural, and peer groups. (For some exceptions, see Kugelmass, 1973; Harburg et al., 1973.)

SOCIOLOGICAL APPROACHES TO EMOTIONS

Although there is no systematic sociological theory of emotions, sociologists from Marx to Homans have dealt with emotions and the kinds of coping response that particular emotions produce. Marx believed that violent social change would result from a process involving the alienation and immiseration of the working class. For Marx, alienation was a psychological condition that resulted from certain patterns of ownership and control of the means of production ("a social relation of production") and was manifested by the fact that the worker "does not fulfill himself in his work, but denies himself, has a feeling of misery rather than well-being" (Marx, 1964b, p. 125). Work that is alienating is also "a labour of self-sacrifice, of mortification . . . [it is] activity as suffering (passivity), strength as powerlessness, creation as emasculation . . . " (Marx, 1964b, pp. 125–126). For Marx, socially produced misery and the ensuing conflict is the paradigm for historical analysis in that "the history of all past society has consisted in the development of class antagonisms, antagonisms that assumed different forms at different epochs" (Marx and Engels, 1959, p. 27).

Whereas Marx's venture into emotions explained the suffering, despair, and the ultimate answer of the mass of producers by the social relations of production of the epoch, Durkheim (1897) examined a type of emotional expression, namely, suicide, from a different view of the structure of social relations. Although some suicides are the result of rational and instrumental choice, many follow from a variety of deeply felt emotions. Durkheim explained certain stable differences in suicide rates between various national and social categories—Protestants, Catholics, Jews; men and women; married, divorced, single; and among occupational groups—as resulting from greater or lesser social integration and greater or lesser social regulation. Integration refers to the sheer number of connections in which individuals are linked by bonds of obligation to others. If there were too few bonds or too many, suicide rates were higher than in the intermediate categories. Regulation, on the other hand, refers to the existence of social horizons of appropriateness and rules and norms for what is just, proper, and sufficient to satisfy the desires. When rapid deregulation occurs—for example, during economic crises or as a result of divorce—individuals lose the sense of limits imposed on them by the social context that regulates their desires and aspirations. Durkheim gave the name *anomie* to these states of social deregulation, and social categories and persons who are exposed to anomie tend toward higher rates of suicide.

Max Weber, third of the great classical triad of sociological theorists, also touched on emotion, but at a very high level of generality. For Weber, the entire trend of Western society was toward "disenchantment," in which emotional and nonrational elements were being purged in favor of a mode of social organizations whose epitome was technical mastery and rational administrative control, in a word, bureaucracy. By contrast with administrative conduct in earlier periods, bureaucratic administration operates "under the principle of *sine ira ac studio* (without anger or bias). Its specific nature, which is welcomed by capitalism, develops the more perfectly the more the bureaucracy is 'dehumanized,' the more completely it succeeds in eliminating from official business love, hatred, and all purely personal, irrational, and emotional elements" (Weber, 1946, pp. 215–216).

Recent sociology contains a greater effort to explicate specific emotions than does the classical sociology just reviewed. Somewhat surprisingly, Homans (1961) discussed emotions more thoroughly than any other recent sociologist. The astonishment stems from the fact that Homans' version of social exchange theory is based on B.F. Skinner's radical behaviorism, which does not investigate the feelings of actors, only their overt acts. Homans, however, was too sensible of the concrete reality of his Person and Other to overlook the emotions we all know accompany social interaction.

Homans was most explicit in his discussion of anger and guilt, although he also dealt with several other emotions. One of Homans' basic propositions is that "the more to a man's disadvantage the rule of distributive justice fails of realization, the more likely he is to display the emotional behavior we call anger" (p. 75). Distributive justice is the principle that one's profits from interaction should be in proportion to one's investments. Investments are factors of whatever sort— education, race, sex, community of origin, and the like—that lead the actor to believe (correctly or otherwise) that he has a right to expect a certain rate of return (cf. Kemper, 1974). To receive less than one believes he deserves according to the distributive justice rule produces *anger*. This proposition not only appeals to common sense, there is also experimental evidence to support it (Stephenson and White, 1970; Pepitone, 1971). However, are there any other situations that lead to anger? Homans did not tell us, since he was not as interested in emotions as he was in distributive justice.

Homans also addresses the problem of guilt, which emerges when the distributive justice rule fails in the direction favorable to the actor: when "he has done better for himself than he ought to have done" (p. 76). Again we are pursuaded in a common sense way that this is one emotion that may be felt, and there is experimental support for this (Berscheid and Walster, 1967). Withal, Homans' view of both anger and guilt is that they are *results of outcomes in social interaction*, a position highly compatible with the theory of emotions offered here. However, Homans puts the matter a little differently: " . . . when we consider, as we must, the stimulus-situations that elicit emotional behavior [f]or men the heart of these situations is a comparison. Besides exchanging rewarding activities with each other, Person and Other do in fact perceive and appraise their rewards, costs, and investments in relation to the rewards, costs and investments of other men . . . And if distributive justice fails, anger arises" (p. 75). Homans might have added *also* guilt in the other party, since if one gets too little, the other may believe he is getting too much. Anger and guilt are thus evoked together for Homans, at least in the paradigm of social exchange.

Emotions other than anger and guilt are not developed much in Homans' work. His notion of *sentiment* is a very modest general concept that in some way embraces emotions. Homans defines sentiment as "the activities that the members of a particular verbal or symbolic community say are the signs of the attitudes and *feelings* a man takes toward another man or other men" (p. 33, emphasis added). Although sentiments are not the feelings themselves, they are overt behaviors that reflect feelings. It is the best we can do with Homans' view of emotion in general, other than for his consideration of anger and guilt. If, however, we seek hard we can find references to *admiration* ("they must have been carried away by admiration . . . " p. 176), *liking* (three different chapters are devoted to this in one form or another), *hostility* ("only when a man behaves worse than he is entitled to will he arouse the hostility of others," p. 247), *anxiety* ("in the presence of two broad status-classes the members of the lower class who stood highest within thir class were most anxious to avoid contact with members of the upper class . . . " p. 333), and *fear* ("a leader, then, is a man who can punish as well as reward, and punishment as we know, arouses a very different kind of behavior from that aroused by reward: punishment is a reason for avoiding and fearing the punisher," p. 300). These examples should suffice to show that even in a (so to speak) behaviorist's account of social interaction, emotions somehow work their way into the analysis. However, they do so under cover of fleshing out what we all know to be the case in an intuitive rather than a systematic way. As seen later, some of Homans' insights on emotion can be viewed as particular instances of a more general theory that examines the social stimulus situation as the key to emotional response.

In another theoretical formulation that is akin to, but differs in some particulars from Homans, Anderson et al. (1969) presented conditions for "embarrassment and guilt" and "anger and dissatisfaction." In a situation in which a person is overrewarded, given his ability, he will feel "threatened or embarrassed" (p. 7) when he is in contact with someone who has both the knowledge of his true level of ability, ergo, what his just deserts are, and who *also* "controls the distribution of goal-objects in the situation" (p. 5). On the other hand, if the person is underrewarded relative to another, "it manifests itself in *anger* and *dissatisfaction* and not (as in the case of over-reward) as *embarrassment* or *guilt*" (p. 8). This formulation, like that of Homans', has the virtue of looking on emotions as a product of interactional outcomes. It suffers, however, from a failure to specify more carefully the conditions under which guilt rather than embarrassment will ensue from a case of overreward, or when they are likely to occur together. I assume that guilt and shame are separate emotions (see Ausubel, 1955; Lewis, 1971). Obviously, too, Anderson et al. were not concerned with explaining guilt and embarrassment as such. These emotions happen to be by-products of certain interactional outcomes and were dealt with as such. Further, the interaction formulation of Anderson et al. is a limited one rather than a general system of social relations that explains a broad spectrum of emotions.

The last recent sociological foray into emotions I examine is by a sociologist from a tradition very far removed from that of Homans or Anderson et al. This is the ethnomethodological work of Garfinkel (1967), who treats *anger* and *embarrassment*. Not surprisingly, these emotions are stimulated in the course of interaction, according to Garfinkel's example. "On the part of the person distrusted there should be the demand for justification, and when it was not forthcoming, as 'anyone could see' it could not be [in the experimental situation Garfinkel describes], anger. For the experimenter we expected embarrassment to result [from the fact that he had to play somewhat the part of a fool in order to carry out his experiment successfully]" (pp. 50–51). Garfinkel has prepared us for these emotions, for he declared his purpose as one of producing "bewilderment, consternation, and confusion [and] the socially structured affects of anxiety, shame, guilt, and indignation since to produce disorganized action should tell us something about how the structures of everyday activities are ordinarily and routinely produced and maintained" (p. 38). We see that in traditions as different as exchange theory and ethnomethodology in contemporary sociology, emotions are seen to result from interactional outcomes. This is neither more nor less than one can expect from any sociological theory of emotions.

However, there are fundamental difficulties with previous sociological approaches to emotions. First, emotions are almost never the subject of main interest, but rather a secondary phenomenon that in some way cannot be avoided in a veristic description of what occurs. This produces a discussion of only those emotions which are specific to the interaction conditions that are the main topic of interest. Thus we have no general statements concerning either a full range of emotions or a full range of interaction conditions that might produce emotions. Second, the situational conditions themselves are not always adequately specified. Homans' discussion of distributive justice is a relatively clear-cut depiction of a situational condition and has the further virtue of stemming from a more comprehensive analytic framework. Thus it is not simply ad hoc. At the other extreme we read that "highly personal experiences and contacts . . . bring about fluctuations in mood" (Kendall, 1954, p. 81), with this being measured by "something happened which put me in a good (bad) mood" (p. 81). The problem of adequate specification of the situation is related to the third, and most important, problem facing any sociological effort to present a comprehensive theory of emotions, namely, before there can be such a theory, there must be a sociological model that embraces all the social interaction conditions that give rise to emotions. This is a problem that partial theories of interaction, such as exchange theory, do not address. A sociological theory of emotions must stand basically on a comprehensive model of interaction, since only by means of such a model can we investigate the full spectrum of emotions that have a social locus.

chapter 2

Fundamental Dimensions of
Social Relationships

The basic argument of this book is that events in the social environment instigate emotions. The most important events are the ongoing or changing patterns of social relations between actors. To predict emotions from patterns of social relations, we need a theory of interaction that comprehends the full scope of relational possibilities. To present such a theory is the work of this chapter.

The theory is based in part on an empirical generalization that has evolved from a large number of studies of interaction. The problem in those studies was to find the *basic* or *fundamental* dimensions of social behavior or personality in the social setting. A remarkably consistent result in those studies is that *social relationships* can be understood as a reflecton of two dimensions of interaction content: *power* and *status* as they are called here. Later I offer a set of postulates about social interaction from which the relational dimensions can be derived.

So as not to impede the forward flow of the presentation and to move as rapidly as possible to the treatment of emotions, I relegate some additional materials to two appendices. The first resolves certain ambiguities in factor-analytic results in which the two-dimensional model* appears to be negated or obscured. The reader who is especially interested in the question of the number of dimensions and the factor-analytic strategy in getting at these dimensions will find Appendix 1 of interest. Appendix 2 elaborates the conceptual aspects of the two dimensions beyond the contents of this chapter. The reader who finds that the ideas presented here about power and status clash with his own or with those of other authors, such as Homans, Blau, and Thibaut and Kelley, will be interested in consulting Appendix 2.

The substantive argument of this chapter leads to what Lopreato and Alston (1970) called a "propaedautic idealization," in particular, a heuristic model of social relationships that is confined to two dimensions. As with all models, it is a lens that focuses attention on some aspects of phenomena while excluding other

---

*I take a terminological liberty in this book by calling the two-dimensional framework of social relationships a "model," although it is probably more accurate to call it a paradigm (Kuhn, 1962).

possible data from view. The model can be of interest, of course, only to the extent that it provides a parsimonious, comprehensive explanation of matters that are important to practitioners in the field. The two-dimensional model is validated in part by its ability to explain a wide variety of disparate results in the factor-analytic approach to the question of the basic dimensions of interaction (see Appendix 1 for an extended discussion of this) and in part by its utility for a wide-ranging theory in the area of emotions.

TECHNICAL, POWER, AND STATUS ACTS

The basic postulate of the sociological approach taken here is that human relationships generally occur within a context of interdependence and division of labor between actors. This is of necessity true because if humans were not fundamentally interdependent there would be no need for them to come together. Interdependence also implies a division of labor, that is, "co-action" (Firth, 1951; Nadel, 1957) directed toward a goal that cannot be attained by the single individuals. In the course of the cooperative activity, a "simple" or more "complex" division of labor emerges in which different persons engage in different parts of the common task (Durkheim, 1933, pp. 124, 212; Kemper, 1972).

Analytically the division of labor seems like the correct starting point for sociological analysis, because any lower level of abstraction would obviate the need for sociology except as a descriptive discipline. Thus it is fairly well agreed that most of the explanation of the complex societies of bees and ants is genetic. Despite the interest we may take in descriptions of bee or ant behavior, if we wish to explain the behavior we do not look to the social organization of these insects but to their genetic code. Social organization for these forms is an expression of the genetic, not an independent explanatory condition. If humans acted largely according to genetic instructions, sociology would merely be a descriptive embellishment on biology. In the same vein, if humans were *all* Robinson Crusoes, capable of surviving and adapting in isolation from others, this might lead us to explain human behavior exclusively by means of a psychological theory. In the case of truly self-sufficient human beings we would need to know only the organism's psychic make-up. Other humans would enter the picture as features of the environment, of much the same significance as plants, animals, mountains, or hurricanes. That is, they are there, but they contribute nothing to the explanation of behavior. This point of view has long been identified as the atomistic fallacy, and we need not spend more time with it.

In the division of labor of the sciences, sociology begins at the point at which human behavior cannot be explained by genetics or individual psychology. The sociologist's task is to deduce the consequences of interdependence and the division of labor—not as mere description, for, after all, bees and ants have a division of labor too—but as an explanation of what humans feel and do.

Participation in the division of labor entails doing certain *technical* things to accomplish the task for which actors are together in the first place. This may involve the exchange of food, tools, materials (both raw and processed), information, even women (and men), as Levi-Strauss (1963, p. 289) has so perceptively suggested. All the great variety of skills associated with formally differentiated occupations, as well as informal roles in social interaction, reflect the elaborate technical activity that actors engage in as participants in the human division of labor.

I suggest as a second postulate that when the division of labor becomes complex—and this may involve only two actors who must allocate tasks between them—there arises a need for a new function, namely, one that will attend to coordination, scheduling and sequencing, deciding priorities when emergency conditions prevail, and so on. For what it is worth, Marx (1964a, pp. 150–151) and Engels (in Marx and Engels, 1959, pp. 481–485) on one hand, and Parsons (1956) on the other, agree that a role we usually identify as leader or coordinator emerges at some point in the division of labor.

More generally the technical exigencies of the division of labor require that the actors sooner or later turn their attention from purely technical activities to a consideration of their *relations* with each other. Bales and Strodtbeck (1951) dealt with the problem as a matter of phase movement, whereas Parsons, Bales, and Shils (1953) identified this as a functional requisite of any social system. Terms such as "sociogroup" and "psychegroup" (Jennings, 1950), "external" and "internal" (Homans, 1950), and "instrumental" and "expressive" (Parsons, 1955) have been used to refer to the technical-relational distinction (cf. J. Israel, 1966).

Illustratively, in the construction of a house the carpenter may hammer and saw, and the plumber tap pipe and solder (these are technical activities), but at some point it may become necessary for either one to be able to request or order the other (relational activities) to stop or to work faster; in the usual case, some third party emerges to handle these questions. At this point it is no longer a question of functionally differentiated specialists, each doing his technical activity in the division of labor, but of the way the actors are oriented to each other, that is, their *relationship*.

The pivotal question in this derivation of the basic dimensions of social relationship can now be broached: How may we explain that individuals *do* comply with the actual or implied desires, requests, orders, or demands of other individuals in the division of labor? Generalized, the question is *Why does A do what B wants him to do?* In answer I propose two analytically independent explanations: either A *does what B wants because A is actually or potentially being coerced to do so by B,* or A *does what B wants because A wants to do it as a benefit to B.*

It is crucial to understand at this point that the question and the answers just given are treated in a very general form and that many different answers of a more specific nature can be given, depending on one's interests. Parsons (1963), for example, puts a somewhat similar question and proposed an answer in the form of a set of mechanisms by which compliance is obtained. He offered a fourfold table whose cells are labeled *inducement, persuasion, activation of commitments,* and *coercion*. It is also possible to answer the question as to why A complies with B's request, wish, order, or demand from the point of view of A's *motives*. Weber dealt with the matter directly and disposed of it:

> In a concrete case the performance of the command may have been motivated by the ruled's own conviction of its propriety, or by his sense of duty, or by fear, or by "dull" custom, or by a desire to obtain some benefit for himself. *Sociologically, these differences are not necessarily relevant* (Weber, 1968, Vol. 3, pp. 946–947, emphasis added).

Although individual motives for compliance may be more important than Weber implies, the interaction model proposed here is concerned neither with specific motives nor with mechanisms to induce compliance, but with the *intentional behavior* of actors toward each other. The emphasis is on the link *between* actors. Action toward others is either *coerced* or *voluntary*. This conclusion also conforms to the two dimensions of relationship between actors that are found in the many factor analyses of interaction available to us. Let us consider now the implications of the two answers offered above to the question of why A does what B wants.

First, compliance based on coercion or the threat of coercion seems to be very much in keeping with Weber's (1946) definition of *power:* "the chance of a man or a number of men to realize their own will in a communal action even against the resistance of others" (p. 180). Actors do not ordinarily use power unless other actors resist givng what is wanted from them or could conceivably resist in the future. What is wanted, of course, are various benefits, rewards, and privileges. Power is thus a mode of social relationship in which compliance, broadly speaking, is obtained from others who do not give it willingly (Kemper, 1974). Thibaut and Kelley (1959, p. 243) also spoke of the "non-voluntary" nature of compliance in power relationships. Despite the attempt by Parsons (1963) to remove the implication of coercion from the concept of power, it is central to a meaningful definition of power (cf. Bierstedt, 1950; Wrong, 1968; Blau, 1964; Tedeschi and Bonoma, 1973). Definitional and terminological quibbles aside, it is incontestable that force, coercion, threat, and the like are significant modes of human interaction, and a comprehensive model of social relationships must acknowledge their existence.

Considering now the second ground for compliance, namely A doing B's will, not because of coercion but because he wants to do it, that is, voluntary compliance, the popular but elusive sociological term *status* is suggested. Thus A's doing B's bidding or responding voluntarily to B's request, order, or command is a reflection of B's status and is one form of the currency in which B's status is paid to him. In a dyad, if B has higher status than A, this means that B receives more in the way of voluntary compliance from A than A receives from B. Ultimately it is possible to rank the actors in a social system according to how much voluntary compliance, or status, they receive on the average from those with whom they interact.

Runciman (1968) also defined these terms essentially as they are defined here (the fact that Runciman's distinction between power and status emerged in the course of a discussion of animal studies does not bear significantly on the issue):

> Animal hierarchies often rest on force, or the threat of force, and this sense are relations of *power*, even where the threats are highly ritualized and thus, serve the function of inhibiting fights to the death. But given ritualization there can be an additional element of what it is perhaps legitimate to call '*status*' in the relationship, as is seen in the gestures of positive and respectful submission shown for example, by wolves and some monkeys toward their superiors, or in the non-coercive leader-follower relationships observed among ducks, sheep and deer (Runciman, 1968, p. 36, emphasis added).

SOME CONSEQUENCES OF THE FOREGOING

According to the model of social interaction just presented, human actors engage in technical activity in the division of labor and relational activity toward each other. The basic content of the relational activity is power behavior and status behavior. At its strongest, the model implies that *there is nothing more to observe when there is human social interaction than technical activity and acts designed to acquire, express, maintain, increase, or upset relations of power and status.* I propose that these are the important elements of interaction for the sociologist.

A comprehensive description of the types of behavior implied by the power-status model includes the following:

Power. (1) A's actions to force B to do what B does not want to do, for example, beating, cursing, screaming, threatening, punishing and so on. Even cruel and hurtful remarks that serve no apparent or immediate purpose create a structural condition of relationship in which the user of such verbal power has so reduced the other's status claims that they are essentially dismissable. The person who is thus demeaned is under constraint to accept the other's definition of his worth. In relational terms, the victim is at a disadvantage and must frequently comply to avoid even further debasement. (2) B's countermeasures, including power acts as above, as well as avoidance and escape acts, for example, warding off blows, jumping out of the way of a blow, leaving the room, and so on. (3) B's acts of compliance should A's power overcome B. These acts are virtually infinite is number and kind, including working in a factory, serving in the army, cooking suppers, accepting sexual intercourse, picking up a scrap of lint, publicly denouncing oneself, doing one's homework, typing a manuscript, and so on.

Status.   (1) A's actions that may elicit status from B, for example, politeness, courtesy, lovingness, competent performance, manifesting any characteristic that matches standards held by B (see Chapters 11 and 12). (2) A's verbalized claims for status: "I have a Ph.D.," "My father is rich," "Of course we're not Jewish," "They elected me by acclamation," "I'm one of the most lovable persons you'll ever meet." (3) B's acts of status accord, virtually infinite in number and kind and equivalent in content to acts of compliance that are coerced [see (3)] except that these are voluntary.

Each category of interactional content is of theoretical interest. In this book, I give attention mainly to A's (or B's) power behavior and to whether B's (or A's) compliance is voluntary, that is, whether given as status. The particular content of the acts of compliance, whether voluntary or coerced, is not examined. Some will find this content an important source of theoretical advance (e.g., Foa and Foa, 1970). I do not deal with this material here. Neither do I give more than passing attention to A's (or B's) verbalized status claims. These are part of what Goffman (1959) has called "front" for purposes of presenting one's self and establishing an identity that others can accept and credit. This is an important mode of establishing the level of status an actor gets from others, but, given the other concerns of this book, I can give only scant attention to it.

An important implication of the power-status model is that *all social relations referred to in common parlance terms, for example, romantic love, international relations, exploitation, collegiality, and so on can be understood as relations of power and status.* (The purely technical activity is ignored for the present. In Appendix 1, I discuss the problem of the overlap of the technical and relational.)

The social relations of common parlance can be depicted quite easily in a two-dimensional space in which one axis represents power and the other status. By placing actors in the space according to their power and status—relative to each other—common parlance terms for any social relationship are usefully explicated. Figure 2.1 shows a number of relationships plotted according to what I believe is a common understanding of their power and status components.*
Thus romantic love is seen as two actors both extremely high in both power and status vis a vis each other. Each lover does what the other wants because he wants

---

*The power and status axes are plotted orthogonally since in virtually all factor analyses the two dimensions were obtained by orthogonal rotation of factors.

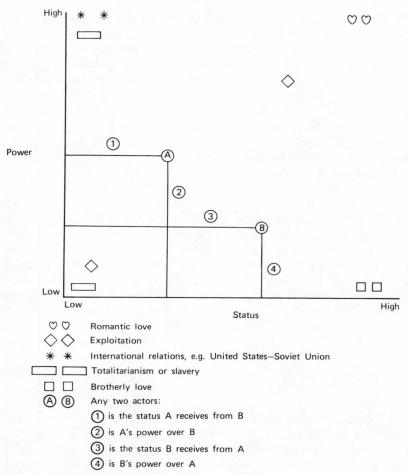

Figure 2–1   Some common relationships as depicted in the power-status space.

to; that is, the level of voluntary compliance or status conferral is extremely high on both sides. Should it turn out, however, that either lover could not or did not comply at the level desired by the other, the other often has the coercive capability, that is, power, to compel the compliance. From this point of view it is clear why romantic love is so volatile and evanescent: the demands on each lover to confer status on the other can be very great and therefore difficult to sustain, while at the same time the potential for coercion is ever present should there be reduced voluntary compliance. (Love relationships are the topic of Chapters 12 and 13.)

In contrast to the perils of romantic love, in brotherly love (see Figure 2.1) the actors are extremely high in status, that is, there is a great deal of mutual voluntary compliance, but there is no coercion. The actors are essentially at the zero point on the power dimension. Given this view of brotherly love, it is easy to see why it remains a utopian concept. Power would have to be dissolved from human relationships. This is perhaps what is meant by saintliness, a quality more easily described than attained. (In Figure 2.1 several other social relationships are plotted according to their putative power and status positions.)

Heuristically, I assume that power and status are the theoretically fruitful relational dimensions for actors at any level, whether individuals, small groups, collectivities, or societies (see Appendix 1). Were this not the case, the analytic dimensions of social relationships would change as the units change. This does not seem to be a reasonable position. I do not mean to say that all macrotheory is identical with microtheory, only that the *relations* between macrogroups may be understood by means of the same set of analytic dimensions that characterize the relations between individuals or small groups, namely, power and status. It is also a very small step to take at this point to propose that the power and status relational model may be applied diachronically (i.e., in historical studies) as well as synchronically.

Should it be objected that power and status are not what actors appear to be doing, but rather talking to each other, exchanging goods and services, making bodily contact, and so on, I propose that these manifest behaviors are sociologically meaningless in and of themselves. Only when a theoretical "lens," so to speak, is interposed between the observer and the phenomenal world is the manifest behavior brought into sociological focus (cf. Simmel, 1950, pp. 3–25). A highly productive lens is available in the specification of power and status as the two relational dimensions of interaction. Such actions as talking, exchanging goods and services, making bodily contact, and so on may be seen as instances of either technical activity that goes on in the division of labor or relational activity (power and status), or both, if there is an overlap between the technical and the relational.

Admittedly, in the relational domain a codebook is required to permit the accurate classification of acts into either power or status categories. Yet this is not an insurmountable task, for actors are continually experiencing power and status behavior directed toward them and are most often fully aware of it. These same actors direct power and status acts to others, and most often the others are fully aware of it. When the other does not "get the point," the behavior or the message is repeated until it is understood. Indeed, one of the functions of any culture is to provide a key to the power-status meaning of concrete behavior.

Thompson and Meltzer (1964) have shown experimentally that research subjects can convey to judges a variety of emotional states by facial expressions alone. This finding merely underscores the fact that there is a cultural codebook, that is, shared understanding about what behavioral gestures signify. What is true for emotional states ought to be no less true for the power and status relevance of behavior. A somewhat more intensive application of this principal is illustrated by the work of Ekman (1964), who found that individuals can match photographs of persons, taken while they were talking, with their verbalizations when the picture was taken. In light of this evidence it is not difficult to assume that most power and status behavior is readily identifiable as such.

Ethnomethodology, to the extent that it is sociological, is devoted to the intensive development of the codebook of social interaction (cf. M. Israel, 1969). The content of the social life whose creation and sustained character the ethnomethodologists investigate may be understood heuristically, if not actually, as the interplay of power and status relations and technical activity (see Schegeloff, 1968; Sudnow, 1967).

I believe there is good theoretical sense in choosing a two-dimensional model in which power and status are the fundamental modes of relationship between actors. This is no new insight. A review of some earlier efforts to explicate the fundamental grounds of human behavior in two dimensions is of some interest now.

Earlier Theory

In the long history of efforts to explain human behavior, one of the more consistent themes involves the concepts of reward and punishment. The notion is found among the pre-Socratic Greeks,* in religious conceptions of heaven and hell, in the Utilitarians' hedonic calculus, in Freud's *eros* and *thanatos*, in the positive and negative reinforcements of contemporary learning theorists, in the cost–benefit analysis of operations researchers, as well as in such works as those of Thibaut and Kelly (1959), Homans (1961), Blau (1964), and Emerson (1971).

That some version of reward–punishment theory is traditional as well as empirical to a large degree (as in the case of the learning theorists) is no automatic warrant for its acceptance. A closer examination of reward and punishment, however, argues strongly for a tempered acceptance, especially given the previous discussion of this chapter.

First, consider punishment in the light of Weber's definition of power—"the

---

*Freud (1937, pp. 349–350) recognized the antique origin of his own two-dimensional—*eros* and *thanatos*—approach. The pre-Socratic Greek philosopher Empedocles had postulated two dynamic forces in the universe: love and strife or hatred (Cleve, 1969). Obviously Empedocles' dimensions can be easily assimilated to the core ideas of status and power, respectively.

chance of a man or a number of men to realize their own will . . . even against the resistance of others." If one must realize one's will against the resistance of others, the others are still opposed, and this requires the use of threat or presentation of aversive stimuli, that is, punishment. Thus power and punishment are clearly parallel concepts.

On the other hand, status implies rewards. To accord status is to give rewards. To have status is to get rewards from others who accord status, whether the rewards are counted in dollars or deference. To have high status in a relationship with another is to receive much reward and gratification from that other. To have low status is obviously to receive relatively little reward and gratification from the other.

By definition, status means that the rewards are given voluntarily. It is quite easy to think of instances in which gratifications and rewards are obtained through power, for example, fraud, theft, or rape. Reward is thus not the *differentia* between the effects of power and status in social relations. It is whether the reward is given freely.

Although the relational model presented here is closely linked to classical and current notions of punishment and reward, these forms are understood somewhat differently from other approaches. Ordinarily, in the individualistically oriented theories in which rewards play an important part, the reward is of interest *because it is gratifying and affects the behavior of the actor who receives it*, who is also the focus of analysis. In a sociological or relational analysis, however, we are interested not only in the actor who receives the reward, *but also in the actor who gives it*. Although the behavior of one actor may be rewarding to another actor, that behavior may be an act of love or the bitterest gall to the actor who performs it. This distinction between actions undertaken voluntarily and those which are the result of coercion is at the core of social relationships. It makes a very great difference for the course of the relationship and the emotions engendered if the "rewarding" behavior is given as status or is coerced by power. By viewing the concept of reward, which I do not abandon, not only from the point of view of the recipient, but also from that of the donor, we can retain the large body of work which has treated rewards only psychologically, that is, as benefits to the recipient; we also enlarge the scope of analysis so that rewards can be considered in the light of their relational significance.

In recent times one of the earliest non-factor-analytic statements of the two-dimensional model was that of Freedman, Leary, Ossorio, and Coffrey (1951). The dimensions were named *Dominate–Submit* and *Love–Hate* and were later incorporated by Leary (1957) in his own work. Brown (1965) also discusses the power-status dimensions but labels them *Status* and *Solidarity*. However, Brown's definitions of these terms reveal that they refer to the power and status dimensions, respectively. More interesting is the fact that Brown derived the two dimensions not from an examination of behavior in interaction, but from forms of linguistic usage (see Appendix 1 for more on this).

Bales' (1970) recent three-dimensional scheme of "up," "down," and "forward or back" may also be understood as power, status, and technical activity, as can Bales' earlier work on interaction process analysis if one analyzes the famliar 12 categories thus: The first three categories, including "shows solidarity," shows tension release," and "agrees" are status–conferral behaviors; Bales refers to this set as "Socio-Emotional Area: Positive." The six central categories beginning with "gives suggestions" and ending with "asks for suggestion" are technical activity; Bales calls the set "Task Area: Neutral." Finally, the last three IAPA categories, including "disagrees'" "shows tension" and "shows antagonism" are equivalent to the power dimension: Bales labels this set "Socio-Emotional Area: Negative." In subsequent work and in the cognate work of Parsons and Bales (1955), Zelditch (1955), and others, the two socioemotional areas were yoked under the rubric "Expressive" and were contrasted with the technical activity labeled "Instrumental." Although this concision may be useful for some purposes, it obscures the very important differences between power and status behaviors.

From the foregoing it is evident that the power-status model is not a novelty, invented ad hoc, or representing a minor vision of human relationship. Power as force, coercion, threat, and the like is an incontrovertible reality of human affairs, and many have seen this. Equally, the accord of status, as congeniality, respect, friendship, and love is also incontrovertibly a mode of human relationship. Many have seen this too. Nonetheless, until systematic empirical evidence suports the power-status model, it remains merely speculation. The technique of factor analysis has been virtually indispensable here.

Empirical Results

For about two decades, in scores of factor-analytic studies of observational and survey data of husband–wife interaction, parent–child interaction, group therapy sessions, military combat teams, work groups, interaction in neonate groups and international relations, and in many factor analyses of personality data that include interactional and relational characteristics, at least a dimension of power and a dimension of status have emerged. That is, researchers universally find a dimension that reflects in some degree coercion, domination, threat, force, control, and the like (power) and a dimension that reflects in some degree voluntary compliance and giving to others as in friendship, support, affection, warmth, and the like (status).

The power and status dimensions are variously labeled, depending on the author and the source of data, as Individual Prominence and Achievement and

Sociability (Carter, 1954), Assertiveness and Likeability (Borgatta, Cottrell, and Mann, 1958; Borgatta, 1964), Authoritarian-Control and Hostility-Rejection (Zuckerman et al., 1958), Control and Affection (Schutz, 1958), Autonomy vs. Control and Love vs. Hostility (Schaefer, 1959), Dominance-Submission and Hostility-Affection (LaForge, in Foa, 1961), Dominance and Friendliness (Burke and Bennis, 1961), Control and Affection (Lorr and McNair, 1963), Psychological Autonomy vs. Psychological Control and Acceptance vs. Rejection (Schaefer, 1965), Power and Leader-Member Relations (Fiedler, 1964), Interpersonal Deprivation and Interpersonal Seeking (Longabaugh, 1966), Tendency to Use Socially Unacceptable Techniques and Tendency to Use Socially Acceptable Techniques (Marwell and Schmitt, 1967), Equal versus Unequal and Cooperative and Friendly versus Competitive and Hostile (Wish, Deutsch, and Kaplan, 1976). Additional sources of similar two-dimensional outcomes are reviewed in Rinn (1965) and Goldin (1969).

Despite the variation in factor names and the nuances of difference implied, two underlying relational themes appear in this list, namely, coercive control of one actor by another and the degree of positive social relations, or, as I call them, power and status.

An examination of the items as well as a consideration of the factor names support the power-status interpretation. Table 2.1 lists the highest loading items under the names assigned by various investigators to the power factors that emerged in their research. Although not every item in each power factor conveys the implications of force, threat, punishment, control, and the like, these aspects of relationships are clearly anchored in the factors in such items as "is authoritarian" (Borgatta, 1964), "authoritarianism" and "aggressiveness" (Carter, 1954), "forceful" and "quick to take the lead" (Wherry, 1950, in Carter, 1954), "attempts to dominate" (Longabaugh, 1966), "threat" and "aversive stimulation" (Marwell and Schmitt, 1967), "many threats" (Rummel, 1966). Even when these are not the highest loading items, they help define the factor. More important, the repeated emergence of such power items indubitably confirms the empirical presence of a power dimension.

In like manner, as can be seen in Table 2.2, status factors are loaded by such items as "is friendly" and "is pleasant" (Borgatta, 1964), "pointed toward group acceptance" (Carter, 1954), "genial" and "cordial" (Wherry, 1950, in Carter 1954), "gives support-approval" (Longabaugh, 1966), "promise (of rewards)" and "liking" (Marwell and Schmitt, 1967). Although actors do manifest such positive orientations toward others inauthentically or because of coercion, it is implausible and cynical to suggest that such actions and sentiments are never genuine. The factor-analytic results thus support the view that actors also relate to each other by giving benefits and rewards to others that are not coerced by power and the threat of its use.

TABLE 2-1   POWER FACTORS AND ITEMS

Assertiveness (Borgatta, 1964)
  Is very active
  Does most of the talking
  Is authoritarian
  Is assertive

Individual Prominence (Couch and Carter, in Carter, 1954)
  Authoritarianism
  Confidence
  Aggressiveness
  Leadership
  Striving for recognition

Forceful Leadership and Initiative (Wherry, 1950, reported in Carter, 1954)
  Bold
  Forceful
  Not timid
  Quick to take the lead

Interpersonal Deprivation (Longabaugh, 1966)
  Attempts to dominate
  Assaults socially
  Symbolic aggression

Tendency to Use Socially Unacceptable Techniques (Marwell and Schmitt, 1967)
  Threat
  Aversive stimulation
  Debt [calling a debt because of past favors]
  Negative esteem [threatening loss of esteem from others]

Conflict Pattern (Rummel, 1967)
  Many threats

When we examine factor names, we find considerable variability in both the power and status dimensions. In the status dimension, for example, factors are named Sociability, Affection, Likability, and so on. These different labels may make it appear that the factors are different dimensions, yet the items reveal that they all refer essentially to voluntary compliance with the wishes of the other, which is at the core of the concept of status. Where the factor names are not simply synonymous, it is not hard to see that the differences reflect different levels of intensity along the continuum of status. Thus Sociability and Likability are somewhat lower on the status band than Affection and Love. Similar considerations affect factor labels of the power dimension.

TABLE 2–2   STATUS FACTORS AND ITEMS

Likeability (Borgatta, 1964)
Is friendly
Is pleasant
Is likeable
Supports others

Group-Sociability (Couch and Carter in Carter, 1954)
Sociability
Adaptability
Pointed toward group acceptance

Successful Interpersonal Relations (Wherry reported in Carter, 1954)
Genial
Cordial
Well-liked

Interpersonal Seeking (Longabaugh, 1966)
Gives support-approval
Gives help
Suggests responsibility

Tendency to Use Socially Acceptable Techniques (Marwell and Schmitt, 1967)
Promise [of reward]
Liking
Positive altercasting

In some cases the whole range of the power or status dimension emerges as a bipolar factor, for example, Hostility versus Affection. This is not, strictly speaking, in accordance with the understanding of status proposed here. When no status is given or received, sociability, affection, or the like is neither given nor received. There is no negative status in this view, nor is there negative power (cf. Hare, 1970). Carter (1954), Borgatta (1964), and Longabaugh (1966) obtained unipolar dimensions with scales that run from zero to some positive amount. On the other hand Schaefer (1959, 1965a, 1965b), Lorr and McNair (1963), and LaForge (in Foa, 1961) obtained bipolar factors. Although the differences between the unipolar and the bipolar solutions are not substantively serious, the grounds of difference between the two are worth discussing.

First, bipolar factors emerge principally when items or scales that are factor analyzed have strong negative correlations with each other. Thus if two items with opposite meaning that measure the same concept are included (e.g., Schaefer's scales labeled "control" and "[permit] autonomy," their oppositeness guarantees that they will form the two poles of a single factor, rather than defining two different factors (cf. Bryson, 1974). By reversing the scoring direction of one of the items, the correlation between them is made positive, and a unipolar factor results.

Second, if some items measure a type of behavior by one actor and other items the type of response the behavior evokes from another actor (e.g., LaForge's measures of "dominance" and "submission"), the chances are very strong that a bipolar factor will emerge. Typologies of personality are very strongly concerned with this form of bipolarity, since it may help identify both proactive and reactive characteristics of the individual.

Because of the circumplex format to which they are amenable, bipolar solutions have the virtue of nicely describing the interfactor space that is blurred by orthogonal factors (see Schaefer, 1959; Lorr and McNair, 1963). The bipolar solution is also metaphorically more appealing, for example, "love *versus* hostility," "control *versus* autonomy." Where the dimensions lend themselves to such polar conceptualizations they are more starkly revealed. Cognitive clarity is known to be enhanced by the double anchoring of scales (Heise 1969). On the other hand, the unipolar solutions have the virtue of being able to represent the relational positions of *two* actors, revealing where each stands in reference to the other on the same dimensions. The bipolar solution presents a somewhat better picture of the behavior and attitudes or feelings of single actors (cf. Lorr, Klett, and McNair, 1963, p. 27). Regardless of whether a unipolar or bipolar factor is obtained, the content of relational factors appears clearly located in either the power dimension or the status dimension. This uniformity overshadows any suggestion that the power-status model can be easily attenuated on the basis of factor polarity.

Based on the persuasive evidence of the factor analyses of interaction and theories of personality compatible with it (e.g., Leary, 1957), many authors now employ the two-dimensional model as an organizing framework. Winch (1958), Couch (1960), Straus (1964), Brim et al. (1962), Cancian (1964), Pepitone (1964), Mishler and Waxler (1968), Carson (1969), Boulding (1970), Triandis (1972), Swensen (1973), Heilbrun (1973), and Benjamin (1974) have used the model in their work. There is thus a broad recognition both theoretically and empirically that two dimensions account for a considerable amount of interactional behavior, personality in social settings, attitudes toward interaction, and even meanings of stimulus objects.

Culture and Epiphenomenal Indicators of Power and Status

Considering the diversity of the substantive interests of the researchers, the variety of populations, and the spectrum of methods employed, the empirical convergence on two relational dimensions of interaction is indeed remarkable. It is also remarkable that the convergence was glimpsed despite the blurring effect of discrepancies between the separate studies in the number and types of factors produced (see Appendix 1). An even more fundamental blurring can occur when we consider cross-cultural differences in the behaviors, indicators, and symbols of power and status. Although I assert a heuristic claim for the universality of the relational dimensions, I do not make the same claim for their concrete indicators. The major axis of variability of the indicators is culture, understood either at the societal or the subsocietal level. The symbols and signs of status in New Guinea are markedly different from those in a United States city, and within the city they are different in a ghetto from what they are in a corporate setting. At corporate headquarters they are different for underlings from what they are for the executive elite. Each category and each group has specific indices and criteria for the acquisition and expression of status and power (Benoit-Smullyan, 1944). This manifest variability is *epiphenomenal*, despite its charm and interest for students of ethnography. I believe that a useful theory of human behavior cannot be developed on the basis of the culturally variable manifestations that greet and blind the eyes of even the scientific observer.

There are two ways in which cultural variability obscures the underlying power and status dimensions. First is the epiphenomenal variability of the behavioral and symbolic indicators just mentioned. Second are the factual and normative patterns of power and status relationships that operate in a given society or subsector of society. Thus in many societies much deference (status) is given to elders; in Western society deference to elders is limited. In Western societies, middle-class children are encouraged to relate to parents in an egalitarian manner; in working-class families the power difference between parents and children is more strictly maintained (White, 1957; Kohn, 1969). Thus the scientific observer who wishes to test propositions about social behavior is confronted with a *doubly* variable set of phenomena, often within the same society. These twin sources of differentiation cause much ambiguity about what is to be systematically analyzed. Because of the double variability the researcher is often confused about what the data "mean." In the end, they are often analyzed in the most shallow fashion, that is, at the epiphenomenal level itself.

Cross-cultural studies of relationships necessarily confront the problem of double variability. Triandis (1972) penetrated the cultural variability and found in addition to a division-of-labor-task factor which he calls Association–Dissociation, two relational factors: a power factor (Superordination–Subordination,) and a status factor (Intimacy). He referred to these as "the fundamental dimensions of human social behavior [that] are obtained with different methods of human investigation" (p. 270). Wish, Deutsch, and Kaplan (1976) also reported a power factor (Equal–Unequal) and a status factor

(Cooperative and Friendly versus Competitive and Hostile) in their analysis of Greek and American views of 44 interpersonal dyads. They commented specifically on the problem of double variability:

> Although the underlying dimensions appear to be the same in the two different cultures, the location within their dimensional space of *specific role relations* and *specific social behaviors* is different . . . [T]hus even though certain dimensions of interpersonal relations may be culturally invariant, the social meaning of particular role relations may vary from culture to culture (p. 419, emphasis added).

This does not mean that the epiphenomena are uninteresting or unimportant as culture-bound indicators of underlying dimensions, but that which is immediately evident and observable makes possible only a very low order of scientific theory. Willer and Webster (1970) cogently analyzed strategies of theory construction in the sciences and concluded that theoretical progress is fostered by working with concepts at the "construct level" as opposed to the level of "observables." The major difference between the two is that, whereas observables are rich with immediate experience, constructs permit the development of cumulative theories. The power-status model is the construct level that grounds the epiphenomenal variability. The factor-analytic results provide a sufficiently strong empirical foundation to warrant a trial of the power-status dimensions as the contruct level at which to build theory.

However, the reader may not wish to accept the results of the original factor analyses or my interpretation of them. It should be noted, however, that I do not offer plausibility as a ground for credibility. Scientific theories are often highly implausible, yet they have worked in the sense that they have led to significant results in research. The power-status model must stand or fall according to whether it can do the same. The technical-relational distinction and the power-status relational model are not treated here as theoretical statements, but as indispensable descriptive constructs that can be used to form theoretical statements. According to Laing (1971), "Unless one can describe one cannot explain" (p. 75). According to Eysenck (1952), "Measurement is essential to science, but before we can measure, we must know what it is we want to measure. Qualitative or taxonomic discovery must precede quantitative measurement" (p. 34).

The reader who finds some merit in the power-status position, but does not feel he can go "all the way" by adopting these as the only relational dimensions need feel no constraint to do so. Some formulation of social relations is necessary for a sociological theory of emotions. For heuristic purposes, I adopt the power-status model. By trying to hold to it consistently in subsequent chapters, I put it to a rigorous test, and its errors and omissions are more easily perceived. Thereby a better theory is possible.

chapter 3

A Sociological Theory of Emotions: Structural Emotions

The ingredients for a sociological-theory of emotions are available to us. All social relations between actors can be plotted in the power-status space, and this is the key to the theory of emotions presented in this and succeeding chapters. Here I propose the general hypothesis that *a very large class of emotions results from real, imagined, or anticipated outcomes in social relationships.* To account for emotions that have a social locus, we must be able to specify the full range of real, imagined, and anticipated relational outcomes. For this purpose an astonishingly simple formulation suffices.

The theory begins with a dyadic model of relationship. Later this is expanded to include a third party, but at this point, since there are two actors who relate to each other in the two dimensions of power and status, this gives rise to four relational channels. From the viewpoint of each actor, there is his own power, the other's power, his own status, and the other's status (see Figure 2.1 on page 32 for depiction of these channels for any two actors A and B). Given this format, 12 logically possible relational outcomes can result from any interaction episode. Figure 3.1 shows the complete set for two actors, A and B. A and B may gain power, or they may lose power; A and B may gain status, or they may lose status; both the power and status levels of A and B may continue as before. Logically, every interaction episode produces a relational outcome in each of the four relational channels. Thus A may gain power and lose status, whereas B gains power and status, or A may lose power and gain status, whereas B loses power but his status does not change, and so on. Since neither actor can both gain *and* lose power or status at the same time or continue at the same level while he gains or loses in the same dimension, four changes are the maximum number that can actually occur as a result of a single real, imagined, or anticipated interaction episode. Although there can be as many as four changes of relational standing, there need not be even a single change. However, even where there is no change, intense emotions may ensue, as shown later. Since the A-B, power-status model allows as many as four relational changes to occur simultaneously, this produces our first theoretical benefit, namely, an explanation of mixed or

43

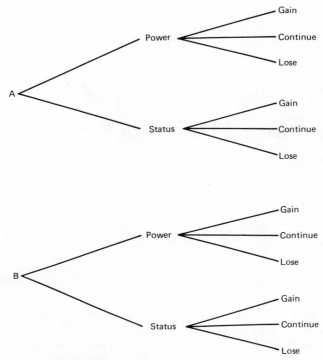

Figure 3-1   Possible outcomes of social interaction.

conflicting emotions. If, as is established later, different emotions follow from changes in different relational channels, simultaneous change in more than a single channel of self and other's relationship automatically produces more than one emotion. For example, we feel both happy and fearful: it means that the outcome of interaction has affected more than one of the four relational channels.

Agency. The four relational outcomes of any interaction episode are always due to an agent. Either *self* or *other* (it is useful at times to adopt the self-other or own and other terminology, since this makes it easier for the reader to view the whole relational scheme from the perspective of a single actor) was responsible or in some sense caused the particular set of outcomes. Agency is understood from the perspective of the actor who has the emotion. If he believes that he was the responsible agent, his emotion is influenced in one way by this, even if objective observers would say he is not the agent. If he believes the other was the agent, his emotion is influenced accordingly, even if objective observers would say the other is not the agent. An actor may assign responsibility for agency to self or other in various ways. Self may accept responsibility for the outcomes in all four relational channels, assign responsibility for all to the other, divide the responsibility by relational channel, or even assign a shared responsibility to self and other for single channels. These manifold possibilities are appropriate for the task of delineating the often puzzling pattern of emotional nuances evoked by social interaction.

The concern with agency is standard. Pastore (1952) helped to introduce the concept in his analysis of the frustration-aggression hypothesis. Aggression follows frustration, he claimed, only when there is an intentional agent of the frustration. Rotter's (1966) internal and external control are also agency concepts, since they allocate locus of responsibility for the outcomes the actor experiences. Those who score high on internal control generally believe they are the agents responsible for what happens to them, whereas those high on external control feel that others determine outcomes for them. Attribution theory (Kelley, 1971; Bem, 1967; Valins and Nisbett, 1971) also relies on the notion of an agent with a certain degree of intentionality to his behavior. The agent, of course, may be the self. Thibaut and Kelley (1959), Ezekiel (1968), and Stokols (1975) also used the concept of agency.

Third Parties. To make the theory of emotions based on relational outcomes fully general, we require the concept of third party as agent. The third party is responsible for outcomes in the A-B relationship that are caused or brought about by an agent outside the relationship. For example, if A and B are peers in an organization and C promotes A over B, the relationship between A and B is changed, although neither A nor B was the agent of the change in a direct sense. The third party is frequently a concrete individual with whom A and/or B have a relationship, but in the most general case the third party can be an impersonal force, for example, "the system," illness, aging, death, Fate, God, and so on.

Direction of Emotion. The concept of agency in the determination of relational outcomes suggests that, for any given relational outcome, different emotions may be directed toward the different parties involved: self, other, and third party (if there is one). For example, if A loves B but B loses interest in A, A's emotional response varies according to whether he attributes the change to his own shortcomings (self as agent), B's fickleness (other as agent), or to the pernicious intervention of C (third party as agent). Indeed, A may believe that all these are true; thus there is compound agency for the relational change. In the triangular situation described, it is likely that A feels three different emotions: sorry for himself, angry with B, and jealous of C.

When self is the agent of the outcome, one may have emotions toward self and toward other. When other is agent, one may also have emotions toward self and toward other. When a third party is agent, emotions may be directed toward self, other, and third party. Figure 3.2 shows the sevenfold set of possibilities when agency and direction of emotion are considered together.

Summary Postulates. The sociological theory of emotions is founded on the following postulates:

1. Relationships between actors can be characterized by locating the actors relative to each other on the two relational dimensions of power and status.
2. In any interaction episode, up to four possible relational changes can occur simultaneously.
3. Relational changes are understood as gain or loss in the power and status positions of the actors vis a vis each other.

Agent	Direction	Emotion
S	S	
	O	
O	S	
	O	
T	S	
	O	
	T	

S = Self
O = Other
T = Third party

Figure 3–2   Agency and direction of emotions.

4. Continuity of the existing levels of power and status of the actors is also a possible outcome of an interaction episode.
5. When a relational change occurs or when there is continuity, some agent is responsible for the outcome.
6. Agents can be self, other, or third party.
7. One can feel different emotions toward self, other, and third party (if there is one) as a result of the same relational outcome.

A THEORY OF EMOTIONS

There are many definitions of emotion (see Arnold, 1970, for statements by different authors). What is important in a definition is that it be adequate for the data the theory purports to explain. I define emotion thus:

Emotion is a relatively short-term evaluative response essentially positive or negative in nature involving distinct somatic (and often cognitive) components. This definition does not seek congruence with others, but it is not at variance with generally held ideas about emotion (cf. Arnold, 1970). I do not wish to bog down in specifying narrowly what is meant by short term. Emotion is relatively transitory, depending in part on the type of emotion, its intensity, and the circumstances instigating it. "Positive" and "negative" must be understood quite plainly as gratifying or aversive. Thus joy differs from fear in the basic primitive sense that the former is sensed as "feeling good" and the latter as "feeling bad." As to what it means to feel good or feel bad, ultimately we must rely on the actor's own report. This is unavoidable, but it is useful to know that there is often considerable agreement among actors as to what stimuli feel good or bad. There is also disagreement, as acknowledged in Chapters 1 and 2, but this cannot stand in the way of a general theory that accounts for the undeniably modal character of emotional responses within defined cultures, subcultures, groups, roles, and the like.

"Distinct somatic components" implies such measurable and observable events as changes in heartbeat, pulse, respiration rate, facial flush, perspiration, motoric activity, and the like. "Cognitive components" consist of verbal judgments or labels that identify the emotion, for example, "I feel *angry*," "Am I ever *happy*!" or "I feel I'm in *love*." The cognitive aspect of emotion can arise through explicit appraisal of the stimulus situation and its significance for the person, for example, it is threatening or pleasing (cf. Arnold, 1960, 1970; Lazarus, Averill, and Opton, 1970). The cognition can also arise from explicit appraisal of one's somatic state, for example, "My hands are sweating, I must be *anxious*" (cf. Schachter and Singer, 1962). Cognitive awareness and labeling of the emotion are not necessary, although they are frequent components of the experience of emotion. This does not negate the part cognition may play in the arousal of emotion. It merely says that the person responding with an emotion need not be aware of it, nor of its conventional label. Infants in a rage do not "know" it. Similarly there need not be direct awareness of the stimulus situation that is cueing the emotional response, but there is always a stimulus situation, even if it is proprioceptive or imaginal (Wolpe, 1973, pp. 14–15). Emotions do not occur simply at random; they are always a response to a stimulus or cue.

There are other organismic-psychic states that resemble emotions and probably ought to be distinguished in name. The discriminations can be quite extensive. Young (1961, pp. 352–353) made eight: *simple sensory feelings, persistent organic feelings, emotions, moods, affects, sentiments, interests and aversions,* and *temperaments.* Although a sorting as fine as this is valuable, a coarser gradation is used here. The important distinction is between short- and long-term emotions. In a short-term emotion, the stimulus event produces the emotion, and after some relatively short period the somatic and cognitive components die out and the individual can no longer be said to be experiencing the given emotion. In a long-term emotion, the individual is repeatedly activated to the same emotion by a continuous or recurring stimulus situation (e.g., a disturbed relationship with a spouse) which is often labeled as such, and the emotion is understood to be ongoing. This expectation for reactivation and recurrence is distinctive of the long-term emotion. Feelings of love, for example, are activated again and again in the presence of the other and are reactivated frequently in action concerning the other even when the other is not present. Hostility also has this character. Long-term emotions retain their force by virtue of the fact that the basic stimulus—the relational pattern—remains the the same from occasion to occasion. I call these more enduring emotions *affects* or *sentiments,* but most often the term emotion is used with the short- or long-term implications implied by the context (cf. Arnold, 1960, pp. 199ff).

The most general statement of the sociological theory of emotions is given at the beginning of the chapter, but it bears repeating: *a very large class of emotions results from real, imagined, or anticipated outcomes in social relationships.* Real and anticipated outcomes are different bases for the production of emotion, and separate classes of emotions are considered for these later. Real outcomes include relational events extending backward from the present (what happened a moment ago) to the distant past, biographically, or socially by virtue of enculturation to the relational outcomes in the history of one's group. According to accepted canons of consensual judgment, the supposed events did actually happen or are transmitted as true in the socialization process. The actor may experience emotion upon recollecting a relational outcome of the past. An important question is whether the actor is consciously aware of the relational event that is cueing the emotion. However, I do not treat this question to any significant extent, since the distinction does not materially affect the emotions that result from the relational outcomes. Imagined outcomes refer to relational events that have not happened in the past or may possibly happen in the future, although conditions are not as clearly set for them to attain the relatively high probability of anticipated outcomes. Imagined outcomes may also be misperceptions—simple or motivated—of relational events. Where imagined outcomes are plainly fictitious or have very low probabilities of occurrence in the future, they are day dreams or fantasies.

Structural, Anticipatory, and Consequent Emotions.   I propose that a sociological analysis dictates three kinds of emotions: *structural, anticipatory,* and *consequent.* This may be understood thus: our analysis of the relationship between actors begins at a certain point in time, often a point of equilibrium. This means that the relationship is relatively stable, with little change of power-status pattern from interaction episode to episode. However, even if each new episode of interaction changes the distribution of power and status, the analysis begins with the current state of the relationship, that is, the actors' power-status positions after the last episode. Obviously there is very little restriction here, but some device is necessary to bring the analysis to bear on the relational positions of the actors.

Whether the relationship is in equilibrium or not, I propose that each actor is either satisfied or dissatisfied in some degree with his own and the other's positions on the power and status dimensions. This is expressed by a class of emotions I call *structural,* since they result from the relatively stable structure of the relationship—in power and status terms. The structural emotions vary according to the specific relational bases for satisfaction or dissatisfaction.

Since human actors have the capacity to plan, hope, and adumbrate the future of their relationships and to anticipate that there will be certain outcomes as a result of subsequent interaction episodes, I propose that there is a second important class of emotions that are responses to how the actor views the future state of the relationship. I call these *anticipatory* emotions.

Since relationships are ongoing, the next interaction episode soon occurs. Thus there is a class of emotions that are consequences of the relational outcomes of the interaction episode and are the culmination of the chain that links the structural and anticipatory emotions to the actual results of interaction. I call these the *consequent* emotions. In this chapter I discuss the structural emotions, in the next chapter the anticipatory emotions, and in Chapters 5 and 6 the consequent emotions.

STRUCTURAL EMOTIONS

Structural emotions are broadly positive or negative in tone, but this can be specified further since different relational channels give rise to different emotions. First I examine the two relational channels pertaining to self, namely *own power* and *own status*. One may feel content or discontent with one or both of these. Contentment arises as the feeling that one's power and status are adequate in the relationship. Discontent, however, can arise in two different ways: either there is a felt *excess* or a felt *insufficiency* of power and status. Excess or insufficiency is perceived as such by virtue of both subjective cum cultural* definitions of what is and is not excessive or insufficient power or status. In chapter 1 I discussed various conditions that tend to homogenize particular meanings and definitions of situations for large categories of persons, thus reducing individual differences. Here we are concerned with the emotions that result after the definitions are applied.

Second, I examine the structural emotions that pertain to the power and status of the other. The emotions are still those of the *self*, for we have emotional responses not only to our own but also to the other's power and status in the relationship. The power and status of the other can also be evaluated in terms of adequacy, excess, and insufficiency.

Own Power

One's own structural position in the power channel of a relationship with another can be adequate, excessive, or insufficient. When it is viewed as adequate, I refer to the emotion or affect as *security*. This is a positive feeling of comfort and ease, because one feels assured of winning in any showdown or confrontation with the other. The benefits and rewards one enjoys in the relationship are thus generally guaranteed. Although the outcome of any actual power conflict with the other may lead to defeat or a serious withdrawal of voluntary compliance (i.e., status) even if the rewards continue, or even a termination of the relationship, these are secondary possibilities of power. At the surface, power creates security.

Power also affords a sense of ease concerning vulnerability to attack from the other. One's structural power acts as deterrent. The sense of ease afforded by

---

*The subjective and cultural definitions may be in conflict. Thus one may feel something the cultural norms forbid or give one no right to feel, for example, if one finds oneself in love with the wife of a friend or intensely disliking one's children. This is a very important problem in the study of emotions, but it is not dealt with explicitly in this work.

adequate power may not be conscious, except when it is challenged or could conceivably be challenged. A number of theorists have suggested a security or safety affect (Harlow, 1962; Strasser, 1970; Jacobs, 1971). Later I discuss how security is related to the power of the other as well as to one's own power. This provides a certain economy in the overall taxonomy of the structural emotions. For the present, however, security stems from the felt adequacy of one's own level of power, that is, the ability to win, as Weber (1946, p. 180) said, despite resistance by the other.

Excess Power.   When an individual senses that he has a structural position of excess power over the other in the interaction dyad, I propose that the emotion most persons feel is *guilt*. Guilt involves painful feelings of remorse and regret, a peculiar physical discomfort associated with the recognition that one has wronged another. All subjective reports of feelings of guilt indicate that it is uncomfortable and unpleasant (Hayward and Taylor, 1964; Lewis, 1971, pp. 215–274). Ausubel (1955) defined guilt as "a special kind of negative self-evaluation which occurs when an individual acknowledges that his behavior is at variance with a given moral value to which he feels obligated to conform" (Ausubel, 1955, p. 370). Overwhelmingly, moral values refer to relational conduct: the Decalogue, the Sermon on the Mount, the teachings of the Buddha. The transgression of moral values—killing, assaulting, stealing, lying, and the like are violations of relational standards concerning the use of power. Excess power may take the form of noxious hurt to the other, or it may be exercised as status withdrawal, that is, the punitive witholding of customary or legitimate rewards and gratifications. Here the mode of power use would include insults, disrespect, deprivation of accustomed goods and services, and so on. These are all instances of *process* power, actions that are employed to overcome the actual or possible future resistance of the other (see Appendix 2).

A felt excess of *structural* power also leads to feelings of guilt. This is in part the result of the process power that may have been used to win benefits in the past, but is mainly due to the sense that one has won too much or too often at the expense of the other. This may involve inequitable distributions of benefits that one enforces on the other or continual violations of the norm of reciprocity or of the rule of distributive justice that one accompanies by force, punishment, or threat (Homans, 1961; Gouldner, 1960; Stephenson and White, 1970).

Obviously it is the actor's own view of his power that produces the feeling of guilt. An objective observer might disagree entirely. A whole society may sanction a particular behavior, for example, killing in wartime, yet the individual may feel guilt. I am concerned here only with the person's own sentiment. Of course, the most heinous crimes and the most wanton use of power may not evoke guilt in the perpetrator. Classical psychopathy is said to involve just such indifference (McCord and McCord, 1964; Hinsie and Campbell, 1970). For present purposes, the psychopath does not experience guilt. Most persons, however, are socialized to values that set limits on the use and enjoyment of power over others. When those limits are overstepped—under conditions that do not permit justification—the emotion we feel is guilt.

Leventhal and Bergman (1969) estimated that social knowledge of the relationship between wronging another and feeling guilt is widespread. In an experiment in which extreme inequity of distribution of rewards was forced on subjects, many reduced their rewards to zero. Leventhal and Bergman deduced two possible motives for this action: either subjects wanted to demonstrate their complete independence of the other, or, by worsening the outcome for themselves, they would induce painful feelings of guilt in the other. The details of the experiment do not actually permit us to infer guilt induction exclusively, since shame is also a possible consequence, depending on which relational consideration was activated in the extreme beneficiaries of the reward distribution (see the discussion of shame later).

By introducing the concept of *agency*, we obtain a useful sense of how guilt and the other structural emotions can become differentiated. Essentially, emotions can be directed inward toward the self—*introjected*, or they can be directed outward—*extrojected*.* I propose that introjection occurs when self is viewed as the agent of the relational condition and extrojection when other is seen as the agent. Fundamentally, however, the core emotion is a response to the relational condition; agency only differentiates the core response. The two modes can be thought of as acting "out" and acting "in."

Self as Agent. I hypothesize that when self is seen as the agent of excess power use, the emotion is introjected and experienced as guilt in the classical sense—an uncomfortable feeling of regret, remorse, and self-blame which can develop ultimately into a desire for punishment as a means of expiation. According to Sarnoff (1962), "punishment is the only kind of response sufficient to reduce the tension of guilt" (p. 351). In this highly rationalistic epoch, the desire for expiation may seem curiously antiquated, for few today seem willing to accept or indeed welcome the punishment merited by ill deeds. A reluctance to accept punishment as morally valid and psychologically sound apparently stems from an historically revised view of personal agency and responsibility. To the degree that

---

*To retain a direct link with the standard term *introjection*, I have created the term *extrojection* to stand for the process of casting off an emotion by attributing its origin or agency to another person. This is different from projection, which means attributing one's own emotion to another. I shall later use the terms *intropunitive* and *extropunitive* to refer to punishment directed toward the self or toward the other respectively (see Chapter 10).

individuals are seen as responsible for their own actions, they are judged more culpable and more deserving of punishment by others and themselves. Nettler (1959) asked a large sample of persons engaged professionally in dealing with youth offenders—social workers, educators, ministers, and the like—to indicate how severely they would punish young people for various offenses. He found that they recommended more severe punishments the more they attributed "free will" and responsibility to the delinquents, that is, to the extent the offenders were the agents of their own difficulties. However, if external forces are seen as responsible for the harmful behavior—the agent is not the self—there may still be a feeling of guilt, but one that is sharply severed from a desire for punishment.

Walster, Berscheid, and Walster (1973) do well to remind us of Aesop's compelling insight that "the injuries we do and those we suffer are seldom weighed on the same scale" (p. 153). If we do not treat our own misdeeds as seriously as the misdeeds of others, the punishment we deem just for ourselves will usually *not* fit the crime according to the views of others. Nonetheless the desire for expiation is no mere curiosity. Numerous investigators have found that when research subjects have harmed another subject without justification, the subjects subsequently behaved in an expiatory manner that would lead to an inference that they had experienced guilt. Brock and Buss (1964) found that subjects acknowledged their guilt feelings directly. Berkowitz and Holmes (1960) and Pepitone and Reichling (1955) found that subjects who had expressed or acted in a highly aggressive manner in an experimental situation, without provocation to do so, later rated their victims favorably. Expiatory responses, such as volunteering to experience a series of painful shocks or to undergo extra effort for the benefit of another are also assumed to reflect prior feelings of guilt (Freedman, Wallington, and Bless, 1967; Wallace and Sedalla, 1966; Carlsmith and Gross, 1969; Regan, Williams, and Sparling, 1972). The severity of the harm, aggression, or punishment previously administered to the other also affects the likelihood of expiatory response. Holz and Azrin (1961) argued that when punishment is severe, there is greater likelihood of compensating for it by a positive response to the other. This too suggests a greater need to expiate guilt.

Galtung (1958) also supported the idea that expiation is a mode of adaptation in situations in which guilt is prominent. He found that prisoners who face long sentences sometimes view their incarceration as an expiation for the wrong they did—and thus appropriate in consequence of their guilt. Particular cultures, especially in their form of religious expression, affect the psychological disposition both to experience guilt and to accept punishment as the mode of cleansing the guilt. Murphy, Wittkower, and Chance (1970) found that guilt, as an aspect of the depression syndrome, is particularly prominent in cultures that adhere to Catholic or fundamentalist religious doctrine. The agent of excess power use in all these instances of remorse and desire for or acceptance of punishment must be seen as the self.

Other as Agent. If we believe that the other is responsible for our excess of power, I hypothesize that, instead of remorse, the emotion is extrojected in a form of anger and hostility toward the other that suggests *megalomania*. Indeed, megalomania is the sense or feeling that one is aggrandized, magnified, and powerful in relation to others (Hinsie and Campbell, 1970). Self-aggrandizement makes it possible for the megalomanic to operate with false justification in the power channel. Clinical and historical records of megalomania support the view that it is most directly associated with coercion. Since extreme coercion is contrary to the moral code of most persons, the actual or anticipated use of large amounts of power engenders the feeling of guilt. However, if the agent deemed responsible for one's own use of excessive power is the other, the coercion is somehow justifiable as retaliation, retribution, or deserved assault (Harburg et al., 1973). The important point is this: were there no feeling of revulsion over the doing of wrong, there would be no basis for the megalomanic alternative. Like remorse and the desire for expiation, the megalomanic reaction is an emotional response *in* guilt. Schurman (1935) also pointed out in his analysis of the Nazi regime the double alternative of expiation and megalomanic-sadistic cruelty that reside as possibilities in feelings of guilt (p. 288ff).

There is considerable evidence that victims of excess power are often derogated or blamed (Ryan, 1971). Lerner and his colleagues (Simmons and Lerner, 1968; Lerner and Matthews, 1967) saw this response as stemming from the desire to believe in a "just world." If the other is punished or hurt (whether or not the actual harm is administered by the self), the other must somehow deserve the punishment. Thus the other is the agent of his own troubles.

In a typical experiment (Lerner and Matthews, 1967), research subjects observed a young woman being mistreated or hurt. The subjects are later asked to evaluate the innocent victim. Astonishingly, instead of expressing positive sentiments of compassion and status enhancement, the subjects had a tendency to derogate the victim, thus adding insult to injury. Perhaps this can be explained by the fact that guilt is induced in Lerner's subjects. The guilt is extrojected, however, because it is too uncomfortable to contemplate one's own responsibility for the wrong that is being done before one's eyes.

In none of Lerner's experiments did the subjects themselves use power on the victim, but in other experiments subjects did actual harm. In the study by Heilman, Hodgson, and Hornstein (1972), subjects were led, accidentally, to cause some hurt to another person. Subsequently some subjects denied responsibility for their own actions by blaming the victim or an unnamed other, or they attributed the mishap to chance. Self-exculpation was more likely when the damage was "great" and "unrectifiable." These results are interpretable only if we assume that the experimental condition that would ordinarily induce greater guilt also induced a desire to avoid the conventional consequences of guilt—

namely, regret and remorse. This was done, at least by some, by casting asper-sions on the victim. Since guilt was not measured in this experiment, the in-terpretation must be tentative.

Perhaps the most complete dissection of the phenomenon of guilt in both of its alternative response modes of expiation and megalomania is the literary depic-tion by Dostoyevski in *Crime and Punishment*. Raskolnikov, the main character, has spent months in rationalizing his prospective crime. It comes down to a self-projection as a "great" man, who must dare to do a "small" evil so that he may then do a "great" good. An old pawnbroker is ultimately dehumanized by Raskolnikov so that killing her is justified, but during the long, feverish process of self-aggrandizement so that he may have the power of life and death over another, Raskolnikov must constantly struggle against feelings of self-revulsion that can only be understood as guilt. Even after carrying out the planned crime and an unintended second murder, Raskolnikov long contends that the two victims were of no matter—indeed, he saw the first as a positive evil of whom the world was well rid. She was thus in a sense the agent of her own execution. Raskolnikov castigates himself not as a murderer, but as a bungler who lost his nerve and acted stupidly when he should have been cool and efficient. Although this rationalization never sits well with him, only at the very end of the tale, virtually the last page, does he begin to accept his actions as his own responsibil-ity. Although it is not a whole-hearted remorse, he accepts that he has done wrong and that he deserves punishment. He has become, finally, the responsible agent in his own eyes.

Although guilt is the primary emotion in situations of felt excess power, anxiety is also a strong possibility. Anxiety is discussed extensively later; for now I define it as the emotion of fear aroused by the threat of possible retaliation by the other (Berkowitz, 1962; Walster, Berscheid, and Walster, 1973). Unless the power imbalance is extremely great, there is always the chance that the other may strike back. Many studies of interaction sequences indicate that power-plays by one actor lead to power reciprocity by the second (Rausch, 1965; Epstein and Taylor, 1967; Michener et al., 1975). Although the experimental studies usually pit equals against equals, we know more broadly from the case of guerrilla warfare that power inferiors are not loath to strike at superiors as long as they are not under constant surveillance. Thus, as a fundamental possibility, in addition to guilt, power invites counterpower and anxiety (Harsanyi, 1962).

Insufficient Power. The structural condition of insufficient power also gives rise to an emotion. I call this emotion *fear-anxiety*. There is some debate over whether fear and anxiety ought to be discriminated according to whether their object is realistic (fears) or imagined (anxieties), or whether one is aware (fear) or not aware (anxiety) of the source of the threat or danger (Freud, 1936;

Lazarus, 1972; Cattell, 1972). I ignore these distinctions for now, since my interest is in the relational condition that gives rise to either fear or anxiety. This is the felt insufficiency of one's own power (or, as discussed later, the excess of the other's power). In his classic discussion of anxiety, Freud (1966) clearly saw a relational basis for this emotion. He distinguished between two sources of anxiety. One is generated by repression of libidinal energy, especially in regard to sexual drives; for example, coitus interruptus or enforced sexual abstinence induce anxiety as an id response to the repression. The second type of anxiety is generated by the ego, as in the case of separation or castration anxiety. Freud here reversed the relationship between repression and anxiety. In the id type, repression causes anxiety; in the ego type, anxiety causes repression. Thus one forgets that some initially aggressive impulse (oedipal hostilities, perhaps) may have initiated the castration anxiety. It is clear that the ego-generated anxiety described by Freud is fundamentally relational in nature and that the basic relational mode is power. Indeed, Freud (1966) explicitly put the issue in these terms:

> On what occasions anxiety appears—that is to say in the face of what objects and what situations—will of course depend to a large extent on the state of a person's knowledge and on his sense of *power* vis-a-vis the external world (p. 394, emphasis added).

A real or imagined deficit of power is at the root of anxiety, and we must look there to understand this emotion. To have insufficient structural power means that ordinarily the other can win when there is a crucial showdown. Thus one must surrender and comply with the wishes of the other when one does not want to comply. Insufficiency of one's own power also means that one cannot ordinarily force the other to comply when he does not want to. Since structural power is calculated as an empirical probability based on the results of previous confrontations (see Appendix 2), the recognition of one's own insufficiency projects the likelihood of loss onto future occasions of confrontation. This makes the future both uncertain and uninviting, suitable conditions for fear-anxiety.

Self as Agent. When the agent is believed to be the self, this implies that one's lack of power is due to one's own incapacities and deficiencies. I hypothesize that fear-anxiety is introjected in the classical mode: a feeling of impending doom, destruction, and disaster (e.g., Davitz, 1969, p. 36, pp. 54–55). Something terrible is imminent, and the emotion is the cognitive and somatic response in acknowledgment of the doom awaited. The relational condition anticipated is power use by the other. The power may take the form of a noxious stimulus, or status loss or deprivation. In either case, one feels helpless to prevent the oncoming blow.

The structural condition of insufficient power means that the other can exercise power at will, and the uncertainty of what the other may demand or when this demand will be made gives rise to the painful character of the emotion. Samuel Johnson's famous dictum that "if a man knows he is to be hanged tomorrow it clears his head enormously" does not ring entirely true, but it is a recognition of the time factor in anxiety. Several experiments have shown that timing is important. Nomikos et al. (1968) showed a film in which there were suggestions of an impending accident. Indicators of anxiety were highest in viewers in the period prior to the scene showing the accident itself. Other experiments, in which research subjects were shocked, also showed a timing effect (Lazarus and Averill, 1972). When the time of shock was uncertain, anxiety levels, as indicated by various autonomic measures, were highest. Whatever contributes to uncertainty about how much or when the other will exercise his power amplifies the level of fear-anxiety. With self as agent, the focus is on one's own weakness and inability to deter the other.

In a direct test of some of the hypotheses of the theory of this book, Myers (1977) surveyed 326 persons about their power-status relations with their supervisors at work. He factor analyzed 44 items of relational behavior and obtained six factors reflecting various power or status configurations, among them one factor he labeled "supervisory process power." The highest loading item of this factor was "He/she 'rides' a person who makes a mistake." Self-agency is clear in this situation, as is the structural power and power behavior of the supervisor. Myers found a correlation of $+.44$ between scores on this factor and scores on a fear-anxiety factor.

Other as Agent. When other is seen as the agent of one's own insufficiency of structural power, the emotion is still fear-anxiety, but it has a different outcome. To view the other as agent is to assign to him the intent and will to overcome us and to benefit thereby. This leads, I hypothesize, to extrojecting the fear-anxiety as anger and hostility against the other. This takes the form of an effort to destroy the other's power or the bases of that power. I call this type of fear-anxiety response *anarchy-rebelliousness*. Indeed, anarchy literally means "without rule," and those who are confronted with a power disadvantage in which other is seen as the agent are disposed to destroy the ruling power that is inducing the fear-anxiety. In his theory of "psychological reactance," Brehm (1966) indicated a strong power reaction in response to another's imposition of control over previously "free" behaviors. Stokols (1975) also offered some conditions similar to the power-agency notions to discriminate between what he called "subjugation" (fear-anxiety introjected) and "rebellion" (fear-anxiety ex-trojected). The first condition is that there be "personal thwarting" which is a "negatively viewed activity, person, group, or culture." When no alternatives to the thwarting are perceived, the consequence is subjugation; when alternatives are available, the result is rebellion.

When the other is in a position of authority, the anxiety response is man-ifested in rebelliousness against orders, commands, and requests, which are ignored, disobeyed, and avoided. Two classic cases involve the adolescent in rebellion against the demands of the parent and the employee who resists the legitimate orders of a superior or employer (Feuer, 1969; Levinson, 1964). Resis-tance is not necessarily due to disagreement with the technical adequacy of the order or request, but to the fact that the other has requested an action that violates one's sense of self-determination in the circumstance. But this is pre-cisely related to the amount of one's power. When this response pattern is well set, it frequently operates in an anticipatory manner. Thus even prior to a command or order, the fearful-anxious person in this mode may engage in fantasy conflicts with the other (Levinson, 1964). The anarchy-rebelliousness response has no relationship to the political program of anarchism, although both are responses to social relations involving a deficit of power—one at the societal, the other at the interpersonal level.

Fear-anxiety in which other is the agent also operates in a preventive mode to guard against the power encroachments of others. Thus we build nuclear deter-rents and arm our children for social life by teaching them to combat aggression (i.e., exercise of power) by counteraggression and urge on them the wisdom that this is a language that bullies understand. Patterson, Littman, and Bricker (1967) found that when children who were targets of aggression retaliated against their tormentors, the rate of aggression against them declined sharply. Rausch (1965) also found among groups of children that "submissive antecedent acts of one child were strongly associated with immediately dominant acts of another (while) dominant antecedent behavior tended to be followed by submissive acts, but at a much lower level of probability" (p. 494). This suggests that when a child reveals that he does not or cannot fight back, he will be bullied or dominated. Pisano and Taylor (1971) investigated how the power level of response by one actor to another actor's aggression affected the intensity of the succeeding round of ag-gression by that actor. They found that the optimum strategy for getting the other to reduce his level of aggression was to match the aggressor's previous power behavior in each round of interaction (cf. Pilisuk and Skolnik, 1968). Taken together these experimental and observational results suggest that a controlled use of counterpower can make the other desist from using power, and that lack of power to "match" or return the other's power plays leads to high levels of power use and domination by the other. As in the case of guilt, the extrojection of fear-anxiety turns the emotion into a basis for power exercise against the other.

Own Status

Since one obtains one's own status in the relational model proposed here only from the other, and since status conferral is defined as the voluntary giving of rewards and gratifications, when one receives status in adequate amounts one should "feel good." There are many terms for the feeling of adequate status, including happy, content, joyful, glad, esteemed, rewarded, approved, accepted, liked, loved, and so on. I use the term *happy*. Whether one can ever feel happy *enough* is a question that some have asked. Durkheim (1897) suggested that the desire and capacity for gratification in humans ever renews itself as we obtain new levels of satisfaction. Yet Durkheim also agreed that when there are definite social horizons that provide standards of appropriatness for the level of our "just deserts," so to speak, we can be happy in the sense that we feel that we receive enough. The concept of "relative deprivation" (Stouffer et al., 1949) is also applicable, for it suggests that we may lose our sense of happiness if we learn that others who are similar to us in an important comparative sense are obtaining more rewards than ourselves. This has been shown for wage comparisons (Patchen, 1961) and in a general way in the development of "equity theory" (Adams, 1965; Leventhal, Allen, and Kemelgor, 1969; Walster, Berscheid, and Walster, 1973). It also resides at the heart of Homan's (1961) proposition regarding distributive justice. Satisfaction ensues automatically in Homan's formulation when one receives rewards commensurate with one's "investments." In general, exchange theory is not fully appropriate for deriving the emotion that obtains in the relational condition of adequate status. This is because exchange theory is implicitly based on power relations, not status relations (Blau, 1964; Emerson, 1971, 1972a, 1972b). I treat this important aspect of exchange theory in Chapter 13. Nevertheless, since many experiments have been conducted using the exchange model, many results on emotions are available; where compatible, I use them to support hypotheses proposed here.

Excess Status. Just as with excess power, a specific emotion is evoked by receiving excess status. I propose that when an actor accepts more status than he feels he deserves the emotion is *shame*. Since status is defined as the amount of reward, recognition, and gratification that others give to us voluntarily without threat or coercion, it is important to understand the basis on which such voluntary reward is given. In Chapter 11 I elaborate the view that status is given for meeting standards for competence or achievement in the division of labor or in social relationships. When one claims more competence than is the case or others mistakenly assume this and more status is given and accepted than is deserved, the resulting emotion is shame (cf. Goffman, 1967a).

Shame is ordinarily a brake on insatiability, the overweening desire for more and more benefits from others—even when one does not deserve them. Norms

and standards that guide manners and appropriateness are devoted almost exclusively to delineating the mutually deserved signs and symbols of status: who
deserves and gets how much. To feel that one has received more than one's due
is a ground for shame. To be exposed as one who has accepted more status or
honor than is due is to be dishonored. Since honor is a grant of status in the first
place, one deserves less if one has accepted too much.

Garfinkel (1961) has provided a tortuously complete analysis of the formal
process of reducing a previously credited person to a lower status level. The
ceremony involves the careful annihilation, destruction, or removal of the conventional social insignia of status, for example, medals, braid, signs of rank, and
the like. Garfinkel's analysis indicates the relational process of status withdrawal.
The emotional correlative must be assumed, under most circumstances, to be
shame.

Even momentary lapses of authentic competence or in the grounds for honor
subject us to shame, although a frequent term here is embarrassment (Ausubel,
1955; Goffman, 1967a; Weinberg, 1968; Modigliani, 1968). Whether momentary or long lasting, the lapse causes "self-depreciation vis-a-vis the group" (Ausubel, 1955, p. 382) or "loss of self-esteem" (Modigliani, 1968, p. 315). Since
esteem is given by others and is one of the currencies in which status is paid, the
loss of self-esteem is tantamount to the notion that one did not deserve the
amount of status that was given. Ergo there is shame.

A significant factor here is public exposure; thus those who provide the status
become aware of the falsity of the status claim. All fraudulent self-presentations
potentially evoke shame when they are exposed (Goffman, 1959). Failed claims
of competence—whether in intellect, virtue, bravery, probity, or technical skill
of any kind—expose the claimant to shame. Those who are impervious to the
emotion are excluded, but instances of nonfraudulent claims are included. Thus
one may honestly claim competence but fail, in which case many persons feel
shame.

In ordinary discourse there is often confusion between guilt and shame, and
some authors dispute the significance of any distinction between the two (e.g.,
Bandura and Walters, 1963). According to Ausubel (1955) there is a certain
degree of conceptual overlap; thus "moral shame" may be a component of guilt.
From the relational perspective taken here, the two emotions are analytically
distinct, but shame and guilt may co-occur. A person who feels he has used
excess power feels guilt and, in addition, may feel the shame of his failed claim to
the good opinion of others, that is, the status he claimed as a person of virtue who
does not hurt others. Similarly the person who initially feels shame due to excess
status may also experience guilt if it turns out that his undeserved status caused
hurt to others. The "white liberal" has grounds for feeling both shame for

enjoying his relative affluence when others who deserve as much are deprived and guilt to the extent that he acts in ways that perpetuate the unjust arrangement; that is, he is both the agent and beneficiary of an exploitative (excessive) use of power. The conceptual confusion between guilt and shame is enhanced by the empirical correlation between the two. For example, assuming valid measures, Wood, Pilisak, and Uren (1973) found a relationship of $r = +0.59$ $(p < 0.05)$ between them.

Self as Agent. When self is felt to be the agent responsible for the excess status, that is, one believes that one is lacking in competence and true grounds for social credit, and that the status has been taken under false pretenses, the resulting emotion is introjected and appears as *embarrassment-humiliation*, the feeling of actual or imminent exposure of one's faults of competence. The reaction that follows has several possibilities: either *acceptance* of the lower status level or *withdrawal* from interaction, thereby canceling the credit arrangement by ceasing to draw on it at all, or *compensation*, which is the effort to prove, against the available evidence, that one is indeed worthy of the status one previously received. This is the more difficult course, since all future status claims will be regarded with suspicion by those who are aware of the previous discrepancy between promise and performance. Yet there is a certain lure to compensation as the coping response in shame, for to do it successfully usually earns status over and above the substantive grounds for the original status claim. Thus the truly reformed criminal or the former coward who acts heroically evokes a special grant of status because of the recognized difficulty of the task. Attribution theory (Kelley, 1971) also supports such a view. The reasoning is that since the previously shamed person is the agent of his own embarrassment-humiliation, he must overcome a strong personal disposition that is a handicap to earning status. Thus when he does in fact show true probity, reliability, courage, and the like, it is worthy of extra credit.

Recompense as discussed here differs from the punishment that may be desired to expiate guilt. Although recompense may be costly and in that sense "punishing," it is actually a form of social trading: status is earned by displaying status-worthy traits. Punishment, on the other hand, that is accepted by those who feel the remorse of guilt, is not social in the ordinary sense. It deals fundamentally with the delicate balance by which punishment cancels a psychic debt.

Since claiming or heedlessly consuming undeserved status is a form of power behavior against the others who were defrauded into giving the status, guilt may also be engendered, and the compensatory action that cleanses away the shame may also operate to eradicate the guilt. The distinction between guilt and shame nonetheless prevails: guilt when the *other is harmed* by one's actions, shame when *one has benefited* beyond one's due. Indeed, although both may occur, the emotions felt depend on how much the person is concerned with the excess power and how much with the excess status.

Other as Agent. I propose that when other is seen as the agent of one's excess status, the emotion is still shame, but extrojected into a form of anger and hostility toward the other. If one actor sincerely and regularly inflates the status of the other, the apparent benefit of this becomes a torment if the beneficiary is not merely cynical. To be continually exposed to the contrast between what one believes oneself to be and the higher estimate of the other must ultimately create a demand on oneself to be as good, able, and praiseworthy as the other supposes. But this may be impossible. Yet the implied demand continues unabated, and the unpaid debt, so to speak, accumulates. The discrepancy between what one is and what one receives credit for evokes shame; but the other, through his un-realistic evaluation, is the agent of this outcome. The discomfort of this must turn into hostility toward the other for insisting on the invidious difference.

There is an experimental literature that supports the view that we ordinarily feel comfortable in accepting from others only as much as we can reciprocate lest we be placed under obligations we cannot meet or repay (e.g., Gergen et al., reported in Gergen, 1969, pp. 77–80). Blau's (1964) position is that when we have received excessive benefits from the other which we cannot repay in kind, we repay by according the other "power." Ordinarily, this should be the least preferred solution, for it mortgages our future.

Another important possibility in regard to excess status occurs when the other has acted as agent to expose the discrepancy between what we are and what others credit us to be. Again, the fundamental emotion is shame, turned outward again against the other as anger and hostility. In an imaginative experiment, Aronson and Mettee (1968) found that subjects whose self-esteem had been temporarily lowered were more likely to cheat in a card game than subjects whose self-esteem had been temporarily elevated. This is an unusual but compelling display of how shame, which is tantamount to loss of self-esteem, can lead to power behavior to recoup something of one's former level.

The retaliatory motive that activates aggression in situations of shame has been studied experimentally by Deutsch and Krauss (1962), Hornstein (1965), and Brown (1968). Goffman (1959) proposed that aggression is especially preva-lent when one's prestige or status has been devalued in public. We may even feel fundamentally competent, but minor vagaries of interaction can suddenly high-light a well-hidden weakness or make it appear that we are less than what we claim to be, as in a momentary inability to "top" someone's witty remark made at our expense. The anger felt here against the other may take a particular turn at first, regardless of what may ensue after the initial interchange. Since the exposure by other of one's excess status can be viewed as a power act by other, I suggest that a frequent response is a power act of the same type. This is peculiarly apt, since depriving the other of *his* wonted status reequilibrates the status system, even if it is at a lower level for both. If A and B have, hypothetically, eight and nine units of status, respectively, and if A's act of shame-exposure caused B to lose 3 units, the relational system is reequilibrated if B can cause A to lose 3 units of status. This is not difficult to do, since all are vulnerable. It only requires finding the weak point. A counterwitticism at a later point cuts A down to size—in this case a unit below B.

Where the other is seen as the agent in the manner described, there is a tendency toward *hypercriticism* and *perfectionism* toward the other. This reduces the other's status to the same low level of one's own status. In effect hypercriticism says: "If I did not deserve the status I received, neither do you." Ford (1963) and Thibaut and Kelley (1959) noted this technique of status reduction as a response when shame is evoked. Brown (1970) proposed the concept of "face-restoration," which is defined as an "attempt to seek redress from another after the other has caused him to look foolish" (p. 256). In an earlier experiment, Brown (1965) found that experimental subjects were willing to pay out of their monetary winnings in the experimental situation for the opportunity to retaliate against an adversary who had ostensibly reduced their status by making them look foolish.

Hypercriticism-perfectionism is, of course, power behavior. Thus it has something in common with megalomania as power behavior. Yet it is important for an adequate understanding of these responses to see that one is a mode that stems from the felt excess of one's own power, whereas the other results from the felt excess of one's own status.

Insufficient Status.   I propose that when voluntarily given benefits and compliance from the other are inadequate, the emotion experienced is *depression*. A. A. Lazarus (1968) discussed depression explicitly as a condition of inadequate rewards. Since most important rewards for humans are social in origin, regardless of whether they are material or symbolic, depression is the emotion that accompanies the relational condition of the insufficiency of these rewards. Depression may result from rejection by a loved one, loss of a loved one through death, rejection of one's contribution in the division of labor and ergo the recognition that might have come with its acceptance, and so on. Structural insufficiency of status means that one is not receiving from the other enough of the benefits and rewards that one either required as a result of human existential interdependence or that one has come to depend on in that relationship (see Chapter 13 for a discussion of existential and relational interdependence).

There is a general consensus that depression ensues from a deficit of gratifications. Freud (1966) expressed the psychoanalytic view of depression in terms of "object loss" and the consequent awareness of helplessness, incompleteness, and failure (Bibring, 1953). The failure and incompleteness are experienced as the result of inadequate status, that is, a deficit of rewards voluntarily given by others. Freud (1936) also discriminated between *anxiety*, which is provoked by the danger or threat of loss of an object, and grief or *depression*, which results from the actual loss of the object (p. 119). Rushing (1969) proposed that "interaction loss, particularly loss that is due to social rejection, tends to produce depression" (p. 72). Price (1968) viewed depression as related to the dominance hierarchy of groups, wherein "elated behavior has evolved (in the genetic sense) in connection with a rise in the hierarchy and depressive behavior in connection with a fall" (p. 48). In a more extreme order of depression that we consider in this chapter, namely, depressive illness, Price suggested:

> We should consider the hierarchical position of our depressive patients. This does not, of course, refer to their social class, but to their standing within their own group acquaintances . . . Grant (1965) has shown that the cues and responses may be very subtle—a glance, a tone of voice, a few degrees variation in posture. Grant was able to observe one change of status made deliberately by the nursing staff, and this resulted in depressive behavior lasting two or three weeks on the part of the patient whose status was lowered (p. 46).

The convergence of virtually all perspectives on the assessment of depression as reward deprivation is seen again in the behavioral definition of depression by MacPhillamy and Lewinsohn (1974): the "depressed person is considered to be on a prolonged extinction schedule . . . as a function of (1) the number of events which are potentially reinforcing . . . (2) the number . . . which are available . . . and (3) the skill of the individual in eliciting (them)" (p. 651). In research with clinically depressed and nondepressed persons, MacPhillamy and Lewinsohn found that the depressed were significantly lower on "obtained pleasure," an index created by multiplying the *frequency* by the *enjoyability* of a large number of social and other recreational activities.

   Self as Agent.   I propose that when self is felt to be the agent of the deficit of status or if one feels there is no hope of remedy because one does not have the capacity or the means to change the situation to evoke status conferral from the other, the depression takes its classic form as despair, apathy, or hopelessness. One must go through the motions of relationship, but there is not enough in it, and one is incapable of changing the relational structure. Fishman (1965) found that when self, as opposed to other, is seen as the agent of a status loss, even though another is involved in the interaction, greater aggression will be expressed toward self than toward other. I take this to mean a higher degree of depreciation of the self as a result of shame. However, the next effect is depression, since status is denied to the self, in the first instance by another and secondarily by self. There is also considerable theory and evidence for the relationship between hostility turned against self and depression (Freud, 1917; Gottschalk and Gleser, 1969; Schless et al., 1974).

In the work of Myers (1977) discussed earlier, the "supervisory process power" factor was correlated with a scale Myers named "anger-depression." The latter consisted of such items as "I am unhappy," "I am annoyed," "I am depressed." The principal item of the supervisory power factor was "He/she 'rides' a person who makes a mistake." The second highest loading item was "He/she criticizes people in front of others." These two items establish the self-agency and status-withdrawal aspects, respectively, of the relational situation. Myers found a correlation of +.49 between scores on this factor and the anger-depression scale.

Other as Agent. I propose that if responsibility for the status insufficiency is assigned to the other, the fundamental expression of depression is extrojected in the form of anger and hostility. When we feel ourselves worthy, but the other denies us benefits, recognition, respect, approval, or love—in a word, status—animosity is released against the other. I propose that the primary emotion of depression—the hunger for the status and benefits denied—is still present. The anger is not a substitute but rather a way of expressing the depression that is seen to result from the agency of the other. Cattell (1972) also saw the implicit relationship between anger turned outward and depression when there is status loss:

> Frustration may produce pugnacity (sometimes loosely called "aggression") and, if demonstrated to be irremediable, it leaves (a) undischarged ergic tension and (b) depression (p. 48).

In numerous studies of depression, the classic syndrome includes despair and hostility (Schless et al., 1974; Wessman and Ricks, 1966; Reimanis, 1974). Although some of this hostility is turned outward—indubitably an expression of resentment against the other's agency in causing the status loss—anger turned inward is also a frequent condition. Schless et al. (1974) employed a large number of measures of hostility and depression and found consistently that the more severely depressed patients in their sample were also more *inwardly* hostile. Others have also reported similar findings (Gottschalk and Gleser, 1969). These results support the classic description by Freud (1917) in which depression is accompanied by hostility turned inward. However, I disagree with the causal link that Freud proposed. In his view, depression was caused by the fact that one was hostile toward another person—perhaps a loved one—with whom one identified.

If the other activated the hostility, it was in part directed toward the self by virtue of the identification. In Freud's "hydraulic" model, the hostility directed toward oneself energizes the self-punitive, self-denying condition experienced as depression.

I offer an alternative explanation of the relationship between depression and hostility directed toward the self. First, the basic depression stems from hunger for the gratifications denied or lost. Other is *always* the necessary donor or mediator of these gratifications. Even if the agency is assigned to oneself, other is in some way accountable too. This would ordinarily produce anger when we lose status. However, if the other is powerful by virtue of our dependence for yet other gratifications, would retaliate with a noxious stimulus if we expressed our anger, or it would make us feel shame or guilt to express our anger, we do not do so. In most cases this failure to seek redress for felt injustice, especially in interpersonal relations, can be viewed as cowardice. We simply do not have the courage to stand up for what is rightfully ours. Although courage and cowardice belong to a moral vocabulary of an earlier time, they are still important to those whose self-worth is in question.

I propose that when felt hostility is not expressed toward the other when the other has done us injury, we suffer not only from the actual loss of what was denied us, but also from the loss of self-esteem by virtue of cowardice in taking the injury lying down, so to speak. The anger is just, but since we do not have the courage to express it, we must judge ourselves unworthy on that account, in addition to our other deprivation. If this view is correct, we should find that the more severely depressed are also more anxious, which indicates the fears that sap courage in the first place. Indeed, although we have good reason to distinguish the two states, anxiety is often high among the depressed (Schless et al., 1974; Cattell, 1972; American Psychiatric Association, 1968).

It is also important to recognize the distinction between the anger of anxiety and the anger of depression. The anarchy-rebelliousness response to insufficient power is directed against power or its bases with the object of destroying or nullifying that power. In the case of insufficient status, hostility is directed toward the status of the other, and the hostility is often manifested by withholding status from the other. To be unfriendly or cold and aloof to others denies them their due, just as they have denied us ours. Anxiety and depression are emotional foundations for the use of power against others, but the focus of the power exercise, when it comes, is different in the two types, as is the cause.

Although depression is usually discussed as a clinical and psychiatric phenomenon, the relational model suggests that it is a general condition that follows from a structural deficit of status (cf. Klinger, 1975). Depression need not attain levels that require or demand psychiatric attention.

To summarize, six structural emotions are outcomes of ongoing relationships when one's own relational channels (own power and own status) are the focus of attention: *security* when own power is adequate, and *guilt* and *fear-anxiety*, respectively, when own power is excessive or insufficient; *happiness* when own status is adequate, and *shame* and *depression*, respectively, when there is an excess or insufficiency of status received. I look now at the emotions experienced by self that have their source in the other's power and status.

Other's Power

As hinted earlier, own power and other's power are yoked in zero-sum fashion for the purpose of the structural emotions. This does not mean that power is a zero-sum concept (see Appendix 2). In interactional and relational analysis it is important to know how much power each actor has, but in the analysis of the structural emotions, I suggest that when own power is adequate, this is generally equivalent to feeling that the other's power is adequate, although this probably also means that other's power is less than one's own. When the other's power is adequate (rather than excessive or insufficient), this should elicit the same emotion as when own power is adequate, namely, *security*. In like fashion, I suggest that when one feels that own power is excessive, this is the structural equivalent of feeling that the other's power is insufficient and should produce the same emotion, namely, *guilt*. To complete the parallelism, when one feels that own power is insufficient, this is structurally equivalent to feeling that the other's power is excessive and also gives rise to the same emotion, namely, *fear-anxiety*. This structural equivalence between own power and other's power makes possible a welcome economy both here and in the elaboration of the consequent emotions in Chapters 5 and 6.

Other's Status

The last of the relational channels, other's status, also gives rise to structural emotions felt by self. I propose that when we give adequate status to the other, we feel that we are fair, equitable, and just; regardless of how little the status may be in absolute magnitude, we feel a positive affective response of satisfaction or contentment with self. I frankly speculate that in quality the emotion is indistinguishable from the feeling of *happiness* that results from *receiving* adequate status. The literature on distributive justice and equity (Homans, 1961; Adams, 1965; Walster Berscheid, and Walster, 1973) has generally dealt with the effects of injustice and inequity. However, there is a strong implication that doing right by another precludes negative emotions—for example, guilt, shame, anxiety, and anger. I infer that the fairness and justice of the action—its fitness—also makes one "feel good." This leads to an important conclusion, namely, that we can attain happiness by giving status to others as well as by receiving it from them. I consider this further in Chapter 11.

Excess Status. For one actor to accord excess status to another appears to be an anomaly, since I have defined the giving of status as voluntary compliance. In addition, providing excess status to another is a defect that is easily corrected. It is not likely to become a structural condition if we are clear that we mean true, voluntary compliance when we use the term status. Thus excess status accord is probably a null cell as far as structural emotions are concerned. Although excess status conferral virtually never occurs if the facts are known, excess *reward* conferral does, as in flattery. That is, there are relational conditions that promote our giving rewards to others when we do not want to or when we would not if we knew the true value of the other. An explicit power threat by the other or manipulation and deceit (covert power) are frequently the source of excess conferral of rewards (not status). Of course, we may even deceive ourselves or be mistaken about the status-deserving qualities of the other. When we are enlightened, the emotions may range broadly from astonishment, shame (at oneself for gullibility), anger (at the other), since we may attribute some intent to deceive, and contempt which indicates our distaste or disgust for the inappropriateness of the other's excessive status claim (see Chapter 6).

Insufficient Status. To accord less status to another than he deserves is to deny the other his due. This is a form of exercise of power—the withholding of status—and like all use of power that is excessive, the emotion evoked is *guilt*. In addition to guilt, however, there may be *shame*, since the excessive use of power may negate claims to probity, decency, fairness, and the like, that the actor has previously made. Thus a combined emotion of *guilt-shame* is probable when one gives less to another than he deserves (cf. Walster, Berscheid, and Walster, 1973).

Equity theory also provides some insight into the emotions that are evoked by insufficient status accord to another. There is the very strong suggestion that not only are guilt and shame a likely outcome, but also fear of retaliation, which stems from the sense that one has wronged the other (Walster, Berscheid, and Walster, 1973; Lerner and Matthews, 1967; Lerner and Simmons, 1968).

Self as Agent. I propose that if one accepts the responsibility for the failure to provide the other with the status the other deserves, the emotions of guilt and shame will be felt in their introjected modes: remorse, regret, and the painful recognition of the distance between one's claimed and deserved status. Whether this leads to expiation and compensation, as in the case of excess power use and excess status, is another matter. If self and other are competing for the same status resources—whether these are material or symbolic—it may appear that the only way to retain enough for oneself is to deny them to the other. Blau's (1964, pp. 43–47) discussion of competition for prestige points to this dilemma.

Other as Agent. Where other is assigned responsibility for one's own failure to accord deserved status, we have another instance of rationalization of guilt and shame; derogation of the other and hypercritical-perfectionism will likely appear. This is discussed extensively in an earlier section.

In summary, I propose that when self considers the status given to the other to be adequate, the structural emotion is *happiness;* when insufficient status is given, the emotion is a compound of *guilt* and *shame.* A true excess of status conferral to the other is possibly a null cell.

The intensity of the structural emotions depends on the degree to which the four relational channels are favorable or unfavorable to the actor—either objectively and according to common standards and particular conditions of the relationship, or subjectively, according to a more idiosyncratic interpretation of what is favorable and what is not. Obviously it feels good to receive status; it also feels good to give status to the other, as long as this is in appropriate amounts. In general, too, it is good to have power, as long as one has more of it than the other, since it is a partial guarantee that the rewards one gets will continue to flow from the other and that punishments from the other are deterred. On the other hand, when the other has power, especially more of it than one has oneself, it does not feel good. For power is based on coercion, force, and punishment, and if one is actually or potentially the recipient of these, it cannot feel good. As to whether it does feel good to receive rewards and bad to receive punishment, no less an authority than Wittgenstein (1961) supported this view: "And it is also clear that the reward must be something pleasant and the punishment something unpleasant" (p. 146).

The alternatives of the structural emotions are depicted in Figure 3.3. Since the 12 outcomes shown are the possible structural emotions of a single actor—corresponding to his own and other's relational positions—it can be seen that when the emotions are all positive, the person must be quite content in that relationship. The intensity of each positive emotion depends on the favorableness of the particular relational condition. When all emotions are negative, the person must be quite discontent. Again, the degree of unfavorableness of the relational channels affects the intensity of the felt emotions.

Although it is possible to analyze the degree of contentment or discontent with a relationship according to the four components of self and other's power and status, this is not a conventional mode of thought for most persons (despite the fact that it is analytically useful and illuminating). Nonetheless, something of this sort is done whenever the structural emotions are mixed in tone. Some

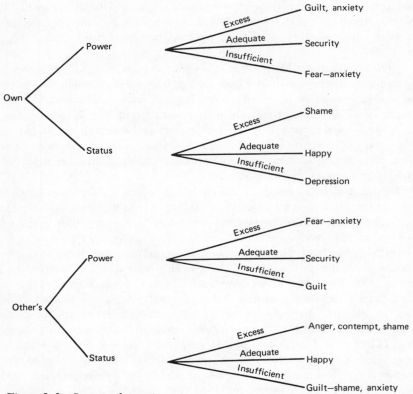

Figure 3–3   Structural emotions.

things about the relationship are pleasing, while others are not. I suggest that the analysis of the relational bases of what is and is not liked in recurrent interactions with others can easily be assigned to the distribution of power and status in the relationship. The two most important relational modes are these: For contentment, one should be receiving sufficient status (cf. Byrne, 1971; Lott and Lott, 1974), and the other should be using very little power (Barry, 1970; Bradburn and Caplovitz, 1965). Discontent occurs when the values of these two dimensions are reversed, that is, inadequate status received and too much power use by the other. Although the notion of mixed emotions is not original (Izard, 1972; Plutchick, 1962; Arnold, 1960), the power-status model captures the complexity of emotional response in real life, and at the same time systematically allocates the mix of conflicting emotions to particular relational sources. This is new.

The several sources of structural emotions can be of varying significance even for the same level of intensity. Miller (1944) has shown that the gradient of avoidance is steeper than the gradient of approach, and this can be applied here to predict that discontent in *power* relations probably weights overall dissatisfaction more heavily than discontent with *status* relations, other things being equal. In general, I suggest that the overall structural sentiment of contentment—discontent aggregated over the four relational dimensions is an easily locatable mathematical (regression) function of the four relationally based emotions. A least-squares solution would give us some sense of the parameter values associated with each relational condition. Hamblin and Smith (1966) and Hamblin (1971) have provided some useful illustrations of both method and theoretical utility. (Hamblin and Smith's study is discussed in Chapter 12.) Bradburn and Caplovitz's (1965) work on the structure of psychological well-being also points to the need to consider positive and negative conditions separately. Those investigators obtained two factors of psychological well-being, one containing "good" things, the other "bad" things that might happen. Overall happiness was determined not only by having the good, but by having fewer of the bad: in other words, by receiving enough status and having enough power.

chapter 4

Anticipatory Emotions

When *security* and *happiness* are the structural emotions, there is ordinarily little desire for a change of relational position for self or other. When the structural emotions are *guilt, shame, fear-anxiety,* or *depression,* it is no surprise if relational change is desired. Negative emotions are a strong incentive to look to the future of a relationship and evaluate the possibilities for improvement. Even if we feel only positive structural emotions, occasionally our thoughts must turn to the future: Will the desirable state of affairs continue?

I propose that the orientation toward the future of the relational system has either a positive or a negative feeling tone, depending on whether the future is seen as prospectively good or prospectively bad. These are the *anticipatory* emotions. I believe it is useful to view the anticipatory emotions in terms of two elements. One comprises the results of all *past* experience, the second the situational indicators of probable success or failure in the *present* relational setting. Success is defined as retaining or improving the relational conditions that promote security or happiness, failure as the opposite of these.

The Effect of Past Experience. Relational experiences cumulate to provide the basis for a subjective estimate of probable success or failure in any new interaction episode. The residue of the relational past is summed up as *optimism* or *pessimism.* Freud (1966) describes the emotional tone of pessimism:

> A general apprehensiveness, a kind of free-floating anxiety which is ready to attach itself to any idea that is in any way suitable . . . [W]e call this "expectant anxiety" or "anxious expectation" . . . [Where there is] a tendency to an expectation of evil of this sort . . . one calls people over-anxious or pessimistic (p. 398).

Thibaut and Kelley (1959) suggested that optimism and pessimism are reflections of the individual's "actual effectiveness vis-a-vis his environment" (p. 98). Stotland (1969) proposed that failure and success have a cumulative character: "the effects of successes and failures early in life seem to show that they have lifelong effects, so that a person is consistently optimistic and successful or pessimistic and failing" (p.75). Supporting Stotland's view, the large literature on levels of aspiration confirms that success produces higher levels of aspiration—indicating optimism—and failure leads to a lowering of aspiration—indicating pessimism (Lewin et al., 1944; Feather, 1962; Mischel and Staub, 1965). Hull's (1943) analysis of learning also supports this view. His concept of *fractional anticipatory goal response* signifies that as one approaches a goal, the cues for imminent reinforcement become stronger, and these are consumed along the way, so to speak, and assist the organism to reach the goal. Anticipatory responses are probable when one has passed along the route to the goal (or one like it) in the past. If the past experience has been successful—for example, status was gained, or other's power was reduced—the fractional responses are positively toned, providing grounds for optimism; if the past experiences have been unsuccessful, the fractional responses evoke pessimism. In any given relational situation, whether change is desired or not, the strength and direction of the optimism— pessimism component of the anticipatory emotions depend on the record of past outcomes in similar relational situations.

The Effect of Present Circumstances. The second constituent of anticipatory emotion depends on the circumstantial evidence for probable success or failure in the next interaction episode. The affective result is *confidence* or *lack of confidence*. Confidence or lack of it is based on whatever resources, interests, rules, conditions, personalities, and so on are known or believed to operate in the situation. The knowledge of particular formal conditions of a situation may dispose one toward confidence about a preferred relational outcome. Formal conditions include existing law, bureaucratic rules, terms of a contract, and the like, which suggest the high probability of the enforcement of a positive outcome—even though that may currently be denied due to the arbitrary actions of the other.

A second factor that may affect confidence is a judgment concerning the character of the other or oneself in light of certain norms of equity, reciprocity, fairness, and the like. If one believes that the other holds such norms and will act on them, this engenders confidence that structurally negative relations will change for the better. If one intends to apply those norms to one's own conduct when one is knowingly the agent of the other's discontent, this is reason for confidence in the outcome ahead. We think things over after an argument and conclude that we were at fault and decide to apologize. This alone can induce confidence concerning the future positive course of the relationship and our own feelings. If, on the other hand, one's knowledge of self or other suggests that the appropriate norms of equity or fairness will not be applied, then these are grounds for a lack of confidence in a preferred outcome.

A third factor that can determine the direction and intensity of the confidence aspects of the anticipatory emotions is the amount of resources at hand for effecting change. If one has weapons and the will to use them to change disadvantageous power relations, these are grounds for confidence—assuming that the use of these weapons will not bring retaliation so damaging as to nullify the gains. Relational weaponry, however, need not always be destructive. In the channel of status relations, the "weaponry" or technology of attainment of rewards from others is to do what evokes status from them. Blau (1964, pp. 39–40) suggested that respect is attained by showing novel opinions, competence, or courage. Homans (1962) said that we gain prestige by providing group members with important services they cannot provide for themselves. Goffman's (1959) analysis of the "presentation of the self," with its "front " and "backstage," its "performances" and "arts of impression management," is an elaborate manual of some formal aspects of relational technology for gaining and maintaining status. Structural discontents can be rectified by the accumulation of resources (e.g., guns, money, education, emotional health, etc., depending on which of the relational channels is defective) and by their utilization to change adverse relations or maintain satisfactory ones. If one is dissatisfied with the amount of status one is giving to the other—it may be too much or too little—one may use money for behavior modification or psychotherapy, which will improve one's ability to relate to the other in a manner more in keeping with one's goals for ideal relational behavior.

When the two components of the anticipatory emotions are cross classified—*optimism–pessimism* by *confidence–lack of confidence*—we obtain a set of possibilities such as those found on the left in Table 4.1. Optimism and confidence are the bases for a state of what can be called *serene confidence*, obviously a pleasant anticipatory emotion. When optimism is combined with a lack of confidence, there is still a positive affective tone to mitigate the unattractive prospect. It can be considered *guarded optimism* or *hopefulness*. Hope is indeed a function of past experience, but it only comes into play when the objective indicators of the present situation are negative (cf. Stotland, 1969). When pessimism is combined with a positive set of circumstantial indicators that warrant confidence, the compound effect is a *grudging optimism*, rather uncharacteristic of the pessimist, since his past experience has given him little ground for optimism. Finally, when pessimism is combined with a view of current circumstances that dictates lack of confidence, the affective result is *hopelessness*. Nothing in either past or present warrants more than this.

In popular discourse one of the most common anticipatory emotions is anxiety. This signifies a fearful anticipation of a negative future outcome and can emerge either as pessimism or lack of confidence. Often the undesirable outcome anticipated will result the from the present inadequacy of one's own power or excess of other's power. Thus this anticipatory emotional state can be simply the direct carry-forward of the structural condition that gave rise to the emotion (see Chapter 3). In other words, the pattern of past interactional outcomes now

TABLE 4–1 OPTIMISM, CONFIDENCE, OUTCOME, AND EMOTION

Optimism	Confidence	Anticipatory Affect		Outcome	Emotion
High	High =	Serene confidence	+	Favorable	Mild satisfaction
				Unfavorable	Consternation
High	Low =	Guarded optimism (anxiety)	+	Favorable	Strong satisfaction
				Unfavorable	Mild disappointment
Low	High =	Grudging optimism (anxiety)	+	Favorable	Mild satisfaction
				Unfavorable	Mild disappointment
Low	Low =	Hopelessness (anxiety)	+	Favorable	Astonishment
				Unfavorable	Resignation

crystallized in the structure of the relationship has its most salient emotional thrust in the threat of unattractive future outcomes. Thus as a structural emotion, anxiety already has an anticipatory aspect. Furthermore, all the anticipatory emotions other than serene confidence have some anxiety attached to them. This is true even if fear-anxiety is not a structural emotion. Merely the threat of power or status insufficiency in the future is enough to engage anxiety. .

Anxiety as an element of anticipatory emotions must be distinguished from *anxiousness* which can be understood best as impatience or the wish for reduced waiting time for some event, positive or negative. Anxiousness is viewed here as a state or trait personality characteristic unrelated to social interaction as such, having perhaps to do with discomfort due to speed, duration, and intensity of autonomic arousal (see Cattell, 1972, pp. 160–165). Anxiety, anxiousness, and anticipatory affect can occur together, given the proper relational and dispositional configuration.

ANTICIPATION AND OUTCOMES

It is useful to examine the interplay between the anticipatory emotions and actual outcomes, since, depending on outcome, a set of emotions related only to the state of anticipation will be induced. These emotions are additional to the substantive emotions that are directly instigated by the particular relational outcome. I propose that the emotion that results from the interaction of anticipatory affect and relational outcome acts as a multiplier of the intensity of the emotion ordinarily produced by the relational outcome. The right-hand side of Table 4.1 shows anticipatory affect combined with different outcomes conditions and the multiplier emotions hypothesized to result in each case.

Serene confidence and a positive outcome should not act very strongly as a multiplier, since the gratifying result was never in doubt and does not particularly stand out from the previous pattern of successes. Since physiological activation appears to result from novelty or difference, this combination does not provide any ground for such emotional augmentation (Sternbach, 1966). Should serene confidence meet with disappointment or defeat, however, there should be considerable confusion, disbelief, and dissonance. The past, instead of being recaptured, is disconfirmed. We should expect a strong emotional response to be activated. Several studies have shown the magnification affect of a contrast between *expected* positive and *actual* negative outcomes, particularly when the relational conditions prompt anger as the consequent emotion (e.g., Austin and Walster, 1974). Anger is considerably intensified in such circumstances. Pastore (1952) also found an increasing monotonic relationship between "expectancy" and the strength of reaction to frustration. This is also one of the classic conditions for the arousal of cognitive dissonance (Festinger, 1957). Not only does novelty leads to activation here, but in addition the concentrated mental effort to discover an explanation for the unexpected outcome leads to physiological arousal (Lacey, 1967). I call this emotional state *consternation*, keeping in mind that the magnitude of consternation is due in part to the discrepancy between what was serenely expected and what actually happened, as well as the salience of the relationship as a whole. (The idea of salience is introduced here in recognition of the fact that each relationship has a place in a hierarchy of relationships of varying importance to the individual.)

The guarded optimist who obtains a favorable outcome must feel *relieved*, *pleased*, and *happy*. He did not stake highly, since he lacked confidence in the immediate circumstances, but the confirmation of residual optimism must be satisfying. Should there be failure for the guarded optimist, the multiplier effect due to anticipation is not strong, since a positive outcome was doubted in this particular instance. Austin and Walster (1974) proposed, on the basis of earlier work of Austin (1972), that "expectation of an unpleasant event . . . ameliorates the distress a person experiences when the threatened event eventually occurs" (p. 215). In an experiment involving equity considerations, Austin and Walster found that subjects who were prepared to expect a poor outcome were less distressed than those who prepared to expect more, but received less. There is nonetheless a sense of *disappointment*, since those who hope do so for a positive outcome, even when they doubt its objective likelihood.*

When the grudging optimist obtains a favorable outcome, he too is no doubt *pleased* (Verinis, Brandsma, and Cofer, 1968), but with a somewhat incredulous air. He may attribute the outcome to luck as opposed to the real interplay of operating elements in the situation or to his own merit. In the case of an unfavorable result, the grudging optimist must derive some small measure of *satisfaction*, because the outcome confirmed his residual pessimism (McClelland et al., 1953). However, this will be offset by the *disappointment* of the actual failure in a situation of high confidence. When satisfaction and disappointment are combined in this way, we can get what is called "grim satisfaction."

Two bodies of experimental work shed additional light on the anticipatory emotions of guarded optimism and grudging optimism. Rotter (1966) and his colleagues (Rotter, Chance, and Phares, 1974) discussed two main types of orientation toward source of control over personal outcomes: *internal* and *external* locus of control. Internal control is akin to guarded optimism which flourishes even in the face of circumstances that are foreboding. External control suggests grudging optimism. Those high on internal locus of control believe that outcomes are subject to skillful manipulation and that results are affected by their own abilities. On the other hand, high external control persons judge that events are subject to unpredictable forces, and that luck or chance determine outcomes more than skill. When past outcomes have been generally successful, there is a tendency toward the kind of active efforts to gain success and avoid failure that lead to the sense of internal control. The fact that internals have higher achievement than externals supports this view (Crandall, Katkovsky, and Crandall, 1965; McGhee and Crandall, 1968; Weiner and Kukla, 1970). On the other hand, those who attribute their good outcomes to forces external to themselves are more likely to have experienced failure—due in part to lack of active effort.

The guarded optimist has had sufficient success in the past to make him an internal, whereas the grudging optimist, who is fundamentally a pessimist, has had sufficient failure to make him an external. When events confirm the residual tendencies, the resulting emotion should be congruent with the residual character of both the optimist and the pessimist. Thus when the guarded optimist succeeds, he should feel pleased, but not at all pleased when he fails, despite the fact that he expected failure in this situation. On the other hand, the grudging optimist should feel less pleased by the same level of successful outcome, because

---

*There is a hint in McClelland et al. (1953) that the confirmation of an expected disappointment brings a slight positive affect that derives from the satisfaction of being right.

it was not his doing—as an external, his success and failure are due to chance and luck—and when he fails, there should be some degree of satisfaction, in contrast to the total displeasure of the internal in the same situation. The satisfaction comes from confirmation of long-standing expectancy.

In the final type of anticipatory emotional state, in which pessimism and lack of confidence combine to produce hopelessness, when the anticipatory affect is disconfirmed by a positive outcome, the emotion should be one of *astonishment* and incredulousness. Furthermore, since hopelessness is one of the strongest indicators of depression (Stotland, 1969; Klein, 1974), if the anticipatory hopelessness is an aspect of the structural emotion of depression carried forward into the future, any positive outcome is less pleasing than would otherwise be the case. In general, depressed persons suffer not only from lower frequency of satisfying activities, but they also find them less enjoyable than do nondepressed persons (MacPhillamy and Lewinsohn, 1974). This point was made more strongly by Costello (1972), who asserted that depressed people are not so much lacking in positive reinforcement, but suffer from a reduction in the positive effects of their usual rewards. Although there is not complete identity between depression and the anticipatory emotion of hopelessness, there is enough overlap to warrant the conclusion that a positive outcome is less pleasing to the hopeless than to those with other anticipatory emotions.

When the outcome in the state of hopelessness is negative as expected, the resulting emotion should reflect *passive resignation*. In a study by Loeb, Beck, and Diggory (1971), depressed persons had lower aspiration levels than normals prior to undertaking a task. Experimental conditions were manipulated so that half the depressed subjects were told they had succeeded at the task, and half were told they had failed. In the failed group, the level of aspiration was even lower for a second task. Thus each new negative outcome for the depressed (the hopeless) drives them further back in hopelessness.

An experiment by Houston (1972) also brought out the condition of resignation when a low expectancy of success is combined with failure. Subjects were high in either internal or external control (Rotter, 1966). The experimenter informed half of each group that they could avoid shock by avoiding mistakes in an experimental task. He told the other half of both groups that they would be shocked unavoidably. The external control group in the unavoidable shock condition showed the lowest amount of physiological arousal as measured by heart rate. Temperamentally pessimistic, as indicated by the high external-control score, this group also had no circumstantial evidence to buoy even a grudging optimism. When the shocks were administered as expected, there was no astonishment and little arousal. In other words, they were passive and resigned to their fate.

It is useful, finally, to be aware of the hypothesis that the anticipatory emotions and their interactions with actual outcomes do not produce the "main effects," so to speak, but serve to amplify or suppress the emotions that result from the relational outcomes of interaction. The relational outcomes instigate the consequent emotions, which I now discuss.

chapter 5

Consequent Emotions: I

Emotions are defined earlier as responses to outcomes of social interaction. Some of these outcomes are of relatively long duration and constitute the structure of the relationship between the actors. This structure gives rise to what I call the *structural* emotions. Each relationship, emerging from its past, also has a future. The *anticipatory* emotions are the subjective estimates of how the relationship will develop, whether it will improve, deteriorate, or simply continue as before. In ongoing relationships there is further interaction that takes place within the context of both the existing relational structure (and its associated structural emotions) and the relational anticipations and emotions. The results of the interaction are that power and status have either increased, decreased, or remained the same. These relational outcomes give rise to the *consequent* emotions.

The articulation of interaction outcomes with structural conditions, although simple to formulate systematically, gives rise to a large number of combinations. Figure 5.1 shows the full development for self-*status*. This relational channel can be structurally excessive, adequate, or insufficient. Three outcomes can be articulated with each of the three structural possibilities: gain, loss, or continuity of status. Thus, depending on the initial condition, there are nine possible outcome conditions, as shown in Figure 5.1. However, each of these must be multiplied by the sevenfold agency-direction matrix of Figure 3.2, page 46. Thus in considering self-status only, we must conceive of nine × seven = 63 possible emotions, depending on initial structural condition (excessive, adequate, or insufficient status), interaction outcome (gain, loss, or continuity), and agency and direction of emotion (self, other, or third party). When we proceed in the same fashion for self-power, other's status, and other's power, we add three × 63 = 189 more outcome cells, for a total of 252. Does this shake the reader's faith in the utility of this effort to predict emotions by means of a social relational model? Indeed, the end is not yet in sight, and although a full treatment of the problem greatly amplifies the number of cells, I introduce some modifications that reduce the number of emotions that must be discussed.

First, to do the analysis full justice would require 1701 cells. This comes about as follows: Each interaction episode that gives rise to a consequent emotion

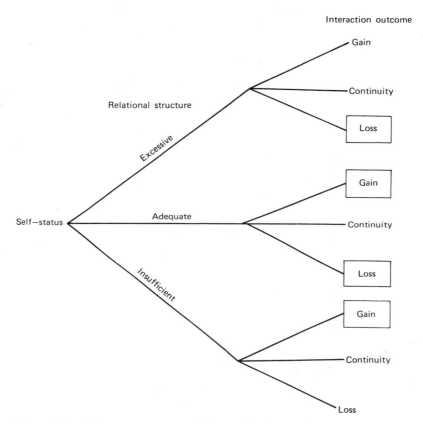

Figure 5–1   Self-status: structure and interactional outcomes.

occurs within the context of an existing structure of relationship and its appropriate emotions. Since relationships are constituted of four channels—own power and status and other's power and status—a complete account of the structural context of each interaction episode that gives rise to a consequent emotion would include each of the relational channels. For example, the structural levels of own power, other's power, and other's status also affect the consequent emotions that result from the interaction episode that has affected the structural level of self-status. The same considerations hold for each relational channel as it is considered in turn as the central focus of outcome. Since each of the four relational channels—own power, other's power, own status, and other's status—has three structural conditions—excess, adequacy, or insufficiency—a full set of structural combinations would lead to $3^4 = 81$ contexts. These must be multiplied by the three interaction outcome possibilities—gain, loss, or continuity—to give 243. This number is multiplied in turn by the seven agency-direction possibilities, and the grand total comes to 1701, a number that may evoke *consternation* among those who have, up to this point, favored this effort at a sociological theory of emotions, and mere *resignation* among those who have had no hope for it from the beginning (see Chapter 4 for a discussion of these emotions). Yet it would be cowardly to turn away from a logical outcome, despite its apparent complexity.

Some instructive examples from other sciences about complexity can help us over this possible crisis of confidence. First, complexity is not indicated by the sheer number of outcomes. Indeed, if we can generate a large number of results with a very small number of operations, instead of complexity, we have attained simplicity. Simplicity resides in being able to comprehend Nature's great diversity by means of a few principles. This not an argument for parsimony—which some do not like—but rather an assertion that any science, even if it is not dedicated to parsimony, engages in reducing the apparent complexity of phenomena to the principles of a generative grammar, so to speak. By the rules of the grammar, a nearly infinite set of combinations is sometimes made possible. This is the case for the generative grammer of linguistic utterances as elaborated by Chomsky (1965). His notion is that the relatively few rules of the grammar make it possible to generate all possible sentences, a number much larger than the 1701 emotions that are admittedly so terrifying to contemplate here.

Consider also Mendeleyef, who provided the basic understanding of the Periodic Table of Elements. Indeed, he did no more than provide a grammar by which it would be possible to generate the various cells in which elements with given properties were (or should be) found. Since Mendeleyef's day, new elements have been added to the basic table he constructed. Yet they fit into the scheme according to the several principles on which he constructed the original table. A final example of simplicity in apparent complexity is found in the work of Einstein on the general theory of relativity. In his 1915 paper, the theory was summed up in 10 equations, an appealingly small number considering the magnitude of the problem he was treating. Yet the 10 equations were adequate for his purposes, since they were drawn from a branch of mathematics known as tensor calculus. In that discipline, each briefly stated equation can stand for a whole system of terms. One of Einstein's tensors in fact represented more than a million terms (Hoffman, 1973, pp. 121–124), but the entire theory was adequately represented by the 10 equations that Einstein published.

Nonetheless we can still be cowed by the problem of spelling out 1701 emotions. It is difficult enough to find suitable terms for the emotions of a greatly reduced number of cells. It is impossible at present to find terms for the full set. In the future two developments may help resolve the problem: either there will be a body of empirical data (currently nonexistent) that will specify the emotions associated with each cell, or a new, simplifying principle will eliminate the need to elaborate the scheme into 1701 cells. In the meantime, however, we must proceed.

Having admitted the impossibility of dealing with the complete matrix of 1701 consequent emotions, I resort to what is perhaps the ultimate device of any science for reducing an unmanageable complexity while making forward progress possible: the simplifying assumption. Among the most widely known examples of this are those used by Galileo in his presentation of the problems of acceleration in free-fall and of motion along an inclined plane. In the first case he assumed that objects were falling in a vacuum, undeterred by air resistance. In the second case he assumed a frictionless plane. In the social sciences, too, simplifying assumptions can make science possible.

I now introduce three simplifying assumptions to reduce the scope of the matrix with which we must deal. First, I do not attempt to formulate the consequent emotions in terms of the full set of $3^4 = 81$ structural conditions. Instead it is reasonable to work with only a single structural channel at a time, for example, self-status, as in Figure 5.1. Yet, as we consider each relational channel in turn, the remaining three structural dimensions can be included in a simplified way. So as not to lose the effect of the additional channels on the consequent emotions, we can dichotomize the consequent emotions into a set that operates when self "likes" the other and a set that operates when self "dislikes" the other. How do liking and disliking bear on the problem of the missing structural channels in each case?

Liking results from the relational competence of the other (see Appendix 2). Relational competence can be understood as the other's giving us adequate amounts of status and not using excessive amounts of power. Those who voluntarily reward us in adequate amounts and do not punish us elicit liking (Berscheid and Walster, 1969; Lott and Lott, 1974; Clore and Byrne, 1974). Further, our liking for the other affects how much power we exercise and how much status we give to the other. Thus without specifying the precise structural conditions each time in the three omitted channels, we can assume that particular distributions of self and other's power and status are associated with liking or dislike. For each consequent emotion agency-direction-outcome cell associated with the three possible structural conditions of a given relational channel, we can attempt to specify the emotion further on the basis of liking or dislike for the other. This enables us to take account of the 27 relational structure possibilities that are omitted.

Instead of $3^4 = 81$ structural contexts that are multiplied by three possible interaction outcomes and seven agency-direction possibilities to produce 1701 cells, we now have the following: each relational channel has three structural possibilities (excess, adequate, or insufficient). These are multiplied by the two liking–dislike alternatives that replace the 3^3 structural contexts to be omitted each time. Thus we have $3 \times 2 \times 21$ (interaction outcome agency-directional possibilities) = 126 cells *for each relational channel*. Since there are four relational channels (own power, own status, other's power, and other's status), we obtain 504 cells, certainly an improvement, but still far too many. A second simplifying assumption permits a further reduction in the number of cells that should be given primary attention.

In Figure 5.1 nine outcomes are shown: gain, loss, and continuity for each of the three structural conditions—excess, adequacy, or insufficiency. Without great loss we can exclude five of these and examine only these outcomes: *loss* when there is a structural condition of excess, *gain* and *loss* when there is a structural condition of adequacy, and *gain* when there is the structural condition of insufficiency. These outcomes are shown boxed in Figure 5.1. Although we may miss some emotions by this strategy of looking only at four of the nine structure-outcome possibilities, certain likelihoods mitigate the loss. In the case of structural excess, the outcomes of continuity or gain would appear to lead to a higher intensity of the feelings associated with excess (Verinis, Brandsma, and Cofer, 1968). Similarly, the outcomes of loss and continuity in conjunction with the structural condition of insufficiency would also act to aggravate the sentiment already present. Finally, when the structural condition is adequacy, the outcome of continuity should not lead to any different emotion than that already present due to adequacy. By adopting this simplifying assumption, we reduce the 504 cells by 5/9. This gives 224, a number that is still not easily manageable.

The third device by which we can reduce the matrix of consequent emotions was broached in the previous chapter when we considered the structural emotions, namely, the isomorphism—for certain purposes—between own power and other's power. As discussed in Chapter 3, own-power adequacy is isomorphic with other's adequacy, own excess with other's insufficiency, and own insufficiency with other's excess. This parallelism reduces the matrix again by a quarter. When we apply the three types of reduction to the full matrix of 1701 cells, we arrive at a matrix of 3 (relational channels) $\times$ 4 (structural condition-interaction outcomes) $\times$ 7 (agency-direction cells) $\times$ 2 (states of liking or dislike for the other). This equals 168. Even this reduced number of cells is troublesome, for reasons to be set forth later, but readers should take heart. We have reduced a matrix of 1701 cells to less than one-tenth the size by a series of reasonable assumptions. Furthermore, as will become evident, we need not deal with 168 discrete emotions. In fact, we are focusing attention not on 168 emotions, but on 168 agency-directional possibilities for emotion in light of certain relational outcomes, given certain structural conditions. Similar emotions often emerge in different cells. For example, whether other or third party is the agent of our power loss, the emotion ought to be the same. Numerous duplications of this kind appear.

Nonetheless, because of some further difficulties in the present state of knowledge of emotions, it is not possible to discuss each of the 168 cells. I present hypotheses for many cells, and, for a limited portion of the matrix, I attempt a complete discussion. At least my method of analysis at this stage of development of the theory will be clear.

I deal with two matters before discussing the consequent emotions. A glance ahead at Tables 6.1 to 6.6 in the next chapter shows that many of the cells do not contain a label for an emotion. This is an admitted defect of the presentation, but there are some mitigating factors that touch intimately on our present state of knowledge in the study of emotions. These are considered immediately below. The final matter before turning to the consequent emotions involves the translation of experimental paradigms and results into a language compatible with the power-status model. I examine several common experimental situations and inductions to see whether they make sense within the power-status framework. If they do, the experimental results can be used as evidence to support hypotheses about the consequent emotions that are derived from the power-status model.

LABELING EMOTIONS

One issue that dominates the study of emotions is naming them. In the investigations involving recognition of emotions from photographs, this is tantamount to identifying the basic set of emotions (see Frijda, 1969). In the basic dimensions approaches (see Chapter 1), the task is done when a label is attached to a particular psychophysiological-cognitive-motoric state. In that way we have identified an "emotion." Yet agreement on what emotions are expressed in photographs is not very high, nor is there perfect agreement on the synonymity of words presumed to express given emotions (Schlossberg, 1954; Osgood, 1966; Davitz, 1969; Stringer, 1973). Perhaps, too, *there are more emotions than we have labels for at present.* Very important emotions have probably not escaped our attention. However, our perceptual-cognitive apparatus, through which we first receive the external stimuli that produce emotions, may be more discriminating than the language we use to label the emotions that the perceptions and cognitions lead us to experience.

Gibson (1966) differentiated between what is perceived and what is labeled, "between perceptual cognition or knowledge of the environment, and symbolic cognition, or knowledge *about* the environment. The former is a direct response to things based on stimulus sources produced by another human individual" (p. 91, emphasis in original). It is a matter of conjecture whether any language community has coded all possible human social encounters. As evidence I refer to the accepted untranslatability of certain terms with an emotional referent (e.g., *Gemütlichkeit, Weltschmerz, élan,* etc.) between one culture or language community and another. Gibson's point, however, is quite far reaching in the domain of emotions, for it suggests that we *feel* more than we know, and the reason we do not *know* is that we do not have the language to label our feelings.

Osgood (1966) has also commented on the inexactitude of labeling emotions. Referring to the results of the recognition studies and the low reliability of naming emotions, he attributes this to " . . . confusability among labels. If such confusions were random, confusability would be identical with unreliability— but they are not. Rather, they are reasonably systematic, reflecting the loose mapping of names onto things, and the existence of conventionally determined quasi-synonyms" (p. 29). Lazarus and Averill (1972) also indicated our language difficulties with emotions: "Any verbal expression [of emotion] is subject to a variety of constraints as part of a linguistic system which is not particularly well suited to the expression of affect" (p. 244). Firestone, Kaplan, and Russell (1973), discussing fear and anxiety, acknowledged that "subjects' vagueness in the use of verbal labels for the two emotional states . . . [is] . . . hardly surprising in the light of psychologists' overlapping use of these concepts" (p. 411). Young (1961) provided another explanation of the confusion that attends the labeling of emotional states. He saw emotion as constituted of three elements: "a conscious experience that is felt," "emotional behavior," and "physiological process" (p. 354). Given these diverse responses, there is understandable difficulty in giving single, reliable labels that make coherent the three qualitatively different response phenomena. Young also offered a list of eight distinctions in levels and degrees of affective process (see page 48). This proliferation places an extraordinary burden on language to identify clearly and carefully the specific quality and intensity of emotion at each level.

Although our stock of labels for emotions may be relatively meagre, this does not mean that we lack the sense of how to elicit emotions by our actions. Here again we know more than we can sometimes say. In an experiment involving high temptations to wrong a partner for one's own benefit, Bonacich (1972) found that subjects reacted to evidence of cheating with a long list of pejoratives, such as "cheat, screw, fink, liar," and the like, in association with ideas designed to elicit feelings of guilt in the wrong doer. Bonacich concluded that "one kind of social control is to label the non-cooperative act as negative and immoral so that the non-cooperator will punish himself through lowered self-esteem and feelings of guilt" (p. 366). There is also some evidence that practical knowledge in eliciting emotions is better developed in the case of negative as opposed to positive emotions (Kahn and Young, 1973).

The clinical recognition of "affectlessness" as a symptom of emotional disorder illuminates from yet another direction the problem of adequate labeling of emotions (Hinsie and Campbell, 1970). In varying degrees, normal individuals may also lack affect in certain situations, which would indeed seriously hamper their own and others' ability to label the emotions that modally and normally occur in those situations. Affectlessness can be either a form of repression or a failure to learn the proper labels of one's own emotion as well as the emotion of others. When parents are ignorant or repress affect, they fail to identify emotions adequately for their children, thereby perpetuating the inability to label emotions. A closely related difficulty is the mislabeling of emotions. Schachter (1967) proposed that obesity may result from fat persons' inability to label correctly different states of physiological activation, in particular mistaking gastrointestinal for true "emotional" arousal. Schachter claimed that this might happen in individuals whose emotions were misidentified by their parents, as when the parent feeds the child who is fearful. Fear is then identified with feeding and leads to the refrigerator instead of to flight or other means for self-protection. Although Schachter's hypothesis depends on his view of the undifferentiatedness of physiological arousal for all emotional states (a position to be discussed in Chapters 7 and 8), it is easy to see that the mislabeling of emotions can easily occur, particularly if parents are not able to distinguish emotions in themselves or in their young children, whose communication is mainly motoric and autonomic instead of verbal. Indeed, one of the reasons first-born children may be more "emotional" or sensitive to emotional display (Schachter, 1959) may be because they have not been given an adequate emotional vocabulary with which to cognize and reflect on their emotions. The deficit may be attributable to parents who could not recognize the emotions of their first-born children, although this is less of a problem with later-born children (Adams, 1972).

In the next chapter I attempt to label the emotional consequents of given social relational outcomes. Yet some cells in the table of emotions remain empty, not because I believe there is no emotion, but because I cannot name it. This means either that I was badly brought up to know the emotional vocabulary and am thus ill equipped to provide the labels, or that my culture is deficient in linking labels to emotions and emotions to social relational events. There is some reason to believe the latter alternative is at least partly true. Wolman et al. (1971) studied how children locate emotions as they mature, particularly whether the emotions were felt to be "internal" or "external." Wolman and his colleagues correctly reasoned that younger children more than older children would depend on external cues and that for them "the locus of the initiation of an activity or situation occurs outside the child and is rooted in the external world" (p. 1290). The children ranged in age from 5 to 13 years, and the emotions about which they responded were hunger, thirst, sadness, sleepiness, happiness, anger, fear, and nervousness.* As hypothesized, younger children

---

*These are not all emotions as usually understood, but I retain the terminology used by Wolman et al.

were more likely to attribute emotion to external instead of internal conditions. Wolman and his colleagues comment that "the movement from external to internal of the child's description of what provokes a feeling is consistent with theories of personality development and the growth of the self-image" (p. 1292).

The irony is that such consistency goes far to rob us of what children still know, namely, that emotions are most often socially cued and that when one is happy, sad, angry, frightened, and so on, it is because some transaction with the environment has produced the feeling. If we have some tendency to idyllize the "childlike," it is perhaps because children still see clearly the connection between social cause and personal feeling. Personality development as suggested by Wolman and his colleagues means to lose the child's *sophisticated* understanding of the connection between social relations and tears, laughter, joy, fear, and the like. By various processes, including parents' and teachers' active suppression of much emotional display, emotions and their labels are internalized, and this separates the person who experiences the emotion from the situational conditions that gave rise to it. No wonder we cannot label the emotions that follow from particular relational outcomes. No wonder that we so often cannot say what we feel, or when we do know what we feel, do not know why.

EXPERIMENTAL FORMATS AND POWER-STATUS RELATIONS

In the next chapter I label the emotions that follow from social relational outcomes in one of two ways. Principally I hypothesize relevant emotions from an understanding of the empirical findings or existing theory about emotions. Where neither theory nor empirical studies are available, I rely on a phenomenological role-taking method and hypothesize heuristically the emotion that I believe fits the social relational conditions specified. Although the frankly speculative character of this residual method of labeling is ordinarily deplorable, the empirical study of the social relational precursors of emotions is so scant that this empathic approach can perhaps be accepted at this stage.

Where there is empirical work that deals either directly or indirectly with emotions, the results provide *evidence* to support *hypotheses* about specific emotions. The studies I cite are almost universally of a single type: an experimental manipulation causes an emotion (either measured, inferred, or inferrable) to be induced. However, before we can adopt the results of these studies for our purposes, we must examine carefully the experimental inductions themselves, for they serve the theory only to the extent that they adequately reflect the power and status relational conditions and outcomes that I hypothesize give rise to emotions.

Although there is little *systematic* inquiry into the sociological or relational precursors of emotions, many researchers have unwittingly investigated particular emotions from this framework. This must indeed be the case, since many emotions usually occur only when there is a relational cue or stimulus. When investigators study emotions experimentally in the laboratory (or coping responses such as aggression that are assumed to follow an emotion), they must supply a suitable stimulus to instigate the emotion in research subjects. This suggests that, even without a coherent, inclusive framework for relational analysis, researchers know, practically, a good deal more about the social stimuli that produce emotions than has been systematically set down.

When researchers wish to induce anger, they often use the technique of insulting their subjects (Konecni and Doob, 1972; Ax, 1953; J. Schachter, 1957). Other investigators use the technique of shocking the subject (Brock and Buss, 1962; Berkowitz and Holmes, 1960). Sometimes anger is induced by having someone—usually a confederate of the investigator—deliver shocks in preference to some milder form of noxious stimulus, thus adding insult to injury and assuring the victims that there was intent to hurt them (Baron, 1974; Baron and Ball, 1970). When the experimental problem is fear or anxiety, researchers have also found situational methods to induce these emotions. Anxiety can be induced by threatening the subjects with noxious stimuli (S. Schachter, 1959; Frankenhaeuser and Rissler, 1970) or by threatening to deliver a noxious stimulus, but delaying it. During the "build-up" period, high levels of anxiety are induced (Nomikos et al., 1968). Guilt has been induced many times merely by getting the subject to do some hurt or harm to another (Wallace and Sedalla, 1966; Regan, Williams, and Sparling, 1972). When the emotion under study is shame, the researchers have been equally facile. Very often individuals are given tasks they cannot possibly complete, and they are informed of their failure. The indicator of shame—which is not always of direct interest to the investigator—can be an explicit expression of shame and embarrassment, or it maybe lowered self-esteem (Firestone, Kaplan, and Russell, 1973).

Despite the lack of a sociological theory of emotions, experimenters have been quite ingenious at devising the sociological stimulus conditions that induce various emotions. As to whether the specific emotions of interest are in fact induced, there is evidence from the subjects themselves, who, by verbal report, paper-and-pencil tests, observable behavior, or physiological response, indicate the motoric, cognitive and autonomic signs of the various emotions of interest. Indeed, we must conclude that more knowledge is available to substantiate a sociological theory of emotions than might have been guessed at first.

It is useful to review carefully some of the experimental inductions just cited. If the laboratory or field manipulations can be comfortably accommodated to the power-status relational model, the experimental results can be regarded as the basis for hypotheses about the consequent emotions. It is evident from the studies examined that the experimental formats employed to induce various emotions are simply variations on the power-status theme.

A frequent means of inducing *anger* is to insult the subject. In a typical experiment induction of this type (Konecni and Doob, 1972),

> . . . the confederate . . . started off by saying; "Haven't you finished yet?" and went on in this fashion, saying that the subject was slow, that the anagrams were easy to solve if one had any brains, and that everything about the subject was somehow phoney. He commented on the subject's clothes, wondered aloud how the subject had managed to get accepted to the university, said he felt sure that the subject had been getting poor grades, etc. The confederate naturally varied the procedure some-what from subject to subject, pursuing the line that seemed to disturb the subject the most. The purpose of this was to annoy every subject as much as possible (p. 383).

Indeed, after confederates pursued such a line, we may wonder that some did not go home with fat lips while others went to the infirmary with broken jaws. That nothing of this kind was reported by the researchers may suggest that perhaps the experimental induction did not take as was intended. Yet the experimental results were in the predicted direction, and subjects apparently did not see through the procedure. My interest, however, is in the *relational* implications of the induction. First, the subject and the confederate, even if only barely intro-duced, are in a relationship. There is apparent mutual dependence in some task in the division of labor that has been set by the experimenter. Although little of a relational character may have occurred up to the point at which the confederate begins his diatribe, it is clear that the confederate has turned his attention away from the task and is directing it to the subject himself. As indicated in Chapter 2, this is the fundamental condition of relationship—that actors be oriented toward each other rather than (or in addition) to the task. In what relational channel is the confederate operating? Clearly it is the power channel. He is punishing and hurting the subject and is doing so by means of status withdrawal.

This must be understood further. The subject presented himself for the experiment (and for the interaction in the division of labor with the confederate) in what might be termed "all innocence." That is, he expected he would be accepted at face value and at his apparent worth—a student at a ranking univer-sity, which implies a certain intellectual stature, personal character, and the like (cf. Goffman, 1959). These characteristics are indeed worth something—not awe, nor deep reverence—but certainly ordinary politeness—that is, a moderate amount of status. Instead he is lambasted for a dummy, and virtually everything about him except his forebears is subjected to denigration. This is severe status withdrawal with the purpose, of course, of provoking an emotion—anger—and the type of behavior that usually follows anger, namely, aggression. For the present it is enough to see the experimental induction—the insult—was a use of power in the mode of status withdrawal. Later we see that the experimental induction worked.

In other experiments anger is induced by shocking the subject as a form of judgment on his competence. Here is a typical procedure (Berkowitz and Geen, 1966):

> . . . the experimenter described the experiment as dealing with problem-solving ability under stress. One person, and the experimenter indicated that the subject was to take this role, would have to work on a problem knowing the other person (the accomplice) would judge the quality of his solution. The accomplice would evaluate the subject's performance by giving the subject from one to ten electric shocks; the poorer the solution, the greater the number of shocks that the subject was to receive . . . Later the experimenter returned, picked up the subject's written solution, and strapped the shock electrode on to the subject's arm . . . One minute later the accomplice in the adjoining room administered either one shock (*non-angered* condition) or seven shocks (*angered* condition) (pp. 526–527, emphasis in original).

What is the relational situation created here when the subject is evaluated by the method of shocks? As in the case of the subjects who were insulted in the Konecni and Doob (1972) experiment already discussed, the student subjects came to the experimental situation with their self-esteem more or less intact, possessed of certain characteristics worthy of at least ordinary respect and surely not punishment. Quite unexpectedly, they are informed that they did poorly on a task that they were given no previous reason to suppose they could not complete adequately. Berkowitz and Geen did not tell us the nature of the problem given to the students, but we must assume that the students probably thought they had done it reasonably well. They were evaluated and the evaluation was both injury and insult, namely, the accomplice used power (literally, in this case) to reduce the status of the subjects by telling him that his performance was less than competent. We must assume that seven shocks measures considerable displeasure and status withdrawal on a scale of one to ten. Indeed, the subjects of Berkowitz and Geen's experiment thought so too, as was evident by their responses.

In accordance with the well-known frustration-aggression hypothesis (Dollard et al., 1939), many researchers have frustrated their experimental subjects to see whether they would subsequently act in an aggressive fashion. I examine some of these frustrations from the point of view of the power-status relational model. Inductions of frustration can be effected by the actual relational behavior of confederates in an experiment, but research subjects can also be asked to recapitulate or imagine their responses to apparently frustrating relational outcomes. Pastore's (1952) study of arbitrary frustration is of this kind. Pastore asked a group of respondents about the degree to which a set of "frustrations" was justified. Some of these are shown in Table 5.1. How do they look when viewed through the power-status lens?

When the bus driver intentionally passes you by (item 1, Table 5.1), this is a direct withdrawal of status. Admittedly the prospective passenger expects little status in some absolute sense from the bus driver, but obviously one thing is important, namely, that the driver stop the bus when he sees you waiting. To pass by *intentionally* does more than simply violate the exchange relationship between the bus company and the public that the company has pledged to the local transit commission that it will honor. It is a direct affront to the prospective passenger, because it suggests that the passenger is somehow discreditable and therefore not fit to be carried on public transport with other persons, that the passenger's interests, which would be served by his being carried to his destination, are of little account and can be ignored, or that the bus driver has the right to judge the worth or the person of the passenger—a privilege that is not included in the bus company's franchise. Any of these and many other possibilities may lie behind the interpretation of status withdrawal, but they are all instances of it.

Similarly it is status withdrawal when "an intimate friend" (item 2, Table 5.1) spreads uncomplimentary and unjustified stories about one. Similarly the dilatory repair man (item 3, Table 5.1) exhibits little regard for the customer when, after promising to complete work on the broken object by a certain date,

---

TABLE 5–1   INTENTIONAL AND UNINTENTIONAL FRUSTRATIONS[a]

A.   Intentional
1.   You're waiting on the right corner for a bus, and the driver intentionally passes you by.
2.   You have heard that an intimate friend spread rumors about you that were unjustified and somewhat uncomplimentary.
3.   You left an article of yours in a repair shop. You call for it at the appointed time, but the repair man informs you that he has only just begun to work on it.

B.   Unintentional
1.   You're waiting at the right corner for a bus. You notice that it is a special on the way to the garage.
2.   You have heard that an intimate friend, while drunk, spread rumors about you that were unjustified and somewhat uncomplimentary.
3.   You left an article in a repair shop. You call for it at the appointed time, but the repair man informs you that it isn't ready because of a death in his family.

---

[a]Items from Pastore (1952, p. 729). Copyright 1952 by the American Psychological Association. Reprinted by permission of publisher and author.

---

has not done so. It is an iron law of social life that when the customer is important enough (read: has high enough *status*) that the utmost will be done to render the service promised within the time specified. To fail to complete the promised work is to suggest that the repairman deemed that the customer did not deserve enough status to require him to exert himself.

Items 4, 5, and 6 (Table 5.1) recapitulate the three situations just discussed, but slight changes in emphasis create a quite different relational picture and thereby a different kind and degree of frustration—this is precisely Pastore's point. Obviously the bus on the way to the garage implies very little in the way of status withdrawal for the passed-by passenger. Were the prospective passenger to become angry—the hypothesized emotional response to status withdrawal—it would not be toward the bus driver, but toward the dispatcher or the "company" in the abstract which runs its buses on an inconvenient schedule. (Pastore did not, in fact, include this possibility of anger toward the company.) Also, the case of the talkative friend in his cups might lead to anger, because the victim of the rumor might judge that the friend should have had enough regard for the victim to protect him, either by not becoming drunk or by not paying any heed to the rumors in the first place. Nonetheless, the status withdrawal implied by rumor spreading when drunk is somewhat less than that implied by spreading rumors when sober. A whole body of literature in the area of Attribution Theory (Kelley, 1971; Jones and Nisbett, 1971) stands behind the view that the injury is felt to be much greater when it is seen as intended (cf. Baron, 1974; Greenwell and Dengerink, 1973). Finally, virtually no one except a person of megalomanic arrogance would feel that any personal injury, that is, status withdrawal, was intended by the repair man whose work was delayed by a death in the family. Clearly the differences between the first three items and the last three in Table 5.1 is precisely that *intended* status withdrawal is a plausible inference from the behavior of the frustrators of the first three situations, whereas it is not in the last three situations.

I suggest that perusal of the experimental literature in which anger and aggression is induced reveals that even without a systematic social relational theory, researchers have employed status withdrawal as the primary stimulus condition. It should also be clear that there are virtually infinite ways to withdraw status from another, but these are merely epiphenomenal, as argued in Chapter 2. To develop an adequate theory, the concrete cases of insult, pain, bother, annoyance, irritation, frustration, and the like set up by ingenious laboratory investigators for their subjects must be seen as specific instances of a general type of relational outcome, namely, status withdrawal.

It is instructive to examine other laboratory inductions for their relational structures. Freedman, Wallington, and Bless (1967) created this situation: A confederate of the experimenter reveals to the naive subject information about the experiment in which the subject is to participate. Shortly after, the experimenter appears and addresses the subject:

> This is a Remote Association Test developed by Professor Mednick at the University of Michigan. Since we are testing a slightly different hypothesis, we must make sure that you have not taken this test or heard about it from friends (p. 119).

The interesting result here is that "in all cases except one the subject said he had not heard about it . . . thus the . . . manipulation consists of eliciting a direct lie from the subjects. All subjects say they have not heard about the test, but those in the lie condition actually have just been given a complete description of it. They are lying . . . " (p. 119).

Without pausing to consider the objectives of this experimental manipulation, let us evaluate the subjects' behavior in power-status terms. The experimenter purposely (since this is precisely what is at stake) put herself in the power of the subject, and in all but one case—for reasons that are not given and do not concern us here—the subject used the power. In Chapter 2 (and Appendix 2) lies and deceptions are defined as power acts. Here is an experimental instance. Since power is punitive and hurtful when it is exercised, the experimenter would indeed be hurt by the subject's lie if the stated facts about the Remote Association Test were true. This is evident in the instructions to the subject just above. If the subject knows about the Remote Association Test, the experiment will be a waste of the experimenter's time, and, worse, the results will be wrong and perhaps damaging to the experimenter's career, and beyond that to the science of psychology itself. It is perhaps too much to think that the subjects who lied thought of all that. However, the strong moral injunction against the use of power by lying is designed to encompass all such possibilities. Thus the induction is another instance of power use, this time by the subjects of the experiment.

Let us now examine another experimental induction of power use in the study of Brock and Buss (1962).

> [T]he subject is told to play the role of an experimenter and to administer shock to another "subject" whenever the latter makes an incorrect response . . . There are ten shock buttons . . . the first button gives shock just about the touch threshold; 2 and 3 are painful; and 5 is an extremely noxious stimulus . . . In the high schock condition subjects were instructed to use only the shocks at levels 6-10, nothing below . . . [For realism] the victim gasped loudly every time the shock was 6 or higher" (pp. 197–198).

There should be no ambiguity about this straightforward relational condition between subject and "victim." It is, of course, a power relationship, mediated by noxious electric shocks, the intent of which, as far as the naive subject is concerned, is to evoke correct responses from the victim. Although it is only a laboratory situation, the use of noxious power to gain compliance (or "correct" responses) is so widespread as to be considered an ineluctable part of the human condition (Lorenz, 1966; Freud, 1918; 1951). Sensing this, Brock and Buss created a relationship in the power mode to elicit in their subjects a particular emotion and its behavioral consequences.

Some additional variants on the experimental induction of power relationships are also instructive. Berscheid and Walster (1967) arranged to induce high power use by the following complex field manipulation: Some women (seemingly by chance) were appointed as supervisors in a two-woman partnership that could win smaller or larger prizes (in the form of a number of "green-stamp" books) by correctly predicting how well the teammates would fare *individually* on a test of knowledge about their home region. The supervisor receives a communication ostensibly from her partner in which the latter claims to have very little knowledge and therefore requests that a low estimate be given by the team. This low estimate, the partner says, would be just enough to gain the prize she would like to have. The supervisor, however, is falsely induced to believe that a high estimate (or quota) is possible. "Which quota to set poses a problem for the subject. On the one hand she wanted to set a low quota as her partner has suggested. On the other hand she was anxious to win as many green stamp books as possible for herself" (p. 438). What were the results? "All but four of our subjects did disregard the confederate's suggestions and did set a fairly high quota . . . [later] it was evident that this strategy had been a mistake" (p. 438). In the words of Berscheid and Walster, "all subjects inflicted harm on another person" (p. 436). Indeed, to inflict harm on another where the intention is to gain a benefit for oneself while the other is thereby denied a benefit is to exercise power as defined in Chapter 2.

Another laboratory version of an exploitative power relationship is found in the work of Lerner and Matthews (1967). The subjects were informed that they would be working in pairs; one person was to learn certain words and the other was to punish the learner by electric shock for every mistake. Actually all subjects were assigned the task of training and shocking the ostensible partner. In one experimental condition,

> some subjects were presented with the alternatives of negative reinforcement, positive reinforcement and a control condition [in which the subject merely shocks the learner]. Again, all subjects were led to believe they would be in the desirable [reinforcement] condition. If, in addition to causing the other to suffer, the subject benefits herself at the expense of the other, then this might elicit a different reaction to the victim than when the subject merely avoids the suffering herself . . . (p. 320).

Again there is a victim, and even when there is the sanction of the psychological experiment, the one who delivers shock to a victim is in the position of exercising power. A fortiori this is true when the subject not only punishes the victim for her errors, but is the sole beneficiary of the victim's *correct* answers. Who can deny that this arrangement is unjust? Nor can the prevalence of such arrangements of power and exploitation in real life be denied.

In some experiments status accord is induced in the laboratory. Nemeth's (1970) subjects were paired in an apparent study of work performance and interview techniques. At the outset each subject and his partner (a confederate) were set to work proofreading two typewritten sheets of paper containing numerous errors. They were informed that if one person finished his task before the other,

> (Voluntary help and refusal condition): You may if you wish help the other person with his task. Of course you are under no obligation to do one thing or the other; or (Compulsory help): Please help the other person with his task. It is important that we have enough time to finish the experiment; or (Compulsory refusal): Please do not help the other person with his task. It is important that each of you work on your own task alone (p. 305).

The purpose of the experiment was to examine the differential effects of voluntary and compulsory helping and refusal to help. Obviously the voluntary help condition is status accord. Indeed, the term voluntary in the experimental instructions is exactly congruent with the definition of status as voluntary compliance with the needs, wishes, or interests of the other, as described in Chapter 2 and Appendix 2.

Another example of status accord is illustrated in the experiment by Lerner and Lichtman (1968). Subjects volunteered to participate in an experiment on learning in which one person ostensibly takes the part of the learner while the other takes the part of a trainer whose principal task is to administer a painful shock to the learner when the latter makes an error. The experimenters wished to manipulate the conditions under which each subject assumed her role. The subjects were presumably assigned the learner or trainer role by randomly choosing a number that allowed either the subject or the partner to select which role to play. In one condition, called the "gracious act," this induction occurred:

> The subject was told that the other subject's number had been selected, but that when asked which condition she wanted to be in, she had "hesitated and then said that her choice was for you to make the choice—that she would prefer to let you decide." The subject was then asked to make her choice [of whether to take on the role of trainer and give the shocks to the other, or to assume the role of learner and receive the shocks] (p. 229).

By allowing the subject to choose which role she preferred, despite the fact that the procedure permitted the partner to make the choice, a considerable status enhancement was conferred on the subject in that situation. Indeed, it was literally deference, and since it was also uncoerced, it could only be regarded as status gain by the subject and was so intended to be understood by the experimenters.

A condition of threateningly high power residing in the other has also been experimentally induced. In his famous affiliation experiment, Schachter (1959) had his subjects enter "a room to find facing them a gentleman of serious mien, horn-rimmed glasses, dressed in a white laboratory coat, stethescope dribbling out of his pocket, behind him an array of formidable electrical junk" (p. 12). The induction proceeds by having the white-coated gentleman introduce himself as "Dr. Gregor Zilstein of the Medical School's Department of Neurology and Psychiatry." He goes on to say:

> We would like to give each of you a series of electric shocks. Now I feel I must be completey honest with you and tell you exactly what you are in for. These shocks will hurt, they will be painful . . . (p. 13)

There is no indication whether "Dr. Zilstein" looked kindly and spoke softly, despite his obviously threatening remarks, but at one point in the description of the experimental procedure, Schachter wrote, "Zilstein paused ominously . . . " (p. 13). There can be no question that the relational situation was one in which the other had power and promised to use it. Although this is not very great power and the subjects are obviously free to leave the experiment without punishment, the induction conforms to the paradigm of power, namely, where one actor can hurt, punish, or coerce another. In no experiments of which I know is a structural power induced that leads to actual noxious consequences for the subjects. The ethics of research do not permit it.

Some experimental approaches have even dealt with the reduction of power. The Prisoner's Dilemma game is a particularly apt format for this, as for other relational conditions. Figure 5.2, reproduced from Wrightsman (1966), shows a

Figure 5–2   Prisoner's Dilemma game [a]

	A	B
X	$3, $3	$0, $6
Y	$6, $0	$1, $1

"Person one chooses between rows X and Y, person two between columns A and B. Person one's payoffs are the first numbers in the box. Person two's are the second numbers" (Wrightsman, 1966, p. 329).

[a]Reproduced from Figure 1, Wrightsman (1966). Copyright 1966 by the American Psychological Association. Reprinted by permission.

typical game matrix. The object is for one player to choose between the rows X and Y, while the other player chooses from the columns A and B. The first number in each cell is the value of the outcome for player 1; the second is the value of the outcome for player 2. If the players choose X and A, respectively, each wins $3. If they choose Y and B, respectively, each wins $1, and so on. If player 1 chooses first and he chooses row X, he has put himself in the power of player 2, because player 2 can decide to choose column B and win $6 in which case player 1 wins nothing. If player 1 chooses row X it must be because he feels that reducing his own power (equivalent in this case to enhancing the other's power) will lead in the long run to good outcomes for both. That is, if player 2 consistently selects column A when player 1 selects row X, they *both* maximize their winnings, that is, $3 each.

The Prisoner's Dilemma format permits not only the reduction of one's power, but also the possibility of *not* enhancing one's own power. This alternative emerges in the opportunities of player 2. If player 1 has chosen alternative X, player 2 can take advantage of him by choosing alternative B. By choosing alternative A, player 2 refrains from a power act.

A detailed analysis of typical experimental formats in which a variety of emotions were elicited shows that the experimental inductions comprise merely varying relational possibilities of the power-status model. This is a crucial point in the development of a sociological theory of emotions. Once it is accepted that experiments induce different emotions in their subjects mainly by manipulating power-status relations, the results of these studies can be taken as evidence in support of the theory. Although it is necessary at certain points to take a more speculative stance—for reasons already discussed—and to suggest emotions corresponding to particular relational outcomes without empirical evidence to support the contention, in the main I try to generate the emotions of the cells of Tables 6.1 to 6.6 in the next chapter by referring to the experimental literature. In this I try to follow (very humbly) Isaac Newton, who said, "*Hypotheses non fingo!*" which can be understood as "I do not speculate." What Newton meant was that he would theorize only on the basis of data. This inductive position was in contrast to speculative approaches to knowledge that deduced the "facts" from certain a priori, nonempirical assumptions. As much as possible I wish to avoid the error against which Newton warned. I have not entirely skirted the pitfall. Nor, apparently, did Newton in some of his work (Shamos, 1959, pp. 58–59). I turn now to the consequent emotions.

chapter 6

Consequent Emotions: II

Interaction produces relational outcomes, and the immediate motoric-autonomic-cognitive responses are the *consequent* emotions. The power-status model, in conjunction with the factors of agency and direction of emotion, generates a matrix of 1701 cells, as discussed in the previous chapter. By means of simplifying assumptions this was reduced to 168 cells. Despite this more than 90% reduction, it is not feasible to discuss completely even this relatively small number of outcome cells.

In this chapter I attempt to support the sociological theory of emotions by hypothesizing an emotion for each relational outcome-agency-direction cell, either on the basis of empirical findings or speculatively on theoretical or phenomenologically plausible grounds. Ultimately, each hypothesis must be tested experimentally. The relational structure and outcome of each cell must be simulated in the laboratory, and the ensuing emotions must be obtained from verbal reports or deduced from coping behavior or physiological and somatic evidence. Where it would be unethical to instigate particular emotions, we must rely on naturalistic observation. This constitutes no serious problem for testing the theory *if there is broad agreement on the power-status implications of the almost infinitely variable set of concrete situational possibilities*. It would be highly unfortunate if those who wish to build a theory of emotions were to bog down in behavioral epiphenomena while the social noumena slip away from us.

The importance of agreement about the power-status significance of concrete behavior cannot be emphasized too strongly, for without it researchers can easily despair over the possibility of a theory of emotion that starts with social stimulus conditions. Even those who favor such a point of departure have expressed doubts: "It is recognized . . . that eliciting conditions by themselves are insufficient for distinguishing between emotional syndromes, in part because people and animals are 'conditioned' and emotions may become attached to a variety of objects" (Lazarus and Averill, 1972, p. 254). This cautionary statement must be understood merely as suggesting that different individuals are conditioned to different concrete stimuli *which stand for the power-status relational conditions*. Clearly, the variable concrete stimuli do not in themselves instigate emotions; they do so only in so far as they signify particular power-status relations. This is in

99

some way self-evident, for if the concrete stimuli were capable of eliciting emotions, this would comprise one of their inherent properties and would therefore elicit the same response from all individuals. To the extent that concrete stimuli evoke different responses they do so because they represent different power and status relational conditions to different actors. Thus when a stimulus elicits emotion, it is the implied power-status configuration that does so, not the concrete stimulus per se.

I wish to avoid at the outset a certain tautological pitfall that seems to plague reinforcement approaches. In particular, I do not want it to appear that I am willing to define a stimulus simply in terms of its effects, that is, that a particular stimulus is "power" because it produces the effect that I theorize a power stimulus should have. Crosbie (1972) confronted the same problem with regard to the concept of reward:

> A "reward" might be conceptually defined as any good or service which Ego perceives to be of benefit to himself. Operationally, reward might be defined as any good or service which Ego indicates he would prefer to its absence. These meanings can be completely independent of the meaning of say, compliance, which might be conceptualized as conformity to Other's wishes, and operationally defined as the probability with which Ego accedes to Other's directives. And it would be a proper test of the assertion "if reward, then compliance" to show that whenever Other offers Ego a good or service (which Ego has indicated he would prefer to its absence) for compliance, the probability with which Ego accedes to Other's directives increases (pp. 208–209).

Mutatis mutandis, if we define power behavior as coercive, punitive, or expressing threat, and if a person identifies a particular stimulus as coercive, punitive, and threatening to him, we can test the hypothesis that power behavior instigates fear. The particular stimulus is immaterial in this example, for it must be "appraised" (Lazarus and Averill, 1972) as coercive before it produces the effect I have hypothesized. The theory must stand supported when, regardless of the concrete character of the stimulus, it is appraised as coercive and it instigates fear.

In this chapter I discuss hypotheses about consequent emotions that result mainly from power loss when own structural power is excessive and status loss when own status is adequate. A few additional cells of the 168-cell matrix are also considered. In all cases the choice of cell for discussion is dictated not by the demands of a complete presentation, but by the availability of evidence to support a credible hypothesis. Even where evidence is available, hypotheses are offered very tentatively. Rarely have researchers actually measured emotions, and more rarely still have they taken into account the structural conditions of the relationship within which the particular interaction outcome occurs. Tables 6.1

to 6.6 list all the hypotheses I have been able to generate by means of empirical evidence or by speculation for the 168-cell, reduced outcome-agency-direction matrix.

RELATIONAL CHANNEL: SELF-POWER

Relational Structure: Excess power for self. *Structural Emotion:* Guilt (introjected). *Interactional Outcome:* Power loss for self.

6.1.1* Agent: *self.* Direction: *self.* Relational Summary: *Liking for other.* †

Hypothesis: When self is the agent of own power loss in the context of liking for the other, the emotion(s) directed toward the self should have a strong positive tone compounded of feelings of *righteousness*, a reversion to *innocence*, and *relief* from the anguish of guilt and any fear of retaliation.

Evidence: There is no experimental evidence that specifically supports the whole cluster of emotions and affects hypothesized. We must tease out support for the hypothesis from studies that approximate some of the structural and relational-outcome conditions. In numerous experiments subjects who have wronged another and are presumed to feel guilt have subsequently engaged in a variety of compensatory and expiatory behaviors, from volunteering for extra work to submitting to electric shocks (Berscheid and Walster, 1967; Freedman, Wallington, and Bless, 1967; Wallace and Sedalla, 1967; Carlsmith and Gross, 1969).

However, Berkowitz (1962) and Walster, Berscheid, and Walster (1973) have proposed that not only guilt, but also fear of retaliation may be one of the primary distressful emotions when one has harmed another. Supporting this, Reimanis (1974) reported a low but positive correlation ($r = +.31$) between survey measures of guilt and anxiety, but the experimental evidence shows that persons who (probably) feel guilt engage in expiatory behavior even when there is no likelihood of actual punishment by the one they have harmed or a third party. Thus a holder of excess power can reduce it from motives of conscience (guilt) alone rather than motives of fear. Clinical evidence strongly supports the view that guilt reduction produces a positive emotional tone, based on a sense of relief and renewal (Sarnoff, 1962; Lewis, 1971).

Since self is the agent of restoring a more balanced distribution of power, the action is voluntary. On the basis of Attribution Theory (Kelley, 1971; Jones and Nisbett, 1971), this suggests that the action is more likely to be judged as an authentic expression of the true motives of the actor than if the behavior were

---

*Numbers preceding hypotheses are keyed to the numbers of cells in Tables 6.1 to 6.6. For example, 6.1.1 means cell 1 of Table 6.1; 6.3.6 means cell 6 of Table 6.3.

†Relational summary indicates the standing of the actors on the three relational channels that are omitted according to one of the simplifying assumptions of Chapter 5.

TABLE 6-1 EMOTIONS HYPOTHESIZED ACCORDING TO STRUCTURE OF RELATIONSHIP AND INTERACTION OUTCOME

Relational Channel: Own Power	Agent	Direction	Emotions When There Is	
			Liking for Other	Dislike for Other
Relational structure Excess of Own power / Interaction outcome Power loss	Self	Self	1. Righteous, innocent, relief from guilt/fear	2. Righteous, innocent, relief from guilt/fear
		Other	3. Liking for other	4. Liking for other
	Other	Self	5. Mixed: relief from guilt, resistance to reduction	6. Some relief from guilt, resistance to reduction
		Other	7. Irritation, suspicion, mild fear, shame	8. Anger, fear
	Third party	Self	9. Relief from guilt; resistance to reduction	10. Resistance to reduction
		Other	11. Mild irritation	12. Anger, fear
		Third party	13. Mixed: liking, some fear and anger	14. Anger, fear.

Relational structure		Interaction outcome	
		Insufficiency of own power	Power gain
Self	Self	15. Potent, self-respecting, confident	16. Potent, self-respecting, justified
	Other	17. Secure	18. Secure
Other	Self	19.	20. Relief from fear
	Other	21. Gratitude, liking	22. Mixed: gratitude, suspicion
Third party	Self	23.	24. Relief from fear
	Other	25. Secure	26. Secure
	Third party	27. Liking, gratitude	28. Liking, gratitude

TABLE 6-2 EMOTIONS HYPOTHESIZED ACCORDING TO STRUCTURE OF RELATIONSHIP AND INTERACTION OUTCOME

Relational Channel: Own Power	Agent	Direction	Emotions When There Is	
			Liking for Other	Dislike for Other
Relational structure Interaction outcome	Self	Self	1. Shame, chagrin	2. Impotent, shame, chagrin, self-pity
Power loss		Other	3. Mild dislike, fear	4. Fear
Own power adequate	Other	Self	5. Betrayed	6. Deep chagrin, impotent
		Other	7. Suspicion, anger, fear	8. Fear, anger
		Self	9. Impotent	10. Impotent
	Third party	Other	11. Fear, anger	12. Fear, anger
		Third party	13. Dislike, anger, fear	14. Dislike, anger, fear

Relational structure	Interaction outcome				
Own power adequate	Power gain				
		Self	Self	15. Guilt, shame	16. Satisfied, justified, vengeful
			Other	17. Secure	18. Secure, contemptuous
		Other	Self	19. Guilt, shame	20. Satisfied, astonished
			Other	21. Trust	22. Suspicion
		Third party	Self	23. Guilt, shame	24. Justified
			Other	25. Secure	26. Secure
			Third party	27. Liking	28. Liking, gratitude

TABLE 6-3   EMOTIONS HYPOTHESIZED ACCORDING TO STRUCTURE OF RELATIONSHIP AND INTERACTION OUTCOME

Relational Channel: Own Status	Agent	Direction	Emotions When There Is	
			Liking for Other	Dislike for Other
Relational structure	Self	Self	1. Worthy, self-respecting, virtuous	2. Embarrassed
Excess of own status		Other	3.	4.
Status loss	Other	Self	5. Resistance to reduction	6. Depressed
		Other	7. Mild anger	8. Anger
	Third party	Self	9. Resistance to reduction	10. Embarrassed
		Other	11.	12.
		Third party	13.	14. Dislike

Relational structure Insufficiency of own status		Interaction outcome Status gain	15. Competent, worthy, proud, happy	16. Competent
Self	Self		15. Competent, worthy, proud, happy	16. Competent
	Other		17. Liking	18.
Other	Self		19. Liked-loved, happy	20.
	Other		21. Liking, loving	22. Suspicion, obligated, irritated
Third party	Self		23.	24.
	Other		25.	26.
	Third party		27. Liking, gratitude	28. Liking, gratitude

TABLE 6-4 EMOTIONS HYPOTHESIZED ACCORDING TO STRUCTURE OF RELATIONSHIP AND INTERACTION OUTCOME

Relational Channel: Own Status

Relational structure	Agent	Direction	Emotions When There Is	
Own status adequate			Liking for Other	Dislike for Other
Interaction outcome Status loss	Self	Self	1. Incompetent, shame, depressed	2. Incompetent, mortified
		Other	3.	4.
	Other	Self	5. Mildly depressed	6.
		Other	7. Anger, astonishment	8. Anger, vengeful
	Third party	Self	9. Mildly depressed	10.
		Other	11. Anger	12. Anger
		Third party	13. Anger, dislike, jealous	14. Anger, dislike

Relational structure	Interaction outcome		Status gain	
Own status adequate				
Self		Self	15. Competent, worthy	16.
		Other	17. Liking	18.
Other		Self	19. Liked-loved, joy	20. Mildly happy
		Other	21. Liking-loving	22. Mixed: suspicion, liking
Third party		Self	23. Liked-loved, happy	24.
		Other	25. Liking-loving	26.
		Third party	27. Liking, gratitude	28.

TABLE 6–5 EMOTIONS HYPOTHESIZED ACCORDING TO STRUCTURE OF RELATIONSHIP AND INTERACTION OUTCOME

Relational structure Channel: Other's Status	Interaction outcome	Agent	Direction	Emotions When There Is	
				Liking for Other	Dislike for Other
Excess of other's status	Other's status loss	Self	Self	1. Mild guilt, shame	2.
			Other	3.	4.
		Other	Self	5. Mild *Schadenfreude*	6. Strong *Schadenfreude*
			Other	7.	8.
		Third party	Self	9. Mild *Schadenfreude*	10. Strong *Schadenfreude*
			Other	11.	12.
			Third party	13.	14.

Relational structure Insufficiency of other's status		Interaction outcome Other's status gain	
Self	Self	15. Righteous, just	16. Righteous, just, noble
	Other	17. Liking	18. Mild liking
Other	Self	19. Captivated, enthralled	20.
	Other	21. Liking-loving, admiring	22.
	Self	23.	24.
Third party	Other	25.	26. Dislike
	Third party	27.	28. Dislike, resentment

TABLE 6-6 EMOTIONS HYPOTHESIZED ACCORDING TO STRUCTURE OF RELATIONSHIP AND INTERACTION OUTCOME

Relational Channel: Other's Status	Agent	Direction	Emotions When There Is	
			Liking for Other	Dislike for Other
Relational structure — Interaction outcome — Status loss by other — Other's status adequate	Self	Self	1. Guilt, shame	2.
		Other	3.	4.
	Other	Self	5. Sadness	6. *Schadenfreude*
		Other	7. Sympathy, pity	8.
	Third party	Self	9. Sadness	10. *Schadenfreude*
		Other	11. Sympathy	12.
		Third party	13. Dislike	14. Liking

112

Relational structure		Interaction outcome	
		Other's status adequate	Other's status gain
Self	Self	15.	16. Shame, self-disgust
	Other	17.	18.
Other	Self	19.	20.
	Other	21. Admiration	22. Envy
Third party	Self	23.	24.
	Other	25.	26. Envy
	Third party	27.	28. Dislike

coerced by the other or a third party. With self as the willing agent of own power reduction, the other can more easily forgive the trespass (Walster, Berscheid, and Walster, 1973). Forgiveness by one's victim can also ease the distress of guilt as long as the forgiveness is not accompanied by overtones of moral superiority, which would comprise a form of retaliation.

The beneficial effects of power reduction as well as the initial propensity to redress the imbalance of power ought to be more probable when the other is liked. Bramel, Taub, and Blum (1968) have suggested that when persons like each other, each tends to give to the other what he thinks the other wants. When one reduces one's excess power, this gives to the other what he more than likely wants, and this should further induce positive feelings in the self. The feelings of innocence and righteousness stem from having done a morally right act, which restores the relationship to a point at which it can start fresh.

6.1.2 Agent: *self*. Direction: *self*. Relational Summary: *dislike for other*.

Hypothesis: As in the previous outcome cell in which other was liked, I hypothesize feelings of *righteousness, innocence,* and *relief* from guilt and fear of retaliation. These emotions should be more intense than where the other is liked, since somewhat more effort must go into the reduction of own power when other is disliked. This would produce a positive tone resulting from the "severity of initiation" effect (Aronson and Mills, 1959; Gerard and Mathewson, 1966). In that literature it was found that the greater the effort involved in the attainment of a goal—particularly involving affiliation with others—the greater the subsequent liking for the others. If one does something positive for a disliked other, the result should be more intense than if one does the same action in behalf of a liked other. The positive emotion may soon pass, and one may return to a consciousness of dislike for the other. This does not negate the positive emotion even if it is present only fleetingly.

Evidence: Although the basic argument for these hypothesized emotions is the same as that for the preceding cell in which the other is liked, some additional evidence is available to support the contentions in regard to the disliked other. In an experiment designed to investigate the conditions under which a person would give in to the threats of an "attractive" (liked) and an "unattractive" (disliked) other, Tedeschi, Schlenker, and Bonoma (1975) found that experimental subjects complied with the demands of the disliked other without regard for the "credibility" level of his threat. Threats were defined as credible only when they were backed up by actual punishment (power) from the other. In the case of liked-other, his demands were met only when his threat credibility was very high, that is, only when he actually used power after issuing a threat. Where the threatener was disliked, subjects apparently "perceived the threatener to be more potent [as well as less liked]" (p. 90). Tedeschi and his colleagues said, "perhaps [dislike] is associated with perceived malevolence, a motive that is clearly relevant to the probability that the [other] will punish [him] for noncompliance" (p. 97). By reducing excess power, one terminates the fear of a seemingly more certain retaliation by the disliked and more "malevolent" other. Thus compared with the previous case of the liked other, it is probable that fear is more strongly involved in inducing the power reduction. I assume that the relief of fear is as welcome to most persons as relief from guilt.

6.1.3. Agent: *self*. Direction: *other*. Relational Summary: *liking for other*.

Hypothesis: When self reduces own excess power, the feelings of righteousness, innocence, and relief directed toward the self are accompanied by increased *liking* directed toward the other. Since voluntarily reducing own power confers a benefit on the other, elevating his status in a sense as well as reducing the power discrepancy, this action stirs up the sentiment of the benefactor, as described by Aristotle (1947): "Benefactors are thought to love those they have benefited more than those who have been well treated love those that have treated them well" (p. 506). Reinforcement theory also provides a rationale for increased liking for the other. We like the other more because he is associated with a reduction in the unpleasant emotions of guilt and, possibly, fear, and we tend to like what is associated either with the increase of pleasure or the decrease of pain (Lott and Lott, 1974, p. 172).

Evidence: There is no precise experimental work that deals with the emotions we feel toward a person we like after we have benefited him by reducing our power. In an experiment that contains some of these elements, however, Hastorf and Regan (reported in Berscheid and Walster, 1969, p. 26) arranged for a lame student to ask other students (the experimental subjects) to pick up some pills for him at the student health service. The request was sometimes made in mild weather, sometimes in poor weather, thus varying the extent of the favor and the benefit conferred. The greater the favor, the more liking the benefactors felt for the lame student (although the result was not statistically significant). Although this experiment supports the general notion that to benefit another induces liking, it does not specifically refer to power reduction under conditions of guilt—although some guilt may have been stimulated by the lame student's handicap (this was not measured)—and there is no indication that there was any special liking for the lame student beforehand. There is evidence that handicapped persons do stir up a variety of feelings involving guilt and anxiety among those who are not handicapped (Wright, 1960; Comer and Piliavin, 1972). At times this leads to more sympathetic treatment of the disadvantaged (Kleck, 1969), sometimes to derogation and rejection (Lerner and Simmons, 1966; Lerner, and Matthews, 1967). In either case, the results of increased liking obtained by Hastorf and Regan suggest that relief from some possibly distressful emotions had been obtained by the greater exertions in the lame student's behalf. This alone would provide the basis for increased liking (Lott and Lott, 1974).

6.1.4. Agent: *self*. Direction: other. *Relational Summary: dislike for other.*

Hypothesis: When other is disliked, I hypothesize conflicting emotions directed toward the other. First, since the other is disliked, the overall relational configuration is unfavorable. In such a case power provides security. Yet excess power may stimulate the fear of retaliation, as discussed in the preceding sections. It becomes politic, therefore, to reduce one's power out of fear of the other's power. One can only dislike more another who, already disliked, is associated with a reduction of our power over him. Yet this increase of *dislike* competes with an increase of *liking*, for the other is also associated with reduced fear and guilt. Since self is the agent and guilt is a feature, I speculate that liking probably just outdistances dislike. Dissonance theory (Festinger, 1957) also supports the liking hypothesis. The uncomfortable state of discrepancy between disliking the other and doing him a good turn can be reduced by minimizing the value of the benefit conferred or by increasing one's liking for the other. Since power reduction is a considerable benefit conferred on others, especially if they are disliked to begin with, I conclude again that the resolution of dissonance is in the direction of liking the other somewhat more.

Evidence: Jecker and Landy (1969) found that when experimental subjects (who were treated in a rude and insulting manner by an experimenter) later did the experimenter a favor—they had a choice whether to do so and therefore were the agents of the favor—they liked him more than did the subjects who did not do him a good turn. Although power reduction was not the explicit purpose of the experimental manipulation in the Jecker and Landy study, power differentiation was provided by the induction. The experimenter indicated his dependence on the benevolence of the subject by this statement: "I wonder if you could do me a favor. The funds for this experiment have run out and I'm using my own money to finish the experiment. As a favor to me, would you mind returning the money you won [in the experiment]?" (p. 374). Since the admission of dependence on the other is an acknowledgment of the other's power (Thibaut and Kelley, 1959; Emerson, 1962; Blau, 1964), this manipulation does induce a power difference in the appropriate relational direction. By agreeing to return the money, the subject reduced the difference in power. It is even possible that the experimental subjects felt a small measure of guilt because of their momentary excess of power over the relatively high-prestige experimenter.

Hokanson and Burgess (1962a, 1962b) found that among experimental subjects who were also insulted by the experimenter as in the Jecker and Landy (1969) study, physiological indices of arousal returned to normal after aggressing against a low-prestige experimenter, but the indices did not return to normal when the experimenter had high prestige. Thus in a structurally disadvantageous relationship, where other ordinarily has higher power, aggression may not provide much relief from anger distress. However, reducing one's power over the other may provide enough relief to enable some liking to emerge.

Another study that provides evidence for the hypothesis is more directly concerned with the manipulation of power. Firestone (1969) arranged to have certain subjects insulted by their partner (the experimenter's confederate); they then had the opportunity to choose or to refuse to work with that partner in a subsequent experiment. After making their decision, those who chose to work with the insulting partner expressed more liking for him than did subjects who chose not to work with him but were assigned to him for the next experiment nonetheless. This result conforms to the standard pattern of such experiments (Zimbardo, 1969). In the subsequent manipulation, the insulting partner gave the subject a noxious stimulus (white noise in the ear); later the roles were reversed, and the subject had the opportunity to administer noxious stimuli (electric shocks) to his partner. Two results of this complicated experiment are of interest. Compared with the subjects who were assigned to the insulting partner in the second experiment even when they did not want to be, those who chose to work with their tormenter gave him fewer and shorter electric shocks in retaliation. In addition, at the very end of the experiment, they expressed greater liking for the insulting partner by indicating they would be willing to work with him in another experiment and that they would be willing to admit him to their circle of friends. (This last result only approached statistical significance, $p < .10$, but it was in the predicted direction.) These somewhat counterintuitive outcomes appear to depend almost exclusively on the factor of agency or "choice" (cf. Glass and Wood, 1969, p. 208). Agency operated in Firestone's experiment in a double sense: first, the subjects could *choose* to work with the offending partner. Second, all who worked with him had the further *choice* of how many shocks and of what duration to deliver. It is not known how many experimental subjects experienced guilt, as required by the structural conditions of this cell. To this extent the experiment does not conform to the paradigm of the present analysis. It does, however, satisfy the condition of excess power reduction. Having the opportunity to give shocks to one's partner does represent power. Choosing to administer fewer shocks of shorter duration indicates power reduction. The result was greater liking, as hypothesized here.

6.1.5. Agent: *other*. Direction: *self*. Relational Summary: *liking for other*.

Hypothesis: The reduction of own excess power when *other* is the agent is quite different from the reduction of own power when self is the agent. In the latter case, reducing one's excess power produces positive emotions toward self and other. When other is the agent, however, the reduction of own power is ordinarily neither voluntary nor contrite, but generally involves some compulsion by the other. Even when we like the other (he ordinarily gives us adequate status and uses little power), when he—rather than we—is the agent of rectification of the wrong we have done to him, a negative tinge must color the emotions we feel. In this situation there are two conditions that operate to make the consequent emotion negative: first is the fact that the other is agent, and this implies that the action is controlled by the other; second, the outcome implies a reduction in a benefit or capacity, that is, having a relatively high amount of power, even if unjustly. On the other hand, there are also two positive elements: first, we rid ourselves of the guilt and anxiety that accompany the excess power, and second, we like the other and therefore want to please him. Under the circumstances the emotional tone must be mixed.

I introduce here the general principle of *resistance to reduction*. Whenever we have a benefit or a means to obtain that benefit, even if there is a price that must be paid for it (guilt, in this case), there is some resistance to reducing the benefit or to giving up the means to obtain it. Since power is a means to obtain benefits, there ought to be resistance to its reduction. Although resistance to reduction is overcome when self is the agent, the resistance should stiffen when other is the agent.

Homans (1961) suggested that when the rule of distributive justice fails to a man's "advantage rather than to his disadvantage . . . he may feel guilty rather than angry" (p. 76). This structural emotion is, in fact, the context of the present analysis of consequent emotions. However, Homans went on: "But he is less apt to make a prominent display of his guilt than of his anger. Indeed a man in this happy situation is apt to find arguments convincing himself that the exchange is not really to his advantage after all" (p. 76). Although Homans dealt with one form of the excess power relation, namely, withholding benefits deserved by the other in an exchange transaction, the principle can be generalized: there is a steeper gradient for the negative emotion when we have too much of a benefit or advantage over another than when we have a deficiency of it. Thus it is harder to feel guilt than anger. This principle should also lead to the following: we ordinarily resist giving up a benefit, even if excessive and undeserved, since more good than troubled feelings come from having it.

Blau (1964, p. 147) dealt with the same question from a somewhat different perspective. He pointed out that persons develop expectations about the reliability of existing levels of benefits, and any attempt to reduce the benefits below the expected level meets with considerable resistance and dissatisfaction. Adaptation level theory (Helson, 1959) and level of aspiration theory and experiments (Lewin et al., 1944) also produced the same conclusion concerning resistance to a reduction of benefits. The tendency to resist a reduction of benefits has been framed in a number of approaches as the need to protect self-esteem (Snygg and Combs, 1949; Goffman, 1959; Freeman, 1973; Kaplan, 1975). Although excess power use may threaten self-esteem by rousing guilt, which usually lowers self-esteem, the extrojection of guilt, as discussed in Chapter 3, can maintain both the benefits gained as well as the high self-esteem.

Evidence: Glass (1964) studied persons of high and low self-esteem who, despite previously stated compunctions, agreed to shock someone in an experi-

ment. The subjects with high self-esteem reported less liking and more derogation of their victims than did the subjects with low self-esteem. The former had
more self-esteem to lose for having violated their own principles; thus they
resisted reduction by casting aspersions on their victims. In a variation of the
experiment, with a victim who was "liked," the subjects with high self-esteem, in
contrast to those with lower self-esteem, even went so far as to evaluate more
positively the use of shock as an experimental procedure (Glass and Wood,
1969). Since excess power usually confers a benefit or is used in the service of
obtaining or maintaining a benefit, it is easy to see that there is some reluctance
to giving up what the power gained.

Even when there is reason to think that the person is feeling guilt, resistance
to reduction appears. This can be seen in the fact that a variety of extraneous
conditions arise easily to prevent the compensation of the victims of excess power
use. Walster and Prestholdt (1966) found that if those who had done harm to
another were publicly committed to their positions (by having signed their names
to a harmful evaluation they gave of the other), they were less likely to compensate for their wrong doing when given an opportunity to do so. Berscheid and
Walster (1967) also found that if the amount of compensation available to restore
"equity" after having deprived another somewhat unfairly was either too little or
too great, there would be considerable resistance to repaying the other for the
wrong done. This result was also found by Lane and Messé (1972). Lawler
(1968) also found that when underqualified subjects for an experimental task
were overpaid, they attempted to compensate at first by being more productive,
but soon they were producing even less than the equitably paid subjects.

In the experiments just cited, the agent was always the self, since the subject
was always the judge of whether to reduce the inequity or the discrepancy. When
other is the agent, the resistance to reduction is strengthened. Michelini and
Messé (1974) found that there was less liking and preference for the other when
the other asked for an equitable distribution of benefits by means of a threat than
by means of a suggestion, even if the request was considered fair. Since threats
cost more to make than simple requests (Harsanyi, 1962), those who make them
are considered to be more purposeful and intentional in their behavior (Kelley,
1971) and thus would be seen as the agents of the induced change.

Although guilt is generally understood to involve uncomfortable feelings that
can be relieved by accepting punishment or compensating the victim, there are
circumstances in which the guilt is relieved and the discomfort dissipated by
discovering a ground for justifying the offense and "blaming the victim" (Ryan,
1971). This can operate as another tactic of resistance to reduction of benefits.
Berscheid and Walster (1969) remind us of Tacitus' assertion that "it is a principle of human nature to hate those whom you have injured" (p. 15). Dostoyevski
also offered the same proposition to explain why the elder Karamazov only truly

began to hate "Dirty Lizavieta" after he had injured her by making her pregnant. More recently, Ryan (1971) discussed the pattern of self and other judgment that prevails among the white, more affluent majority in the United States in regard to the nonwhite poor. The latter are condemned and blamed for their own condition. Jews, too, have been condemned for having been the victims of the Holocaust (Arendt, 1963).

Attempts to explain this phenomenon have centered on dissonance theory, which suggests that individuals try to maintain consistency between their behavior and their attitudes (Festinger, 1957). "Since most individuals think of themselves as kind and fair persons, if they are led to injure another person, they should experience dissonance. One way the harm-doer can reduce his dissonance is by convincing himself that the victim deserved to suffer" (Berscheid and Walster, 1969, pp. 15–16). Unfortunately, the dissonance approach would make it appear that the realignment of attitude with action is simply a cognitive phenomenon without an affective component. As suggested above, dissonance arises as an uncomfortable *feeling* that something is amiss. The discomfort may be the result, in part, of the logical inconsistency between self-concept and behavior, but that ought to be relatively minor compared with the discomfort that flows directly from one's judgment of the behavior itself; when one has hurt another, the feeling ought to be one of condemnation of self, that is, guilt. Since guilt is probably a more uncomfortable feeling than dissonance, because it threatens or invites punishment, which logical inconsistency virtually never does, the whole package of uncomfortable affect can be retired, so to speak, by finding a ground for justifying the hurt to the other by "blaming the victim." Although the theoretical result is identical with the outcome of an analysis by means of dissonance theory, the significant element here is the discomfort of a relationally induced emotion in addition to the discomfort of logical inconsistency.

In this connection, Lerner and his colleagues have shown that awareness of the suffering of another, even though one has not caused the suffering, frequently leads to derogation—a further punishment—of the one who has been hurt. Lerner and Simmons (1966) found that the more the victim was apparently being hurt, the more she was rejected by being found less attractive. Lerner and Matthews (1967) undertook to vary the amount of responsibility felt by the experimental subjects for the victim. They found that the more the subjects felt responsible for the fact that the other was subjected to pain—even though they themselves were not administering the hurt—the more they derogated the victim. When additional injury was added by having the experimental subject benefit by receiving money while the victim received only punishment, derogation was even greater. Lerner has argued that these untoward findings result from the fact that individuals want to believe in a "just world," and, to maintain such beliefs in the face of injustice, they must find some way to justify the victim's suffering. They do this by attributing undesirable characteristics to the victim, who then deserves the fate he gets because this is a "just world." Here, as in the case of other dissonance-based analyses, we can see how feelings of guilt also help explain the pattern of rationalization that heaps blame on the victim. However explained, there is considerable evidence that guilt does not necessarily lead to efforts to reduce the power that caused the guilt, but may produce even further use of power, particularly if there are benefits whose reduction is to be resisted.

On the other hand, the resistance to reduction principle ought to be mitigated somewhat when the other is liked, even if other is the agent. Thus power reduction ought to be easier when a friend initiates the reduction. Swingle and Gillis (1968) found that experimental subjects played more cooperatively with a friend in a prisoner's dilemma game than they did with persons they disliked. Brehm and Cohen (1962) discovered that "aggressors" in their experiment did not usually add insult to injury by also derogating their victim if he was a friend. In an experiment that tested for conditions of altruism, Goranson and Berkowitz (1966) found that a greater amount of help was given to those who had previously volunteered their help to the experimental subjects (and were therefore liked) than to others who had also helped previously, but had not done so voluntarily. Simmons and Lerner (1968) found that their experimental subjects were more willing to accept a role in which they themselves would receive shocks, instead of giving them to the other, when the other had "graciously" allowed the subject to have the first choice of which role she would like to play.

In sum, the evidence suggests a pattern of mixed emotions: *resistance to reduction* of the benefits of high power, perhaps offset by the *reduction in guilt* due to the reduction of excessive power; some *fear* due to loss of power, even though it was unwarranted power, balanced somewhat by the feeling that the other will not press the issue too far (he is liked); some *anger** due to reactance (Brehm, 1966) against the other's agency in instigating the power reduction. Only a direct experimental attack on the problem can help us understand the full range of emotions and the mix engendered by this particular structural-outcome situation.

6.1.6. Agent: *other*. Direction: *self*. Relational Summary: *dislike for other*.

Hypothesis: If there are grounds for resistance to the reduction of benefits when one likes the other, there should be even stronger grounds for resistance when the other is disliked. One may feel guilt because one has used excess power, but if the other has also used excess power and/or given too little status

---

*Fear and anger are emotions directed toward the other. They are considered in cells 6.1.7 and 6.1.8.

(thereby leading to the dislike in the first place), a reduction of one's power initiated by the other cannot help but produce some *fear*, moderated only by the benefit of the *relief* from guilt.

Evidence: In addition to the many studies cited in the preceding section, two experiments by Michener and his co-workers apply here. Michener and Schwertfeger (1972) asked respondents to indicate the level of power tactics they would use in conflict with someone they liked as opposed to someone they disliked. Stronger tactics were selected when the other was disliked. This implies that when the other is disliked, we are less likely to give up our own power, which often means augmenting the other's power. In a second experiment (Michener et al., 1975), participants engaged in bilateral conflict with opponents of both greater and lesser power. The experimental situation "portrayed the altercating sides as having a history of belligerent relations" (p. 66), which implies dislike. The findings very clearly indicate that those of high power offer fewer concessions to the other side than those of low power, and that they are more likely to use their power. Other investigators have also found that having power at one's disposal leads to its employment in conflict, and the more one has, the more one tends to use (Epstein and Taylor, 1967). The experimental studies cited do not portray the holder of relatively high power as feeling guilt; thus they are not precise analogues of the relational and emotional situation we are treating here. Nonetheless, the data of these experiments suggest that having more power than the other when the other is disliked leads not to power reduction, but to its expanded use. A fortiori this is the case when the other is disliked, and he tries to reduce our power. However, resistance to reduction is mitigated somewhat by a reduction in the structural emotion of guilt.

6.1.7. Agent: *other*. Direction: *other*. Relational Summary: *liking for other*.

Hypothesis: When the other aims to reduce our power, we are impelled to resist, as already discussed. But what do we feel toward him? Since the outcome is a reduction of our power, we must respond to his capacity to get us to do what we did not wish to do—or at least wished only mildly to do to rid ourselves of the discomfort of guilt. However, as soon as the other begins to compel us, guilt can easily be dissolved in *shame, anger,* and *fear*. Shame arises because we are exposed as someone who did not have the character to do what we should have done. The other is not only reducing our power; by inducing shame he also lowers our status. Anger is the emotion that follows from a decrease, withdrawal, or withholding of status when other is seen as the agent. (This is discussed later.) Fear emerges because the other is able to reduce our power, which, for many purposes, is the equivalent of increasing his own power. Since power is based on actual or potential coercion and hurt, we are afraid when we find ourselves in the power of the other. Although there is no necessary intimation that anything more than equilibration of the power relationship has occurred—that is, bringing it back to where it was prior to our own excessive structural power—the fact is that it has been moved some distance by the agency of the other. This is prima facie evidence that the other may be able to move it even further to gain a power advantage for himself. Mitigating both anger and fear, but not shame, is the past experience of the relationship, the result of which is that the other is liked. This signifies that he has not used power excessively in the past, nor has he lagged in according status. There ought then to be a considerable tempering of the anger and fear responses. Instead of intense anger, some irritation; instead of fear, uneasiness, which is only a prelude to fear.

Evidence: I defer discussion of the evidence for the evocation of anger until we reach the topic of *status loss*. Fear or anxiety has been evoked in a number of studies, although outright fear has not been investigated experimentally as often as anger. Fear may be a more dangerous emotion than anger in that its effects may last longer, and it is possibly more difficult to reduce once aroused. By informing experimental subjects that their tormenter was a confederate of the experimenter who did not truly intend to insult or abuse them, anger is apparently easily dissipated. It is not clear that the same is true after fear arousal. Anger also differs from fear in that it is praiseworthy in certain situations to show anger, for example, where one's honor is at stake. It is almost never praiseworthy to display fear. Research on animals, however, is not subject to these constraints, and much of what we know about fear is derived from such studies (see Gray, 1971, for a review of many studies.) In animal studies and in research on fear in humans (e.g., Ax, 1953; J. Schachter, 1957; S. Schachter, 1959) a common experimental paradigm is to subject the victim to imminent danger from a noxious stimulus—frequently in the form of electric shock. In relations with others, fear emerges when it appears that others can harm us by a noxious stimulus. To do so they must exercise power over us. Furthermore, they must not be deterred by considerations of our own counterpower.

In the interaction outcome we consider here, the other has actually reduced our power, which is equivalent for certain purposes to the elevation of his own power. This ought to arouse some concern over how that power will be employed henceforth. If the uneasiness does not develop into fullblown fear, this is due in part to the fact that we like the other and therefore *trust* him.

Trust is an affect that relates to both power and liking. "Trust is a decision to be dependent on other people" (Riker, 1974, p. 65), and dependence is a condition that puts us into the power of the other (Thibaut and Kelley, 1959; Emerson, 1962; Blau, 1964). Trust also involves risk (Riker, 1974, p. 65); thus withdrawal of trust, or suspicion, suggests that the other has acted in a manner to make the risk too great. According to Hamsher, Geller, and Rotter (1968), distrustful subjects disclose "feelings of being manipulated by others, being at the mercy of chance factors and 'powerful others,' and respond with a marked suspiciousness toward a variety of authorities" (p. 214). An experimental analogue of trust and suspicion can be found in the structure of the prisoner's dilemma game (see Figure 5.2). Those who are able to choose first and select row Y can be deemed lacking in trust or are suspicious of the other, for if they select row X they put themselves in the power of the other, who has the option to select column B, in which case he gains all while the first gains nothing (Wrightsman, 1966). Depending on the values in the cells, a misplaced trust can lead to great loss instead of merely no gain. This is the type of hypothetical situation for which the prisoner's dilemma was originally developed (Rapoport, 1960; Deutsch, 1960).

When we like another we tend to trust him more. The degree of self-disclosure is positively correlated with liking (Levinger and Snoek, 1972; Jourard, 1964), and self-disclosure is a matter of trust because it elevates the other's power over us by virtue of his having information he can use to attack our self-esteem. Because we have liked and trusted the other, the potential fear of the other's reduction of our power is much mitigated.

Another factor that enters into moderating anger and fear is that we do not read a power-oriented intent into the actions of the other. Several experiments have shown, in the case of anger, that the intent of the other instead of the actual hurt determined the magnitude of the emotion. In an experiment designed to test the effect of "perceived" as opposed to "actual" levels of attack, Greenwell and Dengerick (1973) found that experimental subjects responded primarily to the "symbolic" level of the attacks made on them, as expressed by the intent of the aggressor, rather than to the actual degree of noxiousness of the attack in the form of electric shocks. Baron (1974) and Baron and Ball (1970) also found that when subjects were given electric shocks by a confederate who could just as easily have administered a less noxious stimulus, the subjects became highly incensed against their attacker. These findings bear on our present discussion insofar as self views other's efforts to reduce our power as having the intent merely of rectifying a wrong rather than permanently changing the distribution of power in the relationship to our disadvantage. The past record of liking operates to modify the affects of agency and reduce the anger and fear that would be instigated under a different construction of intent. A final consideration is that, despite some mild distress, there is the major gain of relief from the reduction of guilt caused by our having hurt someone we like.

6.1.8. Agent: *other*. Direction: *other*. Relational Summary: *dislike for other*.

Hypothesis: When other is again the agent of reducing our excess structural power, but the relationship is one in which we dislike the other, the emotions directed toward him are *anger* and *fear*. The occurrence of these two emotions together may be what we mean by the term *hate*. The emotions are fullblown here because the structure and history of the relationship is one in which the other is known to use high power and give insufficient status, the relational conditions of fear and anger. The interactional outcome is merely more of the same, except that anger may be mitigated to some extent because the injury we receive from the other is a way of expiating our guilt. Nonetheless, with a disliked other we would hardly want to expiate the guilt by being paid back in kind. *Lex Talionis* indeed does not apply, except if it is to measure out a penalty deserved by the other.

Evidence: Berkowitz (1962) wrote that "fearful events signify noxious consequences, and as a result of these events the individual anticipates either physical or psychological damage to himself; [additionally] the . . . individual sees himself as having low 'power' relative to that of the [other]" (p. 43). The experimental laboratory has rarely induced high fear of this kind in naive subjects, because ethical standards prohibit it. Berkowitz cited the work of Janis (1951) on the fear reactions of survivors of World War II bombing and the terror of those who fled when they heard the famous Orson Welles "Invasion from Mars" radio program in 1938 (Cantril, 1940). Berkowitz also discussed the relationship between fear and anger, which is pertinent here. In his formulation, any frustrating event instigates anger, but as the noxiousness of the frustration increases, it also induces fear. The relationship between them is that fear reactions rise more rapidly than anger reactions.

For Berkowitz, low power is a constitutive element of the fear reaction, for when we have the power to deter, resist, or overcome the other, we need not be afraid. In the relational situation under consideration, the disliked other has brought about the reduction in our own power. This suggests that the other has power of his own, which is demonstrated to be capable of reducing our power. Where the other is disliked, we have not trusted him nor is there a basis for thinking that he will be "fair," just as we would not necessarily be fair with him. In general, when there is dislike, there is a weakened responsiveness to the positive moves of the other. Tedeschi, Schlenker, and Bonoma (1975) and Swingle and Gillis (1968) have shown the relative invariance of response to the actions of a disliked other as opposed to the actions of a liked other. The former appears to evoke fear and distrust regardless of what he does, whereas the latter receives a more differentiated reception, since his intentions are deemed less invariably harmful to us (Tedeschi, Schlenker, and Bonoma, 1975). If the other has expended greater effort in his capacity as agent in reducing our power—which is likely given the condition of dislike—we tend to attribute greater power to him, which is an additional factor in augumenting our fear (Kelley, 1971; Mogy and Pruitt, 1974).

6.1.9. Agent: *third party.* Direction: *self.* Relational Summary: *liking for other.*

Hypothesis: When third party is the agent of the reduction of our excess power, it should lead to the same emotions toward self as those which occur when other is the agent, namely, the discomfort of resistance to reduction, modified in part by relief due to reduction in guilt.

Evidence: There is no experimental evidence available for this hypothesis.

6.1.10. Agent: *third party.* Direction: *self.* Relational Summary: *dislike for other.*

Hypothesis: Third party reduction of our excess power should produce somewhat stiffer resistance to reduction when other is disliked.

Evidence: There is no experimental evidence in favor of this hypothesis.

6.1.11. Agent: *third party.* Direction: *other.* Relational Summary: *liking for other.*

Hypothesis: A third party has intervened to reduce our power, to the benefit of the other. Regardless of what we may feel or do about the third party, the situation strongly suggests a "scapegoating" response. The third party has caused some injury to self in which other is a highly appropriate target for displaced aggression. Two conditions, however, mitigate the intensity of the *anger* and aggression directed against other: the third party's action has reduced our guilt—to the extent that this is possible without having ourselves initiated the corrective action; second, the other is liked. Since other is blameless, the reaction against him, even if negative, should be relatively moderate.

Evidence: The basic notions of the displacement of aggression stem from Freud (1951), who believed that the instinctual pressure toward expression of aggressive impulses would find an outlet whether appropriate or inappropriate. These views were taken over and systematized by Dollard et al. (1939) in their famous frustration–aggression theory. Considerable experimental work has shown that when A causes B some injury, B often takes it out on C. This can happen even when B and C are friends. Miller and Bugelski (1948) found that individuals who were frustrated by a third party subsequently rated their friends less favorably than did control subjects who were not frustrated. In the case in which the other is neither liked nor disliked—for example, a stranger—the angered person vents his anger on the stranger, even though the latter had nothing to do with the instigation of the anger. Konecki and Doob (1972) found that experimental subjects administered about as many shocks to innocent strangers after they had been shocked by a third party as they did to the third party himself. However, liking for the other does make some difference in the degree to which third party frustrations affect one's behavior toward the liked other, as shown later when we consider the data in which displaced aggression occurs toward a disliked other (Berkowitz and Holmes, 1959, 1960).

6.1.12. Agent: *third party.* Direction: *other.* Relational Summary: *dislike for other.*

Hypothesis: When other is disliked, there is a very much more compelling basis for the release of negative affect toward that other, for example, *anger*, and resentment, even if the other is not directly responsible for the relational outcome that has stimulated the emotion of the moment. If other and third party as the agent are known or believed to be allies in a coalition against self, this may also lead to *fear*. When the other is disliked, the relationship has a very high potential for deterioration along power lines. In this relational case, other is not only disliked, he is also the beneficiary of generally resisted relational change: the power difference was reduced in his favor. There may be a certain cycling here: initial excess power, now reduced by a third party, leads to new excess power against other as a way of discharging resentment.

Evidence: Berkowitz (1962) has argued that among the conditions that should lead to displaced aggression are certain attributes of the "victim." If the victim is disliked, any barriers against aggression should be relatively weakened. An analysis of aggression against minority groups suggests that this is the case. Disliked groups seem more vulnerable to aggression after third party frustration than liked groups (Bettleheim and Janowitz, 1950; Allport, 1954). In an important series of laboratory studies, Berkowitz and his colleagues found that disliked persons are more likely to be aggressed against than liked persons. In the experiment by Berkowitz and Holmes (1959), subjects were assigned to a task in pairs. As part of the experiment, each subect was to be judged and shocked by his partner. In the "dislike" condition, the partner earlier gave the subject a relatively large number of shocks, which produced dislike for the partner. Later, the experimenter—in the role of third party—insulted the subjects. In the final phase of the experiment, the original partners were brought together again to work as a team on a task. The subjects then completed personality evaluation forms about their partners. These were compared with personality ratings of the partners garnered as "first impressions" at the start of the experiment. As predicted, greater change in the direction of hostility occurred toward the partner in the dislike condition than in the control condition of relative liking for the partner. The effect of the third party's insult was to increase aggression toward the disliked other. The greatest amount of hostility toward the disliked partner was expressed in the condition in which hostility toward the insulting experimenter (the third party) was also high.

In other experiments (Berkowitz and Homes, 1960; Berkowitz and Green, 1962) hostility toward the disliked other also correlated with the number of shocks given to that other under the condition of third party frustration (again insult, as in the preceding experiment). It was also found that the disliked other was subjected to greater displaced hostility than a neutral other when there was third party frustration. Although these important experiments do not exactly match the relational conditions we are considering—which includes guilt over excess power in the relationship with the other—nonetheless they provide evidence that liking and dislike bear strongly on the quality and intensity of the affect that is directed toward the other when there is frustration by a third party.

I now turn to a discussion of emotions involving own status.

RELATIONAL CHANNEL: OWN STATUS

Relational Structure: *adequate:* Structural Emotion: *happy:* Interactional Outcome: *status loss.*

6.4.7–6.4.8 Agent: *other.* Direction: *other.* Relational Summary: *liking or dislike for other.*

Hypothesis: When we believe the other is the agent of our status loss, whether by insult, intentional infliction of pain, ignoring us when we have a right to be attended to, or depriving us of goods, services, money, or approval that we have earned or deserve according to our own understanding—that is, whatever form the status currency may take, and whether we have been accustomed to having it or whether this is to be the first occasion—if the other intentionally deprives us of it, the immediate emotional outcome of the interaction is *anger.* This is to be distinguished from the longer-term deprivation of status that may also engender anger that is frequently rekindled, but more usually results in depression, as a form of hunger for the status denied. This is discussed as one of the structural emotions in Chapter 3. Here we are concerned only with the emotion that is directly consequent to a status loss when other is the agent. When there is a serenely confident anticipatory orientation toward receiving the accustomed or expected status, the loss also produces *astonishment* which should cause anger to blaze even higher (see Chapter 4).

Evidence: Anger is one of the best researched emotions. It is very easy to induce in the laboratory, and it has the virtue, unlike fear, of being easily dissipated by postexperimental debriefings. To be more accurate, anger *per se* has not stimulated theoretical or empirical interest as often as *aggression.* This is a behavioral response that frequently follows the emotional response of anger. Berkowitz (1962) linked the two by suggesting that a frustrating stimulus can produce an *"instigation* to aggression . . . termed *anger* (p. 47, emphasis in original). Although Berkowitz also proposed that aggression can occur without anger, simply as a learned response to certain cues (p. 35), I proceed heuristically on the basis that, when other is seen as the agent of status loss to the self, anger mediates any subsequent power behavior intended to hurt the other or to compensate oneself for the original loss. By accepting this inclusive approach, we can examine many studies in which not anger but some aggressive action contingent on a prior deprivation of status by another was measured.

Homans' (1961) proposition on distributive justice provides a convenient starting point. The proposition reads, "The more to a man's disadvantage the rule of distributive justice fails of realization, the more likely he is to display the emotional behavior we call anger" (p. 75). Since there is a zero-sum character to exchange transactions—what I lose you gain, and vice versa—we have a simple system in which agency is transparently clear. In the exchange dyad, other is the agent if he keeps more than his share according to the distributive justice rule. Indeed, the other may not see that he has violated the rule, but if self believes this to be the case, the relational-agency matrix for anger is satisfied. Anderson et al. (1969) proposed a slight variation on the distributive justice theme: when an actor similar in capability to ourselves is rewarded more than we are, we probably feel "hostile" (p. 7) toward the other. (I interpret this as anger.) When the other is dissimilar to us by virtue of lower ability but is rewarded more than we are, the resulting emotion is also "anger" (p. 8). The relational-agency condition that both Homans and Anderson et al. imply is that other has directly or indirectly deprived us of status we believe we deserve.

Pepitone (1971) set out explicitly to test the role of Homans' justice requirement in the distribution of rewards. By experimental manipulation, he managed "arbitrarily" to deprive some subjects of a reward they deserved. (The arbitrary action establishes other as the agent of the deprivation.) Pepitone then gave subjects an opportunity to select from various alternative patterns of distribution between self and other in a prisoner's dilemma game. The highest proportion of "self-maximizing choices" were made by the arbitrarily deprived group. Although the experimental details strongly suggest that these subjects felt angry, Pepitone fortunately provides us with some direct insight into the emotions of his subjects: "According to our informal observations there is an affective context surrounding each player's choices. The person who was denied the initial reward arbitrarily . . . maximized in an spirit of righteous indignation or anger" (p. 154). Similar responses to arbitrary deprivation were obtained by Pepitone et al. (1970) in comparable experiments done with Italian subjects. Stephenson and White (1968, 1970) also found that the "unjustly deprived" were most likely to cheat when given an opportunity to do so in an experiment in which they saw others of lesser merit rewarded.

In another tradition of research, in which the intention of the other is the primary focus of interest (Baron, 1974; Baron and Ball, 1970; Greenwell and Dengerink, 1973; Jones and DeCharms, 1957; Mogy and Pruitt, 1974), it has been found that, when the other is understood to *intend* the injury or can be assumed to act intentionally to injure one, there is greater anger. In several of these experiments, the actual injury consisted of the other (a confederate) administering electric shocks in relatively large numbers. In each case the other was understood to have administered *more* shocks than he need have. Status loss in these experiments consisted of the apparent low regard the confederate expressed for the subject by choosing to deliver shocks he could have withheld. In these cases the insult hurt more than the injury. In a similar study (Jones and De-Charms, 1957) the other inflicted status loss by not rewarding as much as it was understood he could have.

In yet another tradition of research (Berkowitz and Geen, 1966), anger was instigated by the other's administering many shocks as an excessively harsh judgment on the subject's task effort. The results are clear: "directly relevant to the arousal of emotion, after receiving the shocks each subject also rated his mood on a brief four-item questionnaire. The only item yielding a significant effect by analysis of variance was the measure of how 'angry' or 'placid' the subject felt; the men given seven shocks reported themselves as being reliably angrier than the men shocked only once" (p. 527).

In the famous experiments by Deutsch and Krauss (1960) involving control of a "trucking route" whose ultimate payoff is money*, when one party closed a gate to prevent the other player from reaching his goal and realizing a profit, the deprived player would respond with "hostility toward the threatener and . . . with counter-threat . . ." (p. 182). Not unrealistically, money loss has often been used in experiments to induce anger or aggression in the persons subjected to the loss (Hokanson and Burgess, 1962a; Buss, 1963). A vivid demonstration of the developing process of anger induction in a money-loss experiment was provided by Chadwick and Day (1972). Their experimental subjects were scheduled to solve matrix problems in groups of three under an appointed leader (actually a confederate). Correct solutions would gain the whole team a sum of money; if the solution were incorrect, no one on the team would win. The confederate was "programmed" to interfere with the group's obtaining a correct solution, and the anger level in the naive subjects rose in a definite series of stages:

1. *Suggestions.* These remarks are proposed solutions to the group's task. Examples from the tape include: "Let's try violet again." "I suggest we try F."

2. *Evaluations.* These remarks directly or inferentially place a positive or negative value on previous suggestions. They are offered in a fairly detached manner carrying neutral affect to encourage but not demand a choice among alternatives. Examples: "I think it is our best bet right now." "Green has the highest number in it, so I think we should choose it to maximize our chances."

3. *Pressure Attempts.* These remarks, in verbal content and/or emotional tone, clearly make an attempt to urge, push, or demand the other person to alter his behavior. In contrast to the detachment of evaluations, pres-

---

*Money is frequently, but not always, a form of status currency (cf. Parsons, 1954a).

sured remarks are imbued with moderate affect in voice tone, but do not imply a desire to punish the other. Examples: "This system has proved itself seven out of seven times." "Explain yourself. You can't give me a logical reason why you made that choice."

4. *Indirect Aggression.* These remarks imply a desire to punish the leader through sarcasm, ridicule, or cynicism, and involve higher degrees of negative affect, but do not explicitly punish the target. Examples: "Oh Christ, what happened, you agreed with me." "You're supposed to be a leader?"

5. *Direct Aggression.* These are remarks that overtly and directly attack and punish the target person. Examples: "You're an idiot!" "You're so stupid, it's unbelievable!" "You bastard!" (pp. 242–243).

Subsequent analysis showed that 89% of the statements by the naive subjects followed the hierarchical pattern of movement from suggestion to direct aggression; that is, statements indicating one level of anger were almost always preceded by remarks from the level just below it in intensity. In only 11% of the statements was a preceding level skipped over. Berkowitz (1962) also proposed that anger is cumulative and that irritations "summate with repeated thwartings" (p. 62). Furthermore, the larger the irritation, deprivation, or status loss, the greater the subsequent anger (Berkowitz, 1962; Holmes, 1972). This helps to explain, in part, why anger and aggression seem to be more intense in highly integrated and interdependent groups than in groups whose members are less dependent on each other (Berkowitz, 1962). The grimmest evidence of this is found in the statistics of homicide in which the highest percentage of homicides occur among persons intimately known to each other (Wolfgang, 1958).

There are both individual and social-categorical differences in what constitutes status loss. Buss (1963) has shown that different resource losses produce different amounts of aggression. In Buss's experiment self-esteem loss (via failure at a task), loss of grade points, and loss of money induced progressively higher amounts of anger and aggression in male student subjects, but not in females, for whom the three types of loss produce approximately the same level of anger. Apparently the cultural significance of these bases of benefit are more differentiated for males (in Buss's sample) than for females. Although in general males were more aggressive than females, they were less aggressive against females, whereas females made no distinction between males and females as targets of aggression, again revealing a more differentiated anger pattern for the males.

Geen (1968) provided some insight into the difference between status loss due to self-agency and other-agency. Experimental subjects were assigned to one of three conditions. In the first they were asked to solve an insoluble puzzle (any loss of status would be due to self as agent); in the second, the puzzle was soluble, but a confederate of the experimenter undertook to distract the subject (loss was due to self and other); in the third, the confederate simply insulted the subject (loss was due to other). Geen found a linear increase in the amount of anger felt by subjects in the three conditions. In addition, the anger instigated aggressive responses only in the insult condition.

A final consideration is the effect of liking or dislike of the other on anger. When other is liked, this ordinarily makes the other's action of status withdrawal unexpected. If, after the first shock or astonishment, the facts are ascertained to be as they are, the contrast between what was expected (status giving) and what was obtained (status loss) should intensify the magnitude of anger. Some support for this relationship between anticipatory and consequent emotions is given by Pastore (1952), who found an "increasing monotonic relationship between the strength of the [frustrated] expectancy and the strength of the reaction to frustration" (p. 346). Berkowitz and his colleagues (Berkowitz, 1960; Berkowitz and Holmes, 1960) also found that aggression (and anger) increased with the level of the expectation that was frustrated. Experiments by Aronson and Linder (1965) also support this view. They found that there was greater dislike for someone who was at first friendly but turned hostile than there was for someone who was consistently hostile. Indeed, the disliked other acts in ways that lead to dislike, but since this is no surprise, there is no special amplification of emotion caused by the sense of betrayal. I turn now to the final cells to be analyzed in this chapter. The reader is reminded that we are in the relational channel of *own status*.

Relational Structure: insufficient or adequate status. *Structural Emotion:* Depression (introjected) or happy. *Interactional outcome:* status gain for self.

6.3.21 and 6.4.21. Agent: *other.* Direction: *other.* Relational Summary: *liking for other.*

Hypothesis: When other is the agent of our status gain, whether we have had adequate or inadequate status, the net result must be an increase of *liking* and positive feeling toward the other if we like him or if his actions in enhancing our status can be attributed to the other's genuine good intentions.

Evidence: Goranson and Berkowitz (1966) found that subjects in an experiment were more willing to help a partner who had previously given help to them voluntarily than when the partner had been compelled to help. Schopler and Thompson (1968) and Lerner and Lichtman (1968) also found that altruistic actions to the other, which we must assume were based on positive feelings of gratitude, occurred when the other's initial act of status increment was judged as authentic. Otherwise, the reciprocal behavior tended to be equally power oriented and selfish. Tesser, Gatewood, and Driver (1968) specifically tested three components of gratitude in a paper-and-pencil inquiry: intentionality of the benefactor, cost to the benefactor, and value of the benefit to the recipient. These elements establish both the authenticity and the amount of status increment the other gives. High amounts of the three components elicited significantly more gratitude than either medium or low amounts.

A further determinant, however, includes some aspects of the previous relationship with the other. Kiesler (1966) found that when a partner shared winnings in a cooperative game situation, there was more liking for the other than when the other shared winnings after a competitive game (see also Solomon, 1960). Consistency with previous disposition also determined liking for the other in the experiment by Schopler and Thompson (1968). They found that, although the obligation to reciprocate for a favor was often honored, this was not accompanied by liking if the benefactor's behavior did not accord with an understanding that the benefactor had positive intentions. These results, which differentiate the effects of other's agency in providing us with status gain, are consistent with results that differentiate power responses to the other according to whether the other is liked or not (Swingle and Gillis, 1968; Michener and Schwertfeger, 1972; Tedeschi, Schlenker, and Bonoma, 1975). I now discuss one final emotion that pertains to six different cells of the matrix detailed in Tables 6.1 to 6.6.

Schadenfreude.   Whether we like it or not, it is possible to experience "joy at the misfortune of others" (as the dictionary defines the word *Schadenfreude*). This is especially true in the case of those we do not like or who have hurt us in the past. Berkowitz, Green, and MaCaulay (1962) found that angered subjects in an experiment reported feeling better when they heard that their previous tormenter (a confederate of the experimenters) had himself performed poorly on a task than when they heard he had performed well. Bramel, Taub, and Blum (1968) also found that there was a reduction in hostility, aggression, and unpleasant affect in subjects who learned that an experimenter who had previously insulted and antagonized them was himself suffering in another experiment. In contrast, subjects who heard that the insulting experimenter was experiencing euphoria in the other experiment did not indicate the same reduction of distress. Schadenfreude is hypothesized for six different interaction outcome cells: 6.5.5, 6.5.6, 6.5.9, 6.5.10. 6.6.6, and 6.6.10.

A Note on the Work of Jacobs, Skultin, and Brown.   There have been numerous attempts to discover the basic set of emotions, as discussed in Chapter 1. Jacobs (1971) reported an effort that is particularly interesting because it includes some conceptual dimensions akin to the ones used in this book. Jacobs' work, conducted with Skultin and with Brown, began with a test of Mowrer's (1960) theory connecting conditioning to emotions. This entails four emotions: anticipation of a conditioned aversive stimulus produces *fear*; anticipation of the omission of a conditioned aversive stimulus produces *relief*; anticipation of a stimulus conditioned to avoidance of danger produces *hope*; anticipation of the omission of such a stimulus (while the danger continues) produces *disappointment*. Some experimental results by Skultin and Jacobs (Jacobs, 1971, pp. 140–141) showed that Mowrer's formulation was too simple. Principally, Skultin and Jacobs concluded that "positive affective states were more closely associated with reward or incentive motivation conditions that with those of aversive reinforcement" (p. 141). This led to an elaborated scheme in which positive and negative reinforcement contingencies were linked to predicted emotions as follows: (1) danger signal on: *fear*; (2) danger signal off: *relief*; (3) safety signal on: *security*; (4) safety signal off: *apprehension*; (5) reward expectation: *elation*; (6) termination of reward expectation: *disappointment*; (7) signal that there will be no reward: *frustration*; (8) termination of the no-reward signal: *hope*.

Jacobs attempted to order his and Skultin's experimental results and hypotheses into a comprehensive model of "affective states generated by reinforcement contingencies" (p. 144). It included or closely approximated several of the conceptual dimensions of the theory of this book (although in other language): *power* ("aversive reinforcement") and *status* ("reward"), *agency* ("reinforcement from others" and "from self"), and *anticipatory emotions* ("uncertainty, anticipation"). All in all, the effort produced a number of results that are quite like those hypothesized here (e.g., Brown found that *depression* resulted from "justified attack"—that is, self is the agent of the status loss—but not from "unjustified attack"—that is, other is the agent of the status loss; *guilt* results from aversive reinforcement delivered by self; *hope* emerges from uncertain anticipation of positive reinforcement).

Ultimately Jacobs acknowledged that his synthesis leaves "many blank spaces" (p. 143). This is, of course, no disgrace in any effort at a comprehensive embrace of the domain of emotions at this time. Without detracting from the work of Jacobs and his colleagues, I believe that the relational approach of this book, although less general than "reinforcement contingencies," has the advantage of bringing the analytical focus much closer to the existing body of experimental and naturalistic data from which it is possible to infer the conditions that elicit emotions. I also believe that the relational model permits easier entry into a discussion of meaningful changes of reinforcement contingencies because it is closer to natural language. For example, "status loss" more nearly identifies the relational situation of "insult" than does "danger signal onset" or "no-reward expectation onset" (Jacobs, 1971, p. 142). The relational mode also allows for the relatively easy partitioning of emotions into *structural, anticipatory,* and *consequent,* since it invites the application of the temporal frame of reference to the relational situation. This gives a cleaner set of results than Jacobs was able to obtain. Finally, the relational approach also implies the presence of multiple or mixed emotions, which the reinforcement-contingency approach does not. In sum, the relational mode affords a more adequate vehicle for detailing the complex reality of emotional outcomes, despite the apparently more comprehensive formal language of reinforcement theory.

ADDITIONAL MODES AND PARAMETERS

The foregoing discussion of emotions appropriate to some of the relational-interaction outcome cells indicates how the theory of emotions can be slowly built up on the basis of experimental or naturalistic evidence. There is no alternative, I believe, to the systematic accretion of evidence. In time it should be possible to provide well-supported generalizations for all the cells.

In the remainder of this chapter I introduce some additonal considerations to flesh out the theory at certain bare spots in the framework. These are intended as amplifications rather than new modes of analysis.

Simultaneous Output in Four Channels.   In the analysis of particular outcome cells or particular emotions pertaining to a given cell, I must limit the perspective to a given structural-relational outcome, but it bears repeating that a veristic description of what emotions *a given individual* is experiencing must take into account all four channels of relationship: own and other's power and own and other's status. Every interaction episode produces a relational outcome in each of these channels relative to the previous structure and the preceding anticipations. When the respective agencies and directions of emotion are also considered, the whole result can be quite complex. Sometimes it is indeed difficult to know what we feel, since the feelings are mixed by virtue of the mixed nature of the structural-relational outcome pattern.

Several students of emotions have noted the possibility of mixed emotions. Plutchik (1962) pointed out that the study of emotions is plagued by this difficulty, although he did not see the specific relational basis for the mixing. Izard (1972) clearly implied the relational problems faced by experimenters who attempt to deal with isolated emotions:

> One emotion can almost instantaneously elicit another emotion that amplifies, attenuates, inhibits, or interacts with the original emotional experience. When a person begins cogitating the situation that has evoked the original emotion and while he waits in anticipation [in an experiment] for some noxious stimulus, other emotions are almost certain to be elicited. For example, as a subject contemplates the possibility that the experimenter is playing games with him by manipulating the painful event that may or may not happen to him, he may get angry instead of afraid even though the coming event is presumably threatening and fear producing (p. 77).

I am not as certain as Izard about the manner in which emotions interact with each other, but it should be clear that there is often more going on relationally in the experimental situation than experimenters are aware of. Before we accept that one emotion drives out another—although this is entirely possible—we should look at all four channels of the interaction situation. Some coexistence of emotions is doubtless possible, although some theories suggest a "reciprocal inhibition" between certain emotions (Wolpe, 1973).

Izard (1972) also proposed that emotions occur in "patterns" as a result of "constantly changing elements of the perceptual-cognitive field" (p. 103). For example, anxiety is viewed as a *compound* of various other emotions: fear, guilt, shyness, disgust, surprise, contempt, distress, anger, and fatigue. These aggregated in Izard's data somewhat differently as various anxiety "situations" (e.g. fear, distress, guilt, shyness, and anger situations) were described. Although this recognition of the complex nature of emotion is highly valuable, it would appear useful to examine these compounds carefully in terms of the four-channel *relational* conditions that constitute the situation that instigates the various components Izard pieced together into the single "second order" (p. 109) emotion of anxiety.

Arnold (1960) provided another partial recognition of the multiple channels of relationship that produce the emotional configuration an individual experiences at a given time. In her view "simple emotions" are "aroused when an object or situation is appraised under a single aspect . . . [but] a complex emotion is a compound of many emotions, all directed toward the same object, but aroused by various and often conflicting aspects of the object . . . like jealousy [which] includes love, a fear of loss, anger at the beloved [and the third party] . . . and many other emotions, all of which depend on the various aspects of the situation that are emphasized and evaluated" (pp. 197–198). Whether the resulting emotion is in fact a compound of the several emotions instigated by the relational configuration or whether the emotions produced remain discrete and co-present is a question that must be investigated.

Status Claims.   Although the structural-relational outcome model accounts for a large number of emotions, there are yet some which stand outside anything presented thus far. This necessitates a further understanding of the fundamental behavioral dimensions. At the outset (Chapter 2) I suggested that behavior between actors could be understood as either task or relational. As part of the relational content I included behavior we may call *status claiming*. Goffman's (1959) work on the "presentation of self" dealt with the techniques of staking a claim for status, that is, a certain level of deference and respect from the other. Just how the claim is made is of some interest. First, it is carried forward by means of a "line," which Goffman (1967) defined as "a pattern of verbal and non-verbal acts by which (the actor) expresses his view of the situation and through this his evaluation of the participants, *especially himself*" (p. 5, emphasis added). In some of his earliest work Goffman (1959) discussed techniques by which lines are maintained. Principal among them is "front," which translates into "the insignia of office or rank; clothing; sex, age, and racial characteristics; size and looks; posture; speech patterns; facial expressions; bodily gestures; and the like" (pp. 14–15). These aspects of appearance, manner, and style are the means by which the status claim is made. Some of these are ascribed characteristics about which we can do very little—"passing" is an exception (Goffman, 1963)—whereas some are achieved and are susceptible to improvement, embellishment, or suppression—from which the tailor, hairdresser, cosmetician, voice coach, charm school, and plastic surgeon earn their livelihoods. The method of claiming status may be trivial (dress, for example), or invidious (wearing one's Phi Beta Kappa key), yet they are equally aspects of what can be called *relational technology*, which comprises the battery of techniques by which status and power are claimed and acquired.

Power and status differ somewhat in regard to relational technology. Status accord and the techniques of claiming status are largely nonoverlapping, except when status is claimed by virtue of displaying that one knows how to accord it, as in etiquette and acts of consideration for others. Power, however, is virtually always acquired by displaying it—at least at first. The threat, the kick, the sharp word, the critical gaze—these acts of coercion are the relational technology of power. They demonstrate to the other that his will can be overcome (Weber, 1946, p. 180) and that resistance will be either painful or futile. Since relational technology designed to claim status usually differs from actually giving status, it does not fit into the structural-relational outcome matrix discussed above or shown in Tables 6.1 to 6.6. Nonetheless, it may produce emotions.

An other makes a status claim on the basis of his "front," and we either give it credence and accord the status, or we do not. Goffman suggested that except where the claim is unusual—given the setting and the customary norms and rules that govern status claiming—there is a tendency to take the other at his face value. "This means that the line taken by each participant is usually allowed to prevail, and each participant is allowed to carry off the role he appears to have chosen for himself" (Goffman, 1967, p. 11). However, what if the other claims too much status? Here, I believe, is the origin of the emotion of *contempt*. This emotion is elicited when the other claims to be worthy of status equal or superior to our own, but lacks the credentials or "front" to support the claim. The parvenu experiences the contempt of his status superiors in stratification systems because he does not meet the requirements for status as they prevail in that social group—old money, "blood," education, and the like. These are frequently the barriers of front that cannot be penetrated by cash alone (Weber, 1946, p.

186ff.). In this sense, any political formula that creates equality also removes contempt as an emotion with social structural implications. Contempt, of course, is a private emotion that still thrives, but probably less so than in the past. This dying out of contempt is due in part to the homogenization of culture and style; thus larger and larger numbers of individuals are tuned to the same standards for the making of status claims. It is also due to a loosening of standards for the making of claims—dress norms in the United States for example, became much more flexible in the decade 1960–1970. This makes it harder to commit a gaucherie which is a signal to others that the status claim is hollow and thus worthy of contempt.

On the positive side, when the claim the other makes is accepted at its face value, the emotion varies greatly, depending on how much status has been claimed *relative* to the status of the one who has accepted the claim. If the accepted claim is relatively very great, it produces *awe* and *reverence*; if it is on a par with one's own status, the emotion of mild *liking* is produced; if it is very much beneath one's own status level, *pity* or *compassion* are produced, especially if the claimant once deserved better. In general, when the interaction conveys not simply status content, but a claim for status, special emotions are evoked at the moment at which the claim is most sharply in focus.

Depersonalization and Transcendence.   The sociological view of emotions proposed here does not especially look beyond human encounters, but the other may transcend the human. This can have its positive and negative sides. On the positive side are the emotions of awe, wonder, adoration, and worship that are familiar in the language of prayer and in addresses to the Diety. These are all aspects of status conferral, entailing emotions that emerge when intensified by the larger-than-life character of the other. Durkheim (1915) suggested that the sacred is precisely that which is set apart from the ordinary, and in this sense is larger than life. In certain nonsocial situations—for example, benign panoramic vistas that are unusual to behold, such as the vastness of the Grand Canyon, or the imposing peaks of the Alps—*awe* and *wonder* are also instigated. Again, it is the larger-than-life character of the setting that elicits these feelings.

When the other is clearly mortal, but participates in whatever small way in the social life that transcends our own—and this is true of anyone with an institutionalized status higher than our's—the same emotions of awe and wonder are elicited. This, I believe, is the emotional core of the experience of the *charisma* of the other (Weber, 1947, pp. 358–363). The other need not be of great, historical significance, as long as he has a status that transcends our own. When the other has extremely high status relative to our own, the charismatic emotions are magnified. However, if we also have extremely high status the effect is greatly diminished.

By conceiving of social life in this way, we can understand how world leaders are able to deal with each other. Since they are accustomed to great status and/or great power, the power or status claims of others do not appear to be so demanding or impressive. Indeed, for this very reason, the others do not cast images larger than life as each of the leaders knows it. Thus they are not in awe of each other, and interaction can proceed on a basis of relative equality.

When others appear larger than life they are to some extent depersonalized. They are not attributed ordinary needs and wants, and it is perhaps this which exaggerates the shock when a public figure does so ordinary a thing as die. Depersonalization, however, can work in the opposite direction. Sykes and Matza (1957), in their discussion of "techniques of neutralization," included "denial of the victim" as a means by which one can justify aggressive behavior toward the other. The other's status is effectively lowered and his pretensions for fair, equitable treatment so far reduced that he can be treated with contempt, as previously described. In this case, too, the other has been depersonalized, and the emotion elicited is appropriate to the status claim of one who is *smaller* rather than larger than life. A similar pattern of reducing the other is found in the many studies that show that in certain situations the victim is derogated (Lerner and Matthews, 1967; Lerner and Lichtman, 1968; Ryan, 1971).

Vicarious Interactions and Emotions.   Although the theory proposed here can account for emotions that occur during the course of social interaction, it seems less able to account for emotions that occur when one is merely an observer or a recipient of information about the outcomes for others in social interaction. When we read of a particularly gruesome murder, multifatality accident, daring escape from danger, and the like, we experience some emotion. Also, when our child, parent, spouse, or friend experiences particularly good or bad outcomes in social interaction we feel an emotion even though we are not directly involved in the interaction. Finally, when we are audience to a play, film, or novel in which fictitious characters display their interactions and relationships, we also feel emotions, although we are merely onlookers. Obviously, some additional concept is needed to link the sociological theory of emotions to the reality and intensity of vicarious emotions.

Identification is the concept nearest at hand for this purpose. We feel sympathetic emotional resonance with others because when we identify with them we are open to "vicarious affective experience" (Kagan, 1958) through them. Similarity seems to promote identification. Role taking and empathy are easier with those who are similar to us than those who are different. For one thing, we already have knowledge of the role and some positive motivation to take it. Thus wherever there are grounds for a common identity, we are to that extent better able to share imaginatively the other's experience, even though we have not had it ourselves. Sometimes the thread of unity is minimal—simply common humanity in a predicament that has been or may someday be our own. Sickness and accident are two events that unite all persons by their common occurrence.

At a more focused level of similarity, the serious young person who searches for the "meaning of life" and the proper direction and accent for experience finds in Holden Caulfield (*Catcher in the Rye*, Salinger, 1951), Yossarian (*Catch-22*, Heller, 1961), and in the hero of *Siddhartha* (Hesse, 1951) exemplars of similar yearnings, aspirations, and, more important, solutions. Thus one need not be a New York teenager, a World War II bomber pilot, or a Hindu prince to read their lives as if they were one's own, for, indeed, in the relevant aspects, they are our own.

When identification takes place, it allows us to participate imaginatively in the relational structures and interaction episodes of others. In this way, the other's status loss is our loss and the other's status gain is our gain, although only in imagination. Thus vicarious emotions are stirred by the same interaction conditions that stir any of the emotions that have a social origin. (Some additional distinctions concerning identification are discussed in Chapter 8).

The Effect of Initial Values.   Initial values refers to the absolute levels of power-status of the parties to the relationship at the outset of the analysis. Relationships in which one or both actors are located in extreme corners of the space (except where both are positioned in the low power-low status corner, at lower left in Figure 2.1, p. 32) should produce emotions of higher intensity than relationships positioned elsewhere in the space. This follows from the understanding of the power-status dimensions that when power is high, feelings of fear and/or dependency on the other also run high; when very high status is accorded, this can stir very intense emotions of gratitude; when very high status is withdrawn, this must be seen and felt as a great loss. In a number of studies, formal differences of status (and power) have been investigated for their effect on anger and aggression. Hokanson and his colleagues found that the status of the instigator of anger significantly affects certain autonomic indices of anger—particular heart rate changes and systolic blood pressure. In a specimen study of this kind, Hokanson and Burgess (1962a) arranged to have experimental subjects either insulted and badgered or (in another version) arbitrarily denied $4 they had earned for a laboratory task. The instigators were either "high status"—a faculty member—or "low status"—a student assisting the experimenter. In general, the high status instigator produced greater effects on heart rate and systolic blood pressure than the low status instigator. Even when the subjects had an opportunity to retaliate against the instigator by means of a questionnaire in which they could rate his "competence as an experimenter" and his "ability to relate to people," the subjects displayed greater return to a normal cardiovascular rate if the instigator was of low rather than high status. Thus anger and its aftermath depend not only on the fact that one actor has withdrawn status from another, but also on the initial locations of the two actors in the power-status space.

In a similar experiment designed to investigate the effects of the status of the other on autonomic and other response shifts, Reiser, Reeves, and Armington (1955) conducted half their experiment with their soldier-subjects under the direction of a *"captain-*psychiatrist," the other half under a *"private-*physiologist." After a series of experimental manipulations, they reported "the main emotional change during the experimental interviews in experiment one [captain-psychiatrist group] was relief of uneasiness and tensions, whereas the main emotional shifting distinguishing the experimental subjects in experiment two [private-physiologist group] appeared to be the discharge or release of angry, resentful feeling" (p. 198).

Other studies (Cohen, 1955; Graham et al., 1951; Thibaut and Reicken, 1955) also have shown that when the one who deprives the other of status has either higher power or status (depending on the relationship induced experimentally), the "victims" showed less aggression and expressed less anger toward him than toward deprivers of lesser status and power. In yet another tradition of research, the positive emotion of liking, expressed as a sociometric choice of the other, is found almost universally to move in an upward direction toward those of higher status (Jennings, 1950; Riley et al., 1954). Thus it is clear that the initial standing of each of the parties to the interaction in the various experiments cited weighs heavily on the emotional and coping responses that ensue from the interactional outcome.

Desire.   Human interdependence is the first postulate on which this work is based (see Chapter 2). It means that actors require certain actions from others. Some of these are necessary for survival, others merely for comfort, ease, or adornment, and others because they realize an ideal state of affairs. However, the actions of others are not merely required mechanically or dispassionately, they also acquire emotional tone by our *desire* for those actions. If we treat the actions of others as benefits to us, desire is the *anticipatory-consummatory* emotion that accompanies our need and interest in the benefits. Desire may range from a mild attitude of preference to an overmastering craving. In general, social benefits stemming from the relational actions of others, such as approval, power, income, love, and the like, are desired in proportion to their perceived likelihood of satisfying us. However, social standards of appropriateness and moral obligation also impose sanctionable limits on desire. Thus each of the classical seven deadly sins may be understood as excessive (and in one case, insufficient) desire for a benefit: *pride* is the excessive regard for self, which does not countenance status reduction through admission of error or acceptance of a lesser role; *covet-*

ousness is the greedy desire for what belongs to another; *lust* is sexually oriented desire which trangresses rule, or right, or propriety; *gluttony* is excessive desire for food, an elemental benefit; *envy* is excessive desire for benefits that would bring one to par with others; *anger* is the excessive sense of deprivation and loss when benefits we have previously received or now believe we have a right to receive are denied to us; and *sloth*, although defined as "apathy and inactivity in the practice of virtue" (Gove, 1958, p. 2368), can also be understood as the defect of insufficient attention or interest in obtaining the benefits that are available through effort, particularly the good opinion of others through valued contributions to the community.

Desire, whether within or out of social bounds, can be seen too as the emotional concomitant of virtually all status-claiming behavior and of a significant portion of power behavior (defensive power behaviors are excluded). In making the status claim, which constitutes a form of self-recommendation, the actor desires some benefit, depending on the status currency in the setting: social approval and deference, money, sexual access, and so on. Desire energizes the claim. When status claims fail, power is often employed to get what was desired but denied: thus we have deception and dishonest self-presentation to obtain the esteem of others, robbery or embezzlement to obtain money, and rape to obtain sexual access. Desire, which stands generically for all the emotions relating to the preference or need for benefits, is related theoretically to the concept of drive that appears in both psychoanalytic (Freud, 1966) and learning theories (Hull, 1943). In drive-oriented theories, behavior is undertaken to reduce the discomforts that unsatisfied drives (desires) engender. Desire is thus the emotional surface of the concept of drive.

Theoretical Principle of Emotions

Only direct empirical tests can ascertain whether the sociological theory of emotions is adequate as a predictor. Thus far I have formulated the theory inductively, relying heavily on experimental results or outcomes in natural settings for the hypotheses presented. Yet it would be useful if the theory could stand on more general theoretical ground, in addition to the empirical support adduced for it. In this sense I am looking for a principle that can perform the same function as *gravity* in classical mechanics. Nothing so neat will be offered here. I rely on some well-known ideas, namely, evolutionary functionalism (Darwin, 1873; Plutchick, 1962; Lazarus and Averill, 1972; Hamburg, Hamburg, and Barchas, 1975), and on the originating postulate of this work, namely, human interdependence. The most pressing need for theoretical principles, as opposed to empirical generalizations, is to enable us to explain why different social relations produce different emotions: some produce fear, others anger, and others love.

The evolutionary motive of *survival* suggests two emotions that are immediately functional: *fear* and *anger*. Fear serves to drive the organism away from the presence of a noxious stimulus. Fear mobilizes both the physical and psychic energy and effort to flee danger. In small amounts, fear induces caution, which also helps survival. In larger amounts fear conduces to flight. In extremely high amounts, fear leads to freezing. For some species and in some circumstances this is adaptive, but generally it is maladaptive. The relational situation in any of these cases is clear, namely, inadequacy of own power to deter or protect oneself against the power of the other.

Although anger can also be instigated by the noxious power of the other (Berkowitz, 1962, p. 43), it results mainly from the deprivation of benefits rather than noxious threat. Whether the deprivation is of food, territory, sexual objects, or the like, it can be just as detrimental to survival as a noxious threat if it is passively accepted. Ethological work supports the view that the dominance hierarchy among animals operates to provide some animals with more and some animals with less access to the values and necessary benefits for survival—food, territory, and sexual objects (Eibl-Eibesfeldt, 1972). Dominated animals are less likely to survive. The dominance hierarchy represents the structural fixing of the unequal distribution of benefits. In the process of creating it, some animals had necessarily to take away benefits from others. Anger-aggression reactions generally ensue. These emotions are engaged when survival is threatened by a deprivation of the benefits that make for survival. Once the dominance hierarchy is settled, the status levels are set; each party more or less adapts to them, and relatively little anger is manifested. At first, however, deprivation threatens the possibility of total loss of status and evokes anger. Later, depression and apathy resulting from the loss and, in many cases, fear of punishment, inhibit a further display of anger and conflict. It is clear that anger has some survival value for the organism just as fear does. It is also clear that it is the relational conditions between organisms that stimulate anger, just as they stimulate fear.

It is conceivable that a social structure can operate entirely on the basis of power. Whoever is stronger acquires the benefits he wants, and others simply give ground as they must. Animal groupings often appear to be founded on the power principle (for exceptions, see Runciman, 1968, p. 36, quoted earlier p. 30). This would guarantee survival for the strongest or most cunning individuals of a group, but in succeeding generations, because of the survival of the strongest only, conflicts would become so savage in intensity that both winners and losers might sink dead from mutual wounds or exhaustion. Thus the power principle, if applied without moderation, would not guarantee survival for either individuals or groups. In this way, a truly Hobbesian world of out-and-out conflict would eventually disappear. Here may be a significant difference between animal and human groups. In the animal group, an individual once beaten is ordinarily out of contention for dominance, nor does *revenge* seem an applicable concept to nonhuman species. However, among humans, even the weakest can topple the strongest in a moment when the latter is off-guard or asleep. It therefore becomes functional for both the stronger and the weaker to subscribe to a moderation of the principle of power as the sole determinant of outcomes.

I derive from this the idea that *guilt* which accompanies the excessive use of power is the adaptive emotion *for the social group* which prevents unlimited use of power. In Freud's (1922) view it resulted from the primal crime, the murder of the father by the band of brothers. The effect of guilt was thus to prevent parricide. More generally, guilt, if experienced in anticipation of action, frequently prevents the action. Ordinarily the action would have entailed the use of power against another. Similarly, *shame* serves a social group by limiting status claiming. Thus, if there is any shortage of benefits—a condition of scarcity—although guilt prevents one from using power to get as much as one desires, shame limits the horizon of desire by imposing rules of appropriateness with regard to how much benefit one legitimately deserves, based on one's qualities in relation to the qualities of the others who also desire benefits. To this extent, guilt and shame are functional, for group survival, since they both serve to stay the hand that would take more benefits than is good for the group as a whole.

If we now add to evolutionary survival the principle of interdependence, we can deduce a basis for some positive emotions. The incontrovertible fundamental interdependence is sexual. Since human reproduction and group survival are contingent on sexual relations, certain emotions are functional by facilitating sexual activity. First, there is generalized sexual desire without a particular object. This is adequate to ensure that the basic procreative needs of the group will be satisfied. Yet, perhaps especially—although not exclusively—among humans, because of the long infancy and dependency of the human organism, mere random couplings based on generalized sexual desire might depress survival of both individuals and the group. Some additional emotions are of use here, namely, *loving* and its reciprocal, the feeling of being *loved*. Loving helps in survival by linking a particular female with a particular male, a particular parent with a particular child. To love the other is to want to give gratification to the other. When the other is in need, loving is the emotional foundation on which support and giving to the other are founded.

From an evolutionary and interdependence viewpoint, therefore, certain emotions "make sense," and they do so firmly within the broad assumption that the major source of positive and negative stimuli that produce emotions are the actions of other humans. To speak of evolution, however, implies certain genetic attributes of the organism. These are rooted in the biological cell structure, and this serves to remind us that emotions have a physiological locus as well as sociological and psychological aspects. If emotions help the species in adapting to social relational vicissitudes and requirements, it seems likely that some evidence of this might be found in the physiological substratum of emotions. In the next two chapters I consider how social relational events and physiological structures and processes actually dovetail to produce the adaptive emotions required by interdependence and survival needs. Just as social relational contingencies instigate different emotions, so are there specific physiological structures and processes available to trigger the bodily counterparts of the relational conditions of emotion.

chapter 7

Toward a Sociophysiology of Emotions: I. The Evidence for Specificity

Real, imagined, or anticipated outcomes of social interaction produce emotions; the emphasis thus far has been on how the relational dimensions—power and status—articulate with emotions. However, for many readers something may appear to be missing. This is the clearly recognized fact that emotions have not only a *relational* but a *physiological* locus.

Emotions are indubitably accompanied by autonomically guided physiological processes—blushing or pallor, gastric contractions, muscle tensions, perspiration, change of heart and respiration rates, enlargement of the pupils of the eyes, and so on. Studies of the brain also show certain local activities associated with the production or experience of emotion. No comprehensive approach to the study of emotions can omit these nonrelational aspects.

I do not, however, examine the literature on the physiology of emotions for its own sake, merely because emotions and physiology are coterminous. Rather my interest is in the connection between (1) the social relational outcomes, (2) the emotions as experienced, and (3) the physiological responses that accompany both emotions and relational outcomes. In other words, I am interested in a *sociophysiology* of emotions.

This type of inquiry is in no sense original. Psychosomatic medicine (Alexander, 1950) is largely based on the premise of an implicit relationship between the social-psychological conditions of the organism and physiological processes. The very term sociophysiology is preempted and is more than 20 years old (Boyd and Di Mascio, 1954). Some time ago Kaplan and Bloom (1960) reviewed a number of studies in sociophysiology and imaginatively outlined further studies in this area. In one of the finest theoretical efforts to integrate sociological and physiological concerns, Dohrenwend (1967) presented an exemplary model of the relationship between social stress and myocardial infarction. There is also a cumulating body of work that reflects the specific interest in social stress, and this research effort continues strong (Appley and Trumbull, 1967; Levine and

146

Scotch, 1970). Yet from the inception of interest in sociophysiology, the hoped-for integration implied by the label has not occurred. Various reasons can be advanced for dilatory progress in this area of considerable promise.

The first reason is that sociologists are doubtless loath to learn physiology, a technical field with a large and challenging literature. It is understandable that psychophysiology is well established, since in both cases the unit of analysis is the organism. This unity of focus is obviously absent for sociophysiology, thus requiring a very broad reach indeed to embrace the social as well as the organismic.

A second reason sociophysiology has failed to develop is the absence of an extended body of theory to unite the two disciplines. Kaplan and Bloom (1960) spoke of the need for "common concepts . . . accepted and utilized by members of the cooperating disciplines" (p. 128). I take this to mean that both sociologists and physiologists would be willing to work with the same concepts as their counterparts in the other discipline. A prior requirement is that within each discipline practitioners have settled on a useful set of concepts that can stimulate significant research problems when introduced into the other discipline. Where there is lack of clarity within a discipline, there is naturally some reluctance to enter into work in the domain of the other discipline.

Kaplan and Bloom (1960) discussed two possible approaches when the question is approached from the sociological side.

> First, assuming the lack of an adequate typology of social relationships, a population of subjects may be tested in a variety of social relationships in which the subjects normally find themselves by means of a battery of physiological tests. An examination of the results might reveal the existence of homogeneous physiological behavior in certain of the relationships as opposed to others. In such a manner the experimenter might be able to isolate clusters of social relationships on the basis of like physiological responses, thus providing a foundation for an empirical typology of social relationships.

> The second possibility demands the prior existence of a typology of social relationships . . . Once having developed a small number of well-defined dimensions [of relationships], we may derive the finite number of combinations and permutations thereof, and then gather physiological data for subjects engaged in each of these types of social relationships . . . Such data might lend support to the initial typology and might provide the physiologist with data of strategic importance (pp. 129–30).

It should be apparent that the power-status model permits us to move into studies of the second kind, in which physiological data support and validate the conceptual and theoretical results at the sociological level. It is perhaps less apparent that the power-status relational framework may also provide support for physiological theory and clarify ambiguities in the findings at that level. Indeed, the purpose of this chapter and the next is to present evidence for the mutual support that certain sociological and physiological theories can afford each other.

Ordinarily it is assumed that sociology is the "softer" science, thus in need of considerable aid, whereas "harder sciences, such as physiology, are less in need of assistance, particularly not from a soft science. Yet I propose to examine a significant problem in psychophysiology which has for years arrayed the field into partisan viewpoints and is not yet resolved. This is the problem of physiological specificity, first posed in the work of Lange (1885) and William James (1893). Do specific emotions have specific visceral-physiological concomitants? Those who follow Lange and James say yes. The antispecificity position stems from the work of the great physiologist Walter Cannon (1929), who appeared to refute successfully the James-Lange position. Yet the question is not finally settled, and there is evidence favoring both sides. In recent years, however, the antispecificity view has gained ground, due in large part to the work of Stanley Schachter and his associates in psychology (Schachter and Singer, 1962; Schachter and Wheeler, 1962), and of Levi (1972) and Frankenhaeuser (1971a, 1971b) and their associates in physiology. In two recent ventures by sociologists into some aspects of sociophysiology (Moss, 1973; Mazur and Robertson, 1974) the antispecificity position was endorsed largely on the basis of the work of Schachter and Singer, Levi, and Frankenhaeuser.

My position, on the contrary, is that the specificity hypothesis is supported by both the psycho- and sociophysiological evidence and that one reason for the failure of many psychologists and physiologists to realize this is that they have not had an adequate understanding of the sociological conditions of their experimental paradigms. One of the crucial failures here is in the work of Schachter and Singer (1962), which dominates discussions of the specificity question today. Their major experiment is treated extensively in the next chapter.

Lest it be thought that a sociologist is engaging in disciplinary oneupmanship by pointing a finger at the failings of psychology and physiology, it is important to emphasize this: Sociologists bear the primary responsibility for developing an adequate general model of social relationships and sociological conditions. It can hardly be expected that other disciplines do their "home work" and do sociology too! Yet comprehensive models of social relationships have been conspicuously absent until recently in sociological theory. As suggested earlier, the study of emotions must be seriously hampered until comprehensive sociological models are available. The power-status model, with its "finite number of combinations and permutations" (Kaplan and Bloom, 1960, p. 130), permits us to undertake studies of emotions not only at the level of "felt" emotions, but also at the level of the physiology of emotions. The power-status model permits a revealing insight into the specificity hypothesis and the startling possibility of a solution that is facilitative for both disciplines.

I believe that one reason psychologists and physiologists have not conclusively resolved the specificity problem is that they are "too close" to the data. If sociophysiology is of any value it is because certain phenomena at the physiological level cannot be understood adequately without taking into account the sociological context. Clearly, the argument also cuts the other way: a full understanding of social relationships is not possible without the physiological base, for, although we usually ignore the fact, social relations cannot occur without physiological precursors and concomitants. This chapter and the next are intended to suggest not only what sociology can do for physiology, but also what the latter can do for the former. Indeed, I hope the results will provide a firmer basis for fruitful understandings in both disciplines.

I now discuss some theory and findings in psychophysiology and am sensible at this point of two kinds of readers: those who are acquainted with the basic concepts of psychophysiology and those who are not. The latter are more than likely sociologists, the former those with training in any of the psychological sciences. Because of the technical nature of the material, sociologists who shun internal analysis of the organism, particularly below the molar level of the personality system, may hesitate to read on. I believe that the important results obtained by a rigorous application of the "sociological method" very much warrant the required investment of attention. I hope that the sociologist-reader will not skip to the next chapter unless the materials presented seem logically or empirically unsound, not merely technically unfamiliar. Psychologists, on the other hand, will find the materials on psychophysiology comfortably familiar.

First I present a very brief introduction to the central nervous system (CNS) and the autonomic nervous system (ANS). Then I review evidence supporting a specificity theory of emotions. In the next chapter I review the evidence against specificity. There I pay particular attention to pivotal studies by Schachter and Singer, Levi, and Frankenhaeuser and her colleagues. I conclude with an assessment of the implications of specificity theory for sociological analysis and of sociological theory for the physiology of emotions.

THE NERVOUS SYSTEM

The nervous system is composed of two branches, the central nervous system (CNS) and the autonomic nervous system (ANS). The CNS consists of the brain, the brain stem, and the spinal cord (Sternbach, 1966). The CNS largely controls the voluntary muscles and organs, for example, legs, arms, fingers, and jaw, which the person flexes or extends at will. Nerve impulses from the brain travel along the pathways of the CNS to the various muscle sites, and the muscles perform according to the commands received from the brain.

The autonomic branch of the nervous system (ANS) controls the involuntary muscles and organs, for example, heart, stomach, sweat glands, adrenals, veins, and the like. These organs and muscles operate by and large indifferently to conscious instructions from the brain. For example, we do not tell our stomachs to digest food, nor consciously direct our veins to dilate or contract to reduce or increase blood pressure. These processes occur more or less outside our control. The name autonomic conveys the sense of this. In recent years there has been some work on the conditionability and even concious control of certain organs previously considered immune to such control, for example, studies of biofeedback (Miller, 1973; Blanchard and Young, 1973). It appears that we do have a somewhat greater command of these processes than was previously thought. This discovery, however, does not directly affect the substance of the discussion.

To complicate matters somewhat, the ANS is itself comprised of two branches: the sympathetic nervous system (SNS) and the parasympathetic nervous system (PNS). Structurally the SNS sends nerve fibers in great quantity to the various peripheral organs of the ANS (e.g. heart, lungs, stomach, veins, etc.). Functionally when the SNS is activated it produces a diffuse response in the organs of the ANS; that is, heart, lungs, stomach, and so on, are all stimulated. In general the SNS accelerates the heart, deepens the oxygen capacity of the lungs, contracts the veins, enlarges the pupil of the eye, stimulates the secretion of epinephrine (adrenaline) from the adrenal gland, and otherwise produces a state of general arousal or excitation.

Structurally the PNS connects to virtually the same set of organs as the SNS, except that when the PNS is activated, it operates more selectively than the SNS. The SNS has been referred to as operating on a "shotgun" principle, whereas the PNS operates like a "rifle." Functionally the PNS produces a more or less opposite effect from that of the SNS in any given organ. Thus if the SNS accelerates heart and pulse rate, the PNS reduces them. Obviously the SNS and PNS by and large maintain homeostasis in the various peripheral organs. When the stimulation of either the SNS or the PNS does not exceed certain limits, each system can successfully modulate the other, thus preventing a "blow up" or a total "winding down" of the organs involved (cf. Lex, 1974).

It is of considerable importance for what follows that the SNS and the PNS trigger the peripheral organs by different chemical messengers, known as neurotransmitters. The SNS neurotransmitter is a substance called norepinephrine (noradrenaline) which is subsequently referred to as NE. A small amount of epinephrine (E) is involved, too, but the principal agent is NE. The PNS neurotransmitter, on the other hand, is understood to be acetylcholine (ACH). The differentiation of neurotransmitters and their associated autonomic systems is an important aspect of the specificity debate.

Although much more can be said about the CNS, ANS, SNS, and PNS and about E, NE, and ACH, the foregoing suffices as a general introduction to the physiological systems and chemical transmitters that are heavily (although perhaps not exclusively) involved in emotions. Some additional materials emerge in the succeeding discussion.

The basic argument of this chapter and the next is that the power-status social relational model supports specificity theory at the physiological level and can clarify the ambiguity in which the specificity hypothesis is currently mired. Reciprocally, the physiological evidence for specificity of visceral processes in the stimulation of specific emotions provides important support for the power-status relational model. This mutually supporting evidence builds a bridge between the two very distant domains of analysis and offers support for an overarching formulation that comprehends the physiological at one end and the sociological at the other.

Lest the point be misunderstood, I emphasize that my position has nothing to do with reductionism, whether one likes reductionism or not. Generally sociologists do not like it, because they feel it threatens the independence and validity of sociological analysis. There need be no fear of reductionism in the ensuing argument. Sociological concepts are emergents that cannot be reduced to physiological processes. For example, power is a relational concept connecting two organisms, whereas all physiological concepts are local to single organisms. Thus there is neither the intent nor the possibility of reducing power, status, or any other sociological concept to a physiological condition.

Having disavowed reductionism, I acknowledge that sociological concepts do have individual level and organismic correlates. When A exercises power over B, A's emotions and physiology are activated, as are B's emotions and physiology. I believe it is possible to proceed in a straight line from the relational facts to emotional physiological facts. The integrity of neither discipline is violated, but their points of contact and parallelism can be displayed for the purpose of augmenting the grip of each discipline on its own proper level of analysis.

THE EVIDENCE FOR SPECIFICITY

William James (1893) proposed a theory of emotions that said essentially that we *experience* emotions—fear, anger, joy, and so on—when we become aware of certain physiological processes and somatic responses. For example, if we are walking along a street and suddenly see an automobile jump the sidewalk and careen toward us, the heart might suddenly begin to race, the pulse increase, and so on. According to James' theory, the perception of these physiological events leads us to the recognition that we are "afraid." In other circumstances another configuration of physiological responses would occur and produce the sense that we are having a different emotion. Stripped to its core, *specificity* theory says that different emotions are associated with different physiological response configurations.

The antispecificity position is that a common set of physiological processes underlies all emotions. An especially attractive formulation of antispecificity theory for sociologists is that, although the underlying physiology of emotions is the same for all emotions, we experience different emotions because of what we cognize in the situation. To an important extent, as developed later, the cognitive position is correct. We must be clear, however, about what is cognized. Here the antispecificity theorists have erred, I believe. Equally important, the specificity theorists have not known how to interpret the evidence for specificity in the work of their detractors.

Funkenstein, King, and Drolette (1957) provided both a review of the early evidence for specificity, as well as an important experiment that supports the specificity hypothesis. Consider the following:

Funkenstein (1956) was experimenting with the effects of injections of a chemical called mecholyl with psychotic patients. Among these patients were some with high blood pressure, which is a result of high SNS activity. Ordinarily mecholyl reduces blood pressure by activating the PNS, which counterbalances SNS effects. Funkenstein found that the patients with elevated blood pressure reacted in two distinct ways to the injection of mecholyl. The findings are worth citing in the original:

> In one group there was only a small drop in the blood pressure after the injection, and the pressure returned to the usually high level within three to eight minutes. In the other group the blood pressure dropped markedly after the injection and remained below the pre-injection level even after 25 minutes. Not only were the physiological reactions quite different, but the two groups of patients also differed in personality and in response to treatment. Thirty-nine of 42 patients whose blood pressure was sharply lowered by mecholyl improved with electric shock treatment, whereas only three of 21 in the other group improved with the same treatment. Further, the two groups showed distinctly different results in projective psychological tests such as the Rorschach.
>
> All this suggested that the two groups of patients might be differentiated on the basis of emotions. Most psychotic patients in emotional turmoil express the same emotion constantly over a period of days, weeks or months. Psychiatrists determined the predominant emotion expressed by each of 63 patients who had been tested with mecholyl, without knowing in which physiological group they had been classified. When the subjects' emotional and physiological ratings were compared, it turned out that almost all of the patients who were generally angry at other people fell in Group N (a small, temporary reduction of blood pressure by mecholyl) while almost all those who were usually depressed or frightened were in Group E (sharp response to mecholyl). In other words, the physiological reactions were significantly related to the emotional content of the patients' psychoses (pp. 75–76).

Funkenstein (1956) later found that the two types of mecholyl response prevailed among normal, healthy persons as well. Thus, for as yet unexplained physiological reasons, the SNS was differentially modulated by the PNS. The solution to Funkenstein's problem lay in an important discovery concerning chemical neurotransmitters that had been established just a few years before the work with mecholyl began. This was that not one, but two neurotransmitters operate in the SNS. It had long been known that epinephrine was a neurotransmitter. The more recent work established another substance, norepinephrine (NE), as a transmitter with somewhat different functions and mode of operation. (Von Euler, 1951, summarized the important evidence.)

Both E and NE produce rises in blood pressure—Funkenstein's original problem—but by different means: E acts to accelerate the pumping of blood by the heart, whereas NE acts to contract blood vessels in general and perhaps to enlarge the vessels of the heart (Frankenhaeuser, 1971a). Conceivably, the differential mecholyl effects were related to which of the chemical transmitters was mainly operative in producing the elevated blood pressure. Further experiments established that when blood pressure elevation was caused mainly by E, the response to mecholyl was to reduce blood pressure permanently; when the blood pressure elevation was caused mainly by NE, the mecholyl effect was to depress blood pressure for a brief time, after which it rebounded to the previous, elevated level.

The most important conclusion that Funkenstein derived from the whole series of studies was

> that anger directed outward was associated with the secretion of NE, while depression and anxiety were associated with the secretion of E (p. 77).

Funkenstein, King, and Drolette (1957) set out to test the hypothesis more extensively with a normal sample. In a very carefully done experimental study with college students, they found that students who characteristically responded to stressful or frustrating situations with anger directed outward and casting of blame on others were also more likely to show physiological responses like those associated with NE. On the other hand, students who characteristically responded with anxiety or depression, or anger directed inward, tended to respond physiologically as in the pattern associated with E.

In a related experiment, Ax (reported in Funkenstein, 1955) learned that when persons were provoked to anger (by an experimental manipulation somewhat like those reviewed in Chapters 5 and 6), they reacted physiologically in the NE pattern; when the same persons were experimentally induced to feel fear, they reacted physiologically with the E pattern. Ax's (1953) own report of these experiments suggests a somewhat more complex pattern than Funkenstein reported, but one that is consistent with differentiated physiological patterns in fear and anger. Considerable ancillary evidence supports the specificity hypothesis. Much of it confirms the E-fear, NE-anger connection.

Von Euler (1951) reviewed data on the E and NE content of the adrenal glands of various animals. Interpreting the pattern of findings, Reusch (1953) suggested that animals such as the lion, which are high in aggressive activity, have adrenals that are relatively high in NE, whereas animals such as the rabbit, which are low in aggressive behavior and flee from danger instead of combatting it, have adrenals relatively high in E.

In an ontogenetic analysis, West (cited in Funkenstein, 1955) found that NE predominates in the adrenal glands of infants, whereas in older children E predominates. This is compatible with the hypothesis that anger and rage, associated with NE, are more primitive emotions ontogenetically, whereas fear, associated with E, is learned and emerges later. This also conforms with the general understanding that, by and large, the neonate is "fearless." One result of the Funkenstein studies was the stimulation of extensive investigation of the relationship of E and NE to fear and anger, respectively. This was done by investigation of both human and animal behavior and physiology.

Cohen and Silverman (1959) investigated the effects of human centrifugation on blood pressure response to the mecholyl test (which, as already discussed, distinguishes between an E- and an NE-type physiological reaction) and the effects of personality and mood on the outcome of centrifugation. The process involves subjecting the person to an increase in gravity (G-load); thus one feel "heavier" than ordinary. Some persons responded with fear, some with anger, and these were correlated with increases in E or NE secretions, respectively. The mecholyl results were also consistent with the mood of fear or anger that the subject may have been experiencing just prior to centrifugation. Indices of more stable personality characteristics also correlated with the fear-E and anger-NE responses.

In something of a replication of Ax's (1953) experiments in which fear and anger were experimentally induced to establish physiological configurations for these emotions, J. Schachter (1957) found these patterns in his subjects: When fear was induced, 35 of the 48 subjects showed E-like physiological reactions. Subsequently, when the same subjects were intentionally insulted and deprecated to induce anger, 19 of the 48 manifested NE-like physiological reactions, whereas 22 showed E-like reactions, and the remaining seven gave mixed reactions. Several reasons can be advanced for these seemingly ambiguous results with regard to anger. First, the anger induction took place *after* the very successful fear induction; subjects had already had one high-E experience in the laboratory setting. The anger induction may have lead simply to some general arousal, which E promotes. A second explanation is that when anger becomes very intense, the whole body is mobilized for "fight," and this requires E-induced physiological acitivity. In the classic words of Cannon (1929) this involves:

acceleration of the heart, contraction of arterioles, dilation of bronchioles, increase of blood sugar, inhibition of activity of the digestive glands, inhibition of gastrointestinal peristalsis, sweating, discharge of adrenin [adrenalin or epinephrine], widening of pupils and erection of hairs (p. 351).

Thus high levels of anger should yield, finally, to a mobilization of the body characterized not only by NE, but also by E.

J. Schachter (1957, p. 24), indeed, found a stronger E than NE reaction among those subjects whose expressed and reported anger was "high." He also found a somewhat larger E-type physiological reaction when anger was "low." Schachter speculated that this may be explained by anger turned inward, which Funkenstein, King, and Drolette (1957) had found to produce E-like reactions. Funkenstein and his associates theorized that supressed anger signified *fear* of expressing anger. In sum, these results do not neatly support the E-NE fear-anger distinction, but they are sufficiently consistent to make them favorable.

In an important series of studies, Elmadjian, Hope, and Lamson (1958) examined the urinary secretions of E and NE among hockey players, amateur boxers, and psychiatric patients, among others. Hockey players and boxers engage in activities that induce fear and anger in varying degrees; the psychiatric patients manifest personality dispositions reflecting either anger (aggression) or fear (anxiety) in excessive amounts. Among the hockey players, there was a sixfold increase of NE and a threefold increase of E over pregame levels. Two injured men who did not play showed only a 50% increase in NE and a two- to threeefold increase in E. One player who was ejected as a result of a fist-fight showed a ninefold increase of NE and a 20-fold increase of E. Elmadjian and his colleagues did not ask the hockey players about their emotions, yet it is obvious that hockey is a very aggressive sport in which players are often involved in hurtful body contact with each other. Anger is the underlying emotion in an aggressive display of this type (Berkowitz, 1962). Even if the aggressive stance is instrumental at first, it soon appears to become expressive, as indicated by the many serious personal battles that break out on the ice. In addition to aggression and anger, the game involves considerable uncertainty over both personal safety as well as team outcome. In relational terms, the hockey game is a power struggle whose outcome is uncertain. This appears to be a perfect matrix for generating anger and fear. The elevations of NE and E, respectively, are the physiological indicators of this.

Among the boxers, Elmadjian and his colleagues reported that "the high NE prefight values were noted in fighters who engaged in shadow-boxing . . . [T]he highest prefight E excretion was found in the fighters who showed the greatest degree of anticipation preceding the fight . . . [I]ncrease in the postfight samples over the prefight samples of E were observed in those fighters who had to fight the distance for decision in close contests" (p. 535). These results are congruent with the E-NE fear-anger hypothesis if we assume that shadow boxing is a form of self-induced aggressive behavior whose underlying emotion is anger (Berkowitz, 1962), that "high anticipation" is best understood as uncertainty over outcome, the corresponding emotion of which is anxiety or fear (Graham, Cohen, and Schmavonian 1967), and that anxiety and fear are most likely to accompany protracted conflicts in which the outcome is uncertain.

Among the psychiatric patients, a combined motor-activity-aggression score was positively correlated with secretion of NE. Patients with "passive, self-effacing emotional display had normal levels of NE" (Elmadjian, Hope, and Lamson, 1958, p. 536). The more active-aggressive patients had higher NE levels and generally displayed higher E excretion as well. E and NE levels were obtained for each patient immediately following a staff interview. Each patient sat "across from a psychiatrist in the presence of some 20 members of the hospital staff . . . [T]he setting is serious and to the patient it is very important, because on the basis of his performance decisions are made which affect his immediate future" (p. 538). The results showed that, compared with E and NE secretions during a control period (the following day at the same hour) NE secretions were not elevated as a result of the interview, but E secretions were elevated.

Elmadjian and his colleagues concluded that their "results support the hypothesis that active aggressive emotional displays are related to increased secretion of NE, whereas tense, anxious, but passive, emotional displays are related to increased excretion of E in association with normal excretion of NE" (p. 550). Discussing these results, Elmadjian (in Elmadjian et al., 1958, p. 552) dismissed the idea that the increased NE is due to activity per se, citing evidence that activity as such may raise E but not NE levels. This point is not, in fact, entirely clear, and more research must be devoted to clarifying the relationship between E, NE, and motor activity. In further discussion of this point, Von Euler (Elmadjaian et al., 1958, p. 553) asserted, "I think one can safely say that there was no emotional factor involved in this long series of studies made on athletes." If Von Euler was including the studies of hockey players and boxers, he was plainly wrong. It is common knowledge among those who have played vigorous body-contact sports that fear and anger are frequent concomitants of the contest. The very fact that it is a contest in which the outcome is uncertain is sufficient to generate anxiety.

Graham, Cohen, and Shmavonian (1967) provided further evidence for the E-NE emotional distinction with particular emphasis on the role of E in situations of uncertainty. In an experiment with human subjects requiring trials on two days, measures of excreted E on day 1 were considerably higher than those on day 2, whereas measures of NE were more stable. The authors explained the E variability by suggesting that E was higher on day 1 when the experiment was most unfamiliar to the participants. Of course uncertainty can easily lead to a state of fearful anticipation and the stimulation of E secretion.

Although comparative analysis of E-NE effects can only be suggestive, a number of animal experiments support the distinctive emotional effects of these substances. Two investigations most directly parallel studies with humans. Mason and Brady (1964), working with monkeys, noted differential E and NE concentrations in the blood under these conditions: "marked E changes were apparent . . . during brief intervals preceding the start of an experimental session in which the performance requirements were varied and unpredictable" (p. 14). On the other hand, NE elevations with little or no change of E occurred in these two situations: first, the monkeys received brief electric shocks every 20 seconds. The shocks could be avoided if the animal pressed a lever. Second, the monkeys received occasional electric shocks, preceded by a warning bell, when pressing a food-dispensing lever. The animals learned to avoid pressing the lever.

In the last two situations, the conditions suggest frustration and perhaps some pain, rather than uncertainty. Frustration has, of course, been linked to aggression many times, and the emotional precursor of frustration-induced aggression is anger (Berkowitz, 1962). Compatible with the human experiments, the monkeys showed higher E concentrations in the situation of uncertainty in which we would expect fear or anxiety and higher NE concentrations in the frustration situation in which we would expect anger.

In another experiment, Bronson and Desjardins (1971) found that the adrenal glands of mice exposed to "trained fighter" mice increased in size in proportion to body length, whereas there was little increase in the adrenals of dominant or trained fighter mice. The adrenal medulla is the main source of circulating E. The mice exposed to the dominant fighter could be expected to be more fearful and therefore to show high E levels. Structure follows function as the adrenals grow in size to accommodate the increased demand for E. This is an important finding, since one of the frequent criticisms of the specificity hypothesis is that methods for measuring amounts of E and NE through analyzing urinary secretions or blood plasma levels are inexact (Kety, 1972; Frankenhaeuser, 1971b). The structural change in the adrenal glands augments the findings from studies of urinary and blood levels of the neurotransmitters and provides multimethod support for the specificity hypothesis (Campbell and Fiske, 1959). Welch and Welch (1971) also reported increases in E secretion among the mice in their experiment who were exposed to "dominant" fighters.

Brain E and NE.   The data cited so far discuss the specific role of E and NE in the activation of various organs of the SNS. These substances are known to have specific loci of origin as far as the SNS is concerned. NE is produced primarily at the nerve endings that connect with the organs, for example, heart, lungs, blood vessels, and the like (Gellhorn, 1967; Frankenhaeuser, 1971b). Although there may be some E at these points, the major source of E is the adrenal medulla (Gellhorn, 1967; Frankenhaeuser, 1971b). Similarly some NE may be produced by the adrenals. According to Stein (1967), any stimulus that causes the release of NE at the end organs also causes the release of E from the adrenals, and vice versa. Thus NE and E production in the sympathetic nervous system are somewhat linked.

However, they have some temporal separation. Gellhorn (1967) proposed that when there is painful stimulation, for example, NE is released first at the nerve endings to activate the organs of the SNS. One of these organs is the adrenal gland itself. The subsequent flow of E from the adrenal gland passes by means of the blood stream to various parts of the body, including the brain and the various organs of the autonomic system. Here the E may augment or fine-tune the organismic response. These processes are not clearly understood, particularly in regard to what happens differentially in the brain when it is excited by E and NE.

Sternbach (1966), in a review of the evidence concerning E, suggested the involvement of the hypothalamus, and the reticular formation in the brain. Sternbach proposed that stimulating the reticular formation leads to "cortical and behavioral effects of arousal" (p. 62), and, since the reticular formation is sensitive to circulatory E,

> it is possible for cortical activity to stimulate the reticular formation which then produces more generalized cortical arousal and increased autonomic tone, which results in the increase of circulating E, which in turn serves to maintain the reticular activity and thereby the cortical activity (p. 63).

Although all the details of the feedback loop between the brain and SNS are not yet clear, the general outline of the process appears to be known.

There appears to be a somewhat larger role for NE in the brain than for E. Different parts of the hypothalamus can be stimulated to release stored E and NE (Von Euler and Folkow, 1953; Jarvick, 1973). According to Schildkraut and Kety (1967), NE predominates considerably over E in the hypothalamus. Relatively low concentrations of NE in the brain are associated with depression. One of the known brain effects of electroshock therapy, used to combat depression, is that it increases the synthesis of NE in the brain (Kety, 1972). NE in high amounts in the brain also appears to be related to rage, and drugs that inhibit NE also inhibit rage (Kety, 1972). Thus brain NE also plays a role in anger, as does the neurogenic NE that is released at the effector organs.

In a number of studies with mice (Eleftheriou, 1971; Welch and Welch, 1971) brain NE relocation is one of the consequences of defeat or subordination. Eleftheriou found that the total amount of brain NE did not change, but shifted toward the frontal cortex. The exact significance of this relocation is not known.

However, Welch and Welch found that in defeated mice, NE moves from the nerve cells, where it is manufactured, to the nerve terminals where, they speculate, it can be more readily invested when combat occurs. Since the same concentration does not occur in the dominant mice, it can be supposed that the defeated mice require more NE or easier access to the arousing effects of NE to maintain their ability to defend themselves when under attack. The total collapse of aggressive defense on their part would lead to even greater damage than is done to them as losers.

Bronson and Desjardins (1971) also found that testosterone function was reduced in mice subject to daily defeats by trained fighter mice. The relationship of testosterone, produced in the testicles, and aggression is well known (Ehren-kranz et al., 1974). One effect of reduced testicular function is a reduction in the production of gonadal steroid hormone. This hormone stimulates the production of cortisol, which in turn regulates the production of monoamine oxydase which decomposes NE (Broverman et al., 1974). The net effect is that defeat leads to increased metabolism of NE. A low amount of NE is associated with depression (Kety, 1972). It is also possible that the relocation of NE as found by Eleftheriou (1971) and Welch and Welch (1971) results from a systemic effort to counteract the lower level of functioning that depletion of NE, as manifested in depression, brings about.

When NE is released by verious cells, whether in the brain or at the effector organs, it is subject to reabsorption by the cells in a process called reuptake. Cocaine has the property of preventing reuptake of NE, thus prolonging the presence of NE at the sites at which it acts and apparently contributes to cocaine "excitement" in this manner (Gellhorn, 1967). NE in higher concentrations is thus associated with anger, pain, and euphoria (the cocaine reaction). NE in lower concentrations is associated with depression.

SOCIAL RELATIONS AND PSYCHOPHYSIOLOGY

It is appropriate to summarize the findings for specificity at this point. Although there are some ambiguities in the data and the methods of data collection have been criticized (Frankenhaeuser, 1971b; Kety, 1972), there is a consistency in the pattern of findings across subject populations, phylogentic levels, and methodological approaches that can only be regarded as impressive. At very least, these studies support a specificity hypothesis, even if they do not support an incontrovertible theory. The most important findings are that the neurotransmitter substance NE is associated with anger and the hormonal substance E is associated with fear or anxiety.

The physiological differentiation of the emotions suggests a close parallel to the relational differentiation in the social stimulus conditions for emotions.

Specifically, as developed in Chapters 3 and 6, *deficits of power produce fear or anxiety, and loss of status produces anger and/or depression.* The physiological evidence suggests that NE in the SNS is related to incidents of status deprivation and anger; high levels of NE in the brain are also related to anger or to manic excitement, whereas very low levels are associated with depression—the effect of a long-term deprivation of status. On the other hand, E is related to situations of uncertainty and threat that are most pronounced when one has insufficient power or the other has excessive power.

It could be mere coincidence that there are two different chemical substances involved in these important emotions and that there are also two relational dimensions, but this would be to ignore the tendency for the integration of the various organismic systems (Bertalanaffy, 1956). Since relational conditions lead to emotions and behavior, and behavior and emotions imply physiology, I believe there is sufficient evidence for us to assume a theoretical arc from the physiological to the relational, linking the two levels by means of the intervening medium of the emotions. I have now stated the most important hypothesis that emerges from this joint consideration of the sociological and the physiological. We must now look at some additional data in the light of the hypothesis.

Although I have written as if only two chemicals are associated with emotions, this is not, strictly speaking, accurate. Many other substances are found in the brain and nervous system (e.g., serotonin, dopamine, ACTH, etc.). Except for ACTH and some related substances, none has been found to be systematically associated with emotions in the same way as E and NE. ACTH, appears to be involved in general arousal regardless of specific emotion, but it is undifferentiated with respect to any particular emotion. Much has been made of the primary significance of ACTH in crisis situations and in what is known as the general adaptation syndrome (Selye, 1956; Moss, 1973). Although ACTH apparently acts to protect or repair damage in the organism and to mobilize somatic resources for survival, it does not bear especially on the problem of specific emotions. Only E and NE have been found consistently to be *differentially* associated with specific emotions. This is the crucial distinction that allows us to build a conceptual and theoretical bridge between physiology and social relationships.

Even if E and NE are incontrovertibly related to fear and anger, respectively, this hardly settles the matter as far as physiological specificity of emotions is concerned. Indeed, one of the criticisms leveled by antispecificity theorists against specificity is that there can hardly be as many distinct physiological configurations as there are emotions (Cannon, 1929; Smith, 1973; Moss, 1973). Schachter and Singer (1962) said, "the variety of emotion, mood, and feeling states are by no means matched by an equal variety of visceral patterns" (p. 380). This statement assumes that there is a very large number of different emotions. Perhaps there is not.

A simple division can be made between distressful emotions, such as anger and fear, and pleasant emotions, such as contentment, security, satisfaction, and the like. Anger and fear involve the differential stimulation of the SNS. The various physiological symptoms of anger and fear—increased heart rate, dilation of pupils, constriction of peripheral blood vessels, decrease in skin resistance, and the like (I do not distinguish between E and NE effects)—all result from the actions of the SNS. On the other hand, pleasant emotions such as those accompanying relaxation, digestion, and tumescence of sex organs, are related to the activation of the PNS. As discussed previously, the SNS and PNS are reciprocally inhibitory in an extensive way. Thus physiological balance is maintained. Each branch of the ANS, however, achieves a pronounced effect of its own before the other system functions to restore autonomic balance. On the SNS side, the correlated emotions are distressful; on the PNS side they are pleasant and satisfying. Given the apparent specificity of the neurochemical activators of fear and anger by the SNS, it is not surprising to find a similar specificity in regard to PNS activation of the pleasant emotions, namely, acetylcholine.

From a relational point of view, it appears that when there is deficit of power (producing fear) and/or when there is deficit of status (producing anger), the SNS is activated. When there is a sufficiency of power (producing security) and of status (producing the feeling of pleasure and gratification), the organism is in a state of satisfaction and contentment. Although two distinct physiological processes seem to be involved in the distressful emotions—anger and fear—only one process is apparently involved in the satisfying emotions. This requires explanation.

An approach to such explanation can be obtained from the famous lines by Tolstoy at the beginning of *Anna Karenina*: "Happy families are all alike. Unhappy families are each unhappy in their own way." Tolstoy's insight suggests that satisfaction and happiness can result only when the power and status relational dimensions are *both* adequate. A deficit of either produces a decay of happiness, in the form of anger or fear. Bradburn and Caplovitz's (1965) studies of happiness confirm this view of the two-dimensional nature of this state. There must not only be a sufficiency of good circumstances that bring gratification (*status*, broadly understood), but also a relative minimum of bad conditions (which signify insufficient *power* to deter disliked outcomes). Studies of marital happiness also show a two-dimensional basis (Orden and Bradburn, 1968; Barry, 1970). Recent studies of happiness and adjustment among the aged in New York City also show the two-dimensional pattern: happiness results from presence of good conditions *and* the absence of bad (Wilker, 1975). The immediate emotional effect of status loss is anger, and of the sense of inadequate means (power) to forestall harm or injury, fear. When status and power are adequate, they produce happiness and security. There is no need for the marked physiological activation by E and/or NE.

One further development, however, is possible. Gellhorn (1967) and Gell-horn and Loofbourrow (1963) suggested the possibility of what they call "tuning" when either the SNS or PNS are subjected to stimulation powerful enough to overcome the capacity of the other system to return the ANS to a more balanced state. The tuning of either system occurs in three stages. First, because of a persistent, unremitting stimulus, a given system is continuously activated, and the opposite system is prevented from achieving its customary balancing effect. In the second stage a renewal of the nontuned system occurs, and stimuli that previously activated it now operate to augment further the activation of the tuned system. For example, the presence of food in the stomach ordinarily leads to PNS activity to digest the food via acid secretion, and so on. If the SNS is tuned, however, the presence of food in the stomach produces the SNS effect, namely, withdrawal of blood from the stomach and decrease of digestive activity. In the third stage, the breakdown of the reciprocity relationship between the SNS and the PNS continues; thus both systems discharge simultaneously. This is the state called "mixed discharges" (Gellhorn, 1967). Lex (1974) provided a very convincing argument for the effects of tuning in cases of "voodoo death." In this case social relational stimuli overactivate the SNS and the PNS until the result is a damping down of the physiological activity of the organism to the point of death.

Because of the possibility of tuning, Gellhorn suggested that any simple parallel between emotions and either SNS or PNS discharges is not likely. He also proposed that there is a level of integration of somatic, autonomic, and brain systems that together comprise a unity for the purpose of determining emotion. The SNS system and its associated brain and somatic (especially muscle tone) aspects is called the *ergotropic* (ER), and the corresponding PNS integrated system is called *trophotropic* (TR) (Gellhorn and Loofbourrow, 1963). The ER system entails high muscle tone, desynchronized EEG rhythms in the cerebral cortex, and activation of the SNS. The TR system involves relaxed muscle tone, synchronized rhythms in the cerebral cortex, and PNS dominance.

Gellhorn (1967) and Gellhorn and Loofbourrow (1963) proposed the involvement of both the SNS and the PNS in particular configurations for such emotions as anger, fear, depression, and anxiety. In anger, surprisingly, there is an increase in *both* SNS and PNS activity. SNS activity (mainly NE at first, I assume) produces increased heart rate, higher blood pressure, less blood through the kidney, whereas the PNS effect causes the face to flush and the stomach to engorge with blood. Fear, on the other hand, seems to involve mainly SNS activity, supported by E secretion; PNS action is reduced. For example, blood leaves the stomach, as found in the observations of Wolf and Wolff (1947) of the stomach of a person with an open wound. PNS involvement in anger is unexpected. Why should the "contentment" branch of the autonomic nervous system be activated in the course of an obviously distressful emotion? I wish to offer a speculative hypothesis that sheds light on the physiological process from the distant standpoint of social relations.

Anger can be elicited in a variety of circumstances, as indicated in Chapters 3 and 6, but the paradigmatic instance involves status loss. Accustomed benefits and rewards are reduced through the arbitrary action of the other. For present purposes, an actor's status level involves a "set" or anticipation of the usual or promised amount of reward. If these are structurally sufficient, they should produce a pleasant affective tone. In a word, the PNS is already active in providing the actual and anticipated feeling of well-being. However, when status is lost, denied, or withdrawn, this happens in the context of an active anticipation of satisfaction. If this were not true, the denial of status would have no immediate effect, for the flood of anger would appear to be possible only when the disappointment is contrasted with a state of anticipated satisfaction.

If this analysis is correct, the PNS must itself be at least moderately active for anger to occur. The SNS is activated when the status loss occurs, and for a time both systems are active. In Chapter 4 I cited evidence from Pastore (1960), Austin (1972), and Austin and Walster (1974) that indicated the role of prior expectation in the amplifying or modulating responses to frustration and status loss. The confident expectation of a positive outcome must activate physiological processes associated with a consummatory state; thus the PNS must be active even before there is anything to consume. We all know how the mere thought of tasty food can make the mouth water, a PNS response. It is not astonishing, then, that we find the PNS involved along with the SNS in the emotion of anger.

Here we must taper off the discussion of the specificity of physiological response in conjunction with emotions. A great deal of work at the physiological level remains to be done, especially to clarify the interactions of the SNS and the PNS in the production and modulation of different emotions. The problem of the relationship between brain levels of E and NE and the activation of the SNS and the PNS is also a challenging and important part of the knowledge still to be won.

Nonetheless, the evidence for physiological specificity in the production of emotions is highly appealing from the point of view of an integrated theory embracing social relationships on one side and physiological processes on the other. There is a danger, of course, in succumbing to the charms of theoretical closure when the data do not warrant it. In the matter of specificity in the theory of emotions, there is indeed a countervailing view.

Working primarily with cats, physiologist Walter Cannon (1929) showed, in a series of careful experiments, that a variety of emotions—pain, fear, and rage—were accompanied by physiological arousal indicative of E secretion. (Furthermore, extremely minute injections of E could produce this broad spectrum of emotions.) Thus Cannon attacked and appeared to destroy the specificity position taken by James (1893) and a similar theory proposed independently by Lange (1885).

Of course, Cannon worked only with cats and did not study positive emotions—contentment, joy, love, and the like. Nonetheless, Cannon seemed to have established a common physiological basis for fear and rage, and this in itself was quite damaging to the specificity position. Surely fear and anger are different emotions, yet if there is no specific physiological differentiation possible between them, the difference between these emotions must reside elsewhere. On the other hand, Funkenstein (1955), Ax (1953), Cohen and Silverman (1959), and Elmadjian et al. (1958) certainly provided evidence that fear and anger are physiologically distinguishable. Thus we appear to be at an impasse. At such points in a science, the crucial experiment takes on a significance that is well deserved. Schachter and Singer (1962) undertook an important investigation bearing on the question of specificity and using human subjects. The results, as interpreted by Schachter and Singer, appear to suggest that a large number of emotions, including anger, euphoria, amusement, love, fear, and so on, are associated with an identical state of activation of the SNS, particularly with the flow of E. Although Schachter and Singer carefully disavowed the conclusiveness of their experiment with regard to specificity ("Obviously, this study does *not* rule out the possibility of physiological differences among the emotional states" (p. 397, emphasis in original), the results have been accepted as conclusive by a number of others:

In 1962, Schachter and Singer provided an important perspective on the problem by demonstrating that when the social and cognitive aspects of the experimental conditions were appropriate, E intensified a variety of emotional states. Thus emotions are specified by environmental cues and the experience of the organism. E does not elicit any emotion, but E intensifies all emotions. This relationship of nonspecificity between emotions and E was also the relationship established by the work correlating E excretion and spontaneous or experimental emotional states . . . (Smith, 1973, p. 327).

A sociologist (Mazur) met the specificity question head-on by contrasting the results of Schachter and Singer (1962) with those of Funkenstein, King, and Drolette (1957):

A straightforward explanation of Funkenstein's results would say that different hormones cause different emotions; that NE causes the emotion of anger toward others, and that E causes the emotion of anger toward self, or anxiety. That this is not the case was amply demonstrated by Schachter (1964) who showed that one hormone, E, could contribute to two different emotions: anger and euphoria (Mazur and Robertson, 1972, p. 102).

Indeed, one of the interesting by-products of the results of Schachter and Singer is that one does not hear any more of experiments with human subjects that support the anger-NE and fear-E findings of earlier studies. The Schachter and Singer findings are too difficult to explain away. I turn now to a consideration of the work of Schachter and Singer and the antispecificity position.

chapter 8

Toward a Sociophysiology of Emotions: II. The Evidence Against Specificity

Since Schachter and Singer's experiment now has the undisputed status of a classic that determines the direction of work in the field, I review it at some length. I contend that Schachter and Singer wrongly interpreted their findings. Their error makes it appear that a similar state of physiological arousal produced by injected E underlies emotions as different as anger and euphoria. Actually, a more plausible interpretation is that *individuals feel the emotions that are appropriate to the social relational conditions in which they find themselves.* This becomes apparent from an analysis of the details of their experiment.

SCHACHTER AND SINGER'S EXPERIMENT

Schachter and Singer first considered some findings for specificity and discussed these with the suggestion that "recent work might be taken to indicate . . . that the variety of emotion, mood, and feeling states are by no means matched by an equal variety of visceral patterns" (p. 380). They assumed that there is a great "variety" of emotions, without, however, indicating how various are the emotions. Schachter and Singer's central thesis is as follows:

> Granted a general pattern of sympathetic excitation as characteristic of emotional states, *granted that there might be some differences in pattern from state to state,* it is suggested that one labels, interprets, and identifies this stirred up state in terms of the characteristics of the precipitating situation . . . [A]n emotional state may be considered a function of a state of physiological arousal and of a cognition appropriate to this state of arousal . . . It is the cognition that determines whether the state of physiological arousal will be labeled as "anger," "joy," "fear," or whatever (p. 380, emphasis added).

It is clear that, although Schachter and Singer hedged somewhat by admitting the possibility that distinct physiological patterns are associated with particular emotions, they were persuaded that the major determinant of the qualitatively different emotions is the *cognition* of the precipitating events.

From the point of view of a sociological theory of emotions, the position of Schachter and Singer is, in a major respect, welcome, because the precipitating events must in many cases be the real, imagined, or anticipated outcomes of social interactions: we are threatened, applauded, insulted, enticed, and so on. Thus a cognitive approach to emotions comes at least to the boundary line between the organism and the social environment. Schachter and Singer did not discuss systematically the social content of the cognitions that determine the different emotions, but their work serves—although for the wrong reasons—as one of the strongest endorsements of a sociological view of emotions. Of course we can agree with Schachter and Singer that precipitating situations produce emotions. We can also agree that one must cognize, in the sense of interpret, the external situation in a particular way before a given emotion is elicited. Other cognitively oriented theorists of emotion, such as Arnold (1970) and Lazarus, Averill, and Opton (1970) have placed greater emphasis on the interpretation or "appraisal" than did Schachter and Singer. However, in all cognitive approaches to emotion, the gaze is appropriately directed outward to the environment.

Since Schachter and Singer had neither a theory nor a model of the environment, they were reduced to treating it in a curiously detached way: one merely *compares* oneself to what one perceives in the social environment. This overlooks the much more compelling connection we have with the environment, namely, the *relationships with others*. These are relationships of power and status, described extensively in earlier chapters. This does not mean that we may not also be spectators of others who are in situations similar to ours (cf. Kemper, 1968a), but where there is a relationship, it serves better to explain emotions than to assume that one simply puts on the emotions of others with whom we have little or no relationship.

Schachter and Singer obtained their undeveloped view of the environment as a field for comparison from the work of Festinger (1954), who earlier proposed the notion of "social comparison processes" whereby individuals in ambiguous or uncertain situations attempt to obtain cognitive clarity by comparing themselves with others. Schachter and Singer adopted this process for their purposes as a paradigm by which to explain emotions.

They declared that emotions are evoked by both physiological arousal and by a cognition that is attached to the arousal, thereby explaining the arousal. To prepare us for their experimental manipulation, they proposed that when there is physiological arousal but no appropriate explanation for it—for example, if a person has been fed epinephrine (E) covertly and is feeling the usual symptoms, such as "palpitations, tremor, face flushing"—this

would lead to the arousal of "evaluative needs" (Festinger, 1954), that is, pressures would act on an individual in such a state to understand and label his bodily feelings—How would he label his present feelings? It is suggested of course that he will label his feelings in terms of his knowledge of the *immediate* situation. Should he at the time be with a beautiful woman he might decide he was wildly in love or sexually excited . . . [A]t a gay party he might, by comparing himself to others, decide that he was extremely happy and euphoric . . . Arguing with his wife, he might explode in fury and hatred (p. 381, emphasis added).

Thus the *immediate* situation determines the cognition, according to Schachter and Singer, but we see later that this is not necessarily the case for them. It is also noteworthy that in the three examples given cognition is based only once on a comparison (the party setting), whereas in the case of the beautiful woman and the argument with the wife, the cognition is based on what self is doing to other or what other is doing to self in a social relationship. Thus Schachter and Singer did not provide a consistent interpretation of their theory in terms of social comparison processes, but unwittingly included the more highly probable causal effects of social relationship, that is, what A does to B. It is also noteworthy that, although Schachter and Singer began judiciously and "granted that there may be some [physiological] differences from [emotional] state to state" (p. 380), the formal statement of their position included the following: "To the extent that cognitive factors are potent determiners of emotional states, it could be anticipated that *precisely the same state of physiological arousal* could be labeled 'joy' or 'fury' or 'jealousy' or any of a great diversity of emotional labels depending on the cognitive aspects of the situation" (pp. 381–382, emphasis added).

In sum, Schachter and Singer said that when there is physiological arousal but no appropriate explanation, the individual will "label" his feelings according to the cognitions available to him. When there is an appropriate explanation for a state of physiological arousal, there is no "need" to seek an alternative explanation via immediate cognitions. Finally, "given the same cognitive circumstances" (p. 382), the individual does not experience emotion if there is no physiological arousal. Obviously, if this is valid, the specificity approach to emotions is highly questionable, despite the earlier data adduced in favor of it. How did Schachter and Singer support their view?

Because of the highly complex nature of the experiment and because my critical approach to it is based on specific details of the experimental manipulations, a detailed account of the "procedure" based on the most complete report of this work (Schachter and Singer, 1962) is given here.

Schachter and Singer's Experimental Procedure

The basic purpose of the experiment was to test the effect of cognition on the labeling or identification of emotion under two conditions: when there was and was not an "appropriate" explanation for physiological arousal. Three experimental and one control group were created. Regardless of group, all subjects, who were male students in introductory psychology classes at the University of Minnesota, were given the impression that they were participating in a study dealing with the effects of a vitamin compound on vision. All were told this would require that they be given a "small injection" of the vitamin "Suproxin" which was "mild and harmless." All were given the opportunity to refuse to participate, but only one of 185 subjects withdrew at this point. The four groups were

1. *Epinephrine informed* (E-inf). Immediately after agreeing to receive the injection, the subject was told about possible side effects: "they will only last about 15 or 20 minutes . . . your hand will start to shake, your heart will start to pound, and your face will get warm and flushed" (p. 383). A physician then appeared, repeated that the injection was mild and harmless, described the side effects once more, and injected ½ cc of a 1 : 1000 solution of epinephrine.

2. *Epinephrine misinformed* (E-mis). This treatment was identical to that of the E-inf group except that the subjects were given erroneous information concerning side effects. Instead of hand tremor and so on, they were told, "your feet will feel numb, you will have an itching sensation over parts of your body, and you may get a slight headache" (p. 383). The purpose of this group was to control for the effects of giving any information at all about side effects.

3. *Epinephrine ignorant* (E-ign). Immediately after agreeing to participate, these subjects were given the epinephrine injection. However, the physician repeated "that the injection was mild and harmless" and added that it "would have no side effects" (p. 383).

4. *Placebo* (Pl) The subjects in this group were given "precisely the same treatment as subjects in the E-ign condition,"(p. 383) except that their injection consisted of a neutral, saline solution that produces no side effects.

Two experimental inductions were designed to provide "cognitions" the subjects in the various groups might use to identify their "emotions."

1. *Euphoria Induction.* Immediately after the injection the experimenter returned to the room with another subject, actually a confederate of the experimenter, and asked both to wait 20 minutes until the injected "vitamin" could take effect and the vision tests begin. The experimenter apologized for the condition of the room which "had been deliberately put into a state of mild disarray" (p. 384). He said that he "didn't have time to clean it up" and that the two subjects could help themselves to "scratch paper or rubber bands or pencils" (p. 384). The experimenter then left.

Now the confederate began a programed sequence of 14 steps in which he engaged in doodling on paper, crumpling paper and "shooting baskets" at a waste-paper basket, making and flying a paper airplane, flying the paper plane directly at the naive subject, using rubber bands to make a slingshot and using "ammunition" from paper torn from the previously constructed plane, building a "tower" out of manila folders and shooting the paper ammunition at it until it fell, trying some gyrations with one of two hula hoops that were near at hand, twirling the hoop wildly on his arm; finally sitting down with feet propped on a table.

All through this routine, the confederate made such comments as "This is one of my good days. I feel like a kid again" and other remarks designed to invite the naive subject to join him in his activities. The confederate did not know the experimental group of the subject. Two hidden observers, also ignorant of the subject's experimental group, coded the naive subject's behavior in terms of *type* and *time duration* of his participation in the activities to which he was invited by the confederate (e.g., doing nothing, shooting baskets, flying plane, using hula hoop, etc.). An index of participation was created by multiplying a variable weight for type of activity by the duration of the activity.

2. *Anger Induction.* Immediately after the injection, the experimenter returned with another subject, actually a confederate, and asked both to fill out a questionnaire while they waited 20 minutes for the injection to take effect. The confederate sat directly across from the naive subject and paced himself so that he and the subject appeared to be working on the same question at all times.

The questionnaire, five pages long, begins "innocently requesting face sheet information and then grow[s] increasingly personal and insulting" (p. 385). The stooge keeps up a running commentary on the questions. These comments "start off innocently enough, grow increasingly querulous, and finally [the confederate] ends up in a rage" in which he "rips up his questionnaire, crumples the pieces and hurls them to the floor saying, 'I'm not wasting any more time, I'm getting my books and leaving,' and he stamps out of the room" (p. 385).

As in the euphoria induction, neither the confederate nor the two observers behind the one-way mirror knew the experimental group of the naive subject. The observers monitored the subject's behavior for the degree to which he agreed or disagreed with the confederate's protests and irritation or remained neutral or ignored the confederate. These observations provided the basis for an anger index score.

When the euphoria or anger session was finished, the subject was given a questionnaire designed "to measure mood or emotional state" (p. 382). The two "crucial questions" were

1. "How irritated, angry or annoyed would you say you feel at present?" The five response alternatives ranged from "I don't feel at all irritated or angry" to "I feel extremely irritated and angry."

2. "How good or happy would you say you feel at present?" The five response alternatives ranged from "I don't feel at all happy or good" to "I
feel extremely happy and good."

The responses to these two questions were the basis for the self-report of mood.
An index score was created *by subtracting the subject's score on the "anger"
question from his score on the "happy" question.*

Finally, all subjects were asked two open-ended questions "on other physical
or emotional sensations they may have experienced during the experimental
session" (p. 387). In addition to the data thus far described, the physician or the
experimenter took the subject's pulse twice—just before the injection and just
after the session with the confederate.

In sum, there were two experimental inductions—*euphoria* and *anger*–and
four types of groups: E-inf, E-mis, E-ign, and Pl. Each of these was subjected to
both the anger and euphoria manipulations, except for the E-mis group, which
was omitted from the anger condition. It should be apparent from the details that
the experimental inductions were applied to one subject at a time. Each subject
received only a single induction. I believe this is an accurate summary of the
imporant procedural details of Schachter and Singer's experiment.

The results of the experiment were

1. *In the euphoria condition:* both self-report and behavioral measures appear to show that the E-inf are least euphoric, that the E-mis are most
   euphoric, and the E-ign and Pl groups are next most euphoric in that
   order.
2. *In the anger condition:* both self-report and behavioral measures appear to
   show that the E-inf are least angry, the E-ign are most angry, the Pl group
   is inbetween. All the results are given in Table 8.1 which is taken from
   Schachter and Singer's Tables 2,3,4, and 5.

There are only some slightly bothersome failures of prediction that are dealt with
quite handily by Schachter and Singer, for example, why should the E-mis show
greater euphoria than the E-ign? And why should the Pl group show more
euphoria and anger than the E-inf group?

From the point of view of specificity theory, the major implication of the
study is that E, which had previously been shown to be associated with fear and
sometimes anger, but *never* with euphoria, is apparently a physiological trigger
for virtually any emotion. This interpretation of the findings of Schachter and
Singer's results was given by Bandura (1969), Gray (1971), Frankenhaeuser
(1971b), Smith (1973), and Mazur and Robertson (1972), among others. Is it a
valid one? Before turning to this important question, it is useful to look at some
further experimental results that stem from Schachter and Singer's conclusion

TABLE 8-1   RESULTS OF SCHACHTER AND SINGER EXPERIMENT[a]

Experimental Group	Self-report Index	Activity Index
Euphoria Condition		
E–inf	0.98	12.72
E–ign	1.78	18.28
E–mis	1.90	22.56
Pl	1.61	16.00
Anger Condition		
E–inf	1.91	−0.18
E–ign	1.39	+2.28
Pl	1.63	+0.79

[a]Results shown in this table are from Tables 2, 3, 4, and 5, Schachter and Singer (1962). Copyright 1962 by the American Psychological Association. Reprinted by permission.

concerning the nonspecificity of the physiological basis of emotion, and emotional specificity provided by cognition.

In a number of studies, Valins and his colleagues (cited in Nisbett and Valins, 1971) tried to show that the importance of cognition extends not only to the external environment and the precipitating events for emotion, but also to the physiological symptoms themselves. By an ingenious method, Valins supplied experimental subjects with false data on their own physiological responses. This was done with heartbeat sounds, which are speeded up or slowed down as the experiment requires, while the subject is exposed to a particular stimulus, for example, something he fears (Valins and Ray, 1967) or pictures of nude persons (Valins, 1966). According to the reports by Valins, the subjects' "emotional" responses were strongly associated with the false physiological data; that is, their reported emotions presumably corresponded with their false cognitions rather than their true physiological state. Thus a cognitive theory of emotions is apparently supported, and a physiologically based theory is apparently nullified once again.

Valins' work has not escaped criticism. Wolpe (1973) provided a capsule summary of some of the criticism as it relates to Valins' work on densensitization, which is also based on the false cognition principle:

> Traditionalists have seized on the suggestion by Valins and Ray (1967) that the basis for desensitization may be, not emotional reconditioning, but changing the subject's

cognitions about his internal reactions to the feared object. Obviously, this will not be possible if we are correct in regarding neurotic fears as conditioned habits involving the emotional centers of the midbrain, since these would not be altered merely by changing cortical associations. Valins and Ray provided some snake phobic subjects with false heart-rate feedback while viewing slides of snakes. Because [they] . . . subsequently approached closer to a snake than a control group did, Valins and Ray concluded that cognitions about internal reactions might be responsible for successful desensitization. Their study, however, has a variety of internal weaknesses (Wolpe, 1969, 1970). Recent and better controlled replications of the study by Sushinsky and Bootzin (1970) and by Kent, Wilson, and Nelson (1972) have failed to demonstrate any significant effect of cognitive manipulation on avoidance or emotional behavior. Furthermore, a psychophysiological experiment by Gaupp, Stern, and Galbraith (1972) indicates that whenever the cognition, "That stimulus has not affected me internally," is induced in relation to the Valins and Ray snake slides, it is veridical in nature and based on actual reduced physiological responding (p. 101).

Valins' cognitive approach was also criticized by Goldstein, Fink, and Mettee (1972), who carefully replicated and extended one of Valins' experiments and showed, as did Gaupp, Stern, and Galbraith (1972), that emotions are veridical to true physiological arousal:

In an emotional situation, physiological arousal serves as much more than a cognitive cue, since, as we have shown, false cognitive cues contradicting one's state of physiological arousal are overridden in determining one's reported emotional state. In highly emotional situations, there is no physiological mimic of non-veridical cognitive cues (i.e., false heartrate feedback) and these false cues have little effect on reported emotion, but rather actual physiological arousal determines largely the level of reported emotion (p. 51).

In another study in which it was possible to test some of the nonspecificity notions implied by Schachter and Singer, Barclay (1969, 1971) found that arousal induced by the presentation of an aggressive scene did not generalize to a higher need for achievement or a higher need for affiliation, although it did elicit higher levels of sexual motive. Barclay's point was that hostility induces sexual motives, and sexual arousal induces hostility (cf. Zillman, 1971). These are specifically related according to a specific arousal theory propounded by Freud (1955) and MacLean (1965) who, according to Barclay, "indicated that this connection may be due to linked circuitry within the limbic system of the brain. His research showed that aggressive, oral, and sexual impulses may share common circuits so that the onset of one motive can energize one or both of the other two areas" (p. 483). Thus in at least two lines of work that would seem to depend on the nonspecificity conclusions of Schachter and Singer for positive findings, the opposite effects were found.

The most pressing and crucial need with regard to the Schachter and Singer results is a replication. This has not been done, to my knowledge, and the credence with which the findings have been greeted is somewhat surprising in light of the absence of confirmatory results from another experimenter *in which exactly the same findings were sought*. It is not astonishing, however, that the replication has not been done, since there has been a change in attitude toward research with human subjects since the time (about 1960) at which Schachter and Singer injected their uninformed and misinformed subjects with E, a substance that causes tremor, palpitations, and facial flush among other symptoms of sympathetic nervous system activation. Today a good deal more sensitivity to the effects of research procedures on human subjects is in evidence. It is possible that in many universities permission would not be granted easily to undertake a replication of the Schachter and Singer experiment. This is unfortunate. Notwithstanding, the major flaws of their work do not depend on a possible failure to replicate, but on a faulty interpretation of what actually was happening, to which we now turn.

REINTERPRETING SCHACHTER AND SINGER'S RESULTS

The crucial problem of interpretation in Schachter and Singer's study is their failure to conceive of the experimental subjects as having a social relationship with the experimenters and their confederates. The experimental groups do not differ merely in terms of whether they have been given E or a placebo and whether they have been given accurate or inaccurate information about their physiological symptoms; they differ also according to how much *trust* they can repose in the experimenters, how much *regard* they can feel the experimenters have for them, and how much *regard* they owe the experimenters. These are relational questions of power and status that by far supersede in importance the comparison models of frivolity or irritation presented by the confederate.

Schachter and Singer were aware of the *relational* aspects of their experimental situation, but only after the fact. Although they provided the summary data on self-reported anger in the anger manipulation, they discussed these data with this explanation:

> In the situation devised, anger, if manifested, is most likely to be directed at the experimenter and his annoyingly personal questionnaire. As we subsequently discovered, this was rather unfortunate, for the subjects, who had volunteered for the experiment for extra points on their final exam, simply refused to endanger these points by publicly blowing up, admitting their irritation to the experimenter's face or spoiling the questionnaire. Though as the reader will see, the subjects were quite willing to manifest anger when they were alone with the stooge, they hesitated to do

so on material (self-ratings of mood and questionnaire) that the experimenter might see and only after the purposes of the experiment had been revealed were many of these subjects willing to admit to the experimenter that they had been irked or irritated (p. 391).

Thus according to Schachter and Singer, the anger manipulation, with its increasingly insulting questionnaire, did produce *real* anger in the subjects, although, according to the data, *differentially*, depending on experimental group. Schachter and Singer believed the difference was due to the differential need to interpret one's physiological arousal. I believe that the difference is due to the different relationships created between the subjects in the different groups and the experimenters themselves. Real anger was directed against the experimenters because they were the authors and perpetrators of the insults and status withdrawal of the anger manipulation. (I discussed the relationship between anger and status withdrawal in preceding chapters.) Let us now look at the differentiated set of relationships that were actually present in the study.

E-inf.   Before agreeing to the injection, subjects in this experimental group were assured that the injection was "mild and harmless." After agreeing to the injection they were given an explicit description of their probable symptoms—tremors, palpitations, facial flush; they were told that the symptoms are "transitory" and *twice* that these will last but "15 or 20 minutes." While the physician was giving the injection, the E-inf subjects were again told that the injection was "mild and harmless" and given a second description of the side effects.

Let us imaginatively put ourselves in the place of subjects who have received these reassurances and information. Indeed, as Schachter and Singer claim, we would have a completely "appropriate explanation" of our bodily symptoms, but, more than that, we would feel that we were in competent hands; that when we experienced exactly what the researchers predicted, we would be certain that they knew what they were doing. Finally, competence, especially where extrapolated to the high levels manifested in scientific research—of which this experiment is an instance—deserves status accord, our voluntary compliance for the greater human good. The researchers deserve our respect. And we would give it.

In the euphoria manipulation, someone (the confederate) who obviously has little regard for either the experimenters (whom we respect) or for science (which, by virtue of the accuracy with which our symptoms have been predicted beforehand, we also respect) carries on in a frivolous fashion that is demeaning to the serious purpose of the research. Can we join him in his tomfoolery? Probably not. We have no reason to, for to do so would violate the basis of the relationship we have with the experimenter. He has shown us good faith, that is, accorded us

our full due of status; must we not do the same? Given this relational interpretation of the position of the E-inf subjects, it is not astonishing that they did not get
caught up in the frivolity. Table 8.1 shows that they are lowest in self-reported
euphoria of "emotional state in the euphoria condition."

Considering now the anger manipulation, the results show the highest satisfaction and the lowest amount of "angry" behavior for the E-inf group. In fact,
the minus sign in Table 8.1 indicates that the E-inf "have failed to catch the
stooge's mood at all" (p. 392). Here Schachter and Singer might have wondered
why not, since other experimental groups caught that mood. It does not seem
theoretically cogent to suppose that merely having an "appropriate" explanation
for one's physiological arousal prevents one from responding with anger to a
situation in which "many of these subjects [were] willing to admit to the experimenter that they had been irked or irritated" (p. 391).

Rather, is it not a more compelling explanation of this failure to become
angry that the E-inf subjects were simply prepared to go quite a length in their
trust and regard for the experimenters because they had already shown that they
deserved such trust and regard? The E-inf group could afford to sit back, await
developments, and suspend disparaging judgments, for even the insulting questionnaire must be part of some larger scientific purpose. After all, had the
experimenters any intention *really* to insult, degrade, or hurt him, they would
not have been so careful to assure him of the harmlessness of the injection and to
forecast *so accurately* what the side effects would be. Let us see how the *relational*
situation differs for the other groups.

E-ign.   Before agreeing to the injection, the E-ign were assured that it was
"mild and harmless." At the time of the injection the physician repeated that the
injection was "mild and harmless" and added that it "would have no side effects"
(p. 383). Yet in a matter of 3 to 5 minutes, the subject became "aware of
palpitations, tremors, face flushing and most of the battery of symptoms associated with a discharge of the sympathetic nervous system" (p. 381).

These are not common or ordinary bodily signs; they are experienced only
under conditions of *very strong* emotion. Let us now imagine ourselves in this
experimental group, and, after being twice assured about the harmlessness of the
injection and once informed that there were no side effects, we do experience
marked physiological changes. Would not our first thought be that the "Suproxin" *injection* had somehow not agreed with us and caused this marked reaction?
(Schachter and Singer discussed cases of what they call the "self-informed". I
treat these below.)

Indeed, the E-ign subjects at this point must have experienced a bolt of true
fear or anxiety concerning their well-being; recall that they were experiencing
very marked symptoms. Would it not be entirely natural to focus on the experimenters and at least wonder what they might have done to cause the reac-

tion? Perhaps they gave the wrong injection. (Such mistakes are known to happen even at the best hospitals.) Perhaps they should have examined us first to ascertain whether we could safely take the injection. Does not this indicate slovenliness of procedure or disregard for us? In the matter of carelessness on their part, we withdraw status from them; in the matter of disregard for us, it means they have accorded us very little status in the first place. The compelling conclusion is that the E-ign subjects had a social relationship with the experimenters quite different from that of the E-inf subjects. It was not merely that the E-ign subjects were not given an "appropriate" explanation for their physiological state. The lack of explanation significantly changes their relationship with the persons who must be considered mainly responsible for the physiological state, namely, the experimenters.

What is the relationship? First, the surprising symptoms, as they are referred back to the experimenters, suggest that we are in their power. They have done something to us that is making us feel strange. Second, they have withdrawn a considerable amount of status from us by not regarding our safety and welfare adequately, treating us like guinea pigs (?), fooling us into participating in an experiment and lying to us about the effects of the injection they gave us. This all signifies that the experimenters accord us very little status. In the face of this provocation, we quite naturally respond by becoming angry. This is real anger. It is fundamentally initiated by the failed trust between us and the experimenters, and it is aggravated by the rather insulting questionnaire we must complete.

The greater anger of the E-ign group in the anger manipulation (see Table 8.1) is much more likely due to the real anger felt against the experimenters rather than merely 'catching the mood' of the confederate when there is a cognitive deficit and, by means of social comparison, an adequate label for feelings is available. Schachter and Singer (p. 391, already quoted) acknowledged that the anger manipulation induced real anger in many subjects. Should we not suppose that the concern over the symptoms would also induce feelings of anger against the perpetrators—the self-same experimenters? If the confederate had an effect it was certainly not to suggest a label for a feeling, but to provide cues and a social sanction for expressing the real anger that was felt.

Indeed, Schachter and Singer discuss the early work of Maranon, who injected subjects with E and asked them to introspect. In most cases, the reported emotions were couched in terms of feeling "as if" the person were afraid, or happy, or sad. In a few cases, apparently real emotions were produced, but these required Maranon to speak to his "patients before the injection of their sick children or dead parents" (in Schachter and Singer, 1962, p. 381). Schachter and Singer comment: "Apparently, then, to produce a genuine emotional reaction to adrenalin (E), Maranon was forced to provide such subjects with an appropriate cognition" (p. 381).

Indeed, it is pressing the affective neutrality of the term "appropriate cognition" a little far to refer to the recall of one's sick children or dead parents as mere cognitions. Children and parents are others with whom we have affective *relationships* of the highest intensity and significance. To recall them does not merely provide cognitions for the labeling of emotions. In this regard, the emotions felt by the E-ign subjects were also real, because they were also experiencing a relationship, primarily with the experimenters. The emotion was anger, and in the anger manipulation it was further amplified by the insulting questionnaire. The expression of anger was sanctioned by the presence of the confederate who publicly displayed anger. Berkowitz (1962) has discussed at length how aggression, whose precursor is anger, is facilitated when there are anger cues present. Indeed, the behavioral indicators of anger in the experiment were aggression precisely in Berkowitz's sense.

The actions of the E-ign subjects in the so-called euphoria situation can also be understood as aggression. Indeed, they must, because the precursor relational conditions for the E-ign subjects in both the anger and euphoria manipulations were identical. How does Schachter and Singer's euphoria reflect anger in the behavior of the E-ign subjects?

First, it is well known that many forms of humor—for example, wit, irony, satire, farce, and slapstick—although accompanied by laughter and various types of gaiety, are very often hostile displays. Someone is always the butt or target of the clever remark, the broad lampoon, or the pie in the face (Freud, 1905; Bergler, 1956).

Consider the situation of the E-ign subject. He is feeling side effects from the injection and wondering about the good sense and probity of the experimenters. Not only have they failed to predict his side effects, they are slovenly in their housekeeping, which is apparent in the condition of the waiting room, for which the experimenter (somewhat lamely) apologizes. Append to this the frivolous routine performed by the confederate. The setting in which this takes place is one of the rooms devoted to psychological experiments, in this case an experiment with even stronger overtones of *science* since it supposedly deals with the effects of a vitamin on vision. This involves physiological processes which are "harder" science than psychology. In this setting the confederate begins to cavort and carry on in a manner hardly in keeping with the seriousness of both science and the nature of the experiment. To say nothing else, the actions of the confederate are bizarre. Attribution theory (Kelley, 1971) would suggest that those who act in a bizarre fashion would not be judged to have proper regard for the usual symbols of the conventional wisdom, in this case, science.

As far as the E-ign subject is concerned, the ludicrous behavior of the confederate in a setting that is serious is a way of ridiculing that setting. It is also a way of expressing anger in a highly acceptable manner, since it was virtually sanctioned by the parting remarks of the experimenter: ". . . if you need any scratch paper, or rubber bands or pencils, help yourself" (p. 384, already quoted). Furthermore, given the fact that the experimental subjects had the capacity to be angry at the experimenter (as Schachter and Singer acknowledged) but apparently did not have the courage to express that anger directly, this covert hostility in which the experimenters' pretensions are demolished and their sacred symbols demeaned is indeed a good way of getting back at them, of avenging oneself.

The data reported by Schachter and Singer are somewhat ambiguous on this point, and there is also some confounding of the anger in the relationship between the E-ign subject and the experimenters with the anger of the E-ign subject toward the confederate. The latter occurs at number 7 of the confederate's routine previously cited. For the first and only time, the confederate involves the subject directly in his antics by throwing a paper plane at him. This can be variously interpreted. If one is angry with A and B comes along and is annoying, there is evidence to suggest that the anger toward A will enhance the anger expressed toward B (Berkowitz, 1962; Konecni and Doob, 1972). When the confederate flies the plane directly at the E-ign subject, the latter is already annoyed. The response to such a provocation in the usual case would be to pick up the object and throw it back. Thus if the E-ign subject does throw the paper plane back in anger, he is releasing that anger toward the confederate and is at the same time displacing some of his anger and aggression from the experimenters (Konecni and Doob, 1972; Geen, 1968).

Yet this *angry* act will be scored as three points contributing to the activity index that indicates "euphoria." These three points are further increased by multiplying them by the "amount of time the subject spent" (p. 391) flying the plane. The exact weighting scheme involving the time component is not given in the published report. In any case, we see that the E-ign subject has no reason to engage in the so-called euphoric activities, except as they provide an opportunity to discharge hostility against either the experimenters—by virtue of demeaning their pretensions—and against the confederate—by retaliating against him for his directly annoying behavior.

If this interpretation is correct, I would expect that when the subject was asked about "how good or happy he feels" immediately after the encounter with the stooge, he would indeed "feel good." He has, after all, retrieved some of his self-esteem by discharging hostility against the experimenters and somewhat vicariously against the confederate. There is much experimental evidence to suggest that the release of aggression is satisfying and reinforcing (Berkowitz, 1962; Hokanson and Burgess, 1962a, 1962b). Thus it is highly understandable that the E-ign subject should indicate that he feels good.

However, the peculiar way in which Schachter and Singer reported their data obscures something important about *how* good the E-ign subjects felt and also, importantly, *how angry they still feel*. The self-report of euphoria score was obtained by subtracting the score on the "irritated, angry, annoyed" question from the feeling "good or happy" question. Thus the E-ign subjects could have obtained their high scores on euphoria, so-called, by having a fairly high score on anger and an even higher score on feeling good. This is a question of "elevation" of scale (Cronbach, 1955), and the data presented do not allow us to conclude anything about differential elevation. (Plutchik and Ax, 1967, also criticized Schachter and Singer on this point.) In addition, not only should there be differential euphoria among the different experimental groups, there should also be differential anger. Among the groups, the E-ign might be the highest in anger directed toward the experimenter. The E-inf group should be the highest in anger directed toward the confederate. Neither the E-mis nor the placebo groups were likely to feel as much anger toward either the experimenter or the confederate as did the E-inf and the E-ign subjects.

In sum, the E-ign subjects were injected with E and were not informed about side effects. In both the anger manipulation and the so-called euphoria manipulation they manifested apparently higher scores on anger and euphoria, respectively, than the E-inf subjects. I believe the reason is that in both manipulations the underlying emotion was true anger. It is highly likely that instead of E producing the physiological basis for the quite different emotions of anger and euphoria—which would confute a specificity theory of emotions—the injection in conjunction with the relationships with the experimenter and confederate produced a secretion of NE. NE is related to anger, as many studies have shown.

I cannot conclusively prove this interpretation on the basis of the data given by Schachter and Singer, particularly since the only physiological measure was pulse rate. However, I suggest that this interpretation is at least as plausible as the social comparison cognitive-label theory provided by Schachter and Singer. Indeed, I believe it is a more cogent theory, because it takes into account the relevant precipitating events in the social environment that bring on real emotions, not pseudoemotions that are tacked on to physiological symptoms because of an "evaluative need" for cognitive clarity.

Although my theory offers a more plausible explanation of the self-report and behavior of the E-ign and the E-inf subjects, can it handle the fact that in the so-called euphoria manipulation, the highest amount of euphoric behavior and self-report was associated with the E-mis, those who were injected with E but misinformed about the side effects?

E-mis.   The E-mis group was included in the experiment to control for the possible effect of giving information about the effect of the injection. Whereas the E-inf subjects were told precisely what to expect, the E-mis subjects were given incorrect information. Instead of tremors, palpitations, and facial flush, they were told to expect numbness, itching, and headache. By some strange quirk, the E-mis subjects reported fewer of the false symptoms in some respects than the other groups who were not told to expect them: less numbness than the E-ign or placebo groups, less itching than the E-inf, and less headache than any of the other groups (see Schachter and Singer, 1962, p. 388). So much then for the power of suggestion! Yet these curious results lead us directly into a consideration of the relational situation of the E-mis subjects.

Like the other groups, the E-mis subjects were told that the injection was "mild and harmless." Unlike the E-inf subjects, presumably the principal comparison group, they were miscued about the side effects. If the E-inf subjects were able to feel that they were in good hands, that the experimenters were treating them with some respect, and that the experimenters deserved respect in turn, the E-mis subjects were certainly different in an important way. From their point of view, the experimenters must have "goofed" in some way, or they did not take adequate precautions to screen out subjects who would have "funny," that is, unpredictable, reactions. How good, competent, or serious could those experimenters be in the first place? Was the "physician" who gave the injection really a physician? Is psychology really a "science"? Is the whole thing to be taken seriously?

The answer should be "No!" At least we must judge so from the behavior and self-report of this group. Unexpectedly, the E-mis subjects in the euphoria condition obtained the highest score on the index in which anger was subtracted from feeling good. Schachter and Singer justified this on the basis of a difference in what they called being "self-informed" (discussed later), but a clear relational explanation is available. For the E-mis subjects, the whole experiment must be something of a farce. The "doctor" did not seem to know what she was doing; the experimenters and their room were sloppy; their fellow subjects were kooky— what the hell! The whole thing was a joke. If the E-mis subjects participated in the frivolity it was for different reasons than those of the E-ign subjects. The latter were anxious and angry because the experimenters deceived them, and ridicule is a form of counterpower. The E-mis subjects, however, must not have been very angry, merely dubious about the competence of the people behind the whole setup. Since, as everyone knows, science is a serious business, when it is done with such little attention to detail as this experiment, the whole thing must not be serious. Gerard (1964, p. 44) has commented on the refractoriness of subjects in social psychological experiments. This is true even under the best conditions, but with the E-mis subjects, the lid is off, so to speak.

Unfortunately, the E-mis subjects were not included as an experimental group in the anger manipulation. I speculate that their relational situation, as described, would not have led them to manifest as much anger as the E-ign subjects, who had, of all groups, the most about which to be angry. However, the

E-mis subjects would have been more angry than the E-inf subjects, who had relatively little about which to be angry, except for the annoyance of the stooge.

Straits, Wuebben, and Majka (1972) conducted research that bears on the interpretation I offer concerning the E-mis subjects' perception of the "unscientific" aspect of Schachter and Singer's experiment. They asked college students to evaluate three descriptions of social psychological experiments according to 10 bipolar adjectives (e.g., scientific–unscientific, valuable–worthless, fun–boring, professional–unprofessional, etc.). The 10 responses were factor analyzed for each of the three experiments, and two factors emerged each time: one was defined by scales such as scientific–unscientific, real–fake, and professional–unprofessional and was labeled "value to experimenter" (p. 509). The second factor contained scales such as fun–boring, cold–warm, and pleasant–unpleasant and was labeled "value to subject" (p. 509).

The student subjects judged the "scientific value" of an experiment as significantly greater under conditions in which the experimenter's conduct was deemed to be professional as opposed to unprofessional. This is no more than we would expect. Yet it is useful to see how Straits, Wuebben, and Majka described the unprofessional experimenter:

> [He] comes in holding a cup of coffee . . . shuffles through a large pile of papers on his desk and seems to have trouble finding the right one . . . [and says] "I guess the experiment is over. I can't seem to find any more pictures" (p. 504).

This is strikingly redolent of the haphazard performance of the experimenter in the euphoria condition of the Schachter and Singer experiment: the apologetic tone, the sloppy condition of the room, and the curious and unwonted invitation to subjects to help themselves to rubber bands and pencils, which are usually among the most carefully guarded office supplies.

Straits, Wuebben, and Majka concluded their study thus:

> Within the context of an experiment, subjects are apparently willing to forego "hedonistic" considerations for "altruistic" goals such as advancing science and helping the experimenter . . . [S]uch a motivation is extremely unstable, however, as experimental events which do not fit subjects' preconceived models may relatively easily shift their motives (p. 516).

Elsewhere these authors (Straits and Wuebben, 1973) provided an even stronger and more detailed statement of the tenuous and frangible relationship between subjects and experimenters. Subjects, they said, appear to believe that:

> [E]xperimentation is scientifically worthwhile and will benefit mankind, that serving as an experimental subject is not always an interesting or pleasant experience, *that*

experimenters are persons to be respected and trusted, and that sometimes experimenters should be feared for their "psychological powers" of personality insight. If the events of an actual experiment tend to depart from the subject's preconceived model of the experiment as an "orderly" affair, various components of subjective motivation may be intensified, and the subject may exhibit unintended (from the experimenter's standpoint) behaviors (pp. 382–383, emphasis added).

Schachter and Singer, however, introduced a new consideration to explain the larger degree of euphoria of the E-mis than any other group.

We would attribute this difference to differences in the appropriateness dimension. Though, as in the E-ign condition, a subject (E-mis) is not provided with an explanation of his bodily state, it is, of course, possible that he will provide one for himself which is not derived from his interaction with the stooge. Most reasonably, he could decide for himself that he feels this way because of the injection (p. 390).

Schachter and Singer also reasoned that the E-mis subjects were less likely to hit on such an explanation than the E-ign subjects because the former had been cognitively disoriented, so to speak, by the misinformation given to them. Indeed, Schachter and Singer reported that answers to open-ended questions administered at the conclusion of the experiment suggested the correctness of this explanation, since "28% of the subjects in the E-ign condition made some connection between the injection and their bodily state compared with the 16% of subjects in the E-mis condition who did so" (p. 390). (Actually, calculations based on their Tables 6 and 7 (p. 394) in which Ns of these "self-informed" subjects are given, show the percentages of self-informed among the E-ign and E-mis to be 23% and 20%, respectively. Notwithstanding this reduction in the power of the "self-informed" explanation of the greater euphoria of the E-mis subjects, it is clear that for Schachter and Singer, *the* explanation must be a cognitive one. That is, one seeks information about and/or explanation of one's physiological state.)

It is noteworthy, however, that Schachter and Singer retreated somewhat from their earlier contention (and examples) about how the "immediate situation" (p. 381) affects the labeling of the emotion. Schachter and Singer acknowledged one departure from the effects of the immediate situation on emotion when they explained that the self-report data in the anger manipulation were essentially unusable because the subjects were angry with the experimenter— who was not present, even though his annoying questionnaire was. However, the confederate was *immediately* present, and if the subjects were *angry* it was not with him. This moderation of the principle of immediacy in the resolution of cognitive uncertainty is useful, because it permits the introduction of another principle I believe is more appropriate, namely, *relational relevance*. Regardless of the immediate situation, the conditions of the relevant relationships trigger the particular emotion. Often, other(s) in the relevant relationship are present in the immediate situation, which is why immediacy seems to be so compelling an explanation. However, immediacy obscures the more important condition of relational relevance.

I turn now to the last of the major findings in Schachter and Singer's experiment, involving the results for the E-ign and E-mis subjects who were "self-informed" about the connection between their bodily state and the injection. From open-ended questions, Schachter and Singer were able to partition their experimental groups into self-informed subjects and those who apparently were not self-informed. The results show that in the anger manipulation, the three out of 23 E-ign subjects who were "self-informed" had a *negative* anger index compared to the 20 others who had a *positive* index. In the euphoria manipulation the eight E-ign subjects who were self-informed had about half the "activity index" of the remaining 17, whereas among the E-mis, the five self-informed subjects also showed about half the activity level of the remaining 20 subjects.

Schachter and Singer reasoned that the self-informed had been provided an "alternative cognition" by virtue of the "experimental procedure of injecting the subjects" (p. 394). An alternative explanation of these results is also possible. First, in the anger condition, a negative index "indicates that the subject either disagrees with the stooge or ignores him" (p. 392). Schachter and Singer did not provide breakdowns of exactly how much subject behavior falls in the "disagree" and the "ignore" categories. I suggest that if the self-informed were affected by their "alternate cognitions," as Schachter and Singer put it, one logical concomitant of this is that they paid somewhat more attention to their internal thought and physiological processes than the non-self-informed. In a word, they *ignored* the immediate environment and were therefore less likely to be emotionally "tuned" to it. Although this does not explain all the data, because, apparently, the scoring method indicates that there was more than ignoring going on, possibly they angrily (?) asked to be left alone to concentrate on themselves and the relationship of principal relevance, namely, with the experimenter. Just how this would be scored is not indicated. Also missing is the self-report data from this condition, broken down by self-informed and non-self-informed. Although those data are compromised, as already described, they might have been of some use in further supporting or negating the alternative explanation proposed here.

In the euphoria condition, in which the E-ign and E-mis self-informed were only half as busy at frivolity as the non-self-informed, I propose a similar explanation, namely, they were too busy figuring things out, so to speak, to pay much attention to the confederate's performance, even to fly the paper plane back to him. Also missing here are the self-report data broken down according to self-informed and non-self-informed categories. There is a plausible argument to be made that the self-informed in the E-ign condition were actually more angry (at the experimenter) than those who are not self-informed. However, the published data do not permit a test of this surmise. It is puzzling to think that *any* of the subjects in either the E-ign or E-mis group should *not* have been "self-informed." In what Schachter and Singer characterize as a "fairly dramatic" situation, the sharpest image of which must be the injection itself, would not all subjects have connected their tremor, palpitations, and facial flush to the injection? Even prior to 1962 (when the experiment was published), there was general knowledge of "allergic reactions" to drugs. Surely most subjects must have made such a connection. Apparently, however, only those who *explicitly* mentioned it in response to an open-ended question were assigned to this category for purposes of internal analysis of the data. It is, in fact, consistent with the relational explanation offered here that virtually all subjects should have linked their bodily state with the injection; by that route they would be able to view the injection and its aftermath in its relational light. I seriously demur from the view that only as few as 16 out of 73 subjects (in the relevant experimental groups) were able to discern the connection.

In summary, I see the important contribution of the Schachter and Singer study to be its pronounced influence on directing attention to social factors in the determination of emotion (despite the fact that Schachter and Singer, I believe, identified the wrong factors). It is important for the development of a sociophysiology of emotions that their work does *not* show, as has often been alleged, that E is physiologically associated with such widely differing emotions as anger and euphoria. I believe a more adequate interpretation is that the E injection produced physiological side effects that, because of their being anticipated or not, reflected on the relevant relationship between the experimental subjects and the experimenters. In the case of the E-inf subjects, the experimenters deserved status, and they got it. In the case of the E-ign subjects, the experimenters deserved anger and aggression, and they got it. Finally, in the case of the E-mis subjects, the experimenters deserved low status and some contempt, and they got that too.

In a recent critique of cognitive approaches to the study of emotions that is not specifically directed toward Schachter and Singer's work, Izard (1972) soundly, I believe, pointed out the rapid change of emotions that may occur in experimental subjects:

. . . pure emotions are rare and difficult to obtain in the laboratory. If one is obtained, it is probably only a matter of seconds before that emotion elicits other emotions and interacts with cognition. Indeed, such is the nature of anxiety. The first emotion elicited in the anxiety situation may be fear, but fear may quickly elicit distress, shame, or anger . . . For example, as a subject contemplates the possibility that the experimenter is playing games with him by manipulating the painful event that may or may not happen to him, he may get angry instead of afraid, even though the coming event is presumably threating and fear producing (pp. 76–77).

This cuts very close to home, I believe, because it reflects on the emotions *elicited by Schachter and Singer* in their experiment. Plutchik and Ax (1967) also raised a question about the purity of the emotions Schachter and Singer believed they had aroused in their experimental subjects. Stein (1967) also suggested several modifications in the interpretation Schachter and Singer have given: (1) Since E has a very short half-life before it is reabsorbed, "any effects of the exogenous E may have subsided before the manipulation took place" (p. 148). This may or may not bear on the results, although Schachter and Singer initiated anger and euphoria manipulations with the subjects "within one minute" (p. 384). (2) A more important criticism by Stein (also offered by Plutchik and Ax, 1967) is that, because there was not *continuous* monitoring of a number of physiological indices, instead of only a single before–after measure of pulse rate, the experiment

> does not disprove or prove the hypothesis or assumption of an identity between a physiological and emotional state. The study showed that following an injection of E a variety of emotions can be manifested . . . The results did not demonstrate that there were or were not specific physiological or biochemical differences in the specific emotions manifested (p. 150).

Thus citations of Schachter and Singer to disprove the specificity hypothesis are unwarranted in Stein's view because of lack of evidence. Stein also entertained a possible reinterpretation of the Schachter and Singer experiment:

> For the sake of this discussion, let us say that the E in the uninformed subjects produced arousal. The arousal plus specific cognitive input resulted in a specific emotion such as anger or euphoria. The response or specific emotion could be accompanied by specific physiological or chemical processes, or the response might even function as stimuli evoking specific bodily responses. These responses, in turn, might be involved in some type of feedback mechanism concerned with the original stimulus of E arousal (p. 151).

I have suggested almost exactly what Stein proposed—naming the emotions and the social relational and physiological processes: E caused arousal; in E-ign subjects the arousal produced anxiety or fear, with, consequently, real E secreted, and anger, with NE secreted; in the E-mis subjects the arousal produced perplexity, uncertainty, and finally contempt for the experimenter. Probably no very strong emotion was induced. More likely, the SNS arousal was soon moderated by PNS arousal and the E-mis subjects proceeded to have a good time. The PNS, of course, is associated with mild satisfactions and pleasures.

Schachter and Singer should have the penultimate word:

> Obviously this study does not rule out the possibility of physiological differences among the emotional states . . . however . . . given precisely the same state of E-induced sympathetic activation, we have, by means of cognitive manipulations, been able to produce in our subjects the very disparate state of euphoria and anger (p. 397).

Of course my point is that they have not. To prove that E can produce euphoria and anger, a somewhat different experimental design is necessary. At a minimum, four *additional* experimental groups would have been required, namely, E-inf, E-ign, E-mis, and placebo, except that members of these new groups would have been left to sit alone for a period equal to the period required for the anger or euphoria manipulations. With these new experimental groups, it might be possible to sort out emotional effects due to the presence of the confederate and those due to the *relevant relationship*, namely, with the experimenter. At least, these new groups would give us a greater opportunity of investigating the effect of that relationship. It would be possible to see whether anxiety and anger are induced in the E-ign isolated subjects, as I suggest. Additional and perhaps continuous physiological measurements could also be taken in the replication, at a minimum the amount of urine or plasma E and NE, as in the experiments of Elmadjian and colleagues (1958) and Cohen and Silverman (1959).

FRANKENHAEUSER'S EXPERIMENTS

Although Schachter and Singer's experiment is widely cited by those who wish to refute specificity theory, there is an additional body of antispecificity evidence that has cumulated in several research laboratories in Sweden. The two principal investigators are Marianne Frankenhaeuser and Lennart Levi. Both have investigated the question of specificity by means of experiments in which the basic criterion variables involve the amounts of E and NE secreted under given experimental conditions. In two review articles, Frankenhaeuser (1971b, 1976) reported a number of findings by herself and other members of her research group which, she believes, negate a specificity point of view.

Frankenhaeuser and Rissler (1970) studies the effects of punishment by means of electric shock on male subjects. Both E and NE were found to increase, but when the subjects were given an opportunity to avoid the shock, "the rise in E but not in NE was contracted by [this] increased degree of situational control" (p. 382). This pattern suggests that anxious or fearful anticipation of the shock, which is a consequence of other's high power (literally) combined with one's own low power in that one cannot prevent the shock or retaliate, produced the high E secretion. Anger directed toward the experimenter, because of the delivery of the shock in the first place, produces the rise in NE. When "situational control" is obtained, E secretion and fear are reduced because other's arbitrary power has been reduced. However, even when fear has dissipated, one can and often does remain angry at the other for the pain and injury inflicted. Also, to avoid shock, the subjects had to work extra fast pressing a button. Despite this, 40% of the button presses failed to avoid shock. This is a perfect paradigm for anger and NE: being told that one can avoid a noxious stimulus if one exerts oneself, but having this expectation of safety frustrated a significant proportion of the time. Unlike Frankenhaeuser, I conclude from a relational analysis of the experimental conditions that the specificity hypothesis is supported. There was high E secretion when relational conditions promoted anxious anticipation and lower E secretion when the power imbalance was reduced. NE secretion remained high, however, because power use by other, where other is the agent, ought to induce anger (see Chapters 3 and 6). In the second part of the experiment, some insult was added to injury when the subjects discovered they had been deceived into falsely believing they could actually control the number of shocks they received.

In another experiment, the intensity of shock and E excretion correlated positively with subjective estimates of stress and skin conductance—a physiological indicator of fear—whereas the results for NE were much less regular and less marked (Ekman et al., 1964). Indeed, again, increasing intensity of a noxious stimulus ought to be correlated with increasing fear and E excretion. As for NE, the earliest shock could easily have generated the anger, and increasing shocks would have done little by way of further augmenting anger and NE. Even a small hurt can produce great anger, but a small pain is not likely to produce great fear. As the pain increases, however, the fear should increase as well, hence the positive correlation between shock intensity and subjective stress and between these two and E excretion.

The same pattern of E reduction with NE remaining elevated was found in a study by Frankenhaeuser and others (1962) in which subjects were placed under a 3-gravity load in a centrifuge. This device is used experimentally to produce stress, and Frankenhaeuser found that subjective response and E excretion showed "striking agreement," which is what we would expect if the centrifuge produces a fear reaction. At successive sessions, E levels were not as elevated and indicated a habituation to the centrifuge stress. From the work of Mason and Brady (1964) and Graham, Cohen, and Shmavonian (1967) I deduce that fear was reduced by virtue of familiarity with the stress experience. As for NE, although this also rose in the first session, it did not habituate or diminish with succeeding sessions. It may be understood as the physiological counterpart of the anger that was maintained against the experimenter.

In yet another experiment (Frankenhaeuser, 1971a) 40 subjects were subjected to "fear anticipation." E secretion was found to be three times the level of E during a period of relaxation; NE, however, was only slightly elevated. It is apparent that fear stimulated E secretion. However, NE was not secreted because there was nothing to be angry about yet. Although the anticipation of a frightening event is uncomfortable and if it goes on long enough may produce anger, it is highly likely that the short period of the experiment was simply not enough to generate anger at, for example, the inconsiderateness of the experimenters.

Under certain conditions, NE level is increased, whereas E is apparently unaffected. Patkai (1967) reported that experimental subjects were asked to work on some (insoluble) mazes. To simulate a real work setting, "an accompaniment of workshop noise was played . . . [while a 'supervisor' criticized] the subjects for being too slow . . . " (p. 50). Patkai identified four groups of subjects who differed in NE excretion levels. Increasing NE was associated positively with a mean difference in performance. Of course, by now we should not even need to mention that the criticism, if not the distracting noise, should have produced anger. Apparently the angrier subjects, if we can assume a positive relationship between NE excretions and amount of anger, were intent on refuting the criticism. They could do so most effectively by increasing performance efficiency, and so they did.

In another study Patkai (1971) compared E excretion among subjects in a variety of situations "designed to evoke pleasantness vs. unpleasantness." These included a game of chance, taking a psychological test, watching a surgical film, and engaging in neutral activity, like resting. Patkai found that the highest E excretion occurred during the game session, which was also rated the most pleasant of the four activities. Frankenhaeuser (1971b) viewed this as a distinct blow to specificity theory, for it appears that once again E has been identified with both positive and negative emotions, just as presumably found by Schachter and Singer. Frankenhaeuser also cited the results of Levi (to be discussed separately later), who found high E excretion during the showing of both a horror film and a slapstick comedy.

The fact is that games of chance are distinguished by *uncertainty*. Some degree of uncertainty is tonic and creates both challenge and interest. In a game of chance, however, the uncertainty is at a maximum. Who has not felt a faster heartbeat when drawing a card in poker or watching the steel ball bounce and listening to its click and rattle on its way to its final resting spot on the roulette wheel? These are situations frought with uncertainty and, if not anxiety, the physiological simulacrum of anxiety: the palpitations, the tremor, the facial flush. But it is, after all, only a game, therefore "fun." What if the physiological response is so intense as to leave one "rung out!" It is certainly an activity preferable to the other three alternatives in Patkai's experiment. (As for slapstick comedy in Levi's experiment, this would appear to be pure hilarity and gaiety. Yet, as we see later, comedy of all kinds depends on uncertainty, even anxiety, to be successful.)

Notwithstanding what I believe are obvious relational explanations of the results that would support specificity, Frankenhaeuser said:

> According to the so-called Funkenstein hypothesis E release would be specifically associated with anxious emotional state, while NE excretion would be associated with an aggressive emotional state. However, the empirical evidence now available shows that while E secretion is related to the intensity of emotional reactions, the quality of the emotion is determined by other inferences, such as cognitive and situational factors. In respect of NE secretion, a low positive correlation with emotional intensity is generally found, but no correlation with emotional quality (1971b, pp. 27–28).

On the contrary, I suggest that in each of the studies in which E elevation was found, the components of fear, anxiety, or uncertainty were also found. Furthermore, in each of the studies in which NE elevation was found, the relational conditions for anger were also present. This supports the so-called Funkenstein hypothesis. It is clear that one of the reasons Frankenhaeuser and her colleagues have not seen this is that they lacked a theoretical appreciation for the relational conditions of their experimental designs and how these frequently provided a matrix for anger, thus explaining the NE outcome. Since fear or anxiety can be produced outside social relational conditions (e.g., one notices a large stone rolling down a mountain toward oneself), the various experiments in which fear, anxiety, or uncertainty produced E excretion did not always show an immediate relational context (e.g., the Patkai (1971) experiment involving the game of chance). Nonetheless, the principle condition in these experiments was to produce the emotions or sentiments associated with the secretion of E.

LEVI'S EXPERIMENTS

I turn now to the last large body of recent data that attacks specificity—the studies by Levi and his colleagues. In a highly ambitious investigation, Levi (1972) recruited a group of female subjects for a four-session experiment. On four successive days the subjects saw a movie and gave before and after specimens of urine and pre- and post film self-evaluations of mood. The data were examined to see whether a particular type of film was related to a specific pattern of E, NE, or creatin* excretion, and whether these neurohumors, secreted while the sub-

*Creatin is a hormone that may be involved in emotional response.

jects were watching the films, were associated with particular moods, supposedly induced by the films. The four movies, in order of presentation, were (1) a neutral film of nature scenes, (2) "Paths of Glory" (an early Stanley Kubrick film depicting a World War I episode in which several French enlisted men are accused of cowardice, court-martialed, and shot, to cover up the bungling of a vainglorious and incompetent general), (3) "Charley's Aunt" (a comedy in which the male lead capers about in woman's garb to avoid censure for some supposed breach of family propriety) and (4) "Mask of Satan" (a horror film in which there are various gruesome killings and other scariness).

The results—involving pre- and postfilm levels of E and NE excretion and self-reported moods—appear to disconfirm the specificity hypothesis once again. At least Levi interpreted his findings this way, and Frankenhaeuser (1971b) did the same. The principal results that led to their conclusion are these: E excretion was elevated after each of the last three films, but not after the first (neutral) one. Each film that produced an increase in E presumably reflected a *different* emotion. Thus "Paths of Glory," about war and combat, was supposed to activate feelings of anger and hostility; "Charley's Aunt," about happy highjinks among nice young people, a good feeling; and "Mask of Satan," about cruel and threatening matters, a feeling of fear. According to the specificity hypothesis, E secretion ought to increase only during the fear film. Contrary to this, Levi found elevated levels of E after the anger and hilarity films as well. Thus we have another apparent case of dilution of the specificity position, on virtually the same basis as Schachter and Singer's (1962) effort.

Another of Levi's results was that, whereas Funkenstein and others found NE associated with anger and hostility, NE was not found to be particularly elevated after the showing of the putative anger film, "Paths of Glory." On the other hand, NE was significantly higher after the screening of "Mask of Satan," when it presumably should not have been. Finally, the self-reports of mood on such scales as "frightened," "uneasy," "agitated," "aggressive and angry," "despondent," "amused, happy and cheerful," "laughing," "bored," and "tired," clearly supported Levi's views about which films were supposed to induce which emotions: "Paths of Glory" produced anger; "Charley's Aunt," laughter and amusement; and "Mask of Satan," fear.

Films as Stimuli in Experiments

Before addressing the findings, I want to pose questions about the use of films in Levi's study. According to Sternbach (1966, pp. 92–93) we have no precise understanding of the stimulus properties of films in psychological experiments. It is too facile, I believe, to say that a comedy film produces only pleasant emotions, or that a tragedy produces only unpleasant ones, despite the subjects' self-reports to this effect.

A film, regardless of content, is a dramatic form, and if it is successful as an aesthetic object, it must induce at least two emotions: *anxiety* and *satisfaction*. The audience must spend most of the 90 to 120 minutes of the film suffering more or less anxiously over the outcome. The film must contain uncertainty, dramatic irony, doubt, surprise, plot twist, and the like. Otherwise it rarely gets "out of the can," so to speak. Every writer, director, and producer knows this and strives to create a sense of uncertainty in the viewer regardless of the content of the film. This is true even for comedy. In a review of the Italian film, "All Screwed Up," directed by Lina Wertmuller, *New York Times* film critic Vincent Canby (1976) wrote:

> Its a noisy, angry, relentlessly paced comedy that leaves one exhausted. Miss Wertmuller is a risk-taker, which creates a certain amount of tension in the audience. Will she or won't she pull it off? (p. 28)

Uncertainty has been found in numerous experiments to produce anxiety or fear and is accompanied by elevated levels of E (Mason and Brady, 1964; Graham, Cohen, and Shmavonian, 1967; Frankenhaeuser and Rissler, 1970). This is no less true in viewing films than in real life or psychological experiments.

However, if films induced only anxiety, there would probably be no movie industry. All drama must also resolve the uncertainty in a satisfying way. One of the oldest aesthetic theories is that tragedy succeeds when it produces catharsis, a purging of the emotions "pity and fear" which are induced by the details of the plot (Aristotle, 1947, p. 639). Catharsis is no less required in comedy, for, as discussed later in connection with "Charley's Aunt," the essence of comedy is suspense, and this must be resolved.

My second question about the film as stimulus is whether the induced anxiety and satisfaction are the same emotions for tragedies as for comedies. The three dramatic films in Levi's repertory all induce anxiety by their very natures, but is the anxiety the same in each case? Each film has also a more or less satisfying denoument and conclusion. Are the feelings of satisfaction the same? I believe the answer in both cases is yes, because the emotions induced by films, or any other artistic depiction, are not "real" in some sense. Aesthetic theorists have treated this question. Clive Bell (1949) spoke of the "aesthetic emotion" which is different in kind from other emotions and is evoked only in response to artistic representations. Suzanne Langer (1942) flatly declared that the emotions induced by art are not the genuine emotions of real life. She indicated that music, for example, carries listeners through a number of different moods as the rhythm and tempo change from movement to movement of a work. If the moods were real, could we adapt so readily and quickly? The arts seem to have precisely this capacity to induce and dispell emotions in rapid succession, because the feelings have an aesthetic, not a real, origin. Berlyne (1971) pointed to the capacity of aesthetic productions to inhibit what he called "the aversion system"; what would be very unpleasant in real life is somehow not entirely unpleasant in art. Otherwise how could we bear to witness dramas of tragedy and horror, the scenes of which we would shun in real life? We may even shriek or cry when watching drama, but ordinarily the characters whose actions evoke these expressions are themselves neither shrieking nor crying. As Berlyne (1971, p. 120) indicated, numerous aestheticians have differentiated between aesthetic responses and responses in real life by the fact that the former are merely for enjoyment, whereas the latter are for action.

My third question about the film as stimulus concerns audience identification. To the extent that an audience member can experience the emotions of the different characters, he must somehow identify with them. For the most part, we take the point of view of a single character—the hero or heroine. Here authors and directors help us out by clearly delineating heroes from villains and sympathetic from unsympathetic characters. Great artists, however, give life to even morally unfit characters; we are able to identify to some extent with them, if not as much as with our favorites.

The anxiety we feel because of the uncertainty of the outcome is different from the anxiety we may feel through identification with a character in the drama. The latter involves the character's fate, the former our own fate as viewers. That the two are different can easily be seen in the following: In the famous story by Frank Stockton, "The Lady or the Tiger," the character with whom we identify opens one of two doors and meets his fate. There the story ends, without revealing what was behind the door. Years after we have forgotten who the character was and virtually all the details of the story, the uncertainty and suspense still remain with us as *readers*. If only we could resolve that, a certain chapter could be closed. Of course, it can never be closed, and the uncertainty will remain with us for our whole lives.

Similarly, the satisfaction we feel from the aesthetic resolution of the suspense of the story line can be quite different from the satisfaction we may obtain from the resolution as it affects a character with whom we identify in the drama. The aesthetic resolution of the plays *Hamlet* or *King Lear* may be very satisfactory, even though we may be very unhappy about the fate of the prince in one and the king in the other of those dramas.

In sum, all dramatic films create anxiety through suspense, and, if successful, satisfaction. These are quite apart from the vicarious emotions that can be evoked through identification with one or more of the characters. All things considered, films are complex, multivalent stimuli. No simple relationship can be inferred between the manifest content of the film and the emotions that are physiologically alerted and cognitively denoted.

As if these considerations were not enough to raise doubts about a facile interpretation of Levi's results, I note three final points about Levi's procedures.

(1) The subjects of Levi's study were women. In Funkenstein's investigations and numerous other studies, the subjects were men. This raises the possibility that certain of the stimuli that were assumed to convey certain specific emotional connotations were interpreted differently by the female subjects from the usual interpretation given by the male subjects. This does not invalidate the emotions the women felt, but it does raise on yet another ground the question of whether it is methodologically sound to compare certain of Levi's results and the results of previous studies.

(2) The same subjects were used for each of the four films. We may wonder whether the experiment began to assume a certain "demand character" (Orne, 1962; see also Wuebben et al., 1974). Although the subjects could not directly affect their production of E or NE, they could nonetheless reflect on what mood to report in the postfilm survey. Just how much this affected some of the results cannot be determined, nor would disclaimers from the subjects themselves be adequate to retain full confidence in the self-report data. Certainly by the fourth session the pattern of the experiment must have been clear to many subjects.

(3) The self-reports of mood were collected immediately after each film ended, when the dramatic resolution of uncertainty had already occurred. Thus the data on mood are, to some extent, ambiguous. Do they reflect the emotions felt during the film, or after it? We do not know. Let us turn now to the specific findings that must be considered in the light of the specificity hypothesis.

Levi's Results

First, why do films that are presumably capable of stimulating different emotions—anger, fear, and laughter—produce increased excretion of E? Indeed, Frankenhaeuser (1971b) made much of this point in her citation of Levi to support her own argument against specificity. As I have proposed, all dramatic films contain conflict, uncertainty, and suspense, and these produce a certain level of anxiety and its concomitant physiological arousal.

Obvious suspense films like "Paths of Glory" and "Mask of Satan," in which danger and imminent death are substantial plot devices, should produce considerable anxiety. The self-report and the E-excretion data confirm this. The difficulty, however, is with "Charley's Aunt," the comedy. Why is E excretion high, when the self-report (and the experimenter's belief) is that this film gives rise to only pleasant emotion?

Laughter, of course, is not limited to situations that are pleasant. There is grim laughter, laughter at someone's expense, nervous laughter, and the like.

Laughter is also understood to be something of a relief (Hertzler, 1970); that is, the laugh occurs when something has been resolved. A case can be made that all comedy, if effective, is comprised of a rapid interplay of uncertainty and a sudden, but satisfactory, end to uncertainty. This would seem to be why jokes are "funny," why wit is effective, and why satire, farce, and slapstick "work." There is an incongruous situation that builds uncertainty, but the resolution harmonizes the conflicting, incongruous elements that have bred the uncertainty. Although the build-up to the resolution produces anxiety, the resolution itself is pleasant. For example, in "Charley's Aunt" the hero is finally able to doff his female attire, win the girl, get back into the good graces of his family, and so on. It is good comedy because, despite the suspense of its highly circuitous route, it ends as we would have liked it to end had we been there ourselves (Freud, 1905; Bergler, 1956; Berlyne, 1969; Hertzler, 1970).

Shurcliff (1968) reviewed the place of anxiety and uncertainty as a component of humor and conducted an experiment on the degree to which humor is related to the previous build-up of anxiety. He created three experimental groups. In the first (low anxiety), subjects were shown some cages with live rats and were instructed to pick up one of the rats, hold it for five seconds, and return it to its cage. In the second group (moderate anxiety) subjects were instructed to draw a drop of blood from one of the rats to stain a slide. In the third group (high anxiety) subjects were instructed to draw 2 cubic centimeters of blood from a rat by means of a syringe. The difficulties of the task were stressed for this last group. When subjects in each group started on their respective tasks, they found that the animal was a toy. This had previously been hidden from view. Immediately after the discovery, the subjects completed questionnaires concerning how funny they felt the denouement to be, how anxious they had felt prior to the discovery of the "joke," and how surprised they were by the outcome.

The results of Shurcliff's experiment strongly support the hypothesis that humor depends on the relief of previous levels of anxiety and on surprise. The findings held between groups as well as for individual, self-reported anxiety regardless of group. The point is clear. Although "Charley's Aunt" can produce a mood of amusement, happiness, and cheerfulness, *this is after the fact*. The resolution is the happy one that we would look for were we in the situation ourselves, but while we are going through the situation that is ultimately judged as humorous, it is not entirely pleasant. Where is the joke, after all, until the "punch line?" There are, of course, also the minor build-ups and discharges of uncertainty, which produce the laughs that punctuate comedy performances. However, the overall structure of the plot builds the uncertainty to a crescendo, which is finally resolved. Along the way the little uncertainties that cue laughter are part of the build-up, for the major uncertainty of the plot is in contrast to the continual little resolutions that each "funny" spot represents. E can indeed flow during films that produce laughter and are later followed by a good mood. I turn now to the results for NE.

The Funkenstein position would presumably predict the highest NE excretion for "Paths of Glory." Yet the only significant increase of NE was found for the horror film, where fear, not anger was presumably the major stimulus value of the film. On the other hand, self-reports showed a significant increase of anger after "Paths of Glory." Furthermore, this was the only film to produce such an effect. What are we to make of this apparent disjunction—if Funkenstein's version of specificity is correct—of physiology and cognition?

I propose that the discrepancy is due to the ambiguity of the film "Paths of Glory," as a stimulus object. There is plenty about the film to arouse angry feeling—the dishonesty of the officer corps, the injustice of the outcome—but this is intellectual anger, the kind we think, but do not feel. It would take a very strong identification with an angry character in the film to elicit a true feeling of anger. Even the quasi-hero, played by Kirk Douglas, who is legal counsel for the doomed men, does not engage in extremely angry outbursts. He is at least as cynical as he is indignant. I believe we are justified in concluding that physiology is more telling about emotion than is self-report in this case.

The self-reports on another emotion seem much more appropriate to the context of the film. "Paths of Glory" produced the highest mean score on "despondency" of any film, and this was even higher than the mean score for anger for this particular film. Thus if the emotions can be compared, depression exceeded anger for "Paths of Glory." Indeed, the details of the film—the slow grinding toward death for the innocent soldiers while their superiors cover up for each other—are an understandable basis for depression: the hopeless condition in which one's loss cannot be compensated, in which deprivation will occur, and one is helpless.

Physiologically depression is associated with low levels of NE in the brain (Kety, 1972). Although brain NE does not cross the brain-blood barrier and therefore does not contribute to NE found in the urine, brain NE may operate on the hypothalamus which in turn activates other SNS structures that directly trigger neurogenic NE release. The latter would show up in urine specimens. Low brain NE could therefore be associated with low NE levels in the SNS. A final point about the low NE, high despondency response to "Paths of Glory" is that this "war film" was viewed by an audience of women. This particular stimulus may not activate the same kinds of combative identifications among women as it does among men. We need only mention differential socialization in childhood, the war toys that boys enjoy from early childhood, as well as the anticipations of war service that reside in the psyches of males. Thus, although the anger the women reported was perhaps intellectual anger at injustice, it was not the anger of aggression that might have been tapped in a male audience.

There is evidence that women respond to aggression cues and stimuli differently from men. For example, Bandura, Ross and Ross (1961) found more modeling of physical aggression by boys than girls. Bond and Vinacke (1961) and Tedeschi, Lesnick, and Gahagan (1968) found that women play more cooperatively than men in the early phases of a prisoner's dilemma type game. This indication of lesser initial aggressiveness does not receive universal support (cf. Rapaport and Chamah, 1965), but indicates that there may be some differences in anger and anger release between the sexes. On a specifically physiological question relating to sex differences and aggression, Hokanson and Edelman (1966) found that female subjects reacted differently to an opportunity for catharsis than did males. After retaliating against the somewhat annoying experimenter, the males' systolic heart rate returned to normal, but the females did not. This suggests that aggression by females, or perhaps even its recognition, is inhibited by various factors, including hormonal (e.g., lower testosterone) and cultural (i.e., stronger prescriptions against aggression) factors.

The presence of high NE levels after "The Mask of Satan," a film whose content was not expected to evoke anger, is the last important divergence from the specificity hypothesis in Levi's results. Indeed, self-reports indicated very little anger, contrary to the NE data. These results are the most difficult to explain. Although several lines of speculation are available, I let the anomaly stand. (Perhaps some helpful insight might be obtained from viewing the film so that its character as stimulus could be understood better.)

My interpretation of Levi's film studies differs markedly from those of Levi and from Frankenhaeuser. I am not entirely satisfied with the reinterpretation, although it relies on what I believe is a more acceptable view than that of Levi of the dramatic film as a stimulus. One point about films is clear: they are not relational outcomes. The theory of this book attempts to explain emotions that result from interaction, not other stimuli, particularly one as complex as a dramatic film. This brings me to my final point about Levi's film studies. The psychophysiological correspondence between E fear and NE anger has been found in experiments in which the appropriate power-status relational conditions were present. There is no way at present to translate those relational conditions into movie language, although the task is inviting. This means that the Funkenstein hypothesis is not precisely addressed by experiments such as that conducted by Levi in which the appropriate relational conditions were absent. It also means that that hypothesis about specificity cannot be criticized on the basis of Levi's studies.

Some other work by Levi did include the relational format and provides a final example of the difficulties of an experimental approach to the study of emotions that is uninformed by an appreciation for the relational signficance of the experimental design. In this case the result was to overlook data that clearly support the specificity hypothesis. Carlson, Levi, and Oro (1972) examined the effects of stress on the production of E, NE, and other hormones. They designed an experiment to produce stress. As criterion measures, they asked their subjects about the "pressingness" and the "unpleasantness" of the experience. Unfortunately, these are highly undifferentiated with regard to the two important stress emotions, fear and anger, but let us evaluate the experimental situation for its relational properties:

> the task involved sorting small shiny steel balls of four very similar sizes in the presence of a loud industrial noise, variations in the intensity of a dazzling light, rush due to lack of time, and standardized criticism. The criticism was presented in writing 13 and 28 minutes after the beginning of the work period, the subjects being blamed for slowness and carelessness respectively at these times (p. 94).

It should be apparent that the experimental manipulation could have induced anger only, by means of the constant annoyances, irritations, and status withdrawals of the two critical memos. Following the specificity hypothesis, we would expect an increase in NE caused by anger. Since anger was not measured, I cannot assert positively that anger was induced, but NE excretion was significantly raised in the experimental group, just as the Funkenstein hypothesis would hold. Levi and his co-workers, however, did not cite this experiment as supporting the specificity viewpoint. Indeed they cannot, because they have no relational-emotional framework by which to see that physiological specificity in the manner proposed by Funkenstein is supported by their results.

This long excursion into a possible basis for sociophysiology is now at an end. I believe that the application of the power-status relational model and the sociological theory of emotions to the ambiguities of the specificity hypothesis helps to clarify the psychophysiological issues and makes specificity a more highly probable scientific hypothesis than it has seemed in recent years. I believe too that without the power-status relational model, the task of sorting out the evidence for and against specificity would be greatly hindered. If sociology has thus aided a faraway discipline to solve one of its problems, the debt has been repaid immediately. The E-fear and NE-anger data that are central to the psychophysiological understanding of specificity are also highly compatible with the power-status relational model and provide an unexpected source of support for it. If this mutual support can stand up to the results of the many sociophysiological experiments that must be done to test fully the implications of this insight, a very large step has been taken in the integration of disciplines devoted to the study of society and the human organism.

chapter 9

Distressful Emotions and Emotional Disorders

Of all the emotions considered to this point, the quartet of *guilt, shame, anxiety,* and *depression* are especially distressful. We all feel these emotions in the course of particular structural, anticipated, or consequent outcomes of social relationships. In moderate degrees they can even be useful. Thus an active capacity for guilt can deter us from harming others (Mower, 1966; Hoffman, 1970). If we can feel shame, we can restrain ourselves from egregious claims for esteem and thus avoid becoming contemptible to others. Anxiety, when not excessive, has a tonic effect, and the evidence shows that it helps augment certain types of performance (Hebb, 1955; Paul and Bernstein, 1973). Even depression can be useful, since it is both a necessary phase in the decathexis and termination of an old commitment (Klinger, 1975) as well as the inducing condition that energizes the search for new sources of gratification (Wolpe, 1973). In this chapter, however, I deal with the more distressful experience and expression of these emotions. These occur especially when the emotions become detached from the immediate conditions of social relationship. Instead of being relatively transient states, they endure and resist lability as relational situations change (Spielberger, 1972). In effect, this means a breakdown in the normal relationship between immediate social interaction and emotional outcomes. Thus the person becomes *characteristically* anxious, depressed, guilt ridden, or ashamed.

When these emotions develop into lasting traits, we speak of *neurotic* responses that are inappropriate to relational conditions. When guilt, shame, anxiety, or depression become very intense, there appears to be a warping of both self and interaction conduct—intrusive thoughts, hallucinations, delusions, apathy, withdrawal, extreme aggression, obsessive and compulsive noninstrumental activity, bizarre interactional behavior—that is, the whole spectrum of experience and behavior associated with emotional and mental disorder. Indeed, it is commonly known that guilt, shame, anxiety, and depression are among the most frequent emotions of persons who are experiencing emotional or mental disorder and come under psychiatric purview, whether by self-selection or through imposition by social control agents. It is natural then that we should pursue the question of how these emotions relate to standard psychiatric categories of nosology. This in turn leads to an inquiry into the etiology of the major emotional and mental disorders. I offer some hypotheses about a link between the psychiatric conditions, the distressful emotions, and certain relational antecedents that are congealed in these emotions. This leads to a final consideration: there is a large literature on the social epidemiology of mental and emotional disorders. The findings are highly suggestive about how the relational conditions of large social structures are associated with these illnesses, and I suggest how these findings can be made more serviceable by viewing them through the power-status lens. In sum, I propose to show how the distressful emotions relate to psychiatric diagnostic categories and to articulate the theoretical model of this book with major bodies of research on the etiology and epidemiology of mental and emotional disorder.

The conjunction of certain patterns of guilt, shame, anxiety, and depression in the syndromes of major psychiatric conditions encourages a far-reaching heuristic surmise: to the extent that the disorders are not organic or genetic, but have an interactional basis, the ailments that are labeled schizophrenia may be essentially disorders of *power relations,* and ailments involving mainly depression may be essentially disturbances involving *status relations.* This is not to say that power disorders and status disorders are mutually exclusive. Indeed, they readily interlace and mutually aggravate each other, since disturbance in one relational dimension often activates disturbance in the other. Nonetheless, etiologically and symptomatically it may be possible to assign a particular disturbance predominantly to the power mode or the status mode, or both, where that is the case. Indeed, therapeutic intervention may be more effective if the specific relational content underlying the disorder is known. Symptoms might best be studied as indicators of relational precursors. There has been much criticism of psychiatric diagnostic categories (e.g., Costello, 1970; Draguns and Phillips, 1971), and although numerous approaches to revision have been suggested, including the abolition of the entire category system (see Zigler and Phillips, 1961), virtually no attention has been given to a diagnostic system based on a theory of social relationships.

SCHIZOPHRENIA AND POWER

If schizophrenia results particularly from failed power relations, the existing body of research on this disorder should be interpretable in these terms. This excludes, of course, those types of illness which are clearly caused by organic deficiencies or disease (e.g., paresis resulting from syphilis). I assume that whether or not there are physical-organic determinants or genetic disposing factors in schizophrenia, there are also social and interactional conditions that can cause this illness alone (cf. Heilbrun, 1973) or in conjunction with other factors. The data of many studies are too heavily weighted toward this view to warrant its abandonment at present. I suppose also that although social intervention does act to label and perhaps exacerbate what Scheff (1966) has usefully called "residual deviance" and thereby create a full-fledged case of schizophrenia, the residual deviance itself is very frequently accompanied by psychic pain and chaotic mental and emotional processes, and these too must be explained (cf. Gove, 1970, 1975).

Schizophrenia is seen here as an unwelcome set of emotional, cognitive, and behavioral characteristics that comprise a certain type of breakdown of personal and social functioning. Despite the welter of conflicting diagnoses and the possibility that schizophrenia is a congeries of different afflictions (Al-Issa, 1970; Zigler and Phillips, 1961), I proceed on the assumption that a common pattern of relational elements, particularly involving excess power, is associated with the origin and expression of the ailment. To investigate this, I shall examine findings on schizophrenia in these areas: family factors, performance factors, social structural factors, and symptom factors. The first three are concerned with etiology; the last concerns nosology. My basic contention is that both etiological and nosological factors reflect a social relational pattern in which *power* is the fundamental relational mode and *anxiety* the chief emotion. Anxiety, as discussed in previous chapters, is the emotion that ensues from a deficit of one's own power or an excess of other's power.

Often enough, anxiety is accompanied by guilt, shame, depression, and anger. In schizophrenia some combination of these emotions is either manifest or strongly believed to be present although repressed (see American Psychiatric Association, 1968). Schizophrenia, however, is not a particular constellation of emotions, but rather a global disorganization of cognitions and behavior along with the emotions. Together these put the organism into a particular pattern of relationship with its social environment. The social environment also operates to induce the particular cognitive, emotional, and behavioral configuration. When the environment is excessive in its impress of power, the organism's response can be the disorder we call schizophrenia.

A Further Discrimination of Power.   Before examining the various family, performance, social structural, and symptom factors in schizophrenia, I want to emphasize again the bifurcated forms of power. I distinguished earlier (and in Appendix 2) between two forms of process power: the *noxious* stimulus that leads to an avoidance or escape response, and *status deprivation*, that is, the nondelivery of a gratifying stimulus that is usual, expected, desired, or needed. Status deprivation does not ordinarily lead to an escape response. Rather, depending on agency, there is either depression or anger. Although some points of contact appear between the noxious and status-deprivation forms, they are analytically and, frequently, empirically distinct in their expression and consequences. In some cases, however, one type of power blends into the other. A child who screams at a parent not only inflicts the noxious stimulus of unpleasant sound, but also indicates significant status withdrawal: respectful children do not scream at parents. In the other direction, a parent may angrily send a child from the table during a meal. This is a form of status withdrawal both symbolically and actually, by virtue of the fact that the accustomed meal is denied. The child suffers some pangs of hunger and perhaps anger, but ordinarily is not afraid. However, were the parent to withhold meal after meal, the child would have reason to fear the parent: the status deprivation would be transformed into a noxious form of power. The most important response tendency would be to escape the noxious stimulus.

My point is that the lack of the basic gratification in sufficient degree can become the basis for anxiety and fear and avoidance behavior, if that is possible. Therefore, when I speak of power in the following discussion of etiological factors in schizophrenia, I refer mainly to noxious power—either through direct infliction of immediately painful stimuli or through the accumulated effects of the loss of usual, deserved, or necessary gratifications that are initially experienced as status loss or deprivation but become noxious as the magnitude of the loss increases.

Family Factors in Schizophrenia

The major relational precursor of schizophrenia is power, whether by outright cruelty, blatant rejection, or casual indifference. According to Betz (1966), schizophrenia is an "authority problem," in which the schizophrenic feels incapable of self-direction.

> As he sees it, others hold the reins, set the rules, call the signals. Their power is exercised, not altruistically, but coercively or exploitively. . . . Others are often viewed as predators, like jungle animals actively or potentially on the prowl, and he is the prey (p. 48).

The family is the usual locus of the excess power. Dependent for survival and basic nurturance on parent figures, the person also requires that they respond to his active efforts to master the world and people in the world. If parental figures, whether directly by coercion or indirectly by rejection, thwart this effort at mastery, the person develops only a very weak sense of his or her own capacity to affect the environment, to realize his or her own will, to set his or her own goals, and to reach these goals.

One aspect of the schizophrenic patient generally agreed on is that he feels dominated by authority, especially external authority. He feels, in disagreements with his
parents that he was always defeated and was never able by use of his cognitive and
intellectual powers to win . . . He was never listened to when he attempted to present
his side of the conflict (Donnelly, 1966, p.150).

One of the frequent findings in the study of the family relations of schizophrenics
is the role of the mother as a relatively dominant, rejecting figure, exercising
power over the child through inordinate amounts of supervision and overprotec-
tion and through the maintenance of dependency long after this ought to have
terminated (Mark, 1953; Gerard and Siegel, 1950; Freeman and Grayson, 1955;
Reichard and Tillman, 1950; Cheek, 1964; Heilbrun, 1974). Fathers, in contrast, are often, although not always, found to be relatively weak, dominated by
the mother, or isolated from the family and thus playing a role that can only
slightly moderate the power of the mother (Wolman, 1965; Jacob, 1975).
Sociological theory strongly supports the view that where the father is also strong,
he can exert a moderating effect on the excessive power of the mother (Simmel,
1950; Caplow, 1968). That the mother has very great power over the child is
incontrovertible, given the usual cultural pattern of the mother as the major
source of gratification and status. This is due to the conventional division of labor
in which the mother has more to do with the nurturance functions relating to
children than does the father. Where the father is relatively weak or isolated in
the family, not only does the mother control the nurturance (status) supply, but
she also becomes the major dispenser of noxious power. In a series of experiments Henry (1956, 1957) showed that when the mother controls both status and
noxious power, children are more likely to control their own aggression, turning
anger inward, rather than expressing hostility outward toward others. Moulton,
Liberty, and Bernstein et. al (1966) also obtained this finding.

Anger turned inward may not be expressed outwardly for two important
relational reasons: either one is afraid of the power of the other and the punishment that would ensue if the anger were expressed (Berkowitz, 1962; Walster,
Berscheid, and Walster, 1973), or one anticipates guilt reactions, which are not
only painful in themselves but also may be relieved only through punishment
(Sarnoff, 1962; Galtung, 1958). Anxiety and guilt are of course the two distressful
emotions related to impaired power relations (see Chapter 3). The reader may
wish to add that anger can also be suppressed out of love for the other. Although
this appears to be true, a closer analysis suggests that the anger is suppressed out
of dependency on the other in the love relationship, which returns us to the
relational fact of the power of the other (see Chapters 12 and 13 for discussion of
this).

Although Henry's work dealt only with the problem of aggression control, we
can see that when the mother is very powerful because of the isolation or

weakness of the father, the child is reduced to a virtually complete dependence on the mother. Dependence is the obverse of power, as Thibaut and Kelley (1959), Emerson (1962), and Blau (1964) have seen, and when the dependence is accompanied by scant affection and status, the classic pattern for schizophrenia is prepared. Many studies have shown this to be the case, but a jarring note of inconsistency must also be taken into account: After reviewing the literature dealing with familial correlates of schizophrenia, Frank (1965) concluded that in many studies normal adults also reported family patterns very much like those of schizophrenics, but were nonetheless free of illness. Furthermore, the differences between normals and ill persons in these family variables were often small (even if statistically significant). Jacob's (1975) review of observational studies of interaction in families with and without schizophrenic children also showed the pattern of findings to be far less consistent concerning the mother's role than do clinical and retrospective studies of the "schizophrenogenic mother." The pertinent data still suggest, however, that fathers in normal families are more dominant than fathers in families in which there is a schizophrenic child and that the pattern is reversed for mothers. Jacob also indicated that there may be some confounding in these results with social class differences in parental dominance (p. 61). This is discussed later.

The mother's extremely high power is obviously not a sufficient condition for the development of schizophrenia. Furthermore, laboratory studies with schizophrenics are not entirely consistent in showing that, compared to normals, schizophrenics are more sensitive to "social censure" (Rodnick and Garmezy, (1957) from mother figures. Buss and Lang (1965); and Lang and Buss (1965), suggest that *any* "affective stimuli," whether related specifically to parental censure or not, are more likely to influence the schizophrenic than the normal person. In this view, the problem becomes one of cognitive and attentional disorganization and of set and perseveration, rather than disturbed emotional response to a particular constellation of parent figures. However, it must be understood that, although schizophrenics may be disabled initially by the excess power relations of parents, particularly the mother, the difficulty can easily generalize in an insidious process involving components of anxiety, incompetence, failure, and withdrawal; thus many initially unconditioned stimuli are drawn into the net of the schizophrenic's disordered view. Heilbrun (1974) referred to this as a process of "pathological circularity" (p. 151). Furthermore, the very facts of institutionalization, labeling, and the high levels of social control to which diagnosed schizophrenics are subjected constitute a special set of conditions that may affect the diffuse findings of the experimental studies (Goffman, 1961b; Scheff, 1966). The idea that disturbed power relations are causally related to schizophrenia is a heuristic hypothesis. The studies reviewed by Buss and Lang (1965) do not support the hypothesis and in part seem to negate it, but this may be due in part to factors that have intervened since the onset of the illness.

The "double-bind" hypothesis specifically offers the familial pattern as an explanation of the subsequent cognitive problem. Bateson et al. (1956) and others of this group in subsequent work (Jackson, 1967) suggested that the schizophrenic's disordered cognitions and expression are due to a particular form of "illogic" practiced by the parent—usually the mother. Specifically, the parent communicates contradictory messages to the child, for example, urging independence, but subverting it by maintaining control; declaring love for the child, but acting in a cold, punitive manner; and so on. Furthermore, the child is forbidden to comment on the discrepency between the two messages. This is the "double bind," in which each message is logically contradicted by the other, and the illogic is basic to the socialization of the child. Jacob (1975) found differences reported in the literature between communication patterns in normal families and in those with a schizophrenic child, with the latter "exhibiting less clarity and accuracy than the normal families" (p. 55).

Despite its appealing integration of many elements in the schizophrenic pattern, the double-bind hypothesis receives little support from empirical studies (see Schuham, 1967, for a review). One possible reason for this is that most investigations have focused on the cognitive aspects—the model of contradictory communication—rather than the emotional concomitants. Underlying the cognitive difficulty in resolving discrepant communications is the *emotional* response to the double-bind.

In their discussion of case material, Bateson et al. (1956) cited the large amounts of anxiety, guilt, and depression that are induced in the victims of the double-bind. Indeed, in the double-bind, in which one message is communicated verbally and the other by behavior, the problem may not be one of ambiguous communication that provides the child with a model of distorted thought and logic and later appears as a symptom. Rather, the problem may be one of emotional distortion. The contradiction between the parent's verbalizations and behavior has this effect: since the behavior is rejecting, punitive, and controlling, the child responds with anger. However, since the verbalizations are loving, the child must suppress the anger, but also feels guilt for contemplating harm to the "loving" parent. This is the emotional pressure-cooker that the double-bind heats up in the child. This is not all. Since the parent's behavior is not loving, the child suffers depression from the hunger for the support and affection that are withheld. Finally, the parent's controlling behavior is a clear demonstration of power. Thus anxiety is added. For a time, doubtless, the anger is knowingly directed toward the parent, because to the child the source of the punitive and rejecting behavior is manifestly the parent, and punitive rejecting behavior does ordinarily elicit anger when other is seen as the agent. However, with repeated avowals by the parent of his or her love for the child, the child can ultimately come to doubt the parent's culpability and agency and is forced to assume that he himself is the agent. The anger is now repressed. In its place are the introjected forms of anxiety, shame, guilt, and depression (see Chapter 3). The development of this syndrome is assisted if one parent is both the source of control and of whatever rewards are available, however niggardly their disbursement. This fixes the child's attention to that parent, interferes with the authentic expression of anger, and makes self the agent of all noxious outcomes. Since identification, involving both imitation and sex-role identity, is also induced by the single parent, the configuration is especially dangerous for boys whose mothers doubly-bind them and dominate the parental relationship (Moulton, et al., 1966; Heatherington, 1965).

Lidz and Fleck (1960) also offered a theory that directly involves high power in family relations a a causal factor in schizophrenia. Families may become "skewed," in that one parent (usually the mother) is extraordinarily dominant. This appears to be especially dangerous for sons, as discussed earlier. An alternative form of family disturbance is the "schism." There the parents are in constant battle, denigrating each other, competing for the loyalty of the children, rejecting a child when he or she shows interest in the other parent. Girls appear to be especially vulnerable to illness from this form of family disorder. In both types of family the child is reduced to extreme dependence, the obverse of power relations. In yet another approach (Wynne et al., 1958) dependence is also a prominent feature as a result of parental needs to maintain the fiction that family functioning is adequate when it is plainly not. The child is prohibited from seeking relationships outside the family that might clarify the cognitive unreality the child is forced to accept. In both the Wynne and the Lidz perspectives, emotions are distorted in the process of controlling cognitive discrepancies from reality or mastering prohibited impulses such as incestuous feelings that result from failure to attain a proper sex-role identification (Lidz and Fleck, 1960).

Thus several approaches contend that specific constellations of family relationships that emphasize high parental power (of mothers especially) are related to schizophrenia. However, parental rejection does not occur in a vacuum. There is evidence that much of it emerges in relation to the child's adaptive effort in which competence is the main criterion of evaluation. In some cases parental rejection takes the form of insufficient interest to set standards for competence. In other cases, the standards are so high that failure and rejection are inevitable. I now turn to these considerations.

Performance Factors in Schizophrenia

A common finding in schizophrenia is "performance" or "cognitive" deficit (Hunt and Cofer, 1944), that is, failure to perform at adequate levels relative to normal persons. I suggest that excess parental power mainly affects the child's sense of competence and mastery. Since competence, broadly speaking, is the main source of status (this is developed in Chapter 11), failure to attain competence also guarantees failure to attain status—in the family and outside. A lack of competence, however, earns a full measure of noxious power. Thus performance in which competence is required becomes a conditioned stimulus for high anxiety. This depresses performance, as many studies have shown (Paul and Bernstein, 1973; Shakow, 1963), and punishment for lack of competence is given once again, thus initiating a new cycle.

The competence theme is explicit in discussions of schizophrenia (Zigler and Philips, 1962; Philips, 1968; Lu, 1962; Turner, 1972; Heilbrun, 1973; McCreary, 1974). From the work of these and other investigators it is apparent that schizophrenics are more subject to conditions that lead to lower levels of competence than normal persons, *while at the same time the expectations for performance and the sanctions for incompetence remain high.* This leads to a large gap between expectations and achievement, while frequently precluding the relief of reducing one's aspirations to bring them more into line with achievement. This too is a form of "double-bind" that parental enforcement of very high performance standards helps to build in.

Lu (1962) and Stotland (1969) formulated the question more precisely as a discrepancy between general parental expectations for high performance and the failure of parents to provide specific techniques by means of which to achieve the high goals. Lu found that schizophrenics, in comparison to normal siblings, were more dependent on their parents (thus more accessible to parental power and rejection) and were given more responsibility and higher achievement standards. In many cases the illness occurred when a sudden increase in responsibility demanded a new level of performance competence that the person could not give. Lu's data were collected from schizophrenics of working-class origins. She speculated that the aspiration-achievement discrepancy may be particularly stressful for this group in that, although they are often provided with middle-class aspirations and values for achievement, independence, and responsibility, the actual socialization is for the more typical working-class pattern of obedience and dependence. Kohn (1969) has shown how the usual demands of working-class occupations—obedience and conformity—carry over into socialization goals the parents pursue with their children.

Numerous laboratory studies have shown that the threat of failure is strongly related to anxiety in schizophrenics and that trials of competence among the highly anxious, even if not schizophrenic, are especially threatening. Reviewing a long series of reaction-time studies involving schizophrenics, Shakow (1963) concluded that "when the schizophrenic is made aware of his responsibility for a situation, he does most poorly. However, when he is unaware that he is in a situation of autonomy he does surprisingly well" (p. 296). In the usual experiment, subjects could be assigned to an *autonomy* condition (in which they have the freedom to choose the preparatory interval preceding the trial and when to initiate each trial), a *control* condition (in which subjects are told the length of the preparatory interval, and trials are initiated by the experimenter), or *control-blind* condition (in which subjects are told nothing). Schizophrenics do best in, and prefer, the control-blind condition in which responsibility is minimal, whereas normals do best in, and prefer, the autonomy condition. Other results in Shakow's studies suggest that schizophrenics have a much narrower range than normals within which optimum reaction-time performance occurs. This narrowing of optimum performance range is also shown in an experiment by Ludwig and Stark (1973), who found that, compared to normals and other psychiatric patients, schizophrenics preferred a much narrower band of sensory (light and sound) experiences, reacting more sharply against both overload (noxious) and underload (deprivation) conditions.

These results suggest high levels of anxiety in response to failure. Indeed, Saltz (1970) proposed that the underlying orientation of the highly anxious is sensitivity to failure, whereas the perspective of the low anxious is sensitivity to pain. In a complex experiment by Shimunkas (1970), high and low anxious persons were given a manual dexterity task under conditions of either success or failure and of certainty or uncertainty of task. Subjects were asked to estimate their performance level on the last task in the series, after experiencing various combinations of success–failure and certainty–uncertainty. The high anxious in the failure condition expected the lowest performance level for the last task and gave especially low estimates in the high uncertainty condition. Shimunkas concluded that "anxious individuals overreact to recent experience, especially failure" (p. 40).

In childhood, failures of competence ordinarily earn parents' attention. This means that parental power is often focused on failures and that anxiety over impending power is conditioned to occasions of performance that must meet parental standards. In an extensive study of "fear of failure," Birney, Burdick, and Teevan (1969) found that this fear was associated with high levels of felt *external control* and with greater *hostile press* from the environment. Subjects with high fear of failure scores also had higher MMPI scores on the psychasthenia, depression, mania, introversion, and lie scales. These subjects just missed having statistically significant higher scores on the schizophrenia scale. Birney, Burdick, and Teevan hypothesized that an important parental influence in the development of high levels of fear of failure is the mother's role in relation to the child's performance: when the mother punishes failure to meet expectations, the child experiences high hostile press, and fear of failure becomes the dominant perspective on future performance.

High fear of failure may lead to breakdown along two different routes. In one, the fear induces great effort to avoid failure, and this, not surprisingly, can bring success (Birney, Burdick, and Teevan, 1969). However, success may be at so great a price—a form of overachievement—that any additional demand precipitates a crisis, as found by Lu (1962). On the other hand, the fear of failure may inhibit a serious effort to develop competence. This only exacerbates the hostile press.

Rodnick and Garmezy (1957) examined the causal links between maternal power and depressed competence levels in schizophrenics. In a series of laboratory studies, they found that schizophrenics' performance in various laboratory tests significantly deteriorated when stimuli signifying maternal censure were also present. Buss and Lang (1965) criticized this work on the ground that schizophrenics are generally less able than normals to persevere in the face of any obtruding stimuli. Although this is true, it does not negate the hypothesis concerning the maternal source of the anxiety that hampers performance (cf. Wagener and Hartsough, 1974).

In an ambitious and single-minded research program, Heilbrun (1973) and his colleagues pursued the evidence for the high-power mother's contribution to the development of the schizophrenic child precisely through her effect on the child's anxious orientation to performance and its deleterious effects on competence. Heilbrun conceptualized the relational position of the mother in terms of both types of power: high control (noxious) and low nurturance (status deprivation). From the results of a number of experiments, Heilbrun developed the following postulates:

1. High Control-Low Nurturance mothers inhibit the development of personal initiative and sense of competence in the child.
2. The child's inability to act independently binds him to the mother as a critical agent.
3. The child comes to anticipate critical and rejecting responses from the mother.
4. The most likely adaptive responses of the child to anticipatory failure or to actual maternal criticism are of the avoidance or withdrawal nature.
5. Avoidance may take the form of the child's avoiding commitment to a potentially evaluated act or, given commission of the act, evading the source of evaluation. Withdrawal may take the form of terminating the act once initiated or placing physical or psychological distance between himself and the evaluator during the course of the evaluative interaction.
6. In addition to anticipatory failure response and learned adaptive avoidance-withdrawal response, emotional responses such as fear, anger, shame or frustration become conditioned to cues associated with real or anticipated evaluation (pp. 98–99).

These postulates by Heilbrun summarize very well the circular pattern of the relationship between the high power parent, the failures of the child, and the further exercise of power by the parent. Central to the process is the development by the child of a very strong fear of failure, since failure is one of the most likely triggers of parental power and rejection. Heilbrun's work generally confirmed this view as well as adding a second pattern in which the child, instead of withdrawing, excessively invests himself in the actions of mother. The anxiety is expressed as over-attention and ultimately causes a breakdown by blocking adaptive competence at a later stage than among those who respond by withdrawal. The two patterns are also related to the process-reactive distinction discussed below.

The high control-low nurturance parent, mother or father, can perhaps be distinguished in all cases by the fact that he or she is virtually never pleased by what the child does. Indeed, to be pleased would mean to give status as a reward for competence. If standards and expectations are set too high, every effort is doomed to be judged a failure and therefore rejected. This pattern, as Heilbrun and Birney, Burdick, and Teevan pointed out, is likely to develop high levels of anxiety over failure and cause a reduction in performance effort. If, alternatively, parental rejection takes the form of ignoring the child's efforts, the child obtains inadequate confirmation of its capacity to deal with the environment and again enters on a course of anxiety, failure, and further rejection.

Symptom Factors: Types of Schizophrenia.   According to standard nosology (Hinsie and Campbell, 1970), there are different kinds of schizophrenia—simple, catatonic, hebephrenic, paranoid, undifferentiated, and so on. These are not mutually exclusive and are as much diagnostic as they are etiological problems. In recent years another classificatory approach has taken hold that is more analytic than diagnostic. This is the *process-reactive* distinction. The major differences are as follows. Process schizophrenia has an earlier age of onset and a poor premorbid social and sexual adjustment pattern marked by withdrawal. No identifiable precipitating event is associated with the emergence of the deviant pattern of emotions, cognitions, and behavior, and the prognosis for recovery is relatively poor. Reactive schizophrenia, on the other hand, is marked by a later age of onset and relatively good premorbid social and sexual adjustment. There is ordinarily a distinct traumatic event that precipitates the psychotic break, and the prognosis is relatively good. These two patterns were were first labeled by Kantor, Wallner, and Winder (1953) on the basis of an intensive investigation of case histories. A summary of additional criteria is given in Herron (1962). Although the process-reactive distinction has mainly a diagnostic-prognostic purpose, it can be viewed etiologically as well. If the heuristic hypothesis that schizophrenia is an illness of impaired power relations is to hold up, process and reactive types must *both* reveal this relational pattern. Heilbrun (1973) examined the question extensively and brings our attention to focus on two forms of mother dominance. Heilbrun refered to the process-reactive types as "closed" and "open-style," respectively.

The closed-style or process pattern of schizophrenic development involves a high control–low nurturance mother whose power and rejection of the child is definite and unequivocal. The child develops a protective pattern of avoidance of anxiety in the usual fashion of classical conditioning. By avoiding the mother, anxiety is kept defensively in check. Meanwhile, since the mother's dominance and rejection are clear, the child has little need to scan the environment for cues. This leads to increasing privatization and failure to seek feedback. The "pathological circularity" (p. 151) is set in motion, for incompetence leads to further maternal rejection. Emotions are repressed, and details about the self are not disclosed to the manifestly hostile mother. Striving deteriorates, since there is no hope of winning approval.

The open-style or reactive type of schizophrenia, on the other hand, is fostered by a high-control–low nurturance mother whose dominance works indirectly, through covert forms of power: manipulation, claims of martyrdom, and guilt induction. Less manifestly punitive, this type of parent constitutes a puzzle to be solved by the child. This requires a great amount of "external scanning" and processing of cues, with low tolerance of ambiguity. One way to please this mother is to conform, strive, and meet expectations.* Involvement with the environment is required for this, and competence and achievement levels are higher. Birney, Burdick, and Teevan (1969) also pointed out that one way to avoid the discomforts of a fear of failure is to strive especially hard and succeed.

In this description of mother dominance in the closed (process) and open (reactive) styles of adaptation in schizophrenia, we find that the power relationship has not changed; only the style of control changes. These power styles are correlated to some extent with social class, and with the openly dominant mothers more likely to be found in lower-class families and the covertly controlling mother more likely to be found in the middle class (B. Allinsmith, 1960; Bronfenbrenner, 1958). Myers and Roberts (1959) found this pattern among mothers of male schizophrenics. This invites us to consider the hypothesis that process and reactive types of schizophrenia are associated with lower and middle classes, respectively. I defer consideration of this question until after the presentation of some of the data and theory on social class and schizophrenia.

Social Class and Schizophrenia

The most consistent finding in the social epidemiology of schizophrenia is that the highest rates are found at the lowest social class level (Dohrenwend and Dohrenwend, 1969; Mishler and Scotch, 1963; Rushing, 1969; Levy and Row-

*Heilbrun worked almost exclusively with normal (nonschizophrenic) subjects to test his theory of "closed" and "open" style responses to a high control-low nurturance mother. He justified this on the ground that normality and illness lie on a single continuum. Whether or not this is so, the results he obtained show that closed and open styles are related to overtly and covertly dominant mothers, two types that have been previously identified among mothers of schizophrenics.

itz, 1973). Just how schizophrenia relates to the remainder of the class structure is somewhat less clear. One possibility is a linear increase from highest to lowest class levels. Another is some increase as one descends the class structure, with a significant jump in the rate at the lowest class level. This pattern is the most common (Hollingshead and Redlich, 1958; Rushing, 1969; Turner and Wagenfeld, 1967). The findings, however, have their critics. Miller and Mishler (1959) and Mishler and Scotch (1963) raised important methodological questions that make us pause before we try to derive etiological conclusions from these studies. First, the case finding procedures are not independent of social class; that is, more lower-class persons may be included in the incidence or prevalence counts, because, for example, public rather than private hospitals are used, or because at private hospitals, which are more likely to be used by middle- and upper-class persons, a diagnosis of schizophrenia may be less likely (Mishler and Scotch, 1963). Second, diagnosis and treatment type and duration (which would affect prevalence figures) may be affected by the social class of the patient. Hollingshead and Redlich (1958) acknowledged the possible bias that may be introduced when middle-class psychiatrists—who create cases by attaching diagnostic labels to persons—deal with lower-class patients. The diagnosis of schizophrenia may be a result of culture gap rather than symptom. Finally, measures of social class in the various studies are quite variable, making a valid comparison of the results of different investigations difficult (Mishler and Scotch, 1963)*. Despite these caveats, the consistency of the results is so impressive that there is the widespread assumption that schizophrenia is positively related to membership in the lowest social class.

Since the investigation by Faris and Dunham (1939), who were among the first to find an inverse relationship between schizophrenia and socioeconomic standing, the explanations have come down to two: *social causation* and *social selection*. If social causation is valid, it means that certain conditions unique to lower-class life produce more schizophrenia than in other classes. On the other hand, if social selection is operative, two alternative routes are possible by which the highest rates of schizophrenia are found in the lowest class: one involves *intra*generational, the other *inter*generational, downward mobility.

Intragenerational mobility means a change of social standing from one's own previous level. In the social selection hypothesis it means either that those of higher social class "drift" down as a result of increasingly difficult personal and occupational failures until they develop a full-blown case of schizophrenia when they reach the bottom, or that higher-class persons already suffering from schizophrenia fall to the lowest class level. In either case, intragenerational downward mobility inflates the rate of schizophrenia at the lower-class levels.

---

*See Appendix 3 for additional methodological problems in epidemiological studies of emotional disorder.

Intergenerational mobility, on the other hand, means change of social standing from the level of one's parent, usually the father. In particular, young adults from middle- and upper-class homes who are not able to match their parents' occupational achievement level (mainly for males) or who contract disadvantageous marriages (mainly for females) move down from parental level in the class structure and thereby contribute to the lower-class rates when they become ill.

If the social causation hypothesis is correct, it means that we can significantly alleviate or prevent schizophrenia by changing the conditions of lower-class life. If the social selection hypothesis is correct, something other than differential life chances in the social class structure are operating. Proponents of the drift viewpoint have contended that this implies a *genetic* factor in schizophrenia because of the likelihood of a uniform distribution of the schizophrenia genes in the population, somewhat indifferent to social class. Other explanations are also possible, as discussed later.

Dohrenwend and Dohrenwend (1969) proposed an ingenious competitive test of the social causation and social selection hypotheses. They reasoned as follows: if the social causation hypothesis is true, there should be higher rates of disorder in the lower class, because of the harsher conditions of lower-class life, and there should also be higher rates of disorder among more disadvantaged ethnic groups (e.g., Blacks and Hispanics). On the other hand, if the social selection (or genetic) hypothesis is true, abler lower-class members of *non*disadvantaged ethnic groups (e.g., Irish and Jews) will rise out of the lower class, leaving behind a more highly concentrated group of the genetically incapacitated and thus a higher rate of illness in the ethnically nondisadvantaged lower-class groups. In contradistinction, in disadvantaged ethnic groups at the lower-class level, abler members will be prevented from rising out of their class because of ethnic discrimination. Thus their presence will dilute the rate of illness in this group. Wallace (1972) in fact found this to be the case in the results of a mental health inventory in a survey conducted in Philadelphia. On the other hand, Dohrenwend (1975) reviewed evidence from two studies (Dunham, 1965 and Robins, 1966) that appear to support the social causation hypothesis.

Although the Dohrenwends' investigative strategy is highly persuasive, it addresses itself to mental illness in general, not to schizophrenia in particular. A number of studies of social mobility patterns among schizophrenics have addressed the causation-selection issue in this group more directly. The results show that very few studies support the intragenerational version of the downward drift hypothesis. A recent exception is the Levy and Rowitz (1973) analysis of Chicago ecological data for 1960–1961. They noted that

First admissions appear to be fairly randomly distributed throughout the city, crossing freely racial, ethnic, and socio-economic boundaries . . . Downward drift in the social structure after the onset of this disorder seems very likely in a competitive society . . . Data [do not support a drift hypothesis] for manic depressive psychosis, psychoneurotic, psychophysiological, personality disorders or alcoholism (pp. 60–61).

This statement stands virtually alone. Faris and Dunham (1939), Tietze, Lemkau, and Cooper (1941), Hollingshead and Redlich (1958), and Clausen and Kohn (1960), among others, refuted the intragenerational drift hypothesis.

On the other hand, there is evidence favoring the intergenerational version of the social selection hypothesis. Goldberg and Morrison (1963), Dunham (1964), and Turner and Wagenfeld (1967) took the position that the failure of children of middle-class families to duplicate the class level of their parents is responsible for swelling the lower-class rates.

In one of the more carefully controlled studies, based on a psychiatric register of all cases in an upstate New York county, Turner and Wagenfeld (1967) found some contribution from social causation in that the fathers of schizophrenics were *over*represented in the lowest class. However, this did not account fully for the very high rates of illness at the lowest class level. Further analysis showed that schizophrenics are more downwardly mobile than normals, and that the largest part of this downward mobility is accounted for by failure to attain parental levels. Thus Turner and Wagenfeld concluded that both social causation and intergenerational downward mobility best explain the overrepresentation of the lowest class in schizophrenia rates.

The Genetic Contribution.   The occasional finding of intragenerational drift downward among schizophrenics and the more common finding of intergenerational descent into the lowest class (as in Turner and Wagenfeld, 1967) encourages those who count on an important contribution from genetic factors in the explanation of schizophrenia. Mechanic (1966, 1972), among sociologists, has long held the view that the genetic evidence is compelling and that social causation is very limited. Kohn (1972a, 1972b) is another recent sociological convert to a form of the genetic hypothesis. Kohn attempted, as have others, to explain the very high rates at the lowest social class level. He posited three interacting conditions: First, lower-class children are socialized to a highly conformist view of life, and this causes them to respond in an inflexible manner to conditions of stress. Second are the conditions of lower-class life which produce more stress than do conditions at other social class levels. The conformist orientation is ineffective in handling the difficulty, and this exacerbates the stress. Neither conformist orientation nor stress would be sufficient to bring about a schizophrenic reaction without the third factor, a genetic disposition to the illness. The theory is interactive, in that all three components are necessary for the illness to strike.

Mechanic (1972), however, raised a number of questions about this argument, principally whether the conformity and stress components—which reflect the role of social environment—are worth investigating in the first place. Mechanic's point is that the genetic argument is so powerful that social causation in any respect is highly unlikely.

> To establish that a relationship exists between social class and the occurrence of schizophrenia is logically prior to developing and testing formulations as to the reasons underlying the relationship. [There are] recent and carefully executed studies that strongly suggest that the association between social status and schizophrenia is a product of social failure or limited mobility potential resulting from the disabilities associated with the condition . . . [Therefore] it is hardly clear that there is a phenomenon worthy of social explanation at all (Mechanic, 1972, pp. 305–306).

In light of this strong rejection of a social causation approach by a sociologist, who among social scientists should be perhaps most likely to pursue such explanations, it is useful to deal directly with the genetic argument and the evidence for it.

The influence of genetic factors in illness is usually studied by means of concordance rates among monozygotic twins. Since these twins have identical genetic features, a high concordance rate—that is, both twins suffer from the illness—indicates very strongly the genetic contribution. This is especially true when rates for dizygotic, or nonidentical, twins are found to be generally very low (see Gottesman and Shields, 1972).

The results of twin studies depend in part on the accuracy of the precedures that establish monozygotism. Fingerprints and blood typing are the usual methods. In recent years the accuracy of identification techniques has improved, as have the research designs and case-finding procedures. It is interesting that these improvements are associated with an important change between the levels of concordance found in earlier and more recent studies. Stabenau and Pollin (1970) and Gottesman and Shields (1972) have reviewed the studies and conducted research of their own. They found that until approximately 1961 the concordance rates ranged between 44 and 88%, whereas since then the reported concordance rates range between 6 and 50%. This is still a sizeable degree of concordance in illness rates of monozygotic twins and supports the view that there is a genetic infrastructure to the illness. The recent results also indicate that there is greater latitude than was earlier thought for environmental factors.

It is fair to conclude that even if a genetic predisposition is *necessary* it is not *sufficient* to explain any given case of disorder. If the genetic basis for the illness were sufficient, it would lead to illness in *all* monozygotic siblings if one became ill. That it does not bespeaks some other factors. Possibly the genetic factor in some way brings certain environmental factors into play. This has been considered by Stabenau and Pollin (1970), who speculated that early somatic or other physical differences between twins may dispose the mother to respond differently to the weaker or more temperamental twin; thus her treatment helps to induce the illness in that twin only, *even though both twins may be genetically suscepti-ble*. Among nontwin children, some apparent weakness or difficulty may also dispose the mother to act differently from what might otherwise be the case, again helping to precipitate the illness. Gottesman and Shields (1972), who strongly support the genetic position, also entertained this possibility. If this were indeed the case, a causal model would approximate the following: the genetic predisposition→some weakness or difficulty→differential treatment→illness. Clearly, the illness can be obviated by avoiding any link in the chain. Thus, if the genetic disposition is lacking, the illness does not occur. This is as far as those who favor the genetic hypothesis have been willing to carry the matter. Mechanic (1972), for example, offered that "there is a very great variety of situations that may trigger schizophrenic episodes among genetically vulnerable persons" (p. 308). This appears to be an invitation to abandon the search for underlying commonalities that make sense of "the great variety of situations." Although the support so far obtained from family studies is not very strong, there are sufficient differences in interaction and structure between families with an ill person and normal families to warrant further pursuit of this line of work (Mish-ler and Waxler, 1968; Jacob, 1975).

However, Mechanic (1972) depreciated efforts to identify "family factors in schizophrenia." He concluded that the research "literature provides little to build upon despite years of effort among serious and talented investigators" (p. 308). Jacobs' (1975) recent review of studies of the interaction in normal families and in families with a schizophrenic child appears at first to support Mechanic's position, for it concluded that substantive results "have been tentative at best and mixed or almost entirely nonsignificant at worst" (p. 56). Yet this is not the full assessment. Jacobs went on to point out that the studies available for comparison are very different in respect to "diagnostic status of experimental groups, mea-surement techniques used in assessment of particular domains, data analysis procedures by which results are evaluated, and demographic characteristics of family groups" (p. 57). Methodological heterogeneity is so striking, as recorded by Jacobs (pp. 57–62), that the degree of consistency actually found among these studies is itself striking. It is difficult to conclude other than that methodologi-cally sound comparative studies of family factors have yet to be conducted in large enough number to warrant Mechanic's pessimistic evaluation of the sub-stantive results of such undertakings to date.

If the genetic factor induces a change in parent behavior, as discussed, we must be aware of what aspects of that behavior act to aggravate the genetic disposition which then leads to a full-blown case of illness. This is a crucial effort in the study of schizophrenia. If the genetic and the environmental factors must operate together to produce illness, the lack of illness in those genetically disposed to it must also be due to environmental factors—that is, a set of social conditions that support, buffer, or otherwise protect against the triggering effects of environment. At least we must continue to pursue this hypothesis against the "random effects" hypothesis offered by Mechanic (1972).

I believe there is still some room for sociological and social relational explanations at precisely those points at which the genetic hypothesis would seem to enjoy its strongest support, namely, at middle- and upper-class levels. Even if some supporters of the genetic view concede that stressful social conditions may ordinarily be required to precipitate a case, their concession would seem to apply only at lower-class levels at which "bad" conditions prevail (cf. Kohn, 1972a, 1972b). Since there are indubitably cases that occur at middle and upper levels of the social structure, the question that a social causation approach (in conjunction with the genetic vulnerability contingency) must address is, are there "bad" social conditions at middle- and upper-class levels too?

From the point of view of certain objective comforts and amenities and the opportunities for experience, knowledge, and leisure, the answer must be no. However, there is one fundamental demand that confronts middle- and upper-class children, namely, to do as well as or better than their parents. The important social controls are devoted to creating the most enduring and impermeable of barriers between one's social position and lower positions. Status ascription by social class reference points has exactly this purpose and result (Kemper, 1974). Schooling—whether elite, private, or suburban—is dictated by this consideration (Mills, 1956; Baltzell, 1965; Clark, 1960; Collins, 1971). Friendships and dating patterns are guided and facilitated on these grounds (Hollingshead, 1949; Waller, 1937; Scott, 1965; Larson and Leslie, 1968). The values that parents espouse are devoted to these interests (Kohn, 1969; Hyman, 1966; Wright and Wright, 1976). In sum, the major orientation of middle- and upper-class parents is toward building in a barrier against downward mobility. The severe antagonism between middle-class parents and their radicalized or "hippie" children in the 1960s can be understood in part in the light of the break in the supposed covenant of the generations—that what ever else may change, for example, morals, tastes, or religion, at least there will be no loss of class position (Keniston, 1968; Liebert, 1971, pp. 126–127). I do not mean that the parents were simply cynical defenders of class interests. Rather, it is in the very nature of middle- and upper-class life to view it as better than anything below it and to desire that one's children not lose this grace. In addition, for upper-class groups the maintenance of power depends in part on a secure basis for succession, namely, one's children. For middle-class groups, there are both horizons of aspiration for the next generation and the need to maintain a comfortable distance from one's inferiors,

218 DISTRESSFUL EMOTIONS AND EMOTIONAL DISORDERS

lest one be mistaken for them. These are obviously not genetic factors, yet they can converge, I believe, with family dominance patterns to foster schizophrenia at the middle and upper levels. If we keep in mind that the central focus of middle- and upper-class parental exertion is to *prevent downward mobility*, we have a clue to how it can be produced.

The focal institution of American society has for long been the occupational structure, mediated by the school system (Parsons, 1954a; Blau and Duncan, 1967). Education is the best predictor of occupational prestige (Blau and Duncan, 1967; McClendon, 1976). This linked educational-occupational basis for prestige and social standing means that competence and achievement are among the most significant socialization values (Rosen, 1959; McKinley, 1964, p. 96). The middle- and upper-class parents who intend to prevent downward mobility must do so through cultivating competence and achievement interests in their children, since these are the attributes that make for a successful educational-occupational career. Yet the anxious or troubled parent may subvert these goals through setting the demands too high or too soon.

I believe that it may be possible to integrate some of the elements of the preceding discussion into a comprehensive theoretical statement on social class and schizophrenia. The elements include social conditions, performance standards, parental power, and type of illness—process or reactive.

Process Type Schizophrenia

An attractive but extremely treacherous hypothesis, methodologically, is that the good premorbid, open-style, reactive schizophrenics derive mainly from middle-class backgrounds, whereas the poor premorbid, closed-style, process schizophrenics derive mainly from lower-class families. Several studies have reported this to be the case. Allon (1971) found that when patients' socioeconomic status (measured by an index consisting of mean family income, housing expense, educational level, and occupational prestige) was dichotomized, in the upper socioeconomic status (SES) group, 63% were found in the reactive and 37% in the process category; in the lower SES group, the figures were 44% and 56% respectively. There were no social mobility differences between the groups. With race controlled, the results remained virtually unchanged for Whites, but lower SES Blacks exhibited a marked trend toward the process category. With only 7% upper SES Blacks in the sample, the results for that group cannot be interpreted. Lane (1968) also found higher "process" scores for Blacks than Whites. Since race is correlated with socioeconomic status, these two studies suggest that a "process" diagnosis is affected by SES for both Blacks and Whites, with an additional component due to race.

On the other hand, Chapman and Baxter (1963) and McCreary (1974), using scores for patients' *parents'* socioeconomic background, found the reverse of the Allon results: process types were either more likely to come from higher SES families, or there was no difference in SES background between process and reactive types.

The disparity in these results is unfortunate and not easily resolved. The problem is caused in part by the measures used to identify process and reactive types—McCreary (1974) found intercorrelations ranging from .44 to .78 between four different measures (samples sizes varied between N = 68 and N = 99). Allon (1971) used yet a fifth measure. Even if the dependent variable were measured in a uniform way, there are also differences in the way SES is measured in the various studies (cf. Mishler and Scotch, 1963). Most damaging, however, is the argument presented by Chapman and Baxter (1963), which premonitors the later statement by Dohrenwend and Dohrenwend (1969) concerning the dilution and concentration of certain subgroups in the population of the ill (see p. 213). In mitigation of their failure to find the hypothesized relationship between upper SES and the reactive category, Chapman and Baxter pointed out:

> If the hospital is one to which middle-class patients are not usually taken for their first admission, one would expect that these middle-class patients who tend to remit will already have been selected out of the middle-class sample by the time they enter the hospital. As a result, the middle-class sample which enters the hospital will be more chronic, and therefore should have a lesser likelihood of recovery, than the original middle-class group (p. 357).

I wish to offer an additional perspective on the social-class-related factors in the process and reactive types of schizophrenia. Even when social class and illness type are found to be related, the magnitude of the association is weak (e.g., Allon, 1971). Other than low reliability, this suggests that an additional factor or factors may be involved. I propose that this includes the level of *performance standards*. These can vary from too low to too high, where too high may mean too soon. That is, a standard is set before capacities have matured enough to allow success according to the standard.

Table 9.1 contains a summary view of the relationship I propose between social class, the process-reactive typology, and the level of performance standards. It can be understood as follows: Process schizophrenia is essentially a long-term problem of underachievement. In the working class, this type is fostered by "bad" social conditions and in the middle class by familial disorganization that approximates the bad conditions that are more usually the case in lower-class families or by the invocation of rigorous demands for achievement too soon.

Reactive schizophrenia, on the other hand, is essentially a problem of over-achievement. The etiological factors are approximately the same in both lower

TABLE 9-1 SOCIAL CLASS, ACHIEVEMENT STANDARDS, AND
PROCESS-REACTIVE ILLNESS: A HYPOTHESIZED RELATIONSHIP

	Working Class	Middle Class
Process-type illness (Underachievement)	standards too low	standards too high too soon
Reactive-type illness (Overachievement)	standards too high	standards too high

and middle class: An unrelenting demand for achievement that sets the standards
too high.

Working-Class Process Disorders.   From K. Marx to Sennett and Cobb
(1972), many authors have contrasted the life conditions of the lower and working classes invidiously with those of higher classes. Dohrenwend and Dohrenwend (1969) presented a list of what they call "security" stressors that might afflict
individuals regardless of class. Among these are loss of job, divorce, illness,
failure in one's job, loss of responsibility, and the like. Dohrenwend and
Dohrenwend concluded that members of the lower class are more likely to
experience these security stressors than members of higher classes. Although the
experience of stress certainly tests every person's ability to maintain psychological
equilibrium, if the stress is added to a developmental biography of shaky competence and failure, one stress event too many may indeed cause a psychotic break.
The most dangerous consequence of poor social circumstances ramifies through
the family of orientation.
    Lu (1962) found that in the low socioeconomic status families from which
her schizophrenic sample came, the parents had often experienced more financial difficulties and greater interpersonal tension at the time of birth or during the
infancy of the child who later became schizophrenic than during a similar age
period for normal siblings (cf. Stabenau and Pollin, 1970, pp. 114–116). Lower-
class cultural patterns of role differentiation between husband and wife also foster
a more isolated father and more dominant mother in the home. This is due in
part to the stronger residue of traditional role allocation, but in part to the fact
that the working-class husband is not a "success." Wife dominance, ergo mother
dominance, is negatively associated with the husband's occupational prestige and

income (Blood and Wolfe, 1960; Goode, 1964; Centers et al., 1971). Thus the classic pattern of the dominant mother is fostered by lower-class economic and cultural patterns.

In the matter of standards and expectations for attainment, there is evidence to suggest that the lower-class pattern is to have lower levels of aspiration (Hyman, 1966; Wilson, 1959; Rodman, 1963; Della Fave, 1974). There are realistic grounds for lower expectations for attainment in the working class: one simply will not have the resources to "see it through." Although these barriers can depress expectations, it is even worse when parents ignore the need for, or are incapable of, setting standards for performance. Myers and Roberts (1959) found that the working class mothers in their small sample of both schizophrenic and neurotic patients "had little time to spend with the patients [and] showed little concern for [their] personality development" (p. 270). In the schizophrenic subgroup, "patients . . . were left on their own with little concern shown by their parents" (p. 270). There appear to be developmentally appropriate stages for the acquisition of certain skills (Breckenridge and Vincent, 1966; Johnson and Medinnus, 1974, pp. 89–90.) These may be omitted or overlooked. When standards and expectations and associated training efforts are pitched too low, a discrepancy opens up between ordinary, everyday levels of social demand—in the family, in school, among peers, in the community—and the capacity to meet the demand. Failure to meet social demand, as already discussed, leads to punishment and status withdrawal. This can initiate a cycle of privatization and consequently an even lower capacity to meet demand until there is a clear pattern of idiosyncratic cognitive and behavioral activity. This would be a basis for the development of a process type of illness.

All this is more likely as a lower-class than a middle-class pattern because of lesser knowledge of child-rearing requirements (White, 1957; Bronfenbrenner, 1958; Brim, 1959), immaturity of the mother due to earlier age of marriage (Burchinal, 1959; Bumpass and Sweet, 1972), poorer health and strength to cope with children (Cole and Lejeune, 1972), the mother's absence at work without adequate surrogate care for the child (Kadushin, 1970, pp. 74–127), greater demands on the mother's time because of the more probable absence of spouse due to separation, divorce, or nonmarriage (Kephart, 1955; Cutright 1971). In effect, everything that contributes to less interaction between the mother (or an adequate surrogate) and the child in which developmentally appropriate standards and expectations and the skills to meet them can be learned contributes toward the schizophrenic outcome.

The failure to set standards and to hold the child to them would seem to lead inevitably to performance and cognitive deficit. A particular kind of cognitive disorder has been found in the process type of illness. DeWolfe (1974) distinguished between "idiosyncratic" thought in the process illness and "fragmented" thought, which he found more prevalent in the reactive type of illness. If a link also exists between the type of cognitive disorientation and social class, this would help us understand better the nature of lower-class socialization patterns and process illness. In a study devoted to the analysis of class differences in disordered speech among schizophrenics in Puerto Rico, Rogler and Hollingshead (1961) found that even where age, marital status, prior treatment history, and other types of mental illness were controlled, lower-class schizophrenics were more idiosyncratically incoherent and disordered in speech than ill members of higher classes. Rogler and Hollingshead concluded:

> Class V individuals live in dismal and wretched environments . . . Stressful problems tend to be cumulative . . . Incoherence in communication may be a social-psychological reaction to sociocultural stress. The afflicted individual moves from an unpleasant world into an unreal world of fictions (p. 188).

A final important feature of lower-class life involves the lesser use of cognitively oriented control of disobedience and undesirable behavior. Hoffman and Saltzstein (1967) have shown how such "inductions" lead to greater conscience and moral development among middle-class children. Lesser amounts of such use of reason were found in the lower-class families of their sample. Although there has been a long-standing acceptance of the conclusion of Bronfenbrenner (1958) that lower-class parents are more likely to use physical punishment, this has recently been challenged by Erlanger (1974). However, even if Erlanger's critique is correct, there may still be an accompanying pattern among lower-class families of failing to develop explanations and cause–effect relations in the general process of socialization. These would create some cognitive deficits among lower-class children that would militate against their competent performance (cf. Elder, 1963).

In sum, there are more than a few factors in the social conditions of lower-class life that militate against orderly, reasoned, cognitively enhancing patterns of mother–child relations and the patient training of the child to conform to the ordered pattern. These same factors also operate to elevate the mother to a position of control over both noxious and gratifying stimuli. This disposes toward considerable anxiety in the child, as discussed in the section on family factors. The schizophrenogenic circle is completed, I believe, if an ignorant or incapable mother uses high levels of power in relations with the child, especially in contexts relating to performance, by the infliction of noxious punishment. A possible variant pattern is simply to ignore any efforts, which leads to noxious effects through the cumulative inadequacy of status conferral.

Middle-Class Process Disorder.   In the middle class, I believe the underachievement pattern of the process disorder develops in a different way. If anything, the greater amount of time, knowledge, and interest in the details of child rearing can lead to a pattern of overdemand and the setting of standards for performance that the child cannot meet. This would follow from the social structural pressure on middle-class families to maintain their status, to ensure success, and to validate the middle-class moral investment in effort for its own sake. The middle-class ethic of effort and performance shows demonstrable results. For any family to produce less than this through its offspring is regarded as both tragic and shameful.

If the particular family structure disposes the mother toward the dominant role, for example, as a result of victory in long-term husband-wife conflict or, as is likely in the case of husband's comparatively inadequate career attainment (Blood and Wolfe, 1960)—these may dispose her toward a particularly stringent exercise of power in the parent–child relationship. This, in combination with standards that are excessively high because they are imposed too soon, may lead directly into the "closed-style" pattern described by Heilbrun (1973) and reviewed above.

Myers and Roberts (1959) found that among middle class families in their sample of patients 92% of the mothers were "rigid perfectionists," as opposed to only 17% of the mothers in the lower class, and that the middle class mothers were also more likely to emphasize "the patients' character and personality development" and were more likely to have "frustrated mobility aspirations and [be] ambitious for the patients' social advancement" (pp. 270–271). Middle-class schizophrenics in Myers and Roberts' sample were more likely to come from families that suffer from various forms of disorganization that are usually more prevalent in the lowest class. This finding is important, because it offers a heuristic basis for examining middle-class process schizophrenia in terms of family dynamics. Although various indices of family disorganization show a greater prevalence of such disorganization in the lowest class, such as divorce, separation, inadequately supervised child care, families stigmatized by parental deviance, and the like (Matza, 1966), middle-class families are not immune to these patterns. Although middle-class families have more financial and cultural resources to mitigate the effects of disruption, they cannot escape all the consequences of instability and trauma. Thus one additional source of middle-class process illness may be found in the same structural conditions that help to precipitate the illness in lower-class families.

Reactive Type Schizophrenia

The reactive type of schizophrenia in which there is good premorbid competence and performance strongly suggests a pattern of overachievement. As Birney, Burdick, and Teevan (1969) and Heilbrun (1973) found, achievement and anxiety can go very well together, along with the parental dominance that promotes the very high level of anxiety.

Working-Class Reactive Disorder.   The good premorbid adjustment is bought at a very high price. The lower-class pattern would be to set very high standards, perhaps as a conscious basis for upward mobility. Deviation from parental norms and standards for achievement are not tolerated and are set ever higher as attainment reaches the previously set goal level. Since the mother's dominance is less overt in this type, I suggest that the father plays a stronger role, too, but one that is highly power oriented relative to performance. The cumulative effect is to propel the individual into achievement beyond his capacity, but the tenuousness of the whole structure is revealed when a new heavy demand for performance finally stretches the person too thin (Lu, 1962).

Middle-Class Reactive Disorder.   In the middle class, the reactive pattern also involves overachievement, with very high standards set to guide attainment. The father probably plays an important role, overtly punitive (unlike the mother's covert control), but also low in nurturance. The parental standards may focus particularly and explicitly on the demand to do as well as or to exceed the father's own high attainment level. In the course of striving to meet the parental demands there are real attainments, but they fail to be integrated into a stable sense of a competent self. Thus there is everpresent anxiety lest one slip back to a lower level. This fuels the need to strive even harder (Myers and Roberts, pp. 148–149; Heilbrun, 1973). Among Blacks, Parker and Kleiner (1966) found "psychotics" were more subject to "goal striving stress," a function of discrepancy between aspiration and achievement as modulated by the subjective salience of success or failure. As in the lower-class case, the pressure to achieve at increasingly higher levels leads to overload and a breakdown. Significant points of overload may occur during the late phases of advanced schooling and the establishment of a stable working career. The additional stress of this period might take a significant toll among middle-class children, preventing them from attaining the class levels of their parents. This would tend to swell the ranks of lower-class schizophrenics with persons of middle-class background, as found by Turner and Wagenfeld (1967) and Goldberg and Morrison (1968).

The goal of this discussion of schizophrenia and power is to demonstrate certain elements of power relations that are implicated in the development of the disorder and its differentiation both by type (process or reactive) and social class. There is a great deal of evidence for the particularly heavy involvement of a high-power mother at the core of the schizophrenic development in both types. The mother's power style is also differentiated by social class, and this gives us a clue that the process and reactive types may also be differentiated to some extent by class. I propose, however, that an important intervening condition is the enforced level of the standard for competence and performance. The structural conditions of lower-class life enhance the likelihood of minimum standards in combination with high, overt mother power. The structural condition of middle-class life, particularly in terms of the pressure to maintain or exceed the present level, can lead to excessively high standards set too soon. A variant middle-class precipitating pattern occurs when the immediate familial situation approximates the structural conditions of lower-class life.

Where working class fathers exert very high pressure toward mobility in combination with the shared mother-father power pattern, the result can be a tenuous, fearful, overachievement effort that disintegrates when new demands cannot be met and anxiety rises to levels so high they can be relieved only by breakdown. In the middle-class version of the reactive disorders, there is a similar pattern of high demand and high parental power, which drives the individual to and fear-ridden exertions that also fracture under a heavy demand. It is not astonishing that the lower-class and middle-class conditions for the development of the reactive illness are about the same. This is because the goals of both sets of parents—achievement—are the same.

Although I have developed this model of power and schizophrenia as if illness type, mother dominance type, social class, and type of standards were dichotomous variables, this was only a convenience for the purpose of setting forth the theory. I believe these are continuous variables, and the data therefore give a less well-defined picture of the relationships I claim here.

STATUS AND DEPRESSIVE DISORDERS

Depression results from the deprivation of status, either as a loss of status previously accorded or a failure to attain status that was expected or thought to be deserved. It is a "hunger," as discussed in earlier chapters, not merely for gratification, but for *status*, that is, benefits and rewards that others give voluntarily. Since others cannot be coerced into giving status, they give it in recognition of worth and merit. When status is lost or withheld, it is not merely gratification per se that is lost, but the implication for self-worth.

Since one's developing conception of self-worth or esteem is dependent on the evaluations of others, evidence of a serious loss of such evaluation is clear grounds for a loss of one's good opinion of oneself. A common symptom in the depressive syndrome is a sense of low self-worth and low self-esteem. Thus when relational loss occurs, depression threatens. In the following I review epidemiological and cross-cultural data that provide further ground for allocating the relational root of depressive disorders to problems of inadequate or lost status.*

*Although it would be useful to review depressive disorders according to exactly the same categories I used for schizophrenia, this is precluded by different styles of research and different problem emphasis between investigators of the two disorders. Becker (1974, p. 121) acknowledged that relatively little research has been done on depression that would permit a type of analysis comparable to that of schizophrenia.

Status and Relative Deprivation.   Status loss is *relative*. This means that when status is lost, the felt intensity of the loss is relative to the relationship as it was or as we anticipated it would be. We can also feel status loss when we compare ourselves to others who have gained what was denied us. The general concept is captured in the idea of reference groups (Hyman, 1942; Merton and Kitt, 1958; Kemper, 1968) and in the notion of "distributive justice" (Homans, 1961). In Homans' theory, denial of one's due in social exchange produces anger. This is correct, I believe, in exchange relationships, since other or a third party is always the agent of the loss. However, in the broad field of human relationships that extends beyond exchange, the agent of loss—as discussed in earlier chapters—can be self. Despite our "investments" (Homans, 1961), we did not evoke status conferral or we lost it by our own fault. The result is the classic form of depression.

Social Structure and Depression.   My basic hypothesis is that differential position in the social structure poses a differential threat of deprivation or status loss relative to others who serve as a standard for comparison. I review data on depression in relation to social class, race, and sex. The next section reports cross-cultural evidence.

The data on social class show three patterns: rates of depression are (1) higher at higher social class levels (Faris and Dunham, 1939; Levy and Rowitz, 1973) or (2) about evenly distributed through the social class structure (Munro, 1966) or (3) show higher rates of depression for the lowest class, but not at the same disproportionate levels as schizophrenia (Mintz and Schwartz, 1964; Warheit et al., 1973). The depressive pattern differs, then, from the schizophrenic pattern by its greater prevalence among those of higher social position. It also occurs with considerable frequency among those at lower class levels.

I believe the general pattern can be explained thus:

(1) Depression at middle and upper levels of the class structure strikes those who have failed to keep pace with those in their comparison reference group who have succeeded. For males this usually happens in the occupational system, in which competition is intense and evaluation is frequent. At a certain point, while some members of the comparison group are still moving ahead—being promoted to higher levels, marked for new professional or community distinctions, and the like—one's own contribution is rejected or one is passed over for promotion or recognition. This process of sorting out those considered more meritorious from those considered less meritorious is the inevitable result of a vertical ranking system. When we are the ones who are sorted out from our cohort and we feel we are the agent, by virtue of our having reached the outer limit of our capability, the emotional result is depression.

An important ancillary emotion in the depression syndrome is shame, because the rejection can easily raise doubt as to whether one truly merits the status level attained until the point of rejection. A second ancillary emotion is anxiety, generated by concern for the possible loss of the status level thus far attained. Others may use their power, which we are possibly too weak to prevent, and we will be deprived of even more status. The basic relational fact, however, is a failure to move higher.

(2) I propose that at lower-class levels depression is evoked differently. Given the strong stress on achievement for all social classes, even if average levels of aspiration may be lower at the lower-class levels (Hyman, 1966; Della Fave, 1974), there are many lower-class individuals who strive upward. Indeed, there is considerable mobility (Blau and Duncan, 1967), but those who have prepared themselves for mobility through education or the cultivation of the personal traits of higher classes and who expect thereby to attain higher class status, *but do not*, are subjected to the loss of anticipated status, which produces depression.

At the higher-class levels, the comparison group for the depressed is *those who have succeeded*. One has not kept pace with them. I propose that at the lower-class levels, the comparison group for the depressed are *those who have not prepared themselves to succeed*. Even though one is more deserving, one does not outpace them. The result is depression.

I am supposing two general principles for the selection of comparison reference groups (Kemper, 1968a) in suggesting that middle class depressives compare themselves with those in their class who continue to succeed, whereas lower class depressives compare themselves with others in the lower class, not in the middle class. The first principle is that comparisons are made with those in one's own social class. This should be so because one has more knowledge and occasion to be aware of relevant conditions at one's own level. Thus, lower class depressives compare themselves with others in the lower class, not in the middle class.

A second general principle is that one selects the majority of one's group for purposes of invidious comparison. The comparison group in the middle class, where most are assumed to be rising or doing well, must be those who are succeeding. In the lower class, where most are assumed not to be rising or doing well, the comparison group must be those who are not succeeding. Comparison with the majority in each case facilitates the self-agency attribution that is necessary for the classic depression syndrome. If middle class depressives compared themselves with other members of the middle class who were not succeeding, this would provide no basis for the invidious comparison that leads to depression. If lower class depressives compared themselves with the relatively few lower-class successes, I believe this would lead to the attribution of other as agent, and the depression would be expressed as anger and hostility at unjust deprivation (see Chapter 3). On the other hand, if the comparison is with the relatively many who do not succeed, I believe a self-agency attribution for failure to succeed would be more likely. That is one is likely to assume common causes for common outcomes: They didn't succeed, nor did I. Though I am better prepared than they are, there must still be something wrong with me. For both upper- and lower-class depressives, the malady results from a failure of *upward* mobility, a failure to earn more status. This is in sharp contrast to the schizophrenic pattern, which can be understood as a malady of failure premised on *downward* mobility, actual or anticipated.

This view of depression is compatible with data that show that the incidence of depression among Blacks in the United States is lower than for Whites. There are fewer middle- and upper-class Blacks, proportionately; therefore they do not count heavily among those who fail to show continued upward mobility at that level. At the lower levels of the social structure, racism and the visible barrier of color have kept many blacks from seriously aspiring much beyond their fellows. In this way they do not court failure. Thus depression rates among Blacks should be low. In fact, McCarthy and Yancey (1971) argued that it is mistaken to assume that Blacks have lower self-esteem or self-worth than Whites, because Blacks do not use Whites as their "significant other" or comparison group. When Blacks fail to attain upward mobility, they may blame "the system" rather than themselves. McCarthy and Yancey cited Cloward and Ohlin (1960) on this point:

[The] individual who locates the source of his failure in his own inadequacy . . . feels pressure to change himself rather than the system. Suffering from loss of self-esteem, he must either develop mechanisms which protect him from these feelings of personal inadequacy or work toward eliminating them by developing greater personal competence. By implication, then, attributing failure to one's own faults reveals an attitude supporting the legitimacy of the existing norms (p. 112).

Thus, although discrimination exposes Blacks disproportionately to the condition of social power deficit, which engenders schizophrenic disorder, it also serves to protect Blacks from depressive disorders.

Yet Blacks do suffer from depressive disorders and increasingly so. The most recent studies, in contrast to past reports, suggest a rise in depression rates among Blacks so that they equal those of Whites (Warheit et al., 1975; Simon et al., 1973) or are higher than those of Whites (Tonks, Paykel and Klerman, 1970). A part of this increase may be attributed to better enumeration of Blacks in psychiatric censuses (Warheit et al., 1975). At least one other factor that explains increasing rates of depression among Blacks is the rise in Black expectations over the past two decades. Although relative shares of income of Blacks and Whites have converged somewhat during the period (Matras, 1975, pp. 25–27), this must be viewed in the light of a very striking increase in Black expectations for status and benefits (National Advisory Commission on Civil Disorders, 1968, pp. 226–227). This, I believe, would lead more Blacks to higher levels of education and expectation for more lucrative and prestigious involvement in the conventional occupational structure. Since actual mobility has been much slower than the rise in expectations, there is a correspondingly stronger likelihood of depressive outcomes among those who have prepared themselves for mobility but have not achieved it.

Depression in the classic sense requires that self be viewed as the agent of the status deprivation. Some light is shed on this by Heiss and Owens (1972), who examined the McCarthy and Yancy (1971) hypothesis for two different types of traits: *local-role* characteristics, such as being an adequate parent, child, spouse, conversationalist, and the like, and *instrumental* traits such as IQ, trustworthiness, mechanical ability, and the like. Heiss and Owens found that, whereas Black self-esteem was as high as Whites' on the first set of traits, it was lower for the second set. This exhibits the high degree of concern of Blacks with dimensions that are salient for occupational success. Where residual discrimination, as reflected in hiring patterns, promotions, and so on, sets back the ambitions and hopes of Blacks who have prepared themselves to move upward, residual sentiments of instrumental deficit can promote the self-as-agent judgment and consequently, depression, as well as the anger noted by McCarthy and Yancy (1971).

A similar pattern can be noted among women, who, like Blacks, have reached for full equality in recent years. Since the feminist movement has struggled somewhat longer than the Black movement to attain its goals, we could expect that the effect on emotional disorder would have been felt sooner. Gove and Tudor (1973) pointed out that prior to World War I, males exceeded females in rates of major psychoses. Since then, however, females have exceeded males. Dohrenwend and Dohrenwend (1976) demur on methodological grounds from Gove and Tudor's conclusion concerning overall rates of disorder, but agree that women are more likely to manifest depression. Depression rates for Blacks have begun to approximate those of Whites only much more recently, indicating the lag relative to women in large-scale Black mobility efforts, the frustration of which has sharpened the sense of relative deprivation and has increased depression. In regard to depression or its cognates, Yancy et al. (1972) found that, although females in their sample registered higher self-esteem scores than males, they also had lower Midtown scores. The Midtown scale measures general psychological well-being (Langer, 1962; Seiler, 1973). Uhlenhuth and Paykel (1973) and Warheit et al. (1973) found women more depressed than men in separate samples. These data fit the basic pattern of inadequate status relative to institutionalized expectations concerning what is appropriate and due. In traditional societies woman's role was clearly defined, and few women ventured into nontraditional paths. Furthermore, and crucially, there was very little expectation that other roles and increased status were possible. As soon as aspirations increased, however, without the corresponding increase in opportunity, the stage was set for an increase in depression among women.

The data on depression among women and Blacks support a general hypothesis that any underclass is vulnerable to depression as soon as institutionalized expectations for mobility increase but relatively few members of the underclass succeed. Where the discrepancy between aspirations and attainment is explained as a result of the power discrepancy between the underclass and its overclass, anger in the form of rebelliousness and hostility rather than classic depression are the more likely outcomes (see Chapter 3). Weber (1946, p. 184) has cited this "transparency" of the connection between the power relationship and the deprivation as one of the necessary conditions for class action. Except where such ideologies are clearly and explicitly disseminated, rebelliousness and hostility are not the usual route of the emotions when expectations for success are not satisfied in a situation of presumably open opportunity. The depressive response is probably heightened in transition periods, when opportunities are expanding, but not rapidly enough to provide mobility for all. Durkheim (1897) saw such periods as leading to heightened vulnerability to suicide, an extreme solution in depressive disorders.

Linsky (1969) tested the hypothesis that a discrepancy between *aspiration* and *opportunity* is positively associated with depression. He examined rates of depressive disorders in relation to occupational opportunity in 27 communities in the state of Washington. The results show a higher incidence of this illness in communities in which opportunities for upward mobility were relatively limited, given the educational level of residents.

CROSS-CULTURAL STUDIES OF EMOTIONAL DISORDER

The many studies of emotional disorder in other cultures can also give us a perspective on the hypothesis that power and status defects are related to schizophrenia and depression, respectively. Until relatively recently, there was a broadly shared consensus that, by and large, the depressive disorders were relatively rare in non-Western societies (e.g., Al-Issa, 1970; Opler, 1956; Tooth, 1950). Opler suggested that this is due in part to the lesser role of individualism and free will in such societies, leading individuals to associate disappointment or inadequate status with their group rather than themselves. In support of this view, Arieti (1959) and Becker, Spielberger, and Parker (1962) found that rates of depression are lower in "other-directed" societies or in transition to "other-direction." In the well-known typology of "tradition-oriented," "inner-directed," and "other-directed" societies (Riesman, Glazer, and Denny, 1953), personal responsibility for achievement is highest in the inner-directed type, and, consequently, failure to attain the levels that one's internalized standards demand would be most likely to produce depression. In both tradition-oriented and other-directed societies, the individual is less personally accountable: in the former a fixed social code is followed, and in the latter one tunes in to the changing requirements set by the social environment. In both cases, self-agency is considerably less than in the inner-directed period. Rawnsley (1968) also referred to differences in "self-accountability" as a way of distinguishing between societies with higher and lower rates of depressive disorders.

The absence of strongly institutionalized conceptions of self-agency in traditional societies removes one vital element in the conditions that lead to depression. The other element is actual status loss or deprivation. In traditional societies, the major benefits of status are obtained through ascription. This is fixed and supported by custom and can neither be denied nor lost. Achievable elements of status, such as wealth, prestige, or authority, are simply not available in sufficiently abundant supply to make them worth aspiring to. Such wealth as there is is limited to very few persons, and it is not realistic to seek it. A wide distribution of prestige and authority depends also on a highly differentiated and professionalized labor force—precisely what is lacking in such societies. Since the opportunity structure is so limited, aspirations are circumscribed. Thus there is very little chance of discrepancy between the two, compared to more developed societies. Indeed, traditional Indian society has translated necessity in this regard into religious conviction. Lest one aspire to the unattainable, the classic Hindu religion teaches that the external world is *maya* or illusion, thus not worth striving for.

Although ascription is a guarantee of status that cannot be lost, the status of most members of traditional society is very low. Yet power differences, including those based on status, can be very great (Kemper, 1974). Disorders of power, however, lead to schizophrenia rather than depression. Connor (1970) provided some evidence for this. He suggested that schizophrenic-like disorders such as *latah*, *susto*, *inu*, and *amok*, occur in those societies in which social roles and status are more often ascribed than achieved. In such societies, a threat to the self and to one's identity would be of greater consequence than in more complex societies in which an individual has a multiplicity of roles to enact. Ascriptive societies are also much more likely than Western societies to suffer from real and imagined arbitrary power and social control that is divorced from a rational basis (Lenski, 1966; Weber, 1947). Furthermore, the determination of social position and social reward on grounds other than merit, that is, according to ascriptive reference points, is a masked form of power that benefits those who are ascribed high positions and deprives those ascribed low positions (Kemper, 1974). Thus schizophrenia is a more likely disorder than depression in ascriptive societies.

Ordinarily the high social cohesion of traditional societies is beneficial for the avoidance of depression. Wechsler (1961) pointed out that communities in which there is rapid population growth, that is, in which cohesion is breaking down, also have higher rates of depressive disorder. Both elements in the etiology of depression—self-agency and status loss—operate in such situations of change. Cohesive societies are usually based on ascription, and thus status is assured. When the population grows rapidly, especially by immigration, the original residents lose their homogeneous basis of status conferral, and the newcomers must also cope with an environment that is alien to their own language of status. Ordinarily, too, the break up of cohesive communities in today's world results from the introduction of modern ideas (Inkeles and Smith, 1974). One of the most important features of this development is an orientation toward achievement by one's own efforts—in a word, self-agency.

The loss of cohesion in traditional societies also upsets some conditions that mitigate losses when they occur. Stainbrook (1954) suggested that, in traditional communities, the extended family structure provides emotional support in times of crisis. Somewhat related is Tooth's (1950) view that institutionalized rituals for mediating grief (often involving the kinship structure) are more elaborate in non-Western than Western societies, thus operating to cushion potential depression when it stems from the loss of close family members.

On the other hand, some traditional communities manifest high rates of depressive disorder. Eaton and Weil (1955) found this among the Hutterites and explained it psychoanalytically, suggesting that in very highly cohesive communities hostility must be turned inward. This traditional Freudian explanation is also supported by Chance (1964) and Cohen (1961). By and large, however, the Hutterite findings are contrary to the pattern of most other studies of traditional communities, and this suggests that a special factor may be operating. One possibility is that the Hutterites are specifically a religious community in which the principal obligation is to attain individual perfection. However laudable the goal, it presents great difficulties if taken seriously, for one is privy to one's own less than perfect thoughts and desires, and it will seem that one is very far away indeed from the goal—regardless of what may appear to external view. Thus shame and guilt are ever present possibilities, along with the sense of one's own unworthiness and the hopelessness of attaining the religious aim. Looking at one's neighbors, however, may only exacerbate this sense of personal unworthiness, for all one can see is what they appear to be—upright, God-fearing, and succeeding in reaching the common goal. Who can look into their hearts? Furthermore, given the nature of the goal—perfection—who can know when he has attained it? There is no signpost to announce that one has been judged worthy. Weber (1958) proposed that the uncertainty of salvation that afflicted the early Calvinists produced great psychological strain and tension. A similar tension of uncertainty may afflict those who aspire limitlessly high and can never attain their goals no matter how high they climb (cf. Durkheim, 1897). Data on depression in other communal groups would be useful here. Solidarity and cohesion based on grounds other than the common striving for perfection probably would not produce rates of depression as high as those found among the Hutterites. Kramer (1957) suggested yet another possibility to explain Eaton and Weil's data, namely, that the Hutterite community has a high proportion of older persons, among whom there is generally a higher incidence of depression.

Another finding of high depression in a traditional society is also instructive. Although depression in most African societies is low, Savage and Prince (1967) reported that depression is a noticeable phenomenon among the Yoruba, thus appearing to contradict the general pattern of data. They reported, however, that depression afflicts three groups primarily: barren women, menopausal women, and students attending the Western-oriented university. Indeed, these results support only more strongly the position on depression taken here. First, the major form of status acquisition and recognition for women in Yoruba society is to bear children. A barren woman, therefore, is unable to fulfill her traditional role and thus does not gain the status that is the common lot of her peers. Second, menopausal women, whose previous status depended on child bearing, are now biologically obsolete and no longer qualify for status. Third, the students at the Western-oriented university are being socialized to a set of aspirations for which the opportunity structure simply does not exist in their society. More narrowly, however, the rigorous demand for performance at the university introduces the competitive standards and comparison-group striving that can easily lead those who sense they cannot compete to suffer their loss as depression. Indeed, the Yoruba study offers strong confirmation of the part played by disordered status relations in the genesis of depression.

Before introducing the data of a final study, I consider some rhetorical objections to the position I take on the relative paucity of depression in traditional societies. Weinberg (1965), for example, attributed the low rates of depression to prejudice among Western psychiatrists who believe that depression is rare among Blacks, the technologically underdeveloped, and those of low socioeconomic status; to the erroneous application of European and Western diagnostic categories to different cultures; and to the lesser likelihood of hospitalization, ergo less likelihood of inclusion in the illness rates, among the more traditional peoples. These arguments are considered in reverse order.

First, if traditional peoples are less likely to use hospitals for relief of any ailment, it must be explained why they do so for schizophrenic disorders, for which rates are relatively high. If, on the other hand, depressions are simply not so intense as to require hospitalization, the original case, which Weinberg attacked is in fact proved. Second, if Western diagnostic categories are inappropriate for traditional peoples, this means very simply that the signs, symptoms, and syndrome of depression—apathy, despair, and the like—do not exist among traditional people, in which case the original argument is again proved. The findings of Murphy, Wittkower, and Chance (1970) bear on this question and are discussed later. Finally, there is no special reason for Western psychiatrists to believe a priori that depression is rare in traditional societies.

Fabrega (1974), Waxler (1974), and Kiev (1972) also doubted the conclusion that depression is less likely in primitive societies. Fabrega proposed that since higher rates of depression in such societies have been found since 1957 (Prince, 1968), it is possible that the earlier low rates were due to poor data collection. Indeed, if poor data collection were at issue, it must be asked why this did not affect the rates of schizophrenia, which is the main form of emotional disorder. Fabrega also suggested that traditional societies may have culturally different methods for treating the depressed. This would be useful to know, since the efficacy of such methods would prevent the cases from reaching the intensity that requires hospitalization. On the other hand, it is puzzling why these same cultures are not equally efficacious with schizophrenic disorders. Granting Fabrega's point for argument's sake, it may also be conjectured whether the solutions, if they exist, are not successful because they are dealing with less intense types of depression. If this is the case we must ask why depression in traditional society is less intense than in modern society. Indeed, it could be because of stronger cohesion that cushions the disappointments of life, or it could be because the aspiration-opportunity gap does not open as wide in traditional societies. In either case, this would explain *actual* low rates of depression, just as the earlier diagnostic reports have shown. If the incidence of depression in traditional societies has increased since 1957, I believe this can be explained by the fact that these societies virtually everywhere have set themselves on the road to modernity, with all its blessings and shortcomings. Among the latter are the elements that create personal despair for many. As Durkheim (1933) pointed out, civilization does not make us all happier. Suicide rates increase.

Finally, Fabrega, and Waxler (1974) cited the well-known matter of differential diagnosis by psychiatrists as evidence of the high unreliability of diagnostic procedures. Fleiss et al. (1973), in an important series of studies that compared the work of United States and British psychiatrists, found that the British psychiatrists were more likely to diagnose depression than their American counterparts (see Appendix 3). Fabrega and Waxler wondered whether this was not a function of the psychiatrists rather than the patients, again raising the question of how differential rates of depression are a function of diagnosis rather than social relations.

If the data on differential rates of depressive disorder in Britain and the United States can be taken at face value, several implications are possible. One of these, drawn by Fabrega and by Waxler, is to cast doubt on diagnostic reliability and validity. This is so notable a problem that I do not intend to defend psychiatry in this respect except to say that, although diagnostic agreement rates may not be very high (Draguns and Phillips, 1971), they are not random. More important, however, is a second possible explanation of the differential British and American depression rates, namely, that despite the common language and other shared elements of culture heritage, Britain and the United States are different societies with different social structures. The latter determines both aspirations and the opportunity structure, and, as we have seen, these elements enter markedly into the likelihood of depression.

Runciman (1966) dealt with some structural issues in British society that may help us resolve the discrepancy. He suggested that social structure can be understood in terms of the three stratificational dimensions of class, status, and power, approximately following Weber (1946). These can be understood from a personal ("egoistic") or social class ("fraternalistic") perspective. Runciman said that the sense of relative deprivation in the areas of class (economic benefits) and power (national legislative and governmental policy control) has been much reduced in the period since World War I, because of considerable strength of British unions and the Labor Party. On the other hand, the sense of personal deprivation of status (recognition of one's social worth, in Runciman's terms) continues to be high. Here indeed is a ground for high rates of depression as caused by inadequate status.

Murphy, Wittkower, and Chance (1970) provide us with a final perspective on the cross-cultural diagnosis of depression. To determine whether there is a common syndrome of depression across cultural boundaries, they surveyed psychiatrists in 30 countries. They inquired about the prevalence of 27 symptoms that are included in classic descriptions of depressive disorders. Their conclusion, based on psychiatrists' reports (not patient counts), was as follows:

The basic symptoms of the particular depressive syndrome studies must therefore be taken as depressive mood, fatigue, insomnia and loss of interest in the social environment, with diurnal mood swings as a probable fifth. Weight loss, despondency and diminution of sexual interest may prove to be primary symptoms also, but a decision on this must await their investigation in the particular cultures mentioned. All of the remaining symptoms enquired about vary so much from one reported sample to another that they cannot be considered to be essential features of psychotic depression as it was conceived for this survey, though they may be essential features of some secondary cluster or syndrome. This conclusion is not all original, being similar to those arrived at in many earlier clinical studies. Its discovery here, however, may add weight to the argument that any search for the origin of depression should focus on these basic features and not on the more dramatic features of self-accusation, hypochondria, preoccupation with poverty, etc. Investigation of the latter symptoms can be valuable in elucidating the secondary processes in depression, but insofar as psychotic depression can frequently occur without these symptoms, they cannot be assumed to be part of the primary process (pp. 480–481).

Murphy et al. indicated that the failure to find certain of the secondary symptoms in some societies may explain "why to some observers it has appeared that true depression was virtually not present at all" (p. 479). However, they also conclude that, although there is a basic depressive syndrome, "this is not to say that it occurs with equal frequency in all cultures, and there are indications that it may be relatively rare in some (p. 492).

I have sought in this chapter to interpret schizophrenia as a disorder of power relations and depression as a disorder of status relations. Even if the basic premise is true, there is a considerable gap between the etiological processes and the symptomatic reality of either disorder and its cure once it is present. Here the general theoretical notions articulating social relations and illness may not seem to be of much assistance. In slight mitigation of this impression, I cite what has been named, after its discoverer, the "Fairbairn shift." Fairbairn (1952) reported that when a schizophrenic patient's ego begins to reintegrate, the patient also manifests serious symptoms of depression. This, in some sense, is unaccountable, for it seems merely the exchange of one set of symptoms for another. Yet from the point of view of the relational theory propounded here, the shift means that the patient has turned his attention *from problems of power to problems of status, from the problem of how to avoid destruction to the problem of how to acquire gratification.*

Indeed, in the usual hospital setting, with its minimal opportunity to obtain status, it is no wonder that the patient who awakes from the anxiety that has centered on survival becomes depressed. To become depressed is to get better, because problems of power and security are more fundamental than problems of status and satisfaction (Maslow, 1954, pp. 80–92). If the power disorder cannot be resolved, there is no point in seeking status.

The Fairbairn shift is confirmed in a recent experiment that appears to be independent of Fairbairn's work. Donlon and Blacker (1971) reported that when schizophrenic patients were removed from drug therapy, those whose condition deteriorated did so in four stages: (1) denial and anxiety, including a felt loss of control, (2) depression and intensification of defenses, (3) panic and horror and the appearance of primitive fantasies and images, and (4) psychotic disorganization and relief from subjective pain. The most crucial finding for our purposes was that when drugs were readministered, the patients who had passed through these four stages went through *the same four stages in reverse order* as they reintegrated. Depression meant improvement, as Fairbairn proposed (see also Ricks and Berry, 1970).

chapter 10

Parameters of Punishment and the Distressful Emotions

In the preceding chapter I proposed that certain configurations of power and status relations underlie the major psychiatric disorders. The affective key is the set of distressful emotions: guilt, shame, anxiety, and depression. Here I examine more closely how individuals acquire the distressful emotions as characteristic responses. I believe that guilt, shame, anxiety, and depression are acquired as a result of particular patterns of punishment in the socialization process. I see the development of these emotions in terms of several considerations. First, what type of punishment is used? Second, is the punishment proportional to the transgression, or is it excessive according to the understanding of the child. Third, what is the structure of the relationship between the parent and the child within which the punishment pattern occurs? I present a relatively simple model involving binary branching to account for the distressful emotions. Branching each of the three considerations produces $2^3 = 8$ outcomes. These eight correspond to the first eight emotional and coping responses discussed in Chapter 3, that is, the responses to excess or deficit of own power or status, with either self or other as the agent.

TYPE OF PUNISHMENT

Researchers have sought for some time to develop an adequate typology of punishment. W. Allinsmith (1960) proposed the distinction between "corporal" (spanking, whipping, slapping, and beating) and "psychological" (shaming, appeals to pride and guilt, and expressions of disappointment) punishments. Whiting and Child (1953) offered "love-oriented techniques" (rewarding by praise, punishing by isolation, or withdrawal of love) and other techniques (including physical punishment). Sears, Maccoby, and Levin (1957) also discriminated between "love-oriented techniques" and a variety of "object-oriented techniques" (including physical punishment, tangible rewards and incentives, and deprivation of privileges). Aronfreed (1961) introduced further variations in his distinction between "sensitization") including physical punishment as well as

237

verbal assaults such as yelling, shouting, and bawling out) and "induction" (i.e., asking the child why he behaved as he did, insisting that he correct the damage, and giving the child an opportunity to display moral initiative). Hoffman (1960) discriminated between "unqualified power assertion" (e.g., peremptorily ordering the child to obey without explanation), "qualified power assertion" (offering justification or legitimation for the order, or offering compensation or a quid pro quo for compliance), "persuasion" (which enlists the child's conscience or self-esteem or interests in desire for physical comfort), and finally, "suggestion" (which Hoffman did not further elaborate). In later work, Hoffman and Saltz-stein (1967) divided punishment into "physical," "love-withdrawal," and "induction" (which involves indicating that the child's behavior has hurt the parent or some other person). Other versions of punishment typologies have been developed in laboratory studies including "aversive" (e.g., ringing a high-decibel buzzer), love withdrawal (e.g., omitting approving remarks), withdrawal of material goods (e.g., taking away candy previously given), and reasoning (e.g., explaining why a particular behavior must be avoided). Although there is no dearth of typologies, the results obtained from their use are inconsistent (cf. Hoffman, 1963), and it is clear that we still lack a theoretically adequate taxonomy of punishment.

In a rare empirical effort to sort out some of the issues, Roberts and Cooper (1967) factor analyzed a set of scores reporting mothers' and fathers' use of 15 disciplinary practices. These included tangible rewards, praise, negative criticism, indicating good models, indicating bad models, physical punishment, deprivation of privileges, physical isolation, withdrawal of love, ridicule, reasoning, scolding, lecturing, nagging, impulsive action, threats, and follow-through on threats. The results suggest that parental discipline is more complex than the typologies that have been offered to explain it. For example, physical punishment and withdrawal of love are positively correlated with the same factor for girls, but not boys. This negates in part the distinction between the two that has been suggested by many investigators (W. Allinsmith, 1960; Whiting and Child, 1953; Sears, Maccoby, and Levin, 1957; Hoffman and Saltzstein, 1967). Further, Roberts and Cooper found that praise and withdrawal of love load the same bipolar factor with *opposite* signs, negating another frequently espoused notion, namely, that love-oriented techniques, including praise and withdrawal of love, are positively correlated. Withdrawal of love also loads the same factor as tangible rewards, ridicule, scolding, and threats of punishment—another pairing of love-oriented techniques with other types that violates some classic notions (e.g., Sears, Maccoby, and Levin, 1957; Aronfreed, 1961).

Indeed, Roberts and Cooper's factors are encouraging to theoretical interests only in regard to reasoning. This disciplinary behavior loads the opposite end of a bipolar factor from tangible rewards, negative criticism, indicating bad models, withdrawal of love, ridicule, scolding, impulsive actions, and threats of punishment. By and large this is the division between "induction" and "sensitization" suggested by Aronfreed (1961), but is even closer to the distinction made by Hoffman and Saltzstein (1967) between "induction" and "withdrawal of love."

Despite departures from ideal-typical models of parental punishment, the results of Roberts and Cooper do not actually undermine the theoretical cogency of any of the existing typologies. These will stand or fall according to whether they adequately identify factors in parent punishment behavior that are causal as far as relevant dependent variables are concerned. Thus if the love-oriented versus corporal punishment classification successfully predicts outcomes, it is a useful distinction. The contribution of Roberts and Cooper is that parents apparently have not taken the theoretical distinctions into account as much as the theorists have. Few parents apparently punish according to a theoretically pure mode of punishment, and, on reflection, it is difficult to see how they could. For example, withdrawal of love is usually preceded by anger. Yet expressions of anger also accompany physical punishment, deprivation of privileges, scolding, and numerous other punishment practices, with the *possible* exception of reasoning (W. Becker, 1964; Berkowitz, 1962).

Simply examining the *mode* of punishment either assumes or ignores many punishment parameters, including intensity, duration, frequency, timing, consistency, and overlapping of punishments (e.g., hitting may always be accompanied by shouting), and the relationship of any given punishment to the "normative punishments used in the subculture" (Feshbach, 1970, p. 228), among others (Church, 1963). The most prevalent assumption is perhaps that physical punishment is more painful than "psychological" punishment. Aronfreed (1969), however, argued that "reasoning" can be more painful than physical punishment because, although the latter usually terminates the consequences of the transgression, reasoning requires that some uncertain form of behavior change must take place before the positive relationship with the parent can be reinstated (cf. D. Miller, 1962; Hill, 1960). The anxiety developed by psychological punishments can be very intense and therefore highly aversive, whereas physical punishment may be more acceptable in the same situation. There is even a question as to whether physical punishment, when it is effective, derives its potency because of the physical pain it causes. Walters and Parke (1967) suggested that physical punishment may work because "it is perceived by the child as signifying a threat of withdrawal of affection" (p. 181). The views of Aronfreed and Walters and Parke caution against a facile acceptance of the surface features of punishment as indicative of the basis of their effectiveness. The punishment situation is very complex, and punishment can even *enhance* the production of the responses it is designed to suppress (Bandura, 1962; Church, 1963).

I now wish to propose a formulation of punishment which, like Aronfreed's and Walters and Parke's, obliterates some conventional distinctions between manifest categories. The fundamental consideration is that punishment is *relational* behavior. It is a power act in either the noxious or status-withdrawal mode. Furthermore, it ordinarily follows or is an acknowledged response to a stimulus act by the child. The child's act may have been a power act in its own right, or it may have been a failed technical response (an error) that may have had relational implications for either the parent or a third party. Both the parent's power act (the punishment) and the child's initial transgression have a certain intensity (or, in the case of an error, had a certain degree of manifest consequence). On the basis of these interactional conditions of the punishment situation, I wish to draw two important distinctions.

The first distinction is whether the punishment—regardless of manifest type—provides primarily an experience of hurt and pain and thereby locates it for the child in the dimension of (parental) power, or, alternatively, has the principal effect of raising for the child the question of his or her deservingness or worthiness of rewards and gratifications—in effect locating the biting edge of the punishment in the dimension of the child's own status. The second distinction concerns how the child understands the ratio between the magnitude of the punishment and the magnitude of the transgression or error; that is, regardless of type, to what extent does the punishment fit the crime? I propose that these two considerations may be sufficient to explain the differential evocation of guilt, shame, anxiety, and depression. A further relational distinction discussed later should determine whether the emotions are introjected or extrojected.

POWER PUNISHMENT AND STATUS PUNISHMENT

It may appear that the distinction between punishments that are directly felt as the expression of the power of the parent and those that only raise questions of status is merely one of intensity. The difference is more fundamental, and the intensity question is better handled, I believe, in evaluating whether the punishment is in excess or in proportion to the transgression. This is discussed in the next section.

I propose that *any* punishment, running the gamut from physical to reasoning, can be viewed from either the power or the status perspective. A power punishment causes pain directly to the recipient (or anticipation of pain very broadly understood), whereas a status punishment, although painful, more pointedly raises questions of competence and deservingness of status. This distinction is important because it provides a basic relational context for the meaning of the punishment and thus a cue and a commentary to the child concerning the relationship between the precipitating act and the punishment. In this sense, the punishment conveys *information* in a situation sharply reduced in information potential (Parke, 1969). I propose that if the punishment is primarily felt as power, it provides the child with the basis for an inference that his or her own previous behavior was itself a power act hurtful to another and is being treated as such. It is in effect a lesson in one of the most primitive theories of punishment, namely, *lex talionis:* You are done to as you have done to others. By inducing pain, the punishment can evoke the child's concern with the harmful effects of the trespass or the amount of damage done.

On the other hand, if the punishment activates the status mode, the amount of hurt or damage previously done is less important than what the trespass says about the child's own worthiness. By punishing the child in such a way as to raise the question of worthiness, the parent turns the child's view inward to his or her own capabilities, both present and prospective. The status type of punishment is not without distress or discomfort, but it touches a different motive—the hope for reward instead of the fear of pain.

The distinction between hope for reward and fear of pain (or failure) has been made in the achievement literature (Atkinson, 1964; Birney, Burdick, and Teevan, 1969). Piaget (1932) elaborated the distinction between concern for the damage done ("moral realism") and concern for intention ("moral independence"). Kohn (1969) also touched on parental concern in different social classes with damage done (in the working class) as opposed to loss of self-control (in the middle class). Some consequences of this are discussed later.

Now the task is to sort out those punishments which convey the noxious-power message and those which convey the status-adequacy message. Prima facie, it may seem that physical punishment is the epitome of the power type and reasoning the essence of the status type. However, as noted, Aronfreed (1969) argued for the greater painfulness of reasoning in certain circumstances. Walters and Parke (1967) argued against the view that the efficacy of physical punishment is due to the actual pain inflicted, and several experiments have shown that perceived intent of someone exercising power is more important in arousing an emotional response than the actual pain inflicted (Baron, 1974; Baron and Ball, 1970; Greenwell and Dengerink, 1973).

I approach the question thus: there are relatively few instances of punishment that do not have a *cognitive* aspect. That is, a parent who punishes, even physically, is rarely silent. Some declaration, assertion, or label concerning the meaning of both the trespass and the punishment is virtually always conveyed, regardless of whatever else may happen. In the case of pure reasoning, only the verbal component appears. In the case of physical punishment, there is also likely to be a verbal component, although it may be reduced. I suggest that the verbal component carries much (but not necessarily all) of the burden of defining the punishment in terms of power or status. Thus if a physical punishment is defined in terms of its status implications, there is some chance that it has this significance. I say *some* chance because, as noted by Becker (1964), physical punishment is often accompanied by anger, and anger might prevent the parent from clearly presenting the status implications of the trespass.

For illustrative purposes, statements that emphasize the power dimension would include: "I told you not to do that; now you're going to get it!" "Why must you always disobey me?" "I'll show you who's boss around here!" Statements that raise the question of the child's deservingness of status would include: "I expected better of you than that," "Don't you pay attention to what you're doing?" "Only a baby would do a thing like that."

In general the *conjunction* of the cognitive elements of punishment and the actual punishment itself has been slighted. In many empirical analyses of punishment, researchers have been interested in the primary mode or type of punishment and have not looked for the pairing of the two (e.g., Aronfreed, Cutick, and Fagen, 1963). I wish to emphasize that the cognitive element of any punishment, which helps to define its power or status implications, is different from reasoning as such or any of the so-called cognitive-type punishments. The cognitive element can be attached to any type of manifest punishment—from physical to reasoning. When the parent is actually using reasoning, it is easier for the cognitive elements to emerge, but they can also emerge when the parent is inflicting physical pain. The important consideration is that the cognitive element identifies the relational context for the child.

Aronfreed (1968) also approached such a viewpoint:

. . . the aversive affective state that punishment induces in the child . . . will assume a number of different forms of qualitative experience for the child *as a function of the cognitive context in which it appears* (p. 285, emphasis added).

This statement notes the differential emotional consequences of punishment, depending on the cognitive context, but *not* depending on the type of punishment. This is precisely the view I espouse: The same punishment can come to signify different things and evoke different emotions depending on how the parent defines the situation at the time of punishment. The major axis distinguishing the type of punishment is whether it reflects the power of the punisher or the status adequacy of the child.

PROPORTIONALITY OF PUNISHMENT

Intensity is one of the most important, yet least understood, aspects of punishment. Intensity is clearly recognized as a factor in the effectiveness of punishment. Muenzinger (1934) found that rats who received mild shock for error behavior learned better. Estes (1944) suggested that when punishment is very intense it suppresses, but does not extinguish, behavior. For punishment to be effective, said Estes, it must be mild enough to permit the punished behavior to be emitted, and when that behavior is not reinforced, it will be extinguished. Holz and Azrin (1961) and Fisher (1955) proposed that high-intensity punishment by parents is frequently accompanied by regret and a softening of attitude which leads to a positive reinforcement for the child. The punishment thus becomes a discriminative stimulus for reward, and the behavior that leads to the punishment is ultimately reinforced. Mild punishment, on the other hand, does not lead to a compensatory reward and therefore helps to extinguish the punished behavior.

Punishment intensity has also been discussed in connection with the so-called cognitive types of punishment. On the assumption that the more intense punishments are frequently physical, Aronfreed (1961) and Parke (1969) argued that verbal punishment conveys more "information" and, since it is couched in symbols, gives the child something to think about, as, for example, the relationship between the trespass and the punishment. There is, I believe, some confounding here between cognitive or verbal expression as *meaning* and as *intensity*. I have suggested that even high-intensity punishments are often accompanied by the verbal signification of the meaning of the punishment and the relationship between the trespass and the punishment. In general, those who favor cognitive-type punishments assume that they are automatically mild. They can be, but this is another matter.*

The question of punishment intensity has also been approached from the point of view of modeling. Bandura and Walters (1959), W. Allinsmith (1960), and Hoffman (1960) pointed out that intense punishment provides the child with an aggressive model whom the child can imitate in a situation of frustration. If the punishment is given for aggressive behavior, the result can be to instigate further aggression through modeling of the parent.

Dissonance theory provides another basis for understanding the effects of punishment intensity. According to Festinger (1957, p. 291), punishment should be "just sufficient" to evoke dissonance to be effective. That is, the punishment should induce the child to go through a process of self-examination to reduce the dissonance created by the punishment. The reasoning might be as follows: "I am a good child but I did X. I was punished for it, which says that I am not good. If I want to be good, I should not do X." Presumably, mild punish-

---

*One difficulty in sorting out the effects of cognitive elements in punishment is that when they are effective, it may not be the cognitive-reasoning-verbal stimuli of the moment that obtain the particular outcome. Rather, reasoning may acquire its potency in part because at an earlier developmental stage it was paired with a certain kind of nonverbal, noncognitive punishment, whether it was physical punishment, love withdrawal, deprivation, or some other. At the later stage, the cognitive or reasoning type of intervention by the parent not only conveys its own information content, but also carries a latent trace of the earlier, nonverbal punishment.

ment does not hinder the reasoning-through of the elements of action, character, and punishment to a satisfactory conclusion. Indeed, various experiments have found that mild severity of threat or punishment is more successful in obtaining behavior change than more intense punishment (e.g., Aronson and Carlsmith, 1963a; Lepper, 1973). Pallak and Pittman (1972) suggested that, since dissonance reduction is a process that requires some duration to be successful, anything that interferes with the completion of the process must ipso facto lead to a failure. High-intensity punishment would comprise one such type of interference. Hoffman's (1970) treatment of punishment intensity suggests that mild punishment allows the child to invest his or her own moral stature in the situation. Since the child has a certain capacity for empathy and conscience, mild punishment allows these to emerge as determinants of future behavior.

The empirical work on the effects of punishment intensity has centered on the capacity to feel guilt in consequence of transgression or on the ability to inhibit behavior that is prohibited. The apparently milder types of punishment (e.g., psychological or love-oriented) are more successful in eliciting guilt over transgression than the apparently more severe punishment styles (e.g., physical). Another punishment mode, deprivation of privileges, whose intensity is largely unanalyzed, is also relatively unsuccessful in developing the capacity to feel guilt after transgression (Sears, Maccoby, and Levin, 1957). In the experimental work on behavior inhibition, such as resisting the temptation to touch an attractive toy, the results regarding apparent intensity have been mixed (LaVoie, 1974; Cheyne et al., 1969).

I wish to suggest that, from the viewpoint of effectiveness, punishment intensity is *relative*, not absolute, as has been implicitly assumed in most studies. In particular I propose that *the effective intensity of a punishment is proportional to the seriousness of the trespass to the child*. An elementary sociological notion is that a norm or rule for behavior is known to exist if there is a sanction attached to it. That is, does nonconformity carry a penalty? Beyond this clear articulation of norm and sanction, the most important issue is whether the sanction is proportional to the magnitude of nonconformity, or, does the punishment fit the crime?

Some attention has been given to the question of the relative intensity of punishment. For example, the debate over the death penalty is devoted in part to whether the penalty is too severe in proportion to the crime. In earlier times the death sentence was widespread even for minor theft. Today we believe that the death penalty for such conduct far exceeds the seriousness of the crime and that this is "cruel and inhuman." Many also believe the same even when the crime is homicide (see Sellin, 1965). Others, however, take the opposite view, and the issue is largely over the appropriateness of the penalty in relation to the crime, not the heinousness of the crime.

The dramatic example of homicide and the death penalty is far removed from the everyday trespass and discipline problems that arise in most families. Yet the fundamental issue is the same: Is the punishment proportional to the infraction? Logan (1973) saw this as one of the basic conditions of effective punishment:

> Punishment that *suits the crime*, administered by an agent who provides a socially acceptable solution to the motivation for punished behavior is highly effective (p. 133, emphasis added).

Berkowitz (1974) formulated the question in terms of equity considerations:

> Even after having been insulted, people often believe that the *punishment has to fit the crime*," and they might think that their frustrator's pain was too severe in the light of his relatively small misdeed. They want their tormentor to suffer to an appropriate degree (p. 171, emphasis added).

Knott and Drost (1972) found a linear relationship between the level of attack and the level of counterattack in a laboratory experiment conducted with adult subjects. If we assume that the attack is equivalent to the trespass and the counterattack is equivalent to the punishment, we have a positive linear function between the two. Strategically, this would make sense from the results found by Pisano and Taylor (1971). The most effective counterstrategy of one who was attacked by another was to retaliate with punishments equal in intensity to the prior aggression. This led to the greatest likelihood of extinguishing attack behavior by the initiator. Greater or lesser intensities of retaliation were less effective control strategies.

There are some reasons, however, why an exchange of equivalents cannot govern the magnitude of the trespass-punishment relationship. The most important of these is that, unlike the laboratory in which it is possible to create graded magnitudes of trespass and punishment along a ratio scale (e.g., electric shocks), there is no such scale for the vast number of possible trespasses and punishments that occur in families. Neither parents nor children could provide such a scale, although it is probable that an ordinal scale of intensity could be created. Shantz and Pentz (1972) asked 6-, 10-, and 13-year-old boys to indicate how much punishment is deserved by boys who verbally or physically aggress against a peer, sibling, or father who had verbally or physically initiated aggression against the boy. The subjects indicated that aggression against father was more deserving of punishment than aggression against siblings or peers. In addition, less punishment was advocated by the older subjects than the younger ones. Thus, although precise standards are absent, children do distinguish between transgressions worthy of greater or lesser punishment, and we must assume that parents do too.

The absence of precise yardsticks and equivalents, however, makes it most likely to overdo or underdo the punishment relative to the trespass.

The importance of the correct proportionality of punishment to trespass is that it affects the justice or injustice of the transaction from the point of view of the child. A great deal of latitude for error exists in the potentially different perspectives of the punisher and the victim on the same question. Weiner et al. (1972) found that in experiments involving varying explanations for failure of task performance, "trainers" gave greater or lesser punishment for failure, depending on whether the failure was attributed to deficit of effort or motivation. Here is a potentially critical source of disjunction in the trespass-discipline formula. Parents, I suggest, are more likely to judge that poor performance—very broadly defined—is due to inadequate motivation, whereas children are likely to attribute their failures of performance to a lack of knowledge or ability (cf. Brim, 1960). Indeed, if this is true in a particular case, the child must find *any* punishment administered by the parent excessive.

A further complication in developing an adequate understanding of the joint magnitude of trespass and punishment is the possibility that certain genetically determined personality characteristics—introversion–extraversion (Gray, 1970) or assertiveness and person-orientation (Bell, 1968)—may operate to determine felt levels of punishment intensity. Bell suggested that the more assertive children induce more punishment, whereas those low in person-orientation (the introverted) induce lower levels of reward.

Punishment schedules that are agreed on beforehand are probably less likely to be viewed as excessive, because they have the legitimacy of prior assent. In addition, since the punishment is clearly known, the child can weigh it against the forbidden act the punishment is supposed to deter. If the child transgresses nonetheless, it is likely to be with the rationale "It was worth it." (See Bandura, 1969, pp. 344–345 for a discussion of such prearranged punishment programs.)

I am not, however, prepared to conclude that when a *known* rule is broken, children are prepared to accept punishment in proportion to the trespass—even assuming the existence of a scale along which to measure both transgression and sanction. Indeed, following the Aesopian view enunciated here several times, namely, that our own misdeeds are not as bad as the misdeeds of others, I suggest that from the point of view of the one who has broken the rule, there is a *coefficient of proportionality* that sets the fair rate of exchange between trespasses and punishments. In all probability, the value of the coefficient is quite low. An experiment by Bersheid, Boye, and Walster (1968) confirmed the view that wrong-doers do not measure punishments on the same scale as trespasses. The experimenters created several groups according to the following criteria: Individuals were randomly assigned to the status of harm-doer or observer. In the case of the harm-doer, the task was to deliver electric shocks to another subject in a stressful learning situation. The observers would merely watch someone else do this. Half of the harm-doers and observers were informed that the learner would later have an opportunity to shock them as a part of the experiment. The other half of both groups were not told this. Two results are of interest. First, when asked about the "fairness" of the experimental procedures to themselves, the harm-doers who were to receive no retaliation judged the experiment as most fair. Although they had apparently hurt another person, they would not be punished, and they thought this just. This result gains significance in light of a second finding: This group provided the lowest amount of denial of wrong-doing, even lower than the observer groups. This is especially interesting in view of the fact that harm-doers often deny doing wrong or underestimate the harm they have done (Sykes and Matza, 1957; Brock and Buss, 1962). In fact, the harm-doers who expected retaliation judged their fate as less fair and denied wrong-doing much more than the nonretaliation group. In effect, the results say that when we do wrong we are happy to escape the consequences, but in so doing, we may more nearly come to recognize the trespass for what it is. In this one-trial experiment the insightful harm-doers expected no punishment. It is conjecturable whether a schedule of no punishment over a long series of trials would enable the insight of wrong-doing to maintain itself.

Some evidence for a coefficient of proportionality between trespasses and punishment is available in the work of Sellin and Wolfgang (1964) in their innovative effort at magnitude estimation of the seriousness of delinquent acts (Figure 10.1). The basic theory of their work, derived from early experiments in psychophysical measurement is that a "power" law of the type $Y = aX^B$ governs the magnitude of response to physical stimuli. Subsequent work has shown that psychological and attitudinal stimuli also follow this law (G. Ekman, 1962). The power law may also be expressed in logarithmic form as

$$\log Y = \log a + B \log X$$

This has the familiar form of a linear regression equation where B, the exponent, is now the slope of the line.

Sellin and Wolfgang evaluated the relationship of maximum penalties imposed by (Pennsylvania) law for delinquent acts of various degrees of seriousness. The power law applied very well, and B, the slope (or exponent), was found to be $+.7$; that is, the penalty expressed as time in prison was not directly proportional to the seriousness of the crime. In respect to crimes of greater than average seriousness, maximum penalties increased much more rapidly than did seriousness. In regard to lesser offenses, the reverse was true: Maximum penalties increased much slower than seriousness, as can be seen in Figure 10.1, which is adapted from Sellin and Wolfgang (1964, p. 328).

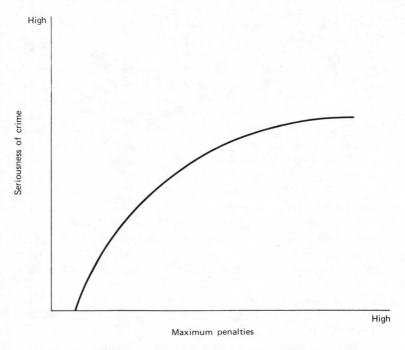

Figure 10–1   Curvilinear relationship between seriousness of crime and maximum penalties in Pennsylvania penal code.

What can we derive from Sellin and Wolfgang's results concerning a coefficient of proportionality that sets a fair rate of exchange between trespasses and punishments? First, it supports the view that punishments and crime are not related in a one-to-one fashion. If we look at the left half of the curve in Figure 10.1, we can estimate that for crimes up to the median level of seriousness, the slope of the curve is approximately .5.* If we interpret the slope as expressing the coefficient of proportionality, it means that maximum penalties are only about 50% of the magnitude of the seriousness of the offense. Second, Sellin and Wolfgang dealt with the *maximum* penalities contained in the law. Very often lesser penalties are imposed; thus the actual coefficient of proportionality is even less than .5. Third, Sellin and Wolfgang dealt with acts that are serious enough to involve the attention of the community agencies of social control. Yet, given this level of seriousness, the coefficient of proportionality is relatively low. Parents usually deal with acts of far less seriousness than those recorded as delin-

---

*Scores were standardized to control for differences in the metrics of the two scales. The slope estimate is therefore independent of scale.

quent by law. Thus we could expect that the coefficient of proportionality would be even lower in the home than the courts. If the ratio of acceptable punishment to actual transgression were about .20, any punishment that enlarges this ratio would be judged excessive. Of course, where no *known* rule existed as far as the child was concerned, any punishment would be deemed excessive.

I recognize the difficulty of discovering the actual magnitude of the coefficient of proportionality. It probably varies by the amount of prior training in moral matters, particularly where explicit delineations of trespasses and sanctions play a part. Furthermore, in the individual case, the calculation of the coefficient occurs unconsciously and probably depends on the past history of trespass and punishment. Cumulative excess of punishment leads to an extremely low coefficient in regard to any new instance of trespass-discipline (cf. Church, 1963, p. 383).

It is easy to see that mild punishments are least likely to exceed the coefficient of proportionality in any case. Indeed, a punishment can be too mild, but this is probably the rarer case. (However, see Schaefer's (1965a, 1965b) discussion of lax discipline.) For this reason, cognitive and verbal punishments that are not accompanied by such "sensitization" intensifiers as shouting, screaming, or physical contact, usually do not exceed the coefficient of proportionality in intensity. I believe that it is in part for this reason (not because of their intrinsic mildness) that cognitive and verbal punishments are effective in producing certain outcomes, whereas other punishments that exceed the proportionality boundary produce different results. It is useful to keep in mind Aronfreed's (1969) discussion of reasoning as more painful than physical punishment in certain circumstances.

What Makes Punishment Punishing?   We must also reflect on what makes punishment punishing. Since one of the principal purposes of punishment is deterrence from further trespass, punishment must carry its effect into the future. According to Mowrer (1960), who has provided one of the central theories, punishment is effective because, on a future occasion in a setting similar to one in which a particular behavior led to punishment, a tendency to act in the same manner evokes *anxiety*. To avoid the anxiety, the behavior tendency is shortcircuited, punishment avoided, and the anxiety dissipated. Aronfreed (1968a) expanded on this view in terms of cognitive and timing factors, but he retained the anxiety basis of punishment effectiveness declaring, however, that anxiety "may assume any one of a number of qualitatively different forms in accordance with its cognitive context . . . fear, guilt, and shame" (p. 54). Aronfreed placed the entire burden of determining the different emotions induced by punishment on cognitive factors, with anxiety as the emotion at the root of all of them. This also follows closely Freud's (1966) view of anxiety as an underlying emotion of guilt, shame, or rage (pp. 403–404). My own view, already expressed, is that cognitive elements help determine the relational mode of the punishment, but the proportionality or excess further denominates punishments into the separate distressful types. To the extent that a given emotion implies a threat to the person who feels it, anxiety may also arise, but this, I believe, follows the original emotion and does not precede it.

Another punishment emotion that has received some attention is *guilt*. Many studies have attempted to discover punishment correlates of guilt (B. Allinsmith, 1960; Whiting and Child, 1953; Grusec and Ezrin, 1972; Sears, Maccoby, and Levin, 1957). Since guilt is difficult to measure directly, numerous indicators have been used, for example, projective test responses indicating guilt or actual self-criticism, confession, or resistance to temptation. Yet these are not all determined by the same independent variables. Grusec and Ezrin (1972) concluded, as a result, that " 'conscience' is not a unitary phenomenon and that behaviors subsumed under it do not all occur in a given individual" (p. 1285). Guilt, however, is so central to classic formulations of response to transgression that it remains of interest. Indeed, since guilt is a distressful emotion, it qualifies as one that might be induced by punishment and to avoid which transgression is avoided.

Given the relative lack of clarity of the distinction between guilt and *shame*, the latter emotion has been little investigated within the same paradigm as anxiety and guilt. Different investigators have variously assigned shaming to "psychological" (W. Allinsmith, 1960) or "sensitization" techniques, depending somewhat on intensity (Aronfreed, 1961). Yet shame is distressful and ought to be a deterrent to transgression. Indeed, some have analyzed the major social control pattern of different cultures according to the guilt-shame distinction (Benedict, 1946; Hsu, 1969). Aronfreed (1969) also indicated that shame, like guilt, can be induced in punishment situations, depending on the cognitive conditions.

The final distressful emotion, *depression*, has received virtually no attention as a possible basis for the effectiveness of punishment. That is, to avoid the depression induced by certain patterns of punishment, the child makes an effort to avoid transgression. Since guilt, shame, and depression can be anticipated, they are often preceded or masked by anxiety. Perhaps for this reason, depression, the emotion researchers least connect with punishment, is ignored in favor of anxiety. More important, however, is that whether or not a parent intends to obtain conformity by the induction of depression, certain patterns of punishment do exactly this.

In sum, I have proposed two important dimensions of punishment, and these can be used to explain the genesis of the four distressful emotions—guilt, shame, anxiety, and depression. The first dimension involves the power-status locus of the punishment, that is, whether the punishment causes the child to focus principally on the immediate pain, loss, or deprivation or to focus on the implications for the future acquisition of status as mediated by the notion of competence or deservingness. I propose that virtually any punishment may qualify for either the power or the status type, depending in part on the accompanying cognitive presentation. There are, however, certain limits: Directly noxious punishments such as hitting or screaming carry very strong power messages that are very difficult to overcome by cognitive means. Other punishments, such as mild reproval within a loving context, are difficult to convert into the power mode. This is not due to the relative intensities—status deprivations that are labeled as such can be very intensely felt—but rather to the different messages that each conveys, one relating to power, the other to status.

The second dimension involves the degree to which the punishment is proportional to the transgression. Here intensity is the major consideration, insofar as it is measured on the scale of the justice of the punishment. I have suggested several grounds for disjunction between the parents' view of appropriate punishment and the child's view. The important viewpoint regarding the emotion that will be generated is that of the child. Together the two dimensions determine the emotion.

Parents do not necessarily restrict their punishments to a single type or mode, although this is also possible. Hoffman (1963), in fact, suggested that, among children with relatively high levels of moral orientation, two types are distinguishable. One is a "humanistic-flexible" type "who in their moral judgments consider extenuating circumstances and invoked principles in support of their [moral] judgments which were based on human need" (p. 311). A second type, labeled "conventional-rigid," consisted of children who "tended not to consider the circumstances and to give principles based more on convention and authority" (p. 311). The parent discipline techniques associated with the two moral orientations are of interest. Hoffman (1963, 1970) reported that, although the mothers (particularly) of the conventional-rigid group tend to use mainly withdrawal of love techniques involving "ego-attack" (e.g., "You ought to be ashamed of yourself" and "Can't you do anything right?"), the mothers of the humanistic group emphasized a different form of psychological punishment (e.g., "I'm disappointed in you") and a broader spectrum of punishments, including physical.

Thus parents may employ different techniques at different times, depending on a great number of considerations. The effect is to evoke the associated emotions, thus giving the child experience with these emotions. Where certain punishment techniques are paramount, the child is especially well trained in the production of the specific emotions entailed. Even if a limited spectrum of punishments is used by the parents, thus stimulating a particular emotion, this can lead to the activation of other distressful emotions in other settings. For example, anxiety generated in the family can contaminate performance in school, which in turn can activate shame and depression. The family, however, is the major developmental source of experience with the distressful emotions.

In Figure 10.2 the two dimensions of punishment are shown schematically, along with the emotions hypothesized for each of the alternatives. When a status-based punishment is in proportion to the transgression, I hypothesize *shame*; when the status-based punishment is excessive, I hypothesize *depression*; when a power-based punishment is in proportion, I hypothesize *guilt*; when the power-based punishment is excessive, I hypothesize *anxiety*. Each emotion can be expressed in an introjected-intropunitive or extrojected-extropunitive style. This entails the third dimension of punishment, namely, the power of the parent with regard to a major type of status dependence, specifically the dependence on the parent for affection. I discuss this before taking up each of the distressful emotions in turn.

THE RELATIONAL CONTEXT OF PUNISHMENT

One of the most consistent findings on the effects of punishment is that punishment is more successful, that is, extinguishes rather than merely suppresses the undesirable behavior, if it occurs in a context of parental affection for the child. This is the essential core of the withdrawal-of-love position in the development of conscience. If there is no love to withdraw, the child has relatively little to lose by continuing the behavior that is deemed a transgression by the parent or by extrojecting the emotion evoked by the punishment in the form of anger and hostility (see Chapter 3). Whiting and Child (1953), Sears, Maccoby, and Levin (1957), Heinicke (1953), and Hoffman and Saltzstein (1967) found higher levels of various indicators of conscience or guilt when punishment occurred in a relationship marked by parental affection for the child. Henry (1956, 1957) found that when the parent who provided the major discipline was also the major source of reward and affection, anger was turned inward. Funkenstein, King, and Drolette (1957) also found this pattern. These studies suggest that when individuals are dependent on another for affection, the emotion engendered by that person's punishment is introjected. When pangs of conscience and guilt (in the usual form of regret and remorse) are felt, this means that the emotion has been turned inward.

Other studies confirm the relationship between introjection and parental control of affection. Eron et al. (1971) found that identification with the father mediated the effects of parental punishment for aggression. Boys who identified were less aggressive than boys who did not identify, even when the parent used physical punishment for aggression. I believe that identification is in part a

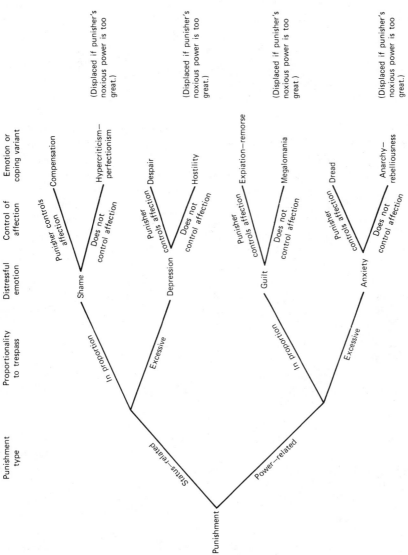

Punishment type	Proportionality to trespass	Distressful emotion	Control of affection	Emotion or coping variant

Punishment

Status-related
In proportion — Shame
  Punisher controls affection — Compensation
  Does not control affection — Hypercriticism—perfectionism
    (Displaced if punisher's noxious power is too great.)

Excessive — Depression
  Punisher controls affection — Despair
  Does not control affection — Hostility
    (Displaced if punisher's noxious power is too great.)

Power-related
In proportion — Guilt
  Punisher controls affection — Expiation—remorse
  Does not control affection — Megalomania
    (Displaced if punisher's noxious power is too great)

Excessive — Anxiety
  Punisher controls affection — Dread
  Does not control affection — Anarchy—rebelliousness
    (Displaced if punisher's noxious power is too great.)

Figure 10–2 Paradigm of punishment and the distressful emotions and their variants.

253

function of dependence on the parent for affection. Mussen and Distler (1959) and Mussen and Rutherford (1963) found stronger identification with the father among boys who saw their fathers as giving affection. Thus punishment for aggression is effective in generating control of aggression when it is mediated by the parent's control of affection. The work of Eron et al. (1971) does not permit us to evaluate the emotion produced by the punishment; we know only that the emotion was introjected rather than extrojected.

The need for approval also indicates dependence on others for affection. In an experiment with college girls, Fishman (1965) found less aggression against another who had arbitrarily aggressed against them when the girls expressed a high rather than low need for approval (Crown and Marlowe, 1964). In addition, girls in need of approval expressed greater aggression against themselves than girls low in need for approval, even though the other actor was clearly the agent of the aggression. This supports the view that the lack of dependence for affection on others leads to greater extrojection of emotions, particularly anger as a response to the power of others. Patterson (1965) found that boys were most sensitive to their father's disapproval when the father generally supported their sons in family arguments. This support is a form of affection by the father.

A final study can be cited to support the greater likelihood of introjection of emotion when there is dependence on the affection of the others. Grusec (1966) found that when children were given the opportunity to express self-criticism after failure at a task, greater self-criticism was expressed by those children who were subjected to a schedule involving high rewards and a form of punishment indicating withdrawal of love ("I am not happy with the way you're playing"). It is reasonable, I believe, to assume that the expression of disapproval was effective in turning criticism inward because of the children's dependence on the approval of the experimenter. Again the particular emotion generated by the punishment is not given, but its introjected mode is clear.

In Chapter 3 I discriminated the introjected and extrojected forms of the distressful emotions according to *agency*: introjected if *self*, extrojected if *other*. There is a logical link between agency and control of affection. If the parent controls affection—and this does not necessarily mean that it is given often, merely that it is given enough so that the child is dependent on the parent for it—I suggest that in general the child attributes good intentions to the parent. This is because, at times (regardless of whether they are few or many), the parent does demonstrate affection. The immediate situation of punishment does not affect this. That is, the parent may be greatly wroth over a particular action of the child, but this does not change the fundamental relational picture. It is like the oft-proclaimed difference between liking and loving. The parent who gives affection presumably always loves but does not always like the child. I believe that when the child receives affection and is actually dependent on the parent for it, the child has an image of the parent as loving, regardless of the immediate level of liking, which can be quite low in the situation of punishment.

The upshot of this is that, even when the immediate situation involves anger and punishment, the affectionate parent gets the benefit of the doubt, so to speak. This means that the child is willing to accept the view that the parent would not punish out of an arbitrary interest in punishment, which would make the other (the parent) the agent. Rather, the child accepts fundamentally that the parent punishes because of what the child did, that is, self is the agent. When affection is absent, there is no basis for good will on the child's part. The parent is simply a malevolent force who is always the agent of the hurt and pain of punishment.

In Figure 10.2 the third branch of the tree shows the alternative introjected-extrojected emotions generated according to whether the parent controls the affection on which the child depends. I turn now to the specific emotions evoked by punishment.

SHAME

A status punishment in proportion to the trespass is the basis of shame. By virtue of the status character of the punishment, conveyed largely by the cognitive component, the child is informed of the relationship between the trespass and the child's worthiness to receive status. Since the punishment is proportional—at least not excessive—it allows the child to focus on the relationship between the trespass and the punishment. This occurs in part because the intensity of the punishment is relatively low; it does not interfere with the cognitive link between the punishment and the previous behavior. Aronfreed, Cutick, and Fagen (1963) found that relatively high amounts of cognitive structure were important in generating self-critical statements. To provide the cognitive structure the experimenter had to speak calmly and quietly. Thus any implied threat was minimal, and the punishments could be considered in proportion (or less) to the transgression. The task, which tested the child's competence, required the child to push a specific doll off a board with a stick without knocking over any other dolls. The central instruction was "The idea is to see how few of the soldiers you knock down when you push the nurse into the box . . . The important thing is to be careful and gentle" (p. 286). When the child inevitably, according to experimental requirements, knocked over some soldiers, the experimenter took away some candy previously given and said, "You knocked down some of the soldiers, so I'm going to take (one, two, or three) tootsie rolls, because that's how careless and rough you've been" (p. 287). The cognitive component of the punishment made explicit the failure of competence and worthiness for status. The tootsie rolls, which were given at the start of the experiment, were the objective correlates of the child's status, the regard in which the experimenter held him. When the child displayed less competence, his status—in tootsie roll terms as well as the implied or obvious regard of the experimenter—was reduced.

It is clear from the details of the experiment that guilt was not induced, since no one was hurt when the child knocked down the soldiers. A relatively pure test of competence is involved, and the verbal instructions make that clear. When, at a later point, the experimenter claimed that the child's carelessness broke one of the toys, the child's self-critical remarks can be understood from the details as a shame response. It is interesting that the availability of a ratio scale of punishment intensity—expressed by the number of tootsie rolls taken away—also afforded the opportunity of examining the effect of proportionality, but this was not part of the experimental paradigm. We must assume from the results that the punishments were not felt as excessive but in proportion to the fall from competence.

Aronfreed and his colleagues (1963), following Mowrer (1960), choose to see the result not in terms of shame, but in terms of anxiety:

> [T]he child, in adopting a socializing agent's critical evaluative responses, reduces the anxiety attached to transgression by reproducing the punitive stimulus aspects of the agent which originally came to serve as cues signifying the termination of the anxiety that accompanied their anticipation (p. 292).

Since neither anxiety nor anxiety reduction were measured in the experiment, it is difficult to know whether this interpretation is correct. If anxiety is a *necessary* feature of shame (Freud, 1966, proposed this), perhaps the Aronfreed interpretation is formally correct. As to what emotion other than anxiety is central to the experimental manipulation, I believe shame is the most plausible. The alternative possibility, guilt, does not seem likely, because no wrong was committed, only a display of less than credited competence. The combination of status-related punishment and proportionality of punishment produces the shame response, because the conditions foster these connections between the transgression and the loss of status. This comes about in a manner described by Lepper (1973):

> People will ascribe attitudes, traits, and dispositions to others from an observation of the others' overt behavior and its controlling circumstances. To the extent that external pressures are perceived as great, one will attribute another's actions to his environment; [but, if they appear weak] one will attribute another's actions to characteristics of that other" (p. 66).

Lepper further suggested that the individual evaluates himself in the same manner. Thus when punishment is severe (excessive), this is an environmental pressure that removes the necessity of judging oneself as the kind of person who does *not* do the punished act. Amending Lepper's formulation only slightly, I suggest that not mildness of punishment but proportionality is more apt to produce the connection between one's act and the punishment. Indeed, if the punishment is too mild, the child does not have to take the matter seriously, and there will be virtually no induced emotion. As discussed in Chapter 3, shame bifurcates into introjected and extrojected types. I propose that introjection, along with the classic sense of embarrassment, loss of face, and the like, occurs when the structure of the relationship with other (the parent) is such that self is dependent on other for affection and other gratifications. If this is not the case, the punishment produces the aggressive hypercritical-perfectionistic response. Indeed, despite the proportionality, ergo the justice of the punishment, the parent has no legitimate ground to punish when he or she has nothing but punishment to give.

DEPRESSION

I propose that if punishment in the status-related mode exceeds the coefficient of proportionality for the trespass, the emotional result is depression. Unlike the case of proportionality, in which the relative mildness permits the child to evaluate the relationship between own action and own status worthiness, in the case of excess status-related punishment, attention focuses on the punishment and its high status-deprivation implications. As discussed in previous chapters, a high magnitude of status deprivation is the relational condition for depression.

The classic syndrome of despair, apathy, and sense of worthlessness is the introjected form of depression. The attribution of fault to the self results from the structural condition of dependence on the status of the other. The effect of an excessive status-deprivation punishment administered by a parent who controls the major affectional and other gratificational rewards must be to raise a serious doubt about the likelihood of receiving such gratifications again. There is indeed nothing incompatible between the parent controlling the major gratifications and withholding them excessively. Here the withdrawal of love in large amounts probably has its strongest effect, especially when coupled with a cognitive overlay that sets the matter in the context of the child's deservingness for love. Various authors have seen withdrawal of love as a generator of anxiety, and I agree that this is entirely possible when the excessive withdrawal of status also elevates the status loss, both present and anticipated, to noxious levels (see Chapter 9 for discussion). However, Cattell (1972) reported that depression, which is often confused in some of its forms with anxiety, is factorially orthogonal to it. When the parent is not a structural source of status in any great amount, punishment that evokes status-related concern leads to the aggressive-hostile outcome discussed in Chapter 3. Other is clearly seen as the agent of the excessive loss.

GUILT

I hypothesize that when the punishment is interpretable in terms of power, particularly the power to inflict pain and loss, yet is in proportion to the transgression, guilt is the emotion activated. Guilt entails the felt sense of wrong done to another. Assuming that the child has used high power against another and caused pain and hurt, the parent's subsequent infliction of pain and hurt permits the inference to emerge for the child that his own use of power caused pain to another, just as the parent's use of power is causing pain to him. By keeping the punishment relatively mild and therefore not exceeding the child's sense of wrong done by him, the parent prevents the emergence of anxiety (to be discussed next). Should that develop, the child is no longer capable of reflecting on the relationship between own act and the punishment. Cognitive components that define the punishment situation also assist in focusing attention on the isomorphism between the child's power act that instigated the punishment and the power act of the punishment.

The preceding discussion assumes a precipitating power act on the part of the child. Yet parents often impose power punishments when the child has merely made a technical error in a task. Ignorance of the requirements or developmental immaturity may be at fault. The power-type punishment, given even relative mildness that maintains proportionality, then attaches to such technical failures a feeling of guilt, despite the fact that no one has been harmed, Obviously any of the other distressful emotions can be inappropriately conditioned to technical inadequacy even when there can be no reasonable expectation of such adequacy. As discussed in Chapter 9, the distressful emotions are often evoked in relation to technical performance requiring competence. If standards are too low, too high, or set too early, performance often reveals a lack of competence. Punishment at those times simply conditions distressful emotions to the failures.

Numerous studies have found that guilt is induced when punishment or threat is mild as opposed to severe (e.g., Aronfreed, 1961; W. Allinsmith, 1960; Heinicke, 1953). In these studies guilt is rarely measured directly. Rather, certain projective test responses or confession (e.g., in Sears, Maccoby, and Levin, 1957) are assumed to reflect guilt. If we can assume that the existing literature supports the hypothesis concerning guilt as the evoked emotion, it also clearly supports the introjected mode of remorse and regret when the parent controls major affectional and other gratifications (Sears, Maccoby, and Levin, 1959; Hoffman and Saltzstein, 1967). I propose that when the parent does not control major affectional rewards, the guilt is induced, but the mode is extroverted, oriented toward self-justification instead of expiation.

ANXIETY

We come finally to anxiety, the emotion most often associated theoretically with punishment (Mowrer, 1960; Aronfreed, 1968a). We must distinguish between the anxiety evoked by the immediate punishment and the anxiety that may arise at some future occasion when there is an instigation or cue to perform the punished behavior. I am concerned only with the punishment-related emotion. I hypothesize that when a punishment in the power mode is excessive, the emotion stimulated is fear-anxiety. There is little opportunity for the child to attach the punishment to his own previous act, as in the case of guilt, since the punishment is too painful to allow the luxury of such concentration (cf. Lepper, 1973; Walters and Parke, 1967). Excessive punishment is usually of relatively high intensity, and this also precludes the parent's necessary concentration on verbal accompaniments that would establish the connection for the child. Instead, there are shouts, bawling out, and the like; these are usually too intense to permit the child to focus on their cognitive content even if they do contain a useful message. First and foremost there is the noxious power of the parent, and when the power of the other is very great, survival itself is threatened. There is no time to look backward at one's own misdeeds. In the research on the family etiology of schizophrenia Heilbrun (1973) has shown the deleterious effects of the high-power, low-status-according mother. It is probable that mothers in this power-status configuration are most likely to generate anxiety due to the excessive response and the strong centering of the child's attention on the mother's power. This does not exclude punishment that also alludes to the child's status worthiness. Rather noxious power is not excluded. Heilbrun, Harrel, and Gillard (1975) found that even normal persons perform worse on a conceptual task when their mothers were relatively high-power, low status according. Poor performance has been explained in many studies (Hebb, 1955; Paul and Bernstein, 1973) by excessive anxiety. Thus we have in indirect confirmation of how the excess power punishment produces anxiety as a characteristic emotion.

The classic anxiety syndrome of dread and sense of doom is hypothesized for the case of excessive power punishment in which the parent controls the major affectional rewards. When the parent uses love withdrawal as the major punishment and this is excessive and couched in power (not status) terms, this produces the anxiety pattern. When the parent punishes in the power-excessive mode, but does not control the major affectional rewards of the child—the child's status is low in the structural sense—we have the high-control low-nurturance parent who generates anarchy-rebelliousness (see Chapter 3). Henry's (1956; 1957) work is again pertinent. The tendency for external aggression is enhanced when one parent gives the major affectional gratifications and the other parent gives the major punishments—interpreted here as power in the excessive mode.

I emphasize again that the anxiety explained here is not the same anxiety referred to by Aronfreed (1968b) in his discussion of the effectiveness of punishment. My effort is to explain *emotions* that occur as a direct result of certain kinds of punishment. It is highly likely that, in anticipation of the commission of a previously punished act, anxiety arises, as Aronfreed said. This is the anticipation of a possible punishment by the parent as a consequence of performing the act. The punishment—if it conforms to the previous pattern—releases a specific emotion, that is, guilt, shame, anxiety, or depression. These are distressful, and one can anxiously anticipate feeling one or another of these uncomfortable feelings. However, in the proposed theory, only when the previous punishment pattern was in proportion to the trespass does the child successfully establish the cognitive path that links his behavior to his distressful emotions, namely, guilt or shame. Otherwise, although behavior may be suppressed because of the anticipatory anxiety, it is not extinguished (Church, 1963).

Displaced Aggression.   The four extrojected, aggressive outcomes of the distressful emotions would ordinarily lead to aggression against the parent, except that in the usual case the parent has considerable reserves of high noxious power at his or her command. This would make aggression against the parent dangerous. However, the aggressive emotion remains, and the parent has provided a model for power behavior (Bandura, 1962). In this case the child who is the more severely (excessively) punished for transgressions and is also given little affection is more likely to displace the aggression and turn it on others. Bandura and Walters (1959) and McCord, McCord, and Howard (1961) found this to be the case with delinquents or boys rated especially aggressive. Eron et al. (1971) also found that high parental punishment leads to aggression against schoolmates. Thus a final deduction we can make with regard to aggression, whether directed toward the punishing parent or displaced, is that, given certain types of punishment and structural conditions, the emotional precursors of aggression are built into punishment itself.

Geen (1972) observed that once the emotional response to punishment is extrojected as a characteristic response, it is difficult to moderate by the usual mechanism of social control, namely, punishment itself. In two experiments, Parton (1964) and Peterson (1971) found that highly aggressive boys were more likely to be aggressive when their behavior elicited an aggressive-punitive response from others than when the response of others was more passive. Punishment by the others appears to induce anger, which in turn produces further aggression.

A TYPOLOGY OF AGGRESSION

An unanticipated result of the preceding analysis is a typology of aggression. Although there is general recognition of the difference between instrumental and expressive aggression (Berkowitz, 1961; Buss, 1961), little has been done to distinguish different types of aggression within the expressive domain (cf. Feshbach, 1970; Cairns, 1972). One of the very few efforts was undertaken by Moyer (1967), who proposed eight types of aggression. His taxonomy was based on observations among nonhuman species and included the following: predator, inter-male, fear-induced, irritable, territorial, maternal, instrumental, and sex-induced. According to Eleftheriou and Scott (1971), these types are "based on separate neuro-circuitry laid down in early development" (p. 9). However, Moyer (1971) did not regard each of these as "necessarily identifiable in man" (p. 234). In addition, Moyer believed that there is no good evidence for a "different physiological basis for the different kinds of aggression in man" (p. 233). This, if true, leaves undisturbed the view developed in the specificity hypothesis discussed in Chapter 7 that a discrete physiological process is involved in human aggression of all types, namely, norepinephrine (NE) dominance in the sympathetic nervous system. Moyer (1968, cited in Scott, 1971) noted that "physiological mechanisms underlying consummatory behavior are similar to those underlying aggressive behavior" (p. 31). This position was also taken by Gellhorn (1967) and others and suggests that certain forms of aggression, if successful, culminate in gratification. The primary forms would be consumption of food or sex, which suggests dominance of the parasympathetic nervous system (see Chapter 7).

Thus the physiological evidence supports the logical view that aggression can be partitioned into two main types: *instrumental*, in which the purpose of the aggression is to gain consummatory gratification, and *expressive* or reactive aggression which results from the prior emotion of anger. Although Berkowitz (1962), Buss (1961), and Gekas (1972) also made this basic distinction, the line of demarcation was not drawn in precisely the same way by each author. My position, following Berkowitz (1962), is that expressive aggression is initiated by anger. Any other aggression is instrumental in that it is initiated by interest in a consummatory goal. Anger, however, is not precluded from instrumental aggression at a later stage, since in the course of such aggression, resistance by the victim can inflict pain, which signifies the power of the other. In such a case, in which other is viewed as agent—as described above—fear and/or anger result.

It is a useful exercise to try to partition Moyer's eight types into those which are instrumental and those which are expressive. I suggest that the instrumental aggressions in Moyer's typology are predator, instrumental, and sex-induced. The expressive aggressions in which anger and possibly some other emotions (e.g., fear) are induced include inter-male, fear-induced, irritable, territorial, and maternal. Each of these, I believe, can be assigned to relational conditions involving actual or potential loss or deficit of power or status. Inter-male is clearly a struggle for dominance and power. Fear-induced is self-explanatory as a function of power threat. Irritable is a generalized category comprehending minor status losses and deprivations. Territorial involves a major status-deprivation threat. Maternal aggression is also interpretable as a reponse to status deprivation. To see this requires only to accept that the mother is the possessor of the children, and until they are grown they are extensions of herself. Among humans this is most probably the result of socialization and identification as discussed in Chapter 6, whereas among nonhuman forms there may be a more determinative biological-instinctual basis (Wilson, 1975). It is also clear that none of Moyer's types can fit into relational situations in which there is excess of own power or status. This suggests the interesting possibility that a major difference between human and other species is the capacity of humans to feel guilt and shame. These emotions also give rise to anger and aggression if the agent is seen as the other. Moyer's list is a useful starting place for a discussion of aggression, but I believe his ad hoc compendium of empirical instances of expressive aggression can be easily integrated into categories of the typology derived from the power-status relational model.

In the preceding discussion of characteristic emotions and in the earlier presentation in Chapter 3 of responses when other is the agent in relational situations of excess and insufficient power and excess and insufficient status, I hypothesized four types of anger responses. These are the emotional antecedents of four different types of aggression. This is not an entirely novel view, since all aspects of the fourfold typology have been individually adumbrated by different researchers.

In regard to the megalomanic aggression of guilt, a considerable literature has accumulated in recent years (Lerner and Matthews, 1967; Ryan, 1971; Walster, Berscheid, and Walster, 1983). With respect to the aggression induced by shame where other is the agent, I have cited the work of Ford (1963) and Thibaut and Kelley (1959). There is perhaps less recognition of the aggression response in anxiety than in the other types, although research by Knott and Drost (1972), Michener et al. (1975), and Tedeschi et al. (1975) can be viewed as supporting the anarchy-rebellion hypothesis. In regard to depression, many investigators have found that anger against others accompanies depression (Gottschalk and Gleser, 1969; Schless et al., 1974). The utility of the power-status mode of analysis is to bring these separate empirical and theoretical insights under the umbrella of a single, comprehensive theoretical formulation.

chapter 11

The Choice of Dependent Variables in the Study of Socialization: An Approach to the Positive Emotions

In the three preceding chapters I applied the power-status model to the problem of distressful emotions and their relational bases and consequences. Distressful emotions are ordinarily of greater interest than their opposites, doubtless because most of us have a stronger motive to avoid or escape our pains than to augment our pleasures. Thus the more we can learn about the causes of distress, the more likely we are to skirt the dangers. Emotional life, however, seems to aggregate as a zero sum. The more we are able to experience love, joy, security, justifiable pride, and other positive emotions, the less likely are we to feel distress, given that relational conditions remain the same. Thus there is good reason to examine the positive emotions and their types and sources.

As in previous chapters, I proceed by drawing out some implications of power-status relations. This leads us to the positive emotions by an indirect route. Although the central focus is on the problem of determining a set of desirable dependent variables of socialization, the result is a logically derived set of preconditions for the avoidance of the distressful emotions and the experience of some of the positive ones.

Convergence on Independent Variables of Socialization

In a highly useful article, Maccoby (1961) examined the choice of independent variables in the study of socialization. Surveying a large body of work by herself and others, Maccoby devoted much of her analysis to a consideration of the effects of varying types and schedules of rewards and punishments administered by parents.

Maccoby's most important finding, from a learning theory perspective or a parent personality or parent-child interaction perspective, was that researchers have largely converged on parental rewards and punishments as the single most important set of independent variables of socialization. Maccoby herself demurred in part from this approach and reported data on the importance of the simple frequency of interaction between parent and child. However, increased frequency of contact also increases the number of rewards and punishments the parents administer. A high frequency of contact may also convey a reward in itself simply because the mere presence of the parent is rewarding to the child. These considerations aside, the reward-punishment orientation in the study of socialization conforms well to the power-status model of interaction, as discussed in Chapter 2 and Appendix 2.

In the socialization literature, the punishment-reward dimensions are identified, respectively, by such names as authoritarian-control and hostility-rejection (Zuckerman et al., 1958), which stresses the negative poles of both dimensions, autonomy versus control and love versus hostility (Schaefer, 1959), control and affection (Lorr and McNair, 1963), psychological control versus psychological autonomy and acceptance versus rejection (Schaefer, 1965a), and independence and affiliation-disaffiliation (Benjamin 1974). These, of course, are also easily understandable in power-status terms (see Chapter 2).

However, convergence on a fruitful set of independent variables of socialization is not yet matched by a similar convergence on the dependent variables of socialization. One difficulty in determining a preferable set of dependent variables is that the possible number is extremely large, involving cognitive and intellective processes (e.g., language learning), basic motor skills for self-management (e.g., self-feeding and toilet training), and social-role learning, especially as related to sex roles and relationships with others. There can be no doubt that each is important, although it is likely that the first two are somewhat less problematic than social-role learning. In the former two domains, there is a relatively high consensus on *what* is to be learned, and the work is devoted to *how* the relevant skills are best acquired. In social-role learning, however, problems of what to learn are as crucial as problems of how to learn. To cite a single case of topical concern, a great deal of attention is now focused on what is to be learned as part of a sex role, which has, of course, large implications for what is to be learned for the purpose of relating socially to others.

In general, although this seems to be especially true in the area of social-role learning, dependent variables in the study of socialization are selected on a more or less ad hoc basis—despite the fact that there is wide consensus that some of these variables are important. Thus in the various handbooks of child development and socialization (Mussen, 1970; Goslin, 1969; Hoffman and Hoffman, 1964, 1966) there are chapters on sex-role learning, moral development, and aggression. There is usually some material, either as a discrete chapter or under larger rubrics, on dependence and on achievement. Intervening processes—in particular, identification, modeling, and reinforcement-contingency learning—often appear in these works. In addition, special topics relating to deviant or pathological outcomes may be appended as items of special interest. I wish to suggest that the usual melange of chapters devoted to independent, intervening, and dependent variables reveals little architectonic form and that the composition of such works is guided more by the unevenly cumulated clusters of work in the field and by fashionable interest than it is by the systematic apportionment of problems according to a unifying theoretical framework.

I propose to draw together, out of the existing knowledge about socialization, as well as some implicatioins of the power-status model, a systematic framework that will enable us to specify with some degree of deductive confidence what dependent variables of socialization might best receive our attention, specifically in the area of social-role learning. The outcome of this heuristic effort at theoretical synthesis can serve to provide investigators with an overarching rationale for a program of work that is, for the most part, well under way. The unifying theoretical framework suggests possible relationships between different areas of socialization and therefore may make researchers sensitive to matters often overlooked when they choose to study one particular dependent variable. There is, for example, little theoretical or even empirical attention to the relationship between different dependent variables, for example, achievement and aggression, independence and aggression, or moral development and achievement. (For some exceptions see Shaw and Grubb, 1958; Weiner and Ader, 1965.) This is true despite the fact that successful socialization in one of these areas may preclude successful socialization in another.

An additional benefit of a unifying framework for the dependent variables of socialization is the understanding it gives of certain interactional preconditions for the experience of positive emotions. In the early chapters I dealt with the emotions that result from on-going power-status structures or immediate power-status interaction. In later chapters attention shifted to long-term emotional dispositions, such as the distressful emotions of mental and emotional disorder. These intense emotions are not tied directly to immediate interaction or relational conditions as experienced by most people. They result, I believe, from long-term exposure to certain power-status relations, especially with parents and very frequently in association with problems of socialization.

I propose that, just as the relational conditions of socialization can dispose individuals toward the experience of distressful emotions, so too can socialization conduce to the appearance of positive emotions. This cannot be accomplished merely by applying a "correct" program of power-status relations. Socialization must, in addition, instill a proper content. In the main this content must prepare the individual to engage adequately in the division of labor and in relationships with others. The proper content shapes the individual's technical and relational actions so that positive emotions arise in the course of doing these actions. Furthermore, both the actions and their associated emotions elicit from others in turn a set of relational responses that initiate an additional cycle of positive emotions. I suggest that the proper socialization content enhances the likelihood that various positive emotions can come to be characteristic of the individual as long-term emotional motifs that prevail at most times and when short-term situational perturbations are discounted.

SOME PRIOR VIEWS

Mine is not the first proposal for a systematic approach to the dependent variables of socialization. We have only to examine Plato's *The Republic* to see how early this was regarded as a critical problem for society. Obviously many subsequent efforts have addressed the issue. Among more recent efforts I detect two lines of attack. In one, represented mainly by psychological approaches, the dependent variables are linked to biological and developmental considerations. In the other, represented mainly by sociological approaches, the dependent variables are derived from considerations of social organization and societal requirements.

Among psychologists Freud stands out for his contribution of the twin concerns of *Arbeit* and *Liebe*—work and love. These both stem, presumably, from the instinctual energy of libido, which is reshaped as "aim-inhibited sexuality" to make love possible and as sublimated sexuality to energize creative expression in work. On the negative side, Freud (1951) posed the important concern for "civilization" with controlling drives for sexual satisfaction and aggression, the latter drive stemming from the destructive instinct he called *thanatos*.

Erikson (1963), in a more elaborate list than Freud's, offered the familiar development octet consisting of basic trust versus mistrust, autonomy versus shame and doubt, initiative versus guilt, industry versus inferiority, identity versus role confusion, intimacy versus isolation, generativity versus stagnation, and ego integrity versus despair. Corresponding to these developmental issues are what Erikson calls "basic virtues" (Erikson, 1963, p. 274), namely, hope, willpower, purpose, competence, fidelity, love, care, and wisdom. Much in keeping with the psychoanalytic tradition from which Erikson's work stems, the eight stages and virtues articulalate closely with physiosexual loci such as the oral-sensory, muscular-anal, and locomotor-genital, or with maturational-temporal foci such as latency, puberty-adolescence, and so on. Thus the systemic nature of Erikson's work involves biological and chronological tables of organismic development.

Sociologists, on the other hand, approach the dependent variables from a consideration of social and cultural demands. Brim (1960) proposed a radical revision in the study of socialization by suggesting that all personality develop-ment might be fruitfully viewed as "role-learning." Different societies and cul-tures require from their members different behaviors, attitudes, and motives as elements of the roles they must play. The socialization process is designed to instill the particular behaviors, attitudes, and motives required. Brim did not treat any specific content, since that is determined by the individual society, but he did address the formal constituents of roles that either fit together in successful role activity or,conversely, lead to deviance when the formal elements are in-adequate to the role demand.

Inkeles (1968) also treated the dependent variables from a societal perspec-tive. He called them the "elements of the personal system developed in any adequate socialization," and they are essentially a mapping into the individual of "requisites for the continued functioning of a society" (p. 83). Corresponding to a dozen or so societal requisites are the individual attributes they entail. For example, the societal requirement of "role differentiation and role assignment" engenders the personal system element of the "self-system; personal identity" (p. 83).

In general, psychological approaches to the dependent variables of socializa-tion are more willing to provide specific content, such as control of sexual impulse (Freud, 1951) or trust (Erikson, 1963), whereas sociological approaches rely either on specific cultures (e.g., Brim, 1960) or broad societal imperatives (Inkeles, 1968) to determine the content. I hope to strike a balance between psychological and sociological perspectives; thus the dependent variables will come closer to the content level of the psychological approach, while at the same time they are systematically derived from social organizational and social rela-tional consideration. I turn to these now.

THE DEPENDENT VARIABLES OF SOCIALIZATION

In Chapter 2, I proposed that the basic and ineluctable condition of humankind is interdependence and that the logical and empirical outcome of such a post-ulate is that when humans interact they divide their labor. The division of labor, which implies differentiated roles and activities for the different members of society, requires socialization of actors to accommodate to the technical differen-tiation in which they will participate and therefore gives rise to the first major dependent variables of socialization.

Second, since socialization with respect to the divison of labor can account only for the technical aspects of human behavior in society and since there are in addition *relational* aspects, four additional dependent variables of socialization are implied and are discussed.

Division of Labor: Sex and Occupational Roles.   Due to the present level of technology involved in the conception, gestation, birth, and early nurturance of human infants, I suggest that the biological division of labor in this process strongly implies the need for some amount of sex-linked role learning. Further, I suggest that the supervening importance for societal survival of human replacement elevates the replacement function to the first rank in the divison of labor. The more primitive the society and the shorter the average life span, the more important this function must be and, consequently, the more attention we may expect will be given to ensuring its accomplishment. Since the biological technology operates through anatomical differences that are not under the control of the organism, societies simply assign each infant according to its potential biological contribution to a sex-role socialization category that has technical and often relational implications (Kemper, 1974).

Even granting the total dedifferentiation of males and females with regard to every single *other* technical or relational element imaginable, the anatomical differences employed in the available biological technology would still require some significant sex-role differentiation in behavior, motives, and attitudes so that the biological tasks of which the different sexes are capable and which society requires can be carried out.

These must be carried out, on the average, somewhat more than twice. This is to say that simple replacement and maintenance of a stable population requires at least two reproductions for each male-female pair, but it actually requires more than twice on the average, because some infants do not survive long enough to produce two offspring of their own. In addition, since some male-female pairs are infertile, others are required to bear additional children to maintain a stable population. (The actual figure for United States society is 2.1.)

It appears inevitable in the light of such considerations that society would seek to inculcate at least a minimum set of characteristics that would make it possible for a female member of society to perform a painful, arduous, and time-consuming role in the biological division of labor. If this implies nothing more than that, whereas, males require nothing special in the way of socialization and females only require something *additional*, it is sufficient to guarantee some differentiation in regard to the socialization of sex-roles.

Clearly the source of the differentiation between the sexes lies precisely in the available technology of reproduction. Should there be a change in this technology, so would there be a corresponding change in the division of labor and of the roles to which actors are socialized. More explicitly, should developments in the technology of extrauterine gestation proceed as at present (see *New York Times*, July 16, 1974), it is wholly conceivable that the role differentiation based on male-female anatomical differences will become obsolete. The technological fillip of Aldous Huxley's *Brave New World* was exactly this. However, whereas Huxley saw that this might mean the end of the family, he did not adumbrate an equally important social change implied by the new technology, namely, the end of sex-role differentiation.

Once infants are gestated outside a human body, most behaviors, motives, and attitudes that are differentially appropriate to males and females today will be unnecessary. Neither one sex nor the other will then be especially suited for nurturing the infant, except if he or she is specifically socialized to provide such nurturance. This could be either an anatomical male or female. It is further conceivable that the usual cross-sex rule in marriage will no longer find its ancient support, for we may assume that rule also relates to the technology of reproduction and the development of characteristics through modeling, which ensures the necessary differentiation in the next generation. Thus with a new reproductive technology, we may have male-male and female-female families, in which the offspring will be half-brothers and half-sisters, instead of full siblings as in the current male-female family. Although there would be resistance to the development of such family forms today, because we sense some need of both same and opposite sex parents to ensure the acquisition of the appropriate sex-linked roles (see Lynn and Sawrey, 1959; Heatherington, 1966), with a new technology of gestation, there would be no need for sex-role learning as such, linked specifically to anatomy. Nurturance functions would still be performed, but with no necessary contingency on anatomy.

This fanciful excursus on another version of *Brave New World* is offered to underscore the significance of biological technology as a determinant of allocation to positions in the division of labor, which in turn requires sex-role differentiation. Obviously, a change in the technology of reproduction would also ensure the end of the last vestiges of differential evaluation of males and females, since males and females would not automatically be assigned to particular functions, and, as the functions are differentially evaluated, so is the category of human actor allocated to the function. The propensity of humans to evaluate their contributions to the division of labor differentially is well known and has a long history in human thought (Dahrendorf, 1968).

Although sex-role learning, in the sense discussed here, is of the first importance in socialization related to the divison of labor in society, other socialized attributes are required by the division of labor. In particular, in societies above the most rudimentary, a specific occupational skill that enables the person to make a contribution for which there is economic compensation is required. In truly primitive settings in which occupational differentiation is scant, the socialization requirement is for the broad range of technical skills that guarantee survival of self and one's dependents—hunting, fishing, agriculture, food preparation and preservation, and so on. Beyond the universal requirement of sex-role learning for reproduction, the specific degree of development of the division of labor in occupational terms determines the particular requirements for socialization of technical skills.

I note finally that, at least since Linton (1945), anthropological analysis of differentiation in human societies has mentioned not only sex, but *age* as a universal basis of role differentiation. This is certainly empirically true, and nothing said here should be taken as a denial of it. Age, however, is not stressed, since, given sufficient longevity, all age grades and their roles will be experienced by all members of society within sex category. Although age grading is a standard social fact, it is not, after childhood, necessarily linked to any particular function in the division of labor as is sex to reproductive roles. Thus it does not have quite the same kind of constraining and inevitable nature as does sex, and although not unimportant, it is surely of lesser importance (cf. Kemper, 1974).

In summary, the major axis of differentiation in all societies at present involves the biological and occupational division of labor and this, in turn, provides the first set of major dependent variables of socialization. Notwithstanding the significance of the technical skills and attributes required by the division of labor, these do not lead to any emotions directly. This is not to say that the process of learning technical competence is not fraught with triumphs and frustrations, pride and tears, but, as should be evident by now, the emotions that accompany technical role learning stem from the *relational* matrix of power assertion or status accord that accompanies the instruction. To identify the emotions that are directly related to dependent variables of socialization, we must turn to the relational dimensions themselves.

Relational Dimensions: Control of Aggression, Autonomy, Competence and Giving-Loving.   The next four dependent variables of socialization can be derived from a consideration of the four channels in the power-status space. In each relationship, each actor has a position along the power axis and a position along the status axis (See Figure 2.1, p. 32). The question now, as it relates to the derivation of the dependent variables of socialization, is, what kind of actors are required who can operate in a social world in which actors have power and status vis a vis each other? I propose that *each actor must have an attribute that corresponds to both his own and the other actor's position in the power-status space.* These are shown in the four cells in Figure 11.1 Each cell indicates a property each of the actors must have to interact in the four channels of power-status relational space. These are now discussed.

Own Power: Learning to Control Aggression.   To have power is to have the capacity to hurt another, at the ultimate to destroy the other. If interaction is to continue between two actors, each must have developed the inner restraints that enable him to control the use of his power when he is impelled to use it, or even when he may legitimately use it. Parents are certainly, and often, angered by some actions of their children, but even if they are extremely angry, they must

	Power	Status
Own	Learning to control aggression	Learning to be competent and achieving
Other's	Learning to be autonomous	Learning to give and love

Figure 11–1 Relational channels and dependent variables of socialization.

somehow be able to prevent that anger from discharging with full force on the child. Children too become angry with their parents, peers, and siblings, and often aggress against them. A significant part of the socialization process involves learning to control that aggression.

Freud (1951) long since pointed out that one of the prices of civilization is the control of aggression, that is, learning to mediate the impulse to strike at the other who blocks our path, frustrates our designs, or denies us what we feel to be our due. Yet Erikson, who also bears psychoanalytic credentials, did not refer to aggression control as a basic problem for the growing human. Some nods in this direction were given in the reference to the "rages of the biting stage" (Basic Trust vs. Basic Mistrust) and in the stage of Autonomy vs. Shame and Doubt, in which the institutional equivalent of the aggression-related personality dimension is found in the "principal of law and order" and the courts.

Of the two sociological perspectives on socialization presented earlier, only Inkeles dealt with the problem of controlling aggression, under the rubric of "moral functioning."* The societal requirement that determines this need is "Effective control of disruptive forms of behavior."

The specific content of the aggression one must learn to control may also be seen in terms of the relational dimensions of power and status. First, there is direct infliction of a noxious stimulus, for example, slapping, beating, shooting,

*This is the most content-specific of Inkeles's dependent variables.

starving, and so on, which are designed to induce pain and fear. Second, there is the denial of anticipated or previously accorded and accustomed status. A third aggression modality consists of manipulations through deception, cheating, outright lies, false innuendoes, and the like, which gain for the aggressor a pseudo-status. That is, the victim is coerced into acts, which, if the facts were known, would be against his will and to which he would not accede if the masked aggression were not employed against him. To teach the young to control their power is a fundamental task of socialization.

Other's Power: The Development of Autonomy. Each actor confronts a problem not only with regard to his own power, but also with regard to the power of the other, especially if the other has not learned to control it. This gives rise to a need for a complex of behaviors, motives, and attitudes concerned especially with the attribute of autonomy, or independence. The basic insight that power and dependence are related is found in Blau (1964), Thibaut and Kelley (1959), and Emerson (1962), but it is Emerson who developed this view extensively. His concise and highly plausible formulation is that A's power over B is a function of B's dependence on A. Similarly, the power of B over A is a function of the dependence of A on B. In symbolic terms:

$$P_{AB} = D_{BA}$$

$$P_{BA} = D_{AB}$$

If D_{AB} is greater than D_{BA}, then P_{BA} is greater than P_{AB}. Where such power imbalance is found, Emerson suggested a number of "power-balancing" strategies, for example, reducing motivational investment in the goals for which one is dependent on the other or the development of alternative sources for the gratification of those goals.

If autonomy is seen as a relational condition in which the actor is relatively free from vulnerability to the force, threat, or coercions of the other, we see that an additional factor in determining autonomy involves not only low dependence on the other, but also direct power resources that can be employed to oppose and nullify the power acts of the other. Thus the child who has been bullied may learn some defensive skills (e.g., boxing, jui jitsu, karate) that can be employed as defense or countermeasure against others who aggress against him. The concept of the "deterrent force" in international relations is, of course, also an example of this principle.

The generalized cultivation of competence over a broad range of activities becomes a firstline defense against the kind of dependence that leads potentially to control by the other, but this is insufficient without the development of a strong motive for autonomy. Knowledge of the common effects of dependence, principally, loss of self-determination, is also an important constituent in developing the motive for autonomy. Competence, however, provides not only the resources to reduce dependence, but also the resources (in a somewhat different sense) that permit the acquisition of counterpower. This will be better understood in the separate discussion of competence.

Two further strategies to neutralize the power of the other suggested by Emerson (1962) involve increasing the other's dependence on oneself, either by increasing his "motivational investment in goals mediated by oneself, or by denying the other "alternative sources for achieving those goals." In both instances, the actor can exercise the power of gratification withdrawal to cause the other to terminate some power act of his own. Both alternatives involve the elevation of one's power by virtue of increasing the dependence of the other. Although this may ensure autonomy, it does so at the price of conflict. This becomes clear when we consider power as a process instead of merely a structural outcome (see Appendix 2). The potential escalation of processual power thus makes it risky as well as costly to attempt to gain autonomy through making the other dependent on oneself.

How much autonomy is enough? Communal and individual views may differ considerably, and many of the pandemic tensions between personal as opposed to social goals revolve around the question of autonomy (cf. Simmel, 1950, pp. 120–121). In some sense the issue is resolved by the goals that the actors are together in the division of labor to accomplish. In another sense, the existing technology determines the degree of interdependence that is necessary. Evaluations of contribution and the ensuing differential placement in systems of rewards and stratification also affect the degree of dependence. Maturational processes and development based on prior learning are also factors. Freud spoke of the major task of young adulthood for males as that of breaking away from the dependence on and the authority of the family and the father. This task of autonomy, which permits self-direction, is not only a requirement of the individual nor a benefit to him alone. I suggest that, by virtue of the relational model from which this attribute is derived, autonomy is a necessary personal goal so that the relationship itself may survive and with it the capacity to achieve the goals all the actors are together in the division of labor to achieve in the first place.

This also logically implies that autonomy must be less than complete; otherwise, the basic assumption of interdependence in the division of labor is nullified, and we are no longer speaking of relationship, but of the activities of atomistic individuals. The Utilitarian tradition in the history of ideas was premised on such a version of completely autonomous individuals joining together to realize their "self-interest." The first great contribution of Durkheim (1933) in *The Division of Labor in Society* was to expose the atomistic-Utilitarian fallacy. I defer further discussion of autonomy until Chapter 13 where it is examined in light of the difference between relational and existential interdependence.

Own Status: Competence and Achievement. In the dyadic model of relationship with which we are working, the status of actor A can come only from actor B, and the status of actor B only from actor A. How may we explain that each actor rewards and gratifies the other *voluntarily*—for that is the differentia specified in the definition of status (see Chapter 2)? I believe a highly useful answer for descriptive purposes lies in viewing the quality of the contributions that each makes in the division of labor. If qualitative ranking of contribution is possible, it may be adopted as a universal maxim that the better the contribution, the more others are willing to reward the actor for it (Homans, 1961; Thibaut and Kelley, 1959; Bales, 1951; Emerson, 1962; Davis and Moore, 1945). This applies to the whole range of human productions, whether we are speaking of accomplishment in art, science, or the practical production of goods or services in the division of labor. In a word, competence earns status. Achievement, which represents an increment over the usual production level of competence, earns even more status (Kemper, 1968).

Competence and achievement behaviors are seen as direct means of obtaining voluntary compliance and gratification from others in the division of labor, but the various forms of status currency are not only gratifying in a direct material sense as products or services to be consumed and enjoyed because they are gratifying per se. At least as important as this direct consumption of status is the enhancement of self-esteem, the sense of worthiness that marks the difference between the enjoyment of deserved and undeserved rewards.

Since gratification is always available through the use of superior force and coercion (i.e., power), there might not seem to be a significant difference between the enjoyment of such forcefully obtained pleasures and those that are gotten voluntarily. The difference is something akin to the difference between rape and freely given sexual intimacy. There is much theory (Mead, 1934; Cooley, 1902) and research (Miyamoto and Dornbusch, 1956; Pepitone, 1968) to support the notion that self-esteem is a product of the conferral of status by others. Since others do not confer gratifications voluntarily without good cause, I propose that the cause resides in the contributions that are made in the division of labor.

There is a class of "contributions" that are not, strictly speaking, competent performance under the control of the actor who makes them, but nonetheless evoke status conferral from others. I refer to inherent biological elements, such as beauty. The actor who manifests extraordinary qualities of beauty is appreciated beyond his fellows, and, since beauty criteria exist in all societies, we must assume that there is a universal contribution to which the mere presence of beauty corresponds. There is evidence that beauty is also regarded as coextensive with "talent" and the kind of ability that wins status for contribution in the division of labor (Landy and Sigall, 1974). Dion (1972) has also shown how status-gaining moral qualities are also differentially ascribed to children of greater and lesser attractiveness. It is conceivable that a concerted campaign of devaluation of physical traits as a basis for status conferral might have some effect, but, since the appearance of those who reward us initially, such as parents, will become assimilated as secondary reinforcements, it is doubtful whether any campaign against response to appearance can succeed entirely.

Much more dangerous, but perhaps more easily eradicated, are the false criteria for status conferral such as age, sex, race, religion, ethnicity, and blood ("blue" or not "blue"). To the extent that these are not necessarily linked *inherently and directly* to competence and the achievement level of contribution in the division of labor, they are bases of misplaced confidence with regard to status accord. The directness of the link is important, for it is imperative to show that the failure to achieve is a direct function of having the given trait, rather than that having the trait is merely used as a social signal to deprive one of the opportunity to achieve, for example, through denial of education (Kemper, 1974).

Reflecting again on the relational basis of the model, each actor must make a contribution before he receives a measure of voluntary compliance from the other. One of the most troublesome questions of social life is how much he will receive for his contribution, depending on its type, rather than its level of competence or achievement. A famous running debate in the theory of stratification between the "functionalists" (Davis and Moore, 1945), and the Marxists and antifunctionalists (Tumin, 1953) focuses on this question. Davis and Moore held that qualitatively different contributions in the division of labor are necessarily evaluated differently—for example, a physician versus a ditchdigger—and therefore the contributors are differentially rewarded. Tumin, on the other hand, said that it is possible to conceive of a system in which competence in whatever contribution is more important than the type of contribution. Put most starkly, the best physician and the best ditchdigger would obtain approximately similar levels of status, as opposed to the extant "functionalist" system in which the best ditchdigger does not attain the status level of even the worst physician. The utopian Marxist solution is to end person specialization in the division of labor, thus making it possible for each actor to occupy several niches in the division of labor at the same time. If the additive combination of status levels corresponding to these niches were about the same for all actors, differential status accord might disappear.

In addition, Marx (1964a, pp. 256–258) adumbrated a stage of social development in which status accord is disjoined from contribution—whether by type or degree of competence—but is rather linked to need, as in the famous formula "From each according to his ability, to each according to his need." In Marx's view the implementation of such a basis for status accord would require not only socialization of the means of production, but also the liberation of production to an extent that would, by and large, eliminate the prime economic category of scarcity. Whether indeed this can be accomplished remains for future societies to discover. To date, scarcity does prevail, and, in the quest for status, contribution is a principal determinant. Even Marx (1964a, pp. 256–258) believed this would prevail in the first stage of socialism.

It can be seen that the acquisition of both sex-role and occupational-role content—the first dependent variables of socialization—are prerequisites for the display of competence and achievement. Without these, no stable basis exists for acquiring status in later life, regardless of how much status may be accorded by doting parents in childhood.

It can be seen also that manifesting competence and achievement obtains the rewards that can be converted into important resources for autonomy. This is true not only because those rich in status resources are able to avoid many situations of direct dependency, but also because status provides the resources for counterpower. Principally this means that others come to depend on one, and their dependence augments one's own power. That power then operates as a deterrent against the other's use of power (Emerson, 1962).

A critical view of the competence-achievement basis of status accord is given by Maslow (1968). He proposed that the "healthy personality" is more prone to "detachment" than to the quest for environmental mastery. This raises a question as to where healthy personalities acquire status and in what currency. It is possible that the early acquisition of status (i.e., love, warmth, and support) from parents in the proper amounts and proper mix with power enables the individual to convey status to himself. Essentially it is a symbolic recapitulation of the love and warmth that were previously received, but it is likely that the early love and warmth were given in large part for the child's displays of environmental mastery. At some point in the socialization process competence and mastery must be fostered. Status accord is a central mechanism for fostering these. Essentially, Maslow's objection may be to competitive status seeking rather than to competence itself.

Other's Status: Giving-Loving. The final dependent variable of socialization to be considered here also emerges from a consideration of the power-status relational model. If one's own status is obtained from the other, it must follow in the dyad that the source of the other's status must be oneself. One must be able to give status, that is, be able voluntarily to confer rewards, benefits, and gratifications on the other for his competence and achievement in the division of labor. The ultimate of such status conferral, which is perhaps divorced from any single overt contribution at all, is love (Kemper, 1972b).

An alternate model of social relations might view the giving of status as an exchange transaction (e.g., Homans, 1961; Blau, 1964), in which each ultimately holds out for the highest gain at the least cost. This is essentially a power model, since capitulation and forced agreement are contingent on dependence and, ultimately, on who has the greater power, as in our previous discussion of autonomy. The relational model proposed here allows for the development of the power-dependence motives and countermotives, but it also proposes that, in addition to exchange, which fundamentally involves a form of coerced compliance, there is also status, which involves voluntary compliance and giving, and that this requires the capacity of each actor to give independently of what he receives. The sociological defect of the inability to give is that one actor then attempts to monopolize all the gratification in the system, and, since both actors must obtain status for their contributions, the failure of one actor to give leads to the destruction of the division of labor and the relationship.

This conclusion is based on the premise that, although one can wrest rewards (for oneself) from the other by coercion and this can continue over a period of time, relationships based purely on coercion are ultimately unstable. When the victim's stock is depleted, he either goes away, dies, or rebels; or one grows weak through indulgence or old age and loses the ability to coerce the other as before. In any case, history records a more or less continuously unfolding development toward greater equity and less power as the standard relational mode, both within and between societies. It was in the light of this that de Tocqueville (1835, pp. 3–6) read the significance of political democracy for both Europe and America. Since his day we have extended the same perspective to the entire globe.

A critical issue, however, is whether the improvement in the equity of rewards has resulted from increases in the power of the previously deprived, or whether those rewards are given as status, that is, voluntarily. From the point of view of a theory of emotions, the difference is connected to the emotions of fear and anger in the first case and to some minimum of respect and liking in the other. If fear and anger are the principal emotions of the giver, the stability of the interaction is again threatened. Respect and liking, however, promise continuity of reward conferral, other things being equal. Of course, the intergenerational transformation of power into status is probably a common mode (see Kemper, 1974).

Ultimately, we must understand how socialization can accomplish the goal of developing in individuals the capacity to give and to love others, where loving is understood as the ultimate form of "giving." I suggest that the capacity to give as an expressive act, that is, the giving is not instrumental as in an exchange theory description, depends on the availability of internalized standards. These standards are activated by the attributes and performances of others, and when these match the standards, giving (or status accord) is triggered automatically. I believe that this explains all voluntary compliance, of moderate or extreme amounts, as in love. Since the question is most sharply focused in love relationships, I reserve a fuller discussion of how standards are related to status conferral for the next chapter, in which I treat love relationships.

Loving, or even lesser levels of giving status, has not attracted much attention from academic students of human development until very recently. Although the concept of altruism, which is, relationally, a conferring of status on another, was proposed and defined by Comte and proposed religiously, philosophically, and ideologically both before and after Comte (see, for example, Isaiah or Kropotkin, 1902), very little actual research on the nature of altruism or the nature of the altruist was undertaken (except Sorokin, 1951) until the murder of Kitty Genovese in Kew Gardens, New York in 1963.

That event received intensive press coverage because it was discovered that as many as 38 persons saw or heard the young woman's plight as she tried to escape from an assailant, but none of the 38 attempted to help her or even call the police. They reported later that they were "afraid" or that they did not want to "get involved". The academic community finally did respond with a substantial number of studies of altruistic behavior. A lengthy review is provided by Krebs (1970).

Altruism is, of course, a form of status conferral, defined as such when another is given gratification at a probable cost to oneself. This makes it a variant on the general theme of giving gratifications voluntarily to others. Other forms would involve both considerateness of others in all social situations through maximization of opportunities to reward others by whatever status currency is available, as well as the capacity to respond to another with love in the interpersonal sense, namely, a valuing of the other at the highest levels. Foote (1953) provided a most useful conception in defining loving as the actions that help another achieve growth.

Most of the relatively meagre research in the area of giving-loving has focused on the relationship between the characteristics of the actor, the situation, and the person to be helped (see the categorization by Krebs, 1970). Since giving-loving is proposed here as a socialization variable, our first concern should be with parent-child relations that contribute to the capacity to give status to others. A very general proposition that will probably find support, with some modifications, is that those who receive status in adequate amounts are probably most able to give it. Felt deficits of gratification will probably be found to be associated with the desire to get from others rather than the capacity to give to them.

Explicit training in the cognitive rationale of giving to others is also important. Cole (1966) found that Peace Corps volunteers who, regardless of other motives, also manifestly sought to help and give to others in need had usually received concrete socialization in values and standards for helping others. Hoffman (1975) also found higher altruism in children whose socialization included specific concern with the effects of the child's actions on others—the "induction" treatment, as discussed in Chapter 10.

A tradition of research that stems from Piaget (1932) and includes Kohlberg (1969) most prominently among others is also relevant to the giving-loving dimension. Although the interest of both these investigators (more so Piaget than Kohlberg) is developmental, the endpoint of both theories of moral development includes concern for the welfare of others, more or less autonomously felt and practised, without external sanctions providing the stimulus.

SOCIALIZATION DIMENSIONS AND POSITIVE EMOTIONS

The reader who has followed this derivation of the dependent variables of socialization may perhaps wonder whether anything new has been said. In some respects, such a conjecture would be entirely correct, for surely sex-role and occupational-role learning, control of aggression, autonomy, competence, and giving-loving have been the subjects of more or less concern by other theorists and researchers. If the preceding discussion is to be appreciated, however, it must be understood that these dependent variables of socialization have never before been derived from a single theoretical perspective. Ultimately, it is the theoretical foundation from which these dependent variables are derived that is at stake.

One direct benefit of this approach to the dependent variables of socialization is that it provides an avenue from which to view the problem of positive emotions. The four dependent variables of socialization derived from the four power-status relational channels—control of aggression, competence and achievement, autonomy, and giving-loving—are behavioral and personality modes by which the satisfactions that underly the positive emotions are obtained.

Guilt and Control of Aggression.   In the earlier discussion of guilt (Chapter 3), I suggested that this emotion stems from a relational condition in which the actor has used excessive power against another. The excess must be felt by the actor involved, and this may be due to the presence of internalized norms or values, comparison with others, and so on. It seems evident that when actors are socialized to control aggression, which is of course in most instances in social life a violation of social norms and values, the actors are helped ipso facto to avoid the emotion of guilt. This formula assumes that the actor has adopted the norm as a serious guide to action. In this sense it has reached the level of internalization that makes the behavior "intrinsically rewarding" (Kelman, 1965, p. 142).

The internalization of prohibitions against aggression can be so powerful that even the mildest affront to another may evoke a strong reaction of guilt, or the internalization may be so weak that virtually no amount of power used against another is accompanied by guilt. It seems likely that cultural norms, with regard to both content and intensity, determine the modal response. Those who fall to either side of the modal response become saints (if their actions totally preclude the emergence of guilt), psychotics (if, regardless of their actions, guilt is nonetheless their paramount emotion), or psychopaths (if, regardless of their actions, they can never experience guilt).

Although there is some utility in labeling the emotion that accompanies the actions that signify the control of aggression, it is difficult to do so. If the aggression is controlled in virtually automatic fashion without even having been evoked as a possibility, the level of emotional arousal may be extremely low. There would simply be calm that is on-going. Yet, if reflection is spurred or if the control of aggression results from a substantial struggle with the impulse to use power, the arousal may reach considerable intensity. Given the dissonance reduction that ought to follow from having resolved the inner conflict, given further the direct rewards of the decision in terms of relief from anxiety and anger (if this relief has occurred), the feeling tone should be a pleasing one. If a single word can capture the sense of the feelings, I propose *righteousness*. This conveys the sense of having done what is right. In virtually all ethical codes the control of the use of excess power against others is so defined.

Shame and Competence and Achievement.   I proposed in Chapter 9 that the distressful emotion of shame results from a felt sense of undeservingness of the amount of status that is accorded to one. The sense of excess, I believe, stems from the disjunction between the appearance of competence (for which the status is given) and the felt sense of lack of competence. It is precisely the socialization for competence that can obviate the emotion of shame. Again, as in the case of guilt, there is the possibility that some will feel shame even when they are competent beyond their fellows, whereas others do not experience shame even when there is an egregious disparity between their performance and their rewards. Social norms also determine the modal response. Standards for performance are rarely absolute, but relative to the available pool of talent. Both over- and undercompetence and achievement are determined by a social yardstick (Kemper, 1968a). If one has been socialized to unrealistic standards for performance, that is, where one's capabilities have been evaluated far above their true measure and therefore performance must always fall beneath the standard, the likelihood of shame is very strong. On the other hand, if one has been socialized to unrealistically low standards of performance (but if social pressure ensures that the performance is at least adequate), shame is rarely felt.

As for the label that may reasonably apply to the feelings that ensue from competence and achievement, I suggest that justifiable *pride* comes phenomenologically closest. As in the case of righteousness, the magnitude of the emotion would seem to depend on the consciousness of the struggle that went into the performance and its resolution in a competent and achieving manner.

Anxiety and Autonomy.   If anxiety, as I have proposed, is the emotion that stems from a sense of the excess of other's power, independence or autonomy in some degree would mitigate anxiety. The useful formula by Emerson (1962) shows this to be the case: $P_{ab} = D_{ba}$. The degree to which one does *not* depend on the other is the degree to which the other's power cannot affect us. This is generally true for the case in which there is dependence for gratifications and status from the other and in which the other can exercise power through status withdrawal. The efficacy of the autonomy strategy is recognized by both Emerson (1962) and Blau (1964).

If, on the other hand, anxiety stems from a concern with the other's use of noxious power, for example, physical coercion, autonomy serves only partially to avoid anxiety, since it operates only to limit the number of occasions of necessary interaction. This may reduce the statistical probability of anxiety, but it does not ensure against the power of the other on occasions when interaction is necessary or the other simply goes on a rampage. In such cases only deterrent capability would seem to stand one in good stead. When the other is aware that noxious power will be met with counterpower, there is a smaller likelihood of his attacking in the first place. When one is free of the fear of attack, the feeling is one of *security*. I have already used this label to refer to the positive emotional tone that prevails in the absence of fear-anxiety (see Chapter 3).

Depression and Giving-Loving.   The most unexpected outcome of this joint examination of the distressful emotions and the socialization dimensions is the preventive role of giving-loving as an offset of depression. If there is empirical validity to the theoretical inference, it provides support for an ancient message: the more we concern ourselves with others, the less we suffer from the lack of concern given to us. Loving, in other words, is the best antidote for the distress of not being loved.

Loving, however, is not an act of will. As I develop in the next chapter, love is a nonvolitional response and thus truly an emotion. Nonetheless, giving and loving behavior can be undertaken because they are "right or "moral" or because duty and obligation bind us, even if the emotional component is largely absent. There is a possible tension between the feeling and form of action that has been noted by several authors. Hoffman (1970) tried most explicitly to sort out the two orientations in the context of "moral" behavior. He reported data (collected with Saltzstein) in which children were found to engage in moral behaviors either because the children spontaneously chose the moral alternative or, on reflection, they chose it because it was the "right" thing to do. Hoffman called the former orientation "humanistic-flexible" and the latter "rigid-conventional." Hoffman's discussion suggests that the humanistic-flexible children responded to situations of moral quandaries with a direct emotional lovingness. The others in the situation evoked status accord spontaneously, and a relatively pure emotion of positive feelings toward the others would seem to underly this orientation. The rigid-conventional children, however, appeared to respond more to anxiety and threat of punishment in their choice of the moral alternative, thereby suppressing their spontaneous impulse, which was not to give or love, but to withhold. Thus the rigid-conventional giving is not precisely status accord as I have defined and used this concept. Rather, it reflects a coercive evocation of rewards in which conscience stands for the earlier parental figures who commanded and coerced obedience to the rule of love and morality.

From the point of view of the dyad, if the on-going interaction must be maintained, it is probably preferable that actors engage in giving and loving behavior even if it is not spontaneous than not to act that way at all. Parents, doubtless, often act lovingly toward their children even though they do not feel it at the moment, and spouses often act so in a similar vein toward their mates. Perhaps social life and personal feelings cannot always be expressively veridical. At the off-times, so to speak, it is useful to have available a superego or concepts of duty and obligation to maintain the giving behavior even though the giving emotion has been temporarily shortcuited. Maslow (1968) sensed the danger in any commitment to total emotional expressiveness and argued that some proponents of "self-actualization"—a movement that stresses greater personal expressiveness—"do not sufficiently warn that most adults don't know *how* to be authentic and that, if they 'express' themselves, they may bring catastrophe not only upon themselves but upon others as well" (p. 161, emphasis in original). In the next two chapters I examine the relational and emotional aspects of giving and loving very extensively and defer until then precisely labeling the emotion.

A final consideration is that, although there is a zero-sum quality to emotional life, the positive emotions are not present simply in the absence of distressful emotions. As discussed in Chapter 3, when we considered the structural emotions, the absence of relational conditions that would provoke distressful emotions leads to contentment and satisfaction; that is, adequate amounts of power and status is the state of relational affairs, and there is little emotional arousal. The contentment is calm. When any of the four relational channels—own power, own status, other's power, other's status—are activated, they become salient for the evocation and magnification of emotions relating to them. Thus the pride of achievement is particularly felt when the contribution is offered and recognized, that is, when status is first accorded for the contribution. Later, the achievement and the relational mode of own status become less salient in one's attention, and a generalized satisfaction takes over. In a sense, the positive emotions are tantamount to the pleasures experienced while consuming well-prepared tasty food. Afterward a pleasing sense of satisfaction takes over that is different from the specific pleasurable sensations that occur during the meal.

chapter 12

Love as a Social Relationship: I. The Status Dimension

Considering the vast appeal of love to both popular and ethical consciousness, it is remarkable that so little theory or research is devoted to the topic. In recent years numerous investigations have dealt with the subject of interpersonal attraction (for a review of many approaches, see Huston, 1974), but because of the temporal constraints of laboratory experiments, the insensitivity of survey instruments, or the reluctance of investigators to apply crude methodologies to deep and delicate emotions, love itself has been largely skirted (cf. Berscheid and Walster, 1974; Carlson, 1971).

Discussions of love are often hindered by the recognition that there appear to be different kinds of love and that different conclusions must be drawn depending on the type with which we are dealing. For example, Marlowe and Gergen (1969) spoke of the "differences among such phenomena as the comradeship felt by members of a team, the respect felt for a powerful leader, sexual attraction for a person of the opposite sex, a mother's devotion to a child, and the gratitude of a person relieved of distress . . . " (p. 622).

Harlow and Harlow (1972), based on their work with primates, proposed five "affectional systems": mother love, infant love, age-mate or peer love, heterosexual love, and paternal love. Fromm (1956), in one of the most widely known discussions of love, discussed brotherly love, motherly love, erotic love, love of God, and self-love. Although we can exclude self-love from consideration here since it is not a social relationship in the same sense as the others, Fromm's is certainly a plausible, but not necessarily exhaustive list, as are Harlows' and Gergen and Marlowe's types of love or relationships in which love may play a part.

Yet until some common framework is available from which the various types of love relationships can be reasonably derived, discussions of love must necessarily be limited. The first objective of this chapter, therefore, is to present a heuristic typology that can provide a comprehensive framework for analytical investigations of love relationships. I derive the typology from a further consideration of the two relational dimensions of power and status. This follows from the recognition that, although love is related to very potent emotions, these are virtually always the result of real, imagined, or anticipated involvement in social relationship. Thus we must look to an understanding of social relationship for a better understanding of love. This leads us, as a second objective, to consider the dynamics of power and status as these affect the arousal and decay of love, both as emotion and relationship. The status aspects of love are treated in this chapter, the power aspects in the next chapter. The next chapter also deals with a number of recent theoretical contributions to the understanding of love relationships— reinforcement-exchange theory, need-fulfillment theory, and the two-factor theory based on the work of Schachter and his colleagues (see Chapter 8.) I shall compare these with the view of love afforded by the power-status model.

In the preceding chapter I derived the ability to give and to love as a critical dependent variable of socialization. This followed deductively as an implication for person characteristics from the adoption of the power-status model of social relationship. I believe that the power-status model also implies a conception of love in what I discuss in the next chapter as its *evolutionary optimum* form. Readers of Fromm (1956) and Maslow (1954, 1968) will find the conception familiar. However, I hope to contribute by articulating their formulations with the systematic relational model of this book.

Before turning to these matters, I wish to indicate certain limits of the analysis presented here. First, few persons in Western culture who reach adult-hood fail to experience the intense emotional arousal and involvement in a social relationship that is ordinarily classified as love. We are all, then, more or less aware of the strength, depth, and astonishment of feelings whose relational aspects we deal with here. However, I defer discussion of the unique *feeling tones* of love until after the analysis of the relational aspects of love and the sources of the loving impetus.

Second, actors are assumed to desire, to like, and to feel good (within the limits of satiation) when they are voluntarily given gratification, reward, and compliance in all their manifest forms—that is, when they are given status. Furthermore, actors are assumed to dislike, to try to avoid, and to feel bad when they are the objects of force, coercion, threat, manipulation, punishment, and so on, either as noxious increments of pain or as the withdrawal or withholding of customary or expected gratifications, that is, when they are the objects of power wielded against them. Particularly in the case of withdrawal of customary re-wards, that is, the reduction of status, the object of such loss ordinarily feels the hurt even if the withdrawal was not part of a purposive power play as such—that is, it hurts to lose customary rewards whether or not the reduction was employed specifically as a coercive tactic to overcome resistance. (The direct emotional consequences of some of these relational changes are discussed in earlier chap-ters.)

Third, this analysis excludes those actors for whom the usual pleasures are painful and the usual pains pleasurable. Thus the actors here are given motive force by their approach to the vast array of usual gratifications and avoidance of the usual kinds of pains.

Fourth, the analysis does not imply that both actors in the relationship feel the same, even if they believe they do. This is a difficult problem in all social relationships, and a great deal more work must be done to clarify it (cf. Weber, 1947, p. 119; Blumer, 1962; Kemper, 1968b). Nonetheless I proceed with the analysis in the hope of capturing its main relational elements and emotions, even if these must be modified in certain cases because of perceptual noncongruence.

A TYPOLOGY OF LOVE RELATIONSHIPS

First, it is necessary to adopt seriously the view that love is a social relationship, actually or potentially. If the relationship is actual, concrete behaviors are directed by the actors to each other; if the relationship is only potential, one actor (or both) imagines or anticipates directing certain behaviors toward the other actor. Although a potential relationship, as defined here, is only minimally social, it does involve an other who is taken account of and who thereby causes alteration in the anticipated behavior of the focal actor (cf. Weber, 1947, p. 88; Jones and Gerard, 1967, pp. 505–512).

If we assume that love implies a social relationship, this suggests that love relationships must be constituted of the same dimensions as other social relationships. In this work I view all social relationships as comprised of the two dimensions of power and status, and I continue in that view. In particular, considering the definition and discussion of status accord in Chapters 2 and 3, I suggest that the status dimension is at the core of social relationships that involve love. Keeping in mind that status accord involves the voluntary giving of gratifications, benefits, rewards, compliance, and the like to the other, I offer this definition: A *love relationship is one in which at least one actor gives (or is prepared to give) extremely high status to the other actor.* Thus, if A loves B, A is giving or is prepared to give extremely high status to B.

How high the status must be is open to question. Does it mean that A would die for B if the circumstances required? That is possible, although for most people this is a rare test of love and does not assist us in defining love for the great mass of humankind. We can perhaps resolve the ambiguity by suggesting that the status ought *implicitly* to be limitless.

The definition just proposed—that a love relationship implies at least one actor according extremely high status to the other—suggests an approach to discovering how many different types of love relationship are possible. This can be done by plotting all the dyadic possibilities between two actors in the power-status space in which one or both actors are extremely high in status received from the other actor. Since the definition is unrestrictive with regard to power, this dimension is free to vary and assists in generating the various types of love relationships. Figure 12.1 shows that there are seven ideal-typical possibilities. These are also found in Table 12.1. In both the figure and the table, a particular love relationship is identified by the same number attaching to the two actors in the relationship. Thus the pair tagged with the number 1 comprise a unique relationship, as do the pair tagged with number 2, and so on to number 7.

An examination of Figure 12.1 shows that only extreme or ideal types are depicted. Except for at least the one actor who is very high in status, the power and status position of the other actor can vary unrestrictedly, as can the power position of the extremely high-status actor. Thus if we consider the pair 5-5, it is conceivable that the actor who has less power and status could have a moderate amount of both rather than none at all. Thus instead of the lower 5 falling at the origin, this actor may be at the X-mark in Figure 12.1. This is probably common and might perhaps be added as an empirical instance of some importance. Also, since the power and status scales are continuous, it is empirically possible for infinite gradations of love relationships to exist that conform to the definition offered. Nonetheless, I do not deal with these variations, because, for practical purposes, we must simplify our treatment; otherwise the analysis would be end-

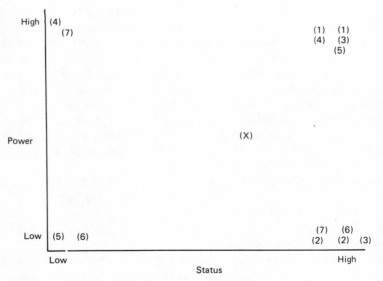

Figure 12–1   Seven types of love relationships.

TABLE 12-1   SEVEN TYPES OF LOVE

Type	Actor A's Power	Actor A's Status	Actor B's Power	Actor B's Status
1–1 Romantic love	High	High	High	High
2–2 Brotherly love	Low	High	Low	High
3–3 Charismatic or discipleship love	High	High	Low	High
4–4 Infidelity	High	High	High	Low
5–5 Infatuation	High	High	Low	Low
6–6 Adulation by fans	Low	High	Low	Low
7–7 Parent-infant	Low	High	High	Low

less. Yet the theoretical value of the ideal-typical set of seven derived here is that they manage to incorporate all the known types (for example, those discussed by Marlowe and Gergen, 1969, Harlow and Harlow, 1972, Fromm, 1956, and Maslow, 1954, 1968). Let us consider these seven types of love relationship.

1-1. Romantic Love.   A reciprocated relationship between two actors, in which both give each other extremely high status, but in which each actor also has high power, appears to be what is commonly designated romantic love. The mutual involvement of the parties is of such an order that each can punish the other severely for real or imagined transgressions to ensure conformity in the future, as well as to assuage the hurt feelings of the past. To be romantically involved is to wield power as well as pleasure and often to be a victim. In this type of love relationship, status and power are maximally interwined. Each actor receives extremely high status from the other, but—as developed in the section on power and dependence in the next chapter—it is the very pleasure that each obtains from the other that becomes the source of the other's power. The "romantic agony," in which the loved object is also a source of pain, is indeed an agony, since it leads to an approach-avoidance conflict and/or cognitive imbalance. The instability of such situations suggests why romantic love is so precarious a relationship. In addition, the fact that romantic love is the only relationship in which both actors are extremely high in both power and status, that is, they are at the very ends of the two relational scales, explains why this type of relationship is so profoundly experienced.

2-2. Brotherly Love.   The millennial hope, as well as a vain dream of humankind, has been to order social life on the basis of what is called brotherly love, when "swords shall be beaten to ploughshares" and "men will not make war anymore." Sociologically, it would entail that all persons accord each other high status and that they are low in power. Compliance would be willing; self-interest would metamorphose into the other's interest; disagreement, should it arise, would be adjudicated by mechanisms that neither invoke nor require power. If there is an abiding problem for humankind it is surely focused here: how to let go of power and accord each other status. Ethical injunctions dating back thousands of years have advised us that this is our salvation, yet they have not provided either the theory or the means by which the transformation from social organization based on power to social organization based on status can be accomplished. It is a bold hope that social science can uncover enough of the well-springs of human action to make it possible to devise the means by which the low-power, high-status goal can be attained.

3-3. Charismatic or Discipleship Love.   There is a type of love relationship in which one actor is high in power and status, and the other is high only in status. I believe that several types of relationships in which the actors are related as teacher-student, master-disciple, and revered leader-worthy follower are of this type. Concretely this would involve relationships in which one gives oneself over to the direction of the other and is received as a worthy apprentice, novice, or follower. The leading partner of this relationship gives status to the follower and receives it in return, but the leader also retains the power to coerce so that the guidance will be effective. Certain phases in the father-son relationship appear to be of this type. Mussen and Distler (1959) and Mussen and Rutherford (1963) found that identification of boys with their fathers was enhanced when the father was seen as both loving and powerful. Although Mussen and his colleagues did not measure the boys' love for their fathers, we assume that the high identification with the father was a sign of love. Although identification, according to some, might also result from *fear* of the aggressor and thus preclude love directed toward the father, Mussen and Distler specifically tested and rejected this hypothesis. Parsons (1955) generalized the notion of the power component as important for the parent in relation to the child so that benefits for the child in the socialization process can be accomplished even over the child's resistance.

In its charismatic form, the leader has a transcendental nexus that is the major resource of his power over disciples and followers, while they both depend on the benefits granted them and return love and adoration to their larger-than-life leader (see Chapter 6).

Another close approximation to a recognized love relationship of this type is psychoanalytic transference. The analysand develops a strong attachment for the analyst, according him very high status in his surrogate role for an earlier love object (Freud, 1912, 1915). Since, from the point of view of the analysand, the relationship is romantic—sexual fantasies, for example, are common—high power is also ceded to the analyst. The analyst may not, theoretically as well as therapeutically, return the love in kind, but the analysand must be valued, and receives a high degree of interest and concern—status—from the therapist. The critical point is that the analysand not be given power, for then he and the analyst are romantically involved, as in the first of the love relationships discussed, and this would destroy the therapeutic relationship. Freud discussed the dangers to both patient and therapist of succumbing to romantic involvement, indicating that, although the analyst may be able to resist "the merely sexual" aspects of the relationship, the real peril in the particular case may lie in the fact that "there is an incomparable fascination about a noble woman who confesses her passion" (Freud, 1915, p. 389).

Ordinarily, the sociological structure of charismatic and discipleship contexts protects against the development of the relationship into fullfledged romantic love as in the 1-1 relationship. This has to do with the usual one-to-many character of such relationships: one teacher, many students; one therapist, many patients; one leader, many followers. Thus, although the disciple or follower has only the single source of status and is dependent on that source, the leader has many sources and therefore need not depend on any single follower. This precludes the development of dependence on the individual follower and the development of that follower's power. In the case of parents and children, the parent can avoid a romantic entanglement with a child by maintaining affectional dependence with the other parent. There are indeed strong norms against parent-child incestuous development in the family, but it can be seen that a homologue to the incest taboo is also a feature of the other leader-disciple relationships (e.g., teachers and students, therapists and patients).

4-4. Infidelity.   An unusual form of love relationship is that in which one party is accorded high status and has high power, whereas the other party is accorded low status, but has high power. An *apparent* romantic love relationship in which there is covert infidelity by one of the partners fits into this category. The duped partner accords high status to the duping one, and because of the overt and manifest signs of high status accorded by the betrayer, the latter also has high power. However, in relationships in which infidelity is treated as a breach of the most intimate trust, the duper has in fact withdrawn a very significant amount of status from the duped. This would be immediately apparent were the facts to become known. Despite the fact that the duper is not exclusively dependent on the betrayed partner for gratification and therefore the latter's power is not quite as high as it might be, the very large number of other details of the relational interdependence—particularly when formalized as in marriage—guarantees a considerable amount of power to the betrayed. That the duped still has a good deal of power is also evidenced by the fact that the infidelity is usually kept secret. Although the concept of "no fault divorce" is gaining some support, the frequently punitive stance of courts in proven cases of infidelity has a long history.

When fidelity is not a valued norm of conduct between the partners, this analysis does not apply. In addition, if exposure of infidelity does not lead to exercise of power by the betrayed to stop it, the latter's structural power crumbles to a significant degree, since it appears that gratifications, that is, high status, will be accorded to the betrayer regardless of what he or she does. The legal concept of *condonation* also applies. This involves the mitigation or elimination of penalties for adultery in those instances in which the betrayed spouse has willingly had intercourse with his or her mate after the latter has confessed to infidelity. In such instances, however, the relationship passes out of this type into the next type to be discussed. In the more common case, when infidelity is discovered the significant amount of status withdrawn by an enlightened and enraged partner from the exposed partner moves the relationship out of the domain of love entirely; that is, neither partner is according the other extremely high status, whether in appearance or reality.

The relationship involving deception again sensitizes us to the need to examine love relationships from the perspectives of both actors. In the case of infidelity, the relationship is one of love only from the point of view of the betrayed, since he or she still truly confers extremely high status on the unfaithful partner. However, from the point of view of the betrayer, as long as the acknowledged norms condemn infidelity, the relationship no longer involves extremely high status conferral on the other—regardless of how much status is apparently conferred. Since deception is a tactic of coercion—the other would not give status voluntarily were the truth known—from the point of view of the betrayer, the relationship is largely one of power, that is, extracting gratifications from the other over the other's (highly probable) opposition (see the discussion of manipulation and power in Appendix 2).

5-5. Infatuation.   As we have just seen in the case of infidelity, in some love relationships there is such a disparity between the status positions of the two actors that the loving is essentially one-sided. Deception, however, is not needed to create the disparity.

In the case of unrequited love, high status and high power exist on one side only, whereas little status and little power are in the possession of the other actor. One-sided infatuations are of this type, in which a mere glance can be sufficient to inflame the sentiments of one person, whereas the other may be unaware of the amount of status the first is prepared to accord, much less of the power he holds vis a vis the first.

The ultimate form of dualism of this kind of love relationship can involve love of God. In various ways men are commanded to love God, and it is intimated that God loves man, but the two can scarcely be equated. To God belongs both the "power and the glory" (status), and these are infinitely greater than those of man according to the doxologies of (at least) the Western religious traditions. Man is both commanded to depend on God, that is, cede power to God, and to love God, that is, grant God's will or give status. Although some religious traditions also broach the question of God's need of man, so that man also gains some power, the disparity between God and man is understood to be so great that the relationship remains highly imbalanced. Conceptions of the God-man relationship can, however, move in the direction of the charismatic or discipleship type (2–2). In that case, God reciprocates man's love, but retains power, whereas man has little or none. Another possible model of the God-man relationship is the 7–7 type discussed later.

6-6. Adulation by Fans   The most attenuated form of love relationship is found in the case in which the power and status of one partner is low and only the status, but not power, of the other partner is high. Prototypical of this form of love is the relationship between fans and their idol. Although one thinks immediately of the crescendos of adulation performers are able to evoke from their fans, the relationship is essentially weak because the bonding is undirectional, marked by the high status of only one of the actors. It is further weakened by the inability of either actor to exert power against the other on an individual basis. Collectively, however, fans do command very great power. When the relationship is seen in that form, it is no longer the same, but moves on to become similar to the parent-infant love relationship discussed next.

Although the adulation-by-fans type of relationship is tenuous, as described, it is yet a very important form of love, inasmuch as it is the way in which most love relationships begin. One person finds value and merit in another and initiates (or contemplates) the accord of extremely high status to the other. I treat this again later in the discussion of the phases of love relationships.

7-7. Parent-Infant.   The newborn infant is, in the overwhelming majority of cases, accorded virtually supreme status. No need is denied the neonate. Every cry is heard and heeded. The other in this case, usually the mother, is bereft of status. Virtually nothing she wants or needs is given or done by the infant. Of course, this is because the infant is not aware of the mother's interest, does not know the appropriate symbol system to be able to detect the mother's wants, and so on. Mother, however, has one resource when all else is lacking, namely, power. Her physical and psychological superiority can in most cases prevail over the infant. This is true to the extent that certain infant tactics that may gain it power, such as prolonged shrieking and crying, do not succeed. If they do, the relationship deteriorates into the pattern of type 4, namely, the infidelity model. As the child grows older, the relationship changes in most cases to one of the other forms (e.g., discipleship) and probably passes through other types as well, not excluding romantic love. The best final outcome from the point of view of both parties, if such an evaluation may be ventured here, is probably brotherly love. All other outcomes are less good for one or both actors, because of the painful effects of the employment of power.

This concludes the discussion of the seven types of love relationship. Heuristically I propose that any concrete love relationship can be adequately located within one of the ideal types.

Comprehensiveness of the Typology

It is useful to see that Fromm's four types of love are contained within the seven types derived from the power-status model, as well as some types that Fromm did not include in his ad hoc presentation. Marlowe and Gergen's (1969, p. 622) types of relationships, mentioned at the outset, can also be understood better at this point. The "comradeship felt by members of a team," if sufficiently intense, would appear to fall into the brotherly love category. This is implied not only by the equality, sharing of burdens, and capacity for self-sacrifice inherent in the notion of comradeship, but is also supported by the very nearly synonymous nature of the words comrade and brother.

The "respect felt for a powerful leader" may be variously understood, depending on what is meant by the term "powerful." If it means only successful and able, the relationship may be that of adulation by fans—something like the public adoration of the triumphant general on his return to Rome (Tacitus, 1942). If "powerful" means the coercive capacity the leader holds over the members of the group, dependence may be implied, in which case some valued rewards are given to the member, even though he has little power himself. This would be the type of transference love. We need not pursue this longer than to suggest that many psychoanalytic studies of leadership have exactly identified the love of the leader with the love of some earlier, usually parental figure (e.g., Freud, 1923; Fromm, 1941). If the term "powerful," on the other hand, does not imply the kind of power that comes from the ability to withdraw the status on which the other is dependent, but rather implies the capacity to inflict noxious stimuli, that is, the totalitarian leader, we have an instance of the infatuation or love of God phenomenon. In regard to this identification of God and totalitarianism, no amount of reverence can conceal that some conceptions of God do indeed attribute the most awesome power to God, and, what is more, that God uses this power! Obviously, only a precise specification of what is intended by the relational term power can provide an adequate basis for understanding Marlowe and Gergen's phrase. However, it is useful to underscore that one of the utilities of the power-status model lies precisely in its ability to differentiate between quite different types of love that involve power.

Marlowe and Gergen's next type, "sexual attraction for a person of the opposite sex," does not, on the face of it, appear to be a type of love at all. This may occasion some astonishment, since popular notions of love certainly understand this attraction as a manifest signal of love. Yet it is useful to reflect on the definition of love offered here, namely, a relationship in which one actor actually or potentially *confers extremely high status on the other actor.* Feeling sexually attracted to another seems to suggest just the opposite kind of situation; that is, one actor feels he can receive extremely high status from the other. It should be clear that the desire to receive status can hardly be the same as the desire to give it. Maslow (1968, pp. 42–43) discussed these two modalities as deficiency-type love and being-type love, respectively, and it is hardly necessary to expatiate further on the fact that the distinction has been known since ancient times and that only the giving or being-type is understood as love by all but the very callowest of persons.

Marlowe and Gergen's next type, "a mother's devotion to a child," fits very obviously into the mother-infant type in which the status conferred on the child is clearly "devotion," since there is no return—that is, no status is received from the child in return. The last type, "gratitude of a person relieved of distress," does not appear to be a case of love, since, ordinarily, the feeling is not translated into giving the other extremely high status as an enduring feature of the relationship. On the other hand, it may attain such a level, in which case it would become a type of love. The type would depend on the status giver's status and the power of both.

Although I have yet to deal with the precise feeling tones of love, it seems obvious that comradeship, respect for a leader, mother's devotion, and gratitude evoke different feelings. I can only note as a heuristic surmise without the full development it requires that the origin of the differences in feeling tone is principally in the differences in the power-status positions of the actors in the different relationships. This view conforms to the general position on structural emotions presented in Chapter 3.

A further reflection on the limitations of this analysis of love is now possible. The reduction of so sensitive an emotion as love to a typology derived from only two dimensions of social relational behavior may offend the reader who senses more variety in loving than proposed here. It is worth noting, then, that the seven types of love relationship are logically, not empirically, derived, and that the number of logically possible love relationships depends on the number of dimensions of social relational behavior initially postulated. For example, if there were a third dimension in addition to power and status, and if the same assumption were retained that at least one of the actors must be accorded extremely high status, while the power of this actor is free to vary, as are the power and status of the second actor—and the position of both actors is free to vary (either high or low) on the third dimension, instead of seven types of love relationship there would be 26 types. Adding a fourth dimension of relationship while retaining the original definition of love would lead to 100 different types of love relationship. (Table 12.2 shows the full set for three dimensions.)

If this is frightening, it ought well to be, and perhaps the parsimony offered by two dimensions may be seen to be acceptable for reasons not previously elucidated. Were it to turn out that there are 26 or 100 or, adding yet another dimension, some 400 types of love relationship, this would surely beggar the capacity of social science to record, much less explain, them all. Oversimplification, of course, may be implied by the seven relationships generated from the two dimensions of power and status. Yet, as has been shown, the seven types can reasonably comprehend the full spectrum of types already suggested (cf. Fromm, 1956; Marlowe and Gergen, 1969, p. 622; Harlow and Harlow, 1972).

Furthermore, as Goodenough (1965) proposed, based on the work of Miller (1956), perceptual and behavioral discriminations of roles may possibly not exceed seven or so in number. The underlying principle, suggested by Miller, is that the human capacity for information processing and discrimination imposes a relatively stringent limit on the number of differences individuals are able to perceive in more or less error-free fashion. Immediately, based on this notion, one might propose that *within* both the power and status dimensions, seven or so discriminations are possible, and thus many additional types of love are possible. These would, in my view, be variations in degree and not in kind. For heuristic purposes, I proceed on the assumption that love relationships can be usefully understood in terms of the relational dimensions of power and status. Not only has this led to a typology of love relationships, logically derived from terms previously defined, but it allows us to examine love relations further in terms of the dynamics of power and status and thereby understand the emotions connected with love.

DYNAMICS OF STATUS CONFERRAL

Although power is intimately involved in all but two of the seven types of love relations I derive, status accord is at the heart of each type. A question of great interest as far as love relations are concerned is, how does status come to be conferred? Although the status dimension pervaded this work, I have not yet dealt with this question. In the context of love it has a peculiarly poignant interest, because it is directly pertinent to the fascinating riddle of how people fall in love, stay in love, and fall out of love. Of course, the question is broader still,

TABLE 12–2 POSSIBLE LOVE RELATIONSHIPS WITH THREE RELATIONAL DIMENSIONS

Type of Love[a]	Actor A				Actor B			Number of
	P[b]	S	X		P	S	X	Types
Romantic (1–1)	H	H	H		H	H	H	
	H	H	H	single type	H	H	L	3
	H	H	L		H	H	H	
	H	H	L		H	H	L	
Brotherly (2–2)	L	H	H		L	H	H	
	L	H	H	single type	L	H	L	
	L	H	L		L	H	H	3
	L	H	L		L	H	L	
Charismatic-discipleship (3–3)	H	H	H		L	H	H	
	H	H	H		L	H	L	
	H	H	L		L	H	H	4
	H	H	L		L	H	L	
Infidelity (4–4)	H	H	H		L	H	H	
	H	H	H		L	H	L	
	H	H	L		L	H	H	4
	H	H	L		L	H	L	
Infatuation (5–5)	H	H	H		L	L	H	
	H	H	H		L	L	L	
	H	H	L		L	L	H	4
	H	H	L		L	L	L	
Adulation by fans (6–6)	L	L	H		L	H	H	
	L	L	H		L	H	L	
	L	L	L		L	H	H	4
	L	L	L		L	H	L	
Parent-infant (7–7)	H	L	H		L	H	H	
	H	L	H		L	H	L	
	H	L	L		L	H	H	4
	H	L	L		L	H	L	

[a]Label of love type applies for two-dimensional analysis.   [b]P = power; S = status; X = a third dimension.

for, whereas love involves the very highest level of status accord, most social relationships entail status conferral in varying amounts. An answer to the question of how extremely high amounts of status come to be accorded can also reveal how lesser amounts are conferred.

Let us recall that in Chapter 2 the status concept was derived from the idea of *voluntary compliance* with the wishes, desires, and interests of the other actor. That is to say, A wants to give benefits to B. He is not coerced to do so by B. I have held steadily to this *relational* conception of voluntary action in the case of status accord.

Now I must risk a certain terminological ambiguity by asserting that, *from the standpoint of the actor who confers the status*, the desire to do so is a nonvolitional response (cf. Hamblin and Smith, 1966, p. 184)*. This statement does not contradict the definition of status as the according of voluntary compliance. What is meant here is that the *inner* impulse or desire to give status to the other is not under the conscious or rational and volitional control of the actor who feels the impulse to give. Thus *from the point of view of the actor*, the impulse or desire to give status is nonvolitional. We cannot, in other words, help whom we love. However, *from the point of view of the relationship*, the readiness to give or the actual giving of extremely high amounts of gratification to the other is voluntary. Otherwise, the gratifications would be accorded because of coercion, that is, the other's power. We have come finally to some sense of the *emotional* quality of love, the nonvolitional, noncentral, autonomic nervous system aspects of the phenomenon. In love relationships, which involve extreme levels of voluntary compliance, the emotional component is nonvolitional as far as the lover is concerned. He has no control over what he feels. The nonvolitional nature of status conferral is akin to what Zetterberg (1966) described in his discussion of love as "emotional overcomeness," the nonvolitional succumbing to feeling for the other.

Yet we must recognize that whether the nonvolitional desire to give voluntary compliance actually leads to overt behavioral expression of the feeling is a separate matter. For example, a man may find himself in love with someone else's wife and come to the very rational decision to contain his feelings and never express them. Thus it is possible to decide volitionally in most cases whether to *behave* toward the other in terms of high status conferral (cf. Hamblin and Smith, 1966, p. 191). Whether or not one *feels* love, that is, the desire to accord high status to the other, in the first place, is, in this view, not a matter under the actor's volitional control.

This insight, which I believe is crucial not only to an understanding of love

---

*Hamblin and Smith actually used the expression "non-voluntary response." I chose to substitute the term nonvolitional response, because it is orthographically more distinguishable from "voluntary response" and is less likely to be confused with it.

relationships but also of the status dimension of social relations in general, comes from the extremely important work of Hamblin and Smith (1966). Their interest was in testing a theory of status prediction. In their empirical study, graduate students evaluated their professors on various characteristics such as merit of publication, merit of teaching, professional demeanor, cordiality, appearance and likability. These bases of evaluation were employed in a multiple regression analysis to predict professorial status as the dependent variable. Hamblin and Smith hypothesized that status conferral might operate homologously to psychophysical responses of a nonvolitional nature, where the magnitude of the response is an exponential function of the magnitude of the stimulus:

$$R = cS^n, \text{ or multivariately,}$$

$$R = cS_1{}^{n_1}S_2{}^{n_2} \ldots S_k{}^{n_k}$$

Here R equals the amount of status conferred on the professor, c is a constant, and S_i are the evaluation stimuli, such as merit of publications and the like, and n is the exponent. When the multivariate multiplicatory equation is transformed into a logarithm, it reads

$$\log R = \log C + n_1 \log S_1 + n_2 \log S_2 + \ldots + n_k \log S_k$$

The exponents are now equivalent to regression coefficients. Hamblin and Smith were able to account for 98% of the variance in the dependent variable, professorial status, by means of this model. Support for the nonvolitional nature of status conferral was provided by this successful application of the psychophysical multiplicative model. This remarkable outcome, however, is no more so than the statement that prepares the ground for it:

> Genuine status giving is problematical because having feelings of approval, respect, or esteem for someone appears to be beyond the individual's direct choice. In fact, the evidence suggests that all feelings, including those of approval, respect, or esteem, are part of a class of non-voluntary responses. As with all non-voluntary responses, these feelings are presumably controlled by the unconditioned or the conditioned stimuli which elicit them. *Apparently, an individual must provide the valued attributes and behavior which produce in the other the feelings of approval, respect or esteem; then and only then may these feelings be communicated as genuine status* (Hamblin and Smith, p. 184, emphasis added).

Status, then, is accorded to a person when he cues it by exhibiting some behavior or characteristic for which the other is ready *to accord status*. This is somewhat like the imprinting phenomenon described by ethologists (Hess, 1959; Harlow, 1962). There, for example, a duck exposed at an appropriate age to a terrycloth facsimile of a mother duck later seeks the presence of the facsimile in preference to its own true, feathered mother.

In their study of status accorded to professors by students, Hamblin and Smith dealt with moderately high levels of status accord, "feelings of approval, respect, or esteem." I believe that the fundamental principle of the evocation of status conferral by means of presenting "valued attributes and behavior" applies to status accord at any level, including the very highest, namely, feelings of love. If this conception is valid, the fundamental dynamics of status conferral involve the automatic (nonvolitional) triggering of the giving response when the behavior, qualities, and attributes of one actor match the values and standards of the actor who can give the status. By values and standards I refer to what Parsons (1960) called "conceptions of the desirable . . . " (p. 122). If the behavior, qualities, and the like are not congruent with the values and standards, or match them poorly, little or no status is conferred. If the matching is negative, for example, the standard is for honesty and the behavior is dishonest, instead of status conferral, the impulse is for status withdrawal. With this perspective on status conferral, we can see that the course of love relations is delicately contingent on the kinds of standards and values that are applied (automatically) by the lover to the attributes and performance of the loved one. The greater the congruence between the standards on the one side and the attributes on the other, the stronger the emotional impulse for status conferral.

Although my own commitment to this view of the status-evoking process is based on the persuasive empirical work of Hamblin and Smith, I find that others also have converged on this position from a clinical or phenomenological direction. One of the most perceptive modern discussions of love, despite its avowed ethical and normative interests, is provided by Scheler (1954), who wrote; "The primary orientation of love is toward values, and toward the objects discernible through these values, as sustaining them . . . " (p. 151). The value component of love is not static, as Scheler saw it:

> Love . . . is a movement pointing from a lower value to a higher one, though it is not necessary for *both* values to be *given* in the process. Usually it is the lower value that is given, either in the intimation of value which produces the love, as in love at first sight, or in a sequel to the occurrence of an act of preference between several given objects. But whichever it may be, "love" for the object or bearer of value concerned only begins with the commencement of that movement toward a potentially higher value in the beloved object . . . (p. 156, emphasis in original).

Although the nature of the "movement" of which Scheler spoke as a defining characteristic of love, is not entirely clear, it may be no more than the recognizable pattern of growth and enlargement of feelings, an implicit developmental notion (cf. Levinger and Snoek, 1972; Murstein, 1972; Centers, 1975). Scheler made very clear that the loved object possesses to an important degree attributes that match the values of the lover. Elsewhere Scheler said, ". . . our appreciation for the value-attributes are governed by our love . . . of the things exhibiting these values; it is not our appreciation that governs our love . . . " (p. 149). This would seem to reverse the causal priority of the process just suggested. Yet even this reversal is understandable as part of a developmental process in which the matching of values and attributes produces feelings of love, which in turn modifies the evaluative criteria as they are *subsequently* applied to the love object. Some evidence for this understanding may be gleaned from the following:

> Love invariably sets up, as it were, an *"idealized" paradigm of value* for the person actually present, albeit conceiving this at the same time as an embodiment of his "true" nature and "real" value, which only awaits confirmation in feelings. To be sure this "paradigm" is *implicit* in the values already disclosed empirically in feeling—and only the fact that it is so implicit keeps it free from interpolation, empathic projection, etc., and hence from delusion. But for all that, it is not empirically latent in them save as an appointed goal, and objective ideal challenge to a better and more beautiful fulfillment of the whole (p. 154, emphasis in original).

Although Scheler projected the full realization of the match between values and attributes into the future, this statement reinforces the view that the match—actually or potentially—is fundamental to feelings of love.

Freud (1915), although not explicitly discussing values, nonetheless intimated them in his assertion that

> Every human being has acquired . . . a special individuality in the exercise of his capacity to love—that is, in the conditions which he sets up for loving, in the impulses he gratifies by it, and in the aims he sets out to achieve in it. This forms a cliche or stereotype in him . . . (p. 312–313).

Freud provided us with an indispensable insight into idiosyncratic elements in the values that are available for matching the attributes of the loved object. I discuss this further in treating the different types of standards and values.

Three Types of Standards and Values

If standards and values are as significant as supposed here in the evocation of the emotional disposition to accord status at the highest levels—that is, to love—it is apparent that the potential of a love relationship depends on the type of values of the lover. I wish to propose three types of values and standards that, although not analytically independent, have some differential bearing on the outcome of love relationships. These are *transient, transference,* and *true* standards and values.

Transient standards and values are relatively superficial in content and relatively quick to evanesce in their ability to satisfy the holder of these standards. There are doubtless value judgments involved as well as systematic variation by culture groups, and it is probably dangerous to assert that a given value is transient in any particular case. Nevertheless, it is likely that persons of little experience, who are younger and therefore less developed in their value choices, are more susceptible to the transient values. These would include most of the external characteristics such as physical appearance and dress, as well as abilities and performances that gain wide popularity, for example, athletics and dancing, but are not based on genuine interpersonal skills or substantial contributions that are valued in the community. The danger of transient values is that they fail to provide a basis for long-term status evocation. This can be for two reasons: first, the standard itself can be quickly satiated. For example, physical attractiveness, although very potent in the intial stages, is soon eclipsed in importance by other characteristics (Levinger and Snoeck, 1972; Murstein 1972). A second difficulty with transient standards is that the love object may lose the capacity to satisfy the standard. If physical beauty is a deeply held standard, it may cause a turning away from the love object as the aging process leaves its mark on the features and figure. There are always younger, more physically beautiful others who can evoke the desire to accord status. Although I have little data to bear out this view, I can point to the higher incidence of divorces among those who marry at a very young age (England and Kuntz, 1975). Although many factors may contribute to such breakdowns in putative love relationships, I suggest that some of these relate to the evocation of feelings of love on the basis of poor or transient standards.

One of the deeper mysteries in the analysis of love relationships is why certain persons are particularly attracted to each other. In the terms of a classic question, it is the problem of "what does he/she see in her/him?" Some have seen in this ignorance a desirable, ineffable mystery at the heart of love. Scheler (1954) spoke of

> the utterly misguided "rationalism" of seeking to account for one's love for an individual person in any such terms as those relating to his qualities, acts, achievements, or dispositions . . . For we always find out in the process that we can imagine every single one of these details to be altered or absent, without being a whit the more able, on that account, to leave off loving the person concerned . . . There is always a surplus we cannot account for (p. 167).

Scheler seemed to negate his previous understanding that love is initiated by the match between the values of one and the characteristics of the other. Yet he was of course touching on a real phenomenon: we often do not know why we love the other. I propose that the answer lies in part in the importance of *transference standards*. These are unconscious and are carried along, as Freud (1915, 1971) discussed, from earlier loves, usually parents or parent surrogates. Indeed, Freud saw all love relationships to be derived in this way. He proposed that the love expressed in psychoanalytic transference

> consists of new editions of old traces and that it repeats infantile reactions, *But this is the essential character of every love* . . . [T]he transference love has perhaps a degree less freedom than the love which appears in ordinary life and is called normal; it displays its dependence on the infantile pattern more clearly, is less adaptable and capable of modification, but that is all and that is nothing essential (p. 387, emphasis added).

Here, I believe, is a substantial answer to the mystery of the "surplus" in love relationships mentioned by Scheler. The lover is unaware of the standards, their source, and the attributes that match the standards, because they are repressed, stemming perhaps from a period prior to the development of verbal symbolization adequate to bind the initial experience as a memory with a language analogue for recall purposes (cf. Dollard and Miller, 1950, pp. 198–199).

Any learning theory with a notion of secondary reinforcement can be integrated with the psychoanalytic view of transference expressed by Freud. The original love object or the object that supplied gratification had certain characteristics and attributes that, by association with the primary rewards of the relationship, were conditioned to those rewards and acquire what are commonly known as "secondary reinforcing" capacity. If the lover is responding to a love object on the basis of standards connected with earlier figures in this manner—a particular color of hair, shape of eyes, turn of head, tactile feel, and the like— these would hardly seem sufficient to evoke love; yet by association with the earlier figure they have the capacity to elicit strong feeling in the present. Berscheid and Walster (1974, p. 356) cited novelist Lawrence Durrell's (1961) reflection on love that suggests essentially that accidental stimuli may be discriminative cues for a whole package of elements that went together in an earlier loved one or were desired from that other. When these stimuli occur in the present, their carrier benefits from the "love by association," so to speak. The operation of transference standards can be seen in this occurrence.

It is clear that, although transference standards have a strong hold because of their association with a potent reinforcer and the fact that they are not ordinarily in awareness, they may also touch on trivial and transient attributes that are not intrinsically satisfying or long lasting in their appeal. This is not a necessary result of the operation of transference standards, since many good and substantial qualities can also be formulated into standards as a result of transference.

True standards are realistic, compassionate and imbued with reason as well as emotion. I hesitate to specify content, although some efforts have been made under other rubrics, for example, Maslow's (1968) "B-values" (p. 83). These are values the person who can love others may hold for himself. The B stands for "being" as is opposed to "D" or "deficiency" values, which are more concerned with how to get the other to give love to us. Fromm (1956) also pointed to true standards and values by his contrast between what he called the "marketing" and the "productive" orientation. The latter includes modesty, adaptability, confidence, loyalty, purposefulness, and tolerance, among others (Fromm, 1947, pp. 120–121). We need a more focused approach to the kinds of values *that pertain to others* that, when matched by the attributes of others, are productive of relatively lasting emotions of love. I pose this as a scientific problem, although the ethical and normative implications of the answer to such a question are clear.* Furthermore, I am aware of the *subcultural* variations that are doubtless legitimate variants on the very broad theme of what may be valued to evoke status (cf. Morris's study of values, 1956). According to Kerckhoff (1974), normative "variations by race, class, and locale suggest that the male-female . . . relationship itself is defined differently by various segments of our society . . . [and] that the characteristics deemed desirable—those that lead to interpersonal attraction—vary depending on the definition of the relationship one anticipates having with the other person" (p. 70). It is possible, however, that some fundamental set of "true" values may be discovered, although they all may not have emerged as a normative set in any single culture. It is also clear that as far as true, transference, and transient standards are concerned, it is doubtless impossible to assure that only true standards will be held. Indeed, I recognize that standards and values evoke hierarchical degrees of commitment from individuals and that what is wanted are hierarchies leaning toward the true standards, rather than purely so. In the next chapter I take up the question of standards again in an effort to explain how particular standards may lead to good and bad outcomes in love relations. Now I turn to the particular emotions of love.

LOVE, AESTHETICS, AND EMOTIONS

Love is not only a relationship of extremely high status conferral, it also entails emotion. Poets have done the most to portray the emotions of love, and in this no social scientist can outdo them. However, poets lack an adequate theory to explain emotions, and here we may succeed. Curiously, we cannot abandon poets entirely when we talk of love. This is because *aesthetics*, which is the formal theory of poetry itself (or of any of the arts), is one of our best entry points into the theory of the emotions of love. I believe there is a remarkable con-

*I acknowledge that an interest in a relatively enduring love relationship is a value judgment. The evidence is very strong, however, that at present the costs of unstable love are so great in terms of personal stress that it is a value with a definite positive benefit attached to it. I acknowledge that even this is a value choice (cf. Westman et al., 1970).

vergence between our present social scientific understanding of status conferral as a function of the match between attributes and standards and the main line of aesthetic theory that has attempted to account for the experience of *beauty*. On this question, aesthetics lacks the empirical basis afforded by the type of work exemplified in Hamblin and Smith (1966), whereas social science lacks a theory that resolves the question of the emotional denouement. Aesthetics is a little ahead in developing the convergence, since many aesthetic theorists have seen the link between love and art in terms of the common medium of *beauty*. However, some psychologists also have favored the connection. Maslow (1954, 1968), perhaps more than others, viewed aesthetic experience as part of a master paradigm for love.

Maslow (1968) asserted that there is a "single description [of] some of these basic cognitive happenings in the B-love experience . . . [and] the aesthetic perception" (p. 73). He called these "peak experiences." Elsewhere Maslow suggested that there are data "which indicate that some of qualities which describe the structure of 'good' paintings also describe the good human being, the B-values of wholeness, uniqueness, aliveness" (p. 95). Further, "these same B-values which exist as preferences or motivations in our best specimens [persons] are to some degree the same values which describe the 'good' work of art, or Nature in general, or the good external world" (p. 169). Although Maslow did not connect the aesthetic perception with the loving perception, it is clear from the tenor of his remarks that the two are akin. Of what value is such an insight?

I believe that an examination of the aesthetic experience can give us a better understanding of the emotional components of loving. One of the major themes of aesthetic analysis is that beauty not only resides in the object, but corresponds also to a characteristic of the beholder. In the view of Plato, who inaugurated aesthetic analysis, the "essential form of beauty, absolute beauty [is] not seen by the eye but grasped conceptually by the 'mind alone' " (Beardsley, 1966, p. 39). Something exists in the mind to accommodate the impress of external stimuli and to experience these with the pleasure that beauty gives. According to Plato, we all have knowledge of "true beauty" prior to birth, but when we are born we forget the prior existence. Nonetheless, by virtue of "recollection," certain objects in the real world remind us of true beauty. The latter is, of course, an "ideal" representation of the object, and the objects of the world are only approximations of the dimly recollected ideal. Yet when a *correspondence* is sensed between the real objects and the inner, recollected ideal, an aesthetic experience ensues. The aesthetic experience is linked intimately to beauty.

The platonic view of correspondence has informed aesthetic analysis to the present day, although the notion of ideals recollected from a time before birth has been dropped. Plotinus elaborated the doctrine by including among the beautiful not only visual and musical experience, but also "minds that lift themselves above the realm of sense to a higher order" (Beardsley, 1966, p. 80). There is thus "beauty in the conduct of life, in action, in character, in the pursuits of the intellect; and there is the beauty of virtues" (p. 80). Thus persons can be experienced as beautiful for more than their physical qualities. Although Plotinus still held to Plato's doctrine of some earlier knowledge that guides the recognition of the correspondence between the object and the ideal, he also appeared to admit some necessary modification of the observer: "You must make yourself beautiful in spirit, morally excellent, to know perfect beauty" (p. 84). This touches the very core of the view expressed earlier that in love we indeed find what we are capable of finding, or, more bluntly, we get what we deserve. If our own standards are flawed, so will the object be whose attributes correspond to those standards.

Plotinus, as others in this tradition, was very explicit about the direct emotional consequence of the matching of standards and attribute: "Our interpretation is that the soul—by the very truth of its nature, by its affiliation to the noblest Existents in the hierarchy of being—when it sees anything of that kin, or any trace of that kinship, thrills with an immediate delight, takes its own to itself, and thus stirs anew to the sense of its nature and of all its affinity" (Quoted in Beardsley, 1966, p. 81). According to Beardsley, "for Plotinus love . . . is always, in every form, a love of beauty, and consequently a love of goodness and of being" (p. 83).

The correspondence theory of aesthetic satisfaction is no less central today than it was two millenia ago. In one of the most graceful and "beautiful" statements of this position, Santayana (1896) wrote:

Beauty as we feel it is something indescribable: what it is or what it means can never be said . . . It is an affection of the soul, a consciousness of joy and security, a pang, a dream, a pure pleasure. It suffuses an object without telling why; nor has it any need to ask the question . . . beauty is of all things what least calls for explanation. But we—the minds that ask all questions and judge of the validity of all answers—we are not independent of this world in which we live . . . The satisfaction of our reason, due to the harmony between our nature and our experience, is partially realized already. The sense of beauty is its realization. When our sense and imagination find what they crave, when the world so shapes itself or so moulds the mind that the correspondence between them is perfect, then perception is pleasure, and existence needs no apology. The duality which is the condition of conflict disappears. There is no inward standard different from the outward fact with which that outward fact may be compared . . . In the heat of (intellectual) speculation or of love there may come moments of equal perfection, but they are very unstable. The reason and the heart remain deeply unsatisfied. But the eye finds in nature, and in some supreme achievements of art, constant and fuller satisfaction. For the eye is quick, and seems to have been more docile to the education of life than the heart or the reason of man, and able sooner to adapt itself to the reality. Beauty therefore seems to be the clearest manifestation of perfection, and the best evidence of its possibility. If perfection is, as it should be, the ultimate justification of being, we may understand the ground of the moral dignity of beauty. *Beauty is a pledge of the possible conformity between the soul and nature,* and consequently a ground of faith in the supremacy of the good (pp. 201–203, emphasis added).

This is how Santayana concluded his classic work on beauty, encompassing the joy of both mind and heart within the aesthetic paradigm insofar as they too reflect the harmony between the inner and the outer. Subsequently Dewey (1934), in *Art as Experience,* the Gestaltist Arnheim (1954), and the philosopher Langer (1942) also viewed the aesthetic response as a correspondence between inner and outer conditions of the organism, a harmony between external stimuli and either innate or learned standards of response. We see that aesthetic theorists not only base their understanding of beauty on the selfsame matching principle as found by Hamblin and Smith (1966), they advance beyond this to the specific emotions that successful matching evokes: *joy, delight,* and *pleasure.* Phenomenal evidence indicates that these are also the emotions of love.

It is useful in detailing the convergence between aesthetics and social science to note that aesthetic theorists—at least in recent years—have couched their discussions of beauty in terms of *values,* which with *standards* are the inner conditions that make possible a response of delight or pleasure to objects that are beautiful. According to Morris (1946), "a value is a property of an object relevant to an interest—namely the property of satisfying or consummating an act which requires objects with such a property for its completion" (p. 134). Jarrett (1957) spoke of "beauty as a kind of value," particularly "inherent value" which "conduces to felt satisfaction" (pp. 31–32). Yet for the value—the beauty—of the object to be felt, the observer must be prepared; that is, he must have acquired standards for appreciation. "Value" said Jarrett, "is ultimately always for somebody. Some organism must have a need or desire, and the object must be such that it answers to that need or satisfies that desire, if value is to be attributed to the object" (p. 33).

Another quality of the aesthetic experience that finds a certain parallel in the experience of love is its disinterestedness (Maslow, 1968, p. 43). Jarrett contrasted aesthetic with other attitudes: the *practical* (or instrumental), which seeks to know the object's utility, the *personal,* which is concerned with utility specifically for the self, the *common sense,* which severely limits the imagination of possibility beyond what is directly given (cf. Scheler's opposite view of love as movement toward a higher value), and finally there is the "an-aesthetic" *analytic* attitude, which is concerned with decomposing the experience into its elements rather than with the experience for its own sake.

Berlyne (1971) elaborated further the difference between aesthetic and other attitudes, and here I demur from the usual aesthetic view. According to Berlyne, "whereas many stimulus situations influence an organism's internal conditions, which in their turn influence outwardly visible behavior, aesthetic stimulus patterns commonly modify internal processes (thoughts, images, emotions) without giving rise to any corresponding action. In other words, the information . . . is transmitted as far as the appreciator's internal state but no further" (p. 43). Thus delight, pleasure, and joy are the emotional responses to the aesthetic object, but action or coping is not. Consider also Maslow's (1968) view: "approval, admiration, and love are based less on gratitude for the usefulness and more on the objective, intrinsic qualities of the perceived person" (p. 36).

Yet the disinterested view of the object that provides joy does seem to produce another emotion that mingles with the joy and negates Jarrett's and Berlyne's rejection of action and Maslow's rejection of "gratitude." This is *appreciation*. If an aesthetic object provides pleasure, it seems to follow that its creator inspires a sense of gratitude we call appreciation. This is a pleasurable emotion that finds release and expression in conferring status on the creator as a provider of delight or joy. If the aesthetic experience is tranquil and not disposed to action, the appreciation emotion seeks expression in the full range of human actions that imply status accord to the creator—from vocal and verbal approval, to symbolic honors, to monetary gifts, to physical-sexual contact.

Aestheticians who have concentrated with such good results on the emotional effects of the match between inner standards and outer stimuli have ordinarily slighted the relational consequences of the experience of beauty. In both love and aesthetic experience there is an "author" of our delight and pleasure, and he or she evokes our voluntary compliance and accompanying emotion of intense appreciation. This is what makes love a social relationship and art potentially so. Ordinarily, in love, the author of our joy is a person to whom we can actually give status. In art the author may be inaccessible or long dead.

Here is a summary and synthesis of the foregoing views of love and aesthetics.

1. Aesthetic experience (of beauty) calls out a response in us.
2. The response is based on our capacity to evaluate the sight, sound, symbol or idea.
3. If we did not have the capacity in our repertoire, we could not respond.
4. Some capacities may be natural or innate—the ability to respond to certain rhythms, colors, and the like; others are culturally induced via socialization.
5. The capacities equal values and standards for appreciation.
6. When a standard is applied and the stimulus is in harmony with it, the experience is directly and automatically one of pleasure, delight, and joy.
7. The harmony itself provides the satisfaction.

8. The harmony is the match between the natural or socialized standard and the stimulus.

9. Whoever creates the object that elicits pleasure, delight, and joy also elicits our appreciation.

10. Love is thus comprised of two emotions: one is the disinterested, aesthetic-like, intrinsic joy and delight in the object, and the second is the happy appreciation and willing gratification of the agent and author of our joy.

11. In regard to persons as objects, both joy and appreciation are part of a single experience when the attributes of the other—physical, psychological, or relational—give us pleasure by matching our standards.

12. Once set in motion, these emotions amplify each other; thus we may have joy in the beautiful (the harmony) and find beauty (harmony) in the works of the person who provides joy.

From the point of view of a theory of emotion, the most important consideration in the foregoing is that once the standards are in place—innate or internalized—the ensuing emotions of joy and appreciation are nonvolitional responses to characteristics and attributes of the other. We cannot compel another to love us; we cannot compel ourselves to feel love. The nonvolitional character of status conferral invites the speculation that we are dealing with a process of the autonomic nervous system. How or in what way is unknown. In Chapters 8 and 9 I presented an argument for the specificity of organ involvement in the emotions of fear and anger and a sociophysiological approach to emotions. To be consistent, joy and appreciation, especially in the magnitudes involved in love, also ought to be assignable to specific physiological response patterns. The work of Olds (1962; 1973) is an important step in this direction, although it dealt only with directly physical pleasure. Maslow (1954, pp. 364–378) called for work in this area; however, it has not been forthcoming.

The intimate tie between the emotions of love and the status dimension of social relations permits us to ask some additional questions. Whereas we can give status to many in even moderately high amounts—we admire, respect, and like them—we love only one or at most a few. This is a pivotal matter. It is conjectural whether the limited extensity of love (Sorokin, 1954) reflects inherent limits on the accord of extremely high status due to the *nature* of humankind or whether a limit is imposed by the fact that, by chance alone, very few others who are capable of cueing the very highest status accord are within our ken at one time. A possible reason for the latter, if it is the true explanation of the limited extensity of love, may be that the other does not release the very highest status accord unless that other conforms to the internalized standards in not merely one but a number of characteristics. Thus he may be not only handsome but also competent, sensitive, and dependable. She is not only beautiful but also modest, loyal, and intelligent. The well-known "halo-effect" may then cast a proper glow over the remaining characteristics of the other. The other emerges as a paragon matching perhaps all the standards of virtue that were internalized. How can one fail to grant extremely high status to such a person? Conclusively, loving that person is in no sense an act of will.

Aesthetic theory can assist us here too. Many analysts of the experience of beauty emphasize the importance of overall *harmony* and *unity* among the elements of the aesthetic object (see Beardsley, 1966; Berlyne, 1971). We may be able to apply the same criteria to the qualities of a person. Our standards—some aggregate of transient, transference, and true—are already unified by *us* by being in us. Although conflict between standards is possible, a large literature attests to the presence of a strain toward consistency (see the review by Glass, 1965). Yet the consistency can take a quite idiosyncratic turn, due especially to the presence of transference standards. When another person appears to match our particular template of standards in one or more important respects, the strain toward consistency is activated by the beginnings of a show of harmony and unity among the elements. When elements are missing or contradictory, if a major part of the pattern is there, the other parts are filled in, "leveled or sharpened" (Klein, 1970) as necessary so that, as in gestalt perception, we *complete* the pattern even though elements are missing.

Although the notion of matching standards and attributes as a basis for status conferral seems to be fundamental to all social relationships, and perhaps most crucially in love relationships, only a little work has been done to develop this line of investigation. A parallel line of inquiry, however, can be seen in the studies of mate selection and marital harmony according to the principle of complementarity of personality traits. The results of these investigations are inconclusive, with some investigators (Winch, 1958, 1963; Kerckhoff and Davis, 1962; Rylchak, 1965) finding that there is complementarity, whereas others find similarity to be more prevalent (Bowerman and Day, 1956; Banta and Heatherington, 1963; Schellenberg and Bee, 1960; Centers and Granville, 1971). Although there is some kinship between personality traits and attributes on one hand and values and standards on the other, the details of these relationships must be explored further before the similarities and differences between complementarity theory and the status-conferral theory can be adequately assessed. It is possible that there is some latitude in the degree to which the same personalities can hold widely differing standards that lead to the highest levels of status conferral, and that the same standard can be held in association with widely different personalities. Thus I believe that personality complementarity theory has only a partial relevance to the explanation of mutual love and regard.

A much closer approach to the status-conferral position is found in the concept of "matching" proposed by Foote (1956). Although Foote was explicitly concerned with matching of "traits of individuals" (p. 24) and with "personality" (p. 25), the essence of his argument touches on the relationship between the standards of one mate and the attributes of the other. In particular, Foote emphasized the developmental character of the standards and the dangers posed by a change of standards to the stability of a relationship:

> Persons who took the initiative in seeking divorce, in explaining their experience, and likewise observers of broken marriages, speak frequently of a mate's having outgrown the other. It is the husband who usually outgrows the wife; the opposite is theoretically possible, however, and in a few cases seems to occur. The husband is exposed to more stimulation and new experience outside the home—not to mention members of the other sex—than is the wife who is confined to domestic affairs. In time a man in business may come to feel that his secretary is closer in step and sympathy with his personal development than is his wife; the irony often is that he married his wife on the same account, and that having married his secretary, he removes her from his office and immures her in his home, there to await the fate of her predecessor (p. 25).

In sum, I have tried to develop the view that, as love and the emotional aspects of loving are experienced in social relationships, the dynamics of love must conform to the dynamics of the fundamental dimensions of relationship. Here we have looked at the status dimension. We now turn to power.

chapter 13

Love as a Social Relationship: II. The Power Dimension

With the exception of brotherly love and adulation by fans, love relations are comprised not only of status accord but also power. This requires us to examine the dynamics of power in love, for as power is activated so too are the emotions that most often flow from the use of power: fear, anger, depression, guilt, and shame—emotions far removed from love. My position is that status accord is the active, giving component of love, but, since human relationships, regardless of label or personal intent, cannot always be loving, power emerges when compliance is not forthcoming voluntarily. Furthermore, when status is withheld or withdrawn, even as a nonvolitional response because the attributes of one no longer match the standards of the other, the deprived partner ordinarily views the withholding of accustomed status as a power play. This pattern bears crucially on how love relationships deteriorate and cause the emotions of love to die, and it is examined below.

Power is also of interest in love relations because it is the obverse of dependence, as discussed in several previous chapters. Since love relationships provide very high levels of gratification, it is easy to see that the recipients of the benefits and pleasures of love can easily come to desire their continuance and to depend greatly on the person who provides them. Thus dependence seems to be a very highly probable accompaniment of love. However, if dependence creates the basis for power in love relationships, it is by that much antagonistic to the continuation of love. This anomaly is explored later.

Finally, power is an important, although sometimes unrecognized, element of a number of theories of love and attraction that view the love relationship from a reinforcement, exchange, or need-fulfillment perspective. These theories lead to a specious view of love. My understanding of love differs from those theories in several important respects, and it is useful for practical, theoretical, and empirical purposes to understand the differences clearly.

POWER AND LOVE

Power, even in putative love relationships, is still defined structurally as domination or control over another, which means the ability to enforce involuntary compliance, and processually as the behaviors that are intended to force, coerce, punish, threaten, deter, or hurt the other. It can be noxious power or status-withdrawal power—the intent is the same.

Emerson's (1962) useful formulation in which power and dependence are inversely related, $P_{AB} = D_{BA}$ and $P_{BA} = D_{AB}$, is a statement of structural power. It indicates the winner when the smoke of battle has cleared, because the winner is less dependent, or has greater noxious power, than the loser. Yet in the course of the struggle in which the structural outcome was decided, B, the more dependent actor for the purpose of this discussion, may have initiated more power acts than A. The rationale is that the more dependent an actor is, as long as he is not in a state of total dependence, the more likely he is to employ power to get what he wants when it is not forthcoming. Ultimately, his greater dependence may require that he settle for what the other is willing to give, but the dependence may provoke him to use more power acts, including noxious power, more frequently (see Appendix 2).

There are two bases of dependence and power in love relationships. The first stems from the dependence on the *joy* provided by the other whose attributes match one's own standards. Any falling away by the other from the maintenance of the proper level of those characteristics can elicit coercion as a means to get the other to reinstate the attributes that produce the harmony and the joy. The second emotional basis of dependence and power relates to the gratifications one receives as an expression of the *appreciation* by the other of one's own attributes. If for some reason the level of appreciation falls, it is likely that dependence on the other for the appreciation leads to coercion to restore giving to its previous level (cf. Casler, 1973, p. 10).

Yet an actor whose gratifications are reduced does not ordinarily use power immediately to reinstate his rewards. He may first try nonpunitive inducements. The somewhat neglected wife may visit the beauty salon, diet to slim her figure, or resort to perfume. These steps are calculated to create an incentive for the husband and to rekindle his flagging level of interest. Only if the husband does not respond to the new hairdo, the trimmer contour, or the enticing scent does the strong probability exist that a power act will occur (cf. Chadwick and Day, 1972).

From the process viewpoint, the formulation is: the probability of A's using power acts against B is a function of the dependence of A on B. Similarly for B, the probability of B's using power acts against A is a function of the dependence of B on A; or PR ($PA_{AB} = D_{AB}$) and PR ($PA_{BA} = D_{BA}$), where PA stands for power act. This result augments the purely structural position on power and dependence presented by Emerson and others. Process power acts are crucially implicated along with structural power in the dynamics of how love relationships degenerate, all too often, into their opposite, namely, conflict and hatred.

Sex, Dependence, and Power

In all social relationships, actors necessarily depend on each other for actions that fulfill their needs. In love relationships the partners ordinarily satisfy a large number of each other's needs. No single need is more central in adult love relationships than that of sexual satisfaction. Freud (1915) minced no words when he wrote:

> The love between the sexes is undoubtedly the first thing in life, and the combination of mental and bodily satisfaction attained in the enjoyment of love is literally one of life's culminations. Apart from a few perverse fanatics, all the world knows this and conducts life accordingly; only science is too refined to confess it (p. 389).

Science has indeed caught up in the investigations of Kinsey and his group (1948, 1953) and Masters and Johnson (1966, 1969). Their discoveries of the rates and frequency of various sexual practices and of the physiological and psychological properties of sexual arousal and pleasure do not, however, touch adequately on the relational quality of sexuality.

If we take Freud seriously, we must conclude that for most persons sexual dependence can be of a very high order. This is probably most true for relatively younger persons in whom the sex drive is very strong, as evidenced by high frequency of sexual activity (Kinsey et al., 1948, 1953). The ideal monogamous relationship, essentially a bilateral monopoly on sexual access, is especially prone to generating mutual dependence in the sexual area, and, by derivation, power. Cultures or communities in which sexual fidelity is neither seriously prescribed nor practiced by either sex do not engender relational power based on sexual gratification. Yet even if fidelity norms are not strongly fostered, individual partners can develop strong sexual dependence on each other, and this gives sex a high potential for implication in power relations.

The interpersonal physiology of sexual relations also disposes toward a strong power connotation to both sexual denial and surrender. Aubert (1965) pointed out that "in the act of love the distinction between giving and receiving is blurred or obliterated" (p. 221). If the receiver denies the giver (the one who initiates the activity) the opportunity for his or her gratification, this denial can be interpreted as a very stringent degree of status withdrawal: the punisher who sacrifices his own pleasure to negate the other's pleasure must be angry or indifferent indeed (cf. Kelley, 1971; Mogy and Pruitt, 1974).

The ambiguity of sexual pleasure in respect to the actual emotions of the actors is also important. If the giver also receives, the receiver cannot know for certain whether the giver gives *in order to give* (i.e., that sex is an expression of status conferral) or *in order to receive* (i.e., that sex is merely a technical activity to ensure a proper return of satisfying technical and relational activity from the other). It happens that once the sex activity has gotten under way and both parties are psychologically and physiologically aroused, each is equal vulnerable and capable of profiting from the deception, if there is one. Yet if emotions are being counterfeited simply to gain one's own pleasure, the activity falls under the heading of power as manipulation (as described in Appendix 2). If, at the outset, the other knew the real state of affairs, the access might not be granted. The counterfeiter of emotions undoubtedly knows this at some level of awareness and therefore obtains compliance involuntarily.

In a more direct way, sex entails power. Freud (1955) and more recently Barclay (1969, 1971) and Zillman (1971) have attested to the relationship between sexual arousal and aggression. Barclay found that of several possible drives and motives—achievement, affiliation, anxiety, sex—only sex was activated in conjunction with aggression. This work supports a specificity theory of emotions, as discussed in Chapters 7 and 8, and also provides evidence for the power aspect of sex. Indeed, in its direct anatomical expression, sex implies ownership and control. The act of enclosing or enfolding another, restricting the other's movements, penetrating or incorporating the other—these all signify possession. However, what we possess we control, and when it resists our control we usually apply force or power to it. The power mode is almost entirely physical, and, although it is not usually carried very far so as not to create great resistance and thus endanger both the giving and receiving of satisfaction, at times it does indeed go far, as in rape.

We see then that sex and power are not alien to each other on a number of grounds and that the emergence of power in love relationships is tied, at least in part, to the satisfactions of sex. It follows that if sexual dependency is decreased, power also diminishes. Burton (1973) reported that "better" marriages are precisely those in which sex activity is somewhat reduced. Maslow (1954) wrote that for the "self-actualizing people [Maslow's ideal humans] the orgasm is simultaneously more important and less important than in average people. It is often a profound and almost mystical experience, and yet the absence of sexuality is more easily tolerated by these people" (p. 242).

It should be clear from this discussion that any need that is strongly satisfied in a relationship can lead to dependence. Indeed, since many needs are usually satisfied, the potential for dependence is great; thus the potential for the emergence of power is also great.

THE EVOLUTION OF LOVE RELATIONS

I now attempt to weave together the various strands of the foregoing discussion to provide a theoretical answer to the question of how love may grow and then die. It is indeed perplexing, and to those involved usually very painful, why two persons bound at first by ties of the highest mutual status conferral can end by hating each other. The power and status derivation of love relationships, the nonvolitional nature of status conferral, and the relationship between structural power, process power, and dependence provide an answer to this question.

The principal assumption is that, in general, to receive status is considered good and desirable by most persons, and that power or punishment, if used against them, is considered undesirable. Excluded from consideration are pathological types, such as masochists, since they represent reversals of the usual response pattern.

Love relationships ordinarily begin, on one side or the other, as an instance of adulation by fans (type 6, Chapter 12). One person, with certain standards and values, finds them matched by another person's attributes. The fit between the standards and the attributes is immediately pleasurable, and the experience induces appreciation of the other as the author of the pleasurable harmony.

In fortunate instances, the adulation becomes mutual, and the relationship passes into the brotherly love model (type 2, Chapter 12). In less fortunate instances, in which the love is not requited, it may die, or, as may happen for a while, since the less attainable the object, the more desirable it may become (see Blau's discussion, 1964, p. 79), the relationship develops into infatuation (type 5, Chapter 12). There, one party gives or is prepared to give in high amounts, whereas the other gives little or nothing. The one who gives, however, is so dependent that even the meagerest rewards—a look, a touch, being called by one's name—are extremely valued; therefore the uninvolved partner in this relationship has a great deal of power. Since the uninvolved is not dependent on the rewards of the other, little or no power develops for the infatuated.

When the adulation is indeed mutual (type 2, Chapter 12), the relationship becomes most poignant, beautiful, and evanescent. It is for precisely such moments—and their duration may be for a literal moment—that the later agonies of love must be felt worthwhile and are revisited again and again by the perenniel circuit-riders of the provinces of love. When there is only giving and caring and no hurting or forcing, when the actions of each in behalf of the other are freely given, each must feel himself fortunate to a degree beyond account. At such moments, the full, free expression of one's love and caring for the other must strike the lover as both ennobling of self, for it is selfless, and transcending, being devoted to a good outside oneself. One of life's great pities is that only in very exceptional cases does mutuality of this kind last.

It is precisely the *threat* of impermanence that propels the relationship into full-blown romantic love (type 1, Chapter 12). Both actors in the drama have both high power and high status. The status is a carryover from the previous stage, but the power—both structural and processual—emerges as each lover seeks to transmute what was a gift into a possession. Each wants to maintain the other's love and ensure that its pleasures and benefits continue. Thus each lover is now dependent on the other, and each is introduced to the structural and processual power of the other. The experience of romantic love, in which there is still the delight of receiving, is provided an extra fillip by the peril of vulnerability and the threat of loss. Although the earlier mutual adulation stage is felt as most beautiful, the romantic stage is experienced as most intense, because it entails fear as well as satisfaction.

There is much subjective evidence that the romantic condition inspires the sentiment that each must love (i.e., confer extremely high status on) the other eternally. There is also much objective evidence to deny this subjective conclusion. The record suggests that instead of taking root permanently at the high-power, high-status mutuality of romantic love, the relationship very frequently develops in the direction of continued high power, with a moderate to considerable loss of status on one or both sides. In the case of one-sided status loss, we have the relationship of infidelity (type 4, Chapter 12); in a large number of cases the infidelity is explicitly sexual, although, of course, it need not be. Although the reduction of the sexual dependence of the unfaithful partner implies a loss of power for the duped one, this is more than compensated by the latter's capacity to punish the betrayer if the infidelity is exposed. In the case of mutual status withdrawal, the relationship can no longer be called love, according to the definition of Chapter 12. Neither party now accords extremely high status to the other.

In some proportion of cases, varying apparently by phases of the life cycle (Rollins and Feldman, 1970), the romantic love relationship reverts to the earlier form of brotherly love in which power is reduced and status conferral remains high on both sides. How this may be achieved is perhaps the most important question that students of love can address. It is obvious from the rising rate of divorce (Leslie, 1976, p. 676) that many married couples—presumably once loving—do not attain power reduction while maintaining continued high status accord. Some understanding of how love relationships deteriorate into a high-power, low-status pattern may suggest a preventive.

HOW LOVE DIES

When love dies, the prevalent emotion is not just a seasonal sadness over the inevitable passing of a transient phase, but deep grief, guilt, despair, fury and often an unforgivingness that ravages both the adamant bearer of spite as well as its victim. These emotions mirror the relational pattern of how love dies. Since love is a social relationship, love dies when the relational bases are either inadequate or noxious to the continuance of the relationship. In essence, either extremely high status conferral is not maintained, or power is excessive, or, usually, both. The heart of the matter is in the standards for status conferral.

Content of the Standards for Status Conferral

If we accord status because the other reflects so many preferred characteristics and acquires more by halo, it is understandable that status is withdrawn if those characteristics are no longer manifested and are not replaced by others similarly valued. Additionally, if the status grantor's internalized standards change in the course of time, status is withdrawn unless the other exhibits deserving behavior or traits in the new areas of evaluation. Finally, in addition to manifesting the panoply of desirable traits that deserve status, a person may neutralize his status value by exhibiting traits that are worthy in the other's eyes only of disesteem. For example, he is handsome, witty, and sensitive, but derives his income from criminal activity, or, despite many good qualities, she is a compulsive gambler or an alcoholic. Just as in the case of status accord, the disesteemed traits lead to a *nonvolitional* withdrawal of status.

Yet another danger to maintaining the match between standards and attributes occurs when the person manifesting the attributes is "overachieving," so to speak, and is not ordinarily as good, able, witty, caring, and so forth as appears at first. The strain of abnormally high performance may then lead to a sharp fall in performance as resources are exhausted or the goal—status and esteem from the other—is attained. This can only lead to a reduction of status conferral, with disappointment in the lover sharpened by the inexplicable failure to continue to match standards as before. Simmel (1950, pp. 326–329) touched on this. Of course, the standards themselves may be "impossible," requiring superhuman capacities to maintain the match between them and attributes, or the structural conditions of institutionalized patterns of love relationships may militate against the maintenance of the match. For example, the conventional division of labor with regard to childrearing may so exhaust or disorient the mother—who is usually the principal child-care agent—that she can no longer manifest those qualities which made her attractive in the childless phase of the relationship (see Baum, 1971).

The most important way in which standards affect the course of love relationships is through their content. To proceed along the route of a well-worn argument, if the impulse to confer status is nonvolitional, the content of the prevailing standards that trigger the nonvolitional status-conferral response ought to affect the probable duration of status conferral. With regard to women, some notoriously unreliable standards have been fostered by the cultural media in Western societies. Their unreliability is manifested in the transient character of the attributes or satisfactions they evoke. The two outstanding offenders are physical beauty and sexual appeal—I treat these as separate for this analysis.* If nonvolitional status conferral is based largely on an internalized standard of physical beauty, the nonvolitional status withdrawal ought to begin as soon as beauty begins to fade or new standards of beauty are acquired and invoked.

Some evidence for this is provided by Murstein (1976), who found, among a sample of married couples, that the more satisfied husbands evaluate their wives as physically attractive, whereas the dissatisfied husbands do not. I believe we can assume that many of the dissatisfied men judged their wives as more attractive at an earlier time. I also assume that for most of them the causal direction is from the fading of the wife's attraction to dissatisfaction rather than the other way around. This is an important question on which entirely too little empirical work has been done.

There appears to be a similar problem of fading arousal in the case of sexual attraction. The how-to-do-it guides to sexual gratification are unanimous in their exhortations to partners to vary coital positions, to innovate (if that is possible), and at least to experiment. These are all designed to ward off satiation and boredom between the partners (cf. Foote, 1954). Thus, remarkable as it may seem, even the highest level of individual and interpersonal gratification can culminate, in time, in ennui. Status conferral that is largely based on sexuality is thus foredoomed, as the moralists have been preaching lo! these millenia.

Of course, beauty and sexual attractiveness are not the only qualities that cue status conferral by men in Western society, nor is there necessarily a negative correlation between these characteristics and other less transient traits of a more reliable nature. The exact magnitude of the correlation is not known, but I suspect that is only moderately positive. Thus a large measure of slippage is possible between the concomitant availability of the more and less transient traits.

When we turn to the qualities of men that cue nonvolitional status conferral by women, more practical considerations prevail than when men select women (Scanzoni, 1972, p. 53). Women appear to give less weight to the transient standards. Thus although women certainly respond to beauty and sexuality in men, these are perhaps balanced by some additional considerations related to prospects for security. It is easy to explain this on the ground that women's virtually total economic dependence until relatively recently has fostered a set of selection criteria that stress such practical matters as financial security and pro-

---

*I assume that sexual attractiveness is an attribute that cues the desire to *confer* status, not merely the desire to receive it in the form of sexual pleasure.

vider dependability. Barry (1970) proposed that marrige usually involves a greater change in life style for women than men; thus women require more supportiveness than men. It is easy to see that the promise of such supportiveness both financially and emotionally can become primary considerations in status conferral. Scanzoni (1972) put the matter in terms of making the best possible "bargain" in an exchange relationship. (This approach is considered later.)

The empirical studies of male and female values and standards for what attributes should evoke status accord to the opposite sex generally support the distinction I suggest between men's and women's standards. There are also indications, however, that we may be in a transitional period, with new standards emerging in American society for both sexes. The on-going disturbance of settled consciousness that is provoked by the Women's Movement is is undoubtedly changing at least surface attitudes. There are some terrible incompatibilities, however. As values and standards change for what I believe are "true" standards, the rate of marriage break-up has also increased. This suggests that there is a lag between the shifting values and the older structural forms of male-female relationship that are incongruent with the newer values. I choose to think that this signifies a transitional phase during which the new values and standards are giving birth to new structural forms.

In regard to physical attractiveness, Christensen (1950) and Coombs and Kenkel (1966) found that this is an important standard males hold for women, but it is not an important female standard for men. Byrne et al. (1970), in a more recent study, confirmed this and found that attitude similarity is more important as a basis for attraction for women. Touhey (1972) further specified the differential standards by sex by discovering that, within the attitude domain, males are more attracted to a woman who shares their sexual attitudes (degree of permissiveness, etc.), whereas women are more attracted to men who share their religious attitudes (belief in God, etc.). More recent studies of physical attraction, however, suggest that there is movement in this standard among women. Walster et al. (1966) and Berscheid et al. (1971) found that physical attractiveness is the strongest determinant of cross-sex interest in both sexes. Both these studies were done with college students, and it is conjecturable whether this reflects a change in cultural standards or only the febrile interests of relatively immature persons of both sexes.

It is obvious that, although the cultural mass media pull standards and values mainly in a "transient" direction, there are restraining forces that reflect more serious interests. The major institutional media of socialization—family, school, religious group—transmit male and female socialization goals that ultimately take their place as the basis for standards and attributes. Obviously, all sex-linked role and personality characteristics are automatically elected to serve as selection standards *for the other sex*. Here, too, although the attributes transmitted are usually more substantial than physical and sexual attraction, the results have disposed toward breakdown of love relationships. The problem has to do with *differential* goals in male and female socialization (beyond the minimum discussed in Chapter 11).

Many cultures have imposed similarly differentiated standards as male and female socialization goals. Barry, Bacon, and Child (1956) found that achievement and autonomy are valued attributes for males in many cultures, whereas nuturance and responsibility are valued for females. Cultures that actually foster such sex-differentiated attributes and roles also foster status conferral for those who conform to the cultural guidelines. The achieving, autonomous male evokes status from females, and the nurturant, responsible female evokes status from males. Langhorne and Secord (1955) confirmed this at least partially in their finding that the women they surveyed desired their husbands to display such characteristics as ambition, energy, and enjoyment of work. Centers (1971) offered one of the most explicit lists of attributes deemed differentially desirable for males and for females. His respondents were 60 engaged couples recruited from among university students. A majority of both the males and females agreed that the following attributes were "more desirable" for males: athletic ability, mechanical ability, leadership, economic ability, observational ability, intellectual ability, scientific understanding, theoretical ability, common sense, achievement and mastery, and occupational ability. A majority of both the males and females agreed that the following attributes are "more desirable" for females: social ability, interpersonal understanding, art appreciation, art-creative ability, moral-spiritual understanding, domestic ability, affectional ability, sartorial ability, and physical attractiveness. Both sexes deemed erotic ability about equally desirable for both males and females. It is not known to what extent this particular set of standards pertaining to desirable attributes of each sex is universal in American society. Doubtless there are variations by region, ethnic subculture, age level, and the like. Yet the list is also apparently congruent with the cross-cultural findings of Barry, Bacon, and Child (1956). Males are expected to achieve and dominate, whereas females are expected to be giving and nurturant.

It is apparent that sex-linked role and personality attributes serve as selection standards *for the other sex.* yet one of the structural difficulties in love relationships in advanced societies is the conflict between appreciation for sex-linked and sex-indifferent or universal standards. Parsons (1954) pointed out that the usual socialization of male and female children does not differentiate until relatively late—approximately high school in the working class and college in the middle class. Thus a long period of universal evaluation standards is subsequently replaced by differential standards. Since the universal standards, however, are ordinarily retained for males, they naturally retain their hold on both males and females as *more* desirable, and therefore worthy of higher status conferral, than the differential attributes, the ones more likely to be assigned to females.

If these considerations are valid, it follows that there is an inherent differential between the sexes in their capacities to evoke status conferral over the long term. Both males and females value male attributes more than males and females value female attributes. This seems to bode ill for relationships that are normatively and ideologically premised on equality of feelings. Thus males evoke more status, in the long run, from females than females evoke from males. If, as is traditionally or classically supposed, women "love" more strongly than men, it can be due in part to the fact that the applicable standards, as culturally induced, provide for this.

It is also apparent, considering Centers' (1971) list and Barry, Bacon, and Child's (1956) socialization attributes, that, given the differential context of the standards with regard to loving itself, that is, the giving, nurturance, and affectional attributes, relational difficulties are fundamentally structured into male–female interaction. Since giving and according status are, by definition, at the heart of love relationships and only one sex is particularly expected to be competent in the performance of this attribute—*although both sexes require it* if the mutuality of the relationship is to be maintained—it is likely that the deficit of affection and love given by men to women will have devastating effects on the relationship. Wives in troubled marriages do in fact report more often than their husbands a lack of demonstrated affection, tenderness, and love (Locke, 1951, pp. 209–212). This is precisely what we would have expected from an examination of the sex-linked differential in standards for status conferral that is an obvious feature of our culture. The important considerations are that love relationships, initially fueled and fired by probably transient physical and erotic standards, are further undermined because of the incompatibility of the other standards that are differentially applied to men and women.

I have suggested two ways in which the standards for high-level status conferral may be involved in the destruction of a love relationship. First, the standards often employed by men may be unsatisfactory because of the transience of the attributes they invoke; second, differences in the way more serious standards are applied to men and women actually work against the maintenance of status accord to women. Given our understanding of power, status, dependence, and nonvolitional aspects of status conferral, what can we predict?

The Devolution of Love Through Power

Let us first examine the case of the couple in which the man has responded according to transient standards. Two bases exist for a relatively rapid decline in the level of male status conferral. The first is the transitory nature of the original status conferral ground, that is, the relatively speedy satiation with beauty and sexuality or the fading of these. The second is the fact that women are generally ascribed lower status than men in American society (Kemper, 1974). Although falling in love may create a surge of egalitarianism or even reversal of adjudged superiority, the attenuation or loss of the grounds for this unwontedly high status reduces the woman to her former, lesser status. Although she may still command higher status from her husband (or lover) than do other women, she is, after all, *just* a woman and partakes therefore in the generally lower status of women.

The withdrawal of status can happen in innumerable ways, from failing to open the door for her to failing to wait until she is ready for orgasm. The withdrawal of status-conferring acts once generously and gladly given is experienced as a loss. It is something like taking a cut in salary (cf. Blau, 1964, p. 147), and the fact that it may happen gradually is no less disturbing. Some empirical support for the decline of status accord by males is provided by Rubin (1969), who collected data from dating and engaged couples.* Although males are more loving in the earliest phase of the relationship, over time they alternate with their girlfriends in who loves more, and by the time the relationship is 18+ months old there is a definite downward trend in the males' love scores (cf. also Pineo, 1961; Marlowe, 1968; Rossi, 1968).

The second phase in the decline of the love relationship is entered when the woman's effort to regain the lost status fails, and she resorts to process power. The flagging attentions of the man are perhaps first commented on (a mild taste of power), complained about (a somewhat stronger taste of power), and, if the former prove fruitless, ignited into tirades (a full-blown taste of power). This sequence follows approximately the one suggested by Patterson, Hops, and Weiss (1975) in their discussion of a "general formulation for marital conflict" (p. 295). However, can the increase in coercion level retrieve the lost status? The male's status withdrawal was as little calculated or volitional as the initial status conferral. Power acts on the part of the woman can only make her less attractive, yet the anger and frustration induced by the loss of the wonted status can drive her to retributive, vengeful acts of power.

Baum (1971) suggested that the greatest strains in marriage occur in those phases of the life cycle at which a man is most involved in working out his career trajectory and a woman is engaged primarily with young children. The husband's career involvement does often mean less time to confer status on the wife (Ridley, 1973), and the wife's depression from long days of inadequate status received from him and from children can lead to aggression against the husband. Age-specific divorce rates tend to substantiate at least the timetable Baum proposed (England and Kuntz, 1975). Nonetheless, the two bases for male status withdrawal, namely, the satiation with initially attractive but often transitory qualities in the woman and the *re*devaluation of female interests, pursuits, and activities, in conformity with the prevailing cultural image, are heavily implicated in the

*Rubin's data are based on different samples of couples at different stages of courtship progress.

interpersonal deterioration that marks what is obviously, for many couples, an admittedly difficult period.

Although we do not have direct evidence for status withdrawal on the part of the husband, data presented by Rollins and Feldman (1970) show that wives are between 50 and 100% more likely than husbands to report negative feelings arising one or more times a month from husband–wife interaction, at least until the fifth phase of the life cycle (oldest child under 21 years). These negative feelings, we can surmise, are due in part to the husbands' status withdrawal (see also Bandura and Walters, 1959).

Phase three is launched by the man's retaliation for the power used against him. This means escalation of conflict. Where he had previously only insulted her, he now adds injury. His perspective on the matter is not rational, but partakes of a common, retributive response pattern, namely, that power is visited on those who employ power against one (Rausch, 1965; Pisano and Taylor, 1971). Where power on the woman's part might have been effective when the couple were in the first stages of a romantic love relationship, they have now slipped first into the prototypical infidelity model, in which he withdrew status from her, and now, if her power response is severe enough, it means a serious reduction of status for him. To recover his previous level of gratification, the male is also wont to use power acts, especially noxious power in which a direct injury is inflicted. Barry (1970) reported that troubled marriages are especially marked by the use of coercion by husbands.

This is the beginning of phase four, and here, by definition, we are no longer speaking of a love relationship. That is, once both partners have reduced status conferral from extremely high and both have retaliated with coercion, we are dealing with another form of relationship, in which not status but power is the pivotal variable. Compliance between the partners is ordered not voluntarily but coercively. If the relationship continues as a series of power exchanges, status conferral is less and less possible or likely. This is simply due to the fact that, as spelled out in a previous assumption, neither men nor women normally like to have power used against them. It is rare that a victim of power (barring pathology) can bring himself to grant status to his tormenter. This is true despite religious injunctions of Western tradition dating back more than 2000 years. There is little left to be said about the devolution of the love relationship into the archetypical pattern of power-driven nation-states (see Figure 2.1). Whether such relationships endure *de facto*, for example, in the case of marriage, depends in part on other matters not discussed here.

This pattern of devolution is supported, in general, by a literature dealing with the sequential effects of positive and negative behaviors toward others and the effects of changes in orientation toward others from positive to negative. In a highly useful series of studies with children, Rausch (1965) reported that over the course of a number of "interaction sequences," there is generally a decline in the proportion of "friendly" acts. Correspondingly, hostile behaviors from the other are reciprocated by hostile behaviors. Gormly, Gormly, and Johnson (1971) found that subjects in an experimental study recalled disagreements with others more than agreements, and that increasing the number of disagreements had a "cumulative negative effect," especially when the overall proportion of agreements was high, as it would be initially in a love relationship. Thus decreased liking for the other was particular manifest when the relationship had been initially positive.

These findings conform to a generally pessimistic view of the effects of introducing positive or negative information into a relationship that is initially of the opposite character: negative information sours a positive relationship more easily than positive information improves a negative relationship (Pastore, 1960; Richie, McClelland, and Shimunkas 1967). Aronson and Linder (1965) also found a tendency for the victim of a positive-to-negative change to like the changes less than when the other had even maintained a consistently negative orientation. Although this result has not been confirmed in an attempted replication (Tognoli and Keisner, 1972), Swingle (1966) did find that in a two-person competitive game, players were at least as willing to retaliate against a known, liked partner who acted in a harmful manner to the subject as they were against a stranger who was equally harmful.

In a small study of marital pairs, Fineberg and Lowman (1975) found that, between adjusted and maladjusted couples, wives in the troubled set were 20% less submissive than wives in the adjusted set. This again suggests the reciprocal, escalating set of conflict behaviors in couples moving toward dissolution of their relationship. Aggression and the use of power also tend to be followed by increased aggression and power use, not only because of retaliation by the other party, but also because the use of power does not apparently universally provide the cathartic effects sometimes attributed to it (cf. Berkowitz, 1974). Straus (1974) also showed that the use of lesser amounts of power, for example, verbal assault, is associated in families with the use of more intense power, expecially physical violence.

Several investigators have found that the use of power by one spouse in marriage more strongly depresses the other spouse's overall satisfaction than the availability of pleasures increases it (Hawkins, 1967; Orden and Bradburn, 1968; Wills, Weiss, and Patterson, 1974). From an understanding of the relationship between power and status withdrawal, it can be seen that as power-use increases, it is likely to invade status conferral; thus pleasures decrease inevitably with the rise in power.

The scenarios presented here for the devolution of a love relationship assume that, whereas the man's standards for status conferral were transient, the woman's were not (nor were they instrumental and therefore inauthentic). In the case in which the woman's standards for status conferral were transient, we would expect the devolution to proceed in the same manner, except that she rather than he would have been the first to withdraw status. Let us now turn to the probable outcome of the case in which the woman's standards are inauthentic because they are instrumental. The ultimate details differ little from what has just been discussed. Only the origin of the devolution differs.

I suggested earlier, and the evidence in Langhorne and Secord (1955), Centers (1971), and Barry, Bacon, and Child (1956) supports the view, that women choose men according to more practical interests—with the opportunity for solid financial support among the most prominent of these. Where such an instrumental concern determines "romantic" interest, we may wish to question the depth of authentic status conferral. There is a distinction between high-level nonvolitional status conferral and simply the acceptance by a woman of a permanent relationship with a male, usually in marriage. Kephart (1967), for example, found that women are more likely to marry someone they do not love than are men. Rubin (1969) also found that men are more "romantic" than women. Security may be so powerful a motive that women may enter into a putative love relationship, such as marriage has become in Western society, without nonvolitional status conferral to their husbands in very high amounts. In such a case, a wife may be dutiful, but she cannot be said to be loving. Any degree of calculation and rational instrumentality in what is otherwise deemed to be an expressive relationship detracts from the full manifestation of the behavioral components of the relationship.

This is obviously not intended to suggest that wives in general do not love their husbands at the outset of marriage as much as their husbands love them. Any deviation from authentic status conferral, however, is likely to have a price in a supposed love relationship. Essentially, such inauthenticity creates a relationship of infidelity (type 4, Chapter 12) at the outset.

If, from a motive of security, a woman marries a man she does not love, although she may like him, this is in part made possible by her perception that she is loved. She can feel secure because he does confer on her unlimited status. That this status may be based on transient standards is usually unknown to both parties. When the status is withdrawn, this is perceived as extremely threatening. This may be understood as follows:

In cases of female instrumental calculation, the relationship does not attain to romantic love but falls immediately into the cell of infidelity. This means that, although the man does not have high status, he does have high structural power because of the woman's acceptance of the dependence. At the outset, she has both high power and status. When, because of possibly transient selection standards and lower status valuation of women, the man begins to withdraw status, the woman's instrumental plan is demolished. Not only is security threatened, but the compensation for the psychic costs of intimacy with a person one does not love is now also diminishing.

If we add to this the possible recognition on the man's part of the inauthenticity of the relationship on the woman's part, that is, the fact that he was never truly granted the status that the culture legitimates, he has immediate grounds for anger, retaliatory status withdrawal, and the use of power. Thus, all the ingredients of relational devolution are present, in a heightened and more advanced stage.

Freud (1914) wrote that in the case of beautiful women especially, they

> love themselves with an intensity comparable to that of the man's love of them. Nor does their need lie in the direction of loving, but of being loved: [But] a large part of the dissatisfaction of the lover, of his doubts of the woman's love, of his complaints of her enigmatic nature, have their root in this incongruity . . . (pp. 46–47).

In sum, the devolution of love relationships is importantly related to the selection standards for status conferral that are employed by the lovers and by the emergence of power as a result of the dependence that each has on the other as a provider of gratification. When the gratification level fails because of nonvolitional status withdrawal, process power erupts. This leads to retaliation and, ultimately, the assertion of structural power. The principal damage is done to nonvolitional status conferral. To say that this diminishes is to say that love itself is less.

It would appear that the solution to the frequent deterioration of love relationships resides in several factors: First, the content of the standards for nonvolitional status conferral must change toward the "true" standards discussed in the preceding chapter. Here an enormous job of reconstituting the themes and lessons of the popular cultural media confronts us. For the media along with the family comprise the most important sources of models for love relationships and standards of selection of love objects. To change the content of the media in respect to these standards may first require a radical change in the structure of society.

Some idea of an emerging pattern of American values and standards for both sexes can be obtained from a large, but unfortunately not representative, survey conducted by the popular magazine *Psychology Today* among its readers (Tavris, 1977). The sample of approximately 14,000 men and 14,000 women is younger, more educated, and more liberal politically than the United States population average, and, importantly, approximately half have never been married. Bearing in mind these caveats, the results showed that among the attributes the men find important in women are: ability to love (90% +)*, warmth, stands up for her

---

*Percentage figures in parentheses indicate proportion of sample endorsing the previously given trait(s) as important for the opposite sex.

beliefs (80% +), gentle, self-confident, fights to protect family (70% +), romantic, soft (60% +), sexually faithful, able to cry (50% +). Only 47% of this sample of men indicated that physical attractiveness was important in the "ideal"women.

Among the women respondents, the important attributes of the "ideal" man were: able to love, stands up for his beliefs (90% +), warm, gentle, self-confident, intelligent (80% +), fights to protect family (70% +), sexually faithful, successful at work, romantic (60% +), able to cry (50% +). Only 29% of the women thought physical attractiveness in the man was important.

Although some differences in standards between the sexes are still present— for example, the greater importance of male occupational achievement—the similarities are more striking, particularly in the very important attribute "ability to love." This bespeaks, at least among this particular social subgroup, a growing appreciation for what I would regard as "true" as opposed to transient standards. We cannot tell whether these self-proclaimed values are actually operative when these individuals confer status on others, but the knowledge of which values and standards are desirable is a step toward acting in accordance with them.

Although knowledge and actual internalization of true standards for status conferral will help, I believe, to assure more stable and enduring love relationships through continued grounds for status conferral, a change in the power dimensions of love relationships is also required. Fundamentally, dependence in love relations must be modified to a level at which some status-withdrawal by the other does not engender process power to get it back and structural power to settle the argument. Here two paths are possible. In one, the division of labor between men and women might be changed. This involves the fuller participation of women in the economic division of labor of society to reduce their dependence on male providers; in addition, the division of labor of expressive relations might change. Marriage contracts written by the partners, "open marriage," agreed to in advance, and other such devices for reducing sexual and emotional dependence also may afford some relief from the high levels of dependence that lead to the growth and display of power (O'Neill and O'Neill, 1972).

The maintenance of love by the reduction of dependence and power looks also to a pattern of socialization that produces persons who do not easily become dependent. Maslow (1968, p. 26, p. 36) for example, spoke of the "detachment" of the self-actualizing individual. This signifies the essential *self*-centeredness of the person who does not become dependent. There is evidence that individuals who are less passionately involved with others and therefore do not experience the sharp vicissitudes to which intense human relationship are subject are also less susceptible to physical illness (Hinkle, 1974). We must learn how to cultivate such persons in the socialization process, since situational opportunities for intense dependence relationships abound. A somewhat detached individual who maintains autonomy does not imply either selfishness or total lack of interdependence, but rather lesser dependence and therefore the lesser likelihood of power in relationships in which he is involved. It can be seen that that the cooler the initial passion, the cooler the argument that succeeds it. Although this may mean living less intensely—an Apollonian rather than a Dionysian style—it does not mean loving less, and it may mean loving longer (cf. Casler, 1973).

Since the lover receives even as he gives and giving pleasure is known to be pleasurable in itself, as Aristotle (1947) proposed in his discussion of friendship in the *Nichomachean Ethics*, and as researchers have recently confirmed by ingenious experiments in the laboratory with pleasure-giving machines (Davis, Rainey, and Brock, 1976), the pleasure of giving might seem to be a sufficient basis for ensuring continuity of giving. Yet, as we know from the case of sexual giving and receiving, even intense satisfaction is not sufficient to prevent the deterioration of love. This implies that those theories of love which are based on naive notions of reinforcement, need fulfillment, or exchange do not tell us how to avoid the death of love relations. They do not consider the deleterious effects of the emergence of dependence and power, nor have they adequately conveyed the importance of the standards and values that provide a basis for status conferral. It is important to place these theories in relation to the theory of this book, as well as to show by contrast what a solution to the power question must consider.

REINFORCEMENT, NEED, AND EXCHANGE THEORIES OF LOVE

I have presented a theory of love as emotion and relationship that is nearest in tone and value to the work of such writers as Fromm (1956) and Maslow (1954, 1968). The central motif in their work is that love is *giving* not getting, although there is obviously something gotten in the love relationship. I have addressed the question of what is obtained in love in terms of the joy that comes from harmony between one's own standards and the attributes of the other. This means that the other is a reinforcer or provides reinforcement, and the second emotion of love, namely, appreciation, is related to this fact. In some respect, then, I have offered a reinforcement theory of love, and there are several proponents of such a view. Lott and Lott (1974), for example, proposed that liking for another (and presumably love) "will result under those conditions in which an individual experiences reward in the presence of that person" (p. 172). This is a quite radical theory; although it allows the attributes of the other, for example, beauty or kindliness to provide the reward, this need not be the case. If the other is simply present "even though not contributing to the pleasure, at a pleasurable event or place, e.g., a party" (p. 172), the other acquires the character of a secondary reinforcer and is liked for it. That is, the other is a discriminative stimulus associated with reward, and we like what is associated with what rewards us. Presumably, although Lott and Lott did not say so, we would like enormously what rewarded us enormously. This would be love.

A similar view was expressed by Byrne (1971) and his colleagues, who have formulated what they call the "attraction paradigm." It holds that attraction is a positive linear function of the proportion of positive reinforcements associated with the other. In many experiments attraction has been found to be related to attitude and personality similarity. Since these similarities presumably give rise to positive feelings, "one likes others who reward him because they are associated with one's own good feelings" (Clore and Byrne, 1974, p. 145).

To the extent that Byrne and Lott and Lott focused on the rewardingness of the other as the *elictor* of positive feelings (joy and appreciation), their view and mine are compatible, although we differ on exactly what is found to be rewarding. For Lott and Lott, Clore and Byrne, and other reinforcement theorists, the other's actions directly reward us. For example, he or she is kind, plays the piano well, is sexually competent, and so on. These are certainly rewarding actions by the other and would be sufficient in ordinary reinforcement theories to elicit interest and attraction.

My view, on the other hand, depends not so much on the immediate satisfactions derived from the "reinforcing" actions of the other, but on the reinforcement from the harmony between the actions of the other and our values and standards. This is more than merely saying that we each have our idiosyncratic reinforcement requirements and that we will love whoever happens to meet them. That is quite possibly adequate for Harlow's (1962) monkeys and for human infants. Rather, my point is that the most important reinforcement in the sphere of loving derives from the harmony between the other's attributes and our own standards. Otherwise it is difficult to explain love relationships in which the actual reinforcements are very low: infatuations with strangers, especially figures in public life, unrequited love, and love for someone who treats us badly.

Theories of love based on *need fulfillment* view the other as a source of rewards that satisfy certain imperative requirements of the organism, such as sex, food, and physical comfort, or of the personality, such as esteem, dominance or abasement, gregariousness, and the like (cf. Murray, 1938, for a list of needs). Orlinsky's (1972) view was that we love others who satisfy our "growth needs," and these may, of course, vary among individuals. Centers (1975), however, proposed five specific needs that are arranged in a hierarchy. These are needs for sexual satisfaction, affectionate intimacy, maintenance and enhancement of sexual identity and role, interpersonal security, and self-esteem. According to Centers (1975), we feel "an affectionate response to one who is instrumental in the gratification of (our) needs" (p. 306).

A frequent theme in need-oriented theories of love involves the need for dependence itself, precisely what I suggest is so deleterious to love relationships. Freud (1914) was among the earliest in this tradition. He developed the view that, although originally humans focus their pleasurable interests on themselves ("narcissism"), "those persons who have to do with the feeding, care, and protection of the child become his earliest sexual objects" (p. 44). Freud labeled these "anaclitic" (literally, "leaning against") love objects. In adult life, the male loves, according to this anaclitic pattern, "the woman who tends" (p. 47), whereas the woman loves, *mutatis mutandis*, "the man who protects" (p. 47). Rubin (1970) also followed this view by including in his scale designed to measure feelings of love items dealing with the fulfillment of affliliation and dependence needs.

We can all agree that humans have needs and require others for those needs to be satisfied, and indeed we even long for particular others to satisfy those needs. However, despite the prevalence of the label love to describe those yearnings for the other, my interest is to explain *loving* not longing. Although the two can exist in the same relationship, as in the case of romantic love, it is unusual for them to coexist for long. The dynamics of power and status militate against it, as described earlier.

A Note on the Two-Factor Theory of Love.   Early in their piece on the cognitive determinants of emotional state, Schachter and Singer (1962) explicitly claimed that if emotional arousal of an unknown source occurs in the presence of a beautiful woman, a man might believe his emotion to be love. This follows directly from their view that the physiological basis of emotion is undifferentiated with respect to particular emotions, and that immediate situational cues impart the meaning of the emotion to the actor. This perspective also underlies Berscheid and Walster's discussion of love. Indeed, they moved forward of Schachter and Singer, indicating that situations that arouse negative emotions— for example, fear—may lead to feelings of love.

> What may be important in determining how the individual feels about the person who is apparently generating these intense feelings is how he *labels* his reaction. If the situation is arranged so that it reasonable for him to attribute this agitated state to "passionate love," he should experience love. As soon as he ceases to attribute his arousal to passionate love, or the arousal ceases, love should die (p. 363, emphasis in original).

Berscheid and Walster acknowledged that "studies have not yet been conducted to test this hypothesis" (p. 363). Indeed, they did cite cognate studies in support of their thesis, but these differ so much from the conditions required for their arousal theory that the evidence can be rejected, I believe (see Berscheid and Walster, 1974, pp. 363–369).

In Chapter 8 I reviewed the work of Schachter and Singer (1962) in detail and concluded that their precise assertions concerning the "cognitive" or labeling features of emotional states are not warranted by the details of their experiment. Thus further theoretical work—like Berscheid and Walster's on love—that depends on that experiment is also questionable. There is, however, a highly restricted sense in which Berscheid and Walster's view is correct. I referred in Chapter 8 to the association that has been found between the emotion of anger and sexual arousal (Barclay, 1971; Zillman, 1971). No emotions other than anger have been found to relate positively to sexual arousal. This is important, for it negates the view that *any* emotion can be transmogrified under the proper labeling conditions into a feeling of love.

If, however, we extend the terms of the analysis somewhat beyond the construction imposed by Berscheid and Walster, based on their appreciation of the work of Schachter and Singer, we can gain some understanding of how a broad range of emotions may be distally associated with feelings of love. For example, in the case of a shared experience of danger that generates *fear*, the denouement may be love, not because the arousal due to fear was labeled as sexual passion, but because a shared experience of peril that is overcome allows for the deep revelation of the status-creditable qualities and attributes of another person, such as honor, courage, intelligence, physical strength, and the like. Thus we may come to love the other because he or she has demonstrated in a crisis qualities that we deeply admire.

In a variant on this situation, where fear is still the primary emotion, if the other rescues us from danger there may be immense gratitude, which may turn into dependence and create a simulacrum of love. This would not necessarily entail status conferral, but only the continued need to receive support from the other. In sum, I believe it is a more useful hypothesis to see love as a response to the match between our standards and the qualities of the other than to the mislabeling of our emotions in a situation of cognitive ambiguity.

Love and Exchange

Exchange theory, since its development by Thibaut and Kelley (1959), Homans (1961), and Blau (1964) and their many disciples, is based on the simple proposition that A *does X in order to get B to do* Y. If Y is a characteristic or behavior that is rewarding to A, then A will want to maintain this reward and will pay B by doing X (assuming that B is pleased when A does X). In the exchange formulation, X is a cost to A.

The exchange position has been applied to the whole spectrum of positive affect toward others, including liking, attraction, love, and marriage. Although the last of these does not necessarily imply positive affect, the Western cultural ideal is to combine the two. McCall (1974) viewed attraction within a framework of mutually adjusting character processes of the two actors. These adjustments entail such market practices and attitudes as "negotiation," "bargaining," "strategic response" and depend on "expected utilities." Indeed, each actor evaluates the other "primarily as representing an opportunity structure for obtaining the many varieties of rewards to which ego is oriented" (p. 225). In particular, each actor finds merit in the other to the extent that the other provides "confirmation of the specific contents of a person's idealized and singular imaginations of himself" (p. 226). Thus, contrary to the view expressed here that love is a response to the qualities of *the other*, McCall saw love as an exchange response to the other's response to the qualities of the self.

Scanzoni (1972) carried this view further and saw American marriage, both before and after the ceremony, as "sexual bargaining." Indeed, "lifelong is the notion of an ongoing quest or seeking for rewards, as the best bargain possible. Therefore, persons today bargain during courtship, during the decision to marry, and furthermore, *they continue this bargaining on through the length of their marriage*" (p. 53, emphasis in original).

Murstein (1972) viewed even the mutuality of the level of physical attractiveness of particular men and women for each other as the outcome of an exchange process. In an experiment in which judges rated the comparative attractiveness of the two partners of engaged couples, the judges attributed greater similarity of physical attractiveness to the partners of actually engaged couples than to randomly paired men and women.

This was interpreted as evidence for the view that marital choice is an exchange-market phenomenon, since each obtains the greatest reward at the least cost by directing efforts toward someone about equal (to self) in physical attractiveness. Pursuing someone more attractive is costly, and pursuing someone less attractive is insufficiently rewarding for what one has to offer. A person of similar attractiveness is therefore most profitable. The analysis conforms to the exchange principles that supposedly govern association as described by Homans (1961). Elder (1969) too employed an exchange formula to account for the fact that upward mobility for lower-class women depends on their attractiveness, which is the commodity they exchange for a higher-status marriage.

Blau (1964) provided the most detailed and hence the most valuable exchange view of love:

A man's intrinsic attraction to a woman (and hers to him) rests on the rewards he *expects* to experience in a love relationship with her (p. 79, emphasis added).

However, a love relationship is "intrinsically rewarding" (p. 15) and therefore different from ordinary exchange relationships in that no specific *quid pro quo* is exchanged. Rather, the rewards are derived from "the association itself . . . It is not what lovers do together but their doing it *together* that is the distinctive source of their special satisfaction . . . " (p. 15, emphasis in original). Blau also asserted that "in the case of intrinsic attraction, the only return expected is the willingness to continue the association" (p. 20).

The association itself, even if a source of intrinsic satisfaction, is still an exchange relationship:

> Exchange processes occur in love relationships as well as in social associations of only extrinsic significance. Their dynamics, however, are different, because the specific rewards exchanged are merely means to produce the ultimate reward of intrinsic attraction in love relations, while the exchange of specific rewards is the very object of the association in purely instrumental social relations. In intrinsic love attachments . . . each individual furnishes rewards to the other not to receive proportionate extrinsic benefits in return but to express and confirm his own commitment and *to promote the other's growing commitment to the association*" (p. 76, emphasis added).

Despite Blau's disavowal that love is not an ordinary exchange relationship, it is hard to see from this and other statements how intrinsic satisfaction differs in principle from extrinsic satisfaction. The "dynamics" to which Blau referred seem to add up to a quantitative difference: in love relationships the rewards are obtained over a broader span of activities and they are sometimes more potent, as in the case of sex. Blau made this explicit: "Ultimately, to be sure, a man's love for a woman depends on her willingness and ability to furnish him unique rewards in the form of sexual satisfaction and other manifestations of her affection" (p. 80). Intrinsic satisfaction seems to be, by this analysis, synonymous with the notion of "diffuse" in Parsons' (1951) pattern-variable alternative of that name.

In certain respects I do not dispute Blau's view of love as a reasonably accurate description of relationships that are frequently designated as love. However, I believe that some aspects of the exchange description of love relationships can be challenged. Although Blau may accurately describe what many would label love, the irony is that the degree to which such relationships are actually based on exchange principles is the degree to which they are vulnerable to the introduction of power and and the deterioration of status conferral, that is, the giving at the core of love.* Although partners in loving relationships do reward each other, much depends on their doing so for reasons other than to receive rewards in return, since this expected reciprocity is the core of exchange relations:

> An individual is attracted to another if he *expects* associating with him to be in some way rewarding for himself, and his interest in the *expected* social rewards draws him to the other (Blau, 1964, p. 20, emphasis added).

---

*According to Blau, power emerges when exchange relations are imbalanced and one actor cannot reciprocate the benefits received from the other. Blau did not specifically discuss how power enters into love relationships.

This points to the essential difficulty that subverts love that is practised according to the exchange conception: it is a *power* relationship. This is because when A does X *in order to* have B do Y, A *depends* on B to do Y. A is prone to use process power at some point to compel B's compliance. Additionally, A's dependence gives B structural power in that B can withhold Y to coerce or punish A. This ought to be more rather than less true in "intrinsic" relationships, since the partners depend on each other for more and thus generate broader bases of power vis a vis each other (Berkowitz, 1962; Holmes, 1972). The breakdown of an ordinary extrinsic relationship may be infuriating but the breakdown of a love relationship is heartbreaking as well.

Some may object that it does not make sense to think of love relationships that do not reflect such dependence. According to some reinforcement theorists with an exchange perspective, the actor need not even be aware of his or her *intent* in giving rewards to receive them. Emerson (1973) integrated the exchange and reinforcement positions and omitted as unimportant the intention of the exchangist.

> The issue, then, is not the prior calculation of the giver—it is the unfolding nature of the *relation* . . . I am led to reject prior calculation of returns as a defining feature of exchange in favor of a much broader base—social *operant* behavior. The latter includes, but is not confined to, the former. Social operant behavior is behavior whose level of performance *over time*, is sustained by reinforcing (rewarding) activity from other people" (pp. 21–22, emphasis in original).

Emerson stepped outside the usual framework of exchange theory by sacrificing the notion of rational calculation. This allowed him to say of love specifically:

> *If* the emotion and accompanying behavior called "love" with all of its "irrational" self-denial in pursuit of other's welfare, is sustained in the long run only by reciprocal love (among other supporting returns) then the love relation is appropriately analyzed within the exchange approach" (p. 22, emphasis added).

Tedeschi (1974) also took this point of view directly into the domain of love relations. One's own attractiveness, labeled "attraction" (when viewed from the perspective of the person attracted) is specifically defined as a "power resource" (p. 204). ". . . [A] person values attraction because of the rewards that a positive liking relationship beings to him" (p. 204). Further Tedeschi said that "to perceive a behavior as altruistic requires that the perceiver be ignorant of the selfish motives such actions fulfill. That attraction is not simply a matter of altruism is demonstrated when failure to reciprocate disrupts a friendship" (p. 211). Finally, "the difference between true love and . . . false love . . . is a matter of timing, illusion, and appearances" . . . (211).

Again, it must be acknowledged that there is a certain plausibility to this formulation, since it certainly describes relationships that are currently designated by some as love. However, the problem of such relationships is that they founder on the power that they conjure up. Yet can there be another type of love relationship? Although Blau (1964) was dubious, there is also some ambiguity:

> Love appears to make human beings unselfish, since they themselves enjoy giving pleasure to those they love, but this selfless devotion *generally* rests on an interest in maintaining the other's love. Even a mother's devotion to her children is *rarely* entirely devoid of the desire to maintain their attachment to her (p. 76, emphasis added).

If "generally" and "rarely" are not merely stylistic qualifiers, this hints at a possible love in which A gives X to B without expectation of return. Tedeschi (1974), too, allowed a modicum of qualification in his unrelentingly "Machiavellian" (p. 211) position:

> As Aristotle (cited in Blau, 1964) said: "*most* men wish what is noble, but choose what is profitable; and while it is noble to render a service not with an eye to receiving one in return, it is profitable to receive one. One ought therefore, if one can, to return the equivalent of services received, and to do so willingly" (p. 211, emphasis added).

Unless Aristotle did not believe in "noble" action and used the qualifier "most" with only an indifferent intent, this indicates that Aristotle (and Tedeschi) believed that some actions—and we would think especially so in putative love relationships—are done without expectation of gain.

There is a clear difficulty here. Human beings are interdependent and therefore require others to provide them goods and services they cannot provide for themselves. This is one of the first postulates enunciated in this book. Even in "true" love relationships, goods and services are given by each to the other, as Blau said, but can things be "exchanged," outside the premise of *exchange theory*? Can we have a case in which A does X but *not* to have B do Y, even though Y is indubitably gratifying to A? The question is considered on several grounds. First I discuss whether all hedonic action, that is, action that gratifies the *doer*, should be defined as exchange when it is directed toward another person. Many theorists, in fact, treat all hedonic action as "exchange," but I believe it is erroneous and leads to a mistaken conclusion about the generality of exchange processes. Second, I propose a distinction between *existential* and *relational* interdependence. This addresses the important question of the extent to which dependence can be avoided and power thereby mitigated. Third, I examine the concept of cost in both exchange and status-conferral theory and suggest that the two approaches to love can be distinguished by the amount and locus of costs that may be experienced in a love relationship. Finally, I suggest that love as a concept and an ideal has evolved over time and that exchange conceptions, although often adequately descriptive of the relationship that many practise under the name of love, are nonetheless misleading by implying that love can be only an exchange relationship. The most highly evolved views of love dispute this.

Hedonism, Exchange and Love

Let us distinguish between *hedonic* action, which is designed to ensure maximum reward and gain to oneself when choosing from a spectrum of possible alternative actions, and *exchange* action, which is designed to ensure maximum reward and gain to oneself *from the action of others*. The two are often confused, but they are not the same. I think it is a very useful assumption that *all* human action is *at all times* hedonic, and, therefore, our actions depend on the most favorable internal, or subjective, balance of the reward-cost ratios. This is true not only for the most venal and greedy persons, but also for the mostly saintly and self-effacing. In exchange action, too, the central concern is to make a profit, but the specific difference is that *in exchange, the rewards must be expected from the actions of others directed toward us as a consequence of our actions toward them*.

Can there be hedonic action that, by defintion, is maximally rewarding to the actor, yet does not depend on the reciprocity of others? Blau (1964), an exchange theorist, offered some clues. First, actions that are impulsive and based on an "irrational push of emotional forces" (p. 5) are excluded from exchange. Indeed, love, conceived as nonvolitional status conferral, may well fit this definition of impulsive action. If this is the case, Blau's earlier discussion of love as an exchange process is now obscure. Perhaps Blau would agree that actions that are truly loving do result from the "irrational push of emotional forces." However, since on-going interactions may pass from one type of relationship to another, depending on the power-status configuration, perhaps Blau's major discussion of love is focused only on the romantic type, which is closest to the dissolution of mutual love. If this is so, Blau's exchange view is not incorrect but simply misleading by not considering the possibility of other types of love, principally the prototypical case of brotherly love.

In his later work, Blau (1968) retreated from his earlier position (Blau, 1964) that even Weber's (1947) category of "Wertrational" action is exchange and acknowledged that actions oriented toward values ought not to be included in the exchange framework.

It is instructive to repeat Blau's citation of Weber's definition of Wertrational conduct:

the action of persons who, regardless of possible cost to themselves, act to put into practice their convictions of what seems to be required by duty, honor, the pursuit of beauty, a religious call, personal loyalty, or the importance of some "cause" no matter in what it consists (Weber, 1947, p. 116).

It is regrettable that Weber did not include love, although he did mention beauty. Yet it is clear that Wertrational action is not guided by what others can do to reward one. It appears to be a matter of standards for conduct, conformity to which is automatic and, fortunately, deeply rewarding in the hedonic sense. It does not appear to be a matter of exchange at all. In fact, there is a sense in which both impulsive and Wertrational action are based on the same nonrational, nonvolitional ground.

Whereas impulsive action is nonrational because it is not shaped by the reflection of its probable consequences, Wertrational action is nonrational because the means suitable to the attainment of the goals are not shaped by reflection of any consequences *except* success. Thus there is no consideration of "cost," as Weber said. In this it is equivalent to impulsive action and can therefore be linked to the kind of nonvolitional response that is at the heart of love.

It is clear that at the moment of action, by virtue of the assumption that, from the point of view of the actor, the action undertaken is maximally hedonic, both impulsive and Wertrational action are the most satisfying available action choices. However, since they are not instrumental in that they are not directed toward expected benefits for the self to be obtained from others, they stand outside the exchange model of relationship. To the extent that loving action is correctly conceived as gratifying to the self even though it is nonrational, it too stands outside the confines of exchange.

The difference between hedonic action and exchange, which Blau's emendations help us see, is blurred by those who view all action in which one derives satisfaction, whether or not it depends on some action or response of the other, and whether or not the actor *intended* to elicit behavior from the other that would gratify himself, as exchange.

In a very useful essay, Huston (1974) considered suggestions by Lerner (1974) and others that the distribution of rewards in exchange relationships can be governed by principles other than maximization of own gain (cf. Meeker, 1971). Thus one can engage in exchanges in which benefits are distributed according to a principle of *parity* (equal shares), *equity* (shares proportional to investment), or *need* (shares proportional to need). Huston commented that "an equity theorist might argue that Lerner's typology represents [only] varied conceptualizations of reward rather than different forms of justice. An individual who makes great sacrifices for another may derive substantial pleasure from enhancing the other's well-being and thus find commensurate reward in the relationship. From the perspective of the investor the *exchange* is 'equitable'" (p. 21, emphasis added).

Indeed, by calling it exchange Huston made precisely the error that views all conduct as exchange because it is hedonic.* Although the "investor" has profited, it is neither from the actions of the other nor at the expense of the other, two conditions that are central to a meaningful theory of exchange relationships.

There is experimental work that supports the view that hedonism is compatible with gain for the other, even at supposed cost to oneself. In a study conducted by Krebs (1975), subjects who empathized with an other because of similarity were able to help the other win money in an experimental game or avoid shock, even though such aid "meant jeopardizing their own welfare" (p. 1144). Krebs concluded that "even if human beings are essentially hedonistic, they need not be selfish. When the pains and pleasures of others become intrinsically tied to the affective state of the observers, it can be to their best interest to maximize the favorableness of the hedonic balance of others to maximize the favorableness of their own hedonic state" (pp. 1144–45). Although this view bases altruism on hedonism and self-interest, it removes it from exchange, which is the principle concern here.

In love relationships, the gain is partly derived from giving pleasure to the other as an expression of appreciation. It gratifies the giver to give, and if appreciation is truly a nonvolitional, therefore emotional, response, it is not given to stimulate reciprocity. Yet it is also true that we cannot give appreciation indefinitely without some return. This fact makes it appear that giving must be based on the prospect of receiving; thus we are back to an exchange view of love. The matter can be clarified by distinguishing between two forms of human interdependence—existential and relational.

Existential and Relational Interdependence

Human beings are by nature interdependent. Indeed, we cannot survive in infancy unless others satisfy our primary needs, and, except in rare cases, we cannot survive in adulthood without social support. Beyond this the existence of the species itself depends on the biological cooperation of men and women. Thus there is a minimum level of interdependence in which we all partake and perhaps gives rise to a common fund of sentiment about our being bound together as a collective humanity. I call this *existential interdependence*.

Beyond this common level of mutual dependence, individuals exhibit greater or lesser "dependence needs" (Goldfarb, 1969; Maccoby, and Masters, 1970). Our happiness and satisfaction with life can become more or less dependent on the presence or actions of some specific other person or persons. This may, for the adult, involve parents, spouse or lover, friends of the same sex, and work

---

*Secord and Backman (1964) also promulgated this view.

colleagues, to name a few of the most important others from whom we may seek explicit solutions to the problems of approval for our accomplishments and benevolent emotional support when we are in difficulty. In addition, given the technical-economic structure of developed societies, most of us are also dependent on a specific employer or union or professional association for the maintenance of our livelihood. These are aspects of what I call *relational interdependence*.

My fundamental thesis is that, although existential interdependence is the common lot, relational dependence varies very widely among individuals. To the extent that we are relationally dependent, by so much are we constrained by the structural power of others and instigated to engage in process power of our own when we cannot obtain that for which we depend on the other.

Equally important, however, I propose that those who are susceptible to high levels of relational dependence are more likely to view their relationships with others, including love relationships, from an exchange perspective. That is, since I require Y from you, I will only give X as long as you give Y. It is not material whether such a formulation is implicit in the personality structure or develops naturally in a given relationship in which certain benefits are found to be very gratifying. The result is the same as far as relational development is concerned: power emerges.

Although it may be argued, following Durkheim (1933), that mutual relational interdependence is a strong ground for solidarity and cohesion, this proposition, which is so appealing at the level of the whole society, fails badly at the level of concrete interindividual relationships. Whereas at the societal level there can be no withdrawal by any part or person from the whole, at the interpersonal level one can survive by finding a new partner or by suspending relational activity *for a while* in certain ways. Indeed, Durkheim dealt with the minimal level of existential interdependence, whereas any concrete interindividual relationship reflects the degree of relational dependence for the persons concerned.

Yet, clearly, some amount of relational dependence is inevitable. The issue is not how to eliminate relational dependence entirely, but to limit its extent. In the same way, Durkheim (1933) realistically assessed the benefits of the regulation of competition in the division of labor:

> It is neither necessary nor even possible for social life to be without conflicts. The role of solidarity is not to suppress competition, but to *moderate* it (p. 365, emphasis added).

In moderating relational dependence, so are the structural and processual aspects of power moderated.

The question of standards and intent is important in the avoidance of relational dependence. If one gives to the other because one has standards that evoke nonvolitional status conferral, the intent is to convey appreciation rather than to elicit exchange reciprocity of benefits from the other. This suggests that relational dependence emerges insofar as giving is not guided by standards. For, even if the standards are transient, they evoke authentic status conferral as long as they last. This is what probably gives even the shallowest love relationship a simulacrum of truth. Yet as soon as the transient standards have run their course, further giving is no longer nonvolitional and authentic, but must be premised on what one can get in return. Another characteristic of transient standards is that they are more likely than true standards to reflect need and evoke relational dependence. The prototypical need of this type involves the sex drive in which the appealing characteristic of the other is effectively expressed in satisfying the self on an exclusive basis (cf. Blau, 1964, p. 80).

True standards, however, are not ordinarily oriented toward exclusivity; standards for compassion, justice, competence, for example, allow the love object to operate in a wider orbit. One loves the other not for what the other does for oneself in particular, which would be relational dependence, but for what the other is or does in general. This generalization of the quality of the other reaches to the level of existential interdependence. If the other's effective qualities and our standards transcend the immediacy of the relationship, we are thereby less personally affected by the normal ebb and flow of the output of the other's qualities. This allows us to mediate better the occasional, inevitable breaks in the display of the attributes that evoke our status accord. Being less dependent in an individual sense, we are less likely to resort to power to have our needs fulfilled or the relationship rebalanced, as if it were an exchange.

Yet, even in relationships founded on true standards, if for whatever reason one actor ceases to give appreciation, the other also soon terminates giving. *Prima facie* this would seem again to support an exchange view, yet deeper analysis shows that this need not be the case.

If, in a relationship of mutual giving according to true standards, B ceases to give to A, A must also eventually terminate giving to B, because sooner or later A must feel existential hunger for the gratifications B provided and must seek them from another source. Although B's qualities may still evoke appreciation from A, the failure of reciprocity must take A out of B's field as part of his search for the minimal set of gratifications that are implied by existential interdependence. Thus, by not being present, A effectively terminates giving to B. *Even if A wished, nonetheless, to continue to give to B*, current forms of social organization, the major paradigm of which is the legal contract (Durkheim, 1933), do not encourage unilateral giving, even from the side of the receiver. To accept benefits with no intention of returning them is considered opportunistic and reprehensible, on one hand, and it creates uncomfortable pressures toward unwilling reciprocity on the other (Foa and Foa, 1974, pp. 244–250).

If we wish to know whether actor A gives to B according to *standards* or the *exchange model*, we find an important clue in the emotion A feels if B terminates giving to A. In general, the emotion is *depression*, due to the hunger for the benefits B formerly provided. If A gave nonvolitionally according to the status-accord model, the depression takes the classic form of a sense of inadequacy, worthlessness, and the like; if A gave for exchange purposes the depression is experienced as anger and hostility. In the former case, self is viewed as the agent of the loss: if one gives because the other's attributes merit giving, one must reason that the other was also giving for the same reason. Otherwise, there would be a flaw in B's character so deep as to have jeopardized A's willingness to give to B in the first place. Thus if the other ceases to give, it must be because one's own attributes no longer meet the other's standards. One may then suffer very keenly from the deprivation of accustomed status benefits, but, since one is responsible oneself for the loss, one is depressed in the classic sense. Where the exchange model prevails and A gave to receive, B's failure to give must evoke the sense that B is the agent responsible for the loss, and this instigates anger. Since anger is a frequent precursor emotion to aggression, as detailed in Chapters 6 and 10, it links theoretically to the dependence-power outcome. This result, however, also relies on the dependence being relational. That is, in this case A specifically depended on B to provide the benefits; that is why A gave benefits to B in the first place. When the return is no longer forthcoming, it is a ground for feeling cheated and angry. Since A has done his part, why cannot B also comply?

If most love relationships move from the mutual satisfactions and benefits of existential interdependence in brotherly love to the relational dependence of romantic love, it is because present forms of social organization and the division of labor between the sexes do not ordinarily emphasize autonomy sufficiently for all. Barry, Bacon, and Child (1956) reported that, overwhelmingly, autonomy is considered a masculine trait in various world cultures. In addition, some of the prevailing ideology of love relationships, as discussed earlier in relation to need-fulfillment theories, is frankly and forthrightly dedicated to fostering relational dependence, despite the fact that it may not be an ultimately satisfactory solution to the problem of existential interdependence. Since psychiatric and psychoanalytic views dominate here, there is perhaps an excess of knowledge and focus on the ineluctable fact of infantile dependence and the clinical picture of its continuation in various forms of neurotic disorder (cf. Maslow, 1954, p. 355). It is a gross error to assume that human adaptation to the minimum interdependence needs of existence must be resolved in relational dependence.

The Cost of Loving

Another clue to whether giving in a love relationship follows the status-accord or the exchange model involves the concept of cost. In economic theory, cost is understood as opportunity foregone in choosing a particular course of action (Homans, 1961). Ordinarily one wants to make a profit, in which case the rewards one gets exceed the rewards one might have gotten from any of the opportunities foregone (Homans, 1961, p. 58). Blau (1964) spoke of profit in love relationships in terms of "net cost" (pp. 102ff) or "costless rewards" (p. 132) (cf. Foa and Foa, 1974, p. 250).

> If an individual obtains gratification from doing something in social interaction that is also gratifying for his associate, he provides the associate with a social reward without any cost to himself. Although there is a cost in time for him, this cost should be allocated to the reward he himself experiences rather than to the one he simultaneously furnishes the other. Such costless rewards are typical of mutual love, where each individual derives gratification in the very process of furnishing it to the other . . . (pp. 101–102).

Now there is no sense in which "objective" cost can be ascertained. That is, estimates of cost and the arithmetic that pertains to them are recognized to be a subjective matter, as in the concept *subjective expected utility* (Lee, 1971, p. 32). Yet, in this subjective sphere, if one chooses the action that gratifies the other, it is also the action that is maximally hedonic for the doer, as discussed earlier. In this sense Blau's "costless rewards" follow from the basic assumption of hedonism at the root of all action.

However, if costs and rewards are to be understood from a consistent application of exchange theory, the costs of giving are experienced as such only if there is insufficient return *from the other* to pay those costs and leave something over. In a social exchange formulation, costs and rewards cannot be charged to the account of the actor as if he were alone. This is "atomism," a view that has long since been thrust out of sociological theory. Indeed, if the hedonic assumption is correct and all action is profitable, the atomistic approach is tautologous. The result must always be that action is "costless" in the way Blau meant us to understand it. This remains true whether the net profit is very high or very low. Even if it is a minus profit, (i.e., there is a loss), the loss is relatively less than that entailed by any other action.

In the status-accord model of loving, on the other hand, cost does not enter to be deducted from gratification-received to obtain "net cost." The position here is that loving is *cost-free*. Scheler (1954) captured the sense of this:

> The feeling of "benevolence" also involves the making of an effort towards the well-being of the others: it is not properly a volition, but an impulsive tendency to self-exertion . . . But *there is no sense of effort in love* . . . Love may give rise to all kinds of effort . . . for the beloved object, but they are no part of it (pp. 140–141, emphasis added).

If joy and appreciation are at the extremely high levels supposed in love relationships, then what is given is given freely. In general, if one accords precisely the amount of status one feels one wants to give, there can be no felt cost, because the match between attributes and standards evokes status conferral nonvolitionally. Indeed, when this match occurs, cost is experienced subjectively only when the circumstances are such that one cannot give because the other refuses to accept the appreciation or is dead or gone and cannot receive. It is in this sense that we must understand Fromm's (1956) statement:

> Immature love says: "*I love you because I need you.*" Mature love says: "*I need you because I love you*" (p. 34, emphasis in original).

Even these costs are not to be charged to the other if the desire to give is truly evoked as status conferral. The costs of relationship from this point of view are counted only from the moment that giving is coerced. When we do not want to give in a particular amount, but feel forced or the other directly forces us to give, the experience of cost is subjectively very great. Thus costs enter a love relationship as soon as power enters.

The exchange view, on the other hand, despite Blau's formulation of it, must view costs in terms of the failure of the other to pay some return for one's efforts. Indeed, this must be so, since an exchange theory that involves *social* exchange does not sensibly deal with actions individuals undertake for their own satisfaction in doing them, but only with the exchange of actions in some form of *quid pro quo* with others (cf. Blau, 1964, p. 20).

An Evolutionary Conception of Loving

Although the exchange model is rejected here as an adequate theory of loving, this is not because exchange is not practised by many who believe themselves to be loving or because exchange does not operate in the interstices of truly loving relationships. Rather it is because there are loving relationships that are not impelled by exchange principles, and, although perhaps rare, they must be analyzed as a form of relationship that ramifies differently from those which are governed by exchange. Most important is the moderation of dependence and power entailed by formulating love relationships in a nonexchange way.

If the nonexchange model leads to such desirable outcomes, it may be asked why it is not practised more. Here we must admit to some puzzlement about the nature of the species, but ultimately some optimism. I believe that the status-accord view of love is an *evolutionary* conception. Love has not always been conceived in the same way in Western culture and understanding. Although the exchange view is a very prevalent model, rooted in the same philosophical soil that gave rise to the notions of social contract and the equality and dignity of the individual in the fifteenth to seventeenth centuries, it is only one step toward the full development in cultural consciousness of a better understanding of loving. It is not likely to be the last stage of that development (Barnes, 1948).

Loving, as I have insisted here, means giving. Love so defined has existed in individual cases virtually from the dawn of human history. Even nonhuman forms—mammals, birds, and the like—that nurture their young until they are ready to fend for themselves enact many behaviors that are manifestly the same as those of the loving human parent. Of course, we attribute consciousness to the human lover and here probably resides not only the difference from lower forms but also the possibility for the evolution of love as an ideal. There are several "natural" histories of love (Gourmont, 1932; Hunt, 1959), and from these we can glean the fact that the earliest cultural conceptions of love in the Western world, with the exception of the parental form, were expressed largely in terms of sex and longing, a conception of love as "getting," the very opposite of the idea of love proposed here. The rhymes of Cattulus, Ovid, and Sappho and the "Song of Songs" in the Bible tell of love that gives full due to passion and virtually none to giving. If Durkheim's (1933) view is correct, in earlier societies in which personalities were little differentiated from group identity there was no institutionalized basis for recognizing the worth and value of the other *qua* unique person.

With the emergence of individualism as an ideology, the conditions are fulfilled for recognizing and valuing others for their own merits. Particularly associated with an age of accomplishment and striving, the newer ideology of love entailed the lover's finding value and worthiness in the love object first and only later an inflamed passion in oneself. The sonnets of Shakespeare bespeak a deeper and broader basis of interest in the loved one than merely sexual attraction, although this is not absent. By the beginning of the nineteenth century— see the novels of Jane Austen—we find the full-blown cultural conception of love as fundamentally giving, regardless of longing, that continues in a clear line until the present.

All this is not to say that no one in primitive societies felt love in the sense of desire to give rather than get. Even primitive societies are not monolithic in their control over their members, and with the model of an unselfish maternal love to guide as well as to shape them, surely some individuals developed the capacity to admire merit and worth and to give. However, such developments were probably rare, and the customary pattern of mating through family-to-family contractual arrangement did much to limit the scope for realizing a valued interest in the the other in male-female relationships. Although the giving kind of love was unusual, all could experience the longing of sexual attraction and view the other as possessing qualities that one needed to satisfy one's own needs.

Yet even in relatively early societies, a significant sense of love as giving emerged as an ethical commandment that expressed the highest principal of social relations. "Love thy neighbor as thyself" does not mean "long for" or "feel need for" the neighbor, but rather give as one would want to be given to. This remains an explicit injunction in the Western religious tradition to the present day. Regrettably, one cannot feel loving on command, though one can be enjoined to act lovingly. Freud (1951) viewed the injunction to love others as foolish, since it went against fundamental human processes rooted in instincts for gratification of self, particularly in regard to sex and aggression. Yet Freud had also to acknowledge that love as giving did occur. His solution was to view it as a transference phenomenon, as discussed in the preceding chapter, or as "aim-inhibited sexuality." Withal, Freud (1918) also acknowledged a progressive advance in the way aim-inhibited sexuality was conceived and expressed. In one of his most pessimistic essays, "Reflections on War and Death," he wrote that civilization exists only as a veneer covering an earlier stage of psychic development in which instinctual and impulse gratification was prepotent.

> There are therefore more civilized hypocrites than truly cultured persons and one can even discuss the question whether a certain amount of civilized hypocrisy is not indispensable to maintain civilization because the already organized cultural adaptability of man today would perhaps not suffice for the task of living according to the truth. On the other hand, the maintenance of civilization even on such questionable grounds *offers the prospect that with every new generation a more extensive transformation of impulses will pave the way for a better civilization* (pp. 28–29, emphasis added).

Although pessimistic, Freud acknowledged further that "the ethical strivings of mankind . . . are an acquisition of the history of man: they have since become, though unfortunately in very variable quantities, the hereditary possession of people today" (p. 61).

Scheler (1954) too accorded the benefit of an evolutionary view to certain qualities that might be thought of as the penumbra of love: "Kindness, goodwill, gratitude, affection . . . are assuredly modes of love which are common to all men and do not depend for their emergence on the level of historical development. But it is otherwise with amiability, courtesy, filial regard, etc." (p. 174). Earlier Scheler commented, "A proportion (sic) of these terms denote attributes which are not part of the basic fabric of human nature, but only exist in the context of a given framework of historical development" (p. 174).

These views deed to culture and history both the source and the opportunity to develop higher ethical conceptions of love as well as the better human beings who can love in accordance with them. Indeed, this is an optimistic conclusion, because it acknowledges progress in the past and possibility for more progress in the future. Culture and suitable forms of social organization and socialization—the creation of certain types of social order and human personality—may perhaps be sufficient for the widespread diffusion in practice of the most evolved conception of loving. Socialist experiments in societal organization have precisely this aim if they are oriented toward realizing certain of Marx's (1964, pp. 247–248) views on how human personality may be developed. We have no evidence as yet, however, concerning the success of those experiments in regard to the most evolved conception of love.

The significance of regarding love, from the point of view of its historical and cultural definition, as an evolving concept rather than a fixed and immutable one is that we may look toward a progressive realization of loving as giving among more and more people. Although love as giving can occur as a relational outcome regardless of cultural sanction, the institutionalization of this definition would doubtless improve the likelihood of its being realized in relationships that are labeled love. Indeed, we would not then label love any relationship that does not attain to the most evolved conception. This reassignment of labels would perhaps save many from the grief of entering relationships that can only turn out badly. That part of socialization which is concerned with the inculcation of standards might then concentrate more realistically on standards that are reliable, stable, and give promise of maintaining status conferral. Correlatively, that part of socialization which is concerned with the inculcation of attributes might concentrate more realistically on attributes that reliably match the true standards the other will hold for them.

chapter 14

Conclusion

I have tried to do two things in this book. One was to illuminate the study of emotions by means of a sociological theory of social relationships. The second was to demonstrate the utility of power-status theory through this concrete application to the field of emotions. The reader will evaluate the adequacy of these undertakings at his or her own leisure. Here I take the opportunity to summarize briefly the work of the previous chapters and to offer my own estimate of its value.

The basic "facts," as I understand them, are the factor-analytic results, presented in Chapter 2 and Appendix 2, which are that many researchers have located two relational dimensions—*power* and *status*, as I call them. This is a very powerful finding, for it promises that social relations are not comprised of so many categories and variables that the whole may ultimately be too complex for our understanding. Rather the finding implies that social life is composed of a relatively simple underlying framework on which we weave our affairs. History, ethnicity, and local conditions may particularize the manifest shape of cultural items that indicate power and status magnitudes, and there may be differential normative and structural patterning of who has how much power and status. The important ground fact for knowledge is that social relations are comprised of two fundamental dimensions that transcend local and temporal distinctions.

The last is, of course, only a heuristic surmise. There is the danger that it outruns the evidence, but science often grows by guesses that are lucky enough to be right. However, I believe there is more than guesswork here. I have been much encouraged by finding that the power-status view of social relations has a long history. Although that guarantees nothing about its validity, it does mean that our present understanding is confirmed by independent observers in different times and places. The earliest efforts were those of philosophers and social philosophers whose judgments were based only on informal observation and evaluation of "the nature of things." Today our efforts are based on systematic observation by trained observers or individuals systematically evaluating themselves and others. The remarkable fact is the virtually perfect convergence of results from the different methods and different ages.

The two-dimensional model of social relations may be thought too simple. Yet it elaborates quickly into a more complex formulation according to the demands of the question. From the point of view of any single actor, there are four channels of relationship when one other is involved: own power, own status, other's power, and other's status. If a third party is added, the number of primary channels increases to eight—by adding the four new own-and-third-party power-and-status channels. Four secondary channels are also possible, involving the power-status relationship between other and third party. Furthermore, when the power-status model is applied to existing relationships, the actors evaluate the state of the relationship out of a set of 12 possibilities—to use only a very crude ordinal scale of measurement: own and other's power and status can be adequate, insufficient, or excessive. The actual situation is a particular configuration of four conditions: for example, own power adequate, own status insufficient, other's power adequate, other's status adequate, and so on. The full set of four conditions comes to $3^4 = 81$, as discussed in Chapter 5. These two examples ought to lay to rest the fear that a two-dimensional approach to social relations cannot comprehend the real complexity of social life.

In applying the power-status model to the problem of emotions, I have tried to develop systematically the implications of the common intuitive understanding that many human emotions result from outcomes in social relationships. I do not claim that all emotion is of this character, nor that any given emotion results only from social relationships. Rather, I have tried to explore the emotional consequences of relational outcomes. The reader can see how important it is for the systematic exploration of this large question to work with a comprehensive model of social relationships. Even with the help of such a model, the work had of necessity to be less than complete because of my own inadequacy and lack of sensitivity about emotions, the cultural disjunction in the mapping between language and emotions, and most crucially, the large lacunae in the empirical literature, in which emotions have rarely enough been studied at the molar level and virtually never with the *explicit* understanding that social relational structures and outcomes produce emotions. Yet the sociological approach to the study of emotions has been implicit in the work of the cognitive theorists (Arnold, R. S. Lazarus and his colleagues, Schachter and his colleagues), the learning theorists (A. A. Lazarus, Wolpe), the clinical and psychoanalytic tradition inaugurated by Freud, and the many social psychologists whose experimental paradigms are simply different encodings of relational conditions that produce emotions.

In referring to the common intuitive understanding that social relational outcomes produce emotions, I do not ignore the fundamental insight of many sociologists that this is the case. Every sociological treatment of emotions arrives at this conclusion, whether it is the work of the classic theorists—Marx, Weber,

Durkheim, Simmel—or more recent theorists—Homans, Blau, Goffman, Garfinkel. Although sociological contributions to the study of emotions will become increasingly important, I believe, they have had little impact on systematic study in this field. This is, for the most part, because sociologists have been content to keep their insights to themselves without troubling to build the necessary bridges of common understanding that would enable them to make contact with students of emotions in psychology. A singular barrier has been the radically different subject matter and context of work on emotions in the two fields. Sociologists have only rarely (some exceptions are Kaplan and Bloom, Moss, Mazur) sought to learn enough about the psychophysiological properties of emotions to enable them to address the main corps of psychologists working in this area. Since I have specifically treated the psychophysiological results, I hope this book will further both the dialogue and cooperation between the two fields.

I have been particularly encouraged by the understanding the sociological viewpoint contributes to the psychophysiological problem of *specificity* (discussed in Chapters 7 and 8). The application of power-status theory to the psychophysiological experimental data accomplishes two things. First, it is very clear that a sociological understanding of the experimental conditions of most research settings necessarily illuminates the question of what emotions to expect in those settings. In many cases, experimenters have proceeded without adequate knowledge of the sociological context of their experimental manipulations. This has led, I believe, to mistaken conclusions about psychophysiological relationships. Indeed, although it is a barbarism to say it, I must conclude that the solution lies in the emergence of a new discipline that would deal with (although perhaps not be called) *sociopsychophysiology*. Indeed, this is what psychophysiology and sociophysiology already are at their best.

The second important result of applying power-status theory to the psychophysiological experimental results was the unanticipated but wholly welcome finding that there are discrete physiological structures and processes that are organismic analogs to the social relational dimensions. The so-called Funkenstein hypothesis, dealing with the differentiated emotional results of epinephrine and norepinephrine, is so intelligently compatible with the two-dimensional social relational formulation that each mutually enhances the plausibility of the other. This was entirely unlooked for at the outset, but I believe the evidence compels the conclusion that there is indeed an unbroken theoretical arc that links the structure and process of relations between actors with the structure and process within actors. I count this result to be one of the most important contributions of this book. There is obviously much work to be done to strengthen our understanding of the relationship between the two domains, but at least it can go forward on both sides on the basis of equally important contributions.

The most difficult and challenging task was to show how relational outcomes determine the *consequent emotions* (Chapter 6). The literature on emotions is so scant that I have sometimes felt myself to be engaged in a task of "emotional paleontology"—that is, reconstructing an entire emotional skeletal structure from a tooth, a toe, or a shin plate, so to speak. Social psychologists have rarely been interested in emotions for their own sake; instead they have dealt with problems of equity, altruism, attraction, aggression, and the like. The research results overwhelmingly have reported *behavior*–helping or witholding help, hurting or refraining from hurting—or *autonomic* results such as heart rate, palmar conductance, or blood pressure. Yet the phenomenological emotion is often unmeasured. Thus I have inferred emotions appropriate to the experimental conditions, as discussed in Chapter 6, on the basis of an untested theory, namely, the one to which this book is devoted. I have no doubt done some violence to the "facts." Yet there is no way to know the facts until experimental work explores the emotions implied by every cell of the multicell table discussed in Chapter 5. More than likely it will not be necessary to investigate every one of the 1701 cells. I suggested some useful concisions that may help to establish quickly some empirical regularities that can be extended lawfully to many untested cells.

There may be a good reason for the extreme paucity of experimental social psychological work on emotions. After all, the end state—aggressive *action*, equitable *behavior*, loving *conduct*, and so on—may be of more consequence as well as more interest than the emotions that energize them. I have not even considered until now whether it is a useful inquiry to predict emotions. Phenomenologically, of course, it is very useful. As a sentient organism, I am aware of the bodily and psychic signs of my emotions, and I want to know more about them. I believe that an important contribution of the theory of this book is that it enhances the phenomenological understanding of emotions. It therefore contributes to self-knowledge, and this is probably desirable for many reasons, not the least of which is that we can better order our relationships with others— both what we do to them as well as what they do to us—in the light of our knowledge of the relational conditions that instigate our emotions. Surely, enough has been said on the subject of authenticity, the need to harmonize intellect and viscera, to require no further discussion of the benefits of self-knowledge concerning emotions.

Many of us wish to do more than know ourselves. We are dedicated to knowing others and to making our knowledge helpful to them. I believe that here too the sociological approach to emotions offers distinct advantages. On the basis of some suggestive shreds of evidence from the psychiatric literature and the derivation of the distressful emotions—guilt, shame, anxiety, and depression— from the patterns of self and other's excess or insufficient power and status, and from the fact that the distressful emotions are central to the mental and emotional disorders, I have proposed that the two major categories of mental and emotional disorder—schizophrenia and depression—can be allocated to disorders of power relations and status relations, respectively. I reviewed many studies to see whether the hypothesis fits; although I do not find the conclusion inevitable, I offer it nonetheless in the hope that it may provoke some next steps that might reject or establish it more compellingly. Among the major difficulties is the assessment of the precise role of genetic factors that may dispose individuals to mental and emotional disorder. Although some investigators strongly favor the genetic hypothesis, there is enough support for some kind of social causation—in the form of difficult interpersonal relations, invidious social structural conditions, or explicit labeling of unusual behavior—to warrant a vigorous pursuit of efforts to locate sociological and relational conditions that contribute to emotional and mental illness. This may be no more than a statement of faith, but it is premised on two considerations: First, sociological and social relational analysis is not yet so sophisticated that it can be said we have done the best that can be done. I believe we must expect that future research into social causation will be sounder both theoretically and methodologically than it has been. I would not have us give up the extremely important hypothesis of social causation without a crucial test that we can fairly well agree is adequate. This remains to be done. The second reason I believe we must still pursue a social causation explanation of mental and emotional disorder is that, if it proves to be true to any degree, to that degree (if we have the will to do so), we may be able to ameliorate or remove the deleterious social causes and thereby prevent the illness. Genetic explanations, to the extent they are valid, do not permit so easy a confidence that a preventive approach can be taken. Genetic engineering may be almost upon us, but it is not yet so.

The chapters dealing with punishment, the dependent variables of socialization and positive emotions, and love also contribute understanding that may enable us to help others. It is surely a principal objective of all studies of socialization to understand the outcomes and consequences of parental conduct toward children. Larger social structures and cultural settings may determine what parents do, in the main, but we must also understand the effects of what they do. In considering punishment, I treated it as *relational* behavior. This means that, from the point of view of emotions, punishment simply elicits the emotions appropriate to the behavior, but, since the child is not a finished product, so to speak, punishment in the course of socialization has the effect of tying particular emotions to particular interaction conditions. These are of two kinds. First, there is the relational behavior of the parent in the punishment situation. Second, there is the technical and relational behavior of the child in the situation that elicited the punishment. Emotions are conditioned to both by virtue of punishment type—does it elicit power or status concern—and by whether it is proportional to or in excess of the damage done by the supposed trespass.

In assigning punishment to either a power or status category, I obliterated some conventional distinctions, such as those between physical and love-withdrawal punishment or between reasoning and deprivation of privileges. These manifest categories, I believe, are not adequate for theoretical purposes. The degree to which they are understandable as *relational* gives us a clue as to their *emotional* significance. The verbal component of punishment helps the child identify the relational significance of the punishment. The proportionality of punishment to trespass helps discriminate the power-status significance of punishment into whether one's own or other's power and status are at issue. I believe that the interaction between punishment type and proportionality produce the four distressful emotions—guilt, shame, anxiety, and depression. Doubtless I have simplified a great deal to get this result. Nonetheless it is the business of a theory to do so, and I believe that, even if wrong in part, some gain in understanding is possible from this view of the punishment situation. The most important benefit, I believe, is that it assigns much of the emotional trauma of childhood to the disjunctions between parent's and child's view of the *seriousness* of a trespass and the *intensity* of punishment for it. Indeed, many actions that are wholly innocent for the child are converted into trespasses in the very act of their being punished. Much has been made of the terror and loneliness of childhood, the fear of abandonment, and the loss of security. These are existential conditions through which we all pass and, since we do not all emerge emotionally scarred or maimed, the specific difference must lie in something beyond the existential traumas. I propose that the parent–child relationship often consists of heavy doses of punishment for the child far beyond what parents even intend. Much of this happens, I believe, in the disproportionality between the child's understanding of what he or she has done and the relatively heaviness of the consequences that parents impose.

Just as the socialization process fosters and conditions distressful emotions, it also provides the basis for positive emotions. In considering the dependent variables of socialization I aimed not so much at the optimum relational conditions of the socialization process, but rather at the socialization outcomes that parents ought to seek. The power-status model does provide an answer to what that content should be: control of aggression, autonomy, competence and achievement, and the ability to give and love. These are derived in a straightforward manner from the four relational channels: own power, other's power, own status, and other's status. I believe that the power-status theory makes a contribution by pointing to these socialization outcomes as particularly important for the realization of positive feelings and emotions. Perhaps the most important deduction stemming from this analysis is that *giving* status—ultimately, loving—is an antidote or preventive of the depression that results from inadequate receipt of status. This implies that beyond a certain level of existential need for status, as discussed in Chapter 13, we can be satisfied by giving status instead of getting it. The irony, of course, is that if we all gave status we all would also receive it in quite high amounts, presumably satisfying all interests and all hungers.

Although I believe that each of the dependent variables of socialization discussed in Chapter 11 is reasonably derived from its respective relational channel, I have not been able to answer the question of magnitude for each of these dimensions. How much control of aggression? How much autonomy? Competence? Loving? We must await future research results to show us how these outcomes are related to each other, what the shape of the joint function is, and what is implied for each dimension as limits are approached in the magnitudes of other dimensions.

In the two final chapters on love I aspired to clarify what is still a mystery—although there is enough theory: what is involved both in coming to love a particular person and in coming to unlove that person. Again I followed the path of the relational dimensions. The emotions of love occur in a social relationship. The power-status dimensions suggest seven types of love relationships, and these accommodate well, I believe, the discursive literature on love. The typology of love relationships also allows us to follow a path as love passes through phases engaging different emotions. The emotions change, of course, as the relational positions of the actors change. Beneath the surface of the daily life of lovers are the nuances of movement and the reflection of standing on the relational dimensions, the actions that harmonize or clash with internalized standards and so release or quell the flow of status toward the other.

I have chosen to call love only those emotions which are part of *status conferral*, not those related to status demand or dependence. Thus desire, longing, and felt need that only the other can satisfy were not my principal concern. Indeed, we need another term to discriminate the relationship that elicits those feelings, and I suggested *oblove* (Kemper, 1972) because it implies, etymologically, the idea of something contrary to, or against, love. Yet oblove is what many theories of love based on "need" or "exchange" seem to be trying to explain. Oblove, however, is not the whole domain of love, as exchange is not the whole domain of social interaction.

Two types of relationships stand outside the exchange framework: one involves pure coercion, in which one actor obtains the compliance of the other only by power while the other actor gains nothing in return; the second involves pure status conferral, in which only voluntary compliance passes between the actors, who have no expectation of return. In neither case do the actors give or comply *in order to receive* (which must be understood as the central reason for any exchange). Over time a relationship between two persons can touch all the possibilities. It may tend toward mutual status conferral, toward exchange, or toward pure power, or it may wobble unstably to and fro among these. In treating love relationships it is important, I believe, to see them in their evolutionary most evolved form, as status conferral. Only then can we offer others a valid vision of human possibility and perhaps obviate at the outset what can otherwise occasion great pain.

Sociological work on emotions is only beginning, and there is a great deal to learn from taking the view that particular patterns of social relations elicit particular emotions. I believe too that the power-status model offers the best understanding at present of the structure and content of social relations. I can hope that the model, which has sustained the entire argument of this book, has merits that exceed its faults. If not, I take comfort in the fact that scientific knowledge is cumulative for the most part, and progress may come even from discovering that a particular approach is mistaken. If the power-status model wrongly construes social relations, I take refuge in the limpid view of Francis Bacon that "Truth emerges more readily from error than from confusion" (cited in Kuhn, 1962, p. 18).

appendix ONE

Factor Analysis and the Fundamental Dimensions of Social Relationships

Three problems concerning factor-analytic studies of social interaction or personality in social settings are considered here. The first is that, despite the noteworthy factor-analytic convergence on power and status as the fundamental dimensions of social relations, other factors emerge. Carter (1954) found three factors; Longabaugh (1966), three; Wherry (1950, cited in Carter, 1954), four; Borgatta, Cottrell, and Mann (1958) and Borgatta (1964), five; Rummel (1966), seven; and so on. Although this troublesome point has been largely ignored by those who favor the two-factor relational solution, the initial credibility provided by the convergence on two dimensions is somewhat vitiated by the uncertainty about how many dimensions there will be when they are all counted. Furthermore, despite the convergence on two dimensions, if we do not know all the dimensions, there is a nagging suspicion that perhaps the most important ones have not been discovered. Thus until the question of the number of basic dimensions and which ones they are is settled, there is an understandable reluctance to commit oneself to any of the solutions offered—whether it is the two, three, four, or more dimensional scheme.

As is well known, the more items one includes in a factor analysis, the more factors one is likely to obtain. Yet the problem is more than merely quantitative, for the additional factors have a right to be interpreted and must have meaning. Why do they also not have a claim to relational relevance, particularly if they emerge in the course of factor analyses of items that deal with interaction? I argue that when more than two dimensions are found, the excess factors are not ordinarily relational, that is, characteristic of the orientations and behavior of actors to each other.

The second problem concerning the factor analyses of interaction arises from studies that have discovered a correspondence between linguistic and perceptual structure on one hand and the structure of personality and social interaction on the other. This raises the question of whether observers and raters of personality and social interaction are actually judging the external world, or merely impose innate perceptual or linguistic categories on it. These categories then emerge as the dimensions found in factor analysis. I argue that there are logical and empirical grounds for accepting the veridicality between factor-analytic dimensions and the external world.

The third problem stems from the fact that some have confused the factor analyses of social interaction with some similar, but not identical, results obtained from factor analysis of semantic differential protocols, thus extending the social relational model to cases to which it should not be applied. Thus we now see critiques of the power-status model that are actually, although unwittingly, addressed to certain erroneous interpretations of it, as in the work of Hays and Sievers (1972). I clarify the model to preclude erroneous applications and confounding with similar, but not identical domains of analysis.

Number of Dimensions

Four independent reasons are discussed for the emergence of more than two factors. Although this is not parsimonious explanation, it must be remembered that the factor analyses are themselves quite variable in their subjects, scales for scoring interaction, methods of observation, and the like. Even more remarkable than the divergences is the fact that, regardless of method, these studies do converge on power and status factors. Before considering the several types of factor-analytic outcomes when there are more than two dimensions, I propose a small elaboration of the power and status model that will better prepare the ground for what is to come.

In Figure A.1 a possible arrangement of two actors in a power-status space is shown. Each actor has both a power position and a status position. Considering power, for example, it is possible to obtain two power factors from the analysis of any concrete relationship—actor A's power and actor B's power. How might this occur? Suppose that when A uses power on B it is always by some physical means, for example, pushing, hitting, and the like. Suppose also that when actor B uses power on A it is always by verbal means, for example, threats, insults, deprecations, and the like. A factor analysis of such data would produce two power factors, one reflecting the physical power acts of A, the second reflecting the verbal power of B. By similar processes, two status factors might emerge, that is, a factor reflecting the specific behaviors by which the status is accorded by one actor (which is the status received by the other) and another factor reflecting the status accorded by the second actor (which is the status received by the first). When the power and status currency, that is, the observable behavior, is identical for both actors, only one power and one status factor should be found. Let us now turn to a consideration of four types of theoretically troublesome factor-analytic outcomes.

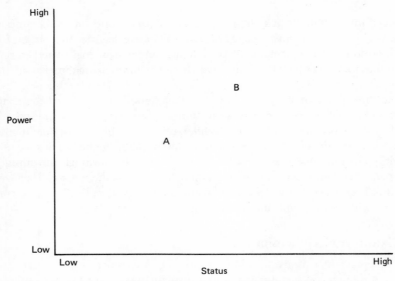

Figure A–1   A possible dyadic power-status relationship.

Additional Factors Are Technical Activity. Carter (1954) was one of the earliest to find at least three factors, both in his own work and in his review of several prior studies. Carter's three factors are *individual prominence and achievement, sociability,* and *aiding attainment by group.* Despite its name, the first factor is the power dimension (it is defined by such scales as "authoritarianism," "confidence," "aggressiveness," "leadership," "boldness," "forcefulness," etc.). The second factor is apparently the status dimension (it is defined by such scales as "sociability," "adaptability," "pointed toward group acceptance," "behavior which is socially agreeable to group members," "sincere," "helpful," etc.). The third factor, however, is not relational in nature. It is defined by such scales as "efficiency," "cooperation," "pointed toward group solution," "effective intelligence," "competent," and the like. These scales refer to the actors' participation in the task to be done and support the theory of Chapter 2 that, in addition to the two relational dimensions of power and status, actors also engage in technical activity in the division of labor. In numerous other factor-analytic studies, one or more technical factors emerge (e.g., Borgatta, 1964; Rummel, 1966). This insight is also found in Longabaugh (1966).

Additional Factors Are Nonsociological. In a study by Borgatta (1964), which produced five factors, a power dimension labeled *assertiveness* (defined by such items as "is very active," does most of the talking," "is authoritarian" and "is assertive") and a status dimension labeled *likeability* (defined by such items as "is friendly," "is pleasant," "is likeable," "supports others") emerged. Of the three additional factors, at least one appears to be a task or technical-activity factor Borgatta labeled *responsibility*. It is defined by such items as "interested in getting things done," "pays attention to the task," "accepts responsibilities," "is conscientious." The fourth factor, called *intelligence*, is somewhat ambiguous in that it may be considered either a technical factor or what may be called a "personality" factor, that is, descriptive of the person without concern for relational behavior. Its defining items include "is intelligent," "is rational and logical," "is clearminded," "is mature." Finally, there is a factor that is very clearly neither relational, as are the power and status factors, nor technical, as is the responsibility factor. It is called *emotionality*, and its principal items are "is very tense," "gets upset easily," "is nervous," "is emotional." It seems clear that this is simply a personality factor that says nothing about relational behavior per se (despite the fact that emotionality is manifested in interaction or results from interaction).

It may appear that some violence is being done to the highly plausible intuitive understanding that, of course, emotionality is an important dimension of interaction, or if not of interaction—since it is a property of the person—it must certainly influence interaction in a significant way. Nothing said here was intended to contradict the view that emotionality is important—only that it is not a dimension of social interaction. This can be seen in the following.

First, Borgatta's subjects were judging each other's *personalities*. Indeed, they could have been asked to judge each other's achievement motivation, religiosity, willingness to take risks, or, obviously, any other dimension of personality. Clearly, not every dimension of personality is interactional. Yet somehow emotionality does *seem* to be one of the interactional dimensions of personality, since it is manifested very frequently in the course of interaction. Although this is so, I contend that whether someone is emotional is very much a feature of the person. Indeed, emotionality can be manifested when one is entirely alone; thus, unlike power acts or status acts, no other is necessarily implied. Beyond this, emotionality fails to be an interactional dimension in its own right, because the emotional person—or the unemotional one for that matter—manifests the relational consequences of emotion of lack of it by the type, style, and intensity of *power* and *status* behavior. That is, emotionality that moves from the emotional actor to others is conveyed not by emotionality as a dimension of interaction, but by the known interaction dimensions themselves, particularly power and status behavior and also technical behavior.

Evidence for this interpretation is found in data presented by Borgatta, Cottrell, and Mann (1958), which is an earlier version of the 1964 work by Borgatta. Although efforts were made to obtain simple structure in the factor rotations of the 1958 study, this was not possible. This resulted in some substantial loadings of some items on more than one factor. It is instructive to examine these joint loadings, as Borgatta, Cottrell, and Mann did. First, it is important to know that the same five factors emerged in that earlier study as in the Borgatta (1964) study under discussion. Factor 1 was labeled *individual assertiveness* and is clearly the power factor, since it highly loads such items as "attempts to dominate others," "disagrees most," "interrupts others," "tends to be antagonistic." Factor 4 was clearly the *emotionality* factor and is defined by "emotionality," "is most tense," "tends to be most nervous," and "makes most emotional responses."

Borgatta, Cottrell, and Mann examined items with the highest joint loadings, that is, when they loaded more than a single factor highly, despite efforts at simple structure. Table A.1 is a reproduction of their Table 13 and shows the joint loadings of their factor 1, individual assertiveness (power) and factor 4 (emotionality). The explication is best given in their own words:

> Items that are loaded in the fourth factor appear to be loaded most commonly also in the first factor . . . In a sense, this indicates that *some degree of individual assertiveness is necessary for a person to be recognized as being emotional.* There are two additional items that are of interest in terms of joint loading with the Emotionality factor. The first of these is . . . Suggestibility, which appears to be defined primarily by a joint loading on Emotionality (.435) and Sociability (.410) [the status factor]. The second of these is . . . Conventionality, which appears to be defined by a joint

TABLE A–1[a]   JOINT LOADINGS ON FACTORS 4 AND 1 IN BORGATTA, COTTRELL, AND MANN

Variable	Loading	
	Factor 4[b]	Factor 1[c]
Emotionality	.591	.625
Is most tense	.558	.467
Tends to be most nervous	.522	.502
Makes most emotional responses	.508	.737

[a]Reprinted with permission of authors and publisher from Borgatta, Edgar F., Cottrell, Leonard S., Jr., and Mann, John H. The spectrum of individual interaction characteristics: an inter-dimensional analysis. Psychological Reports, 1958, 4, 279–319, Monograph Suppl. 4, Table 13.

[b]Factor 4 is labeled *emotionality*.

[c]Factor 1 is labeled *individual prominence*.

loading on Emotionality (.415) and Task Interest (.386) [the technical activity factor]. These identifications appear to be remarkably intelligible in terms of the factor structure (p. 294, emphasis added).

Indeed, the intelligibility that Borgatta, Cottrell, and Mann saw is precisely that the behaviors of emotionality emerge, in this case most strongly, as conjoint items of the power factor and less strongly as conjoint with the status and task or technical factors. This is a conclusive demonstration, I believe, that emotionality, although a legitimate property of persons and responded to as such, operates relationally through the dimension of power and status.

Another case of a nonrelational, nontechnical dimension is found in the factor analysis of internation data by Rummel (1966). He obtained a factor he labeled *South American*. Its principal item is "short air distance from the U.S." Like emotionality, it is clearly neither a relational dimension nor a technical activity.

Additional Factors Include Status Received by Actor and Status Accorded by Actor. In a few cases the theoretically possible outcome of a double status factor, as discussed at the beginning of this section, is found. For example, in the work of Wherry (1950), reported by Carter (1954), four factors are found: *forceful leadership and initiative* (power), *job competence and performance* (technical activity) and two additional factors: *proper attitude toward job* and *successful interpersonal relations*. The items loading the last two factors are, for the "job" factor, "sincere," "helpful," and "cooperative," and for the "interpersonal" factor, "genial," "cordial," and "well-liked." This last item, "well-liked," is the important clue that permits discrimination between the two status factors. *Proper attitude toward job* is essentially the status an actor *accords* to other group members, whereas *successful interpersonal relations* is the status *received* by the actor from other group members.

A more recondite version of the double status dimension is seen in the factor analysis of *inter*nation data by Rummel (1966). Rummel found seven clearly definable factors. They are, along with their highest loading items, as follows: *conflict pattern*: "many threats" (this is the power factor), *participation*: "trade" (this would seem to be a technical activity factor), *popularity*: "large ratio of foreign visitors to population" (this is either a technical activity factor or a status-received factor or, more likely, a case of overlap between the two), *migration*: "large ratio of immigrants to population" (another potential case of overlap between technical activity and status received), *South American*: "short air distance from the U.S." (a nonrelational factor to be disregarded), *aid*: "many U.N. technical assistance fellowships received" (very clearly a factor reflecting status received, but also partly technical), and finally *ideology*: "large net percent of votes with the U.S. in the U.N." (Depending on one's view of current international relations, this can be either a status-accorded factor, reflecting voluntary compliance with the United States, or a power factor, reflecting coercion employed by the United States to line up United Nations votes. Both may be true in different empirical instances.)

In Rummel's data (in which the items are by no means exclusively behavioral and relational) we find the highly complex interweaving of technical activity and status-received by an actor in several factors and at least one probable case of status accorded by an actor. Whether the reader agrees in every detail with the explication of the Rummel factors, it should be clear that the factors do reflect power (i.e., coercion, threat, etc.), status (voluntary compliance and giving), and technical activity (task activity in the division of labor). The multiplicity of technical, status, and power factors results from different patterns of task, power, and status behaviors employed by some actors toward others. Analytically, however, nothing new in the way of dimensions of relationship has been added by these additional factors.

Population Variability. In the work of Schaefer (1965a) three factors are found, two of which, *psychological autonomy vs. psychological control* and *acceptance vs. rejection* are clearly power and status, respectively. The third factor is a peculiar bipolar mix of scales reflecting low power in the form of "lax discipline" and "extreme autonomy" granted to children (the data pertain to parent behavior). At first this seems somewhat perplexing, because the power scales already load the power factor where they should, but the lax discipline and extreme autonomy scales load only the third factor, which is named *firm control vs. lax control*. An examination of the respondents in Schaefer's study provides an explanation of this third factor (Schaefer, 1965a). In one analysis in which this third factor emerged, the sample consisted of 81 girls and 85 boys aged 12 and 13 years from a surburban parochial school. *In addition*, it included 80 delinquent boys in a public institution, ranging in age from 12 to 18. The socioeconomic background of the delinquent group is acknowledged to be lower than that of the normal group. In Mann-Whitney tests of differences between the delinquent and nondelinquent boys on the scales used in the factor analysis, the delinquents' mothers and fathers were found to be significantly higher than the nondelinquents' mothers and fathers on the scales of "extreme autonomy" and "lax discipline" (Schaefer, 1965b).

It appears to be no mystery, therefore, why this third ambiguous factor should emerge. It reflects a sharp disjunction in populations within the group. Had the data been analyzed separately for delinquents and nondelinquents, in all likelihood there would have been no third factor. Since there was very little variance on the autonomy and discipline items *within* either group (Schaefer, 1965b), these items would more than likely not have defined a separate power factor in separate factor analyses. Only because there was variance *between* groups on these items was it possible for them to define a factor (see Guilford, 1952). Goldin (1969) also raised the question of population heterogeneity in Schaefer's data.

In a second sample in which the *firm control vs. lax control* factor also emerged, the subjects consisted of 162 personnel in two Army hospitals and 100 patients in an Army hospital suffering mainly from neuropsychiatric illness (Schaefer, 1965a). Again the heterogeneity of the sample provides ample explanation for the third factor outcome.

Another explanation of the emergence of the *firm control vs. lax control* factor is also possible. Although it does not invalidate the explanation already provided, it rests on a somewhat different analytical base. It is that the factor in question, although couched in the language of power, refers not to power relations but to the provision of a set of guidelines for behavior. Thus extreme autonomy and lax discipline, the scales that load this factor, may refer to failure by parents to provide the rules that might guide their children. In this sense, it might be considered an *absence* of certain requisite technical activity on the part of the parents in the division of labor between parents and children. This would remove the factor from consideration as a relational factor and reflect the level of performance of parents in a technical dimension.

Although this concludes the special analysis of four deviant cases in which factors other than power and status were found, several final points must be raised to indicate that the job of teasing out the power, status, and technical dimensions of interaction, whether in direct observation or factor analysis, can be delicate. One problem resides in the degree of overlap between relational activity, (power and status), and technical activity, as found, for example, in the Rummel (1966) data.

Two examples illustrate some of the possibilities. First, when a child steps off the sidewalk into the path of an approaching car and his mother seizes him roughly by the arm, yanks him back, and then slaps him, the mother's behavior reveals an overlap of power and technical activity. The yanking and slapping are power acts, and they help define the relationship between mother and child on the power axis. They are also technical, in as much as the goal of the actors in the division of labor is to teach the child to obey those parental injunctions which will enable the child to survive.

Second, a kiss may be purely a status act, that is, it has no special technical relevance, or it may be both a status and technical act simultaneously. If a husband comes home after work and says, " Don't cook tonight, dear. We're going out to dinner," the wife's kiss of gratitude is a pure status act, a voluntarily given gratification to the husband without further technical significance. If, on the other hand, the husband comes home and, feeling amorous, begins to kiss his wife with the object of arousing her sexually, each kiss is a status act in that it voluntarily conveys gratification, but it is also a technical act, in as much as kissing is an aspect of the husband's function in the sexual division of labor in which the goal is intercourse.

A further understanding may now be obtained of those studies in which only two factors emerge. These often involve parent–child interaction, therapy group interaction, or strictly interpersonal relations. In such contexts the technical activity is often coterminous with the power and status behavior. In some forms of psychotherapy, for example, transference (i.e., giving status to the therapist) *is* technical activity for the patient. The overlap is such that a separate technical factor need not emerge.

It should not be inferred, however, that when there is no technical factor, there is no division of labor or technical activity. Durkheim (1933, pp. 55–56) explicitly discussed the division of labor of the partners in a friendship, nicely detailing the technical activity that overlaps with the relational. I turn now to another challenge to the validity of the factor-analytic results.

Domains of Analysis

A second problem we confront in deciding whether two dimensions are sufficient to describe relational behavior or personality in the social setting is the following: the dimensions obtained when observers rate persons are identical to the dimensions obtained when persons simply judge meanings of words—without ever attempting to use these words to rate persons. This would suggest that the individuals who rated others for the purpose of providing raw scores for the factor analyses on which the conclusion concerning two relational dimensions is based were *not* providing ratings of what they perceived, but were simply recording the internal structure of perceptual, cognitive, or linguistic categories. This body of work has been offered somewhat critically to forestall the acceptance of the findings of factor-analytic investigations of personality and social interaction (Levy and Dugan, 1960; Mulaik, 1964; D'Andrade, 1965).

Levy and Dugan (1960) were among the first investigators to raise the issue of the relationship between the internal structure of perception and the stimulus world that the raters were judging. Each subject in their experiment rated 15 photographs of 15 different faces on the degree to which each face appeared to manifest a single trait (e.g., nurturance). The subjects then rated another set of 15 faces on a second trait. Eventually, the subjects rated 15 sets of 15 photographs on 15 traits. The ratings were factor analyzed, and a coherent structure with four factors emerged. Since the method assured that any correlation between ratings was *not* due to the attributes of the objects rated—each subject rated

225 *different* faces—Levy and Dugan concluded that "ratings may correlate simply because they represent the same perceptual dimension" (p. 24).

Mulaik (1964) also questioned the external validity of ratings of persons. His concern was the degree to which factors obtained by measurement of phenomenal "surface" characteristics represented underlying or "source" traits, particularly with reference to the work of Cattell (1967), which relies heavily on factor analysis. Mulaik had three samples of raters evaluate three types of stimuli on 76 bipolar trait adjectives. The stimulus sets consisted of (1) 20 persons: 10 known to the rater and 10 who were public celebrities, (2) 20 stereotypical social roles (e.g., housewife, air force general, mental patient, etc.), and (3) 20 trait words other than the 76 bipolar adjectives. The procedures for the rating of the three different stimulus sets approximated the paradigm for ratings by means of the semantic differential in which concepts are rated on bipolar adjective scales (Osgood, Suci, and Tannenbaum, 1954).

Mulaik factor analyzed separately the scores obtained from the three stimulus domains. His interest was in the degree of overlap between the factors from each domain. Were the factor sturctures mainly alike, he could judge that "it is not necessary to rate actual persons in order to determine the personality factors that would be associated with a set of trait words" (p. 509). Indeed, the three separate factor structures produced importantly similar results: Three factors from the three different stimulus domains were largely overlapping, and within each study these three factors accounted for more than 60% of the explained variance. Thus there is evidence that the structure of ratings of persons and roles does not differ from the structure of perceptual or linguistic categories.

Passini and Norman (1966) were next to challenge the validity of factors obtained from ratings of persons. They brought their raters together in groups of six to nine persons. All members of these groups were previously unknown to each other. Interaction in these groups was severely restricted: members were instructed not to talk to each other, and within 15 minutes they were asked to rate the "personalities" of each of the other members by means of a trait-adjective list according to what they would "imagine" them to be. The ratings were factor analyzed and the results compared with an earlier set of factors obtained by Norman (1963) from four different groups in which the length of acquaintance ranged from a few hours to up to 3 years. The remarkable finding was the considerable similarity of the new factors to the ones obtained in the earlier study. Passini and Norman concluded that, in addition to whatever clues to personality their subjects could glean from casual observation in a 15-minute period, it was likely that ratings were being made on the basis of "implicit personality theory" (Cronbach, 1958) which "people eventually and normally build up [and which provides] a notion of the relative frequency of the joint occurrences of various personality attributes and behavior dispositions in persons" (p. 47).

In another frequently cited study in this tradition of research, D'Andrade (1965) found that factor analyses of ratings of stimulus persons and factor analysis of similarity of meaning judgments produced the same set of factors, leading once more to the surmise that perhaps the categories of personality are not in the external world but in the structure of the language that is used to make the judgments. D'Andrade mitigated the conclusion by suggesting that "it is possible that the so-called psychological traits dealt with . . . exist both as components in the terms used to describe the external world, and in the external world as well." (p. 227). Mulaik (1964) and Passini and Norman (1966) also admitted this possibility, but given their result, are inclined to doubt this.

Some work is now considered that provides evidence against the kind of neo-Kantian flirtation with a priorism that the work just reviewed encourages. Still wrestling with the problem, Norman and Goldberg (1966) compared factors of ratings obtained by a random (Monte Carlo) procedure with ratings obtained from judgments by subjects of stimulus persons. Norman and Goldberg concluded that, although the Monte Carlo method shows that ratings *can be* explained wholly without reference to the characteristics of the persons rated, other studies (Norman, 1963) show that the length of acquaintance with the stimulus persons produces two effects that could be expected if the ratings were explained by the ratees. First, increasing the length of acquaintance was associated with a "cleaner" (Norman, 1963, p. 581) factor structure and with factors that were less highly intercorrelated. Second, increasing the length of acquaintance with the stimulus persons produced higher correlations between the raters' judgments and the judgments of themselves made by the persons who were rated. Thus we have some putative support for the view that the factor structures are not merely derived from the structure of perceptual categories or the structure of language.

A final set of logical arguments can be offered. First, if the structure of language and the structure of judgments of personality are identical, it is not reasonable to suggest that the language structure preceded the observational judgment structure. D'Andrade acknowledged that the identical structures "might be the result of the external world affecting first the discriminations made by speakers of a language, who then eventually develop a semantic (meaning unit) structure within the language to encode these discriminations" (p. 228). Second, if there were any considerable degree of discrepancy between the cognitive structure produced by language or by innate perceptual categories (Levy and Dugan, 1960) and the external world, the lack of veridicality would produce enormous confusions in interaction. Individuals would of necessity always act on the basis of their faulty cognitive or perceptual apparatus and fail to act in accordance with the "real" characteristics of the persons with whom they are interacting. Militating against such an interpretation is the fact that the accuracy of judgment improves with the length of acquaintance (Norman, 1963; Lay and Jackson, 1969). That Passini and Norman's subjects were able to make judgments on very short acquaintance says nothing about the accuracy of those judgments; it does say that there exists a set of contingent ideas about what kinds of characteristics tend to go with each other. The existence of such "implicit theories of personality" does not negate the accuracy of judgment when there is adequate evidence on which to base a judgment. Furthermore, although 15 minutes of acquaintance is a very short time, it is not nothing. There is a growing literature that attests to the importance of nonverbal gestures in communication of meaning, affect, and personality (see Scheflen, 1974, for a review of "kinesics, proxemics, metacommunication"). Although we accept that a longer length of acquaintance would certainly have improved the accuracy of the judgments, even short acquaintance sustains some basis for judging others. It is also true that judgments based on quick impressions are a necessary and standard feature of social life: whether to pick up the hitch-hiker who looks like a student; whether to accede to an appeal for a handout; whether to invite the Avon lady into your home, and so on.

I conclude that the two-dimensional relational results in studies of interaction are also veridical representations of the behavior of actors "out there" rather than only representations of what is inside. Yet, even were the two-dimensional structure of relationships ultimately discovered to be only a feature of cognition, perception, or language, this would only more strongly support the need to develop a theory of the effects of such inner two dimensionality of judgment.

An Erroneous View of the Two-Dimensional Model

Another line of work that concerns the two-dimensional relational model comes out of the semantic differential tradition. The effort there has been to obtain universal categories for the judgment of meaning. Some quite strikingly similar factor structures of meaning have been obtained across various cultures (Osgood, Suci, and Tannenbaum, 1954; Tanaka and Osgood, 1965, Heise, 1969). Three factors are generally found: *evaluation* (measured by such scales as "good-bad," "pleasant-unpleasant"), *potency* (measured by such scales as "strong-weak," "heavy-light"), and *activity* (measured by such scales as "fast-slow," "excitable-calm"). Occasionally, the potency and activity factors merge into a single factor called *dynamism* (Heise, 1969). The three semantic differential factors strongly resemble the three-factor solution in interaction studies, namely, activity = the task or technical factor, potency = the power factor, and evaluation = the status factor. If the apparent correspondence is not pushed too far, the result is quite encouraging, because it suggests that the semantic domain is congruent with the domain of interaction and that the technical-power-status scheme has application even broader than interaction itself.

However, some caveats are in order. First, the division between the technical and the relational (power and status) has important ramifications in social interactional analysis. Researchers within the semantic differential tradition are prone to forget this and assume that *all* domains are three dimensional. Second, the three SD factors are not homogeneous with respect to their underlying form. Specifically, potency and activity are properties of the stimulus that is being evaluated. On the other hand, evaluation is a property of the evaluator. Good-bad, pleasant-unpleasant, and the like are how the judge *feels* about the stimulus, not what the stimulus *is* in the sense that it is fast or slow, hard or soft. Thus, although there is some noteworthy parellelism between activity (technical), potency (power), and evaluation (status), the parallelism breaks down at an important point. The technical, power, and status factors refer exclusively to the stimulus, whereas in the SD tradition, the activity and potency factors refer to the stimulus, and the evaluation factor refers to the evaluator or rater. A neglect of this important difference between the structure of the domain of social relationship and the structure of the domain of meaning has led to mistaken efforts to destroy the argument for the orthogonality of the dimensions of the relational model. I turn to this now.

Hays and Sievers (1972) brought together a number of interesting strands of research that appear to them to nullify the orthogonality of the two-dimensional relational model. First they denoted the two dimensions *dominance-submission* and *love-hostility* (from Foa, 1961). They suggested that the dominance dimension is strongly related to the amount of participation in interaction, a result they obtained from the studies of small groups by Bales (1951) and the work by Couch (1960) in which dominance is associated with volume of activity. However, Carter (1954), Borgatta, Cottrell, and Mann (1958), and many other researchers found that authoritarianism also is related to activity dominance. Hays and Sievers reported that in one of their experiments, subjects observed interaction between members of a group by the method of watching lights that represented each member blink on and off when the member spoke. Thus no actual observation of interaction was made except for the blinking lights. Yet, Hays and Sievers reported, their subjects reported "having *affective* feelings about each speaker in addition to obvious judgments one would make from knowledge of the relative prominence [i.e., activity] of each man" (p. 255, emphasis added).

This led Hays and Sievers to conclude that "since only the activity dimension is depicted by the lights in this impoverished treatment . . . and the activity and affective dimensions are supposed according to Foa and others to be statistically independent—the respondents should not have been able to achieve relatively consensual affective judgments about each man" (p. 255). They proposed as an alternative a parabolic relationship between dominance (activity) and the affective response, operationalized as liking-disliking. When activity rate is low, liking is low, when moderately high, the activity rate should be high, and when activity is very high, liking should again be low. The hypothesis was tested with judgments of a series of words whose meanings overlap in varying degrees on two dimensions, "share of participation" (activity) and "favorableness-unfavorableness" (liking). Indeed, as hypothesized, the relationship is parabolic, with favorableness being associated with moderately high activity, whereas very low or very high activity receives unfavorable judgments. The results were replicated for a Spanish-speaking sample and further supported by other studies in which observers of videotape interactions also made favorableness judgments of the actors on the basis of activity according to the parabolic mode. Thus it would appear that the independence of the factors of the two-dimensional model is successfully challenged.

Although the Hays and Sievers study stands on its own merits, those merits have little bearing on the two dimensions of relationship found so often as orthogonal factors. Crucially, the two-dimensional model reports that when actors behave in relationships or their personality is judged in social contexts, the behavior or the personality is found to manifest an orthogonal structure of power and status dimensions. This work does *not* say that when observers report on their favorableness toward the interaction behavior of members of a group, that favorableness is orthogonally related to the behavior observed. Indeed, it is precisely from following the semantic differential model too closely that Hays and Sievers were misled. As noted, the evaluation factor in the semantic differential is *like* the status dimension in the relational factor structure, but it differs importantly in the semantic differential analysis *by being a characteristic of the evaluator rather than a characteristic of the thing evaluated.* Hays and Sievers may indeed have a quarrel to pick with the semantic differential model, but they have not yet begun to examine the relational model. In the relational model the orthogonal factors emerge because they are depictions of the interactional behavior of members of a group toward each other. They are not, as Hays and Sievers misconstrued, an actor's behavior and an observer's affective response to the behavior.

appendix TWO

Power and Status: Conceptual and Methodological Issues

Power and status are not new concepts in sociology and social psychology, but their customary use is notoriously ambiguous. Here I try to clarify some of the issues. First, I examine how the power-status model can provide a useful insight into the requirement for the understanding of *meaning* in several cognitive and interpretive sociologies. Second, I discuss a number of definitional and conceptual issues. Finally, I compare the present use of the power and status concepts with those of the exchange theorists Homans, Blau, and Thibaut and Kelley. These writers used power and status in their work most nearly like the usage here, but there are important differences that lead to quite different formulations of significant problems.

Power, Status, and Meaning in Social Interaction

The methodological position associated with Max Weber and the concept of *Verstehen* stands as a polar orientation to a behaviorist account of social interaction. The central idea was expressed by Weber (1974) as follows: "for a science which is concerned with the subjective meaning of action, explanation requires a grasp of the complex of meaning in which an actual course of understandable action thus interpreted belongs" (pp. 95–96). As examples, Weber cited the observation of a man chopping wood or aiming a gun. We can only understand "in terms of motive in addition to direct observation if we know that the wood-chopper is working for a wage or is chopping a supply of firewood for his own use or possibly is doing it for recreation. But he might also be 'working off' a fit of rage . . . " (p. 95). "Similarly" said Weber, "we understand the motive of a person aiming a gun if we know he has been commanded to shoot as a member of a firing squad, that he is fighting against an enemy, or that he is doing it for revenge" (p. 95).

Although we can have no explanatory understanding of what an actor is doing without knowing the context of the action and its meaning for the

368

actor—which we obtain by empathic understanding *(Verstehen)*—Weber provided systematic delineation of neither contexts or motives. How many of these are there and what types? Since contexts and motives at the phenomenal level can be almost infinitely variable, we are thrown back on the resources of implicit knowledge. As Weber put it, we are helped at times to interpret the actions of another actor by our own susceptibility to the same kinds of actions (Weber, 1947, p. 92). Yet even this is not necessary, since a merely "intellectual understanding" is adequate for certain purposes (Weber, 1947, p. 91). Weber's most specific contribution to aid us in the process of interpretation is the concept of "rational action." Rationality implies that the best means are selected to attain given goals and can be set up as an *ideal type* against which to compare deviations "which will be attributed to such factors as misinformation, strategical errors, logical fallacies, personal temperament . . . " (p. 111). Yet rationality is too embracing a concept to provide adequate grounds for interpretive understanding. It leaves open the entire field of contexts and motives that are so important for an explanatory understanding according to Weber. Although Weber provided a methodological framework within which to approach the question of the meaning of action, he offered too little in the way of substantive content to enable us to delimit the field of inquiry.

By way of contrast to the open-endedness of the Verstehen method, I suggest that a useful delimitation of the scope of inquiry, while still employing a method of interpretive understanding, can be obtained by employing the technical-relational model proposed here. Chopping wood or aiming a gun—even as Weber analyzed there—are either technical activity in the division of labor—and/or relational (or emotional responses to relational) activity. Once the technical-relational lens, so to speak, is applied to the problem of "seeing" what action means, a considerable sharpening of theoretical vision results.

Symbolic interactionism is the contemporary heir of the *Verstehen* approach. Whereas for Weber the observer was required to obtain an explanatory understanding, for symbolic interactionists it is the actor who understands his own situation by means of *Verstehen*. "The actors' responses are not made directly to the actions of one another, but instead are based on the meaning which they attach to such actions" (Blumer, 1962, p. 180).

For Blumer, "behavior, accordingly, is not a result of such things as environmental pressures, stimuli, motives, attitudes and ideas but arises instead from how he interprets and handles these things in the action which he is constructing" (p. 183). "Fundamentally," said Blumer, "group action takes the form of a fitting together of individual lines of action. Each individual aligns his action to the actions of others by ascertaining what they are doing or what they intend to do—that is, by getting the meaning of their acts" (p. 184).

Yet, like Weber, Blumer also failed to tell us "what they are doing" or how we may go about conceptualizing "the meaning of their acts." Surely, not all models of action or intention need be equally good, but at a minimum we must have some tentative hypotheses, even "sensitizing concepts" (Blumer, 1956), so that research may be initiated. Indeed, one reason for the popularity and necessity of field research methods in the symbolic interactionist tradition is that those who are interested in the problem and process of "fitting together individual lines of action" are without benefit of theory or an interactional model to guide even a preliminary formulation of what the actors are doing when they are "fitting together individual lines of action."

As in the case of *Verstehen*, the technical-relational model can prove very useful to the researcher in the symbolic interactionist framework. Technical activity and/or power and status *are* what actors are doing and what they see other actors doing in reference to themselves. By so viewing the content of interaction, the symbolic interactionist researcher can indeed begin to explain *how* the different lines of action—the technical and relational—are fit together.

Among anthropologists and students of ethnoscience the distinction between *etic* and *emic* methods of investigation (Pike, 1967) is parallel to the problem of meaning posed by the *Verstehen* and symbolic interactionist approaches. In the etic approach the investigator measures the important variables from the perspective of his own conceptual theoretical foundation. In the emic approach the investigator presumably abandons his own perceptual-cognitive categories of understanding in favor of learning to see the phenomena of interest through the categories of the persons he is investigating, who are experiencing them first hand. This makes the participant-observer focus primary in the research role.

There is no doubt that many questions must be approached from the emic point of view, particularly in new domains of investigation. Yet it seems excessive to claim that an investigator can bring no prior categories of analysis to the site of his research. As discussed in Chapter 2 in the section on culture and epiphenomena, I believe that different settings employ different indicators and observables to stand for certain more fundamental categories. Even the functional relations between categories can vary depending on the culture. However, the categories themselves are likely to be stable from society to society and culture to culture (Triandis, 1972). Work in the tradition of *Verstehen*, symbolic interaction, and anthropological or participant-observation field studies can be understood in part as the search for the local indicators and observables of the technical-relational or for the particular functional relations that prevail in the local setting between the technical and relational constructs.

Lofland's (1970) critique of field studies under the heading of "analytic interruptus" also falls within the context of this argument. He complained that field students fail to advance knowledge because they omit to think through the field experience sufficiently to come up with analytic categories on which further research can be built. I suggest that those who search for "meaning" as a way of understanding social phenomena, whether they are *Verstehen*, symbolic interactionist, or emic-oriented researchers, can discover a great deal of coherence in what they observe by viewing their data from the technical-relational perspective. Although this means importing what appears to be an etic view into a local situation, I contend that, if properly understood, it will not only *not* conflict with the emic view, but will make that view very much clearer.

POWER

Although power is one of the most popular concepts in sociological theory and social psychology, it is beset with numerous definitional and methodological difficulties. For example, in studies of the family, power can be defined and measured in a variety of ways, and these different definitions give, as one might expect, different outcomes in research (Safilios-Rothschild, 1970; Olson, 1969; Turk and Bell, 1972). Similarly, a debate has raged for many years between proponents of different views on the definition and measurement of power in the study of communities and societies (Hunter, 1954; Mills, 1956; Parsons, 1963; Dahl, 1958; Polsby, 1959; Rose, 1967). There is also the question of whether power ought not to cede to the concept of influence as the most general notion (Wrong, 1968; Tedeschi, 1973). Some believe that power should apply to the capacity to attain goals for a social system rather than the ability to coerce others to obtain whatever goals are desired by those who have power (Parsons, 1963; Dahl, 1958). Some even wish to dispense indefinitely with the concept, substituting the term "force" for certain aspects of power (Goode, 1972). Obviously, further clarification and elaboration of the concept of power as it is used in this work is required.

Intention. Power is *intentional* in the sense that the one who exercises power ordinarily intends to obtain a certain objective when another is opposed and the power wielder's actions are intended to overcome the opposition of the other (Weber, 1946, p. 180; Wrong, 1968). Usually the intention is clear enough to the parties involved. Rarely, an actor does not intend to compel the other to grant what is wanted, but the other believes that compulsion would be used and therefore accedes. This, I assert, is not true of the common run of relationships. Usually evidence exists of the coercive intentions of the power wielder. This definitional postulate is assumed to hold for most cases.

Structure and Process. Power is defined as a *structural* condition of relationship when it is measured in terms of the probability of gaining one's own ends in the relationship when the other resists. Additionally, power as structure is restricted to particular domains (Dahl, 1958; Wrong, 1968); that is, interaction between A and B usually has some specific role content, for example, husband-wife, teacher-student, parent-child, employer-worker, and the like. Within the domain marked out by the role, each actor can attain his objectives to a certain extent and with a certain probability.

Power as structure does not usually come into being without power as *process*. Process power includes all the behavior intended to coerce, punish, sanction, hurt, or deprive the other either prospectively as threat or subsequently as punishment and thereby as deterrent looking toward the next occasion of interaction. Any act that has the intention of coercing, hurting, punishing, or depriving—whether it is a punch, a sarcastic remark, a disapproving glance, or a refusal to live up to a previously committed obligation—whatever the act, it is power as process if there is even minimal intention to punish, deter, or overcome the other (cf. Jacobson, 1972).

Manifesting Power. Structural power is manifested by winning. In many relationships the probabilities associated with winning are relatively stable. It is easy to say for these relationships who has more and who has less power. Even when the relationship is unstable, with frequent shifts in structural superiority, the relationship can be characterized structurally, based on the probable outcome of the next effort by each actor to impose his will.

Process power is manifested in two ways. First is the *noxious stimulus*—the bullet, punch, kick, slap, starvation, imprisonment, and the like. These are all aversive, since the recipient wants, ordinarily, to escape or terminate them.

Second is *reward deprivation*. This includes withholding rewards that have been customary and regarded as a right (Blau, 1964, p. 147) or withholding rewards that were prospective and expected. A child is deprived of a sweet or his mother's smile for misbehavior, an adolescent is deprived of an opportunity to use the family car for failing to meet certain requirements for school performance; an adult is snubbed, reprimanded, insulted, villified, shamed, or ridiculed for violating a social taboo. These sanctions are all forms of withdrawal or withholding of rewards that we previously customary or expected in prospect. It does not matter that some deprivations are of concrete objects, some of opportunities for activity, some of symbolic behaviors (smiles), and some of aspects of one's identity (as in shaming, insulting, snubbing, etc.) Sometimes the deprivation of rewards becomes noxious. Spitz's (1965) "hospitalism" victims were infants denied the handling and holding that appears to be essential to growth at certain stages of development. Many such children sickened and died. When a lover turns away, the loss of love can be experienced as intensely painful and therefore aversive. The withdrawal from drugs is also of this order (cf. Peele and Brodsky, 1975). An important variant on reward deprivation is manipulation.

Although this has long been considered an aspect of power relations (Goldhamer and Shils, 1939; Mills, 1956), it has proven to be quite troublesome, since it also touches on the question of "false consciousness" and ideology (Marx, 1964a; Mannheim, 1936). Manipulation is understood here as a type of reward deprivation and therefore a form of power exercise because it is employed, ordinarily, only in those cases in which the other would not provide what is wanted if the other knew the *real* situation. The forms of manipulation include outright lies, deceptions, and frauds, as well as the propagation of ideologies that are designed to justify that the other cede rewards or not claim them when they would *otherwise* be claimed.

In the preceding paragraph the italicized words "real" and "otherwise" are of some importance. The *real* situation is understood to mean what the situation would *otherwise* be understood to be by the one who is being manipulated, in the absence of the lie, deception, fraud, ideological smokescreen, and so on. There is some question, nonetheless, about the intention of the liar or the ideologue. When social systems have operated over the course of generations, power tends to be transformed by ascription into a "legitimated" relationship in which some receive more and some less (Kemper, 1974, 1976). The beneficiary of such a system may sincerely believe that he deserves more, whereas the deprived may sincerely believe that he deserves less. At this point we have a borderline case. By taking the point of view of an observer who is not party to the relationship, the *real* situation can sometimes be detected and presented. Mannhein (1936) believed that intellectuals in society could perform such a role, since, presumably, they were not parties to the central relationship of manipulation in society, namely, that between the bourgeoisie and the masses. In general the borderline cases of manipulation are not treated here.

Another category of reward deprivation is that of outright theft in its various forms, from the street robbery to the embezzlement of funds in a classic white collar crime. Included here too are the crimes of the marketplace. Thus price-fixing, presenting shoddy merchandise as good quality, unfair labor contracts, and the like are power activities, because they are all categories of theft, either with or without manipulation (lies, ideology, etc.) to gloss over the obviousness of the reward deprivation entailed.

A final category of reward deprivation may be understood in the light of political or state crimes. In political crimes, the citizenry is deprived of its *rights* (benefits and rewards), which are guaranteed either by custom or constitution. These rights comprise an important element in the counterpower of the citizenry. Political crimes, virtually by definition—since political refers to power—are those in which structural power differences are increased between one group in society and another group. The various forms of administrative crime in this context, for example, wiretapping, suborning witnesses, destroying records, and the like, have, when practised, the intention of depriving another of the realization of rights in the institutionalized political system.

   Coercion. From the preceding it should be clear that power requires that the other feel (or would feel if he knew) the *coerciveness* of the power wielder. If the other yields, it must be because of the overcoming of his resistance; even at the moment of yielding, while complying behaviorally, the other does not (or would not) comply attitudinally (Kelman, 1965; Merton, 1959). Presumptive evidence of attitudinal noncompliance is that surveillance is required to maintain behavioral compliance (Thibaut and Kelley, 1959; Tedeschi and Bonoma, 1973).
   Some theorists do not limit their definition of power to the coercive and the punitive, but also include "reward power" (French and Raven, 1959; Raven, 1965). To be consistent, reward is a feature of power only *when it can be withheld or withdrawn.* French and Raven (1959) and Raven (1965) did include this employment of reward quite properly in their discussion of "coercive power." However, they also wanted to include the capacity to reward in the form of positive inducement or incentive as a base of power.
   I adopt the more limited view of power as coercion for three reasons: (1) The punitive and coercive behaviors of actors and the positive, rewarding behaviors of actors emerge in *different* orthogonal factors in many empirical studies, as cited in Chapter 2 and Appendix 1. (2) If actor A offers actor B an incentive (reward) of $100, let us say, to perform an act, and if actor B believes that $100 is a fair price (i.e., he complies attitudinally) and actually performs the act and receives the $100, this appears to be an ordinary marketplace exchange of equivalent values. It does not seem useful to think of A as having *power over* B, despite the fact that actor B had to surrender his time and effort to obtain the $100. If French and Raven's position were acceptable here, it would make just as much sense in this example to say that B has power over A, since by means of the reward of his time and effort he has command of $100 in A's possession. Yet it is just such types of exchange that Raven (1965) would have us accept as instances of the "reward power" of actor A.
   (3) If actor B in the preceding example had a strong need for the $100 and were virtually dependent on actor A for it, the potential reward would indeed become a counter of A's power, because it is needed by B and can be withheld by A unless some act that A desires is done by B. This is the simple case of reward operating as a source of "coercive power" *when it is withheld.* For example, the drug pusher who offers the apparent incentive of cheaper heroin to an addict if he will become a pusher does not have "reward power," but must be seen as coercing the addict because the addict is dependent. This is specially true if the addict does not want to become a pusher.
   Emerson (1962) has usefully formulated the relationship between power and

dependence: the power of actor A over actor B is a function of the dependence of actor B on actor A. It should be seen, however, that dependence implies that the power of a reward comes from the ability of one actor to withhold or withdraw the reward, *not merely from the ability to offer it* as an incentive for some contingent act. In the case of the $100, this would be true if actor A wanted actor B to perform the specified act but were willing, at first, to pay only $10 for it. Actor B, however, refused at that price, holding out for and finally obtaining $100, because of actor A's dependence *on him* to perform the act. This puts quite a different construction on the examples of "reward power" given by Raven (1965).

A further clarification of the role of reward in relations of power is now possible. If we compare the quantities of rewards (resources) available to actor A to dispense and withhold from actor B with the quantities of rewards (resources) available to actor C to dispense and withold from the same actor B, we would probably be correct in surmising that actor A has more power (over actor B) than does actor C—since actor A's resources are greater than those of actor C. However, if actor A has more power over actor B than does actor C, it is because actor B is more dependent in some way on the rewards and resources A can withhold than he is on the rewards and resources C can withhold. In this case we might even say that A has more power than C. Thus "reward" power may be an appropriate concept when the resources of two actors are compared *relative to some third actor* or situation of competition. This type of third-party analysis is not undertaken in this book. Power is understood here as a coercive mode of relationship between two actors.

Relationship Between Structural Power and Process Power. Structural power is represented in the cartesian space of Figure A.1, p. 356, by the position of the actor with reference to the vertical axis. If the Weberian (1946, p. 180) definition of power is taken literally, the power axis can be conceived as a probability scale ranging from 0 to 1.0. The the actor's position on the power axis gives the probability of being able to realize his will "even over the resistance" of the other. The probability figure itself would be determined, as are all empirical probabilities, by examining all previous instances in which the actor had tried to get the other to comply even when the other did not want to do so. Actually, this is impractical and, more than likely, impossible, although the actors themselves doubtless operate with subjective estimates of these probabilities. For certain purposes, we must assume that it is possible to obtain at least a rough estimate of the probability that each actor can get the other actor to do what he does not want to do.

Process power is defined as the whole set of acts that can be used to force others to do what they do not want to do. These include the noxious stimuli as well as the various forms of status withdrawal, manipulation, and so on. Let us further assume that the action is process power as long as there is intent to coerce the other, even if the other does not feel hurt or deprived by the process power act. The classic children's retort to insults is applicable: "Sticks and stones may break my bones/But names will never harm me." Even name calling, however, is considered process power as long as the intent is to hurt and coerce. Now the question of interest is in the relationship between structural power and process power. Let us assume the case of a husband who has greater structural power with regard to the domain X than his wife, but who is generally silent while the wife constantly nags, denies the husband rewards, insults him, and the like. However, when he wants her to do X, he can get her to do it with a certain high probability, even if she does not want to do X. Based on a pure *frequency* count, the wife uses a great deal more process power than the husband, yet this produces a result opposite to the outcome obtained for structural power. To resolve this discrepancy and make structural and process power compatible, we must develop a set of weights that can be applied to the process power acts of both husband and wife. Each weight would represent the amount of noxiousness, aversiveness, or deprivation the given act has for the one to whom it is directed.

Let us assume that the wife employs the following acts of process power: nagging, casting aspersions on the husband's family, and denying sexual access. Let us say that the husband's acts of process power are slapping, public insulting the wife and staying away overnight. Let us now give these actions an arbitrary set of weights on a scale ranging between 1 and 10. The weights, it must be recalled, indicate relative noxiousness *as far as the recipient is concerned.* As to whether we know what hurts the other, there are certain standard vulnerabilities; as knowledge about the other grows in a relationship, a part of the knowledge consists of the other's idiosyncratic vulnerabilities. Self-exposure (Jourard, 1964) is the process of revealing to the other where one is vulnerable. It is an expression of trust, and trust is to put oneself in the other's power. When one does not reveal oneself, it is because one does not trust that the other will not use power precisely where one is vulnerable.

Let us say that the weights are as follows:

Weight
3 nagging (X_1)
4 casting aspersions on husband's family (X_2)
8 denial of sexual access (X_3)
10 slapping (X_4)
8 publicly insulting (X_5)
7 staying away overnight (X_6)

Using these weights two equations can be formed: one to indicate over a given number of occasions in which process power is used how much power the wife has "inflicted" on the husband, and two, the same for how much power the husband has inflicted on the wife. (The number of occasions is arbitrary for present purposes, but in any relationship it begins to cummulate from the very first use of power.) Each act of process power must be multiplied by its frequency of use (f) and by its weight.

$$\text{Process power of wife} = f_1X_1 + f_2X_2 + f_3X_3$$
or, for example, with $f_1 = 7$, $f_2 = 1$, and $f_3 = 2$,
$$7(3) + 1(4) + 2(8) = 41$$

$$\text{Process power of husband} = f_4X_4 + f_5X_5 + f_6X_6$$
or, for example, with $f_4 = 1$, $f_5 = 3$, and $f_6 = 2$,
$$1(10) + 3(8) + 2(7) = 47$$

The results of this example show that cumulatively the process power of the husband was greater than the process power of the wife even though the wife employed power 10 times to the husband's use of power six times. Jacobs (1974) concluded that structurally weaker parties may for a time use intense process power: "Dependents may also use violence in the short run even though they may not have final access to a preponderance of force" (p. 48). As a general hypothesis, I propose that wherever structural power is clearly distinguished, process power is also distributed in such a way that the one who has the greater structural power also has used the greater amount of process power cumulatively.

When it is not clear who has the greater process power, there is continuous conflict. War is such a state of uncertainty. Nations, or spouses, who are certain their process power is less than that of the enemy do not make war but surrender or retire from competition. Even this is not wholly true, for there are other considerations, for example, honor or self-respect, that will stir an individual or group to engage in conflict even when the odds are impossible—sometimes even to win. Ultimately one can die in combat with the other and by so doing prevent him either permanently or for a time from realizing his will. Thus the captured agent accepts torture and dies rather than reveal his secrets. These are interesting, sometimes poignant, borderline cases that may require special theoretical consideration, but do not preclude the development of a theory that comprehends the overwhelming number of cases, in which structural power depends on the greater amount of process power, other things being equal.

STATUS

Status has been used to connote two empirically related but analytically distinct concepts (cf. Barnard, 1946; Zelditch, 1968). The first of these is "functional status" and refers to a position in the division of labor and implies a set of *technical* activities that form a more or less coherent, interlocking contribution with the contributions of other positions in the division of labor. Teacher is a status in this "functional" sense when we consider such technical activities as preparing and presenting materials to a class, examining students, and assigning work for study.

The second connotation of status is referred to as "scalar" and signifies relationship between actors in terms of the amount of rewards, benefits, and compliance they give each other, regardless of the status currency. In the scalar sense of status, some actors have more status than others, rather than simply a different status as is the case in the functional usage. A teacher's status in the scalar sense is comprised of the deference, respect, esteem, salary, and the like he obtains from the members of his role set (Merton, 1957).

The term status is employed only in the scalar sense in this work. If "functional status" is at issue, it is referred to as position or function in the division of labor.

Power was defined earlier as a mode of relationship in which the more powerful gains the *involuntary* compliance of the less powerful in that, against his will, the latter surrenders some object as demanded or undertakes a desired performance or desists from it, as desired.

It seems conceptually economical to maintain parallelism between the power and status modes by defining status as the mode of relationship in which there is *voluntary compliance* behaviorally with the wishes, desires, wants, and needs of the other. Ordinarily, status is not defined to emphasize both the voluntary and the behavioral aspects, nor are cognate terms (to be discussed later) such as prestige, esteem, respect (cf. Thibaut and Kelly, 1959; Homans, 1961; Blau, 1964). Yet the terms that are frequently used to connote status, for example, social approval, positive social evaluation, superiority along a good-bad scale, even deference, have social force only to the extent that they are enacted behaviorally. It would serve little theoretical purpose to think of social approval merely as a pleasant sentiment of passive regard for another that has no active, behavioral consequences. In such a case we would rightly abandon the concept and be none the poorer for doing so. Status and all its cognates entails a certain kind of compliant, supportive, and beneficial behavior directed toward the other. The important consideration about this behavior is that it is undertaken without coercion or fear of punishments that the other might inflict were the behavior not undertaken. Rather, the other is deemed to deserve the compliance and benefits. Since the behavior that comes under the heading of status is beneficial and rewarding to the other, it can also be assumed that the other is desirous, needful, or wants these benefits, and that, whether he explicitly requests or asks for them, when they are given it can be understood as *compliance* with his wishes. Status is accorded when the desires, wishes, and interests of the other are known or suspected, even if unexpressed by the other, and are complied with voluntarily.

Several additional issues to clarify the meaning and usage of the term status must be discussed: the relationship between reward and status, the relationship between status and such terms as prestige, respect, esteem, liking, and authority, and structure and process.

Status and Intention. When actor B accords status, that is, gives voluntary compliance to actor A that compliance can in a general way be said to consist of reward(s) to actor A. The rewards can be paid in a variety of currencies, for example, help and assistance, counsel and advice, an admiring glance or word, a kiss, a word of encouragement, a cash payment, combat on A's side when A is at war with C, and so on. All these are rewards to A and, if provided *voluntarily*, are status provided by B to A. Clearly, most of the rewards mentioned can be obtained by A from B by means of power, that is, by threat, force, punishment, or coercion. Thus it is important to examine not only the actual behavior but also the intentional context of the behavior.

As in the case of power, the point of view is an analytical concern. Here it affects the understanding of intention. For example, B may give rewards to A, which A believes are signs of status accorded to him by B, whereas B may accord the rewards as a result of fear of A's power. This is not an uninteresting or infrequent case and prevails to some extent in every relationship in which power exists. I assume that, in addition to the cases in which A and B have different understandings of their relationship, there are also many cases in which B intends to confer status on A and A accepts the relationship as such. Thus giving status necessarily equals giving of reward, but giving reward does not necessarily equal giving status and is not status unless the rewards are given voluntarily.

Status, and Prestige, Esteem, Liking, and Authority. There are numerous terms in the sociological glossary used to indicate conferral of rewards in a relationship. Status as defined here comprehends esteem and liking fully, whereas it is co-extensive with prestige and authority only to the degree that the actor conferring the rewards that go with prestige and authority does so voluntarily. Some preliminary distinctions are useful. First, there is the difference between interaction that has mainly technical as opposed to relational significance. Prestige attaches to the technical position in the division of labor (Davis, 1950). By prestige is meant that the occupant or performer in the technical position receives a certain amount of reward over and above his economic remuneration and authority in the work, merely by virtue of having that position, for example, physician, mother, or truck driver. The prestige of a position can be very great or very small, even zero, that is, no extra reward at all.

Further within the domain of the technical, *esteem* refers to that noneconomic component of the rewards that are given to the occupant of the position because of the *technical competence* of his or her performance (Davis, 1950). We hold in esteem the *great* physician, the *good* mother, and the *diligent* truck driver. We do so by giving rewards beyond what were allocated on the basis of the prestige of the position. As in the case of prestige, esteem can be zero if the actor does not display any distinctive technical skill compared to others in the same position.

The *relational* competence of the physician, the mother, or the truck driver may evoke liking. We dislike those who are cold, indifferent, make us feel uncomfortable, insult us, and degrade us, despite the fact that their technical positions evoke reward for their prestige, and the performance of them evokes reward as esteem. On the other hand, the physician who seems to care about us personally instead of only about the gall bladder, the mother who knows when to dispense a cookie even if dinner is imminent, and the truck driver who is eager to help a fellow driver in trouble display relational competence, whatever may be the case about the rewards to which their technical positions (prestige) and the way they perform (esteem) entitles them. Thus liking generates an increment of reward over and above the rewards that accrue on the basis of the technical activity. However, nothing has been said about status. Let us incorporate the concept into the foregoing discussion.

Prestige, that is the amount of reward that is given because of the actor's technical position, may be all status (i.e., rewards voluntarily accorded), partially status, or not at all status. If the one who accords prestige rewards believes and wholeheartedly endorses the value and worth of physicians, mothers, and truckdrivers, the prestige accorded is entirely status. On the other hand, one may believe physicians are overrated in importance, question the selflessness of mothers, or doubt the integrity of truck drivers. Nonetheless, some residue of regard may remain for these positions as technical contributions to the overall division of labor. In an interaction episode, prestige rewards accorded to occupants of these positions may therefore be partially accounted for by the true level of positive regard (status) plus some situationally necessary further reward that is coereced by one's dependence on the other. For example, when seeking help from the physician, even though one does not think very highly of practitioners of medicine, it is necessary to show a level of deference that does not alienate the particular physician. The last possibility is that the amount of status given under the heading of prestige may be zero, despite the fact that rewards are accorded. Again, situational necessity may require deference, although it is entirely involuntary and depends on the power of the other to withhold a needed service.

Whereas prestige can vary in the amount that is voluntary reward (status), esteem is entirely status. If another is a competent technical performer and we value competent technical performance, the rewards given are entirely voluntary. Thus they are status. If we do not value competent technical performance, the other can evoke no esteem from us for his competence. If we value competent technical performance and the other is not competent, we can give no esteem (cf. Hamblin and Smith, 1966).

In a similar manner, liking, which results from competent relational performance, entails rewards that are entirely voluntary and are therefore status. These rewards can be added to the rewards that were gained through prestige and esteem, or they can be the only rewards given, should prestige and esteem be lacking.

In Figure A.2 some variant types of aggregated rewards generated by prestige, esteem, and liking are presented. Type (a) shows that the prestige reward is entirely coerced. The reader may have some difficulty conjuring up an instance of this. Yet it applies to the criminal's respectful demeanor *while in the presence of a policeman,* for which position in the division of labor he otherwise has no positive regard. Type (b) shows a mix of coerced and status-based prestige reward. This is a common case and is somehow what we all feel about doctors, lawyers, and teachers—after the ideal visions of childhood have run into the reality of professional practice. These are occupational categories for which we have some honest regard, but some of the deference we display is not a measure of our true

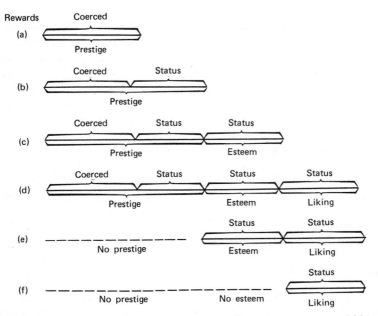

Figure A–2   Coercion and status components of prestige, esteem, and liking.

sentiments. Type (c) shows a case of mixed prestige augmented by esteem for the performer. Type (d) depicts, again, mixed prestige, esteem, and liking. In type (e) there is no prestige—presumably because the activity in the division of labor has no value in our eyes, although the excellence with which it is done is striking and evokes our esteem.* In addition, the person is highly likable because of his relational competence. Finally, type (f) is the case of pure liking, where the technical activity carries no prestige, the performance does not evoke esteem, but there is liking for the other. (Obviously no metric is assumed for the lengths of lines of prestige, esteem, and liking in Figure A.2.)

Status, then, comprehends the voluntary compliance and rewards that are given to others. In social life, the amount of reward transmitted to others is frequently a compound of both status and coerced reward. The exact distribution of the two components in a given relationship is not necessarily immediately apparent, yet it becomes apparent to those in the relationship or to the astute observer. The true distributions of power and status are revealed especially because of the difficulty of simulating status accord when the behavior is evoked by the power of the other. Coerced compliance requires surveillance, and there are many opportunities for even dedicated manipulators of the apparent nature of relationships to fail when they believe the other is off guard. The inauthentic conferral of rewards usually fails at some point, if only because inauthentic behavior is a strain on the performer.

There are methodological difficulties in ascertaining precisely how much of a given amount of reward in a relationship is status and how much is coerced. This is a matter to be worked out empirically. To my knowledge, no such work has been undertaken.

The last of the concepts that can be related to status is *authority*. Sociological interest in authority began with the work of Weber (1947), whose definitions and elaborations of the concept are still at the core of contemporary understanding of this type of relationship. The term that Weber used *(Herrschaft)* has been translated (by Parsons) as "imperative co-ordination," but it is more commonly referred to as authority. Weber defined authority as "the probability that certain specific commands (or all commands) from a given source will be obeyed by a given group of persons" (p. 324). Lest this appear to be merely another definition of power; Weber said: "It . . . does not include every mode of exercising 'power' or 'influence' over other persons" (p. 324). Yet, of course, power is very much at the heart of authority, since the "commands" are not universally and automatically the wish and desire of those who are commanded; nevertheless they are obeyed. Weber provided the solution: "A criterion of every true relation of

---

*An extraordinary instance of this is the real-life character—celebrated in some of the poster art of Toulouse-Lautrec—whose nightclub act consisted of sounding tunes by means of finely modulated flatulation.

imperative control (authority), however, is a certain minimum of *voluntary submission*; thus an interest (based on ulterior motives or genuine acceptance) in obedience" (p. 324, emphasis added). We see, then, that authority is based not only on power, whereby obedience can be enforced, but also on status. Without the element of voluntary compliance, the relationship would be merely one of power.

Weber provided several grounds for this voluntary obedience by members of a group to their superiors: "by custom, by affectual ties, by a purely material complex of interests, or by ideal *(Wertrational)* motives" (p. 325). Weber discounted purely material interests by suggesting that relationships of authority so founded "result, in this as in other connections, in a relatively unstable situation" (p. 325). Thus custom, emotional ties, or ideal motives create a basis for voluntary compliance with the one who exercises authority. Yet even this is not enough according to Weber; lasting authority relations are also based on a sense of *legitimacy*, of which there are three pure types: legitimacy claimed on "rational grounds," "traditional grounds," or "charismatic grounds" (p. 326). Rationally based authority, which is also termed "legal authority," is based on "a belief in the legality of patterns of normative rules and the right of those elevated to authority under such rules to issue commands" (p. 326. This category would include the legitimacy claims of all legally elected or appointed officers and officials of virtually all corporate groups, whether they are political states, political parties, profit-making organizations, voluntary groups, and the like. Traditional authority rests on "an established belief in the sanctity of immemorial traditions and the legitimacy of the status of those exercising authority under them" (p. 326). Here would be included the authority of parents over children and kings (descended from the royal blood) over their subjects. The final pure type, charismatic authority, has claims to legitimacy "resting on devotion to the specific and exceptional sanctity, heroism or exemplary character of an individual person and of the normative patterns or order revealed or ordained by him" (p. 328). This would include all cases of personal leadership enacted by the great figures of history, who frequently claimed divine sanction and not infrequently divine dialogue as well. The leader who inspires reverence, awe, and personal devotion rules on the basis of charismatic legitimation.

It is easy to see the thread of voluntary compliance running through each of Weber's three types of legitimate authority. This conforms very well to Weber's view that "the content of the command may be taken to have become the basis of action for its own sake . . . [yet] the fact that it is so taken is referable only to the formal obligation, without regard to the actor's own attitude to the value or lack of value of the content of the command as such" (p. 327). Despite the latter caveat concerning the actor's own commitment, Weber next said: "Subjectively, the causal sequence [of grounds for obedience] may vary, especially, as between 'submission' and "sympathetic agreement' " (p. 327). Authority consists of some mix of power elements and status elements, sometimes constituted more by one, at other times more by the other—but over time comprehending both.

Structure and Process. The status mode of relationship is understood to have a structural as well as processual aspect, just as power does. From the structural perspective, the amount of status an actor receives may have a certain degree of stability and consists of a probability that certain types and amounts of rewarding behavior will be accorded to him without his having to exert power to obtain that measure of compliance and reward and without the other who provides the rewards doing so because of fear of punishment. Relationships can be quite stable in terms of joint structural levels of status accorded by each actor to the other. However, as in the case of power structures, even sharply changing status relationships can be considered to have structure at a given time.

The processual aspect of status consists of the variety of acts that can be subsumed under the heading of voluntary compliance. At a minimum, mere recognition would constitute one boundary—that is, acting toward another in such a manner as to acknowledge the other's legitimate existence in the particular situation. We can speculate that to offer one's life for the good and welfare of the other is at the outer boundary of status conferral.

Power and Status: Alternative Modes of Obtaining Compliance.   It should be apparent that power and status are alternative modes by which compliance is gained in social relationships. Relationship is defined in terms of the distribution of these modes between the actors. Thus when we wish to discuss the structure or process of activities when the actors are oriented toward each other, as opposed to their orientation toward the technical activities of the division of labor, we can do so in terms of the power and status modes of relationship.

Power and Status in Homans, Blau, and Thibaut and Kelley.   Power and status are commonly used concepts, but the terms are variously interpreted, and some attention to their different uses in some of the more prominent work is of interest. In addition, we can point out where different terminology conceals common meaning.

Homans. For Homans, the term "esteem," defined as "expressed social approval" (p. 149), is approximately what I intend by the term status, except that my understanding of status is that any reward, including social approval, can be employed as status currency. Homans used the term status to refer to the sum of rankable qualities, attributes, performances, and the like that constitute an actor's stimulus value for others. The ranking of these attributes is in terms of higher or lower, better or worse.

Among characteristics that contribute to the person's rank is the amount of esteem he receives. Beyond esteem there is the type of work he does, the clothes he wears, the style of house he lives in—whatever is susceptible to ranking (Homans, 1961, p. 149). Esteem and status levels can be quite different, since esteem refers to the approval the actor receives for providing rare services, whereas the status level depends on all his stimulus properties. He may have stopped providing rare services long ago—even generations ago—but the residual benefits of the esteem provided earlier may still be credited to his account as status.

When one person influences many others "often and regularly he commands . . . leadership, power, or authority" (p. 283). Homans did not distinguish between these three, using the terms interchangeably and referring essentially to the amount of influence one actor has over others. Authority is based on the ability to reward and punish others. "We must never forget that a leader is often able to maintain his position by negative reinforcers, such as threat of physical violence, as well as by positive ones . . . " (p. 291). Authority is usually correlated positively with esteem, since the ability to influence others depends on the degree to which he can (usually) reward them, and the ability to reward others by performances that are generally rare provides esteem. Esteem is something like a "promissory note" (p. 298) which the person who is given esteem can "cash" at a time of his own choosing. This involves requesting or ordering those who have given the esteem to grant some service. By doing so, they have reduced the esteem holder's credit for further cashing of esteem promissory notes. However, if the activities that are entailed when the esteem (or authority) is invoked are successful—that is, they provide additional rewards to the members of the group they could not otherwise have obtained, the esteem credit is renewed and may even be higher than before. Authority, power, and leadership, however, are problematic for the power holder, because he is not generally liked for the costs he must assess those whose obligations he periodically cashes in. In addition to the general costs he causes others to incur in discharging their obligations, he may criticize, blame, disapprove, and otherwise punish those who are recalcitrant, inept, apathetic, and so on.

Although Homans' terminology is not exactly congruent with the power-status language of this book, the underlying dimensions Homans treated very much overlap the power and status dimensions defined here. The essential difference is in the omission by Homans of the significant difference between rewards per se and status, wherein rewards are given voluntarily.

Blau. In Blau's version of exchange theory, power emerges in approximately the same way it does for Homans, namely, when one partner cannot repay the debt incurred by the contributions of the other, the exchange relationship is equilibrated by granting "power" to the creditor. This power enables the power holder to call on the debtor for services that discharge the obligation at some future time. More formally, power is defined as "the ability of persons or groups to impose their will on others despite resistance through deterrence either in the form of withholding regularly supplied rewards or in the form of punishment" (p. 117). Although this accords precisely with my own definition of power, Blau's conception of the power *relationship* does not. Blau saw power as "inherently asymmetrical and as resting on net ability of a person to withhold rewards from and apply punishments to others—the ability that remains after the restraints that they can impose on him have been taken into account . . . Interdependence and mutual influence of equal strength indicate lack of power" (pp. 117–118). This view of power relationship does not take into account the fact that relationships in which both parties have very great amounts of resources that can be used to back up power thrusts, although both parties to the relationship are equal in their resources, are very different from relationships in which neither party has any resources to back up an attempt to impose his will on the other. The model adopted here deals with the absolute power position of each party while acknowledging that in any given encounter it is the relative power of each that bears on the outcome.

Although power was defined in a fairly clear manner by Blau, status was not. Blau said: "Men who make essential contributions to a group as a whole or to its members individually, have an undeniable claim to superior status . . . The obligations of group members to those who make such benefits possible are discharged by according them superior status. They command respect and compliance, which serve as rewards for having made contributions in the past and as incentives for the future . . . " (p. 47). Respect is further defined as "unilateral approval of abilities presumably judged by objective standards" (p. 62). And to further clarify status, "Superior status rests on the respect a person commands in his official position of power" (p. 64). Or "Superior status . . . is firmly rooted in the social structure . . . by generally acknowledged expertness . . . superior power, or . . . position of official authority" (p. 68). Thus we see that, for Blau, status is a generalized concept pertaining to rank relative to others, but that rank can depend on any number of criteria. One of those criteria—respect—is equivalent to the view of status propounded here. The others—power and authority—do not, since they are regarded as separate concepts and modes of obtaining compliance in social relationships, except in so far as they also instigate respect, that is, status.

Ultimately, Blau appeared to reduce the compliance equation to a single term, power, or, when legitimated, authority. He did this by suggesting that groups "successively differentiate respect, power, and dominance" (p. 128). This outcome follows naturally from Blau's view of what happens when individuals come together in interaction. Since they are attracted to each other for the purpose of obtaining rewards in the process of exchange, each member is motivated to "impress" other members with his desirability as an exchange partner. This is done by exhibiting unusual (but desirable) attributes and opinions, or courage, competence, and ability to take risks without manifesting great tension, and so on, that is, "qualities that command admiration (and) respect" (p. 39). Once the respect hierarchy has been established, those with the most respect compete among themselves to establish who will create the greatest number and magnitude of obligations among the remaining group members. This of course gives rise to power. Dominance involves the clear-cut emergence of one member of the group with the greatest power.

Blau did not grant autonomous conceptual validity to the status concept (or to an equivalent), but at several points he implicitly acknowledged the defining characteristics of a status relationship. Thus "In contrast to prestige and authority structures, power structures rest not . . . on social consensus concerning the privileges and rights that must be granted to members of the various strata but on the distribution of resources with which compliance with demands can be enforced" (p. 130). Thus prestige—apparently a nonpower source of privileges—is a version of status. Blau further acknowledged that "a person of superior status in a group . . . usually commands respect as well as compliance (and thereby) exerts two types of influence, only one of which should be designated properly as power to impose his will on others" (p. 130). This is the nearest Blau came to asserting the two different sources of compliance in social relationships. Blau's concern at this point was with influence and the differentiation of the patterns of "following advice" and "following orders." Thus an opportunity to develop the important difference between the status and power modes of relationship was lost.

Despite blurring somewhat the treatment of the status concept, Blau, as did Homans, treated power more or less equivalent to its consideration here.

Thibaut and Kelley. In the earliest of the major statements of exchange theory, Thibaut and Kelley (1958) treated both power and status. Their definition of power was ability "to affect the quality of outcomes attained" by others (p. 101). They saw two types of power: fate control, in which A has power over B regardless of what B does, and behavior control, in which A can make it desirable for B to act in a certain way. Fate control is absolute power, whereas behavior control is more in the nature of strong influence. Fundamentally, power is a function of the dependence of one actor on another. Unlike Blau, who limited power to the net difference in the ability to obtain benefits from others, Thibaut and Kelley acknowledged the presence of "counterpower" by virtue of counterdependence. Power emerges as a result of having rewards to offer to others who come to depend on them and who comply for fear that the rewards may be withdrawn. In addition, there are what Thibaut and Kelley called "non-voluntary relationships" in which forceful constraint or exclusion are employed by power agents. Any aversive environment maintained by some social agent is a manifestation of that agent's power. Thus power results not only from the ability to withhold rewards, but also from the active application of noxious, aversive stimuli, precisely as it was seen by Homans and Blau and as it is presented here.

Status is viewed first as a matter of subjective evaluation of the goodness of one's outcomes relative to those of others. Social status emerges when there is consensus among group members concerning the relative goodness-of-outcomes distribution. There is, however, no single status distribution. Rather, status evaluations and comparisons are made among those with approximately the same amount of "power in relation to those outside agents of control . . . (pp. 224–225). When there is status consensus, "the value that the high status person places on his privileges and rewards is validated by the low-status person's strivings, admiration etc., and in this manner the rewards attained by the high status person are increased" (p. 231). Further, "Low status persons are asked, in effect, to subsidize the outcomes to high status persons by assenting to the value of activities, many of which are exclusively the province of the highs. The effect of this assent is to give lower status persons some power over the higher ones" (p. 231). The increment of power that results from the admiration of those of lower status for those of higher status stems from the fact that admiration is a reward, and, since the higher-status persons can only obtain it from the lower, the lower-status persons have some influence on the quality of the outcomes higher-status persons receive. In a word, lower-status persons gain some power.

Thibaut and Kelley saw the status system, namely, the publicly acknowledged social consensus on relative goodness of outcomes among group members, as having an important social function. The status hierarchy "provides a set of rewards for members who contribute to the group and incentives to spur others to do likewise. The status system constitutes a form of currency with which members upon whom the group is highly dependent can be paid off" (p. 232). It appears to follow from this that "status and power will generally be positively correlated" (p. 232). This is true because power determines the goodness of outcomes for all members of the group, whereas status is some increment of admiration that accrues to those with better outcomes by virtue of the fact that they have had the power to obtain those better outcomes. This does not provide a very vital part for the effect of status in social relations, since power is the determining relational mode. This view is the opposite of Blau's notion in which status, in the form of respect, emerges before power. We can conclude that status plays a decidely secondary part in the view of social relationships propounded by Thibaut and Kelley.

In general, in the work of Homans, Blau, and Thibaut and Kelley, the concept of power is not only more or less congruent among them, but also converges very closely with the way the concept is used in this book. At its core, power is the mode of relationship whereby one actor can coerce another into doing what he does not want to do, either by the infliction of noxious stimuli or by withholding rewards previously given or expected. The concept of status does not fare so well among Homans et al. or between their usage and that adopted here. First, the terminology is different (e.g., Homans used esteem, Blau, respect). This is not a serious problem. More important is that, although the theorists reviewed found some place for the status concept in their formulations—it is too evident to deny entirely—they did not view status accord—defined as voluntary compliance—as a fundamental mode of relationship. This, I believe, is a crucial omission, and one that has important ramifications for the range of questions Homans, Blau, and Thibaut and Kelley can consider.

One of the reasons for the apparent failure of Homans and others to develop an adequate view of the status concept is the implicit dependence of these theorists on a psychological view of rewards, which takes as its central problem the effects of rewards on the actor who receives them, but virtually never examines rewards in light of the whole relational context, which would include the giver as well as the receiver (see Chapter 2 for additional discussion of this point).

appendix THREE

Methodological Issues in Epidemiological Studies of Emotional Disorder

Theory construction in the area of emotional disorder is beset by numerous methodological difficulties that create extensive problems for an inductive approach as well as for an adequate test of existing theories. Some of these problems are set forth here.

True Rates. A precise statement of the social etiology of the major mental disorders must be based on all the cases in the population or a representative sample of all cases. This gives rise to several types of measures. The first is *incidence,* which is the number of new cases that occur in a population in a given time period, for example, a year. There is *true* incidence, which is the actual number of cases of mental disorder, and there is *treated* incidence, which is the number of cases that enter treatment in the time period. Obviously these can be two different figures, and there can be a considerable margin of difference in theories based on true as opposed to treated incidence. The latter rate may be a reflection of how social groups regard the symptoms that accompany or define mental illness (Dohrenwend and Crandall, 1970), or how these groups utilize the variable opportunities available to them for the care and treatment of illness (Mechanic, 1972). Treated incidence, although reflecting these difficulties, is nonetheless easier to obtain than true incidence (Turner, 1972). True incidence requires the psychiatric diagnosis of a representative sample of the population, an extremely difficult set of data to obtain. *Prevalence,* as opposed to incidence, refers to the number of persons who suffer from mental illness in any one time period, for example, a year. This includes not only those who have become emotionally ill during the year, but also those who became ill in previous years and have not recovered. *True* prevalence is the actual number of ill persons at any one time, as distinct from *treated* prevalence, which is the number of mentally and emotionally ill who are in treatment at the given point in time.

Miller and Mishler (1959) and Mishler and Scotch (1963) indicated the difficulties of developing adequate etiological theories on the basis of epidemiological data that do not report true incidence and prevalence figures.

Diagnostic Adequacy. Even if true incidence and prevalence were obtainable, the analysis of epidemiological data would be open to many questions based on the notorious unreliability of psychiatric diagnosis. Simon et al. (1973) found that, whereas hospital physicians diagnosed Blacks as having significantly lower rates of depression than Whites, psychiatrists associated with a research project, who also diagnosed the same patients within 72 hours of intake, found no difference between the rates of depression of Blacks and Whites. Turner (1972) reported that when psychiatrists were aware of a previous diagnosis of schizophrenia, they were more disposed to diagnose schizophrenia than otherwise. In a comparative study of differential diagnosis by hospital-intake psychiatrists in New York City and London, Fleiss et al. (1973) found that New York psychiatrists diagnosed schizophrenia nine times more often than affective disorders, whereas in London the rate was about even. In addition, whereas 90% of patients in New York were diagnosed schizophrenic regardless of presenting symptoms and psychopathology, in London only 70% of those evaluated as disordered were also labeled schizophrenic, and only 20% of the "moody" received this diagnosis. It is unnecessary to review the additional literature on cross-cultural differences in the rates of the schizo and affective disorders, which in part reflect cultural and social structural differences as well as differences in the reliability of diagnosis (cf. Rawnsley, 1968). The effect of diagnostic unreliability is to make very difficult the comparison and interpretation of different sets of results.

Classificatory Adequacy. Even if all diagnoses were based on true incidence and prevalence and the diagnoses themselves were reliable, published reports frequently differ in the classification of the conditions they seek to explain. Often the matter of classification remains undiscussed, and the analysis proceeds to explain rates of psychosis versus neurosis (Hollingshead and Redlich, 1958); schizophrenia versus other psychoses (Turner and Wagenfeld, 1967); schizophrenia versus manic-depressive disorder (Faris and Dunham, 1939), schizophrenia alone (Bateson et al., 1956) or manic-depressive disorder alone (Winokur, 1973). Eysenck (1970), for example, clearly differentiated psychosis from neurosis and provided evidence for this frequently employed distinction. However, others (e.g., Kendall, 1968) reject the distinction for specific illnesses (depression) and endeavor to explain a single spectrum of disorder rather than two discrete maladies. Gove (1970) and Gove and Tudor (1973) are among the very few who have offered any rationale for their classificatory schemes. Their distinction is between the functional psychoses (schizophrenia and manic-depressive disorder) and neurosis on one hand, and personality disorders, and the organic psychoses on the other. Dohrenwend and Dohrenwend (1976) disagree and offer a somewhat different classification.

It is obvious that a very different theory must emerge from considering all mental disorder versus mental health, as opposed to considering only schizophrenia in relation to manic-depressive disorders. This is not a fatal flaw in any single study, since there is no reason why an adequate theory cannot be developed regardless of classification used, even though some classification schemes may prove to be far more amenable for theoretical development than others. The classification problem becomes severe when one is reviewing the results of many studies. In the inductive process of theory construction, which depends on available data, inference is hindered when the various studies have employed different taxonomical schemes to aggregate their data. This failing is endemic in studies in the area of mental health and illness and cannot be resolved easily.

REFERENCES

Adams, B.(1972). Birth order: A critical review. *Sociometry, 35,* 411–439.

Adams, J. S. (1965). Inequity in social exchange. In Leonard Berkowitz, Ed., *Advances in Experimental Social Psychology,* Vol. 2. New York: Academic.

Al-Issa, I. (1970). Culture and symptoms. In Charles G. Costello, Ed., *Symptoms of Psychopathology: A Handbook.* New York: Wiley.

Alexander, Franz (1950). *Psychosomatic Medicine.* New York: Norton.

Allinsmith, B. B. (1960). Expressive styles: II. Directness with which anger is expressed. In Daniel R. Miller and Guy E. Swanson, Eds., *Inner Conflict and Defense.* New York: Holt.

Allinsmith, W. (1960). The learning of moral standards. In Daniel R. Miller and Guy E. Swanson, Eds., *Inner Conflict and Defense.* New York: Holt.

Allon, R. (1971). Sex, race, socioeconomic status, social mobility and process-reactive ratings of schizophrenia. *Journal of Nervous and Mental Disease, 153,* 343–358.

Allport, Gordon (1954). *The Nature of Prejudice.* Reading, Mass.: Addison-Wesley.

American Psychiatric Association (1968). *Diagnostic and Statistical Manual of Mental Disorders,* 2nd ed. Washington, D. C.: American Psychiatric Association.

Anderson, B., J. Berger, M. Zelditch, and B.P. Cohen (1969). Reactions to inequity. *Acta Sociologica, 2,* 1–12.

Appley, Mortimer H. and Richard Trumbull, Eds. (1967). *Psychological Stress.* New York: Appleton-Century-Crofts.

Arendt, Hannah (1963). *Eichmann in Jerusalem: A Report on the Banality of Evil.* New York: Viking.

Arieti, S. (1959). Manic-depressive psychosis. In Silvano Arieti, Ed., *American Handbook of Psychiatry.* New York: Basic.

Arieti, S. (1970). Cognition and feeling. In Magda B. Arnold, Ed., *Feelings and Emotions.* New York: McGraw-Hill.

Aristotle (1947). *Introduction to Aristotle.* Richard McKeon, Ed. New York: Random House.

Arnheim, Rudolph (1954). *Art and Visual Perception.* Berkeley, Cal.: University of California Press.

Arnold, Magda B. (1960). *Emotion and Personality,* Vols. 1 and 2. New York: Columbia University Press.

Arnold, M. B. (1967). Stress and emotion. In Mortimer H. Appley and Richard Trumbull, Eds., *Psychological Stress.* New York: Appleton-Century-Crofts.

Arnold, M. B. (1970). Perennial problems in the field of emotions. In Magda B. Arnold, Ed., *Feelings and Emotions.* New York: Academic.

Arnott, C. C. (1972). Married women and the pursuit of profit: an exchange theory perspective. *Journal of Marriage and Family, 34,* 122–131.

Aronfreed, J. (1968a). Aversive control of socialization. In William J. Arnold, Ed., *Nebraska Symposium on Motivation*, Vol. 16. Lincoln, Neb.: University of Nebraska Press.

Aronfreed, Justin (1968b). *Conduct and Conscience*. New York: Academic.

Aronfreed, J. (1969). The concept of internalization. In David Goslin, Ed., *Handbook of Socialization Theory and Research*. Chicago: Rand-McNally.

Aronfreed, J., R. A. Cutick, and S. A. Fagen (1963). Cognitive structure, punishment, and nurturance in the experimental induction of self-criticism. *Child Development*, 34, 281–294.

Aronson, E. and J. Mills (1959). The effects of severity of initiation on liking for a group. *Journal of Abnormal and Social Psychology*, 59, 177–181.

Aronson, E. and D. Linder (1965). Gain and loss of esteem as determinants of interpersonal attractiveness. *Journal of Experimental social Psychology*, 1, 156–171.

Aronson, E. and D. R. Mettee (1968). Dishonest behavior as a function of differential levels of induced self-esteem. *Journal of Personality and Social Psychology*, 9, 121–127.

Aronson, E. and J. M. Carlsmith (1963). Effect of severity of threat on the devaluation of forbidden behavior. *Journal of Abnormal and Social Psychology*, 66, 584–588.

Atkinson, John W. (1964). *An Introduction of Motivation*. New York: Van Nostrand.

Aubert, Vilhelm (1965). *The Hidden Society*. Totowa, N. J.:Bedminster.

Austin, W. G. (1972). Theoretical and experimental explorations in expectancy theory. Unpublished Master's Thesis, University of Wisconsin.

Austin, W. G. and E. Walster (1974). Reactions to confirmations and disconfirmations of expectancies of equity and inequity. *Journal of Personality and Social Psychology*, 30, 208–216.

Ausubel, D. P. (1955). Relationships between shame and guilt in the socialization process. *Psychological Review*, 62, 378–390.

Ax, A. F. (1953). The physiological differentiation between fear and anger in humans. *Psychosomatic Medicine*, 15, 433–442.

Bales, Robert F. (1951). *Interaction Process Analysis*. Cambridge, Mass.: Addison-Wesley.

Bales, Robert F. (1970). *Personality and Interpersonal Behavior*. New York: Holt, Rinehart, Winston.

Bales, R. F. and F. L. Strodtbeck (1951). Phases in group problem solving. *Journal of Abnormal and Social Psychology*, 46, 485–495.

Baltzell, E. Digby (1965). *The Protestant Establishment*. New York: Random House.

Bandura, A. (1962). Punishment revisited. *Journal of Consulting Psychology*, 26, 298–301.

Bandura, Albert (1969). *Principles of Behavior Modification*. New York: Holt, Rinehart, Winston.

Bandura, A., D. Ross, and S. A. Ross (1961). Transmission of aggression through imitation of aggressive models. *Journal of Abnormal and Social Psychology*, 63, 575–582.

Bandura, Albert and Richard Walters (1959). *Adolescent Aggression*. New York: Ronald.

Bandura, Albert and Richard Walters (1963). *Social Learning and Personality Development*. New York: Holt, Rinehart, Winston.

Banta, T. J. and M. Heatherington (1963). Relations between needs of friends and fiancees. *Journal of Abnormal and Social Psychology*, 66, 401–404

Barclay, A. M. (1969). The effects of hostility on physiological and fantasy responses.

Journal of Personality, 37, 651–667.

Barclay, A. M. (1971). Linking sexual and aggressive motives: Contributions of "irrelevant" arousals. *Journal of Personality*, 39, 481–492.

Barnard, C. (1946). Functions and pathologies of status systems in formal organizations. In William F. Whyte, Ed., *Industry and Society*. New York: McGraw-Hill.

Barnes, Harry E. (1948). *An Introduction to the History of Sociology*, Abridged Ed. Chicago: University of Chicago Press.

Baron, R. A. (1974). Aggression as a function of victim's pain cues, level of prior anger arousal, and exposure to an aggressive model.*Journal of Personality and Social Psychology*, 29, 117–124.

Baron, R. A. and R. L. Ball (1970). The aggression-inhibiting influence of non-hostile humor. *Journal of Experimental Social Psychology*, 10, 23–33.

Barry, H., K. Bacon, and I. C. Child (1957). A cross-cultural survey of some sex differences in socialization. *Journal of Abnormal and Social Psychology*, 55, 327–332.

Barry, W. (1970). Marriage research and conflict: An integrated view. *Psychological Bulletin*, 73, 41–54.

Barth, Fredrik (1969). *Ethnic Groups and Boundaries*. London: Allen and Unwin.

Bateson, G., D. D. Jackson, J. Haley, and J. H. Weakland (1956). Toward a theory of schizophrenia. *Behavioral Science*, 1, 251–264.

Baum, M. (1971). Love, Marriage, and the division of labor. *Sociological Inquiry*, 41, 107–117.

Beardsley, Monroe C. (1966). *Aesthetics: From Classical Greece to the Present*. New York: Macmillan.

Becker, Joseph (1974). *Depression: Theory and Research*. New York: Winston-Wiley.

Becker, J., C. D. Spielberger, and J. B. Parker (1962). On the relationship between manic-depressive psychosis and inner-directed character. *Journal of Social Psychology*, 57, 149–153.

Becker, W. C. (1964). Consequences of different kinds of parental discipline. In Martin L. Hoffman and Lois W. Hoffman, Eds., *Review of Child Development*, Vol. 1. New York: Russell Sage Foundation.

Bell, Clive (1914). *Art*. London: Chatto and Windus.

Bell, R. Q. (1968). A reinterpretaion of the direction of effects in studies of socialization. *Psychological Review*, 75, 81–95.

Bem, D. (1967). Self-perception: An alternative interpretation of cognitive dissonance phenomena. *Psychological Review*, 74, 183–200.

Benedict, Ruth (1946). *Patterns of Culture*. New York: Penguin.

Benjamin, L. S. (1974). Structural analysis of social behavior. *Psychological Review*, 81, 392–425.

Benoit-Smullyan, E. (1944). Status, status-types and status interrelations. *American Sociological Review*, 9, 151–161.

Berger, Peter L. and Thomas Luckmann (1966). *The Social Construction of Reality*. Garden City, N. Y. :Doubleday.

Bergler, Edmund (1956). *Laughter and the Sense of Humor*. New York: Intercontinental Medical Book Corporation.

Berkowitz, L. (1959). The generalization of hostility to disliked objects. *Journal of Personality*, 27, 565–577.

Berkowitz, L. (1960). Repeated frustrations and expectations in hostility arousal. *Journal of Abnormal and Social Psychology*, 60, 422–429.

Berkowitz, Leonard (1962). *Aggression: A Social Psychological Analysis*. New York: McGraw-Hill.

Berkowitz, L. (1974). Some determinants of impulsive aggression: Role of mediated associations with reinforcement for aggression. *Psychological Review, 81*, 165–176.

Berkowitz, L. and D. Holmes (1959). The generalization of hostility to disliked objects. *Journal of Personality, 27*, 565–577.

Berkowitz, L. and D. Holmes (1960). A further investigation of hostility to disliked objects. *Journal of Personality, 28*, 427–442.

Berkowitz, L. and J. A. Green (1962). The stimulus qualities of the scapegoat. *Journal of Abnormal and Social Psychology, 64*, 293–301.

Berkowitz, L., J. A. Green, and J. R. Macaulay (1962). Hostility catharsis and the reduction of emotional tension. *Psychiatry, 25*, 23–31.

Berkowitz, L. and R. Geen (1966). Film violence and the cue properties of available targets. *Journal of Personality and Social Psychology, 3*, 525–530.

Berlyne, D. E. (1969). Laughter, humor, and play. In Gardner Lindzey and Elliot Aronson, Eds., *Handbook of Social Psychology*. Vol. 3. Reading, Mass.: Addison-Wesley.

Berlyne, D. E. (1971). *Aesthetics and Psychobiology*. New York: Appleton-Century-Crofts.

Berscheid, E., D. Boye, and E. Walster (1968). Retaliation as a means of restoring equity. *Journal of Personality and Social Psycholgy, 10*, 370–376.

Berscheid, E., K. Dion, E. Walster, and G. W. Walster (1971). Physical attractiveness and dating choice: A test of the matching hypothesis. *Journal of Experimental Social Psychology, 7*, 173–189.

Berscheid, E. and E. Walster (1967). When does a harm-doer compensate a victim? *Journal of Personality and Social Psychology, 6*, 435–441.

Berscheid, Eleanor and Elaine Walster (1969). *Interpersonal Attraction*. Reading, Mass.: Addison-Wesley.

Berscheid, E. and E. Walster (1974). A little bit about love. In Ted L. Huston, Ed., *Foundations of Interpersonal Attraction*. New York: Academic.

Berscheid, E., E. Walster, and A. Barclay (1969). Effect of time on tendency to compensate a victim. *Psychological Reports, 25*, 431–436.

Bertalanaffy, L. V. (1956). General systems theory. *Yearbook of the Society for the Advancement of General Systems Theory, 1*.

Bettleheim, Bruno and Morris Janowitz (1950). *The Dynamics of Prejudice*. New York: Harper.

Betz, B. (1966). The problem solving approach and therapeutic effectiveness. *American Journal of Psychotherapy, 20*, 45–56.

Bibring, E. (1953). The mechanism of depression. In Phyllis Greenacre, Ed., *Affective Disorders*. New York: International Universities Press.

Bierstedt, R. (1950). An analysis of social power. *American Sociological Review, 15*, 730–738.

Birney, Robert C., Harvey Burdick, and Richard D. Teevan (1969). *Fear of Failure*. New York: Van Nostrand Reinhold.

Blanchard, E. B. and Young, L. B. (1973). Self-control of cardiac functioning: A promise as yet unfulfilled. *Psychological Bulletin, 79*, 145–163.

Blau, Peter (1964). *Exchange and Power in Social Life*. New York: Wiley.

Blau, P. (1968). Social exchange. In David Sills, Ed., *International Encyclopedia of the*

Social Sciences, Vol. 7. New York: Macmillan.

Blau, P. (1974). Presidential address: Parameters of social structure. *American Sociological Review*, 39, 615–635.

Blau, Peter and Otis D. Duncan (1967). *The American Occupational Structure*. New York: Wiley.

Blood, Robert O. and Donald M. Wolfe (1960). *Husbands and Wives*. New York: Free Press.

Blumer, H. (1954). What is wrong with sociological theory? *American Sociological Review*, 19, 3–10.

Blumer, H. (1962). Society as symbolic interaction. In Arnold M. Rose, Ed. *Human Behavior and Social Process*. Boston: Houghton-Mifflin.

Bonacich, P. (1972). Norms and cohesion as adaptive responses to potential conflict: An experimental study. *Sociometry*, 35, 357–375.

Bond, J. R. and W. E. Vinacke (1961). Coalitions in mixed-sex triads. *Sociometry*, 24, 61–75.

Borgatta, E. F. (1964). The structure of personality characteristics. *Behavioral Science*, 9, 8–17.

Borgatta, E. F., L. S. Cottrell, and J. H. Mann (1958). The spectrum of individual interaction characteristics and interdimensional analysis. *Psychological Reports* (Monograph Supplement 4), 4, 279–319.

Boulding, Kenneth E. (1970). *A Primer for Social Dynamics*. New York: Free Press.

Bourne, P. G. (1971). Altered adrenal function in the combat situation in Viet Nam. In Basil E. Eleftheriou and John P. Scott, Eds., *The Physiology of Aggression and Defeat*. New York: Plenum.

Bowerman, C. E. and B. R. Day (1956). A test of the theory of complementary needs as applied to couples during courtship. *American Sociological Review*, 21, 602–605.

Bowers, K. (1973). Situationism in Psychology: An analysis and a critique. *Psychological Review*, 80, 307–336.

Boyd, R. W. and A. DiMascio (1954). Social behavior and autonomic physiology. *Journal of Nervous and Mental Disease*, 120, 207–212.

Bradburn, Norman M. and David Caplovitz (1965). *Reports on Happiness*. Chicago: Aldine.

Bramel, D., B. Taub, and B. Blum (1968). An observer's reaction to the suffering of his enemy. *Journal of Personality and Social Psychology*, 8, 384–392.

Breckenridge, M. E. and E. L. Vincent (1966). What are some of the laws which govern growth? In Morris L. Haimowitz and Natalie R. Haimowitz, Eds., *Human Development*, 2nd ed. New York: Crowell.

Brehm, Jack W. (1966). *A Theory of Reactance*. New York: Academic.

Brehm, Jack W. and Arthur R. Cohen (1962). *Explorations in Cognitive Dissonance*. New York: Wiley.

Brim, O. G., Jr. (1958). Family structure and sex-role learning by children: A further analysis of Helen Koch's data. *Sociometry*, 21, 1–16.

Brim, Orville G., Jr. (1959). *Education for Childrearing*. New York: Russell Sage Foundation.

Brim, O. G., Jr. (1960). Personality development as role learning. In Ira Iscoe and Harold Stevenson, Eds., *Personality Development in Children*. Austin, Texas: University of Texas Press.

Brim, Orville, G., Jr., David C. Glass, David E. Lavin, and Norman Goodman (1962). *Personality and Decision Processes*. Stanford: Stanford University Press.

Brock, T. C. and A. H. Buss (1962). Dissonance, aggression, and evaluation of pain. *Journal of Abnormal and Social Psychology, 65*, 192–202.

Brock, T. C. and A. H. Buss (1964). Effects of justification for aggression in communication with the victim on post-aggression dissonance. *Journal of Abnormal and Social Psychology, 68*, 403–412.

Bronfenbrenner, U. (1958). Socialization and social class through time and space. In Eleanor E. Maccoby, Theodore M. Newcomb, and Eugene L. Hartley, Eds., *Readings in Social Psychology*, 3rd ed. New York: Holt, Rinehart, Winston.

Bronson, F. H. and C. Desjardins (1971). Steroid hormones and aggressive behavior in mammals. In Basil E. Eleftheriou and John P. Scott, Eds., *The Physiology of Aggression and Defeat*. New York: Plenum.

Broverman, D. M., E. L. Klaiber, and W. Vogel (1974). Short term versus long term effects of adrenal hormones on behavior. *Psychological Bulletin, 81*, 672–694.

Broverman, D. M., E. L. Klaiber, Y. Kobayashi, and W. Vogel (1968). Roles of activation and inhibition in sex differences in cognitive abilities. *Psychological Review, 75*, 23–50.

Brown, B. R. (1968). The effects of need to maintain face on interpersonal bargaining. *Journal of Experimental Social Psychology, 4*, 107–122.

Brown, B. R. (1970). Face-saving following embarrassment. *Journal of Experimental Social Psychology, 6*, 225–271.

Brown, G. W. (1974). Meaning, measurement, and stress of life events. In Barbara Snell Dohrenwend and Bruce P. Dohrenwend, Eds., *Stressful Life Events: Their Nature and Effects*. New York: Wiley.

Brown, Roger (1965). *Social Psychology*. New York: Free Press.

Bryson, J. B. (1974). Factor analysis of impression formation processes. *Journal of Personality and Social Psychology, 30*, 134–143.

Bumpass, L. L. and J. A. Sweet (1972). Differentials in marital instability: 1970. *American Sociological Review, 37*, 754–766.

Burchinal, L. G. (1959). Adolescent role deprivation and high school marriage. *Marriage and Family Living, 21*, 378–384.

Burke, R. L. and W. G. Bennis (1961). Changes of perception of self and others during human relations training. *Human Relations, 14*, 165–182.

Burt, C. (1950). The factorial study of emotions. In Martin L. Reymert, Ed., *Feelings and Emotions*. New York: McGraw-Hill.

Burton, A. (1973). Marriage without failure. *Psychological Reports, 32*, 1199–1208.

Buss, Arnold H. (1961). *The Psychology of Aggression*. New York: Wiley.

Buss, A. H. (1963). Physical aggression in relation to different frustrations. *Journal of Abnormal and Social Psychology, 67*, 1–7.

Buss, A. H. and P. J. Lang (1965). Psychological deficit in schizophrenia: I. Affect, reinforcement, and concept attainment. In David S. Holmes, Ed., *Reviews of Research in Behavior Pathology*. New York: Wiley.

Byrne, D., C. R. Ervin, and J. Lambeth (1970). Continuity between the experimental study of attraction and real-life computer dating. *Journal of Personality and Social Psychology, 16*, 157–165.

Byrne, Donn (1971). *The Attraction Paradigm*. New York: Academic.

Cairns, R. B. (1972). Fighting and punishment from a developmental perspective. In James K. Cole and Donald D. Jensen, Eds., *Nebraska Symposium on Motivation 1972*. Lincoln: University of Nebraska Press.

Campbell, D. T. and D. W. Fiske (1959). Convergent and discriminant validation by the multitrait-multimethod matrix. *Psychological Bulletin*, 56, 81–105.

Canby, V. (1976). Lina Wertmuller's comedy of foibles. *New York Times*, January 15, 28.

Cancian, F. (1964). Interaction patterns in Zincanteco families. *American Sociological Review*, 29, 540–550.

Cannon, Walter B. (1929). *Bodily Changes in Pain, Hunger, Fear, and Rage*, 2nd ed. New York:Ronald.

Cantril, Hadley (1940). *The Invasion from Mars*. Princeton, N. J. :Princeton University Press.

Caplow, Theodore (1968). *Two Against One: Coalitions in the Triad*. Englewood Cliffs, N. J.:Prentice Hall.

Carlsmith, J. M. and E. Aronson (1963). Some hedonic consequences of the confirmation and disconfirmation of expectancies. *Journal of Abnormal and Social Psychology*, 66, 151–156.

Carlsmith, J. M. and A. E. Gross (1969). Some effects of guilt on compliance. *Journal of Personality and Social Psychology*, 11, 232–239.

Carlson, L. A., L. Levi, and L. Oro (1972). Stressor-induced changes in plasma lipids, and urinary excretion of catecholamines and their modification by nicotinic acid. In Lennart Levi, Ed., *Stress and Distress in Response to Psychosocial Stimuli: Laboratory and Real Life Studies in Sympathoadrenomedullary and Related Reactions. Acta Medica Scandinavica*. Supplementum 528. Stockholm: Almquist and Wiksell.

Carlson, R. (1971). Where is the person in personality research? *Psychological Bulletin*, 75, 203–219.

Carson, Robert C. (1969). *Interaction Concepts of Personality*. Chicago: Aldine.

Carter, L. F. (1954). Evaluating the performance of individuals as members of small groups. *Personnel Psychology*, 7, 477–484.

Casler, L. (1973). Toward a re-evaluation of love. In Mary Ellin Curtin, Ed., *Symposium on Love*. New York: Behavioral Publication.

Cattell, R. B. (1966). Anxiety and behavior: Theory and crucial experiments. In Charles D. Spielberger, Ed., *Anxiety and Behavior*. New York: Academic.

Cattell, Raymond B. (1967). *The Scientific Analysis of Personality*. Baltimore: Penguin.

Cattell, R. B. (1072). The nature and genesis of mood states: A theoretical model with experimental measurements concerning anxiety, depression, arousal and other mood states. In Charles D. Spielberger, Ed., *Anxiety: Current Trends in Theory and Research*, Vol. 1. New York: Academic.

Centers, R. (1971). Evaluating the loved one: The motivational congruency factor. *Journal of Personality*, 39, 303–318.

Centers, R. (1975). Attitude similarity-dissimilarity as a correlate of heterosexual attraction and love. *Journal of Marriage and Family*, 37, 305–312.

Centers, R. C. and A. C. Granville (1971). Reciprocal need gratification in intersexual attraction: A test of hypotheses of Schutz and Winch. *Journal of Personality*, 39, 26–43.

Centers, R. C., B. H. Raven, and A. Rodrigues (1971). Conjugal power structure: A re-examination. *American Sociological Review*, 36, 264–278.

Chadwick, B. A. and R. C. Day (1972). Responses to persistent social interference: A response hierarchy of influence tactics in social exchange. *Journal of Social Psychology*, 86, 241–246.

Chance, N. A. (1964). A cross-cultural study of social cohesion and depression. *Transcultural Psychiatric Research*, 1, 19–21.

Chapman, L. and J. Baxter (1963). The process-reactive distinction and the patient's subculture. *Journal of Nervous and Mental Disease*, 136, 352–359.

Cheek, F. E. (1964). The "schizophrenogenic mother" in word and deed. *Family Process*, 3, 155–177.

Cheyne, J. A. (1971). Some parameters of punishment affecting resistance to deviation and generalization of a prohibition. *Child Development*, 43, 1273–1288.

Cheyne, J. A., J. R. Goyeche, and R. H. Walters (1969). Attention anxiety and rules in resistance to deviation in children. *Journal of Experimental Child Psychology*, 8, 127–139.

Chomsky, Noam (1965). *Aspects of a Theory of Syntax*. Cambridge, Mass.: Massachusetts Institute of Technology Press.

Christensen, Harold T. (1950). *Marriage Analysis*. New York: Ronald.

Church, R. M. (1963). The varied effects of punishment on behavior. *Psychological Review*, 70, 369–402.

Clark, B. (1960). The "cooling out" function in higher education. *American Journal of Sociology*, 65, 569–576.

Clausen, J. A. and M. Kohn (1960). Social relations and schizophrenia: A research report and a perspective. In Don D. Jackson, Ed., *Etiology of Schizophrenia*. New York: Basic.

Cleve, Felix M. (1969). *The Giants of Pre-Socratic Greek Philosophy: An Attempt to Reconstruct Their Thought*, Vol. 2. The Hague: Martinus Nijhoff.

Clore, G. L. and D. Byrne (1974). A reinforcement-affect model of attraction. In Ted L. Huston, Ed., *Foundations of Interpersonal Attraction*. New York: Academic.

Cloward, R. and L. Ohlin (1961). *Delinquency and Opportunity: A Theory of Delinquent Gangs*. Glencoe, Ill.: Free Press.

Cohen, A. R. (1955). Social norms, arbitrariness of frustration, and status of the agent of frustration in the frustration-aggression hypothesis. *Journal of Abnormal and Social Psychology*, 51, 222–226.

Cohen, S. I. and A. J. Silverman (1959). Psychophysiological investigations of vascular response variability. *Journal of Psychosomatic Medicine*, 3, 185–210.

Cohen, Y. A. (1967). The sociological relevance of schizophrenia and depression. In Yehudi A. Cohen, Ed., *Social Structure and Personality*. New York: Holt, Rinehart, Winston

Cole, D. L. (1966). Intercultural variations in recall of parental reward patterns. *Sociology and Social Research*, 50, 436–447.

Cole, S. and R. Lejuene (1972). Illness and the legitimation of failure. *American Sociological Review*, 37, 347–356.

Collins, R. (1971). Functional and conflict theories of educational stratification. *American Sociological Review*, 36, 1002–1019.

Comer, R. J. and J. A. Piliavin (1972). The effects of physical deviance on face-to-face interaction: The other side. *Journal of Personality and Social Psychology*, 23, 33–39.

Connor, J. W. (1970). A social approach to an understanding of schizophrenic-like reactions. *International Journal of Social Psychiatry,* 16, 136–152.

Cooley, Charles H. (1902). *Human Nature and Social Order.* New York: Scribners.

Coombs, R. H. and W. F. Kenkel (1966). Sex differences in dating aspirations and satisfaction with computer-selected partners *Journal of Marriage and Family,* 28, 62–66.

Costello, Charles G., Ed. (1972). *Symptoms of Psychopathology: A Handbook.* New York: Wiley.

Costello, C. G. (1930). Depression: Loss of reinforcers or loss of reinforcer effectiveness. *Behavior Therapy,* 3, 240–247.

Couch, A. (1960). Psychological determinants of interpersonal behavior. Unpublished Ph.D. Dissertation, Harvard University.

Crandall, V. C., W. Katkovsky, and V. J. Crandall (1965). Children's beliefs in their own control of reinforcements in intellectual-academic achievement situations. *Child Development,* 36, 91–109.

Cronbach, L. J. (1955). Processes affecting scores on "understanding of others" and "assumed similarity". *Psychological Bulletin,* 52. 177–193.

Cronbach, L. J. (1958). Proposals leading to analytic treatment of social perception scores. In Renato Tagiuri and Luigi Petrullo, Eds., *Person Perception and Interpersonal Behavior.* Stanford,: Stanford University Press.

Crosbie, P. V. (1972). Social exchange and power compliance: A test of Homans' propositions. *Sociometry,* 35, 203–221.

Crowne, Douglas P. and David A. Marlowe (1964). *The Approval Motive.* New York: Wiley.

Cutright, P. (1971). Income and family events: marital stability. *Journal of Marriage and Family,* 33, 291–306.

D'Andrade, R. G. (1965). Trait psychology and componential analysis. *American Anthropologist,* Part 2, 67, 215–228.

Dahl, R. A. (1958). A critique of the ruling elite model. *American Political Science Review* 52, 463–469.

Dahrendorf, Ralf (1959). *Class and Class Conflict in Industrial Society.* London: Routledge and Kegan Paul.

Dahrendorf, R. (1968). On the origins of inequality among men. In Ralf Dahrendorf, *Essays in the Theory of Society.* Stanford,: Stanford University Press.

Darwin, Charles (1873). *The Expression of Emotions in Man and Animals.* New York: Appleton.

Davis, D., H. G. Rainey, and T. C. Brock (1976). Interpersonal physical pleasuring: The effects of sex combinations, recipient attributes and anticipated future interaction. *Journal of Personality and Social Psychology,* 33, 89–106.

Davis, K. E. and E. E. Jones (1960). Changes in interpersonal perception as a means of reducing dissonance. *Journal of Abnormal and Social Psychology,* 61, 402–410.

Davis, Kingsley (1950). *Human Society.* New York: Macmillan.

Davis, K. and W. E. Moore (1945). Some principles of stratification. *American Sociological Review,* 10, 242–249.

Davitz, Joel (1969). *The Language of Emotions.* New York: Academic.

Della Fave, L. R. (1974). Success-values: Are they universal or class differentiated? *American Journal of Sociology,* 80, 153–169.

Deutsch, M. (1960). The effect of motivational orientation on trust and suspicion. *Human Relations,* 13, 122–139.

Deutsch, M. and R. M. Krauss (1960). The effect of threat on interpersonal bargaining. *Journal of Abnormal and Social Psychology*, 61, 168–175.

Deutsch, M. and R. M. Krauss (1962). Studiesof interpersonal bargaining. *Journal of Conflict Resolution*, 6, 52–76.

Dewey, John (1934). *Art as Experience.* New York: G. P. Putnam, 1958.

DeWolfe, A. S. (1974). Are there two kinds of thinking in process and reactive schizophrenics? *Journal of Abnormal Psychology*, 83, 285–290.

Dion, K. (1972). Physical attractiveness and the evaluation of children's transgressions. *Journal of Personality and Social Psychology*, 24, 207–213.

Dohrenwend, B. P. (1966). Social status and psychological disorder: An issue of substance and an issue of method. *American Sociological Review*, 31, 14–34.

Dohrenwend, B. P. (1967). Toward the development of theoretical models. *Milbank Memorial Fund Quarterly*, Part 2, 45, 155–162.

Dohrenwend, B. P. (1975). Sociocultural and socio-psychological factors in the genesis of mental disorders. *Journal of Health and Social Behavior*, 16, 365–392.

Dohrenwend, B. P. and D. L. Crandell (1970). Psychiatric symptoms in community, clinic and mental hospital groups. *American Journal of Psychiatry*, 126, 1611–1621.

Dohrenwend, Bruce P. and Barbara S. Dohrenwend (1969). *Social Status and Psychological Disorders.* New York: Wiley.

Dohrenwend, B. P. and B. S. Dohrenwend (1976). Sex differences and psychiatric disorders. *American Journal of Sociology* 81, 1447–1454.

Dollard, John, Leonard Doob, Neal Miller, O. Hobart Mowrer, and Robert Sears (1939). *Frustration and Aggression.* New Haven: Yale University Press.

Dollard, John and Neal E. Miller (1950). *Personality and Psychotherapy.* New York: McGraw-Hill.

Donlon, P. T. and K. H. Blacker (1973). Stages of schizophrenic compensation and reintegration. *Journal of Nervous and Mental Disease*, 157, 200–209.

Donnelly, J. (1966). Short-term therapy of schizophrenia. In Gene L. Usdin, Ed., *Psychoneurosis and Schizophrenia.* Philadelphia: Lippincott.

Draguns, J. G. and L. Phillips (1971). Psychiatric classification and diagnosis: An overview and critique. New York: General Learning press.

Dunham, H. W. (1964). Social class and schizophrenia. *American Journal of Orthopsychiatry*, 34, 634–642.

Dunham, H. Warren (1965). *Community and Schizophrenia: An Ecological Analysis.* Detroit: Wayne State University Press.

Durkheim, Emile (1915). *The Elementary Forms of the Religious Life*, translated by Joseph W. Swain. London: Allen and Unwin.

Durkheim, Emile (1897). *Suicide*, translated by George Simpson. Glencoe, ill.: Free Press, 1951.

Durkheim, Emile (1933). *The Division of Labor in Society*, translated by George Simpson. New York: Macmillan.

Durkheim, Emile (1938). *The Rules of Sociological Method*, translated by Sarah A. Solovay and John H. Mueller. Chicago: University of Chicago Press.

Durrell, Lawrence (1961). *Clea.* New York: Dutton.

Eaton, Joseph W. and Robert J. Weil (1955). *Culture and Mental Disorders.* Glencoe, Ill.: Free Press.

Ehrenkranz, J., E. Bliss, and M. H. Sheard (1974). Plasma testosterone: correlation with aggressive behavior and social dominance in man. *Psychosomatic Medicine, 36,* 469–475.

Eibl-Eibesfeldt, Irenaus (1972). *Love and Hate: The Natural History of Behavior Patterns,* translated by Geoffrey Strachan. New York: Holt, Rinehart, Winston.

Eibl-Eibesfeldt, I. (1974). The expressive behavior of the deaf-and-blind-born. In Mario Von Cranach and Ian Vine, Eds., *Social Communication and Movement.* New York: Academic.

Ekman, G. (1962). Measurement of moral judgment *Perceptual and Motor Skills, 15,* 3–9.

Ekman, G., M. Frankenhaeuser, S. Levander, and I. Mellis (1964). Scales of unpleasantness of electrical stimulation. *Scandanavian Journal of Psychology, 5,* 247–261.

Ekman, P. (1964). Body position, facial expression, and verbal behavior during interviews. *Journal of Abnormal and Social Psychology, 68,* 295–301.

Ekman, Paul, Wallace V. Friesen and Phoebe Ellsworth (1972). *Emotion in the Human Face.* New York: Pergamon.

Elder, G., Jr. (1963). Parental power legitimation and its effect on the adolescent. *Sociometry, 26,* 50–65.

Elder, G. H., Jr. (1969). Appearance and education in marriage mobility. *American Sociological Review, 34,* 519–533.

Eleftheriou, B. E. (1971). Effects of aggression and defeat on brain macromolecules. In Basil E. Eleftheriou and John P. Scott, Eds., *The Physiology of Aggression and Defeat.* New York: Plenum.

Elliott, R. (1964). Physiological activity and performance: A comparison of kindergarten children with young adults. *Psychological Monographs, 78,* (10, whole number 587).

Elmadjian, F. J., M. Hope, and E. T. Lamson (1958). Excretion of epinephrine and norepinephrine under stress. *Recent Progress in Hormone Research.* New York: Academic.

Emerson, R. (1962). Power-dependence relations. *American Sociological Review, 40,* 252–257.

Emerson, R. (1971). Power and position in exchange networks. Paper presented at American Sociological Association meetings, Denver, Col.

Emerson, R. (1972a). Exchange theory, part I: A psychological basis for social exchange. In Joseph Berger, Morris Zelditch, Jr., and Bo Anderson, Eds., *Sociological Theories in Progress,* Vol 2. Boston: Houghton-Mifflin.

Emerson, R. (1972b). Exchange theory part II: Exchange relations and network structures. In Joseph Berger, Morris Zelditch, Jr., and Bo Anderson, Eds., *Sociological Theories in Progress,* Vol 2. Boston: Houghton-Mifflin.

Engel, G. (1963). Toward a classification of affects. In Peter H. Knapp, Ed., *Expressions of Emotion in Man.* New York: International Universities Press.

England, J. L. and P. R. Kuntz (1975). The application of age-specific rates to divorce. *Journal of Marriage and Family, 37,* 40–46.

Epstein, S. and S. P. Taylor (1967). Instigation to aggression as a function of degree of defeat and perceived aggressive intent of opponent. *Journal of Personality, 35,* 265–289.

Erikson, Eric (1963). *Childhood and Society,* 2nd ed., revised and enlarged. New York: Norton.

Erlanger, H. (1974). Social class and punishment in childrearing: A reassessment. *Ameri-*

can Sociological Review, 39, 68–85.

Eron, Leonard D., Leopold O. Walder, and Monroe M. Lefkowitz (1971). *The Learning of Aggression in Children*. Boston: Little, Brown.

Estes, W. K. (1944). An experimental study of punishment. *Psychological Monographs*, 57 (3, whole number 263).

Eysenck, Hans (1952). *The Scientific Study of Personality*. London: Routledge and Kegan Paul.

Eysenck, H. J. (1970). The classification of depressive illnesses. *British Journal of Psychiatry*, 117, 241–271.

Eysenck, Hans J. and S. Rackman (1965). *The Causes of Neurosis*. London: Routledge and Kegan Paul.

Ezekiel, R. S. (1968). The personal future and Peace Corps competence. *Journal of Personality and Social Psychology*, Monograph Supplement 8, 1–26.

Fabrega, H., Jr. (1974). Problems implicit in the cultural and social study of depression. *Psychosomatic Medicine*, 36, 377–398.

Fairbairn, W. Ronald D. (1952). *Psychoanalytic Studies of the Personality*. London: Tavistock.

Faris, Robert E. L. and H. Warren Dunham (1939). *Mental Disorders in Urban Areas: An Ecological Study of Schizophrenia and Other Disorders*. Chicago: University of Chicago Press.

Feather, N. (1967). Level of aspiration and performance variability. *Journal of Personality and Social Psychology*, 6, 37–46.

Feather, N. (1962). The study of persistence. *Psychological Bulletin*, 69, 94–115.

Feshbach, S. (1970). Aggression. In Paul H. Mussen, Ed., *Carmichael's Manual of Child Psychology*, 3rd ed., Vol. 2. New York: Wiley.

Festinger, L. (1954). A theory of social comparison processes. *Human Relations*, 7, 117–140.

Festinger, Leon (1957). *A Theory of Cognitive Dissonance*. New York: Row Peterson.

Feuer, Lewis S. (1969). *The Conflict of Generations*. New York: Basic.

Fiedler, F. E. (1964). A contingency model of leadership effectiveness. In Leonard Berkowitz, Ed., *Advances in Experimental Social Psychology*, Vol. 1. New York: Academic.

Fineberg, B. L. and J. Lowman (1975). Affect and status dimensions of marital adjustment. *Journal of Marriage and Family*, 37, 155–160.

Firestone, I. J. (1969). Insulted and provoked: The effects of choice and provocation on hostility and aggression. In Phillip G. Zimbardo, Ed., *The Cognitive Control of Motivation*. Glenview, Ill.: Scott, Foresman.

Firestone, I. J., K. J. Kaplan, and J. Curtis Russell (1973). Anxiety, fear, and affiliation with similar-state versus dissimilar-state others: Misery sometimes loves non-miserable company. *Journal of Personality and Social Psychology*, 26, 409–414.

Firth, Raymond (1951). *Elements of Social Organization*. London: Watts.

Fisher, A. E. (1955). The effects of differential early treatment on the social and exploratory behavior of puppies. Unpublished Ph.D. dissertation, Pennsylvania State University.

Fishman, C. (1965). Need for approval and the expression of aggression under various conditions of frustration. *Journal of Personality and Social Psychology*, 2, 809–816.

Fleiss, J. L., B. J. Gurland, R. Simon, and L. Sharpe (1973). Cross-national study of diagnosis of mental disorders: some demographic correlates of hospital diagnosis in New York and London. *International Journal of Social Psychiatry, 19,* 180–186.

Foa, U. (1961). Convergences in the analysis of the structure of interpersonal behavior. *Psychological Review, 68,* 341–353.

Foa, U. and E. B. Foa (1970). Resource exchange: Toward a structural theory of interpersonal communication. In W. Siegman and B. Pope, Eds., *Studies in Dyadic Communication.* New York: Pergamon.

Foa, Uriel and Edna B. Foa (1974). *Societal Structures of the Mind.* Springfield, Ill.: Thomas.

Foote, N. (1953). Love. *Psychiatry, 16,* 245–251.

Foote, N. (1954). Sex as play. *Social Problems, 1,* 159–163.

Foote, N. (1956). Matching of husband and wife in phases of development. *Transactions of the Third World Congress of Sociology,* Vol. 4. London: International Sociological Association.

Ford, L. H., Jr. (1963). Reaction to failure as a result of expectancy for success. *Journal of Abnormal and Social Psychology, 67,* 340–347.

Frank, G. H. (1965). The role of the family in the development of psychopathology. *Psychological Bulletin, 64,* 191–205.

Frankenhaeuser, M. (1971a). Behavior and circulating catecholamines. *Brain Research, 31,* 241–262.

Frankenhaeuser, M. (1971b). Experimental approaches to the study of human behavior as related to neuroendocrine functions. In Lennart Levi, Ed., *Society, Stress, and Disease. Volume 1: The Psychosocial Environment and Psychosomatic Diseases.* New York: Oxford University Press.

Frankenhaeuser, M. (1976). Experimental approaches to catecholamines and emotions. In Lennart Levi, Ed., *Emotions: Their Parameters and Measurements.* New York: Raven.

Frankenhaeuser, M., K. Sterky, and G. Jarpe (1962). Psychophysiological relations in habituation to gravitational stress. *Perceptual and Motor Skills, 15,* 63–72.

Frankenhaeuser, M. and A. Rissler (1970). Effects of punishment on catecholamine release and efficiency of performance. *Psychopharmacologia, 17,* 378–390.

Freedman, J. L., S. A. Wallington, and N. Bless (1967). Compliance without pressure: The effect of guilt. *Journal of Personality and Social Psychology, 7,* 117–124.

Freedman, M. B., T. Leary, A. G. Ossorio, and H. S. Coffrey (1951). The interpersonal dimension of personality. *Journal of Personality, 20,* 143–161.

Freeman, R. V. and H. M. Grayson (1955). Maternal attitudes in schizophrenics. *Journal of Abnormal and Social Psychology, 50,* 45–52.

Freeman, H. R. (1973). Effects of positive and negative feedback and degree of discrepancy on responses to test results. *Journal of Counseling Psychology, 20,* 571–572.

French, J. R. P., Jr., and B. H. Raven (1959). The bases of social power. In Dorwin Cartright, Ed., *Studies in Social Power.* Ann Arbor: University of Michigan Press.

Freud, S. (1905). Wit and its relation to the unconscious. In Sigmund Freud, *The Basic Writings of Sigmund Freud.* New York: Modern Library, 1938.

Freud, S. (1912). The dynamics of transference In Sigmund Freud, *Collected Papers,* Vol. 2, translated by Joan Riviere. New York: Basic, 1959.

Freud, S. (1914). On narcissism: An introduction. In Sigmund Freud, *Collected Papers,*

Vol. 4, translated by Joan Rivere. New York: Basic, 1959.

Freud, Sigmund (1913). *Totem and Taboo.* In The Basic Writings of Sigmund Freud. New York: Modern Library, 1938.

Freud, S. (1915). Further recommendations in the technique of psychoanalysis: Observations on transference love. In Sigmund Freud, *Collected Papers*, Vol. 2, translated by Joan Riviere. New York: Basic, 1959.

Freud, S. (1917). Mourning and melancholia. In Sigmund Freud, *Collected Papers*, Vol. 4, translated by Joan Riviere. New York: Basic, 1959.

Freud, Sigmund. (1918). *Reflections on war and death.* Translated by Henry Brill. New York: Moffat, Yard.

Freud, Sigmund (1922). *Group Psychology and the Analysis of the Ego.* London: International Psychonalytic Library.

Freud, Sigmund (1923. *The Ego and the Id.* London: Hogarth, 1927.

Freud, Sigmund (1933). *New Introductory lectures on Psychoanalysis.* New York: Norton.

Freud, Sigmund (1936). *The Problem of Anxiety*, translated by Henry Bunker. New York: Norton.

Freud, S. (1937). Analysis terminable and interminable. In Sigmund Freud, *Collected Papers*, translated by Joan Riviere. New York: Basic.

Freud, Sigmund (1946). *The Ego and the Mechanisms of Defense.* New York: International Universities Press.

Freud, Sigmund (1951). *Civilization and Its Discontents*, translated by Joan Riviere. London: Hogarth.

Freud, Sigmund (1955). *Complete Psychological Works.* Vol 18, Ch. 3. London: Hogarth.

Freud, Sigmund (1966). *The Complete Introductory Lectures in Psychoanalysis*, translated by James Strachey. New York: Norton.

Frijda, N. H. (1969). Recognition of emotion. In Leonard Berkowitz, Ed., *Advances in Experimental Social Psychology*, Vol. 4. New York: Academic.

Fromm, Erich (1941). *Escape From Freedom.* New York: Holt, Rinehart, Winston.

Fromm, Erich (1947). *Man For Himself.* New York: Holt, Rinehart, Winston.

Fromm, Erich (1956). *The Art ot Loving.* New York: Harper.

Funkenstein, D. (1955). The physiology of fear and anger. *Scientific American*, 192, 74–80.

Funkenstein, Daniel, Stanley H. King, and Margaret E. Drolette (1957). *Mastery of Stress.* Cambridge, Mass.: Harvard University Press.

Galtung, J. (1958). The social functions of a prison. *Social Problems*, 6, 127–140.

Gardiner, H. M., Ruth C. Metcalf, and John G. Beebe-Center (1937). *Feeling and Emotion.* Westport, Conn.: Greenwood, 1970.

Garfinkel, H. (1961). Conditions of successful degradation ceremonies. *American Journal of Sociology*, 61, 420–424.

Garfinkel, Harold (1967). *Studies in Ethnomethodology.* Englewood Cliffs, N.J.: Prentice-Hall.

Gaupp, L. A., R. M. Stern, and G. G. Galbraith (1972). False heart-rate feedback and reciprocal inhibition by aversion relief in the treatment of snake avoidance behavior. *Behavior Therapy*, 3, 7–20.

Geen, R. (1968). Effects of frustration, attack, and prior training in aggressiveness upon aggressive behavior. *Journal of Personality and Social Psychology*, 9, 316–321.

Geen, Russell (1972). Aggression. New York: General Learning.

Geen, R., D. Stonner, and D. R. Kelley (1974). Aggression anxiety and cognitive appraisal of aggression-threat stimuli. *Journal of Personality and Social Psychology*, 29, 196–200.

Gekas, V. (1972). Motives and aggressive acts in popular fiction: sex and class differences. *American Journal of Sociology*, 77, 680–696.

Gellhorn, Ernest (1967). *Principles of Autonomic-Somatic Integrations*. Minneapolis: University of Minnesota Press.

Gellhorn, Ernest and G. N. Loofbourrow (1963). *Emotions and Emotional Disorders: A Neurophysiological Study*. New York: Harper.

Gerard, D. L. and J. Siegel (1950). The family background and schizophrenia. *Psychiatric Quarterly*, 24, 47–63.

Gerard, H. B. (1964). Physiological measurement in social psychological research. In P. Herbert Leiderman and David Shapiro, Eds., *Psychobiological Approaches to Behavior*. Stanford: Stanford University Press.

Gerard, H. B. and G. C. Mathewson (1966). The effects of severity of initiation on liking for a group: A replication. *Journal of Experimental Social Psychology*, 2, 278–287.

Gergen, Kenneth J. (1969). *The Psychology of Behavior Exchange*. Reading, Mass.: Addison-Wesley

Gewertz, J. L. (1969). Mechanisms of social learning: Some roles of stimulation and behavior in early human development. In David Goslin, Ed., *Handbook of Socialization Theory and Research*. Chicago: Rand-McNally.

Gibson, James J. (1966). *The Senses Considered as Perceptual Systems*. Boston: Houghton-Mifflin.

Glass, D. C. (1964). Changes in liking as a means of reducing cognitive discrepancies between self-esteem and aggression. *Journal of Personality*, 32, 531–549.

Glass, D. C. (1965). Theories of consistency and the study of personality. In Edgar F. Borgatta and William W. Lambert, Eds., *Handbook of Personality Theory and Research*. Chicago: Rand-McNally.

Glass, D. C. and J. D. Wood (1969). The control of aggression by self-esteem and dissonance. In Philip G. Zimbardo, Ed., *The Cognitive Control of Motivation*. Glenview, Ill.: Scott, Foresman.

Goffman, Erving (1959). *The Presentation of Self in Everyday Life*. Garden City, N.Y.: Doubleday.

Goffman, E. (1961a). Role distance. In Erving Goffman, *Encounters*. Indianapolis: Bobbs-Merrill.

Goffman, Erving (1961b). *Asylums*. Garden City, N.Y.: Doubleday.

Goffman, Erving (1963). *Stigma: Notes on the Management of Spoiled Identity*. Englewood Cliffs, N.J.: Prentice-Hall.

Goffman, E. (1967). Embarrassment and social organization. In Erving Goffman, *Interaction Ritual*. Garden City, N.Y.: Doubleday

Goldberg, E. M. and S. L. Morrison (1963). Schizophrenia and social class. *British Journal of Psychiatry*, 109, 785–802.

Goldfarb, A. I. (1969). The psychodynamics of dependency and the search for aid. In Richard A. Kalish, Ed., *The Dependency of Older People*. Occasional Papers in Gerontology, No. 6. Ann Arbor, University of Michigan-Wayne State University.

Goldhamer, H. and E. A. Shils (1939). Types of power and status. *American Journal of Sociology*, 45, 171–182.

Goldin, P. C. (1969). A review of children's reports of parent behaviors. *Psychological Bulletin*, 71, 222–236.

Goldstein, D., D. Fink, and D. R. Mettee (1972). Cognition of arousal and actual arousal as determinants of emotion. *Journal of Personality and Social Psychology*, 21, 41–51.

Goode, W. J. (1972). The place of force in human society. *American Sociological Review*, 37, 507–519.

Goode, William J. (1964). *The Family*. Englewood Cliffs, N.J.: Prentice-Hall.

Goodenough, F. (1932). Expressions of the emotions in a blind-deaf child. *Journal of Abnormal and Social Psychology*, 27, 328–222.

Goodenough, W. H. (1965). Rethinking "status" and "role": Toward a general model of cultural organization and social relationships. In A.S.A. Monograph No. 1, *The Relevance of Models*. London: Tavistock.

Goranson, R. E. and L. Berkowitz (1966). Reciprocity and responsibility reactions to prior help. *Journal of Personality and Social Psychology*, 3, 227–232.

Gormly, J., A. Gormly, and C. Johnson (1971). Interpersonal attraction, competence motivation and reinforcement theory. *Journal of Personality and Social Psychology*, 19, 375–380.

Goslin, David, Ed. (1969). *Handbook of Socialization Theory and Research*. Chicago: Rand-McNally.

Gottesman, Irving I. and J. Shields (1972). *Schizophrenia and Genetics: A Twin Study Vantage Point*. New York: Academic.

Gottschalk, Louis A. and Goldine C. Gleser (1969). *The Measurement of Psychological States Through the Content Analysis of Verbal Behavior*. Berkeley: University of California Press.

Gouldner, A. (1960). The norm of reciprocity: A preliminary statement. *American Sociological Review*, 25, 161–179.

Gourmont, Remy de (1932). *The Natural Philosophy of Love*, translated by Ezra Pound. New York: Liveright.

Gove, P. B., Ed. (1958). *Webster's Third International Dictionary*. Springfield, Mass.: Merriam.

Gove, W. (1970). Sleep deprivation: A cause of psychiatric disorganization. *American Journal of Sociology*, 75, 782–799.

Gove, W. R. (1975). The labeling theory of mental illness: A reply to Scheff. *American Sociological Review*, 40, 242–248.

Gove, W. R. and J. F. Tudor (1973). Adult sex roles and mental illness. *American Journal of Sociology*, 78, 812–835.

Graham, F. K., W. A. Charwat, A. S. Honig, and P. C. Weltz (1951). Aggression as a function of the attack and the attacker. *Journal of Abnormal and Social Psychology*, 46, 512–520.

Graham, L. A., S. I. Cohen, and B. M. Shmavonian (1967). Some methodological approaches to the psychophysiological correlates of behavior. In Lennart Levi, Ed., *Emotional Stress: Physiological and Psychological Reactions. Medical, Industrial, and Military Applications*. New York: Elsevier.

Grant, E. C. (1965). An ethological description of some schizophrenic patterns of behavior. In *Proceedings of the Leeds Symposium on Behavioral Disorders*. Dagenham, England: May and Baker.

Gray, J. A. (1970). The psychophysiological basis of introversion-extraversion. *Behavior Research and Therapy*, 8, 249–260.

Gray, Jeffrey A. (1971). *The Psychology of Fear and Stress*. New York: McGraw-Hill.

Greenwell, J. and H. A. Dengerink (1973). The role of perceived versus actual attack in human physical aggression. *Journal of Personality and Social Psychology*, 26, 66–71.

Gross, A. E. and C. Crofton (1977). What is good is beautiful. *Sociometry*, 40, 85–90.

Grusec, J. (1966). Some antecendents of self-criticism. *Journal of Personality and Social Psychology*, 4, 244–252.

Grusec, J. E. and S. A. Ezrin (1972). Techniques of punishment and the development of self-criticism. *Child Development*, 43, 1273–1288.

Guilford, J. P. (1952). When not to factor analyze. *Psychological Bulletin*, 49, 26–37.

Hamblin, R. L. (1971). Ratio scaling for the social sciences. *Social Forces*, 50, 191–206.

Hamblin, R. L. and C. R. Smith (1966). Values, status, and professors. *Sociometry*, 29, 183–196.

Hamblin, Robert L., R. Brooke Jacobsen, and Jerry L. L. Miller (1973). A *Mathematical Theory of Social Change*. New York: Wiley.

Hamburg, D. A., B. A. Hamburg, and J. D. Barchas (1975). Anger and depression in perspective of behavioral biology. In Lennart Levi, Ed., *Emotions: Their Parameters and Measurement*. New York: Raven.

Hamsher, J. H., J. D. Geller, and J. B. Rotter (1968). Interpersonal trust, internal-external control, and the Warren Commission Report. *Journal of Personality and Social Psychology*, 9, 210–215.

Harburg, E., J. C. Erfurt, L. S. Havenstein, C. Chape, W. J. Schull, and M. A. Schork (1973). Socio-ecological stress, suppressed hostility, skin color, and black-white male blood pressure: Detroit. *Psychosomatic Medicine*, 35, 276–296.

Hare, A. P. (1970). Four dimensions of interpersonal behavior. Paper presented at meetings of American Sociological Association, Washington, D.C.

Harlow, H. F. (1958). The nature of love. *American Psychologist*, 13, 673–685.

Harlow, H. F. (1962). Development of affection in primates. In E. L. Bliss, Ed., *Roots of Behavior*. New York: Harper.

Harlow, H. F. and M. K. Harlow (1972). The language of love. In Thomas Alloway, Lester Kramer, and Patricia Pliner, Eds., *Communication and Affect*. New York: Academic.

Harsanyi, J. C. (1962). Measurement of social power, opportunity costs, and the theory of two-person bargaining games. *Behavioral Science*, 7, 67–81.

Hawkins, J. (1967). Association between companionship, hostility, and marital satisfaction. *Journal of Marriage and Family*, 30, 647–650.

Hays, D. P. and S. Sievers (1972). A sociolinguistic investigation of the "dimensions" of interpersonal behavior. *Journal of Personality and Social Psychology*, 24, 254–261.

Hayward, M. L. and J. E. Taylor (1964). A schizophrenic patient describes the action of intensive psychotherapy. In Bert Kaplan, Ed., *The Inner World of Mental Illness*. New York: Harper and Row.

Heap, G. and P. A. Roth (1973). On phenomenological sociology. *American Sociological Review*, 38, 354–367.

Heatherington, E. M. (1965). A developmental study of the effects of sex of dominant parent on sex-role preference, identification, and imitation in children. *Journal of Personality and Social Psychology, 2,* 188–194.

Heatherington, E. M. (1966). Effects of paternal absence on sex-type behaviors in Negro and white pre-adolescent males. *Journal of Personality and Social Psychology, 4,* 87–91.

Hebb, D. O. (1955). Drives and the C. N. S. (conceptual nervous system). *Psychological Review, 62,* 243–254.

Heilbrun, A. B., Jr., S. N. Harrell, and B. J. Gillard (1967). Perceived maternal child-rearing patterns and the effects of social non-reaction upon achievement motivation. *Child Development, 38,* 267–281.

Heilbrun, Alfred B., Jr. (1973). *Aversive Maternal Control.* New York: Wiley.

Heilman, M., S. A. Hodgson, and H. A. Hornstein (1972). Effect of magnitude and rectifiability of harm and information value on the reporting of accidental harm-doing. *Journal of Personality and Social Psychology, 23,* 211–218.

Heinicke, C. M. (1953). Some antecedents of guilt and fear in young boys. Unpublished Ph.D dissertation, Harvard University.

Heise, D. (1969). Some methodological issues in semantic differential research. *Psychological Bulletin, 72,* 406–422.

Heiss, J. and S. Owens (1972). Self-evaluations of blacks and whites. *American Journal of Sociology, 78,* 360–370.

Heller, Joseph (1961). *Catch-22.* New York: Simon and Schuster.

Helson, H. (1959). Adaptation-level theory. In Sigmund Koch, Ed., *Psychology: A Study of a Science,* Vol. 1. New York: Mc-Graw-Hill.

Henry, A. F. (1956). Family role structure and self-blame. *Social Forces, 35,* 55–68.

Henry, A. F. (1957). Sibling structure and perception of the disciplinary roles of parents. *Sociometry, 20,* 67–74.

Herron, W. G. (1962). The process-reactive classification of schizophrenia. *Psychological Bulletin, 59,* 329–343.

Hertzler, Joyce O. (1970). *Laughter: A Socio-Scientific Analysis.* New York: Exposition.

Hess, E. (1959). The relationship between imprinting and motivation. In M. R. Jones, Ed., *Nebraska Symposium on Motivation,* Vol. 7. Lincoln: University of Nebraska Press.

Hesse, Herman (1951). *Siddhartha.* New York: New Directions.

Hill, W. F. (1960). Learning theory and the acquisition of values. *Psychological Review, 67,* 317–331.

Hinkle, L. E., Jr., (1974). The effect of exposure to culture change and change in interpersonal relationships on health. In Barbara S. Dohrenwend and Bruce P. Dohrenwend, Eds., *Stressful Life Events: Their Nature and Effects.* New York: Wiley.

Hinsie, Leland E. and Robert J. Campbell (1970). *Psychiatric Dictionary,* 4th ed. New York: Oxford University Press.

Hoffman, Banesh (1973). *Albert Einstein: Creator and Rebel.* New York: New American Library.

Hoffman, M. L. (1963). Childrearing practices and moral development: Generalizations from empirical research. *Child Development, 34,* 295–318.

Hoffman, M. L. (1960). Power assertion by the parent and its impact on the child. *Child Development, 31,* 129–143

Hoffman, M. L. (1970). Moral development. In Paul H. Mussen, Ed., *Carmichael's*

Manual of Child Psychology, 3rd ed., Vol. 2. New York: Wiley.

Hoffman, M. L. (1975). Altruistic behavior and the parent-child relationship. *Journal of Personality and Social Psychology, 31*, 937–943.

Hoffman, Martin L. and Lois W. Hoffman, Eds. (1964). *Review of Child Development Research*, Vol. 1. New York: Russell Sage Foundation.

Hoffman, M. L. and H. D. Saltzstein (1967). Parental discipline and the child's moral development. *Journal of Personality and Social Psychology, 5*, 45–57.

Hoffman, Lois W. and Martin L. Hoffman (1966). *Review of Child Development Research*, Vol. 2. New York: Russell Sage Foundation.

Hokanson, J. E. and M. Burgess (1962a). The effects of three types of aggression on vascular processes. *Journal of Abnormal and Social Psychology, 64*, 446–449.

Hokanson, J. E. and M. Burgess (1962b). The effects of status, type of frustration, and aggression on vascular processes. *Journal of Abnormal and Social Psychology, 65*, 232–237.

Hokanson, J. E. and R. Edelman (1966). Effects of three social responses on vascular processes. *Journal of Personality and Social Psychology, 3*, 442–447.

Hollingshead, August B. (1949). *Elmtown's Youth.* New York: Wiley.

Hollingshead, August B. and Frederick C. Redlich (1958). *Social Class and Mental Illness.* New York: Wiley.

Holmes, D. (1972). Aggression, displacement, and guilt. *Journal of Personality and Social Psychology, 21*, 296–301.

Holz, W. A. and N. H. Azrin (1961). Discriminative properties of punishment. *Journal of the Experimental Analysis of Behavior, 4*, 225–232.

Homans, George C. (1950). *The Human Group.* New York: Harcourt Brace.

Homans, George C. (1961). *Social Behavior: Its Elementary Forms.* New York: Harcourt Brace, World.

Hornstein, H. (1965). The effect of different magnitudes of threat on interpersonal bargaining. *Journal of Experimental Social Psychology, 1*, 282–293.

Houston, B. K. (1972). Control over stress, locus of control, and response to stress. *Journal of Personality and Social Psychology, 21*, 249–255.

Hsu, Francis K. (1969). *The Study of Literate Civilizations.* New York: Holt, Rinehart, Winston.

Hull, Clark L. (1943). *Principles of Behavior.* New York: Appleton-Century-Crofts.

Hunt, J. McV. and C. Cofer (1944). Psychological deficit in schizophrenia. In J. McVickers Hunt, Ed., *Personality and the Behavior Disorders*, Vol. 2. New York: Ronald.

Hunt, J. McV., M. W. Cole, and E. E. S. Reis (1958). Situational cues distinguishing anger, fear, and sorrow. *American Journal of Psychology, 71*, 136–151.

Hunt, Morton (1959). *The Natural History of Love.* New York: Grove.

Hunter, Floyd (1954). *Community Power Structure.* Chapel Hill: University of North Carolina Press.

Huston, T. L. (1974). A perspective on interpersonal attraction. In Ted L. Huston, Ed., *Foundations of Interpersonal Attraction.* New York: Academic.

Hyman, H. H. (1942). The psychology of status. *Archives of Psychology, 269.*

Hyman, H. H. (1966). The value systems of different classes. In Reinhard Bendix and Seymour M. Lipset, Eds., *Class, Status, and Power*, 2nd ed., New York: Free Press.

Inkeles, A. (1960). Industrial man: The relation of status to experience, perception and value. *American Journal of Sociology, 66*, 1–31.

Inkeles, A. (1968). Society, social structure, and child socialization. In John H. Clausen, Ed., *Socialization and Society*. Boston: Little, Brown.

Inkeles, Alex and David H. Smith (1974). *Becoming Modern: Industrial Changes in Six Developing Countries*. Cambridge, Mass.: Harvard University Press.

Israel, J. (1966). Problems of role learning. In Joseph Berger, Morris Zelditch, Jr., and Bo Anderson, Ed., *Sociological Theories in Progress*, Vol. 1. Boston: Houghton-Mifflin.

Israel, M. (1969). Comment on James Coleman's review of Harold Garfinkel's *Studies in Ethnomethodolology*. *American Sociologist*, 4, 335–336.

Izard, C. E. (1960). Personality similarity, positive affect, and interpersonal attraction. *Journal of Abnormal and Social Psychology*, 61, 485.

Izard, Carroll E. (1972). *Patterns of Emotions: A New Analysis of Anxiety and Depression*. New York: Academic.

Jackson, D. D. (1967). Schizophrenia: The nosological nexus. In John Romano, Ed., *The Origins of Schizophrenia*. New York: Excerpta Medica Foundation.

Jackson, D. N. and S. M. Messick (1961). Acquiescence and desirability as response determinants on the MMPI. *Educational and Psychological Measurements*, 21, 771–790.

Jacob, T. (1975). Family interaction in disturbed and normal families: a methodological and substantive review. *Psychological Bulletin*, 82, 33–65.

Jacobs, A. (1971). Mood—emotion—affect: The nature of and manipulation of affective states with particular reference to positive affective states and emotional illness. In Alfred Jacobs and Lewis B. Sachs, Eds., *The Psychology of Private Events*. New York: Academic.

Jacobs, D. (1974). Dependency and vulnerability: An exchange approach to the control of organizations. *Administrative Science Quarterly*, 19, 45–59.

Jacobson, Wally D. (1972). *Power and Interpersonal Relations*. Belmont, Cal.: Wadsworth.

James, William (1893). *Principles of Psychology*. New York: Holt.

Janis, Irving (1951). *Air War and Emotional Stress*. New York: McGraw-Hill.

Janis, I. L. (1966). A behavioral study of psychological stress among surgical patients. In William R. Scott and Edmund H. Volkhart, Eds., *Medical Care*. New York: Wiley.

Jarrett, James L. (1957). *The Quest for Beauty*. Englewood Cliffs, N.J.: Prentice-Hall.

Jarvik, M. E. (1973). The influence of drugs on psychopathological processes. In Muriel Hammer, Kurt Salzinger, and Samuel Sutton, Eds., *Psychopathology: Contributions from Social, Behavioral, and Biological Sciences*. New York: Wiley.

Jecker, J. and D. Landy (1969). Liking a person as a function of doing him a favor. *Human Relations*, 22, 371–378.

Jennings, Helen H. (1950). *Leadership and Isolation*, 2nd ed. New York: Longmans Green.

John, E. R. (1973). Where is fancy bred? In Muriel Hammer, Kurt Salzinger, and Samuel Sutton, Eds., *Psychopathology: Contributions from the Social, Behavioral, and Biological Sciences*. New York: Wiley.

Johnson, Ronald G. and Gene R. Medinnus (1974). *Child Psychology*, 3rd ed. New York: Wiley.

Jones, Edward E. (1964). *Ingratiation: A Social Psychological Analysis*. New York: Appleton-Century-Crofts.

Jones, E. E. and R. DeCharms (1957). Changes in social perception as a function of the personal relevance of behavior. *Sociometry*, 20, 75–85.

Jones, Edward E. and Harold B. Gerard (1967). *Foundations of Social Psychology*. New York: Wiley.

Jones, E. E. and R. E. Nisbett (1971). *The Actor and the Observer: Divergent Perceptions of the Causes of Behavior*. New York: General Learning Press.

Jourard, Sidney M. (1964). *The Transparent Self*. Princeton, N.J.: Van Nostrand Reinhold.

Kadushin, Alfred (1970). *Child Welfare Services: A Sourcebook*. New York: Macmillan.

Kagan, J. (1958). The concept of identification. *Psychological Review, 65,* 296–305.

Kahn, A. and D. L. Young (1973). Ingratiation in a free social situation. *Sociometry, 36,* 579–587.

Kantor, R., J. Wallner, and C. Winder (1953). Process and reactive schizophrenia. *Journal of Consulting Psychology, 17,* 157–162.

Kaplan, H. B. (1971). Social class and self-derogation: A conditional relationship. *Sociometry, 34,* 41–64.

Kaplan, Howard B. (1975). *Self-Attitudes and Deviant Behavior*. Santa Monica, Cal.: Goodyear.

Kaplan, H. B. and S. W. Bloom (1960). The use of sociological and social-psychological concepts in physiological research: A review of selected experimental studies. *Journal of Nervous and Mental Disease, 131,* 128–134.

Kelley, H. H. (1951). Communication in experimentally created hierarchies. *Human Relations, 4,* 39–56.

Kelley, H. H. (1971). *Attribution in Social Psychology*. New York: General Learning Press.

Kelman, H. C. (1965). Compliance, identification, and internalization: Three processes of attitude change. In Harold Proshansky and Bernard Seidenberg, Eds., *Basic Studies in Social Psychology*. New York: Holt, Rinehart, Winston.

Kemper, T. D. (1968a). Reference groups, socialization, and achievement. *American Sociological Review, 33,* 31–45.

Kemper, T. D. (1968b). Third party penetration of local social systems. *Sociometry, 31,* 1–29.

Kemper, T. D. (1972a). The division of labor: A post-Durkheimian analytical view. *American Sociological Review, 37,* 739–753.

Kemper, T. D. (1972b). Power, status, and love. In David R. Heise, Ed., *Personality and Socialization*. Chacago: Rand-McNally.

Kemper, T. D. (1973). The fundamental dimensions of social relationships: A theoretical statement. *Acta Sociologica, 16,* 41–58.

Kemper, T. D. (1974). On the nature and purpose of ascription. *American Sociological Review, 39,* 844–853.

Kemper, T. D. (1976). Reply to Mayhew and Scott. *American Sociological Review, 41,* 383–390.

Kendall, Patricia (1954). *Conflict and Mood: Factors Affecting Stability of Response*. Glencoe, Ill.: Free Press.

Kendall, R. (1970). Relationship between aggression and depression. *Archives of General Psychiatry, 22,* 308–318.

Kendall, R. E. (1968). *The Classification of Depressive Illness*. London: Oxford University Press.

Keniston, Kenneth (1968). *Young Radicals*. New York: Harcourt Brace.

Kent, R. N., G. T. Wilson, and R. Nelson (1972). Effects of false heart-rate feedback on avoidance behavior: An investigation of "cognitive" desensitization. *Behavior Therapy*, 3, 1–6.

Kephart, W. M. (1955). Occupational level and marital disruption. *American Sociological Review, 20,* 456–465.

Kephart, W. M. (1967). Some correlates of romantic love. *Journal of Marriage and Family, 29,* 470–479.

Kerckhoff, A. C. (1974). The social context of interpersonal attraction. In Ted L. Huston, Ed., *Foundations of Interpersonal Attraction.* New York: Academic.

Kerchkoff, A. C. and K. E. Davis (1962). Value consensus and need complementarity in mate selection. *American Sociological Review, 27,* 295–303.

Kety, S. S. (1972). Norepinephrine in the CNS and its correlation with behavior. In A. G. Karczmar and J. C. Eccles, Eds., *Brain and Human Behavior.* New York: Springer-Verlag.

Kiesler, S. B. (1966). The relations of perceived role requirements on reactions to favor-doing. *Journal of Experimental Social Psychology, 2,* 195–210.

Kiev, Ari (1972). *Transcultural Psychiatry.* New York: Free Press.

Kinsey, Alfred C., Wardell B. Pomeroy, and Clyde E. Martin (1948). *Sexual Behavior in the Human Male.* Philadelphia: Saunders.

Kinsey, Alfred C., Wardell B. Pomeroy, Clyde E. Martin, and Paul H. Gebhard (1953). *Sexual Behavior in the Human Female.* Philadelphia: Saunders.

Kleck, R. (1969). Physical stigma and task oriented interaction. *Human Relations, 22,* 53–60.

Klein, D. F. (1974). Endogenomorphic depression. *Archives of General Psychiatry, 31,* 447–454.

Klein, G. S. (1970). The personal world through perception. In George S. Klein, *Perceptions, Motives and Personality.* New York: Knopf.

Klinger, E. (1975). Consequences of commitment to and disengagement from incentives. *Psychological Review, 82,* 1–25.

Knott, P. D. and B. A. Drost (1972). Effects of varying intensity of attack and fear-arousal on the intensity of counter aggression. *Journal of Personality, 40,* 27–37.

Kohlberg, Lawrence (1969). *Stages in the Development of Moral Thought and Action.* New York: Holt, Rinehart, Winston.

Kohn, M. L. (1968). Social class and schizophrenia: A critical review. *Journal of Psychiatric Research, 6,* 155–173.

Kohn, Melvin L. (1969). *Class and Conformity.* Homewood, Ill.: Dorsey.

Kohn, M. L. (1972a). Class, family, and schizophrenia: A reformulation. *Social Forces, 50,* 295–304.

Kohn, M. L. (1972b). Rejoinder to David Mechanic. *Social Forces, 50,* 310–313.

Konecni, V. and A. N. Doob (1972). Catharsis through displacement of aggression. *Journal of Personality and Social Psychology, 23,* 378–387.

Korchin, S. (1967). Comments on Arnold. In Mortimer H. Appley and Richard Trumbull, Eds., *Psychological Stress.* New York: Appleton-Century-Crofts.

Kramer, M. (1957). Discussion of the concepts of incidence and prevalence as related to epidemiological studies of mental disorders. *American Journal of Public Health, 47,* 826–840.

Krebs, D. (1970). Altruism—an examination of the concept and a review of the literature. *Psychological Bulletin, 73,* 258–303.

Krebs, D. (1975). Empathy and altruism. *Journal of Personality and Social Psychology*, 32, 1134–1146.

Kropotkin, Prince (1902). *MutualAid*. New York: McClure Phillips.

Kugelmass, S. (1973). Psychophysiological indices in psychopathological and cross-cultural research. In Muriel Hammer, Kurt Salzinger, and Samuel Sutton, Eds., *Psychopathology: Contributions from Social, Behavioral, and Biological Sciences*. New York: Wiley.

Kuhn, Thomas S. (1962). *The Structure of Scientific Revolutions*. Chicago: University of Chicago Press.

Lacey, J. I. (1967). Somatic response patterning and stress: some revisions of activation theory. In Mortimer H. Appley and Richard Trumbull, Eds., *Psychological Stress*. New York: Appleton-Century-Crofts.

Lacey, J. I. and B. C. Lacey (1962). The law of initial values in the longitudinal study of autonomic constitution: Reproducibility of autonomic responses and response patterns over a four year interval. *Annals of the New York Academy of Sciences*, 98, 1257–1290.

Lacey, J. I., J. Kagan, B. C. Lacey, and H. A. Moss (1963). The visceral level: Situational determinants and behavioral correlates of autonomic response patterns. In Paul H. Knapp, Ed., *Expression of Emotions in Man*. New York: International Universities Press.

Laing, Ronald D. (1961). *Self and Others*. New York; Penguin.

Landy, D. and H. Sigall (1974). Beauty is talent: Task evaluation as a function of the performer's physical attractiveness. *Journal of Personality and Social Psychology*, 29, 299–304.

Lane, E. A. (1968). The influence of sex and race on process-reactive ratings of schizophrenia. *Journal of Psychology*, 68, 15–20.

Lane, I. M. and L. A. Messé (1972). Distribution of insufficient, sufficient, and oversufficient rewards: A clarification of equity theory. *Journal of Personality and Social Psychology*, 21, 228–233.

Lang, P. J. and A. H. Buss (1965). Psychological deficit in schizophrenia: II. Interference and activation. In David S. Homes, Ed., *Reviews of Research in Behavior Pathology*. New York: Wiley.

Lange, C. G. (1885). The emotions: A psychophysiologial study. Translated by Istar A. Haupt. In Carl G. Lange and William James, *The Emotions*. New York: Hafner, 1967.

Langer, Susanne K. (1942). *Philosphy in a New Key*. Cambridge, Mass.: Harvard University Press.

Langhorne, M. C. and P. F. Secord (1955). Variations in marital needs with age, sex, marital status, and regional location. *Journal of Social Psychology*, 41, 19–37.

Langner, T. S. (1962). A twenty-two item screening score of psychiatric symptoms indicating impairment. *Journal of Health and Human Behavior*, 3, 269–276.

Langner, Thomas S. and Stanley T. Michael (1963). *Life Stress and Mental Health*. New York: Free Press.

Larson, R. F. and G. R. Leslie (1968). Prestige influences in serious dating relationships. *Social Forces*, 47, 195–202.

LaVoie, J. (1974). Type of punishment as a determinant of resistance to deviation. *Developmental Psychology*, 10, 181–189.

Lawler, G. C., III (1968). Effects of hourly overpayment on productivity and work quality. *Journal of Personality and Social Psychology, 10,* 306–313.

Lay, C. H. and D. N. Jackson (1969). Analysis of the generality of trait inferential relationships. *Journal of Personality and Social Psychology, 12,* 12–21.

Lazarus, A. A. (1968). Learning theory and the treatment of depression. *Behavior Research and Therapy, 6,* 83–89.

Lazarus, R. S. (1967). Cognitive and personality factors underlying threat and coping. In Mortimer H. Appley and Richard Trumbull, Eds., *Psychological Stress.* New York: Appleton-Century-Crofts.

Lazarus, R. S. (1975). The self-regulation of emotion. In Lennart Levi. Ed., *Emotions: Their Parameters and Measurement.* New York: Raven.

Lazarus, R. S. and J. S. Averill (1972). Emotion and cognition: With special reference to anxiety. In Charles D. Spielberger, Ed., *Anxiety: Current Trends in Theory and Research,* Vol 2. New York: Academic.

Lazaarus, R. S., J. S. Averill, and E. M. Opton, Jr. (1970) Toward a cognitive theory of emotions. In Magda B. Arnold, Ed., *Feelings and Emotions.* New York: Academic.

Lazarus, R. S. and E. M. Opton, Jr. (1966). The study of psychological stress. A summary of theoretical formulations and theoretical findings. In Charles D. Spielberger, Ed., *Anxiety and Behavior.* New York: Academic.

Lazarus, R. S., J. C. Spiesman, A. M. Mordkoff, and L. A. Davison (1962). A laboratory study of psychological stress produced by a motion picture film. *Psychological Monographs, 76,* No. 34 (whole No. 553).

Lee, Wayne (1971). *Decision Theory and Human Behavior.* New York: Wiley.

Leary, Timothy (1957). *The Interpersonal Diagnosis of Personality.* New York: Ronald.

Lenski, Gerhard (1966). *Power and Privilege.* New York: McGraw-Hill.

Lepper, M. (1973). Dissonance, self-perception, and honesty in children. *Journal of Personality and Social Psychology, 25,* 65–74.

Lerner, M. (1974). Social psychology of justice and interpersonal attraction. In Ted L. Huston, Ed., *Foundations of Interpersonal Attraction.* New York: Academic.

Lerner, M. and G. Matthews (1967). Reactions to the sufferings of others under conditions of indirect responsibility. *Journal of Personality and Social Psychology, 5,* 319–325.

Lerner, M. J. and R. R. Lichtman (1968). Effects of perceived norms on attitudes and altruistic behavior toward a dependent other. *Journal of Personality and Social Psychology, 9,* 226–232.

Leslie, Gerald R. (1976). *The Family in Social Context.* New York: Oxford University Press.

Leventhal, G. S., J. Allen and B. Kemelgor (1969). Reducing inequity by reallocating rewards. *Psychonomic Science, 14,* 295–296.

Leventhal, G. S. and J. T. Bergman (1969). Self-depriving behavior as a response to unprofitable inequity. *Journal of Experimental Social Psychology, 5,* 153–171.

Levi, L. (1972). Sympathoadrenomedullary responses to "pleasant" and "unpleasant" psychosocial stimuli. In Lennart, Levi, Ed., *Stress and Distress in Response to Psychosocial Stimuli: Laboratory and Real Life Studies in Sympathoadrenomedullary and Related Reactions. Acta Medica Scandanavica.* Supplementum 528. Stockholm: Almquist and Wiksell.

Levi, Lennart (1975). Ed., *Emotions: Their Parameters and Measurement.* New York: Raven.

Levi-Strauss, Claude (1969). *Structural Anthropology*. Garden City, N.Y.: Doubleday.

Levine, Sol and Norman Scotch, Eds. (1970) *Social Stress*. Chicago: Aldine.

Levinger, G. and J. D. Snoek (1972). *Attraction in Relationships: A New Look at Interpersonal Attraction*. New York: General Learning Press.

Levinson, Harry (1964). *Emotional Problems in the World of Work*. New York: Harper and Row.

Levy, L. H. and R. D. Dugan (1960). A constant error approach to the study of dimensions of social perception. *Journal of Abnormal and Social Psychology*, 61, 21–24.

Levy, Leo and Louis Rowitz (1973). *The Ecology of Mental Disorders*. New York: Behavioral Publications.

Lewin, K., T. Dembo, L. Festinger, and P. Sears (1944). Level of aspiration. In J. McVickers Hunt, Ed., *Personality and the Behavior Disorders*. New York: Ronald.

Lewis, Helen B. (1971). *Shame and Guilt in Neurosis*. New York: International Universities Press.

Lex, B. W. (1974). Voodoo death: New thoughts on an old explanation. *American Anthropologist*, 76, 818–823.

Lidz, T. and S. Fleck (1960). Schizophrenia, human integration and the role of the family. In Don D. Jackson, Ed., *The Etiology of Schizophrenia*. New York: Basic.

Liebert, Robert (1971). *Radical and Militant Youth: A Psychoanalytic Perspective*. New York: Praeger.

Linsky, A. (1969). Community structure and depressive disorders. *Social Problems*, 17, 120–131.

Linton, Ralph (1945). *The Cultural Background of Personality*. New York: Appleton-Century-Crofts.

Locke, Harvey J. (1951). *Predicting Adjustment in Marriage: A Comparison of a Divorced and a Happily Married Group*. New York: Greenwood, 1968.

Loeb, A., A. T. Beck, and J. Diggory (1971). Differential effects of success and failure on depressed and non-depressed patients. *Journal of Nervous and Mental Disease*, 152, 106–114.

Lofland, J. (1970). Interactionist imagery and analytic interruptus. In Tamotsu Shibutani, Ed., *Human Nature and Collective Behavior: Papers in Honor of Herbert Blumer*. Englewood Cliffs, N.J.: Prentice-Hall.

Logan, F. A. (1973). Self-control as habit, drive, and incentive. *Journal of Abnormal Psychology*, 81, 127–136.

Longabaugh, R. (1966). The structure of interpersonal behavior. *Sociometry*, 29, 441–460.

Lopreato, J. and L. Alston (1970). Ideal types and idealization strategy. *American Sociological Review*, 35, 88–96.

Lorenz, Konrad (1966). *On Aggression*. New York: Harper.

Lorr, M. and D. M. McNair (1963). An interpersonal behavior circle. *Journal of Abnormal and Social Psychology*, 67, 69–75.

Lorr, Maurice, James Klett, and Douglas M. McNair (1963). *Syndromes of Psychosis*. New York: Macmillan.

Lott, A. J. and B. E. Lott (1974). The role of reward in the formation of positive interpersonal attitudes. In Ted L. Huston, Ed., *Foundations of Interpersonal Attraction*. New York: Academic.

Lu, Y. (1962). Contradictory parental expectations in schizophrenia: Dependence and responsibilities. *Archives of General Psychiatry, 6*, 219–235.

Ludwig, A. M. and L. H. Stark (1973). Schizophrenia, sensory deprivation, and sensory overload. *Journal of Nervous and Mental Disease, 157*, 210–216.

Lynn, D. and W. Sawrey (1959). The effects of father absence on Norwegian boys and girls. *Journal of Abnormal and Social Psychology, 59*, 258–262.

MacClean, P. D. (1965). New findings relevant to the evolution of the psychosexual functions of the brain. In John Money, Ed., *Sex Research: New Developments*. New York: Holt, Rinehart, Winston.

MacPhillamy, D. J. and P. M. Lewinsohn (1974). Depression as a function of desired and obtained pleasure. *Journal of Abnormal Psychology, 83*, 651–657.

Maccoby, E. E. and J. C. Masters (1970). Attachment and dependency. In Paul H. Mussen, Ed., *Carmichael's Manual of Child Psychology*, Vol. 2. New York: Wiley.

Maccoby, E. E. (1961). The choice of variables in the study of socialization. *Sociometry, 24*, 357–371.

Mandler, G. (1962). Emotion. In R. Brown, E. Galanter, E. Hess, and G. Mandler, Eds., *New Directions in Psychology*. New York: Holt, Rinehart, Winston.

Mandler, G. (1975). The search for emotion. In Lennart Levi, Ed., *Emotions: Their Parameters and Measurement*. New York: Raven.

Mannheim, Karl (1936). *Ideology and Utopia*. London: International Library of Psychology, Philosophy, and Scientific Method.

Marchbanks, V. H. (1958). Effects of flying stress on urinary 17-hydroxycorticosteroid levels: Observations during a 22½ hour mission. *Journal of Aviation Medicine, 29*, 676–682.

Mark, J. C. (1953). The attitudes of mothers of male schizophrenics. *Journal of Abnormal and Social Psychology, 48*, 185–189.

Marlowe, D. and K. Gergen (1969). Personality and social interaction. In Gardner Lindzey and Elliot Aronson, Eds., *The Handbook of Social Psychology*, 2nd ed., Vol. 3. Reading, Mass.: Addison-Wesley.

Marlowe, R. H. (1968). Development of marital dissatisfaction of Mormon college couples over the early stages of the life cycle. Unpublished Master's thesis, Brigham Young University.

Marwell, G. and D. R. Schmitt (1967). Dimensions of compliance-gaining behavior: An empirical analysis. *Sociometry, 30*, 350–364.

Marx, Karl (1964a). *Selected Writings in Sociology and Social Philosophy*. T. B. Bottomore and Maximillian Rubel, Eds. New York: McGraw-Hill.

Marx, Karl (1964b). *Early Writings*, translated and edited by T. B. Bottomore. New York: McGraw-Hill.

Marx, Karl and Friedrich Engels (1959). *Basic Writings on Politics and Philosophy*. Lewis Feuer, Ed. Garden City, N.Y.: Doubleday.

Maslow, Abraham (1954). *Motivation and Personality*. New York: Harper.

Maslow, Abraham (1968). *Toward a Psychology of Being*, 2nd ed. New York: Van Nostrand Reinhold.

Mason, J. W. and J. V. Brady (1964). The sensitivity of psychoendocrine systems to social and physical environment. In P. Herbert Leiderman and David Shapiro, Eds.,

Psychobiological Approaches to Social Behavior. Stanford: Stanford University Press.

Masters, William H. and Virginia E. Johnson (1966). *Human Sexual Response.* Boston: Little, Brown.

Masters, William H. and Virginia E. Johnson (1969). *Human Sexual Adequacy.* Boston: Little, Brown.

Matras, Judah (1975). *Social Inequality, Stratification, and Mobility.* New York: Prentice-Hall.

Matza, D. (1966). Poverty and disrepute. In Robert K. Merton and Robert A. Nisbett, Eds., *Contemporary Social Problems.* New York: Harcourt Brace.

Mazur, Allan and Leon S. Robertson (1972). *Biology and Social Behavior.* New York: Free Press.

McCall, G. J. (1974). A symbolic interactionist approach to attraction. In Ted L. Huston, Ed., *Foundations of Interpersonal Attraction.* New York: Academic.

McCarthy, J. D. and W. L. Yancey (1971). Uncle Tom and Mr. Charlie: Metaphysical pathos in the study of racism and personal disorganization. *American Journal of Sociology, 76,* 648–672.

McClelland, David D., John W. Atkinson, R. A. Clarke, and E. L. Lowell (1953). *The Achievement Motive.* New York: Appleton-Century-Crofts.

McClendon, M. J. (1976). The occupational status attainment processes of males and females. *American Sociological Review, 41,* 52–64.

McCord, William and Joan McCord (1964). *Psychopathy.* New York: Van Nostrand Reinhold.

McCord, W., J. McCord, and A. Howard (1961). Familial correlates of aggression in non-delinquent male children. *Journal of Abnormal and Social Psychology, 62,* 79–93.

McCreary, C. P. (1974). Comparison of measures of social competency in schizophrenics and the relation of social competency to socioeconomic factors. *Journal of Abnormal Psychology, 83,* 124–129.

McDougall, William (1933). *The Energies of Men.* New York: Scribners.

McGhee, P. E. and V. C. Crandall (1968). Belief in internal-external control of reinforcements and academic performance. *Child Development, 39,* 91–101.

McKinley, Donald G. (1964). *Social Class and Family Life.* New York: Free Press.

Mead, George H. (1934). *Mind, Self, and Society.* Chicago: University of Chicago Press.

Mechanic, D. (1966). The sociology of medicine: Viewpoints and perspectives. *Journal of Health and Human Behavior, 7,* 1–12.

Mechanic, David (1968). *Medical Sociology: A Selective View.* New York: Free Press.

Mechanic, D. (1972). Social class and schizophrenia: some requirements for a plausible theory of social influence. *Social Forces, 50,* 305–309.

Mechanic, D. (1974). Discussion of research programs on relations between stressful life events and episodes of physical illness. In Barbara S. Dohrenwend and Bruce P. Dohrenwend, Eds., *Stressful Life Events: Their Nature and Effects.* New York: Wiley.

Meeker, B. F. (1971). Decisions and exchange. *American Sociological Review, 36,* 485–495.

Merton, R. K. (1957). Continuities in the theory of reference groups and social structure. In Robert K. Merton, *Social Theory and Social Structure,* revised and enlarged ed. Glencoe, Ill.: Free Press.

Merton, R. K. (1959). Social conformity, deviation and opportunity structures: A comment on the contributions of Dubin and Cloward. *American Sociological Review*, *24*, 177–189.

Merton, R. K. and A. Kitt (1957). Contributions to the theory of reference groups. In Robert K. Merton, *Social Theory and Social Structure*, revised and enlarged ed. Glencoe, Ill.: Free Press.

Michelini, R. L. and L. A. Messé (1974). Reactions to threat as a function of equity. *Sociometry*, *37*, 432–439.

Michener, H. A. and M. Schwertfeger (1972). Liking as a determinant of power tactic preference. *Sociometry*, *35*, 190–202.

Michener, H. A., J. J. Vaske, S. L. Schleifer, J. G. Plazewski, and L. J. Chapman (1975). Factors affecting concession rate and threat usage in bilateral conflict. *Sociometry*, *38*, 62–80.

Miller, D. R. (1962). On the definition óf problems and the interpretation of symptoms. *Journal of Consulting Psychology*, *26*, 302–305.

Miller, G. A. (1956). The magical number seven, plus or minus two: Some limits on our capacity for processing information. *Psychological Review*, *63*, 81–97.

Miller, N. E. (1944). Experimental studies of conflict. In James McV. Hunt, Ed., *Personality and the Behavior Disorders*, Vol. 1. New York: Ronald.

Miller, N. E. (1973). Autonomic learning: Clinical and physiological implications. In Muriel Hammer, Kurt Salzinger, and Samuel Sutton, Eds., *Psychopathology: Contributions from Social, Behavioral, and Biological Sciences*. New York: Wiley.

Miller, N. E. and R. Bugelski (1948). Minor studies in aggression: the influence of frustrations imposed by the in-group on attitudes expressed toward outgroups. *Journal of Psychology*, *25*, 437–442.

Miller, S. M. and E. G. Mishler (1959). Social Class, mental illness, and American psychiatry: An expository review. *Milbank Memorial Fund Quarterly*, *37* (2), 1–26.

Miller, W. B. (1958). Lower class culture as a generating milieu of gang delinquency. *Journal of Social Issues*, *14*, 5–19.

Mills, C. Wright (1956). *The Power Elite*. New York: Oxford University Press.

Mintz, N. L. and D. T. Schwartz (1964). Urban ecology and psychosis: Community factors in the incidence of schizophrenia and manic-depression among Italians in Greater Boston. *International Journal of Social Psychiatry*, *10*, 101–118.

Mischel, W. and E. Staub (1965). Effects of expectancy on working and waiting for larger rewards. *Journal of Personality and Social Psychology*, *2*, 625–633.

Mishler, E. G. and N. A. Scotch (1963). Sociocultural factors in the epidemiology of schizophrenia. *Psychiatry*, *26*, 315–343.

Mishler, Elliot G. and Nancy E. Waxler (1968). *Interaction in Families*. New York: Wiley.

Miyamoto, F. and S. Dornbusch (1956). A test of social interactionist hypotheses of self-conceptions. *American Journal of Sociology*, *61*, 399–403.

Modigliani, A. (1968). Embarrassment and embarrassability. *Sociometry*, *31*, 313–326.

Mogy, R. B. and D. G. Pruitt (1974). Effects of a threatener's enforcement costs on threat credibility and compliance. *Journal of Personality and Social Psychology*, *29*, 173–180.

Moos, R. H. (1969). Sources of variance in responses to questionnaires and in behavior. *Journal of Abnormal Psychology*, *74*, 405–412.

Morris, C. (1939). Aesthetics and the theory of signs. *Journal of Unified Science*, 8, 131–150.

Morris, Charles (1956). *Varieties of Human Values*. Chicago: University of Chicago Press.

Moss, Gordon E. (1973). *Illness, Immunity, and Social Interaction*. New York: Wiley.

Moulton, R. W., E. Burnstein, P. G. Liberty, Jr., and N. Altucher (1966). Patterning of parental affection and disciplinary dominance as a determinant of guilt and sex-typing. *Journal of Personality and Social Psychology*, 4, 356–363.

Mowrer, O. Hobart (1960). *Learning Theory and Behavior*. New York: Wiley.

Mowrer, O. H. (1966). The basis of psychopathology: Malconditioning or misbehavior. In Charles D. Spielberger, Ed., *Anxiety and Behavior*. New York: Academic.

Moyer, K. E. (1967). Kinds of aggression and their physiological basis. Carnegie-Mellon University Report No. 67–12.

Moyer, K. E. (1968). Kinds of aggression and their physiological basis. *Communications in Behavioral Biology*, 2, 65–87.

Moyer, K. E. (1971). A preliminary physiological model of aggressive behavior. In Basil Eleftheriou and John P. Scott, Eds., *The Physiology of Aggression and Defeat*. New York: Plenum.

Muenzinger, K. F. (1934). Motivation in learning: I. Electric shock for correct response in the visual discrimination habit. *Journal of Comparative Psychology*, 17, 267–277.

Mulaik, S. A. (1964). Are personality factors raters' conceptual factors? *Journal of Consulting and Clinical Psychology*, 28, 506–511.

Munro, A. (1966). Some familial and social factors in depressive illness. *British Journal of Psychiatry*, 112, 429–441.

Murphy, H. B. M., E. D. Wittkower, and N. W. Chance (1970). The symptoms of depression—A cross-cultural survey. In Ihsan Al-Issa and Wayne Dennis, Eds., *Cross-Cultural Studies of Behavior*. New York: Holt, Rinehart, Winston.

Murray, Henry A. (1938). *Explorations in Personality*. New York: Oxford University Press.

Murstein, B. I. (1970). Stimulus-value-role: A theory of marital choice. *Journal of Marriage and Family*, 32, 465–481.

Murstein, B. I. (1972). Physical attraction and marital choice. *Journal of Marriage and Family*, 22, 8–12.

Murstein, B. I. (1976). Physical attractiveness and marriage adjustment in middle-aged couples. *Journal of Personality and Social Psychology*, 24, 537–542.

Mussen, Paul, Ed. (1970). *Carmichael's Manual of Child Psychology*, 3rd ed., Vols. 1 and 2. New York: Wiley.

Mussen, P. and L. Distler (1959). Masculinity, identification, and father-son relationships. *Journal of Abnormal and Social Psychology*, 59, 350–356.

Mussen, P. H. and E. Rutherford (1963). Parent-child relationships and parent personality in relation to young children's sex-role preferences. *Child Development*, 34, 589–607.

Myers, Jerome K. and Bertram H. Roberts (1959). *Family and Class Dynamics in Mental Illness*. New York: Wiley.

Myers, Robert J. (1977). Fear, anger and depression in organizations: A study of the emotional consequences of power. Unpublished Ph.D. dissertation, St. John's University.

Nadel, Siegfried F. (1957). *The Theory of Social Structure*. New York: Free Press.

National Advisory Commission on Civil Disorders (1968). *Report*. Washington, D.C.: U. S. Government Printing Office.

Nemeth, C. (1970). Effect of free versus constrained behavior on attraction between people. *Journal of Personality and Social Psychology, 15*, 302–311.

Nettler, G. (1959). Cruelty, dignity, and determinism. *American Sociological Review, 24*, 375–384.

Nomikos, M. S., E. Opton, Jr., J. R. Averill, and R. S. Lazarus (1968). Surprise versus suspense in the production of stress reaction. *Journal of Personality and Social Psychology, 8*, 204–208.

Norman, W. T. (1963). Toward an adequate taxonomy of personality attributes: replicated factor structure in peer nomination personality ratings. *Journal of Abnormal and Social Psychology, 66*, 574–583.

Norman, W. T. and L. R. Goldberg (1966). Raters, ratees, and randomness in personality structure. *Journal of Personality and Social Psychology, 4*, 681–691.

Nowlis, V. (1970). Mood: Behavior and experience. In Magda B. Arnold, Ed., *Feelings and Emotions*. New York: Academic.

O'Neill, Nena and George O'Neill (1972). *Open Marriage*. New York: M. Evans and Lippincott.

Olds, J. (1962). Hypothalamic subtrates of reward. *Physiological Review, 42*, 554–604.

Olds, J. (1973). Brain mechanisms of reinforcement learning. In Daniel E. Berlyne and Karl B. Madsen, Eds., *Pleasure, Reward, Preference: Their Nature, Determinants, and Role in Behavior*. New York: Academic.

Olson, D. H. (1969). The measurement of family power by self-report and behavioral methods. *Journal of Marriage and Family, 31*, 545–550.

Opler, Marvin K. (1956). *Culture, Psychiatry, and Human Values*. Springfield, Ill.: Thomas.

Orden, S. R. and N. M. Bradburn (1968) Dimensions of marriage happiness. *American Journal of Sociology, 73*, 715–731.

Orlinsky, D. (1972) Love relationships in the life cycle. In Herbert A. Otto, Ed., *Love Today: A New Exploration*. New York: Association.

Orne, M. T. (1962). On the social psychology of the psychological experiment: With particular attention to demand characteristics and their implications. *American Psychologist, 17*, 776–783.

Osgood, C. E. (1966). Dimensionality of the semantic space for communication via facial expressions. *Scandinavian Journal of Psychology, 7*, 1–30.

Osgood, Charles E., G. C. Suci, and Percy H. Tannenbaum (1954). *The Measurement of Meaning* Urbana: University of Illinois Press.

Pallak, M. S. and T. S. Pittman (1972). General motivational effects of dissonance arousal. *Journal of Personality and Social Behavior, 21* 349–358.

Parke, R. D. (1969). Effectiveness of punishment as an interaction of intensity, time, agent nurturance and cognitive structure. *Child Development 40*, 213–235.

Parker, Seymour and Robert J. Kleiner (1966). *Mental Illness in the Urban Negro Community*. New York: Free Press.

Parsons, Talcott (1950). *The Social System*. Glencoe, Ill.: Free Press.

Parsons, T. (1954a). A revised analytical view of stratification. In Talcott Parsons, *Essays in Sociological Theory*, revised ed. Glencoe, Ill.: Free Press.

Parsons, T. (1954b). Age and sex in the social structure. In Talcott Parsons, *Essays in Sociological Theory*, revised ed. Glencoe, Ill.: Free Press.

Parsons, T. (1955). Family structure and the socialization of the child. In Talcott Parsons and Robert F. Bales, Eds., *Family, Socialization, and Interaction Process*. Glencoe, Ill.: Free Press.

Parsons, T. (1956). Suggestions for a sociological approach to the theory of organizations. *Administrative Science Quarterly, 1*, 63–85.

Parsons, T. (1960). Durkheim's contributions to the theory of integration of social systems. In Kurt H. Wolff, Ed., *Emile Durkheim, 1858–1917*. Columbus: Ohio State University Press.

Parsons, T. (1963). On the concept of political power. *Proceedings of the American Philosophical Society, 107*, 232–262.

Parsons, Talcott (1967). *Sociological Theory and Modern Society*. New York: Free Press.

Parsons, T., R. F. Bales, and E. A. Shils (1953). Phase movement in relation to motivation, symbol formation, and role structure. In Talcott Parsons, Robert F. Bales, and Edward A. Shils, *Working Papers in the Theory of Action*. Glencoe, Ill.: Free Press.

Parton, D. A. (1964). The study of aggression in boys with an operant device. *Journal of Experimental Child Psychology, 1*, 79–88.

Passini, F. T. and W. T. Norman (1966). A universal conception of personality structure? *Journal of Personality and Social Psychology, 4*, 44–49.

Pastore, N. (1952). The role of arbitrariness in the frustration-aggression hypothesis. *Journal of Abnormal and Social Psychology, 47*, 728–731.

Pastore, N. (1960). A note on changing attitudes toward liked and disliked persons. *Journal of Social Psychology, 52*, 173–175.

Patchen, M. (1961). A conceptual framework and some empirical data regarding comparisons of social rewards. *Sociometry, 24*, 136–156.

Patkai, P. (1967). Catecholamine excretion and performance. In Lennart Levi, Ed., *Emotional Stress: Physiological and Psychological Reactions: Medical, Industrial and Military Applications*. New York: Elsevier.

Patkai, P. (1971a). Catecholamine excretion in pleasant and unpleasant situations. *Acta Psychologica, 35*, 352–363.

Patkai, P. (1971b). Interindividual differences in diurnal variations in alertness, performance, and adrenaline excretion. *Acta Physiologica Scandanavica, 81*, 35–46.

Patkai, P., M. Frankenhaeuser, A. Rissler, and C. Bjorkvall (1967). Catecholamine excretion, performance, and subjective stress. *Scandanavian Journal of Psychology, 8*, 113–122.

Patterson, G. R. (1965). Parents as dispensers of aversive stimuli. *Journal of Personality and Social Psychology, 2*, 844–851.

Patterson, G. R., H. Hops, and R. L. Weiss (1975). Interpersonal skills training for couples in early stages of conflict. *Journal of Marriage and Family, 37*, 295–303.

Patterson, G. R., R. A. Littman, and W. Bricker (1967). Assertive behavior in children: A step toward a theory of aggression. *Monographs of the Society for Research in Child Development, 32*, Whole No. 113.

Paul, G. L. and D. A. Bernstein (1973). *Anxiety and Clinical Problems: Systematic Desensitization and Related Techniques*. New York: General Learning.

Peele, Stanton and Archie Brodsky (1975). *Love and Addiction*. New York: Taplinger.

Pepitone, Albert (1964). *Attraction and Hostility*. New York: Atherton

Pepitone, A. (1968). An experimental analysis of self-dynamics. In Chad Gordon and Kenneth Gergen, Eds., *The Self in Social Interaction: Vol. 1, Classic and Contemporary Perspectives*. New York: Wiley.

Pepitone, A. (1971). The role of justice in independent decision-making. *Journal of Experimental Social Psychology*, 7, 144–156.

Pepitone, A. and G. Reichling (1955). Group cohesiveness and the expression of hostility. *Human Relations*, 8, 327–337.

Pepitone, A., A. Madera, E. Caporicci, E. Tiberi, G. Iacono, G. Dimaio, M. Perfetto, A. Asprea, G. Villone, G. Fua, and F. Tonucci (1970). Justice in choice behavior, a cross-cultural analysis. *International Journal of Psychology*, 5, 1–10.

Peterson, R. A. (1971). Aggression as a function of expected retaliation and aggression level of target and aggressor. *Developmental Psychology*, 5, 161–166.

Phillips, Leslie (1968). *Human Adaptation and its Failures*. New York: Academic.

Piaget, Jean (1932). *The Moral Judgment of the Child*. Glencoe, Ill.: Free Press, 1948.

Pike, K. L. (1967). Language as behavior and etic and emic standpoints for the description of behavior. In Edgar F. Borgatta, Ed., *Social Psychology: Readings and Perspective*. Chicago: Rand-McNally.

Pilisuk, M. and P. Skolnick (1968). Inducing trust: A test of the Osgood proposal. *Journal of Personality and Social Psychology*, 8, 121–133.

Pineo, P. (1961). Disenchantment in the later years of marriage. *Marriage and Family Living*, 23, 3–11.

Pisano, R. and S. P. Taylor (1971). Reduction of physical aggression: The effects of four strategies. *Journal of Personality and Social Psychology*, 19, 237–242.

Plutchik, Robert (1962). *The Emotions: Facts, Theories, and a New Model*. New York: Random House.

Plutchik, R. and A. F. Ax (1967). A critique of *Determinants of Emotional State* by Schachter and Singer (1962). *Psychophysiology*, 4, 79–82.

Polsby, N. W. (1959). Community power: Three problems. *American Sociological Review*, 24, 796–803.

Pribam, K. H. (1970). Feelings as monitors. In Magda B. Arnold, Ed., *Feelings and Emotions*. New York: Academic.

Price, J. (1968). The genetics of depressive behavior. In Alec Coppen and Alexander Walk, Eds., *Recent Developments in Affective Disorders*. Ashford, England: Headley.

Prince, R. (1967). The changing picture of depressive syndromes in Africa: Is it fact or diagnostic fashion? *Canadian Journal of African Studies*, 1, 177–192.

Psathas, George, Ed., (1973). *Phenomenological Sociology*. New York: Wiley.

Rapoport, Anatol (1960). *Fights, Games, and Debates*. Ann Arbor: University of Michigan Press.

Rapoport, Anatol and A. M. Chamah (1965). *Prisoner's Dilemma*. Ann Arbor: University of Michigan Press.

Rausch, H. (1965). Interaction sequences. *Journal of Personality and Social Psychology*, 2, 487–499.

Raven, B. H. (1965). Social influence and power. In Ivan D. Steiner and Martin Fishbein, Eds., *Current Studies in Social Psychology*. Holt, Rinehart, Winston.

Rawnsley, K. (1968). Epidemiology of affective disorders. In Alec Coppen and Alexander Walk, Eds., *Recent Developments in Affective Disorders*. Ashford, England: Headley.

Regan, D. T., M. Williams, and S. Sparling (1972). Voluntary expiation of guilt: A field experiment. *Journal of Personality and Social Psychology, 24,* 242–45.

Reichard, S. and C. Tillman (1950). Patterns of parent-child relationship in schizophrenia. *Psychiatry, 13,* 247–258.

Reimanis, G. (1974). Psychosocial development, anomie, and mood. *Journal of Personality and Social Psychology, 29,* 355–357.

Reiser, M. F., R. B. Reeves, and J. Armington (1955). Effects of variations in laboratory procedures and experimenter upon the ballistocardiogram, blood pressure, and heart rate in healthy young men. *Psychosomatic Medicine, 17,* 185–199.

Reusch, J. (1953). Discussion. In Daniel H. Funkenstein, S. H. King, and M. Drolette, The experimental evocation of stress. *Symposium on Stress.* National Research Council and Army Medical Service Graduate School, Walter Reed Army Medical Center, Washington, D.C.

Reymert, Martin L., Ed. (1950) *Feelings and Emotions.* New York: McGraw-Hill.

Richie, M. H., L. M. McClelland, and A. M. Shimunkas (1967). Relative influence of positive and negative information in impression formation and persistence. *Journal of Personality and Social Psychology, 6,* 322–327.

Ricks, D. F. and J. C. Berry (1970). Family system and patterns that precede schizophrenia. In Merril Roff and David F. Ricks, Eds., *Life History Research and Psychopathology.* Minneapolis: University of Minnesota Press.

Riesman, David, Nathan Glazer, and Ruell Denny (1953). *The Lonely Crowd.* Garden City, N.Y.: Doubleday.

Riker, W. H. (1974). The nature of trust. In James T. Tedeschi, Ed., *Perspectives on Social Power.* Chicago: Aldine.

Riley, M. W., R. Cohn, J. Toby, and J. W. Riley, Jr. (1954). Interpersonal relations in small groups. *American Sociological Review, 19,* 715–724.

Rinn, J. L. (1965). The structure of phenomenal domains. *Psychological Review, 72,* 445–466.

Roberts, M. R. and L. M. Cooper (1967). Patterns of parent discipline. *Journal of Social Psychology, 71,* 257–266.

Robins, Lee N. (1966). *Deviant Children Grow Up.* Baltimore: Williams and Wilkins.

Robins, L. N., G. E. Murphy, R. A. Woodruff, and L. J. King (1971). Adult psychiatric status of Black school boys. *Archives of General Psychiatry, 24,* 338–345.

Rodman, H. (1963). The lower class value stretch. *Social Forces, 42,* 205–215.

Rodnick, E. H. and N. Garmezy (1957). An experimental approach to the study of motivation in schizophrenia. In Marshall R. Jones, Ed., *Nebraska Symposium on Motvation,* Vol. 5. Lincoln: University of Nebraska Press.

Rogler, L. H. and A. B. Hollingshead (1961). Class and disordered speech in the mentally ill. *Journal of Health and Human Behavior, 2,* 178–185.

Rollins, B. C. and H. Feldman (1970). Marital satisfaction over the family life cycle. *Journal of Marriage and Family, 32,* 20–28.

Rose, Arnold H. (1967). *The Power Structure.* New York: Oxford University Press.

Rosen, B. C. (1959). Race, ethnicity, and achievement. *American Sociological Review, 24,* 47–60.

Rossi, A. S. (1968). Transition to parenthood. *Journal of Marriage and Family, 30,* 26–39.

Rotter, J. B. (1966). Generalized expectancies for internal versus external control of reinforcement. *Psychological Monographs, 80,* (1), Whole No. 609.

Rotter, J. B. (1967). A new scale for the measurement of interpersonal trust. *Journal of Personality, 35,* 651–655.

Rotter, Julian B., June E. Chance, and E. Jerry Phares (1974). *Applications of a Social Learning Theory of Personality.* New York: Holt, Rinehart, Winston.

Rubin, Z. (1969). The social psychology of romantic love. Unpublished Ph.D. Dissertation, University of Michigan.

Rubin, Z. (1970). Measurement of romantic love. *Journal of Personality and Social Psychology, 16,* 265–273.

Rummel, R. J. (1966). Some dimensions in the foreign behavior of nations. *Journal of Peace Research, 3,* 201–224.

Runciman, W. G. (1966). *Relative Deprivation and Social Justice: A Study of Attitudes to Social Inequality in 20th Century England.* Berkeley: University of California Press.

Runciman, W. G. (1968). Class, status, and power? In J. A. Jackson, Ed., *Social Stratification.* Cambridge, England: Cambridge University Press.

Rushing, W. A. (1969). Deviance, interpersonal relations and suicide. *Human Relations, 22,* 61–76.

Ryan, William (1971). *Blaming the Victim.* New York: Pantheon.

Rylchak, J. F. (1965). The similarity, compatibility, or incompatibility of needs in interpersonal selection. *Journal of Personality and Social Psychology, 2,* 334–340.

Safilios-Rothschild, C. (1970). The study of family power structure: A review, 1960–1969. *Journal of Marriage and Family, 32,* 539–552.

Sales, S. M., R. M. Guydosh, and W. Iacono (1974). Strength of the nervous system and need for stimulation. *Journal of Personality and Social Psychology, 29,* 16–22.

Salinger, Joseph D. (1951). *Catcher in the Rye.* Boston: Little, Brown.

Saltz, E. (1970). Manifest anxiety: Have we misread the data? *Psychological Review, 77,* 568–573.

Santayana, George (1896). *The Sense of Beauty.* New York: Scribner.

Sarnoff, Irving (1962). *Personality Dynamics and Development.* New York: Wiley.

Savage, C. and R. Prince (1967). Depression among the Yoruba. In Werner Muensterberg and Signey Axelrad, Eds. *The Psychoanalytic Study of Society,* Vol. 4. New York: International University Press.

Scanzoni, John (1972). *Sexual Bargaining: Power Politics in American Marriage.* Englewood Cliffs, N.J.: Prentice-Hall.

Schachter, J. (1957). Pain, fear, and anger in hypertensives and normotensives: A psychological study. *Psychosomatic Medicine, 19,* 19–29.

Schachter, S. (1951). Deviation, Rejection, and Communication. *Journal of Abnormal and Social Psychology, 46,* 190–207.

Schachter, Stanley (1959). *The Psychology of Affiliation.* Stanford: Stanford University Press.

Schachter, S. (1964). The interaction of cognitive and physiological determinants of emotional state. In P. Herbert Leiderman and David Shapiro, Eds., *Psychobiological Approaches to Social Behavior.* Stanford: Stanford University Press.

Schachter, S. (1967). Cognitive effects on bodily functioning: studies of obesity and eating. In David C. Glass, Ed., *Neurophysiology and Emotion*. New York: Rockefeller University Press and Russell Sage Foundation.

Schachter, S. and J. Singer (1962). Cognitive, social, and physiological determinants of emotional state. *Psychological Review, 69*, 379–399.

Schachter, S. and L. Wheeler (1962). Epinephrine, chlorpromazine, and amusement. *Journal of Abnormal and Social Psychology, 65*, 121–128.

Schaefer, E. S. (1959). A circumplex model for maternal behavior. *Journal of Abnormal and Social Psychology, 59*, 226–235.

Schaefer, E. S. (1961). Converging conceptual models for maternal behavior and for child behavior. In J. C. Glidewell, Ed., *Patental Attitudes and Child Behavior*. Springfield, Ill.: Thomas.

Schaefer, E. S. (1965a). A configurational analysis of children's reports of parent behavior. *Journal of Consulting Psychology, 29*, 552–557.

Schaefer, E. S. (1965b). Children's reports of parental behavior: An inventory. *Child Development, 36*, 413–424.

Scheff, Thomas J. (1966). *Being Mentally Ill: A Sociological Theory*. Chicago: Aldine.

Scheff, T. J. (1975). Reply to Chauncy and Gove. *American Sociological Review, 40*, 252–257.

Scheflen, Albert (1974). *How Behavior Means*. Garden City, N.Y.: Doubleday.

Schegeloff, E. (1968). Sequencing in conversational openings. *American Anthropologist, 70*, 1075–1095.

Scheler, Max (1954). *The Nature of Sympathy*, translated by Peter Heath. New Haven, Conn.: Yale University Press.

Schellenberg, J. A. and L. S. Bee (1960). A re-examination of the theory of complementary needs in mate selection. *Marriage and Family Living, 22*, 227–232.

Schildkraut, J. J. and S. S. Kety (1967). Biogenic amines and emotion. *Science, 156*, 21–30.

Schless, A. P., J. Mendels, A. Kipperman, and C. Cochrane (1974). Depression and hostility. *Journal of Nervous and Mental Disease, 159*, 91–100.

Schlossberg, H. (1954). Three dimensions of emotions. *Psychological Review, 61*, 81–88.

Schopler, J. and V. D. Thompson (1968). Role of attribution processes in mediating amount of reciprocity for a favor. *Journal of Personality and Social Psychology, 10*, 243–250.

Schuham, A. I. (1967) The double-bind hypothesis a decade later. *Psychological Bulletin, 68*, 409–416.

Schurman, Frederick L. (1935). *The Nazi Dictatorship*. New York: Knopf.

Schutz, W. C. (1958). *FIRO: A Three Dimensional Theory of Interpersonal Behavior*. New York: Holt, Rinehart, Winston.

Scott, J. F. (1965). The American college sorority: Its role in class and ethnic endogamy. *American Sociological Review, 30*, 514–527.

Scott, J. P. (1971). Theoretical issues concerning the origin and causes of fighting. In Basil E. Eleftheriou and John P. Scott, Eds., *The Physiology of Aggression and Defeat*. New York: Plenum.

Sears, Robert R., Eleanor E. Maccoby, and Harry Levin (1957). *Patterns of Child Rearing*. New York: Row, Peterson.

Secord, Paul F. and Carl Backman (1964). *Social Psychology*. New York: McGraw-Hill.

Seiler, L. H. (1973). The 22-item scale used in field studies of mental illness: A question of method, a question of substance, and a question of theory. *Journal of Health and Social Behavior, 14,* 252–264.

Sellin, Thorsten and Marvin Wolfgang (1964). *The Measurement of Delinquency.* New York: Wiley.

Sellin, Thorsten (1965). Ed., *Capital Punishment.* New York: Harper and Row.

Selye, Hans (1956). *The Stress of Life.* New York: McGraw-Hill.

Sennett, Richard and Jonathan Cobb (1972). *The Hidden Injuries of Class.* New York: Random House.

Shakow, D. (1963). Psychological deficit in schizophrenia. *Behavioral Science, 8,* 275–305.

Shamos, Morris H. (1959). *Great Experiments in Physics.* New York: Holt, Rinehart, Winston.

Shand, A. F. (1920). *The Foundations of Character.* London: MacMillan.

Shantz, D. W. and T. Pentz (1972). Situational effects on justifiableness of aggression at 3 age levels. *Child Development, 43,* 274–281.

Shaw, M. C. and J. Grubb (1958). Hostility and able high school underachievers. *Journal of Counseling Psychology, 5,* 263–266.

Shimunkas, A. M. (1970). Anxiety and expectancy change: The effects of failure and uncertainty. *Journal of Personality and Social Psychology, 15,* 34–42.

Shurcliff, A. (1968). Judged humor, arousal, and the relief theory. *Journal of Personality and Social Psychology, 8,* 360–363.

Simmel, Georg (1950). *The Sociology of Georg Simmel,* translated and edited by Kurt H. Wolff. Glencoe, Ill.: Free Press.

Simmons, C. H. and M. J. Lerner (1968). Altruism as the search for justice. *Journal of Personality and Social Psychology, 9,* 216–225.

Simon, R. J., J. L. Fleiss, B. J. Gurland, P. R. Stiller, and L. Sharpe (1973). Depression and schizophrenia in hospitalized black and white patients. *Archives of General Psychiatry, 28,* 509–512.

Simonov, P. (1970). The information theory of emotions. In Magda B. Arnold, Ed., *Feelings and Emotions.* New York: Academic.

Smith, G. P. (1973). Adrenal hormones and emotional behavior. In Elliott Stellar and James M. Sprague, Eds., *Progress in Physiological Psychology,* Vol. 5. New York: Academic.

Snygg, Donald and A. W. Combs (1949). *Individual Behavior.* New York: Harper.

Solomon, L. (1960). The influence of some types of power relationships and game strategies upon the development of interpersonal trust. *Journal of Abnormal and Social Psychology, 61,* 223–230.

Sonquist, John A. (1970). *Multivariate Model Building.* Ann Arbor: Institute of Social Research, University of Michigan.

Sorokin, Pitirim (1950). *Explorations in Altruistic Love and Behavior: A Symposium.* Boston: Beacon.

Sorokin, Pitirim (1954). *The Ways and Power of Love.* Boston: Beacon.

Spielberger, C. D. (1972). Anxiety as an emotional state. In Charles D. Spielberger, Ed., *Anxiety: Current Trends in Theory and Research,* Vol. 1. New York: Academic.

Spitz, René A. (1972). *The First Year of Life.* New York: International Universities Press.

Stabenau, J. R. and W. Pollin (1970). Experiential differences for schizophrenics as compared with their non-schizophrenic siblings: Twin and family studies. In Merrill Roff and David F. Ricks, Eds., *Life History Research in Psychopathology*. Minneapolis: University of Minnesota Press.

Stainbrook, E. (1954). A cross-cultural evaluation of depression reactions. In Paul H. Hoch and Joseph Zubin, Eds., *Depression*. New York: Grune and Stratton.

Stanley-Jones, D. (1970). The biological origins of love and hate. In Magda B. Arnold, Ed., *Feelings and Emotions*. New York: Academic.

Stein, M. (1967). Some psychophysiological considerations of the relationship between the autonomic nervous system and behavior. In David C. Glass, Ed., *Neurophysiology and Emotion*. New York: Rockefeller University Press and Russell Sage Foundation.

Stephenson, G. M. and J. H. White (1970). Privilege, deprivation, and children's moral behavior: An experimental clarification of the role of investments. *Journal of Experimental Social Psychology*, 7, 144–156.

Sternbach, Richard A. (1966). *Principles of Psychophysiology*. New York: Academic.

Stokols, D. (1975). Toward a psychological theory of alienation. *Psychological Review*, 82, 26–44.

Stotland, Ezra (1969). *The Psychology of Hope*. San Francisco: Jossey-Bass.

Stouffer, Samuel, Edward A. Suchman, Leland C. DeVinney, Shirley A. Star, and Robin H. Williams (1949). *Adjustment During Army Life*. Princeton, N.J.: Princeton University Press.

Straits, B. C. and P. L. Wuebben (1973). College students' reactions to social scientific experimentation. *Sociological Methods and Research*, 1, 355–386.

Straits, B. C., P. L. Wuebben, and T. J. Majka (1972). Influences on subjects' perceptions of experimental research situations. *Sociometry*, 35, 499–518.

Strasser, S. (1970). Feeling as a basis of knowing and recognizing the other as an ego. In Magda B. Arnold, Ed., *Feelings and Emotions*. New York: Academic.

Straus, M. (1964). Power and support structure of the family in relation to socialization. *Journal of Marriage and Family*, 26, 318–326.

Straus, M. (1974). Leveling, civility, and violence in the family. *Journal of Marriage and Family*, 36, 13–29.

Stringer, P. (1973). Do dimensions have face validity? In Mario Von Cranach and Ian Vine, Eds., *Social Communication and Movement*. New York: Academic.

Sudnow, David (1967). *Passing On*. Englewood Cliffs, N.J.: Prentice-Hall.

Sushinsky, L. W. and R. R. Bootzin (1970). Cognitive desensitization as a model of systematic desensitization. *Behavior Research and Therapy*, 8, 29–33.

Swenson, Clifford H., Jr. (1973). *Introduction to Interpersonal Relations*. Glenview, Ill.: Scott, Foresman.

Swingle, P. G. (1966). Effects of the emotional relationship between protagonists in a two-person game. *Journal of Personality and Social Psychology*, 4, 270–279.

Swingle, P. and J. S. Gillis (1968). Effects of the emotional relationship between protagonists in the prisoner's dilemma game. *Journal of Personality and Social Psychology*, 8, 160–165.

Sykes, G. M. and D. Matza (1957). Techniques of neutralization: A theory of delinquency. *American Sociological Review*, 22, 664–670.

Szasz, T. S. (1960). The myth of mental illness. *American Psychologist*, 15, 113–118.

Tacitus (1942). *The Complete Works of Tacitus*. New York: Modern Library.

Tanaka, Y. and C. E. Osgood (1965). Cross-culture, cross-concept, and cross-subject generality of affective meaning systems. *Journal of Personality and Social Psychology*, 2, 143–153.

Tavris, C. (1977). Masculinity. *Psychology Today*, 10, 34ff.

Tedeschi, J. T. (1974). Attribution, liking, and power. In Ted L. Huston, Ed., *Foundations of Interpersonal Attraction*. New York: Academic.

Tedeschi, J. T. and T. V. Bonama (1973). Power and influence: An intimation. In J. T. Tedeschi, Ed., *The Social Influence Processes*. Chicago: Aldine.

Tedeschi, J. T., S. Lesnick, and J. Gahagan (1968). Feedback and "washout" effects in the prisoner's dilemma game. *Journal of Personality and Social Psychology*, 10, 31–34.

Tedeschi, J. T., B. R. Schlenker, and T. V. Bonoma (1975). Compliance to threats as a function of source attractiveness and esteem. *Sociometry*, 38, 81–98.

Tedeschi, J. T., R. B. Smith III, and R. C. Brown, Jr. (1974). A reinterpretation of research on aggression. *Psychological Bulletin*, 81, 540,n562.

Tesser, A., R. Gatewood, and M. Driver (1968). Some determinants of gratitude. *Journal of Personality and Social Psychology*, 9, 233–236.

Thibaut, J. (1950). An experimental study of the cohesiveness of underprivileged groups. *Human Relations*, 3, 251–278.

Thibaut, J. W. and J. Coules (1952). The role of communication in the reduction of interpersonal hostility. *Journal of Abnormal and Social Psychology*, 47, 770–777.

Thibaut, John W. and Harold H. Kelley (1959). *The Social Psychology of Groups*. New York: Wiley.

Thibaut, J. W. and H. Reicken (1955). Authoritarianism, status, and the communication of aggression. *Human Relations*, 8, 95–120.

Thompson, D. F. and L. Meltzer (1964). Communication of emotional intent by facial expression. *Journal of Abnormal and Social Psychology*, 68, 129–135.

Tietze, C., P. V. Lemkau, and M. Cooper (1941). Schizophrenia, manic-depressive psychosis, and socioeconomic status. *American Journal of Sociology*, 47, 167–175.

Tietze, T. (1949). A study of mothers of schizophrenic patients. *Psychiatry*, 12, 55–65.

Tocqueville, Alexis de (1835). *Democracy in America*, Vol. 1. New York: Vintage, 1945.

Tognoli, J. and R. Keisner (1972). Gain and loss of esteem as determinants of interpersonal attraction: A replication and extension. *Journal of Personality and Social Psychology*, 23, 201–204.

Tompkins, S. S. (1970). Affect as the primary motivational system. In Magda B. Arnold, Ed., *Feelings and Emotions*. New York: Academic.

Tonks, C. M., E. S. Paykel, and G. L. Klerman (1970). Clinical depression among Negroes. *American Journal of Psychiatry*, 127, 329–335.

Tooth, G. (1950). *Studies in Mental Illness in the Gold Coast*. London: His Majesty's Stationery Office.

Touhey, J. C. (1972) Comparison of two dimensions of attitude similarity on heterosexual attraction. *Journal of Personality and Social Psychology*, 23, 8–10.

Triandis, H. C. (1972). *The Analysis of Subjective Culture*. New York: Wiley.

Tumin, M. (1953). Some principles of stratification: A critical analysis. *American Sociological Review*, 18, 387–394.

Turk, J. L. and N. W. Bell (1972). Measuring power in families. *Journal of Marriage and Family*, 31, 545–550.

Turner, R. J. (1972). The epidemiological study of schizophrenia: A current appraisal. *Journal of Health and Social Behavior*, 13, 360–369.

Turner, R. J. and M. O. Wagenfeld (1967). Occupational mobility and schizophrenia: An assessment of the social causation and social selection hypotheses. *American Sociological Review*, 32, 104–113.

Uhlenhuth, E. H. and E. S. Paykel (1973). Symptom configuration and life events. *Archives of General Psychiatry*, 28, 744–748.

Valins, S. (1966). Cognitive effects of false heart-rate feedback. *Journal of Personality and Social Psychology*, 4, 400–408.

Valins, S. and R. E. Nisbett (1971). *Attribution Processes in the Development and Treatment of Emotional Disorders*. New York: General Learning.

Valins, S. and A. A. Ray (1967). Effects of cognitive desensitization on avoidance behavior. *Journal of Personality and Social Psychology*, 7, 345–350.

Verinis, J. S., J. M. Brandsma, and C. N. Cofer (1968). Discrepancy from expectation in relation to affect and motivation: Tests of McClelland's hypothesis. *Journal of Personality and Social Psychology*, 9, 47–58.

Von Euler, U. S. (1951). The nature of adrenergic nerve mediators. *Physiological Reviews*, 3, 247–277.

Von Euler, U. S. and B. Folkow (1953). Differentiation of adrenaline and noradrenaline secretion from the adrenal medulla. 19th International Physiological Congress. *Abstracts of Communications*. Montreal.

Wagenar, J. M. and D. M. Hartsough (1974). Social competence as a process-reactive dimension with schizophrenics, alcoholics, and normals. *Journal of Abnormal Psychology*, 83, 112–116.

Wallace, D. B. (1972). Social status and psychological disorder: A crucial test of two explanations. Paper presented at Eastern Sociological Society meetings, New York, N.Y.

Wallace, J. and E. Sedalla (1966). Behavioral consequences of transgression: I. The effects of social recognition. *Journal of Experimental Research in Personality*, 1, 187–194.

Waller, W. (1937). The rating and dating complex. *American Sociological Review*, 2, 727–734.

Walster, E. (1965). The effect of self-esteem on romantic liking. *Journal of Experimental Social Psychology*, 1, 184–197.

Walster, E., V. Aronson, D. Abrahams, and L. Rottman (1966). The importance of physical attractiveness in dating behavior. *Journal of Personality and Social Psychology*, 4, 508–516.

Walster, E., E. Berscheid, and G. W. Walster (1970). Reactions of an exploiter to the exploited: Compensation, justification, or self-punishment? In Jacqueline R. Macaulay and Leonard Berkowitz, Eds., *Altruism and Helping Behavior*. New York: Academic.

Walster, E., E. Berscheid, and G. W. Walster (1973). New directions in equity research. *Journal of Personality and Social Psychology*, 6, 435–441.

Walster, E. and P. Prestholdt (1966). The effect of misjudging others: Overcompensation or dissonance reduction. *Journal of Experimental Social Psychology*, 2, 85–97.

Walters, R. H. and R. D. Parke (1967). The influence of punishment and related disciplinary techniques on the social behavior of children: Theory and empirical findings. In Brenden Maher, Ed., *Progress in Experimental Personality Research*, Vol. 4. New York: Academic.

Warheit, G. J., C. E. Holzer III, and S. A. Arey (1975). Race and mental illness: An epidemiological update. *Journal of Health and Social Behavior, 16,* 243–256.

Warheit, G. J., C. E. Holzer III, and J. J. Schwab (1973). An analysis of social class and racial differences in depressive symptomatology. *Journal of Health and Social Behavior, 14,* 291–299.

Waxler, N. E. (1974). Culture and mental illness: A social labeling perspective. *Journal of Nervous and Mental Disease, 159,* 379–395.

Weber, Max (1946). *From Max Weber: Essays in Sociology.* Hans H. Gerth and C. Wright Mills, Eds., New York: Oxford University Press.

Weber, Max (1947). *The Theory of Social and Economic Organization,* Translated by A. M. Henderson and Talcott Parsons. New York: Oxford University Press.

Weber, Max (1958). *The Protestant Ethic and the Spirit of Capitalism,* Translated by Talcott Parsons. New York: Scribner's Sons.

Weber, Max (1968). *Economy and Society.* Guenther Roth and Claus Wittich, Eds. Totowa, N.J.: Bedminster.

Wechsler, H. (1961). Community growth, depressive disorders and suicide. *American Journal of Sociology, 67,* 9–16.

Weinberg, S. K. (1965). Cultural aspects of manic-depression in West Africa. *Journal of Health and Human Behavior, 6,* 247–253.

Weinberg, M. S. (1968). Embarrassment: Its variable and invariable aspects. *Social Forces, 46,* 382–388.

Weiner, B. (1973). From each according to his abilities: The role of effort in a moral society. *Human Development, 16,* 53–60.

Weiner, B. and A. Kukla (1970). An attributional analysis of achievement motivation. *Journal of Personality and Social Psychology, 15,* 1–20.

Weiner, B. and N. Peter (1973) A cognitive-developmental analysis of achievement and moral judgment. *Developmental Psychology, 9,* 290–309.

Weiner, B., H. Heckhausen, W. U. Meyer, and R. E. Cook (1972). Causal ascriptions and achievement behavior: A conceptual analysis of effort and reanalysis of locus of control. *Journal of Personality and Social Psychology, 21,* 239–248.

Weiner, I. B. and R. Ader (1965). Direction of aggression and the adaptation to free avoidance conditioning. *Journal of Personality and Social Psychology, 2,* 426–429.

Welch, A. S. and B. L. Welch (1971). Isolation, reactivity, and aggression: Evidence for an involvement of brain catecholamines and serotonin. In Basil E. Eleftheriou and John P. Scott, Eds., *The Physiology of Aggression and Defeat.* New York: Plenum.

Wessman, A. E. and David F. Ricks (1966). *Mood and Personality.* New York: Holt, Rinehart, Winston.

Westman, J. C., D. W. Cline, W. J. Swift, and D. Kramer (1970). Role of child psychiatry in divorce. *Archives of General Psychiatry, 23,* 416–420.

Wherry, R. J. (1950). *Factor Analysis of Officer Qualification Form QCC-2B.* Columbus: Ohio State University Research Foundation.

White, M. S. (1957). Social class, child rearing practices, and child behavior. *American Sociological Review, 22,* 704–712.

White, R. (1959). Motivation reconsidered: The concept of competence. *Psychological Review, 66,* 297–333.

Whiting, John W. M. and Irvin L. Child (1953). *Child Training and Personality.* New Haven, Conn.: Yale University Press.

Wilker, L. (1975). Toward a convergence in the measurement of well-being. Paper presented at meetings of Gerontological Society, Louisville, Ky.

Willer, D. and M. Webster, Jr. (1970). Theoretical concepts and observables. *American Sociological Review*, 35, 748–757.

Wills, T. A., R. A. Weiss, and G. R. Patterson (1974). A behavioral analysis of the determinants of marital satisfaction. *Journal of Consulting and Counseling Psychology*, 42, 802–811.

Wilson, A. B. (1959). Residential segregation of social classes and aspirations of high school boys. *American Sociological Review*, 24, 836–845.

Wilson, Edward C. (1975). *Sociobiology: The New Synthesis.* Cambridge, Mass.: Harvard University Press.

Winch, Robert F. (1958). *Mate Selection: A Study of Complementary Needs.* New York: Harper and Row.

Winch, Robert F. (1963). *The Modern Family,* revised ed. New York: Holt, Rinehart, Winston.

Winokur, G. (1973). The types of affective disorders. *Journal of Nervous and Mental Disease,* 156, 82–96.

Wish, M., M. Deutsch, and S. J. Kaplan (1976). Perceived dimensions of interpersonal relations. *Journal of Personality and Social Psychology,* 33, 409–420.

Wittgenstein, Ludwig (1961). *Tractatus Logico-Philosophicus.* London: Routledge and Kegan Paul.

Wolf, Stewart and Harold G. Wolff (1947). *Human Gastric Function.* 2nd ed. New York: Oxford University Press.

Wolfgang, Marvin E. (1958). *Patterns in Criminal Homicide.* Philadelphia: University of Pennsylvania Press.

Wolman, B. B. (1965). Family dynamics and schizophrenia. *Journal of Health and Human Behavior,* 6, 163–169.

Wolman, R. N., W. C. Lewis, and M. King (1971). The development of the language of emotions: Conditions of emotional arousal. *Child Development,* 42, 1288–1293.

Wolpe, J. (1969). How can cognitions influence desensitization? *Behavior Research and Therapy,* 7, 219.

Wolpe, J. (1970). Emotional conditioning and cognitions: A rejoinder to Davison and Valins. *Behavior Research and Therapy,* 8, 103–104.

Wolpe, Joseph (1973). *The Practice of Behavior Therapy,* 2nd ed. New York: Pergamon.

Wood, D., M. Pilisuk, and E. Uren (1973). The martyr's personality: An experimental investigation. *Journal of Personality and Social Psychology,* 25, 177–186.

Wright, Herbert G. (1960). *Physical Disability–A Psychological Approach.* New York: Harper.

Wright, J. D. and S. R. Wright (1976). Social class and parental values for children: A partial replication and extension of the Kohn thesis. *American Sociological Review,* 41, 527–537.

Wrightsman, L. S. (1966). Personality and attitudinal correlates of trusting and trustworthy behaviors in a two-person game. *Journal of Personality and Social Psychology,* 4, 328–332.

Wrong, D. (1968). Some problems in defining social power. *American Journal of Sociology,* 73, 673–681.

Wuebben, Paul C., Bruce C. Straits, and Gary Schulman (1974). *The Experiment As a Social Occasion.* Berkeley, Cal.: Glendessary.

Wynne, L. C., I. Ryckoff, J. Day, and S. Hirsch (1958). Pseudomutuality in the family relations of schizophrenics. *Psychiatry*, *21*, 205–220.

Yancey, W. L., L. Rigsby, and J. D. McCarthy (1972). Social position and self-evaluation: The relative importance of race. *American Journal of Sociology*, *78*, 338–359.

Yarrow, M. R. (1963). Problems of methods in parent-child research. *Child Development*, *34*, 215–226.

Young, Paul T. (1961). *Motivation and Emotion*. New York: Wiley.

Zborowski, M. (1952). Cultural components in response to pain. *Journal of Social Issues*, *8*, 16–30.

Zelditch, M., Jr. (1955). Role differentiation in the nuclear family. In Talcott Parsons and Robert F. Bales, Eds., *Family, Socialization and Interaction Process*. Glencoe, Ill., Free Press.

Zelditch, M., Jr. (1968). Social status. In David L. Sills, Ed., *International Encyclopedia of Social Sciences*. New York: MacMillan.

Zetterberg, H. (1966). The secret ranking. *Journal of Marriage and Family*, *28*, 134–142.

Zigler, E. and L. Phillips (1961). Psychiatric diagnosis: A critique. *Journal of Abnormal and Social Psychology*, *63*, 607–618.

Zigler, E. and L. Phillips (1962). Social competence and the process-reactive distinction in psychopathology. *Journal of Abnormal and Social Psychology*, *65*, 215–222.

Zillman, D. (1971). Excitation transfer in communication mediated aggressive behavior. *Journal of Experimental Social Psychology*, *7*, 419–434.

Zimbardo, Philip (1969). *The Cognitive Control of Motivation*. Glenview, Ill.: Scott, Foresman.

Zola, I. K. (1966). Culture and symptoms: An analysis of patients' presenting complaints. *American Sociological Review*, *31*, 615–630.

Zuckerman, M., B. B. Ribback, I. Monashkin, and J. A. Norton (1958). Normative data and factor analysis on the Parental Attitude Research Instrument. *Journal of Consulting Psychology*, *22*, 165–171.

Name Index

Chance, J. E., 77
Chance, N. A., 53, 232, 234, 235, 236
Chape, C., 20, 54
Chapman, L., 55, 122, 218, 219, 262
Charwat, W. A., 141
Cheek, F. E., 203
Cheyne, J. A., 244
Child, I. L., 237, 239, 249, 318, 320, 324, 340
Chomsky, N., 12, 82
Christensen, H. T., 318
Church, R. M., 239, 249, 260
Clark, B., 217
Clarke, R. A., 77
Clausen, J. A., 214
Cleve, F. M., 3, 34
Cline, D. W., 302
Clore, G. L., 83, 328
Cloward, R., 228
Cobb, J., 220
Cochrane, C., 65, 66, 262
Cofer, C. N., 77, 83, 206
Coffrey, H. S., 35
Cohen, A. R., 141
Cohen, B. P., 23, 24, 129
Cohen, S. I., 154, 156, 164, 187, 188, 192
Cohen, Y. A., 232
Cohn, R., 141
Cole, D. L., 278
Cole, S., 221
Collins, R., 217
Combs, A. W., 118
Comer, R. J., 115
Connor, J. W., 231
Cook, R. E., 246
Cooley, C. H., 274
Coombs, R. H., 318
Cooper, L. M., 238, 239
Cooper, M., 214
Costello, C. G., 200
Cottrell, L. S., Jr., 37, 354, 357, 358, 359, 366
Couch, A., 38, 39, 40, 366
Crandall, V. C., 77
Crandall, V. J., 77
Crandell, D. L., 390
Cronbach, L. J., 12, 180, 363
Crowne, D. P., 254
Cutick, R. A., 242, 255, 256

Cutright, P., 221

D'Andrade, R. G., 362, 364
Dahl, R. A., 371, 372
Dahrendorf, R., 269
Darwin, C., 3, 4, 5, 142
Davis, D., 327
Davis, K., 274, 275, 379, 380
Davis, K. E., 308
Davitz, J., 56, 85
Day, B. R., 308
Day, J., 206
Day, R. C., 130, 311
DeCharms, R., 129, 130
Della Fave, L. R., 221, 227
Dembo, T., 73, 118
Dengerink, H. A., 93, 124, 129, 241
Denney, R., 230
Descartes, 3, 6
Desjardins, C., 17, 157, 159
Deutsch, M., 37, 41, 62, 124, 130
DeVinney, L. C., 59
Dewey, J., 305
DeWolfe, A. S., 221
Diggory, J., 78
Dimaio, G., 129
DiMascio, A., 146
Dion, K., 274, 318
Distler, L., 254, 288
Dohrenwend, B. P., 16, 20, 146, 211, 213, 219, 220, 229, 390, 392
Dohrenwend, B. S., 16, 211, 213, 219, 220, 229, 392
Dollard, J., 91, 126, 301
Donlon, P. T., 236
Donnelly, J., 203
Doob, A. N., 89, 90, 91, 126, 179
Doob, L., 91, 126
Dornbusch, S., 274
Dostoyevski, F., 55, 119
Douglas, K., 196
Draguns, J. G., 200, 235
Driver, M., 132
Drolette, M. E., 152, 153, 155, 164, 252
Drost, B. A., 245, 262
Dugan, R. D., 362, 363, 364
Duncan, O. D., 218, 227
Dunham, H. W., 212, 213, 214, 226, 391
Durkheim, E., 1, 11, 15, 21, 27, 59, 138, 230, 233, 234, 273, 338, 339, 343, 348, 362

Subject Index

447